Now . . . an introductory management text with an important difference

This new basic textbook develops a genuinely integrated model for contingency management

Management: Contingencies, Structure, and Process

Henry L. Tosi,
Michigan State University

Stephen J. Carroll,
University of Maryland

1976, 608 pages, hardbound
ISBN 0-914292-04-8

See page three for information on accompanying volumes

Here is a book which develops fundamental concepts of organizational types and human responses as a basis for describing the management process and prescribing for effective management in specific situations.

Management: Contingencies, Structure, and Process

What It Depends Upon

In the early chapters of this text, the authors describe the characteristics of mechanistic, organic, and mixed-form organizations, how individuals with particular attitudes and abilities come to be associated with various types of organizations, and how organization and individual interact with one another.

In this framework, the book presents comprehensive coverage of management processes—planning and control, decision-making, leadership—and how variations of these processes can be selectively applied to the management of different types of organizations with different problems and different needs.

Managing Types of Organizations

The major feature of the book is a set of chapters dealing specifically with the management of hierarchical, dynamic, and mixed-form organizations (chaps. 12-16). Here, students can see which techniques, which principles, and which approaches are likely to be most effective in particular organizational circumstances. They can develop a strong conceptual understanding of the factors underlying effective management practice in different situations.

Some Values of the Text

"Management process contingency theory" offers a truly integrated structure for organization theory, organizational behavior, and management theory, providing sensible prescriptions for effective management. Prescriptions are based in the major research and theory in the field.

The management coverage is unusually comprehensive. In addition to practical guidance, the text is rich in insights into the manager's role and the things which managers can control or influence. Each chapter is supported by selections from popular business journals—Business Week, The Wall Street Journal, Fortune—to lend realism through contemporary examples of problem situations in modern business defined by contingency theory. Throughout the text, readers will find a strong emphasis on objectives as the basis for planning, decision-making, and getting things done through others.

The Authors

Henry L. Tosi, Professor of Organizational Behavior, Michigan State University, is a Fellow of the Academy of Management and a member of its Board of Governors as well as Past President of the Midwest Academy of Management. He received his M.B.A. and Ph.D. from Ohio State University. He is co-author of *Management by Objectives: Research and Applications,* author of *Theories of Organization,* and co-editor of *Organizational Behavior and Management: A Contingency Approach* and *Managerial Motivation and Compensation.* He has contributed many articles to leading journals and is a major contributor to other books.

Stephen J. Carroll is Professor and Chairman of the Division of Organizational Behavior and Industrial Relations, University of Maryland, and has taught at the University of Minnesota, where he received his M.A. and Ph.D. He is Chairman of the Manpower Management Division of the Academy of Management and has contributed many articles to such journals as *Administrative Science Quarterly, The Journal of Business, The Journal of Applied Psychology,* and *California Management Review.* He is co-author of *The Management of Compensation* and *Management by Objectives* and is co-editor of *The Management Process.*

The Teaching Package   (Available in June 1976)

Instructor's Manual

The manual will include lecture outlines and examination items graded in difficulty.

Readings in Management: Contingencies, Structure, and Process

By Henry L. Tosi

1976, 320 pages, paperbound   ISBN 0-914292-07-2

Compiled to be used as an adjunct to introductory management texts, the articles in this book expose the reader to a wide range of important facets of managing and deal in depth with many of the concepts in the text, **Management: Contingencies, Structure, and Process.** They were selected for readability, for application to the world of the practicing manager, and for the extent to which they invite the reader to see things in the contingency view ("It all depends—and it depends on *this.*")

Part One   The Nature of Managerial Performance

Mahoney, Jerdee, and **Carroll**   Development of Managerial Performance
Mee   Changing Concepts of Management
Bell   Work and Its Discontents

Part Two   Individuals and Groups in Organization

McClelland   That Urge to Achieve
McArthur   Career Choice
Schein   Organizational Socialization and the Profession of Management
Donald F. Roy   Banana Time: Job Satisfaction and Informal Interaction

Part Three   The Design of Organizations

McCaskey   An Introduction to Organizational Design
Child   What Determines Organizational Performance: The Universals vs.
the It All Depends

Continued

Feedback

Please send me   ☐ **Readings in Management**   ☐ Instructor's Manual
Please send exam copies of the   ☐ text   ☐ readings to the following members of my

department _____

Comment

Name _____

Department _____

College or University _____

Street Address _____

City _____ State _____ Zip _____

Litterer   Research Departments within Large Organizations
Mee   Matrix Organization

Part Four   Leadership

Newsweek   Status-Seeking Hormones
Norman and **Von Der Embse**   Six Propositions for Managerial Leadership:
  Diagnostic Tools for Definition and Focus
Shetty   Leadership and Organization Character
Fiedler   Style or Circumstance: The Leadership Enigma
House   Role Conflict and Multiple Authority in Complex Organizations

Part Five   The Management Process: Decision-Making

Karson and **Wrobleski**   A Manager's Guide to Probability Modeling
McCreary   How to Grow a Decision Tree
Herbert H. Roy   Using Computer-Based Control Systems for Decision-Making
Vroom   A New Look at Managerial Decision-Making

Part Six   The Management Process: Planning

Gerstner   Can Strategic Planning Pay Off?
Thomas   Environmental Analysis for Corporate Planning
Mintzberg   Strategy-Making in Three Modes

Part Seven   The Management Process: Control

Vancil   What Kind of Management Control Do You Need?
Campfield   Auditing Management Performance
Koontz   Making Managerial Appraisal Effective

Part Eight   Organizational Change and Development

Burack and **Pati**   Technology and Managerial Obsolescence
Loving   How a Hotelman Got the Red Out of United Airlines
Selfridge and **Sokolik**   A Comprehensive View of Organization Development
Stull   A View of Management to 1980
Steiner   Institutionalizing Corporate Social Decision

Management: Contingencies, Structure, and Process

Management: Contingencies, Structure, and Process

Henry L. Tosi
Michigan State University

Stephen J. Carroll
University of Maryland

St. Clair Press
4 East Huron Street
Chicago, Illinois 60611

Management: Contingencies, Structure, and Process
Copyright © 1976 by St. Clair Press
All rights reserved. Printed in the United States of America.
No part of this publication may be reproduced, stored in a retrieval system, or
transmitted in any form or by any means, electronic, mechanical, photocopying,
recording, or otherwise, without the prior written permission of the publisher.

The material on management by objectives (MBO) throughout this book is drawn
extensively from the authors' book *Management by Objectives: Applications and
Research* (Macmillan, 1973), and "Setting Goals in Management by Objectives," with
John Rizzo, in *California Management Review* (Sept., 1970). Material in chapter 10
on budgeting is based on an article by Henry L. Tosi, "The Human Effects of Budgeting
Systems on Management," in *Business Topics* (Autumn, 1974).

Library of Congress Catalog Card Number 75-43280
ISBN 0-914292-04-8

St. Clair Press
4 East Huron Street
Chicago, Illinois 60611   **Design by Free Chin**

To
Lisa, Kathy, and Jenny Tosi
and
Alisa and Chris Carroll

Contents

Part I   INTRODUCTION

Chapter 1   **The Nature of Management**   2

Managers and Managing   4

    Managers—A Definition

    The Managerial Process

    Areas of Technical Concern to Managers

    How Managerial Jobs Differ by Organizational Level

    Improving Management Skills

Managerial Process Contingency Theory   17

Plan of This Book   19

Chapter 2   **A Short History of Management**   24

Some Antecedents of Modern Management

      Thinking   24

    The Middle Ages and the Renaissance

    The Industrial Revolution

    The Growth of Industry in the United States

Contemporary Management Movements   32

    The Scientific Management Approach

    Administrative Theory

    The Behavioral Approach

    The Management Science Movement

    Contingency Theories of Management

    How We Arrived Here

Items 2.1   Adam Smith

      2.2   Dexter S. Kimball

      2.3   Henri Fayol

Part II   INDIVIDUALS

Chapter 3   **Development of Work Motives, Values, and Attitudes**

Behavioral Model of Human Beings   58

Learning Theory   61
  Positive and Negative Reinforcement
  Reinforcement Schedules
  Behavioral Change
  Reinforcement in Everyday Life
Perception   63
  Stimulus Factors
  Personal Factors
The Socialization Process—Personality
    Development   65
  Early Socialization Experiences
The Unique Individual—The Results of
    Socialization   69
  Skills, Ability, and Knowledge
  Self-concept
  Attitudes
  Values
  Needs or Motives
Frustration and the Inability to Satisfy Needs   76
  Reactions to Frustration
The Development of Orientations Toward Work   79
  Family Characteristics and Work Values
  Occupational Choice and Work Values
  Occupational Socialization
Socialization and Organizational Involvement   82
  The Organizationalist
  Externally-oriented Persons
  The Professional
Organization Socialization—The Psychological
    Contract   91
  Item 3.1   A Nonorganizationalist Top Manager

Chapter 4   **Group Behavior   96**
Groups—Primary and Secondary   97
  Primary Groups
  Secondary Groups

Departments or Permanent Functional Assignments
Committees
Required and Emergent Behavior in Groups
The Effects of Groups at Work—Two Studies
Some Properties of Groups   104
Group Values
Norms
Role and Position
Status
Group Cohesiveness
Some Effects of Membership in Groups   109
Problems of Groups
Intergroup Conflict

Chapter 5   **Motivation and Performance   118**
Motivation—Two Definitions
Job Satisfaction, Motivation, and Performance   121
Factors Affecting Job Satisfaction
Herzberg's Two-factor Theory
Motivation and Performance—A Complex
Relationship
Performance—A Multidimensional View
Basic Input Factors   131
Human Factor Inputs
Technological Inputs
Motivation—The Managerial Function
Motivation by Lower-level Personnel
The Development of Expectancies
Satisfaction—The Result of Performance
The Management of Performance   150
Items 5.1   Incentive Plans
5.2   Job Enrichment

Part III   **THE ORGANIZATION**
Chapter 6   **The Environment and the Organization   154**

The Open and Closed Systems Perspective   154
Organization Subsystems   156
Primary and Collateral Subsystems   157
  Production Subsystems
  Boundary-spanning Subsystems
  Adaptive Subsystems
  Maintenance Subsystems
  Managerial Subsystems
The Relevant Environment of the Organization   166
  The Relevant Environment
Characteristics of the Environment   168
Strategies for Adapting to the Environment   170
The Environment-Organization Linkage   173
Items 6.1   Market Volatility
      6.2   The Technological Environment
      6.3   Changing Structure

Chapter 7   **Organization Structural Alternatives: Adapting to the
             Environment   178**
The Hierarchical, Bureaucratic Organization   180
  Production Subsystems
  Boundary-spanning Subsystems
  Adaptive Subsystems
  Maintenance Subsystems
  Managerial Subsystems
The Flexible, Dynamic Organization   189
  Production Subsystems
  Boundary-spanning Subsystems
  Adaptive Subsystems
  Maintenance Subsystems
  Managerial Subsystems
Technology-Dominated Mixed Organizations   196
  Production Subsystems
  Boundary-spanning Subsystems
  Adaptive Subsystems
  Maintenance Subsystems

Managerial Subsystems
Market-Dominated Mixed Organizations   201
   Production Subsystems
   Adaptive Subsystems
   Boundary-spanning Subsystems
   Maintenance Subsystems
   Managerial Subsystems
The Structure-Environment (SE) Model   203
Items 7.1   A Mixed Organization
     7.2   Boundary-spanning and Adaptive Activities
     7.3   Volatile Technology, Stable Market

Part IV   **THE MANAGEMENT PROCESS**

Chapter 8   **Leadership 208**
Why Do People Comply?   208
   Leadership and Administration in Management
Power—The Basis of Compliance   212
   Organizational Factors
   Skill and Expertise
   Personal Characteristics of the Leader
Leadership, Power, and Dependence   218
Different Perspectives on Leadership
   The Trait Approach
   Behavioral Approach
   Situational Theories
   Leader Behavior—Cause or Result of Effectiveness?
   Can Leadership Style Be Flexible?
   How Leader Behavior Affects Performance
Item 8.1   A Power Base

Chapter 9   **Decision Making   234**
Problem Solving—The Context of Decision
   Making   235
   Problem Solving and Decision Making
The Steps in Problem Solving   236

Step 1—Problem Recognition
Step 2—Identifying Probable Causes of the Problem
Step 3—The Generation and Identification of
   Alternatives
Step 4—The Evaluation and Selection of Alternatives
Kepner-Tregoe Approach to Selecting Alternatives
Decision Theory Approaches to Selecting Alternatives
Decisions under Conditions of Certainty
Decisions under Risk
Decision Making under Uncertainty
Some other Considerations in Comparing Alternatives
Items 9.1 How to Analyze a Problem
     9.2 Decision Making
     9.3 Mathematical Models
     9.4 Decision Making

Chapter 10   **Resource Allocation 276**
Types of Goals 280
   Environmental Goals
   Individual Goals
   Internal System Goals
An Example of the Goal Structure of an
     Organization 282
   Environmental Goals
   Internal Systems Goals
   Individual Goals
The Planning Process and Objectives 285
The Development of Plans 286
   Break-even Analysis
The Development of Operational Plans and
     Budgets 294
   Sales and Profit Objectives
   Production Budgets
   Materials Purchases Budget
   Cash Budgets
   Budgeted Income Statements and Balance Sheets

Planning for Human Resources
Capital Budgeting
Long-range Planning, Capital Budgeting, and Control
The Human Effects of Planning and Budgeting   305
  Planning and Budget Development (Stage 1)
  Plans and Budgets (Stage 2)
  Budget Implementation (Stage 3)
Items 10.1   Planning
      10.2   Planning
      10.3   Planning

Chapter 11   The Implementation of Decisions   312
Effective Decisions   312
  How Quality/Acceptability Affects Decision Making
Management by Objectives   315
  MBO: A Definition
  The Cascading of Objectives
  Problems in Cascading Objectives
Scope and Type of Objectives   319
  Performance Objectives
  What an Objective Should Look Like
  The Action Plan
  Coordination Requirements
  Constraints on Action Plans
MBO and Managerial Control   323
When and How to Use Participation   325
Some Guides to Using Participative Methods   327
  Maier's Decision-making Approach
  The Vroom-Yetton Model
  The Decision Factors and the Vroom-Yetton Model
  Decision-making Behavior of Managers and the
    V-Y Model
  Dangers in the Participation Approach
Values of Managing by Objectives   335
  Management by Objectives—An Organization
    Philosophy

Participation and Organizational Types   338

Part V   MANAGING DIFFERENT TYPES OF ORGANIZATIONS

Chapter 12   Managing Human Resources in the Hierarchical
                    Organization   342
                  Selection of Personnel   342
                    The Personnel Composition of Hierarchical
                      Organizations
                    Selection Strategies in the Stable Organization
                  Compensation   348
                    Methods of Determination of Pay
                  Motivation in Stable Organizations   351
                    Motivational Approaches in Hierarchical
                      Organizations
                  Performance Evaluation   356
                    Performance Evaluation in the Hierarchical
                      Organization
                  Leader Behavior in Hierarchical Organizations
                    Factors Affecting Leadership Effectiveness
                    How a Manager Can Improve Performance
                  Managing Organization Stress in the Bureaucratic
                      Organization   370
                    Ways to Minimize Role Conflict
                    Role Ambiguity
                    Strategies to Reduce Role Ambiguity
                  Managing Conflict in the Bureaucratic Organization
                    Sources of Conflict
                    The Balance of Power
                    Resolution of Conflict in Stable Organizations
                    Formal Mechanisms
                    Nonstructural Solutions

Chapter 13   Decision Approaches in Hierarchical
                    Organizations   382
                  The Nature of Goals in Stable Organizations   382
                    Environmental Goals

Internal System Goals
The Characteristics of Controls
Decision-making Approaches under Risk   385
    Probabilities Mean Maybe
    Utility and Expected Value
A Planning and Control Approach for Hierarchical
        Organizations   389
    Linear Programming

Chapter 14   **Managing Human Resources in a Dynamic**
        Organization   400
Selection of Personnel   400
    The Mixture of Organization Types
    Selection in the Dynamic Organization
Compensation in Dynamic Organizations   403
    Maturity Curves
    The Classification Method
    Executive Compensation
Performance Evaluation in the Dynamic
        Organization   405
    Evaluating Worker Performance
    Evaluating Managers and Professionals
    Who Conducts the Evaluation?
Motivation in the Dynamic Organization   408
    Managerial Approaches to Motivation in the
        Dynamic Organization
Leader Behavior in Dynamic Organizations   415
    Low Task Structure in Dynamic Organizations
    Ways that a Manager Can Improve Performance
    Replace Members with Others of Greater Ability
    Change Position Power
    Change Leader Behavior Style
    Change the Climate
Managing Organizational Stress in the Dynamic
        Organization   421
    Role Ambiguity
    Strategies for Reducing Role Ambiguity

Role Conflict
Strategies for Dealing with Role Conflict
Managing Conflict in the Dynamic Organization   425
Sources of Conflict
The Balance of Power
Resolving Conflict in Flexible Organizations
Item 14.1   The Motivational Setting

Chapter 15   **Decision Approaches in Dynamic Organizations   432**
The Characteristic of Controls
Decision Making under Uncertainty   435
The Pessimistic Criterion
The Optimistic Criterion
The Regret Criterion
The Rational Criterion
A Planning and Control Approach in Dynamic
    Organizations   444
PERT (Project Evaluation and Review Technique)
Time Estimates
The Critical Path
Some Applications of PERT   453
Items 15.1   Resource Allocation
    15.2   Planning

Chapter 16   **Managing the Mixed Organization   456**
Causes of Integration Difficulties   459
Organizational Differences
Differences in Individuals
Integration in the Mixed Organization   469
Matrix Organization

Part VI   **ORGANIZATION CHANGE**
Chapter 17   **Changing Organization Structure   480**
The Emergence of Organization Structure   481
Organization Growth and Structure Change   482
Stage 1: The Small Firm

Stage 2: Dynamic Growth
Stage 3: Rational Administration
Relationship to Organization Models
Adapting to Environmental Changes   493
    Direction of Environmental Changes
Attempting to Change the Conditions of the
    Environment   500
Items 17.1   Transition to Stage 3
    17.2   Environmental Change
    17.3   Moving to a More Compatible Environment

Chapter 18   Changing People in Organizations   506
Prerequisites of Change   509
    Determination of Developmental Needs
Development Techniques   512
    Off-the-job Methods
    The Effectiveness of Off-the-job Methods
    On-the-job Methods
    Effectiveness of On-the-job Methods
    Some Integrated Approaches to Development
    House Management Development Model
    MBO as Development
Item 18.1   Management Development

Chapter 19   The Effective Organization: Present and Future
    Organization Effectiveness
Managing in the Changing World   544
    Growth in Size of Organizations
    Increased Foreign Competition
    Growth of the Multinational Organization
    Technological Change
    Changing Composition of the Labor Force
    Employment of the Disadvantaged Worker
    Changing Societal Values

References   553
Name Index   569
Subject Index   575

Preface

The basic structure of this book is drawn from a wide range of ideas that are part of management and organization literature. The "contingency" theme is of course not a new one. We all know that "It all depends." In this book we try to tell the reader what it depends upon, and what to do when he knows that.

There is a reason for this prescriptive approach. In recent years organization and management theorists have moved away from such an approach. Because of the belief that "There is no one best way," an excessive amount of work in the field is descriptive. But managing requires prescription. In this book we take a very prescriptive position.

We would like to thank all of the creators of the good books of the past—the sources of the ideas that form the substance of our field—but there are so many that it is an impossible task. It is of course upon their ideas that our text is built. What we have sought to do was to draw out essential ideas and weave them into "managerial process contingency theory," a perhaps elaborate way of saying that what a manager should do does indeed "all depend." Sometimes our fabric is smooth, and at other times—we hope not too often—it may be rough, but we hope that the ideas are always developed with reasonableness and logical consistency.

There are many people we can thank directly. Lyman Porter gave one of us a year at the University of California, Irvine, to work on the manuscript. Lynn Mayeda and Gini Nordyke were helpful in effort and spirit. Dorothy Vance and Alyce Kerns at the University of Maryland and Kathy Jegla, Kathy Schumacher, Linda Penrose, and Doris Singer at Michigan State University were instrumental in every stage of manuscript preparation.

We would also like to say a word about our collaboration. The conceptual model underlying this book is Henry Tosi's, but each of us regards the other not simply as a co-author, but as a collaborator without equal.

Finally, a word about our approach to the question of the social responsibility of managers. Much of the substance of a text in this subject, because it deals with widely applicable techniques of management, is not directly related to the treatment of various social ills. Do we think women and minorities should have equal opportunity as managers? Our position is simply that they should. In this book, however, we have generally used the convention of the masculine pronoun because, as many authors have discovered, there is no effective English-language singular that includes both sexes. We have also opted occasionally for female examples, simply to underscore our view that good management is nondiscriminatory.

Students should bear in mind that many management techniques discussed in this book can be applied effectively to various areas of social responsibility, including that of advancing the employment of women and minorities in management positions. Chapter 19, which deals with contemporary management problems, has precisely the purpose of encouraging analysis for that type of application.

It remains to be said that we take responsibility for all errors of logic, omission, or commission. We hope the book works.

Henry L. Tosi
Stephen J. Carroll

Part I

Introduction

We pick the traditional starting point for this book—a definition of the field. Management, as an activity, and managers, as a group, are examined in chapter 1, along with the basic ideas which form the rest of this book.

Chapter 2 shows where the ideas come from. The conventional, incorrect view is that management thinking and writing began around the turn of the 20th century with Frederick Taylor; management practice actually began when human beings formed groups to do things collectively. In chapter 2, we give an historical perspective which tells how we arrived at the state of the field today.

Chapter 1

The July 18, 1975, edition of *The Wall Street Journal* carried a story on page six about federal emission control standards for automobiles. The deadline for reducing emission pollutants to the permissible limits had been extended to 1978–79. From a management point of view, the implications of this action are extensive.

First, it may have an effect on the petroleum and gasoline shortage. Do emission-reduction devices on automobiles increase gasoline consumption? (Auto makers estimate a 5 percent to 30 percent reduction in mileage with 1978's stricter standards.) If they do, who decides what level of increase in fuel consumption is acceptable against what level of reduction in air pollutants? A comparison of costs and benefits is necessary to make a wise decision. This is a management problem and the solution decided upon is one that will affect all of us.

Second, consider the effect of such a ruling on automobile manufacturers. They can now wait until 1977 to have production capability for required emission devices, but what changes must they then make in their assembly lines? And when do they begin training service personnel for the maintenance of the new devices once cars with them are on the road? And how can they plan effectively so that costs are minimized when there are no existing parameters to guide them? (Their estimates of cost increases due to 1978's stricter standards range from $150 to $400 per car.) And what if new legislation is passed extending present standards beyond 1978, as President Ford was recommending late in 1975?

Finally, what effect will such legislation, or even newer legislation, have on the decisions of, say, the owners of firms manufacturing emission control devices? In California, for example, because of its

The Nature of Management

special air quality problems, a law was passed requiring all vehicles manufactured since 1965 to have emission control devices. Later, in response to much pressure from car-owning citizens, California lawmakers decided that such devices would be required only on vehicles when there was a transfer of ownership. Control device firms suddenly lost their market, a market that had been created as quickly.

Driving through Southeastern Ohio on Interstate 70, the traveler is appalled by the devastation left by strip mining. Rolling farmland and verdant woods are gone. In their place are gouges in the land which many feel will never heal over. But the coal taken is energy, and it is a relatively economical form of energy. Some argue that strip mining legislation should require that the land be restored by its devastators. But there are substantial costs involved in such restoration. These costs would ultimately be borne by the society in the form of higher prices.

A husband and wife sit at a kitchen table trying to figure out how much money they need to send the kids away to college. "Can we manage with the old car for two more years?" "How much of the cost of college will the children have to find for themselves?" Basically, they must decide how to allocate the total of resources of the family to reach their goal, a college education for their children. All these problems, from strip mining scars in Ohio to how and where the kids should go to college, have a common theme. They affect people, and they have to do with effective and efficient use of resources.

And that is what management is all about. How can resources be used most efficiently to reach a goal? These goals may be social, such as the reduction of racial and sex discrimination. They may be family goals, such as a college education, a new house, a better way of life. The goals may be organizational goals, such as increased sales, higher profits, or lower costs for a business firm.

The basic task of management is to seek to make efficient use of resources. All resources are limited in supply; therefore they must be managed wisely. We must manage the time, energy, and personal resources we spend in our private lives, as well as in business firms, government agencies, households, universities, restaurants, and so forth. The *management process* occurs when people in organizations attempt to achieve objectives through efficient utilization of resources.

What is the general content of the process of management? It includes activities which:

1. Establish organization objectives, whether that organization is a business firm, a unit in an organization, a government agency, a family unit, and so on.
2. Develop plans to attain these objectives.
3. Assemble resources to carry out the plans.
4. Supervise the execution of the plans by proper direction, providing help and training to those carrying out the plans, and giving other support where required.
5. Evaluate whether or not satisfactory progress toward objectives is being made and initiate corrective action, if necessary.

Management is a necessary activity in any organization. It is an important function for firms in the private sector which produce goods and services to be used in society and return a profit to the owners of the firms. Management is also important in the public sector, governmental organizations controlled through political institutions. The objective of public organizations is also to provide goods and services to society, but these organizations are not concerned with profits—in the sense of economic return to owners. In the private sector, lack of profits can drive a firm out of business while often, for the good of society, public organizations must be, and are, subsidized. But of course, in the public sector, resource allocation decisions must also be made. The implications of decisions within the organization and their effects on other parts of society must be evaluated. Public sector organizations have employees who must be managed, resources which they use, and objectives which they must achieve. Many managers in public institutions do very similar things in their jobs as do their counterparts in the private sector.

Managers and Managing

In this book we are going to concentrate our analysis on *managing*—the process—and *management*—the group of employees in an organization who make and implement resource allocation decisions. The management process is the set of activities carried out in an organization for the purpose of achieving objectives in an efficient way. When we speak of *a manager,* we refer to someone in an organization who has the right to decide how resources are allocated and who has supervisory responsibility for other people.

Managers—A Definition

Managers are a separate and distinct category of employees in an organization. They hold a certain type of job. Approximately 10 percent of the working population in the United States is categorized as a "manager or proprietor." The President of General Electric is a manager. So is the afternoon shift supervisor at McDonald's. There are some important differences, of course, in what they do, how they do it, and the kinds of decisions they make. However, there are some factors common to their jobs.

Frederick Taylor (we will have more to say about him in chap. 2) popularized the idea of scientific management around the early 1900s. One of his basic premises was to separate the activities of *managing* a task from its *execution.* This doesn't mean, necessarily, that one person only managed and someone else only executed. But Taylor reasoned that it would be easier to use resources more efficiently by making this distinction and using it as a basis for the analysis of both managerial and other types of work. It is, of course, possible that the same person may manage and execute some part or all of a particular task.

Those people in an organization who are involved in the execution of tasks, carrying out the activity, doing the work itself are *operative employees.* Their primary assignment is doing the work, not planning or managing it. In an automobile plant, they work on an assembly line. In an airline maintenance facility, they may be highly-trained machinists. In a research laboratory, they might have doctoral degrees in science. Operative personnel work at the lines in steel rolling mills and behind the counters in department stores. Their primary task is making the product or providing the service.

Those who possess high skill levels in a particular kind of job are *specialists,* a particular class of operative employees. Typically, their education and experience make it relatively difficult for them to move about from one type of job to another. A specialist generally is extensively trained in a very narrow area of competence. A long apprenticeship, many years of training, and an intense personal investment of time and resources may be required before one is characterized as a specialist. A specialist may often be a *professional*. Computer programmers, doctors, teachers, personnel technicians, and engineers are specialists who may also be performing operative activities.

A *manager*, or synonymously an executive, in an organization is in a position which has at least two characteristics:

1. *He makes decisions about how other people, primarily subordinates, use resources.* Managers usually have the right to decide how those who work for them can use resources needed to accomplish the operative tasks, the execution of work. Managers make resource allocation decisions which other people must implement. For example, a manager may have to decide whether to spend available funds on new office equipment such as typewriters, or on new office furniture. In some firms managers make decisions about how millions of dollars will be spent for new plants. These decisions, of course, have wide implications not only for company employees but also for the regions where these new plants might be located. A manager of advertising and promotion may have to decide whether the advertising program of a cosmetics firm should be directed at women over 40, or at women under 40. Once such decisions are made and methods formulated to carry them out, the actual work is done by the operative employees.

2. *He is responsible to a higher superior for the supervision of subordinates.* Most people who work in organizations have a superior to whom they make some sort of accounting of how well they do their jobs. Perhaps what most sharply distinguishes a manager's job from that of others in an organization is that the manager not only makes decisions about what resources others can use to achieve objectives, but he is also responsible for insuring that it is done well. This means that he must be concerned with the effective use of human resources as well as physical resources such as plant and equipment. Managers are responsible for the work of other people. Some executives manage operative employees or specialists. Others manage managers.

The Managerial Process

There is, then, a distinction between managerial tasks and operative tasks. One way to increase the effectiveness of organizations is to improve the way in which managers do their jobs, and to do that it is necessary to understand more fully what it is that they do, the components of their jobs. The reason we want to understand the components of managerial work, breaking it down into a set of subactivities, is so that individual skills can be improved. Only when we understand an activity can it be taught to others. Otherwise, doing something well depends upon intuition, or self-teaching. A person who is "intuitive," or a "natural," at any activity—whether it be management, music, or athletics—cannot easily pass the skill on to others. An effective golf teacher knows the components of a good swing and can convey them to a student, but when the intuitive golfer is asked how to hit a particular shot, he is likely to say, "just swing through the ball." That has little meaning to a novice. The senior buyer of women's fashions in a large department store who has a "sense of the market" can only train a new buyer when the premises on which buying decisions are based can be transmitted to the new buyer. Unless the senior buyer is aware of data used to make decisions, and knows how these data are evaluated, improving the performance of another person through training is impossible.

Everyone makes decisions about how to allocate resources of some type. We all manage something—our personal finances, a family, a baseball team. Because of this there is a tendency to believe that management is an intuitive skill, or a matter of common sense. But management is a process and an activity that in its basics can be learned by an individual. Experience, and intuition based on experience, are both brought to bear by the seasoned manager, as they are by the senior buyer with a sense of the market. But the prospective manager can equip himself with a knowledge of certain discrete and basic techniques—for example, of decision making or financial planning— and to these he ultimately will add the wisdom and intuition that are the products of experience. Similarly, a manager can learn to understand human responses, and he can learn to analyze how these responses will occur in particular situations. Again, he can bring the depth of experience to bear ultimately on how well he uses these basic tools.

That is the objective of this book—to analyze and understand the structure and strategies of the management process so that it can be carried on more effectively.

Mahoney, Jerdee and Carroll (1963) conducted a research study in which they questioned more than 450 managers in a variety of companies in an attempt to identify in some detail what it was that they did. They identified eight managerial functions and measured the proportions of time spent on each of them by managers at different levels in organizations (see table 1.1).

These eight functions are components of the managerial process:

1. Planning   5. Coordinating
2. Representing   6. Evaluating
3. Investigating   7. Supervising
4. Negotiating   8. Staffing

TABLE 1.1 Percentage of Workday Spent by Managers on Various
Performance Functions and Areas of Competence (N = 452)

Performance Function	Percent	Area of Competence	Percent
Planning	19.5	Personnel	27
Representing	1.8	Money and finances	9
Investigating	12.6	Materials and goods	15
Negotiating	6.0	Marketing	10
Coordinating	15.0	Methods and procedures	26
Evaluating	12.7	Facilities and equipment	11
Supervising	28.4	Total*	98
Total*	100.1		

*Totals do not add to 100 percent because of rounding.

Those activities in which a manager determines goals, makes decisions about the most effective course of action to take in achieving those goals, and formulates general policies or guides to help those who will do the implementing are *planning* activities. They involve scheduling of work, developing budgets which allocate resources and can be used for control, and setting up procedures to carry out the tasks. In the planning process, goals which may have been stated very generally are translated into standards which will be used in evaluation of performance. Later in this section, we will see that planning occupied a larger percentage of time than any other function for high-level managers and was second in importance only to supervising for managers at middle and low levels.

Though *representing* the general interest of the organization through speeches, consultation, and contacts with others outside the organization proved to be a relatively minor managerial function in terms of the time allocated to it, it is an activity that is apparently important to many organizations. Most of us are familiar with certain of the representing activities of higher-level managers; we hear presidents of large organizations speaking to various groups on many issues. One major public utility actively encourages its managers to participate in such activities as Little League, the Chamber of Commerce, the League of Women Voters, and other public, voluntary agencies. Managers represent their firms in community drives. They may prepare news releases about company activities. They attend conventions. Managers are often actively involved in local service organizations such as Kiwanis or Rotary. They are representing their firm.

The analysis of problems by collecting and preparing information (usually in the form of records, reports, and accounts), is a major part of most managerial jobs. Managers must constantly solve problems, and an important preliminary to problem solving as well as planning is collection of relevant data. *Investigation* involves measuring output, collecting information, and researching possible problem solutions.

Transactions with people outside the organization who provide goods or services is *negotiation*. These functions commonly take the form of purchasing activities or marketing activities. Many managers, however, are involved with negotiations with tax collecting agencies, unions, advertising agencies, or public service agencies which in one way or another affect the work of the organization.

Exchanging information with others in the organization (with the exception of subordinates) to relate and adjust interdependent activities and programs is *coordination*. Advising other department heads about deadlines, determining whether or not other departments will be able to meet deadlines, bringing different groups together at appropriate times, informing superiors about what is to be done, are all coordinating activities. Coordination is an especially important managerial activity, since it is through it that the flow of work can be smoothed out.

Often, alternative ways to solve problems must be considered and only one solution implemented. These are *evaluating* functions, and they are performed by all managers. Managers must judge the desirability of alternative strategies. Having the skill to evaluate financial reports and cost information allows a manager to determine when some corrective action must be taken. The appraisal of employee performance is also done by most managers, and such an appraisal may be the essential factor in the determination of pay increases or promotion opportunities for an individual.

The direction, leading, and development of subordinates to insure that they perform their jobs well is *supervising*. A glance at table 1.1 will show that for the group of managers surveyed, supervision made up one of the two major components of their jobs, and presently we will see that even at high management levels, a very substantial amount of supervisory activity is carried on. Basically, supervision consists in making clear to the individual his work assignment, disciplining, defining relationships with other employees, and handling complaints of subordinates. Supervision also involves coaching and training subordinates to improve their skills so that they can perform up to the standards of their jobs, but it may even go so far as to include counseling of subordinates about personal problems that may be affecting their work.

The activity of maintaining the work force is the *staffing* function. It involves the recruitment, selection, and placement of personnel. Managers very frequently interview prospective candidates for jobs. Even though personnel departments may be active in many phases of staffing, the manager is usually very extensively involved, often making the final determination of which one of several candidates will be employed. Promotion, transfer, and placement of employees in work positions are functions performed, to some extent, by most managers.

These are the particular, personalized aspects of staffing which engage the attention of a manager. In a broader sense, managers are engaged in staffing from the larger perspective of the organizational unit or the firm. As they plan the short- and long-range activities of their units, managers must plan for the use not only of financial and material resources, but of human resources as well. Managers must constantly be concerned with plans and prospects for acquisition of competent people to carry out the objectives of the organization.

Areas of Technical Concern to Managers

Mahoney, Jerdee, and Carroll (1963) also identified the areas of technical knowledge in which these management functions are performed. Of course a manager cannot be expected to have high levels of skills in all of these technical areas. More than likely, an individual will be well versed in one or two and have some limited knowledge about others. These technical areas are:

1. Personnel   4. Marketing
2. Money and Finances   5. Methods and Procedures
3. Materials and Goods 6. Facilities and Equipment

Personnel activities generally include the functions of recruiting, selection, hiring, and promotion of employees. Labor relations activities, such as collective bargaining, are frequently associated with the personnel function. Performance evaluation, promotion programs, and wage and salary administration are part of the area of technical expertise.

Funds that flow in and out of an organization—*money and finances* —are a resource which is used to secure the goods and services needed to exist. At the higher levels of responsibility, managers are concerned with the acquisition, management, and investment of capital resources for the firm. Handling payments of customers and clients, budgeting activities, and the more general area of accounting and controls are among the financial responsibilities of managers at various levels. Many of the activities of this area of technical competence are performed by accounting departments, auditor's office, and cost control departments.

Materials management, ranging from the determination of requirements to acquisition and inventory, is a critical function. Buying materials of too high quality means excess costs are incurred needlessly. Likewise, low-quality raw materials will require more inspection, more control, and higher scrap rates. Inventories of both raw materials and finished goods represent very large capital investments, and the purchasing of *materials and goods,* function is therefore one from which substantial cost savings can be realized. The control, storage, and transferring of inventory from one part of an organization to another, as well as to customers, is part of this technical field.

The *marketing* activities of buying, selling, advertising, promotion, and distribution all require specialized information. The preparation of market forecasts and the development of subsequent marketing plans must be based on extensive knowledge of the customer, pricing strategies, and distribution systems.

Every organization has certain sequenced activities by which certain tasks are performed—their *methods and procedures.* The orderly sequencing of activities to accomplish a particular task is called a "procedure." Procedures may specify the flow of information through the organization. For example, a manager proposing an addition to a general product line may be required to do a return-on-investment analysis of the particular item and submit that analysis, along with a description of the new product, to a committee for approval.

The technology which an organization uses to produce its products usually takes the form of some sort of physical *facilities and equipment.* Assembly lines, computers, artist's boards, typewriters, or audio visual equipment in classrooms are all types of equipment used to produce a product or service. Managers, of necessity, must have some knowledge of and competence with the equipment used by their firm.

How Managerial Jobs Differ by Organizational Level

The percentage of time that the average manager spends on each function and in various areas of competence is shown in table 1.1. Mahoney, Jerdee, and Carroll (1965) also used each manager's functional time allocations to place them in one of eight managerial job types based on how most of their time was spent. The distribution of these job types at different levels of management is shown in figure 1.1. As this figure shows, certain types of managerial jobs are much more likely to be found at some levels than others. For example, the percentage of managers who do planning as their major activity

FIGURE 1.1 Changing Jobs of Managers

Distribution of Assignments at Each Organizational Level
Totals do not add up to 100 percent because of rounding.

Low (N=191)		Middle (N=131)		High (N=130)	
Planner	15%	Planner	18%	Planner	28%
Investigator	8%	Investigator	8%		
Coordinator	5%	Coordinator	7%	Investigator	6%
Evaluator	2%	Evaluator	5%	Coordinator	8%
				Evaluator	8%
Supervisor	51%	Supervisor	36%	Supervisor	22%
				Negotiator	3%
		Negotiator	8%	Multispecialist	5%
Negotiator	6%	Multispecialist	8%		
Multispecialist	6%			Generalist	20%
Generalist	9%	Generalist	10%		

Source: Thomas A. Mahoney, Thomas H. Jerdee, and Stephen J. Carroll, "The Job(s) of Management," *Industrial Relations,* vol. 4, no. 2 (Feb. 1965), 97–110.

increases constantly from the lower levels to the highest levels of management. The percentage of managers who spend the most significant amount of their time in supervising steadily decreases from the lower to the higher levels of management.

Figure 1.2 is an organization chart depicting an industrial organization. The illustration is a manufacturing firm, but it could have as easily been a large government agency. There are three major management levels: (1) supervisory, (2) middle, and (3) top.

Lower or Supervisory Management.   This level is the only one at which a manager does not supervise other managers. A lower-level manager has responsibility for operative employees, or specialists. Plant foremen, heads of secretarial pools, or a supervisor of data processing fall into this category.

FIGURE 1.2   Management Levels in a Large Organization

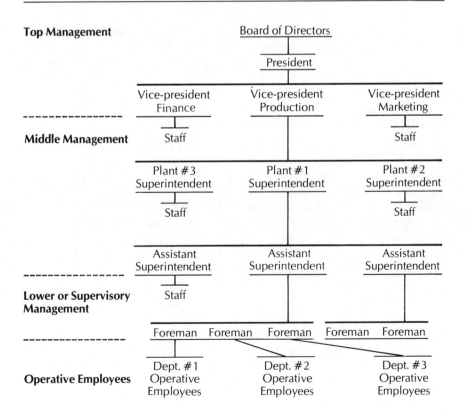

Middle Management.   At this level, individuals supervise other
managers as well as operative employees. They are responsible for
translating general policies made by top management into decisions to
be implemented by the lower echelons. For example, the top management group might institute a policy of cost reduction. The middle
management group decides where and how it can be done. The supervisory level sees that the operative employees carry out the program of
action to achieve the cost reduction.

Top Management.   Top management is the small group of employees
at the highest level of the organization. It includes the board of directors, president (or chief executive officer), and the immediate groups
that make decisions about organization objectives and how to get
there.

   Top management assesses market conditions and translates them
into action steps. It interprets the external environment and attempts
to ease the adjustment of the organization to it. As we will see, this
book takes a contingency perspective, which means that the appropriate way to manage and makes decisions depends upon the external
conditions. Top management's function is to read the environment
(markets, sources of supply, government relations, etc.) and decide
how to deal with it.

Improving Management Skills

There are differences in the way outstanding individuals perform in
any field—art, music, sports, and business—yet in every field there
are some basic guides, approaches, or theories which give some direction to a novice and to which the expert must return when his performance levels begin to deteriorate. These theories, or guides, can be
translated into instructions which are used to teach others how to act
in a particular situation. Such a body of ideas and concepts from
which appropriate instructions can be derived exist in most areas of
human endeavor, and they also exist for management.

   One body of ideas by which management is taught is called the
"principles approach." For many years, management teachers
prescribed what managers should do. The principles approach is
prescriptive and normative. Principles of management are general
guides to handling the problems that an executive encounters in work
situations. In effect, they tell a manager what to do when faced with
problems of designing an organization, making decisions, or dealing
with people. One of the more extensively developed books using this

approach is by Ralph C. Davis. He states a number of principles in his book, *Fundamentals of Top Management (1951)*. To illustrate one such principle, we cite one called the "principle of compulsory staff advice." This principle of management focuses on the relationship between staff units and line executives. Staff units (support or advisory groups) make recommendations to executives which often do not receive proper weighting in decision making. In order to insure that staff units are consulted appropriately, the principle of compulsory staff advice states that:

> No decision or important problem should be rendered or action taken by a responsible line executive until all who may be able to contribute significantly to the success of the mission through advice and assistance have had an opportunity to do so (Davis, 1951).

Principles of management were developed for nearly every phase of the managerial task. There were principles of leadership, of objectives, of single accountability, of unity of command, of equity, of exception —virtually every area with which a manager might be concerned. One of the things the existence of the principles points up is that a great deal of thought has been given to how to manage effectively.

Where did the "principles" come from? For the most part these guides to management decisions and actions were derived from the *experiences* of early writers on the subject. These writers, from the scientific management and administrative approach schools of thought (we will have more to say about these two schools in chap. 2) formulated principles from their own experiences in government and industry. From the early part of this century until about 1955, these significant contributors to management theory all drew upon their own experiences in the work place to formulate "principles." Experience, reflective analysis, and deductive logic were the primary research and theoretical approaches.

In the late '50s and the '60s, however, the principles approach came under severe criticism from a new group of management writers. Principles approaches tended to be "empirically vacuous" said March and Simon (1958), since they were not based on controlled studies, but rather on observation and experience. In fact, many critics noted that in many organizations, principles were violated, but the organization was still effective. Some principles were inconsistent with others. Carzo (1961) shows the contradiction between the "principle of span of control," which says that "no superior can supervise directly the work of more than five or six subordinates whose work is interrelated" and the "principle that there should be as few levels as possible in an organization."

By restricting or limiting the span of control, an organization—especially one that is growing—must increase the number of scalar levels and the administrative distance between individuals. This development inevitably produces excessive red tape and waste of time and effort. Obviously, adherence to the principle of span of control conflicts with the principle that requires a minimum number of organizational levels.

If principles were violated or were inconsistent with each other, how could a principle be a principle? If they were not followed, it did not seem to matter. "Principles" were criticized because they were not based on empirical research, because they were not consistent with other principles, and also because they were too rigid. Some critics of the principles approach rejected it because they argued that principles told managers the "one best way" to manage and there was no one best way. This criticism is, of course, hollow. There is no one best way to do anything. Proponents of the principles approach recognized that not all cases would fall within the guides they prescribed, but, critics generally failed to note these reservations.

Principles are, of course, useful guides to action. They give the manager some place to start when faced with a problem and, if they are not viewed as rigid requirements, they can be very helpful in finding a solution. In fact, Charles Perrow has said that

Though the classical theory was derided for presenting principles that were only proverbs, all the resources of organization theory and research have not managed to substitute better principles (or proverbs) for those ridiculed. . . . These principles have worked and are still working, for they address themselves to the very real problems of management. . . (1970).

Principles are a basic, and an important, component of the knowledge required to be successful in any endeavor. In all fields there must be a basis for the development of additional competence, and competence can only emerge after one has mastered the fundamentals and has the capacity to subsequently use them. Effective managers use the principles of management as they are needed.

But the critics of principles have a cogent point: There are some conditions where a "principle" works and others where it doesn't. That, however, is no reason to ignore the experience embodied in them. In this book, we will try to be as specific as possible about the conditions under which principles, or similar guides, may be appropriate.

Managerial Process Contingency Theory

The application of management fundamentals, principles, or theory, can only be a starting point for learning, application and improvement. How a basic concept is used in practice always depends upon a variety of factors. But to say that "the correct way to apply an idea depends upon the circumstances" says nothing to anyone—it is indeed vacuous. To improve the application of concepts in order to secure better performance, it is necessary to specify the individual and organizational conditions which modify managerial activity; that is, to specify the circumstances on which correct application of a concept depends.

In this book we present our version of management process contingency theory, a theory which integrates the ideas from a wide range of disciplines to make it possible to be more prescriptive about how to manage under different sets of circumstances. The relevant ideas of "principles" theorists are here, as are those from other schools of management and organizational behavior theory, and from the disciplines of psychology, sociology, and economics.

Some Basic Premises

Our major theme is that there are some managerial strategies more appropriate than others in certain circumstances. A managerial strategy is a specific way that an individual carries out the managerial process. For instance, the *evaluation* function involves, in part, determining how well someone performs his job. When a manager evaluates someone, he then gives that person feedback. One manager's evaluation strategy might be to assess quantitative measures of a subordinate's output, such as the volume of sales generated by a salesman. A second manager may be more concerned with evaluating whether or not the salesman acts in an "appropriate" way with customers. In providing feedback, one manager may be very blunt and direct, giving exactly the information he believes a subordinate needs. A second manager may use an indirect approach and act in more of a counseling and advisory fashion with subordinates.

The best way to perform the evaluating function, as well as other managerial functions, depends upon many factors, such as the personalities involved and the requirements of the different jobs being managed. Our approach throughout this book is to specify those things upon which the best way depends. That is what we mean by *managerial process contingency theory*. In deciding which strategy is best, the two factors managers must consider are:

1. The *structure* of the organization
2. The *personnel* in the organization

The management process is performed within the constraints imposed by these two factors. To a great degree, they are significantly affected by forces beyond the control of the manager. He may, in fact, have very little to say about either the structure of the organization or the personalities of the individuals working in it. They represent conditions that the manager has to live with and manage within. To manage well, a manager must recognize that every individual has his own individual outlooks, attitudes, and abilities and will react in different ways to the organization in which he works. The manager must recognize this in in order to be able to anticipate how the individuals he is managing will respond to their work situation and to his endeavors to guide them.

Organization Structure.   The organization structure is the pattern of relationships among the individuals in the organization. The *formal structure* is composed of job descriptions, organization charts, procedures, and other written documents which define and describe how individuals should work with each other. The *nonformal structure* is the pattern of relationships that emerge among people that are not specified in these written documents. It is their behavior.

In some organizations, the work is very repetitive, and the structure is fixed and fairly rigid. To a great degree, it is unchanging. In other organizations the work is more creative and less repetitive, and the structure of the organization is accordingly more flexible, there is more looseness, more freedom in defining what employees do.

The design of an organization's structure must take into account both external and internal pressures. All organizations attempt to adapt to the pressures placed on them, but they differ in the degree to which they successfully adapt.

The external pressures on an organization are especially critical. Customers and clients demand goods and services. Government agencies require compliance with regulations. Unions try to secure benefits for their members. The nature of these external pressures is important, but even more important is their degree of uncertainty. If managers are able to predict with a high degree of accuracy what the demands may be, they then can devise ways to deal with them. For instance, if it is known that consumer demand for a product will be evenly distributed throughout the year, as well as throughout a particular geographical region, then a firm can develop a relatively stable sales and marketing strategy. It can also, if the technology is available, utilize efficient production forms. When there is a high degree of uncertainty, however—when the manager is unable to predict fairly accurately—the firm cannot do this. What it must do, in any case, is adapt itself to its environment, to the particular external pressures upon it.

Some organizations exist in environments characterized by more uncertainty than others. Research suggests that when there is a great deal of environmental uncertainty, a less rigidly structured organization works best (Friedlander, 1970; Burns and Stalker, 1961). In such an environmental setting, the work of individuals will be less repetitive, perhaps more creative. We call this kind of structure a *dynamic,* or *flexible* organization.

When there is a high degree of environmental certainty, a highly structured organization works best. Such organizations, operating in a more certain environment, are called *hierarchical* or *bureaucratic*. In them, work is more routine and repetitive than it is in the dynamic organization.

The Personnel.   Organizations, structured in certain ways, will attract, and be chosen by, individuals with certain kinds of skills and personality characteristics. For instance, people with a need for a great deal of freedom and latitude in determining what they do seek to avoid bureaucratic organizations.

A person's attitude toward work is a function of his experiences at home as a child, and later on in schools. As we have said, the manager must try to understand the personality structures that result from these early experiences in order to deal effectively in a supervisory context with subordinates. The different reactions of individuals in different types of organizations should determine the nature of interpersonal relationships between managers and subordinates.

Plan of This Book

There is, then, always a relationship between the organization structure, its personnel, and effective ways of carrying out the managerial process. Obviously, a manager dealing with a group of operative

employees performing moderately skilled jobs for which little extensive training is required (as would be the case, say, of the supervisor
of a secretarial pool) must of necessity deal with subordinates differently than the manager of a group of highly trained specialists, such as
computer programmers, or engineers. The important question is how
managers can learn to operate effectively in different situations. This
book attempts to show them how they can.

Figure 1.3 shows the basic structure of the book. In chapter 2, we
discuss some of the more important early conceptions of management
and organization thinking and show how the contingency approach
evolved from them. Chapters 3, 4, and 5 deal with different character-

FIGURE 1.3   Plan of the Book

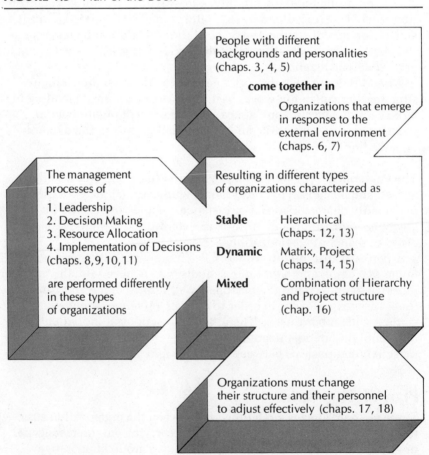

People with different
backgrounds and personalities
(chaps. 3, 4, 5)

come together in

Organizations that emerge
in response to the
external environment
(chaps. 6, 7)

The management
processes of

1. Leadership
2. Decision Making
3. Resource Allocation
4. Implementation of Decisions
(chaps. 8, 9, 10, 11)

are performed differently
in these types
of organizations

Resulting in different types
of organizations characterized as

Stable   Hierarchical
(chaps. 12, 13)

Dynamic   Matrix, Project
(chaps. 14, 15)

Mixed   Combination of Hierarchy
and Project structure
(chap. 16)

Organizations must change
their structure and their personnel
to adjust effectively (chaps. 17, 18)

istics of individuals and groups. In these three chapters, we show how people get to be what they are before they enter an organization, and how they adjust after they are there. This helps us understand the reason for the many differences in attitudes, values, and beliefs among people, differences which affect the way they react to their work situations.

Whether the organization structure is bureaucratic or dynamic emerges as a result of the external environment, and this is discussed in chapters 6 and 7, which deal with the question, "How do organizations get to be what they are?" Chapter 6 discusses the environment of organizations, and examines the degree of uncertainty in the market and technological environment. The way environmental uncertainty is related to the different forms of organization is discussed in chapter 7, in which we define two different types of organizations. The hierarchical, or *bureaucratic*, organization is characterized by relatively fixed relationships among people. Jobs are well-defined and typically are highly routine. Often there is a very heavy capital investment in plant and equipment which takes the form of assembly-line technology. Decision making is centralized at the top management level. The dynamic, or flexible organization, on the other hand, is less rigid. In dynamic organizations, individuals have a great deal more freedom in determining how their work is to be accomplished and usually need to be resourceful and adaptive in meeting varying demands. Personnel may move from one project to another. Authority-responsibility relationships change as the nature of problems changes. These two extremes are not the only kinds of organization, however, and chapter 7 also describes two *mixed* forms, organizations in which one part of the system is hierarchical while the other part is dynamic. Special problems for managers occur in this mixed form perhaps the most important of which is to integrate effectively the different units.

Chapters 8, 9, 10, and 11 describe the general phases of the management process. These consist of the activities of (1) leadership, (2) decision making, (3) resource allocation, and (4) implementation of decisions.

Leadership is a process of influencing other people. Managers must be able to influence those who work for them to meet the requirements of the organization. Influence can flow from the personal characteristics of the manager. It can also result from the position a person is in; in many cases, a person responds to his superior's efforts to influence him merely because he believes it is appropriate to do what he is told by a superior. The right leadership style is a function of the situation and the characteristics of the individuals to be led.

Decision making is another managerial activity. In the context of the
work situation, managers select from various alternatives the course of
action which is most likely to achieve objectives. This requires the
ability to set objectives, predict outcomes, and evaluate alternatives so
that the alternative selected is the one most likely to yield the desired
result.

Resource allocation is a more specific form of decision making.
Once objectives have been set and a plan of action determined, the
manager must acquire and bring together the necessary resources.
These are then distributed, or allocated, to various segments of the
organization which then use them for goal achievement.

Implementing decisions is of course the process of determining—
once decisions have been made—that they are accepted and carried
out by others. In many cases acceptance of decisions by subordinates
is essential if work is to be effectively done. In chapter 11 we discuss
approaches to decision acceptance as well as methods for establishing
objectives for an organization and its members and communicating
objectives to those who will work to meet them.

In chapters 12 through 15 we discuss in detail the most effective
methods of performing managerial functions in view of the type of
organization being managed. We examine more fully the structure and
personnel of bureaucratic and flexible organizations, and we consider
in detail which forms of leadership, decision making, resource allocation, and other management techniques are most appropriate to the
circumstances we have defined. In keeping with the special needs of
these distinctive types, we examine decision-making technology
under conditions of certainty, risk, and uncertainty, and consider how
these techniques might be appropriate to the needs of organizations
operating in particular types of environments.

It should be apparent, as we have noted, that organization structures
are seldom polarized at bureaucratic or flexible extremes. An organization may have both hierarchical or flexible characteristics, and very
commonly bureaucratic and flexible units—for example, the production department and the research department—may be found within a
single organization. Coordination and integration strategies to solve
the special problems engendered in these mixed organizations are the
subject of chapter 16.

Finally, the book examines organization change. The manner in
which the internal structure of an organization may change to adapt
more effectively to its external environment is considered in chapter
17, along with problems associated with growth, organizational strategy, and organizational design. In chapter 18, the focus is on tech-

niques and methods of changing the human factors in an organization. A theory of the development of personnel outlines the basic conditions which must exist to improve individual performance and change attitudes, and some of the more widely accepted methods of organization development, such as the "grid" approach of Blake and Mouton (1964) and management by objectives, are considered.

Chapter 19 provides a brief summary of the book along with a discussion of the characteristics of the effective organization and some of the environmental issues and problems which effective organizations must relate to in the near future.

In sum, then, this book is premised on management contingency process theory, which—to repeat—holds that the appropriate management strategy is determined by the situation. We will show how different situations call for different organization structures, as well as different processes and strategies of management, and what the different situations, structures, and strategies are.

Discussion Questions

1. How does your personal conception of "management" differ from the one presented in this chapter?

2. What differentiates a manager's job from a worker's?

3. Is there a difference between managers and decision makers? If so, what is it?

4. Think about the eight steps of the management process. What other functions would you consider important?

5. Do you believe that a good manager of, say, a marketing sales staff could manage a research laboratory as well? What is the reason for your answer?

6. What are the basic differences in how managerial work varies as a function of organization level?

7. Think about the following statements:
   a) Management is common sense.
   b) Management is an intuitive skill.
   True or false or some of both?

8. What is your understanding of managerial process contingency theory?

9. Of what utility are "principles" to any area of study? Can you think of a field where "principles" are extremely important? Another where they are of no significance whatever?

Chapter 2

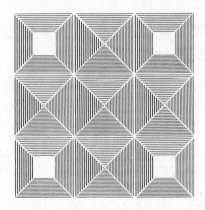

Since man first grouped together, he has tried to organize his own activities and those of others so that they are more efficient. Hoagland (1964), for example, shows how a famous study by Frederick Taylor (who is called the "father of scientific management," because his writings at the turn of the century were seminal to the contemporary study of management problems) can be traced back at least to the Renaissance. One of Taylor's most famous studies centered on the task of "shoveling." Concerned with increasing the productivity of common laborers, Taylor conducted research to determine the most efficient way to perform this task. Hoagland, through historical documents, traces the genesis of this study back to Taylor's teachers in the mid-19th century and farther back to work on the same problem by many others, including Leonardo da Vinci. In this chapter, we present some of the more important historical antecedents of modern management theory.

Some Antecedents
of Modern Management Thinking

In the ancient world, management techniques were used to achieve religious, military, and political goals. (Much of this discussion follows George [1972].) It was in organizations of this type that management thinking originated, and writing on the art of management, as well as the development of various managerial tools and procedures, was about and for such organizations. There were few, if any, economic organizations of the kind we know today. Manufactur-

A Short History of Management

ing, retailing, and distribution organizations of the size we know did not exist.

In ancient Egypt, the pyramids, built for religious and political purposes, were constructed primarily with human labor and crude equipment. One great pyramid contains more than 2 million stones, each weighing about 2½ tons. The individual stones were cut in a quarry, moved by water and land to the pyramid site, and then placed precisely into their assigned positions, often very high. The construction required the labor of 100,000 men working for 20 years, and the problems of planning the work, organizing the work teams, and maintaining such a large work force, as well as the motivation and supervision problems, were obviously tremendous. Egyptian writings surviving from this period make it clear that the pyramid builders thought about these problems and developed management advice for future generations.

Egypt governed a large geographic territory, and the rulers tried various methods of managing their empire until finally settling upon a system which gave local areas autonomy so long as certain key directives from the central government were followed. The Egyptians also invented methods of record keeping, methods they found especially useful in tax collecting, and established rules regulating the activities of individuals engaged in various specialized trades. Similar laws and rules governing economic relationships were developed, and written about in Babylonia, China, Greece, and India. Military operations also required managerial skills of a high order, and the ancient Persians and Romans developed elaborate management techniques for conducting their vast military undertakings.

The Middle Ages and the Renaissance

Complex economic organizations first began to develop during the
Middle Ages. Organizations quite modern in character originated in
Italy during this period, and became especially advanced in Venice by
the 15th century. Many merchants of Venice formed partnerships,
joint ventures, and trading companies. There were some obvious
advantages to this form of economic ownership. Since much business
was in sea trade, losses were often very substantial when ships were
lost. Financing a particular expedition by several families, rather than
by only one, reduced the risks involved in such an undertaking. The
profits were also reduced by spreading the risk, of course, but joint
financing made possible far more extensive undertakings than would
otherwise have been the case.

The Venetians were not only adept in the financing, but also in the
operation of large-scale manufacturing enterprises. The famous
Arsenal of Venice, for example, which was put into operation in 1436
to manufacture arms needed to protect the trade of the city used many
modern production methods and inventory techniques. A form of
assembly-line process was used in outfitting ships. Warehouses were
arrayed on the sides of a canal so that when the ships were towed
along it, parts and supplies from the warehouses were placed on ships
in their proper sequence. Standard parts and an emphasis on efficiency also characterized the production system. Finally, the Arsenal
employed many artisans and manual workers, and used many
personnel techniques, such as performance rating and incentive wage
systems, similar to those used today.

For the most part, however, until the Industrial Revolution
economic organizations were primarily involved in trade and finance.
Very little activity centered on the manufacturing processes as we
know them today. Most production, especially that of consumer
goods, was carried on in the home. True, there were craftsmen in
metals, woods, leather, and so forth, but one factor which severely
limited the growth of manufacturing was the difficulty of harnessing
power.

The Industrial Revolution

The Industrial Revolution came to different parts of the world at
different times. In the late 1700s, it may be said to have begun in
England with the invention of the steam engine. This provided a
simple, flexible means of converting natural materials such as coal

into energy to drive belts, turn wheels, and provide other forms of mechanical motion. Since the steam engine provided such energy anywhere, factories of considerable size could be located in many different places. About the same time came new methods of smelting iron, which also facilitated industrial growth.

The factory system became widespread during the Industrial Revolution. During the early 18th century the domestic system prevailed. To use textiles as an example, with this method of production a farmer and his family would produce cloth on their own loom and sell their finished products at the local fair for whatever they could get. The type of production that succeeded this system was the putting-out system. Entrepreneurs, acting as brokers, contracted for a family's output at a fixed price and supplied the family with raw materials. This turned the farmer into an employee of the broker. When it then became obvious that it would be more efficient to have all of the manpower and the equipment under direct supervision in one building, the factory system began to emerge.

Development and widespread use of power to run machines made the factory possible. A factory, as we know it, requires equipment to be at a particular location, rather than spread through the countryside. Since transportation in the early 19th century was limited and workers had to live close to their jobs, the population started to move from the farm into the cities, where the factories were located. This movement created rapid urban growth, industrial slums, and health and other social problems, some of which are still with us.

The corporate form of ownership also stimulated the growth of the factory system. Investors or owners of a corporation are liable only for the amount of their respective investments, and can thus spread their risks with minimal liability. In addition, the corporate form of ownership is an excellent way to accumulate the capital needed to build and equip a large factory.

But harnessing power with a steam engine was only part of the impetus to economic growth during the Industrial Revolution. About the same time that Watt invented the steam engine, another important event took place that shaped men's thinking about how economic affairs should be arranged. Adam Smith, an economic philosopher published *The Wealth of Nations* (see item 2.1).

This book, along with other ideas about industrial freedom and liberty that were gaining acceptance at this time, spurred a change in thinking that was to have a profound impact on the economic sectors of society. Prior to the late 1700s, it was generally held that economic decisions should be made by the state. Resource allocations were

decided by a small cadre of men around the king, or simply by the
king himself. Smith believed that these decisions were better made by
individuals acting in their own self-interest. Under these conditions,
he asserted, the common good would be enhanced. This concept
forms the basic assumptions underlying classic economic theory of
markets, especially the competitive model.

The concept is based on the conviction that men and institutions
must be free to compete, because competition is in accord with
natural law. Men, institutions, and ideas, through competition, prove
their fitness for survival. Free competition and free markets lead to the
maximum benefit for mankind. The self-interests of various segments
of the economy striving to maximize their own well-being will lead to
a self-regulation of the economic system. There is no need for political
interference. The economy will be guided by the "invisible hand," not
the heavy hand of the sovereign. As Smith put it:

> Every individual endeavors to employ his capital so that its produce
> may be of greatest value. He generally neither intends to promote
> the public interest, nor knows how much he is promoting it. He
> intends only his own security, only his own gain. And he is in this
> led by an *invisible hand* to promote an end which was no part of
> his intention. By pursuing his own interest he frequently promotes
> that of society more effectively than when he really intends to
> promote it.

Smith also convincingly argued that the wealth of a nation did not
rest in the quantities of gold it held. The idea that it did had led to
wars and explorations in which the primary purpose was to increase a
nation's storehouse of gold. Smith showed how the wealth of a nation
could be advanced by increasing the productivity of the capital and
productive components of society.

The new economic philosophy, coupled with advancing technology, shifted the wealth in the society. A new class emerged in England
and in the other countries where similar developments took place.
The new class came into conflict (still not fully resolved) with the old,
landed class for political and economic supremacy. The new industri-
alists had a different set of ideas about "right," "wrong," and "importance" than did the old, landed class. The new class emphasized
individual initiative and individual responsibility. The old, landed
class felt more responsibility for their workers than did the new class.
The newer class had a much stronger work orientation than did the

landed class, and it did not emphasize intellectual, cultural, and recreational pursuits to the same degree as the landed gentry.

ITEM 2.1. Adam Smith

The Revolutionary of Oeconomy

He was the classic absent-minded professor, a philosopher so immersed in his studies that he often seemed to lose touch with life around him. At social gatherings, he would stand alone talking silently to himself, moving his lips and smiling—although, said a friend, if someone interrupted his reverie, "he immediately began a harangue." As a classroom lecturer, he would stutter and stammer for at least a quarter of an hour before hitting his oratorical stride. Contemporaries loved to talk about the night that he got out of bed absorbed in some theory and wandered 15 miles in his dressing gown before thinking to wonder where he was. Altogether, Adam Smith was scarcely the man to whom an ambitious moneymaker would turn for guidance on the intensely practical questions of how prices, profits and wages are determined.

Yet Smith devoted many of his meditations to just such questions, with startling results. He spent at least ten years writing a book that friends despaired of his ever finishing. Smith described himself as an agonizingly slow workman "who do and undo everything I write at least half a dozen times before I can be tolerably pleased with it." He worked out most of the wording on solitary walks along the windswept shores near his home town of Kirkcaldy, Scotland, then often dictated the results to an amanuensis. He finally published the work in March 1776, under the mouth-filling title *An Inquiry into the Nature and Causes of the Wealth of Nations,* and thereby laid the intellectual foundations of capitalism.

It was a rarely equaled example of the detached scholar's ability to explain and influence the world of affairs. Smith's absorption in economics, which he called "political oeconomy," was a product of sheer intellectual curiosity. That curiosity led him to read everything that he could find about money, to study statutes on trade, interview businessmen and visit workshops *(The Wealth of Nations* opens with a detailed description of a pin factory)—but not to practice what he preached. Though he considered the desire to accumulate wealth an overwhelmingly powerful motive for humanity in general, he chose for himself what he called the "unprosperous" profession of scholar and man of letters.

His biography consists of little more than a professor's résumé: son of a collector of customers; student at Oxford; a popular lecturer at Edinburgh University; tutor to the young Duke of Buccleuch; full professor of logic and then of moral philosophy at Glasgow; and author in 1759 of a philosophical treatise, *The Theory of Moral Sentiments.* A bachelor, Smith relied on his mother and a maiden cousin to keep house; if any love affairs ever distracted him from his studies, they have gone unrecorded. "I am a beau in nothing but my books," he once remarked, while showing off his 3,000-volume library to a friend.

Though Smith was a quiet scholar, he was scarcely bloodless. He comes fully alive in his writings as a skeptical observer of human nature, a staunch advocate of political as well as economic liberty, and now and then something of a deadpan Scottish wit. Much of *The Wealth of Nations* is unreadable today, but the browser comes across unexpected bits of phrasemaking—for example, the first description of England as "a nation of shopkeepers." It was no compliment; Smith complained that only such a nation could follow so mean-spirited a policy as Britain's colonial exploitation of its American colonies.

Time, July 14, 1975

Reprinted by permission from TIME, The Weekly Newsmagazine; Copyright Time Inc.

The Growth of Industry in the United States

Before the American Revolution there was little industry in the Colonies, largely because of the sparse population, the lack of capital, and restrictive legislation from England which hindered manufacturing. The Revolution gave some impetus to industry, however, and manufacturing grew slowly until the 1820s, when a number of inventions and technical advances stimulated its growth. In the first half of the 19th century, most U.S. factories were small, and corporate ownership was not nearly as popular as individual or partnership forms. Labor was scarce. In fact, about half of all factory workers were children. In the 1840s and 1850s the construction of new roads, railroads, and canals stimulated industrial growth. About the same time, increased immigration furnished the large labor force necessary for work in factories, railroads, and coal mines.

The Civil War increased the rate of U.S. industrial growth even further, especially in steel, textiles, leather, meat packing, and prepared foods. The railroads opened the West, stimulating demand for many products manufactured in the East, and new inventions and developments also fostered increased industrialization. Two new methods of producing steel, for example, the Bessemer and the open hearth process, were developed in Europe. These were imported to the United States, and the steel industry began its growth to the gigantic size it has today. The oil industry was started when George Bissell was informed by a chemistry professor at Yale that crude oil from western Pennsylvania could be converted into an excellent illuminant, with valuable byproducts resulting from the production process. John D. Rockefeller and others created an oil industry that became one of the world's strongest economic forces.

The steel and oil industries depended on the railroads to transport their products, while the railroads were major purchasers of steel for their tracks. The network of railroads which eventually spanned the country also made it possible to consolidate smaller factories geared to the needs of particular regions, and efficiencies of size became possible.

As in England, the spirit of laissez-faire capitalism characterized U.S. economic life. The owners of large firms became known as "robber barons" and were accused of having little concern for anything except wealth and power. A flaw was becoming apparent in the theory of competition. Adam Smith's argument had been that if individuals were left alone to compete freely, the general well-being would be served, but this conclusion was based on the assumption that there would be a *large* number of buyers *and* a *large* number of sellers. As huge fortunes were accumulated in the United States, many smaller sellers were consolidated into fewer larger ones, and the *monopoly*—a case in which a single firm has almost complete control of the quality and price of its goods and services—emerged. When goods or services such as oil, steel, and rail transportation are vital to the society, those who control them have enormous power, and can misuse it. In time, U.S. monopolies were accused of practices harmful to society: fixing prices, rather than having them result from competitive market forces, and forcing raw material producers to accept the monopolist's price, since there were few other customers.

The Sherman Anti-Trust Act was passed in 1890 as a response to these practices. It prohibited monopoly or tendency toward monopoly. While it is considered by many to be the beginning of a too extensive government regulation of business, the Sherman Act was designed to produce the same result as laissez-faire capitalism— increased social benefits, since the economy, unregulated, was not working as intended in theory. In any event, the Sherman Act significantly affected what an industrialist could do. With its enactment there was no longer unbridled freedom to act only in the best interests of a given firm. There were now some things that a businessman couldn't do, and these constraints made it more difficult to maximize profit. For instance, the Act made it illegal to form a trust to raise prices arbitrarily. As a result, owners had to begin to focus more sharply on managing the resources of the business.

Just as U.S. industry grew after the Civil War, so did the unrest of U.S. labor. By the mid-1870s, workers were beginning to react against extremely difficult and often unreasonable working conditions. Because of increased immigration after the war, there was a vast labor supply available to industry. Because workers had both better working conditions in the United States than they had in Europe, and the promise and hope of more, they tended to be somewhat more tolerant of difficult working conditions. But by the 1880s, poor working conditions, low wages, and an almost total lack of job security were stimulating intensive union activity, especially in the coal-mining industry.

Unions were not widely successful in obtaining contracts, but they were instrumental in bringing about legislation covering working conditions. Like the Sherman Act, these laws were a constraint on the decisions that a businessman could make. Industry was powerful, but abrasive; growing, but inefficient. It drew recklessly on the vast human and physical resources available to it.

It was in this societal and economic milieu of a growing economy, increased regulation, and advancing unionism that the scientific management movement began.

Contemporary Management Movements

The times were ripe, then, for the emergence of people such as Frederick W. Taylor and his colleagues in scientific management. Around 1900 managers began to experiment with ways to use raw materials, men, and equipment more efficiently. When their experiments met with success, their ideas were sought out by others who had similar problems. Since that time, numerous practitioners and theorists have contributed to the present state of the modern art and practice of management. They came from diverse backgrounds, ranging from engineering to journalism, and in a short history it is impossible to give all of them the kind of treatment they deserve. As George (1968) has noted, to "write a history of management is to write a history of man." In this section, we want to point out the major approaches and some of the important contributors to each.

There are five major schools of thought about management: (1) scientific management, (2) administrative theory, (3) the behavioral approach, (4) management science, and (5) the contingency approach. We discuss some of the major ideas of and contributions to each school of thought in this section. Figure 2.1 depicts the development of management thinking since 1900. The primary thrust comes from the *scientific management* movement and the work of Taylor.

The year 1925, with the publication of Henri Fayol's *General and Industrial Management* in France, marked the beginning of the *administrative theory* era. The behavioral approach to management (also called the "human relations" approach) is generally acknowledged to have begun around 1927, with the advent of the Hawthorne studies, while World War II saw the birth of operations research or *management science*. Interdisciplinary teams were brought together to solve major war problems. Psychologists, economists, but especially engineers and mathematicians, contributed to this line of thinking.

The *contingency approach* can be traced back to at least 1949 and Selznick's study, *TVA and the Grass Roots*. Later studies and theory development in this area provided a basis for potential integration of the varied strains of thought from the other approaches.

The major ideas from the five different points of view are discussed here. The reader will note the divergencies. By the mid-1960s, there was a great deal of confusion in management thinking because of the many schools of thought. Perhaps we are closer today to achieving a degree of integration of them.

FIGURE 2.1 Sources of Modern Management Ideas

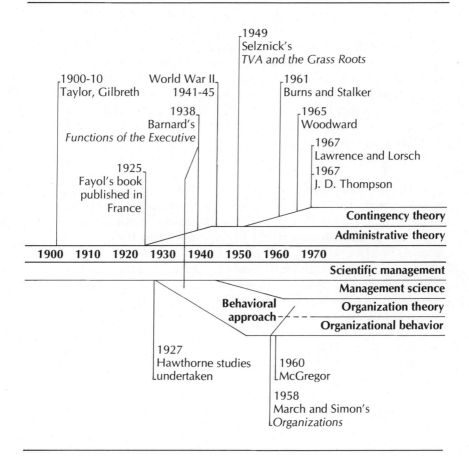

The Scientific Management Approach

Scientific management was focused on the lowest level of the organization, the worker and his boss. The basic question to which most scientific management research was addressed was: "How can the job be designed most efficiently?" Taylor, who was born to a well-to-do Philadelphia family, but who was unable to complete college because of poor eyesight, was the best known of these researchers. He took a job in industry as an apprentice at the Midvale Steel Company in 1878, and quickly rose through the ranks to become chief engineer in 1884, at the age of 28.

Based on his experiences and studies, Taylor developed many ideas to increase management efficiency, and became widely sought as a consultant to other firms. His ideas, when applied, met with considerable success. He presented papers reporting his results to professional engineering societies and later in several books (Taylor, 1947).

Henry L. Gantt was a colleague of Taylor's and worked with him on several consulting projects. Frank and Lillian Gilbreth were also leaders in the scientific management movement. Together the Gilbreths worked to develop scientific approaches to measuring work and designing efficient work practices. Dexter Kimball, whose contribution's are noted in item 2.2, was also active in scientific management. Scientific management is a collection of ideas on management by these, and other writers.

Some of the more important ideas of scientific management are these:

1. *Current management practice was inefficient.* Most scientific management writers believed that the way management was practiced in their time was inefficient. This view of course was a necessary justification for their own work. Taylor argued that the economic success of a firm was not indicative of its efficiency. A firm could be successful, even though inefficient, if it had a patent, a location advantage, or if its competitors were equally inefficient. Gantt felt that the abundance of natural resources in the nation, rather than the quality of its management, accounted for its high standard of living.

2. *Management must adopt the scientific method in industry.* A tenet of Taylor and his colleagues was the use of "scientific method." The scientific method involves solving problems by research, rather than relying on experience or intuition. It requires evaluation of alternatives by making systematic and objective comparisons among them to see which is best. One example was Taylor's famous metal-cutting experiments, which started in 1880 and lasted 26 years. The purpose was to find the optimum method for cutting metal through the use of

science rather than to continue to rely upon experience as in the past. Initially, locomotive wheels were cut, since they were of a uniform hardness and quality. Later other materials were used. More than 800,000 pounds of steel were cut in the study. Twelve variables affecting the cutting process were identified. The relationship of these variables to the cutting of metal were converted to mathematical equations. They were then converted to special slide rules so that this knowledge could be applied by the worker on the job.

ITEM 2.2 Dexter S. Kimball

Author of Management's 'Bible'

Dexter S. Kimball, in 1901 the new works manager of Stanley Electric & Mfg. Co. in Pittsfield, Mass., and only 35 years old, was easy to spot—"a smallish man with a big moustache, and he will be going like hell. That's him," one of the employees explained to a visitor.

Within three years, however, Kimball had settled down in his own particular heaven, Ithaca, N.Y. There he introduced at Cornell's Sibley College of Engineering the first lectures on management to be given in any university in the country. And there he wrote *The Principles of Industrial Organization* (1913)— the "bible of management" for generations of business executives and industrial engineers. . . .

[Fourteen years before he had been working] in the Union Iron Works at San Francisco—then the largest plant on the Pacific Coast, and later to be part of Bethlehem Steel Co. Here young Kimball earned a full journeyman's pay. $3.25 a day, while studying drafting at night school.

Academic Trail. It still wasn't enough. He jumped at the chance to enter Leland Stanford Junior College in 1893, quitting his job on the promise of a position in the engineering department of the company when he graduated in 1896 with an A.B. in engineering. He took it and

soon moved on to designing pumps and presses.

. . . After a couple of years a supervisory position with Anaconda Mining Co., at pay that would permit him to marry, brought him to Butte, Mont.

Butte didn't hold him long. The die was cast that would make him a pioneer teacher of management for half the 20th century when Cornell offered him a teaching position. It lasted three years when the opportunity to more than double his income by returning to business made him works manager of Stanley Electric in Pittsfield. . . .

He faithfully attended ASME meetings. He became well acquainted with scores of engineer-managers in industry—men such as Ambrose Swazey and his partner Worcester R. Warner, the Cleveland toolmakers. He listened to engineers who were trying to extend to organization and to management the scientific approach they took to machinery and materials.

Back to Cornell. In 1903, Frederick W. Taylor presented his first paper on Shop Management, describing his plan of management at the Bethlehem Steel Works. Kimball was completely enthralled. He had already observed that the industrial world was changing fast. . . .

Now, he was convinced, there were "certain phases of the art of management that should form an integral part of any preparation for the industrial world."

Kimball never recovered from his original exposure to scientific management. "No other single document," he later wrote of Taylor's Shop Management, "has had such a profound effect upon American industry and management." The very next year, as soon as he returned to Cornell, he proposed a new course for engineering seniors.

It ended as a course in works adminis-, tration, and out of this grew The Principles of Industrial Organization. . . .

Confirmation.   Kimball's pioneer adoption of Taylor's system of scientific management soon was confirmed. In 1908, even the Harvard School of Business Administration accepted Taylor's methods in its work in shop management. And Pennsylvania State College, influenced by Professor Hugo Diemer, inaugurated a course in industrial management in 1909. . . .

Kimball meantime became full professor of industrial engineering, and in 1920 was named the first dean of Cornell's College of Engineering, in charge of all its schools. His text and his teachings became widely known to working executives as well as to student engineers both in Europe and America. By 1922, courses in management were being given at Columbia, Purdue, Massachusetts Institute of Technology, Pittsburgh, and Yale, among other leading institutions.

When Kimball returned to his favorite subject in a second basic text on management, Industrial Economics (1929), he could claim: "Today it is almost universally accepted that there is a science of business and administration comparable in many ways with any other field of applied science." Only 50 years ago, "no literature bearing on the problems of administration existed." He might have

added that his own contribution was considerable—284 articles and six books.

Writer-teacher.   Though Kimball was a charter member of the society to propagate the new faith in Taylor's vision of a more scientific management, he was never blind or insular in his advocacy. He knew he was not a research scientist himself, so he often was able to counsel moderation among those who knew they personally had found the only answer to all industry's ills.

Instead, he contented himself with writing and teaching, and with public service. He brought Taylor to Cornell to lecture, the father of scientific management stipulating that he be given two full hours to develop his ideas. And he himself went out to spread the doctrine. . . .

. . . "Charlie" Schwab at ASME council meetings liked to refer to him as "the wise guy." President Herbert Hoover entertained him at the White House, and Stanford made him a visiting lecturer on organization at its Graduate School of Business.

Following his retirement from Cornell in 1936, Kimball continued until his death in 1952, at the age of 87, to write and work for better management. Called to Washington by Edward R. Stettinius in 1941, he served in the Office of Production Management, and eased the machine tools and equipment bottleneck in World War II. In 1944, he was lecturing top-level executives at Corning Glass Works on industrial management and organization. And until he died, he returned yearly to teach management in the Postgraduate School of the U.S. Naval Academy, first at Annapolis, then at Monterey, Calif.

Basic Creed.   It was a life full of honors and responsibilities, but Kimball kept his first perspectives. He recognized the basis of modern industry was "mass production, mass ownership, mass management, and mass financing," but there

remained a great unsolved problem—
"scientific distribution" of the wealth
this nation could produce.

Kimball's principles of management
from the start incorporated good human
relations. He knew that the "subjugation
of the worker to supervision" made labor organization "natural." But he concluded: I'm glad that in my industrial life
I had a chance to 'live dangerously.' I

know what it is, when entirely dependent on my own resources, to be out of
work. I know what it is to hunt a job and
try to sell my services to a hard-boiled-
looking factory superintendent." . . .

Business Week, Aug. 14, 1968

Reprinted from the Aug. 14, 1968, *Business Week* by special permission. Copyright © 1968 by McGraw-Hill, Inc.

3. *Specialization should be practiced.* Taylor and his colleagues
believed that each individual in an organization should be a
specialist. This would insure that a person knew his job well and
would make it easier to train and select employees. Taylor believed in
specialization for management as well. For example, he advocated the
use of "functional foremanship," where each employee would be
supervised by several different foreman, each with distinct responsibilities. One foreman would be in charge of machine speeds, another
of discipline, another of planning, and so on.

4. *Planning and scheduling were essential.* In scientific management, there was a very strong emphasis on planning. It was considered to be the essence of management. Everything was to be done
according to a plan. Yearly plans were to be broken down into
monthly, weekly, and daily plans. Plans for a whole organization were
to be broken down into plans for smaller units, and even further to
individuals.

Planning techniques were devised. Gantt devised the "Gantt Chart,"
which not only helped a manager to make optimum use of his
resources by carefully scheduling jobs among available equipment,
but helped to ascertain at a glance whether certain jobs were behind
schedule or not.

Planning and scheduling meant obtaining materials at the right
time, right place, and in the right condition for efficient use. Frank
Gilbreth especially was concerned with this problem. He invented the
movable scaffold so that the bricks could be delivered at the most
efficient height for a bricklayer. Gilbreth even had the bricks placed
on the scaffold with the good side of the brick facing upward so that
the bricklayer could place it without first inspecting it, increasing
speed but not sacrificing quality.

5. *Proper selection should be done.* It was important that the right
man was selected for each job. Taylor believed there were first-class

men, second-class men, and so on, depending upon their qualifications for a task. Just as a draft horse and a race horse were fitted for
particular types of work, in Taylor's view, so were people best fitted
for some jobs but unsuited for others. Taylor advised the use of tests
to identify whether or not a person had the critical attributes for a
particular job. For example, he devised a test for measuring the
perceptual speed and reaction time of quality inspectors.

6. *The standard method should be found.* Scientific management
emphasized finding through research the best way to perform a given
task. Those assigned to that task would then be required to carry it out
in the prescribed manner. This standard method was to be used until
a better one was developed. To improve methods, workers were
studied by observers, or by motion pictures, making it possible to
analyze a task in slow motion. A work method was carefully studied
to see if certain motions could be combined, shifted to another part of
the body, or eliminated, or if the work place could be redesigned for
greater efficiency.

7. *Standard times for each task should be established.* Taylor
believed a primary barrier to greater efficiency was management's lack
of knowledge about what constituted a fair performance level for an
employee. Believing that the output of most workers was below their
capability, he did not think that historical productivity records used
by management could be accurate indicators of how long it should
take to complete a task.

Taylor believed that scientific methods should be used to establish
performance standards for each task, and devised a procedure for
establishing them. First, the best way to do a task would be developed
through work analysis and simplification procedures. Then workers
would be trained to do it in this best way. Next, the workers would be
observed and timed with a stopwatch while performing the task
several times. Then, an average time for each task would be calculated. Each worker would then be rated as to effort and skill. These
effort and skill ratings then were used to adjust the average time,
resulting in a time that reflected what the average qualified worker
could do. Thus, for each task in the organization, a standard time
would be established. This could serve as a means of evaluating an
employee's performance, motivating an employee to perform at a
higher level, and predicting output levels. It could be used in planning a work system. Standard times would be especially useful in
assembly-line operations, since timing is of the utmost importance
when work is interdependent. A part on one line must meet another

part coming down another line at just the right time for the work to flow smoothly through the system.

8. *Wage incentives should be utilized.* A basic premise of most scientific management pioneers was that a man should be paid on the basis of what he does, rather than the amount of time he puts into the job. Many wage incentive plans were devised and implemented. These incentive wage plans generally paid workers a bonus if they reached or surpassed the standard time established by time-study procedures.

Results under Scientific Management.   The application of these scientific management action principles resulted in significant productivity increases. In his most famous case, Taylor significantly improved productivity of the loading of pig iron bars into railroad cars. Working at the time for Bethlehem Steel Company, Taylor observed that about 75 laborers each were handling about 12½ tons of iron a day. He chose a worker, Schmidt—strong, energetic, and known to have a money orientation. He promised Schmidt a raise from $1.15 to $1.85 a day if he would perform the job exactly as Taylor wanted. Taylor's analysis of that job indicated that productivity was highest when the worker was resting almost half of the time. Schmidt picked up the bars, carried them, put them down, and rested *exactly* as Taylor told him. His productivity rate reached 47½ tons a day, a rate he maintained for 3 years. (Interestingly, no other worker similarly trained on this job was able to reach Schmidt's productivity rate.)

In the well-known shoveling experiment, Taylor found, through experimentation, that the optimum size shovel for handling material carried about 12½ pounds of material. This meant that big shovels should be used for light material, such as cinders, and a small shovel for heavy material, such as sand. By varying the shovel to fit the material, careful training of workers in the best method to shovel the material, and the use of incentive wage systems, Taylor was able to increase productivity from 16 to 59 tons of material shoveled per day, while the number of shovelers needed per day was decreased from 500 to 140.

The Gilbreths, in a number of applications of their work redesign methods, also demonstrated spectacular increases in productivity. Frank Gilbreth was able to increase the average productivity of brick-layers from 120 to 350 bricks per hour. This was accomplished in part by decreasing the number of motions used in bricklaying from 18 to 5. While in London at a Japanese-British exposition, Gilbreth observed a female worker in an exhibition booth who was acknowledged to be extremely productive at attaching labels on boxes. She worked at the rate of 24 boxes in 40 seconds. Gilbreth suggested some changes in her methods, and in her first attempt with the new method she disposed of 24 boxes in 26 seconds. In her second attempt, the time was reduced to 20 seconds.

Such results were typical when scientific management was applied, and they led to a strong advocacy of scientific management methods. The analysis and redesign of work was widely applied in industry. As Daniel Bell (1975) says of this movement:

> . . . The prophet of modern work was Frederick W. Taylor, and the stop watch was his rod. If any social upheaval can ever be attributed to one man, the logic of efficiency as a mode of life is due to Taylor. With "scientific management," as formulated by Taylor in 1893, we pass far beyond the old, rough computations of the division of labor and more into the division of time itself. . . .

> There is no little irony in the fact that one of Taylor's chief admirers was Lenin. In a notable speech in June 1919, Lenin urged "the study and teaching of the Taylor system and its systematic trial and adaptation." The logic of efficiency knows no social boundaries.

Administrative Theory

By the late 1920s, a group of managers had begun to write about the job of the administrator. They began to analyze the basic task of management. They were also concerned with the development of principles of management—guides for designing and managing an organization. Most of these writers worked independently of the others but nevertheless came to similar conclusions about management. Two of the more promininent earlier contributors were Henri Fayol (1949) and Chester Barnard (1938; 1947).

Henri Fayol.   Fayol (see item 2.3) distinguished management activities from technical activities, pointing out that managerial activities increased in importance and technical activities decreased in importance as we move from the lowest to the highest level of an organization. He felt that management could, and should, be taught at all educational levels. Only the lack of a management theory, which he would help create, prevented this from occurring.

Fayol proposed 14 principles of management. He stressed the importance of specialization of labor to make the best use of human resources, although he warned that this could be carried too far. Fayol also proposed that responsibility must increase as authority increases, discipline or obedience is essential in any prosperous enterprise, and that organizational members should receive orders from only one superior. He stressed the importance of determining the proper organization level at which managerial decisions are made.

Fayol was concerned about the use of human resources as well. Equality of treatment was to him very important. To facilitate motivation, the wage payment system, he believed, must fit the type of job and situation and that supervisors must encourage initiative among their subordinates.

ITEM 2.3   Henri Fayol

A Business Scientist

From his practical experience Fayol developed a framework for a unifying doctrine of administration that might hold good wherever the art of government had to be exercised. He originated the symbol of formal organization, the organization chart, which, with his organization manual of job descriptions, remains the chief instrument of business management. He produced ideas on human relationships. . . . Not least, he was a firm advocate of the view that management can and should be taught. This was a revolutionary idea when he first propounded it in 1908.

Fayol's first paper on management theory was read to the *Congrès des Mines et de la Métallurgie* in 1900. He followed this with his "Discourse on the General Principles of Administration" at the Jubilee Congress of the *Société de l'Industrie Minérale* in 1908, a paper which appeared in the third number of the *Bulletin de la Société de l'Industrie Minérale* for 1916 and was published as a book by Dunod of Paris. This was translated into English by Conbrough in 1929, and again by Constance Storrs in 1949. It is the latter translation which is in widespread use under the title *Gen-*eral and Industrial Management, and by which Fayol is primarily known to the British and American reader.

Fayol was born in 1841 of the French *petite bourgeoisie. . . .*

His working life fell into four periods. For twelve years from 1860 he was a junior executive interesting himself in the problems of mining engineering, especially fire hazards. Promoted to Manager of a group of pits in 1872, he became concerned chiefly with the factors determining the economic life of the pits in his charge. This not only stimulated him to write a geological monograph but aroused his interest in thinking and planning ahead. In 1888 he was appointed Managing Director of the combine, taking over when the undertaking was on the verge of bankruptcy. He closed uneconomic metallurgical works, replaced exhausted mines with rich acquisitions and expanded the whole organization. When he retired in 1918 the financial position of the combine was impregnable. It had made a contribution of the greatest value to the allied cause in the First World War, and it had an administrative, technical and scientific staff famous throughout France.

In his retirement Fayol devoted his time to the popularization of his own views on management and to the development of theoretical studies. He immediately founded the Centre for Administrative Studies, which had a profound influence on business, the Army, and the Navy in France, and attempted to persuade the French government to pay attention to principles of administration. By invitation of the Under-Secretary of State for Posts and Telegraphs he undertook an investigation of this department. At the time of his death in 1925 he was engaged in investigating the organization of the French tobacco industry. . . .

Fayol's Contribution. Henri Fayol was an able man whose talents had a fertile field for development in the social and economic environment of France between 1860 and 1925. His abilities placed him in the *élite* comprised of those who had attended the *grandes écoles,* the most senior administrators in business, government, the armed forces and in other fields. At the time he commenced his business career the French economy had "taken off" and was passing through [a] period of rapid growth [in which] there was a sense in which French business needed a theory of management, as did American business in a similar stage of development. Fayol's work in France, a country with a long tradition of administration, was complementary to that of Taylor in the U.S.A., a nation which revered the principle of "coming up the hard way". That Taylor worked primarily on the operative level, from the bottom of the hierarchy upwards, while Fayol concentrated on the senior manager and worked downwards, was not merely a reflection of their different careers; it was also a reflection of the political and social history of the two nations.

Fayol's views on management theory contain some weaknesses of analysis and assessment. His principles, elements and duties overlap; he confused structure and process; and there is a vagueness and superficiality about some of his terms and definitions. He hinted at, but did not elaborate, the limitations of his view that management can and should be taught. Senior managers and administrators he imagined as an intellectual élite, a view which could not be supported universally although true of his own circle and still largely obtaining in France today. He placed a higher value on management theory than it could be expected to support, in 1924 addressing a conference on the importance of administrative doctrine as a contribution to peace.

Nevertheless Fayol's contribution to management theory is unique and valuable. He was a generation ahead of his time in proclaiming its significance and he propounded many views which have been attributed to others who followed. While acclaimed for originating the organization chart, the job specification and the concept of management education and training, he has been underestimated. His views on human relationships at work anticipated many of the basic findings of industrial psychology. His idea of flexible planning at all levels lies behind the development of the *Commissariat du Plan* which has played such a significant part in the recent expansion of the French economy.

Although it is clear that he was exceptionally gifted, Fayol maintained that his phenomenal business success was due primarily not to his personal qualities but to the application of simple principles which could be taught and learned. These constituted his theory of management. It exercised, and continues to exercise, a profound influence on efforts to clarify thinking on organization, and is one of the foundations of organization theory. His emphasis on unremitting effort has the flavor of Samuel Smiles of latter nineteenth century Britain, but it is probable that his biological model could only have been produced by a Frenchman. . . .—Norman H. Cuthbert

Journal of Management Studies, 1964– 65

Chester Barnard.   Barnard (1938), another important management theorist, perceived the organization differently than Fayol, who stressed designing an organization in a rational and systematic way and then fitting individuals to it. Barnard paid more attention to human factors. He saw organizations evolving out of the attempt to reconcile organizational needs with individual needs.

Organizations, to Barnard, are systems of cooperative effort and coordinated activities. They are formed, or develop, to overcome the inherent limitations of an individual's capacity; that is, when the task to be done requires more than one person, organized effort is necessary.

Like Fayol, Barnard was aware of the formal, designated structure of organization—but he recognized that what really occurred in the context of any organization was different from the charts, job specifications, and procedures specified by management. He made it clear in his analysis that there were informal organizations that existed side by side with the formal. These resulted from different human needs that could not be dealt with by the formal system.

Barnard, in his exposition of this concept, provided groundwork for later analysis which examined the interrelationship of individuals and groups with organizations. Much of what transpires at work can be accounted for by the formal organization. Much, however, can only be understood if the psychological and sociological aspects of organizational life are more fully considered.

He also examined the structure of organization in terms of decision making. Top-level management set objectives. The next management level established plans to achieve them. Then the next lower level developed more detailed plans, until the operating level was reached.

Barnard, like Fayol, also described what executives must do to manage an organization efficiently. The executive functions, according to Barnard, are:

1. *Maintaining organization communication.* This involves integrating managers and their jobs in the system. Competent managers, compatible to the needs of the organization, should be able to communicate effectively to achieve organization purpose.

2. *Securing the essential services of individuals.* Managers are responsible for recruiting, or inducing individuals to join an organization as well as seeing to it that they produce once they join.

3. *Formulating purpose and objectives.* Managers are responsible for stating, in operational terms, the goals of the organization, then breaking them down into subgoals to be assigned to lower-level units.

The Administrative Point of View.   Some of the major ideas that flow from the administrative approach to management are the treatment of authority, management functions, principles of management, organization structure, and emphasis on objectives.

In the administrative approach, *authority* and *responsibility* are seen as rights and obligations of employees and managers. Authority is the right of a manager to decide about resource allocation. Responsibility is the obligation to perform according to job requirements. Authority and responsibility are associated with a position and should be co-equal; that is, a person should not be responsible for those things about which he has no authority. Line authority flows down, according to the administrative school, from the top of the hierarchy to the lowest managerial level.

An *emphasis on objectives* is required to develop a rational relationship among activities. When goals are clearly defined and stated, other resources can be arranged in such a way as to maximize the possibility of attainment. Managers, the administrative theorists believed, would be able to select the best alternative from those available only when goals are known.

One of the more important contributions of the administrative school to management theory is *organization structure,* or guidance on how to design an organization. Many principles of management deal with this problem. Davis (1951, for example, states the principle of *functional homogeneity.* "Duties should be grouped in a manner which will provide the greatest functional similarity." Such grouping would result in lower costs and better performance. Relationships *between* activities, he said, should be governed by the principle of *complementary functions:* "The functions involved in the completion of a project, and their performance factors, must be related in a manner that will facilitate the cumulation of results into the effective, economical accomplishment of the final objectives" Davis then goes on to detail the things that make functions complementary. This design aspect of administrative theory gives a great deal of help in defining an organization system.

Principles of management were mentioned in chapter 1 as both a strength and a weakness of the administrative approach. Principles were seen by the administrative school as guides to action for managers. Drawn from real-world experiences, they were meant to facilitate high performance. The message from the administrative school was "Follow the principles, and success will very likely come."

Yet many critics, such as March and Simon (1958), attacked these principles because they were based on observation, not research, and they were "proverbs." But many of the principles have extremely sound bases. For instance the unity of command principle states that a person should receive orders from only one superior. This "proverb," based on the experience of the administrative theorists, has a more glamorous conceptual formulation by the social scientist; he calls it avoiding role conflict. Role conflict occurs when a person receives inconsistent demands from two or more others so that complying with one of the demands precludes compliance with another. Research has shown the negative effects on individuals of high role conflict (Rizzo et al.; Tosi, 1970). It was said another way 2,000 years ago: "No man can serve two masters: for either he will hate the one and love the other; or else he will hold to the one, and despise the other."

Management functions are those activities which all executives perform in whole or part. The administrative theorists did the most extensive early analysis of what these functions are. Managerial functions are planning, organizing, and controlling. Planning is the determining, in advance of activity execution, what factors are required to achieve goals. The planning function includes defining the objective and determining what resources are necessary. Organizing is the function of acquiring and assembling resources in proper relationship to each other to achieve objectives. Controlling is insuring that activities, when carried out, conform to plans, to achieve objectives. (The link between these functions developed out of the administrative school and those which we use in our own contingency analysis is discussed in chap. 1.)

The administrative theory school, then, stresses a rational approach to management: If we define our objective, then it is possible to organize resources to achieve it. This is what scientific management was concerned with, also.

The Behavioral Approach

The scientific management movement analyzed the activities of workers; the administrative management writers focused on the activities of managers. The behavioral approach to management sought to understand how human psychological processes—such as motivation and attitude—interact with what one does—activities—to affect performance.

The behavioral approach is probably more fragmented than either the scientific management or administrative management approaches. Behavioralists come from many different social science disciplines (political science, sociology, psychology, and anthropology), and while there are varying emphases among them, they can be generally grouped into two categories. The first category studies *organizational behavior* and considers as a point of focus the individual. Much of the work in this area stems from the Hawthorne studies (discussed below). The second category studies *organizational theory*, and tends to consider the organization as a focal point. Much of the theoretical base for this area derives from the work of social psychologists and sociologists.

Organizational Behavior.   In the early years of the scientific management movement, behavioral scientists were deeply involved. Their concern was with problems such as worker fatigue, boredom, and job design. Quite a different perspective emerged after the Hawthorne experiment at Western Electric in the late 1920s, which gave rise to the "human relations" approach (Roethlisberger and Dickson, 1939).

The Hawthorne experiment was carried out in the Hawthorne plant of Western Electric, an AT&T subsidiary in Cicero, Illinois. The Hawthorne studies (started in 1927) were prompted by an experiment which was carried out by the company's engineers between 1924 and 1927. The engineers, in the best tradition of scientific management, were seeking the answers to industrial questions through research. They studied two groups to determine the effects of different levels of illumination on worker performance. In one group the level of illumination was changed, while in the other it was not. They found that when illumination was increased, the level of performance increased. But productivity also increased when the level of illumination decreased, even down to the level of moonlight. Moreover, productivity also increased in the control group. These results seemed contrary to reason, and so the engineers examined other factors which might have affected the results. The workers in the experiment were the center of attention. They appeared to react as they thought they should react.

The researchers concluded that the way people were treated made an important difference in performance. Obviously, the subjects were not responding *not* to the level of light, but to the experiment itself and to their involvement in it. They were responding in a way that they thought the experimenters wanted and because they were the center of attention. Since that time, this effect in research has been known as the "Hawthorne Effect."

The Hawthorne studies which followed the experiment were conducted by a team of researchers headed by Elton Mayo and F. J. Roethlisberger, from Harvard. The results of these studies are summarized here.

1. *The First Relay Assembly Group.* The first study investigated the effects on worker output of variations in the physical conditions of work, such as rest pauses, hours of work, temperature, and humidity. The study group consisted of six experienced female operators who assembled telephone relays. When each relay was assembled it was dropped down a chute, at which time a mechanism punched a hole in a piece of moving tape. Productivity could be accurately measured by counting the number of holes in the tape and, since it moved at a constant speed, one could later determine productivity levels for any particular time period.

Over a two-year period, many changes were made in the working conditions, especially with respect to rest pauses. Two five-minute, then two ten-minute, then six five-minute rest pauses were tried. Food was served with the rest pauses. The work day and the work week were shortened, first by one-half hour a day, then by one hour, then to a five-day instead of a six-day week. Each change in the physical working conditions was made separately and lasted several weeks.

In addition to these changes, the task was simplified somewhat. Workers in the room were put on an incentive wage plan which enabled them to earn more money if the performance level of the group increased. The approach to supervision in the room was different than in the previous work location. In the relay assembly room, much more attention, interest, and consideration was shown to the workers than on their previous jobs.

In addition, records were kept on temperature, humidity, hours of sleep, food eaten and so on. The data amassed in this study was extensive and detailed.

Over the two-year period, productivity *generally* went up steadily, no matter what changes in working conditions were made. At the end

of the study the investigators formulated five hypotheses to account
for the increased production: (1) improved methods of work, (2)
reduction in fatigue with changes in rest pauses and shorter hours, (3)
reduction in monotony due to rest pauses and hour changes, (4) effect
of a wage incentive plan, and (5) effect of the new method of supervision. The first three hypotheses were rejected by the investigators,
leaving wage incentives and the method of supervision to be tested in
further studies.

2. *The Second Relay Assembly Group.* To test the effects of wage
incentives, a group of workers was selected who remained in the
regular work department, but were taken off the regular wage plan and
put on a group incentive plan. Productivity increased in the study
group by 13 percent, as did their earnings. But the study was terminated after nine weeks because of the resentment of other workers in
the department. The investigators concluded, perhaps unwisely, that
group rivalry was the cause of the increased production rather than
the incentive wage plan.

3. *The Mica-splitting Test Room.* To examine the effects of different
supervision, another group of workers already on piecework was
studied. The change in supervision seemed, at first, to make a difference in performance. But with worsening of economic conditions
accompanying the Depression, productivity declined and remained
stable for a long period of time.

4. *The Interviewing Program.* The investigators had rejected all
their hypotheses about a single cause of the increased productivity.
They decided that employee behavior was the result of a reaction to a
complex social system made up of several interdependent elements.
An interviewing program was initiated in 1928 which lasted several
years, and which involved more than 21,000 interviews with workers
to try to understand some of these complex interrelationships. In this
study, several conclusions were reached:

a) Morale is improved when individuals have a chance to air their
   grievances.
b) Complaints are not objective statements of fact.
c) Workers are influenced in their job demands by experiences
   outside the work situation.
d) Worker satisfaction is influenced by how the employee views his
   social status relative to others.

5. *The Bank Wiring Observation Room.* In this study, 14 male
workers were formed into a work group and closely observed for 7
months. The researchers, in observing the group, saw the emergence

of a social system when these workers were placed together. The social system influenced worker behavior considerably. This study will be described in detail in chapter 4 because it highlights concepts useful to understanding how and why groups affect the behavior of individuals.

Conclusions of the Investigators.   The Hawthorne studies seemed to point up the importance of leadership practices and work-group pressures on employee satisfaction and performance. They downgraded the importance of economic incentives in worker motivation. They also stressed the importance of examining the effect of any one factor, such as pay, in terms of a whole social system, pointing out that employees react to a whole complex of forces together, rather than to one factor alone.

Criticism of the Hawthorne Studies.   While the Hawthorne studies represent the main point of departure for the behavioral approach, both the research methods and the conclusions have been questioned (Carey, 1967; Sykes, 1965; Kerr, 1953; Bendix and Fisher, 1949). For instance, it is said that the research had a management bias, striving to increase productivity without regard to the welfare of workers. Criticism has also been leveled at the research method; for example, that samples were too small, the questions vague. Others criticize the fact that the results were misinterpreted. For example, in the second relay assembly study, production increased with incentives, yet the researchers concluded that group rivalry was the cause. Some questioned the conclusion that management and workers have similar rather than contradictory objectives. Regardless of the merit of the criticisms, the research had a significant impact on thinking about management problems. It provided the impetus for critics of the scientific management movement to argue that any effort to develop a science of management without taking the human factor into account would be fruitless.

Later Work.   World War II intensified the interest of the federal government in management problems research and it funded literally thousands of studies on leadership, job satisfaction, and small-group problems. Psychologists and sociologists gained increased credibility with all groups concerned with management problems. More recent areas of research from the behavioral approach have been in the areas of motivation and job design, much of which, in fact, forms the basis for the content of this book.

Organizational Theory. The administrative theorists were concerned with describing primarily what managers do and proposing "rules" or principles of organization, such as the principle of unity of command. They were concerned with the question of how an organization could be designed to operate more effectively to achieve objectives in a "rational" way. They looked at organization problems rather than at human problems. This broad view could also be found in the behavioral schools, largely based on the work of Max Weber. This German sociologist, whose emphasis was on bureaucracy, was an important influence on writing and theory about the study of organization.

Max Weber's analysis considered organizations as part of broader society (Handers and Parsons, 1947). He described the characteristics of the bureaucracy, which he viewed as the most efficient form for large complex organizations such as business, government, and the military. The bureaucratic form of organization, as described by Weber, uses extensive formal rules and procedures to govern the job behavior of organizational members. Organizational positions are arrayed in a hierarchy, each with a particular established amount of authority and responsibility. Promotion to higher positions is based on technical competence, objectively judged. Weber felt that this type of organization emphasized predictability of behavior and results and showed great stability over time. He suggested that organizations naturally evolved toward this rational form.

Chester Barnard, as we mentioned earlier, was identified with the administrative theory school. However, much of his work had a significant effect on the behavioral approach, especially in the area of organization theory. He added much to the thinking about organization with such concepts as "the linking pin," "the zone of indifference," and "the acceptance theory of authority."

The "linking pin" concept was a way of considering organizational relationships between superiors and subordinates in organizations.

The executives of several unit organizations, as a group, usually with at least one other person as a superior, form an executive organization. Accordingly, persons specializing in executive functions . . . are "members of" or contributors to, two units of organization in one complex organization—first, the so-called "working" unit and second, the executive unit.

The "zone of indifference" and the "acceptance theory of authority" contributed substantially to the view of how compliance was obtained. In the administrative school's view, authority was seen as the right of a superior. Barnard maintained that authority works when it is accepted, and that it is accepted often because a communication from a superior falls within the recipient's "zone of indifference," which means substantially that the person is willing to comply.

Using concepts from Barnard, March and Simon surveyed a wide range of empirical work in psychology and sociology, as well as economic theory to write the book, *Organizations* (1958). This book was stimulated by feelings that the existing research and theory about organization and management were inadequate. The classical principles of management as formulated by Fayol and others were attacked, as we noted earlier; March and Simon contended that such principles were not only logically inconsistent, but oversimplified. They extended the Barnard view of the organization as a social system. Following Barnard, they presented a more elaborate motivational theory for organizational members than the classical writers. They emphasized individual decision making as a basis for understanding behavior in organizations. One of the salient points they developed was that of "bounded rationality." To make the optimal decisions suggested by the administrative theorists, they said, the manager would have to select the best of *all* possible alternatives. But the executive, as an "administrative man," is limited by his own perceptions. He has limited knowledge in making organizational decisions and cannot, therefore, make optimal decisions.

Critics of "Structure."   March and Simon were not the only ones who felt that the principles of management and organization defined by the scientific and administrative schools were limited. There was developing a feeling that the bureaucratic structure was a limited form of organization that would work under some, but not all circumstances. In fact, critics of this persuasion argued that rigid job specifications, rules, and policies stifled the creativity, growth, development, and general effectiveness of the human side of the organization.

Douglas McGregor, in *The Human Side of Enterprise* (1960) said that most managers made a set of incorrect assumptions about those who worked for them. He called these assumptions, collectively, Theory X. Theory X assumed that man was lazy, personal goals ran counter to the organization's, and that, because of this, man had to be controlled externally. In a work context, this meant close supervision and guidance so that management would insure high performance. Theory Y assumptions, on the other hand, were based on greater trust in others. Man was more mature, self-motivated, and self-controlled than Theory X gave him credit for. McGregor suggested that there was little need for either rigid organization or interpersonal controls.

Chris Argyris (1957, 1965) also made a strong case for reducing the amount of organizational control. He believed that many constraints placed by organization structure on human beings were self-defeating to organizational goals of effectiveness and efficiency. The basic thrust of this argument, along with McGregor's, is that the bureaucratic form of organization is incongruent with the basic needs of the healthy individual. Argyris maintains that the bureaucratic form of organization treats lower organizational members like children. This fosters dependence and leads to the frustration of the higher-order human needs. This frustration expresses itself in lack of work involvement and antiorganizational activities such as sabotage.

A concept that embodies these ideas in the management of work organization is the *human resource approach*. It assumes that the job, or task itself, is the primary source of satisfaction and motivation for employees. Tasks, and the organization, should be designed in such a way that individuals have the opportunity to satisfy their higher-level needs through the work itself. This strategy rests heavily on behavioral science techniques to fuse the interests of the organization and the individual. The emphasis in the human resource approach is on individual involvement in the decisions made in the organization.

The Management Science Movement

Management science, or operations research, grew out of World War II research on the application of quantitative methods to military and logistical decision problems. Some of the earliest projects were to increase bombing accuracy, to develop search methods for submarines, to minimize ship loss due to submarine attacks, and to improve methods for loading and unloading ships. This approach to problem solving is interdisciplinary. Problems are attacked by teams, and team members come from a wide variety of fields, though for the most part they are engineers, mathematicians, statisticians, economists, and psychologists.

Miller and Starr (1964) consider operations research to be applied decision theory. It uses "any scientific, mathematical, or logical means to attempt to cope with problems that confront the executive when he tries to achieve a thoroughgoing rationality in dealing with his decision problems." But, how does this differ from some of the other points of view of the scientific management and administrative theory schools? Miller and Starr offer this way of distinguishing operations research approaches from these others:

Management Science differs from Taylor's scientific management in many ways. It is not concerned primarily with production tasks and the efficiency of men and machines. Rather, the efficiency is a secondary achievement which should follow adequate planning. In other words, poor decisions can be implemented in an efficient way.

Thus, the operations research movement tries to marry the concern of the scientific management school with production and efficiency with the planning approach and the emphasis on objectives of the administrative theory school. This is attempted, however, with an eye toward integrating several fields of knowledge and using systematic analytical techniques, especially quantitative methods, to deal with problems facing managers and organizations. Management scientists use models (representations of real life) with computers to make the necessary and often quite complex mathematical computations to optimize the attainment of a given set of objectives. Today, basic techniques such as linear programming, game theory, queuing theory, and statistical decision theory are being applied to many business problems.

However, management science does not eliminate from consideration the effects of behavioral problems. Miller and Starr note that "management science is essentially quantitative; however, the important problems that cannot be quantified are handled qualitatively. Whether quantitative or qualitative methods are applied, operations research is used to produce rational decisions and logical plans of action."

Contingency Theories of Management

At the point we have now reached in our short history, the field of management was in a state of turmoil and confusion. Advocates of one point of view criticized, often mistakenly, other approaches. The administrative theorists argued that the behavioral approach proponents did not understand the realities of the world of business and administration. Critics of "principles" said principles were limited because there were many ways to organize and be successful. Every approach and everyone involved with them were wrong; psychologists were too narrow, sociologists too broad, principles inapplicable, and management science approaches capable of dealing only with trivial problems.

All the critics were right, of course, and all were wrong. The major problem was that critics tended to disparage other contributions without really understanding them. No one took the time to develop an integrated approach to fit together the pieces of the puzzle in a systematic way.

This sorting, sifting, and reformulation of ideas, bringing threads from all the contributing areas and weaving them into a more general approach is what contingency theories of management seek to do. Critics of the administrative and scientific management theorists were correct. There *is* no one best way to manage. But the critics never really told anyone how to proceed to develop a proper managerial strategy. It *did* all depend—but on what?

Some of the answers began to emerge, though in a very seminal way, from a study of the Tennessee Valley Authority by Selznick, *TVA and the Grass Roots* (1949). He showed how various other organizations and interest groups in the outside environment of the TVA affected managerial decisions. The structure of any organization is subjected to many such outside restraints, he claimed, so the organization develops both formal and informal systems which help it to adapt to the outside environment, and thus to survive. Selznick made it clear on what the formal structure depended. Not only that, but he described how and through what kind of strategy the adjustment took place. James D. Thompson (1967), an important organization scholar in this tradition, suggests that the basic task of an administrator is the co-alignment of environmental factors with the internal technology, organizational structure, and human resources.

In 1961, Burns and Stalker published a study of British industry. They found differences in the structures of the firms they studied, and traced these differences to the nature of the technology used and the markets served. When the technological and market environments were uncertain, a loose organization was found. When the environment was more predictable, a more traditional bureaucracy seemed to be most effective. Burns and Stalker not only saw the environment effect as important, but specified more precisely than had been done before what the internal structure should look like, given a certain kind of environment.

Another English study reported by Woodward, following the Burns and Stalker model, showed that the type of organizational structure used was related to a firm's economic performance when type of technology was taken into account.

Lawrence and Lorsch (1967) studied a highly effective and a less effective organization in three different industries: plastics, food, and container. These industries were chosen because they operated in environments which differed with respect to rate of technological change for the products they produced and the production methods used. The industries also differed with respect to the type of competitive situation they were in. These factors led to differences in the amount of environmental uncertainty. Lawrence and Lorsch found that in the plastics and food industry, companies were faced with much change and uncertainty, while the container industry was much more stable and predictable. They concluded that the closer the organizational structure matched the requirements imposed on it by the environment, the more successful was the firm. The effective organization had, for example, a high degree of coordinated effort when the environment required it. And a high degree of task specialization was present in high-performance firms when the environment demanded this. In general, they concluded that organizations in a stable environment are more effective if they have more detailed procedures and more centralization of the decision-making process, while organizations in an unstable environment have decentralization, participation, and less emphasis on rules and standard procedures.

Charles Perrow (1970) another well-known behavioral scientist, has examined this research and other case studies of many large U.S. companies and has concluded that it is very important that a proper fit exist between an organization and its environment, and that one organization's structure and style of management may be effective in one type of environment, quite ineffective in another.

How We Arrived Here

The insights of the contingency view have had a marked impact on the writing of this book. We believe that the studies by Selznick, Burns and Stalker, Woodward, and Lawrence and Lorsch, along with the work of James Thompson, enable the manager to see fairly clearly how the environment affects the structure of an organization. At the same time, the manager must be aware that ideas from the administrative school can be put to good use in management structure and strategy. Planning is important, but it can only be as effective as the amount of information available. Additionally, operations research and decision theory can provide methods both for dealing with certain environments—such as the stable environment faced by the bureaucratic organization—and decision approaches for dealing with greater uncertainty, which may characterize the environment of an organic, or flexible, organization. Finally, motivation theories, developed by the behavioral approach, describe what kind of internal psychological factors seem related to high performance in different types of organizations, and this information, too, can be of great value to the manager. These concepts are all brought into our analysis, and because they are, the approach in this book is termed the "managerial process contingency approach." All of the studies reviewed in this book reveal facets of the problem of managing. We have tried to synthesize the constructs, ideas, and principles that seem to emerge as most effective from these studies—that is, from what is known about organizations, individuals, and managing—and show how this synthesis (from all of the schools of thought on managers and managing) can be effectively applied in the various circumstances in which organizations and individuals find themselves. To conclude our short history, then, the purpose of this book is to specify, as well as can be done at this stage of the art, how a manager can manage effectively.

Discussion Questions

1. If so much thought was given to management problems before the 20th century, what made the Frederick Taylor era the starting point of scientific management?

2. Think about the points of view of the administrative theorists and the scientific management writers. How are they similar? Different?

3. How do you feel about the basic prescriptions of scientific management outlined in this chapter? Do they make sense to you as a manager? As an employee?

4. What is your opinion of the importance of the behavioral approach? How can an understanding of human behavior facilitate the manager's job?

5. Some have said that managers are concerned with manipulation of people. What schools of thought would contribute the knowledge one needs to "manipulate" others?

Part II

Individuals

Technical factors (scientific, technological, and economic) are involved in decision making, but people are the important resource. They harness energy, invent, create. They affect nature—change it to produce something. People make decisions; they work at machines.

Managers get things done through others, but human beings differ widely in skills and knowledge, learning ability, values, needs, personality and attitudes. If people acted as predictably as the solar system, or machines, there would be few human problems. But they don't. The manager must be aware of the wide variations in people. In chapter 3, we show how the characteristics of individuals are shaped by society and how they affect orientations toward work.

People work with others—in groups—and groups have an important effect on individuals. Since organizations (which managers manage) are complex sets of groups, chapter 4 focuses on the kind of problems groups cause for individuals and for organizations.

In chapter 5 we bring together ideas from chapters 3 and 4, along with some additional concepts, and deal with the question: What factors, technical and human, affect the performance of individuals in organizations?

Chapter 3

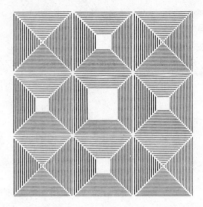

Human beings are involved with their work in different ways. They have different values, outlooks, and attitudes, and these cause different individuals to react in different ways to identical situations. Why is it that when a supervisor gives the same order to two subordinates, one will comply and the other will look for ways to avoid the work? The answer is that they are different people—meaning they have brought different characteristics to the job. This chapter discusses the different kinds of human characteristics which have a significant impact, when brought to the job, on the effectiveness of managerial practices. The manager must understand something about these different characteristics in order to manage well.

First, we will focus on how individuals develop certain attitudes and values. This process is more easily understood if we know some of the fundamental ideas behind learning theory and perception. We will also discuss what some of the individual characteristics are and how they emerge, and we will show how these individual characteristics affect a person's affiliation with work organizations, and how the organization affects different kinds of individuals.

Behavioral Model of Human Beings

Thought of in a behavioral sense, an individual has at least the following: (1) skills, ability, and knowledge, (2) self-concept, (3) attitudes, (4) values, and (5) needs or motives. These are shaped over a person's lifetime, and their content and strength determine not only what a person feels (emotions), but also what he is (behavior), and what he may be (potential). These elements differ between individuals. The differences constitute the uniqueness of each human being.

Development of Work Motives, Values, and Attitudes

Figure 3.1 represents our general behavioral model, considering the human as being made up of, at least, the elements mentioned above. The model is similar to one proposed by March and Simon (1958), and it operates in this way: The individual perceives a *stimulus*, or cue, in the environment. The cue triggers a certain set of values, attitudes, and behavior (the *evoked set*). When a person acts, his action is the *response*. If the response is *reinforced* positively, then the likelihood of that cue triggering a similar response in the future is increased.

Stimuli. A stimulus is a factor or a condition that triggers behavior. It precedes behavior. Stimuli, or cues, are those "aspects of the environment that have a significant impact on behavior in the next time interval" (March and Simon, 1958). A stimulus is perceived by an individual and he reacts to it. The stimulus can be fairly simple—say a whistle that signals a lunch break in a factory. Or it may be complex —a disciplinary interview in which a superior provides information in the form of verbal criticism (what he says), as well as information by how he says it (e.g., with a frown and harsh tone of voice).

Evoked Set. Stimuli act on the individual, but not on all his values, attitudes, and behavioral alternatives. A cue evokes only the particular set of these elements that the individual associates with the cue. The set it acts upon is called the "evoked set," the set that contains the response of the person to the cue. For example, when the lunch whistle blows, it triggers a whole group of attitudes and behaviors— workers pick up their lunch buckets, head for the eating area, and so on.

FIGURE 3.1 A General Model of an Individual

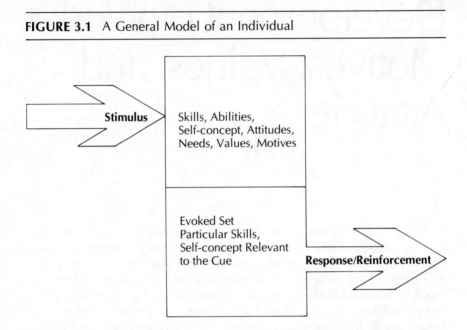

Response. Part of the evoked set contains the response of the individual. The response may be behavior or it may be an emotional reaction. It can be relatively simple (such as going to eat when the lunch whistle blows), or complex (such as changing the way an individual does a job after a disciplinary interview).

Reinforcement. A stimulus induces tension to act—the individual feels the need to do something or say something. (If an inducement of tension does not occur, it is not proper to conceive of the event as a stimulus.) When we respond to a cue with a behavior (verbal or physical) or the expression of an attitude, and the tension is reduced, and we associate this reduction of tension with the cue, positive reinforcement has occurred. (In some instances, however, negative reinforcement may take place. We will discuss the differences between these two types of reinforcement in the next section.)

Over time, as a person experiences reinforcements, patterns or regularities of behavior begin to emerge. A certain behavioral response (behavior or emotion) becomes regularly associated with a cue.

Behavior patterns are learned. An understanding of learning theory will show us how.

Learning Theory

Learning theory is a set of concepts which deals with how individuals respond to cues in their environment. It provides an explanation of how behavioral patterns develop, and this explanation is helpful in many ways. First, we can use it to understand how skills, values, and attitudes are acquired. Second, it is essential to an understanding of why individuals in a work situation behave as they do. Finally, from it, we can gain insights into how to change the environment (cues) or the reinforcements in order to bring about behavior change to improve organization performance.

Positive and Negative Reinforcement

An individual may associate either positive feelings or negative feelings with a particular behavior. Both associations are reinforcements. A response is *positively* reinforced when the probability of its future occurrence with the same cue present is increased. That is, behavior is likely to be repeated in the future if it is associated with a positive result—a reward. A positive reinforcement may be a smile, or a pay increase, or it may be the termination of an unpleasant stimulus (such as the departure from the room of another person who has been berating you). A response is *negatively* reinforced when the probability of its future occurrence is decreased. When a response is sanctioned, or punished (as perceived by the individual) he will try to figure out other ways of responding. A third possibility is *nonreinforcement*. This occurs when neither reward nor punishment follows an individual's behavioral response. Here, as with negative reinforcement, the probability of the response occurring in the future is decreased.

For something to act as a reinforcer, it must be linked to a specific behavior. This means that the individual must perceive the link between the reinforcement and the response. An employee, for instance, may engage in a variety of behaviors which are then followed either by praise or by censure from a superior. Often the employee does not know for sure which of several behaviors resulted in the superior's approval or disapproval. Unfortunately, individuals often believe it was one kind of behavior that solicited approval when actually it was quite another. Therefore individuals often act in ways they believe pleasing to others, when actually those ways are not pleasing.

Reinforcement Schedules

The frequency and rate at which various reinforcements (rewards or punishments) are associated with particular responses is called the *reinforcement schedule*. This schedule affects the speed with which responses are learned, or behavior changes. Rewarding every correct response is 100 percent reinforcement. With 100 percent reinforcement, new behavior is learned very quickly. However, if individuals become used to being rewarded every time they make a certain type of response, they stop behaving that way very quickly if the reinforcement stops. The nonreinforcement is very obvious to the individual.

On the other hand, if the responses of the individual are reinforced or rewarded only intermittently, it takes longer for new behavior to develop, but stopping the reinforcement will not stop the behavior immediately. The individual will continue to anticipate the reward, even though it is not forthcoming, since the nonreinforcement is not obvious. Research has shown that an intermittent and variable reinforcement schedule is slow to bring about new behaviors, but very effective for maintaining a particular type of behavioral response once it is learned (Nord, 1969).

Behavioral Change

An individual may learn to respond in a particular way in one situation, and then find himself in another, similar situation in which the old response is not positively reinforced, or perhaps is negatively reinforced. If now a new behavior, or even the opposite behavior, is positively reinforced, the individual will behave differently. This is, by definition, behavior change. For example, let us say that a student grows up in a household where to the stimulus (or cue) "labor union," the response of expressing negative attitudes toward unions is rewarded with signs of approval. At college, however, when he expresses negative attitudes toward labor unions his position is met with disapproval from his fellow students or from his professors. Since he may wish to elicit approval (rewards) instead of disapproval (punishments), he may begin to express positive attitudes toward labor unions—and at college he may be positively rewarded. Ultimately, in order to justify the contradictory attitudes he expresses in two situations—home and college—he may take a middle position, saying that labor unions have both good and bad features. His behavior in what he *says* about unions has changed because of the contrasting reinforcements he has received.

Reinforcement in Everyday Life

Obviously we are all subjected to reinforcements all the time. Whenever we say something and another person important to us shows approval or disapproval, our behavior is influenced. Whenever we show signs of approval or disapproval of what others say or do, we are reinforcing a particular action of theirs. Of course, what constitutes positive and negative reinforcement lies in the mind of the person reinforcing or being reinforced. A compliment from a hated supervisor may be negatively rather than positively reinforcing. By the same token, an expression of disapproval from a disliked professor may be positively reinforcing to the student, especially when the negative response meets with the approval of other students, with whom he identifies. Since we are often unaware of the perspectives of others, we are often unable to determine when a reaction to a particular behavioral response reinforces it positively or negatively.

Clearly, the concept of reinforcement can provide a manager with a useful motivational tool. These ideas will be discussed in further detail in chapter 5, "Motivation and Performance," and in later chapters on the management of different types of organizations.

Perception

Perception is the way we assimilate and organize the information that surrounds us in the environment. To respond to a stimulus, it must be observed in the world around us. Individuals *perceive* cues. They also perceive reinforcements to a particular response. And, as mentioned, often a reinforcement is perceived to be associated with a different behavior than a manager might intend.

Individuals notice only certain aspects of their environments. Each person's perception of the same situation may be different because of this selective perception. Each of several individuals in a group, or organization, will have a somewhat different perception of the group, or organization, than others. It is, of course, not possible for a person to perceive and evaluate all of the information available from the environment at any one point in time, so he must be selective. This being so, what are some of the factors which influence this selectivity?

Stimulus Factors

Reinforcement has its effect when an event is associated with a behavior. This association of reward or sanction with the behavior is a function of perception. What is it about a cue that is likely to cause it to be seen as a cue? Newcomb and his colleagues (1965) suggest that the characteristics of cues which are related to perception are (1) primacy (2) vividness, and (3) frequency. (The following discussion is based on concepts developed extensively in Newcombe et al., 1965.)

The relative timing by which information about a particular set of circumstances is received is called primacy. Information received early is more likely to have an effect than that received later. First impressions, for example, are likely to be long-lasting and difficult to change. For example, the first time a manager meets someone applying for a job in his department, he forms an impression about the applicant that may affect his judgment about the other person for a long time.

Vividness has to do with the degree to which an event is markedly different from what the individual believes it should be. Circumstances that are unusual, extreme, or that deviate from this notion of "should be" trigger a response. Vividness is not necessarily a function of the magnitude of difference alone, however. It is also related to the extent to which the individual can sense deviations, however small. For instance, an experienced manager might sense that a problem exists, while a less experienced manager in the same situation might believe that everything is as it should be.

Frequency of cues also affects perception. If an event occurs a number of times, especially in some regular fashion, an individual is more likely to be aware of it as something to which he should respond than if it happens less frequently.

Personal Factors

Since perception is defined as an individual, personal process, it follows that individuals perceive or see things differently. Some of the individual factors that affect perception are listed by Newcomb and his colleagues (1965) as follows; (1) the temporary psychological state of an individual, (2) well-established attitudes, (3) the relationship of cues to other specific factors, and (4) the personality characteristics of the individual.

Temporary psychological state refers to the emotional, mental and/or psychological condition of a person at a particular point in time. Human beings are not always hungry, but when they are, food stimuli are more likely to be perceived than other stimuli. If a person is angry, and as a result feels tense and anxious, he may impute meanings to behavior of others that are not intended. A manager, for example, may find that one of his most effective subordinates has failed to follow through on a project, a failure that is not consistent with the subordinate's past behavior. The subordinate, however, may have a major personal problem at home—say a divorce—which is altering his work behavior. The interests and needs of a person influence what he notices in his outside environment. If he is insecure, he may look for information about where he stands with his superior. If he is dissatisfied with his pay, he may try to discover what others are receiving in salary. Sometimes this process is called "selective sensitivity," since the individual is sensitive only to certain aspects of his environment (Costello and Zalkind, 1963).

The well-established attitudes of a person are important because they serve as a frame of reference from which information inputs are organized and interpreted. Individuals with favorable attitudes toward their work and their company will be alert to cues to improve performance. Those with negative attitudes may not sense work-oriented cues, or even if they do, may react in a way different than that intended by the cue-sender.

The relationship of cues to other specific factors, or how an individual perceives data to be organized for him, is important because cues occur in a context, and the individual creates this context. For instance, the behavior of a person who displays gentleness and quietness may be associated by an observer with the general belief—the sterotype—that such traits are those of a weak person. This context will affect the manner in which the cue is interpreted and, consequently, the response of the other person.

The personality of an individual is also important. The personality of an individual refers to their uniqueness; it is often defined in such terms as aggressive, shy, loud, dependent, and so forth. Individuals with dogmatic and structured personalities will usually classify information into categories, rather than trying to see it as it is—as a less-structured personality might. Structured personalities will tend to resist information that would cause them to change previous perceptions. Or, to take another example, individuals with little self-confidence may be unwilling to accept negative information about themselves from the outside world, and therefore they will selectively distort incoming information so that it conforms to a favorable self-image.

The Socialization Process–Personality Development

Socialization is the process by which a culture, or society, or other institution conditions the behavior of individuals. It can be understood in terms of learning theory and perception. Certain responses (behavior or feelings) become associated with particular situations (cues). When the learner perceives a cue, his response occurs. Over time, these responses become regularly associated with the cue by the person. The unique set of values, attitudes, and behaviors of individuals in their adult lives begin their formation in early experiences. From the time a person is born until his death, he is subjected to the pressure of group norms and values, cues, and reinforcements that over a period of time develop and shape his behavior and attitudes. He develops certain modes of adapting to situations he encounters. This *pattern of adaptation* is called "personality." In general, personality is considered to be the unique pattern of psychological and behavioral characteristics of a single individual. The characteristics, as we stated earlier, are: (1) skills, ability, and knowledge, (2) self-concept, (3) attitudes, (4) values, and (5) needs or motives.

Most of those who have studied personality believe that once it is formed, it is resistant to change. They have emphasized the importance of childhood experiences in personality formation; that is, individual psychological and behavioral patterns that persist in the adult reflect the experiences he had as a child. The adult learned then —or did not learn—how to solve some basic problems. There are those who believe personality is set by six years of age. Erik Erikson (1959), the psychiatrist, points out that the orderly development of a healthy personality requires the successive resolution of certain conflicts at each stage of personality development. His life stages and their particular problems are shown in figure 3.2.

Certain aspects of the personality take on special importance in the world of work. For example, people differ in their reaction to authority. This is so because of differences in their early conditioning. And reaction to authority plays a significant role in organization performance. All organizations have authority systems, and authority issues pervade their day-to-day functioning. Reactions to authority learned by a child in coping with demands of parents, teachers, and other authority figures determine, to a great degree, responses as a superior or subordinate later in life.

Early Socialization Experiences

An infant has very simple needs: to be fed and protected. When he is hungry, he cries. Hearing the cry, the parents feed the child. Feeding

FIGURE 3.2   Erickson's Stages of Personality Development

Approximate Chronological Phase	Specific Problem	Resolution
Infancy	Trust vs. mistrust	From and through his parents. the child hopefully concludes that the world is not a hostile or random place, and some people can be trusted.
Young childhood	Autonomy vs. shame Initiative vs. guilt	Again from and through parents. (mainly in the conflict over toilet training and freedom to explore his house), the child should learn that he is an autonomous person who can and should exercise his independence without guilt.
Childhood and adolescence	Industry vs. inferiority	Success in exercising initiative tends to reinforce itself; the young person should become energetic and confident in seeking productive activity and challenge.
Adolescence	Identity vs. confusion	From examples of his elders and personal exploration, the young person should come to know who he is and what he can do.
Young adulthood	Intimacy vs. isolation	Clarity about self should facilitate the ability of the person to enter into close relationships with others.
Adulthood and middle age	Generativity vs. stagnation	With success and maturity, the individual faces the problem of maintaining effort and interest.
Old age	Ego integrity vs. despair	With declining physical and mental states, the individual struggles to maintain a sense of self-worth and optimism.

Reprinted from "Identity and the Life Cycle" by Erik H. Erikson. From *Psychological Issues*, vol. 1, no. 1. By permission of W. W. Norton & Company, Inc. Copyright © 1959 by International Universities Press, Inc.

reduces the tension (reinforcement). The infant learns that crying behavior will result in satisfaction of the hunger need. While a child is being fed, other events also take place. One of these, for instance, may be a display of affection. The infant will in time begin to associate affection with feeding, and, secondarily, with crying. He is getting affection at the same time his hunger need is being satisfied. When he was hungry, he cried. This led to his hunger need being satisfied. But when he cried, he also got affection. Eventually, he generalizes this reinforcement so that affection itself can reduce his anxiety or tension. (affection is reinforcing now, in addition to feeding). So the child learns to cry to get affection. He also learns other ways to get the same reinforcement. He begins to seek the affection of his parents in order to reduce anxiety.

From this relatively simple sequence, a whole range of potential responses may develop. For instance, the child may learn that to get the affection, he may have to resort to what would generally be regarded as "bad" behavior. The child cries. He may become aggressive, but ultimately he obtains some kind of response from his parents, and this may be what he is seeking.

Parents are "authority figures." Authority figures have power. They can give rewards or withhold them. They can administer punishment or refrain from its use. Parents as authority figures can provide a wide range of need gratification to a child by virtue of the way in which they allocate the rewards and sanctions at their disposal.

In his very early years, the child begins to learn how to respond to authority and authority figures. As he grows, he continues to learn how to adapt to and cope with the world. The responses to authority figures learned at home become further developed and reinforced later in churches, schools, and other organizations, such as the Boy Scouts or Girl Scouts.

These early experiences and what is learned from them carry on into later life. A child who has learned that he can obtain affection from his parents by compliance is very likely to do what he is told by teachers in school. If he follows their directions, he will win recognition. He will try to please his teachers. Doing this will result in positive reinforcement, probably praise. This increases the likelihood he will do as he is told later. As he continues to comply with teachers, he continues to be rewarded. A cycle develops. Children who are "good" students are rewarded and reinforced—and they become "better" students. Teachers look for "good student" behaviors to reward. Often they ignore the "bad" behavior of good students. They may selectively perceive only "good student" cues.

There is a reverse side to this coin, and it is the one in which a child is unable to get attention by compliance. Suppose a young girl has a smaller sister. When she is told to be "good," she does so—but sees her parents spending time with her smaller sister, even so. The older child's reinforcement for being good is perceived as having her mom and dad ignore her—no affection. In time she learns that to get reinforcement (attention), it is better not to be "good." She learns that she must compete for her parents' time, and that this can be done most effectively by being a problem, by adopting an alternate mode of behavior from that of complying. She becomes aggressive, a problem child.

When the child goes to school, she carries this pattern of behavior to the classroom. The teacher expects a certain behavior, and this child acts in the opposite way. There may be negative reinforcement of this behavior from the teacher, but the child's fellow students may positively reinforce her. Thus, when the teacher publicly calls attention to her behavior this may, in a sense, be the very recognition she is seeking before her fellow students. This double reinforcement increases the likelihood that her "undesirable" behavior will continue. In time, teachers come to expect her to be "bad," and they will look for that particular behavior and reinforce it accordingly. So will her peers.

Thus, from early life, people develop individual ways of coping with and adjusting to the world around themselves—and to authority figures. As we have said, these patterns of accommodation have special importance in the world of work.

The Unique Individual—The Results of Socialization

The general pattern of individual reaction and response in coping with the world is a manifestation of an individual's personality. We judge another's personality by what we see him do and hear him say. As we have more and more experiences with people, we learn that most of them have patterns to their responses. A person may be energetic, shy, confident, dominant, friendly, truculent, independent, and so on. If a person consistently strikes out at others when confronted with a problem, he is characterized as an "aggressive personality." If he consistently feels that he is the object of intended harm, he may be regarded as "paranoid."

Skills, Ability, and Knowledge

Some people have high levels of competence in certain areas, say mathematics, while others have great difficulty understanding the subject. Others have the ability to perform physical activities well, while others don't. Some people have extremely high finger dexterity, others fumble putting on gloves. Human beings differ widely in the knowledge, abilities, and aptitudes they bring to a job. Knowledge is an acquaintance with facts or principles. Ability is the capacity to do something. Aptitude is the *potential* to develop future skills or knowledge.

Managers (and others as well, of course) often underestimate the magnitude of individual differences. Even within a group of ostensibly similar people there may be wide differences among individuals on some characteristics. In a group of highly trained scientists, for example, there can be substantial differences in the degree *and* the type of knowledge. The widest differences, however, are typically found in lower occupational groups, since in higher-level occupations, minimal ability standards may be a requirement for admittance. In one study, for example, intelligence test scores varied between 100 and 170—a spread of 70—for engineers, but between 45 and 160—a 115-point spread—for coal miners (Tyler, 1958).

Some aptitudes and skills are inherited. (A person's finger dexterity, for example, cannot be changed significantly by special training.) And while there is a great deal of controversy about the relative effects of heredity and environment on intelligence, it is clear that certain levels of intelligence make it easier to acquire certain levels of specialized knowledge. Thus, intelligence tests are often good predictors of who can successfully complete a particular course of instruction.

Individual differences in tested abilities can be overemphasized on the job, however. Quite often a difference in aptitudes, skills, or knowledge in one area has no effect on performance because that area is not relevant to the task. Differences in intelligence, say, in applicants may not be relevant on a job which requires only finger dexterity. Also, the differences may not be extensive enough to matter. A person with an IQ of 140 may perform a job no better than one with a score of 130.

Research shows that the typical individual varies, within himself, from one aptitude to another (Tyler, 1958). Thus, one person may be very high on finger dexterity, medium on color discrimination, and low on intelligence. What is important to management is that characteristics relevant to a job be determined and that they be measured specifically and accurately.

Self-concept

A person's self-concept is the way a person perceives and evaluates himself. Individuals bring a self-concept with them to the job which can have an effect on how they perform. Some see themselves as competent and are willing to undertake tasks which have an element of uncertainty in them. Others see themselves as leaders and attempt to dominate interpersonal relationships. Others may not evaluate their abilities very highly. They may be afraid to assume certain responsibilities. These self-perceptions are, of course, formed over a person's lifetime, largely on the basis of how others react to him. The individual obtains feedback from others about his impact on them and this information is used to find out about himself. Also, at work, some people assume a self-concept which is congruent with their stereotype of an occupation, such as "research scientist," say. Such a person may feel a responsibility to behave as he believes a research scientist should in a particular set of circumstances.

Attitudes

An attitude refers to an individual's feelings and beliefs about other persons, objects, events, and activities. Attitudes are learned, or develop, over time. These feelings and beliefs about persons, objects, events, and activities can be positive or negative and are the *affective component* of an attitude. The affective component is the emotion generated by the object or event. It means simply that we feel some preference—like or dislike toward an object. This affective component develops because we associate, or "perceive," positively, or negatively, the reinforcing circumstances of the object.

What we see and evaluate is the *cognitive component* of the attitude. It is what we believe to be true or not true about the object. So if we find that a certain behavior is positively reinforced, not only is it likely that we will respond similarly to a similar cue, but we will also develop stronger feelings toward the object and the circumstances. We develop a positive, or favorable attitude toward the situation when there is positive reinforcement, or tension reduction.

Attitudes are learned in a variety of ways. In the many groups to which an individual belongs, certain expressed attitudes are continually reinforced positively or negatively. In a work group, for example, an employee's peers will show approval and disapproval after the expression of attitudes about management, unions, work procedures, performance standards, and other matters. Since most of us seek social acceptance, it is not surprising that the group has an influence over attitudes. The expression of attitudes was, of course, also reinforced in our homes as children, as well as in our present neighborhood and home situation. Certain attitudes develop out of personal experiences with an event in question. If some object, for instance, has contributed to a person's failure, it is likely that he will have negative attitudes toward that object.

Most managers believe that attitudes have a significant influence on work behavior. They believe that the way an individual behaves toward an object or event is substantially affected by that person's attitudes. Attitudes are thus considered to have an *action* component. The way a person feels about something—and what he believes about it—determines how he will behave toward it. It is assumed that attitudes precede behavior, and indeed some research has shown that the changing of attitudes toward a person can change behavior toward the same person (Zimbardo and Ebbeson, 1970). On the other hand, some students of the subject do not believe that attitudes cause behavior, although it must be recognized that attitudes are difficult to measure accurately and that therefore the validity of this belief is open to question.

Research has also shown that a change in behavior can lead to a change in attitude. For example, in one study a group of workers' attitudes were measured. Later, some of these workers became foremen. They then were acting as managers, not as workers, and when their attitudes were resurveyed they were found to have changed to be more like those of management. Other workers in the study became union officials. Their attitudes became different from that of the workers, more like those of union officials (Lieberman, 1956). Thus, when an individual behaves in a particular way, his attitudes change so that they are consistent with what he does. For example, if an employee finds himself alongside a member of a group toward which he has a negative attitude, but treats the other in a way consistent with a favorable feeling about the person as a person, he is more likely than not to develop favorable attitudes toward the entire group. This is because individuals attempt to maintain some consistency between their behavior and their attitudes (Festinger, 1957). In general, a person must be able to justify his behavior with an appropriate attitude, and that behavior influences the attitude—which in turn influences future behavior. There is, then, a reciprocal relationship between attitudes and behavior.

Human beings have many attitudes toward different things. We have attitudes toward work, politics, education, sex, leisure, and so on. These different attitudes tend to be consistent with each other as well as with behavior. This consistency helps us make sense of the world and to behave consistently. The attitude system is therefore one guide to reality.

Attitudes are important factors in a person's identification with a particular group. Holding attitudes in common with others contributes to a strong sense of unity with them. Because attitudes perform so many valuable functions for us, it is hardly surprising that we strongly resist attempts to change them.

Values

Values are more deeply ingrained and more general than attitudes (which are aimed at quite specific individuals or objects). Values are what an individual considers good or bad, important or unimportant. They serve as a means or a standard for evaluating objects and events and therefore they help a person to deal with his environment. They are especially useful in comparing alternatives, since the alternatives can be scaled against values.

Many values come from an individual's background—for example, his religious and ethical upbringing. Some come from the culture itself. For example, in the United States a high value is placed on competition, while in Japan, the opposite is true (Whitehill and Takezawa, 1968). Values also reflect the individual's physhological needs anad are part of the action component of such needs.

Needs or Motives

Most people who study human behavior believe that a large part of it is goal-directed, that we behave as we do to satisfy some individual human need. Just what is meant by a "need"? Needs, or motives, refer

---

FIGURE 3.3 Maslow's Need Hierarchy

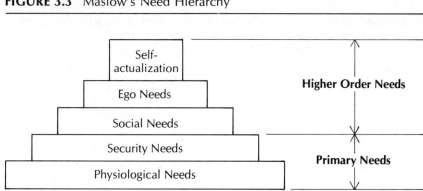

to goal states that an individual strives to achieve. A need exists when an individual determines that his present state of being is not what he desires it to be. When the difference between what is and what is desired is great enough, the person acts to reduce the disparity. This is goal-directed behavior.

There are many ways to conceive of human needs. Some attempts to categorize them describe very specific needs (such as the need for water), while others are more general (relatedness or existence needs). A popular and widely accepted approach to the human need structure is that of Maslow (1943), who describes five categories of needs (see fig. 3.3).

1. *Physiological Needs.* Physiological needs refer to the basic requirements for survival. Man must have food in order to live. He must find some shelter to protect him from the elements. His physical well-being must be provided for before anything else can assume importance.

2. *Security Needs.* Once a person has food and found shelter, he can worry whether or not he will have them in the future. He desires protection against loss of shelter, food, and other basic requirements for survival. The security needs also involve the desire to live in a stable and predictable environment. It may involve a preference for order and for structure.

3. *Social Needs.* The need to interact with others and have some social acceptance and approval is generally shared by most people. For some, this need may be satisfied by joining groups. Others may find sufficient affection from their family members or other individuals, without joining groups.

4. *Ego Needs.* The ego needs have to do with the human desire to be respected by others, the need for a positive self-image. Individuals strive to increase their status in the eyes of others, to attain prestige or a certain reputation or a high ranking in a group. Self-confidence is increased when the self-esteem needs are satisfied. The thwarting of these needs produces feelings of inferiority or weakness.

5. *Self-actualization.* Maslow describes the need for self-actualization as the individual's desire to do what he is fitted for. Individuals want to achieve their potential. This is called the "highest-order need."

A distinction is often made between *primary* and *higher-order needs.* Primary needs usually refer to physiological and security needs. Primary needs are satisfied in fairly standardized ways among people, especially people from the same culture. They are easiest to satisfy in a reasonably active economy, so long as adequate income is provided. That is, an individual with income can obtain the kind of food and shelter that he chooses, within wage limitations, and security needs may be partially satisfied through union contracts or work agreements, as well as social programs such as unemployment compensation and welfare benefits. Letting an employee know what is expected of him also helps satisfy primary needs.

The higher-order needs are more psychological in nature. Different people want different things, and this is precisely the reason why the need hierarchy is difficult to translate into a motivational strategy for the manager. There is no way that managerial strategy or policy can be tailored to meet the very nature of higher-order needs, which include social, ego, and self-actualization needs.

From figure 3.3 it can be seen that an individual's needs form a hierarchy, or ladder. Maslow claims that the higher-level needs are not considered important by an individual until the lower-lever needs are at least partially satisfied. In other words, an individual will not be concerned with social needs if he does not have adequate food or shelter, or if security needs have not been met. Maslow also feels that a person is not motivated by a need that is satisfied. Once a need is satisfied, the person is concerned with the next level of the hierarchy. A person seeks to move up the hierarchy of needs, always striving to satisfy the deficiency at the next highest level. Maslow hypothesized that unsatisfied needs dominate the individual's thoughts and are reflected in what the person is concerned about. (Most attempts to measure needs try to gather information about an individual's thoughts and perceptions.)

A formulation of the Maslow hierarchy has been proposed by Alderfer (1972). Alderfer collapses the Maslow need structure of five into three: (1) existence needs, (2) relatedness needs, and (3) growth needs. *Existence needs* encompass Maslow's physiological needs and some aspects of the security needs; *relatedness needs* include the desire for social acceptance and status in a group; and *growth needs* focus on self-esteem and self-actualization.

From research on how the satisfaction of a need influences its importance and the importance of other needs, it appears that as the need becomes satisfied, it becomes less important, with the exception of the self-actualization needs (Alderfer, 1972). As Maslow predicted, the self-actualization needs do seem to become *more* important as they are partially satisfied.

Finally, research tends to substantiate that if lower-level needs are highly deficient, there is diminished concern for the higher-order needs. The individual is preoccupied with his lower-level need problems (Lawler and Suttle, 1972). This has been shown to be true for individuals who are known to be very hungry, for example, or who have found their jobs threatened, as when a firm faces bankruptcy. Thus, extreme fear or anxiety about lower-level needs precludes thoughts and concerns about higher-order ones. Alderfer's research shows that the relatedness needs may be especially critical for satisfaction of other needs (Alderfer, 1972). If they are not satisfied, the individual may become concerned almost entirely with lower-level needs. If the relatedness needs are satisfied, however, the person becomes primarily involved with the higher-level needs.

An individual's need structure is determined by his socialization, or early learning experiences, and thus there are many differences among individuals with respect to the needs that are important to them. More important, there are many ways in which a particular kind of need may be satisfied. For instance, one person's ego needs may be satisfied by being recognized as the best worker in a department. Another may find this need satisfied by others' recognition of his dress style—being acknowledged as the sharpest dresser in his group.

The specific manner in which an individual satisfies a particular need is learned by reinforcement experiences early in life. We learn through experience that some situations are more desirable (rewarding) than others, and we seek these out. Other situations are ones we seek to avoid. It may be particularly comfortable, for instance, to interact with others of a certain ethnic or religious background, and very uncomfortable to interact with those from other backgrounds.

There is some evidence of differences in needs among occupational groups. Rank-and-file workers generally consider the lower-level needs to be more important in work situations than do managers (Porter, Lawler and Hackman, 1975). Managers, especially those at the highest echelons, consider the higher-level needs more important than the lower-level needs. All this may mean, however, is that lower-level workers may be stating that they are not concerned with higher-level needs as a type of defense behavior, since they have little opportunity to satisfy these higher needs at work. Workers from urban backgrounds seem to be more concerned with satisfying lower-level needs than do workers from rural backgrounds (Locke, 1975). What this means remains open to interpretation, also.

Frustration and the Inability to Satisfy Needs

Behavior is goal-directed. In general, human beings seek to minimize tension by escaping punishment or by obtaining rewards. As we progress from primary to higher-order needs, the particular situations that can positively reinforce, say, ego needs, are different for various people. For example, one person may have his ego needs satisfied when he is promoted, or given a salary increase. The promotion or raise will increase the probability that he will engage more frequently in the behaviors he believes were responsible for obtaining the rewards, and he will do this in the context of the organization where he received the reward. Another person, however, may try to satisfy ego needs away from work by seeking election to an office in the community. If the second person's major orientation is toward, say, a seat on the library board, then a promotion at work will probably not have the same reinforcing strength within the organizational context as it did for the first person.

Perhaps a woman finds that no matter what she does her superior refuses to treat her in a way consistent with her self-concept. She may see herself as a highly effective manager, but she believes her superior treats her as a "simpering female." What happens, then, when tension cannot be reduced or perhaps even avoided? Or, to put it another way, what will a person do when she finds that a particular behavior does not result in need satisfaction? Suppose that the woman wants a promotion very badly but doesn't get it. If she believes her work deserves and has earned recognition, she may continue her past behavior pattern, hoping to be promoted sometime in the future. If she fails to get the next available promotion, however, she will feel *frustration*. Frustration arises from goal blockage when a person is trying to obtain a personal goal, or satisfy an important need but is prevented from obtaining the goal or satisfying the need by some force beyond her control.

The level of frustration may vary with a number of situational factors. One of these is the expectation of failure. The more an individual expects goal blockage to occur, the less frustration he experiences. Whether or not the individual has alternative goals, or means of achieving them, also influences the level of frustration. In addition, frustration is higher the closer the person is to goal attainment when the blockage occurs, when he has had several recent past frustrations, and when the goals he is seeking are important to him (Costello and Zalkind, 1963). Finally, frustration is higher when the blockage appears to be arbitrary, rather than justified.

Reactions to Frustration
The frustrated individual may react in a number of different ways. He may, of course, alter his behavior patterns in such a way that he can

achieve the satisfaction of needs. The manager who desires promotion
may find that he was passed over because he did not have certain
background qualifications, say competence in accounting and financial management. So he goes to school or transfers to another job
where he can acquire this competence. This is constructive behavior.
However, frustration may produce some undesirable effects, such as
aggression, psychological withdrawal, defensive behavior, and alienation.

Aggression is behavior directed at others with the intent of injuring
them. Aggression can take many forms. One is *direct aggression*. For
example, a foreman takes a worker off a job he is trying to finish,
assigning him to another task. The worker goes back to his original
job. After a while the foreman takes him off the job again and assigns
him another task. The worker once more returns to his original job,
and once again the foreman takes him off it. The worker's response is
to solve his problem in a new and more direct way; he flattens the
foreman. Direct aggressive tendencies are not always so extreme, of
course. They may be verbal, as for instance, gossip about another,
spreading malicious stories, or calling another person names. Aggression can also be directed at the organization, and a significant proportion of labor management disputes have their roots in job frustration.
Sabotage, stealing, wildcat strikes, slowdowns, sitdowns, and mili-
tancy and economic strikes may be the result of worker frustration,
and are ways of striking back.

Displaced aggression occurs when the source of the frustration
cannot be attacked directly, and aggression is then directed toward an
innocent third party. At home, an executive frustrated at work may
yell at his wife and children. Conversely, frustrations at home can
result in aggression displaced against innocent individuals at work.

A reaction to frustration in which a person simply gives up and
does not try anymore is *psychological withdrawal*. The level and
frequency of frustration may be so high that the individual says,
"What's the use?" He comes to work late, he stands around doing as
little as possible, he leaves work early. Others may believe that this
worker is uninterested, that he does not like his job.

Perhaps such reactions occur because he is frustrated in his job. He
may have wanted to be promoted, and felt that he deserved such
recognition, but the rewards were never received. This reaction is
seen particularly with underprivileged workers—the subjects often of
discriminatory promotion practices. Several studies suggest that
psychological withdrawal may set in when an initial high level of
motivation is followed by a long series of frustrations (Liebow, 1967).

Sometimes an individual copes with his unsatisfied needs by *defensive behavior*. Such behavior has the function of distorting reality so that self-esteem or esteem in the eyes of others is maintained. It is a result of frustration, especially when failure occurs. Since failure often challenges one's positive self-concept, some method of coping with it must be found. This coping mechanism may take the form of rationalization; that is, finding excuses for failure in the action of others, forgetting mistakes, or blaming others for failure.

The Development of Orientations Toward Work

As we have said, values, attitudes, needs, abilities differ among individuals. Each of us expects something different from work. Nash and Carroll (1975) in reviewing several research studies conclude that lower occupational groups place a higher value on security and money than do higher occupational groups. It must be kept in mind, of course, that there are many differences in work values within any occupational group.

What an individual values in work reflects his psychological needs. For example, employees with higher needs for security place a higher value on having clear work assignments (Carroll and Tosi, 1973). There is also evidence that among managers there is more concern for security in the early years on the job, when the manager is unsure of organizational expectations and perhaps of his own abilities. (Hall and Nougaim, 1968). Security needs for such individuals then decrease as they grow older, but for rank-and-file workers, concern for security increases with age.

Work values differ from culture to culture as well. For example, need for esteem is more important to Italian managers than to U.S. managers, while concern for security is much higher among managers in underdeveloped countries than those in the United States (Haire, Ghiselli, and Porter, 1966). Some research shows much more respect for authority among Japanese workers than among U.S. workers (Whitehall and Takezawa, 1968).

Work values are also a result of what actually happens to a person on the job. If for example, we have worked hard on a task for little money, then we will perhaps convince ourselves that the task has much more intrinsic satisfaction built into it than it actually has. Finally, individuals who have been very successful on a job often come to place a high value on performance itself (Hall and Nougaim, 1968).

Family Characteristics and Work Values

Family background is associated with later work values. The socioeco-
nomic level of the family, for example, is a consistent predictor of
such values. In one study, for instance, being a member of a close
family, having many close friends, being subjected to parental discipline, and having social activities such as dating and taking part in
community projects were all related to placing a high value on job
security, a desire for good working conditions, and a desire for having
good relations with fellow workers (Paine et al., 1967). A stress on
independence and cultural activities in the home, however, was
related to more concern with status, responsibility and independence
on the job. According to Witkin et al. (1962), individuals raised in a
home environment in which independence, achievement, and self-
control were emphasized tend to be more active and have a task orientation as an adult. On the other hand they found that individuals
raised where family ties are emphasized tend to be passive and
socially dependent, and to place a higher value on social acceptance.

Occupational Choice and Work Values

The occupation we choose is also affected by our early socialization
experiences. Although there are many chance factors which affect
one's career choice, it has been shown that the father's occupation is
related to a person's occupation. The sons of individuals in higher-
level occupations, for example, tend to end up in higher-level occupations themselves. The offspring of those in lower-level occupations
tend to take jobs similar to those of their parents. This tendency, of
course, is to some extent determined by the educational opportunities
available, which is most often dependent on the income of the family.

   Which jobs are the high-status jobs? Professional (scientist, engineer, lawyer, physician) and managerial (bank manager, production
manager, etc.) jobs are consistently ranked at the top of the status
hierarchy by the general population (Inkeles and Ross, 1956).

   Individual factors, however, do play a role in occupational choice,
especially in choosing from among occupations with similar educational and experience requirements. One study of those entering the
field of management showed that managerial success (given a high
level of initial ability) was determined by the capacity to understand
one's work environment and demands, competence in handling a
wide variety of tasks, willingness to take risks, and ability to learn
about oneself and then adapt to change as needed (Dill, Hilton, and
Reitman, 1962). Ginzberg (1951) feels that individuals attempt to find

occupations consistent with their values, which make use of their abilities, and are in line with their interests. On the other hand, he feels that an occupation ordinarily does not fulfill all of these requirements, so that an individual must compromise among them to some degree. He sees occupational choice process taking place over a long period of time.

Super (1957) also believes that occupational choice is a result of a long developmental process, during which the individual is learning about himself and developing a self-concept. A person in his earlier years (before 25) is attempting to find out what kind of human being he is and where his strengths and weaknesses are, and he utilizes feedback from others in doing this. His self-concept then becomes an important determinant of his occupational choice. An individual's attempts to establish his identity, however, may continue past the time he makes his occupational choice, especially if he is in certain occupations where the demands appear to require contradictory behaviors, such as pharmacists (businessman or professional dispensator of pharmaceuticals?), military chaplains (army officer or man of religion?), insurance salesman (businessman or financial counselor?).

Chance or luck, as well as parental pressures and individual characteristics also play a role in occupational choice. Chance seems especially important in choosing jobs among the lower occupational levels (Myers and Schultz, 1951). Parental pressures are especially important for individuals who have low self-esteem, or a low self-image (Korman, 1966). Previous investments in certain types of specialized education are also important factors in occupational choice.

Occupational Socialization

For individuals who choose occupations for which specialized training is required, educational experiences may be viewed as a form of socialization for the occupation. For some, occupational specialization begins in professional school, where the would-be professional is first exposed to the perspectives, values, and ways of thinking characteristic to the chosen field. A professional set of beliefs is acquired by participation in informal student groups, from taking courses, and through interaction with teachers. These beliefs are internalized; that is, they become part of the needs, attitudes, values, and self-concept of the individual. The person acts as a "professional" without thinking about it. Reinforcements from teachers are especially influential in shaping the new professional, since in many professions, the professor has much to do with the placement of students. The process

of developing a professional self-image is a slow one, however, and
the student probably does not begin to think of himself as a professional until he is treated as one by those already who have achieved
that recognition.

Socialization and Organizational Involvement

So, what we are is what we have been. Parents, school, college,
friends all shape our personality. We expect certain things from life
and we react according to whether or not we get them. Where we
work, and what we work at is a major part of life. How we react to
work and the work organization is reflective of our personality.

It is possible to categorize various orientations that people have
toward organizations and work that are derived from their experiences. Some people are highly committed to the organization, others
seem to have little or no interest in their work or the organization.
Still others seem to be extremely interested in what they do but have
little commitment to the organization in which they work. Presthus
(1965) categorizes these different orientations as upward mobile,
indifferent, and ambivalent. We have changed the labels in the
discussion that follows, making them more directly refer to individual
organization orientations. These categories are a sort of organizational
personality stereotype, suffering the limitations of any classification
scheme or stereotyping. But they are useful in our later analysis, since
these different personality types appear in different proportions in
different types of organizations. We expect to find more professionals
in some organizations. In others, we expect to find more organizationally-oriented types.

The Organizationalist

Large and small companies, universities, and government agencies all
have highly loyal members who function very well within the system.
A person highly committed to the place where he works is called an
"organizationalist." He does well in the unit in which he works,
seeking organizational rewards and advancement and identifying with
the system. His self-concept is inextricably tied to the organization.
The organizationalist has high morale and job satisfaction. He is likely
to have an extremely low tolerance for uncertainty and ambiguity. He
wants to know what his job is, for what he is responsible, and to
whom he is accountable. The organizationalist is very concerned with
the effectiveness and efficiency of the organization. Organizational

success is important to him because it is reflective of his own success. He is highly committed to the organization's goals. Identifying with a superior, he finds it easy to rationalize organizational pressures for conformity and performance, since he is seeking promotion and other rewards from the system. Status in the organization is very important to him. His life values may be defined, or reflected by, the level he has achieved in the organization. Because this is so important to him, he probably experiences a great deal of status anxiety, or fears that his position in the organization is threatened in reality or potentially. The organizationalist avoids controversy. He is a stickler for maintaining himself within the "channels" of the system, not readily going outside them to handle problems.

The Socialization of the Organizationalist.   How does the organizationalist get to be what he is? The organizationalist develops an early respect for authority figures. His early experiences lead him to recognize the importance of authority, realizing that authority figures have power to dispense rewards and/or sanctions. Presthus (1965) has suggested that the organizationalist comes from a family in which rewards and sanctions are applied primarily by the father.

Externally-oriented Persons

Some people seem to work just for the pay they receive. They find their jobs acceptable but not a critical part of their lives. They perform well but are not highly committed to the organization. They, in effect, act right but feel wrong. They may be managers, lower-level employees, or highly-trained professionals. For some reason or other they do not actively seek the rewards of the organization or strive for higher position. They accept what they have. Given a choice, they would rather be doing other things. They seek satisfaction of higher-order psychological needs outside the organization by doing things that are not related to where they work or what their work is. This is in marked contrast to the organizationalist, who seeks need satisfaction from his connection with the firm. The externally-oriented person generally prefers to withdraw from work. He may be alienated by the tedium of the work itself. He does not get extensively involved with the work organization, and participates in it only minimally beyond work requirements. There are other, more important things in life than the job and the company. Rather then emphasizing the puritan ethic values of work, as does the organizationalist, the externalist seems more concerned with leisure.

He rejects the status and prestige associated with the job. He separates work from what he regards as the more meaningful aspects of life. He is essentially adapting to his work environment by withdrawing from it as much as possible, seeking his psychological satisfaction from neither the work itself nor the organization.

The Socialization of the Externally-oriented.   Presthus (1965) suggests that the externally-oriented person generally comes from the lower middle class. With a limited education, he is restricted in his opportunities for advancement in an organization. If he is in the lower levels of the organization, he is highly likely to stay there.

We must not assume, however, that only lower-level personnel are externalists. Many managers function in this same way. For example, early in a manager's career he may be extremely committed to the organization. He may seek its rewards and want to advance. However, in middle age and in later career life he may find that he has been passed over several times for promotion. Often a person finds that someone else gets the job that he expected to get. When this happens, the person finds other places for positive reinforcement. Thus, it is possible that with their promotion practices organizations may turn managers from highly-committed organizationalists to externally-oriented types. Certainly we would expect to find fewer externalists at higher levels, but it is not uncommon to find them in the higher-management ranks.

Often a person, whether a manager, a specialist, or an operative worker turns the substance of his life to other things. Employees who were once fiercely loyal to the point of following orders without question may change. One such apparent shift in orientation seems to be exemplified in the career of John DeLorean, an ex-employee of General Motors. DeLorean's experiences are described in item 3.1.

We must be careful, however, not to jump to the conclusion that the externalist is a less effective employee than an organizationalist. The externalist orientation is a state of mind. It may be only indirectly related to competence or quality of performance. The externalist may not care as much about the organization as the highly committed person, but, if he has high skill levels, he may be able to perform extremely well. Ability, as well as state of mind, is an important component in determining level of performance.

The Professional

Not all those who look outward from an organization are alienated from their work. Professionals have external orientations but are still preoccupied with their jobs or, more specifically, their careers. While the organizationalist has his self-concept linked to *where* he works, the professional has his tied to *what* he does. The professional has probably been heavily exposed to occupational socialization. In many cases the occupational socialization experiences condition him to believe that he must perform his work extremely well. However, in an organization, there must be compromises with the needs of the system. When the professional is subjected to managerial pressure to conform to organization demands that are inconsistent with his professional values, the professionally-oriented person may believe that such directives are not rational. For instance, a researcher working for a pharmaceutical firm may believe that a particular drug needs more extensive testing before it is released in the market. But there are economic considerations in the decision which must be made. The decision to release a drug might be made by a manager who is less technically qualified than the researcher, and the professional may then believe that a bad decision has been made.

ITEM 3.1   Not All Top Managers Are Organizationalists

Reflections on the Abbreviated Career of John DeLorean, a Nonconforming Executive, at General Motors

Three years ago John Zachary DeLorean, then general manager of General Motors' Chevrolet division, ordered members of his research staff to find him the world's best-handling passenger car. They came back with two Mercedes, and DeLorean ordered his engineers to duplicate their suspension and steering characteristics for the 1973 model of Chevrolet's medium-priced specialty car, the Monte Carlo. When the body of the Monte Carlo was restyled, DeLorean carefully avoided all frills, keeping it distinctively sleek and alive. This year the Monte Carlo is being acclaimed as one of the best-looking, easiest-to-handle cars Detroit has ever produced.

But last spring, while thousands of impatient customers were signing their names on waiting lists for the Monte Car-

lo, DeLorean was walking out of General Motors. At forty-eight, he resigned from a job that paid more than $550,000 in salary and bonuses, ending a career that had seemed to point him toward the presidency of the world's largest and most powerful manufacturing corporation. Instead, he plans to become a Cadillac dealer somewhere.

There is no question that DeLorean's departure was a significant loss to the corporation. Semon E. (Bunkie) Knudsen, who served both G.M. and Ford in high capacities and is now chairman of White Motor Corp., considers him one of the smartest automobile engineers he knows. And Richard C. Gerstenberg, G.M.'s current chairman and chief executive, pays him this tribute: "He was highly regarded by his colleagues and by his dealers. He was good in marketing, too. That's surprising, because he was an engineer, and you don't always find the two going together."

• • • •

In view of his achievements and seemingly brilliant future, DeLorean's departure was not only a surprise, but a mystery.

• • • •

His own stated reason is that he was sick of life at G.M. "The automobile industry has lost its masculinity," he says. "Management's not the same type as when I came here."

The substance of his complaint seems to be that encroaching government regulation has taken the fun out of the business, reducing it to the status of a utility, and that G.M.'s sheer size has led to mind-dulling bureaucratization, which left no room for an individualist like John DeLorean.

• • • •

Lanky, six-feet-four, with friendly blue eyes and a rich, commanding voice, DeLorean practiced the art of nonconformity at G.M. with an intemperance that was downright exuberant. Now that he is out, his daily uniform around Bloomfield Hills, Michigan, is an open-necked sports shirt, faded blue denims, and a well-worn pair of black loafers.

• • • •

He travels in a glittering world of sports stars and movie makers—a group that is decidedly *not* General Motors. Although one divorce is now considered permissible at the company, DeLorean has been married three times, on the last two occasions to actress-models who were in their early twenties.

"A square fellow when I hired him." The child of parents who separated, DeLorean spent half his boyhood in Los Angeles, his mother's home, and half in Detroit, where his father was a set-up man in a Ford foundry. A gangly youth, he doesn't remember winning any school-yard fights, but in other ways he

soon developed an intense, almost uncontrollable drive to attain perfection. Something of a loner, he stuck to activities in which he excelled, giving up saxophone and clarinet lessons because he realized he would never be a great musician.

After getting an engineering degree at the Lawrence Institute of Technology in 1948, DeLorean went to work for Chrysler. It was an era when automobiles were seen as a glamorous product; schoolboys vied to win the Fisher Body Craftsman Guild design contest, and aspired as much to be president of G.M. as to be President of the U.S. DeLorean saw the business as an important calling, a way to give Americans mobility, and he still retains that view to some degree.

• • • •

By 1952 he had grown restless at Chrysler. "It was too big for me to be noticed," he says, and he switched to Packard.

Four years later, when he was head of research and development, Bunkie Knudsen, then general manager of G.M.'s Pontiac division, offered him a similar post with Pontiac. "He was a pretty square fellow when I hired him," says Knudsen. By then married to a secretary from northern Michigan, DeLorean wore his hair short, and his suits came off the rack.

In 1961, DeLorean became chief engineer, and four years later, at forty, the youngest general manager in Pontiac's history. He was also named a vice president of the corporation.

Building on the momentum Knudsen had created, DeLorean led the division to its most successful year. A rock-music enthusiast, he developed a feeling for what young people wanted. "Automobiles are a fashion thing, like clothing," he says. "And the people who set fashions are really the young people, people up to thirty-five." He crafted his idea of what the young wanted into two fast specialty cars, the Firebird and the Grand Prix.

• • • •

Pontiac became known as just about the best-engineered car in the business. DeLorean tightened the pressure on the dealers, and sales leaped from 688,000 in 1964 to 877,000 in 1968, a record that still stands. The Firebird and the Grand Prix accounted for half the increase.

After a triumph of this magnitude, one might think DeLorean would have been immeasurably happy. But he had begun to have misgivings. Back around 1960, Knudsen had taken him to a Pontiac dealers' conference at the El Dorado Country Club in Palm Springs. The late Harlow Curtice, G.M.'s retired president and chief executive, was vacationing nearby and DeLorean met him at the festivities. A powerful executive, Curtice had run the company almost as a monarchy, and he had done so with spectacular success. "I looked at this guy almost as a god," DeLorean recalls.

Talking with the club's golf pro the next day, DeLorean mentioned Curtice. "That's the loneliest human being who ever lived," said the pro. "He comes into my golf shop for a couple of hours every day and talks to me and my assistant about the automobile business. We don't know anything about the automobile business, but we listen to him. He just seems to want to talk so badly."

DeLorean was shaken. Recounting the episode recently, he said, "You realized he never had been regarded as a human being, but only for his job." Like many other G.M. executives, Curtice had devoted all his hours to The Corporation; his friendships were corporate, even his interests and knowledge were pretty much limited to the affairs of General Motors. Now that G.M. was in the hands of others, Curtice's world had rolled away without him. "What is life all about?" DeLorean asked himself. "You work forty years, and what have you got?"

As DeLorean climbed at General Motors and his annual income broke through the quarter-million mark, he gradually shed any attributes Bunkie Knudsen might have considered square. He was beginning to wear turtleneck sweaters and wide lapels, and he grew his hair long.

• • • •

As his own life changed, DeLorean began questioning what he calls the cloistered life at G.M.'s upper levels. As he saw it, the senior officers spent most of their days confined to meetings on the fourteenth floor of the corporation's headquarters in Detroit. Most executives worked ten-hour days, leaving for home around 7:00 p.m., lugging bulging briefcases. On Saturdays many reappeared in the office, this time in shirtsleeves, to put in a few more hours.

Most G.M. executives lived in Bloomfield Hills or neighboring Birmingham, where they socialized together. When they weren't playing golf with suppliers or dealers, they frequently formed foursomes with one another at the Bloomfield Hills Country Club, because few made close friendships outside General Motors. While debate was allowed within the company, it was never to be aired in public, and since G.M. dominated the field, this meant there was little open self-criticism in the industry. Dinner conversations with G.M. executives, DeLorean felt, tended to concentrate on narrow interests—automobiles or finance or engineering—and to exclude such subjects as films or music.

DeLorean wondered if the kinds of friendships that developed around G.M. were really meaningful. In 1968, when Bunkie Knudsen left to become president of Ford, Knudsen became a nonperson at G.M.—despite the fact that his father had been a president of the company and Bunkie himself had built some lifelong associations there. DeLorean made a point of continuing his friendship with the Knudsens, and spent a lot of his time outside the G.M. community with people whose style of life blended with his own.

• • • •

On January 25, 1969, a Saturday, DeLorean was summoned from the twelfth hole of Palm Springs' Thunderbird Country Club by an urgent call from Roger Kyes, then vice president for the car-and-truck group and DeLorean's boss. Kyes told him to catch the first plane back to Detroit and meet him at President Edward N. Cole's house in Bloomfield Hills at eight o'clock the next morning. There Cole told DeLorean he wanted him to become general manager of Chevrolet.

Chevrolet was in trouble. As one G.M. executive describes it, using a metaphor that DeLorean himself is supposed to have coined, "You were looking at the Penn Central of the automobile industry." Chevy's profits were falling, hundreds of dealers were losing money, and the division's market share was shrinking, from 26 percent in 1965 to 22 percent in 1968. Yet Ford was retaining most of its share, even under the battering of imports. As one Chevy dealer says in retrospect: "G.M. got so conservative and so conscious of the corporate image that Ford was beating them with new products people wanted."

Communications among some of the division's major departments were erratic, primarily because each lived in a state of secluded autonomy. The marketing department had launched an ad campaign for the four-cylinder Nova with little warning to the manufacturing department, which had no chance to plan and had to go on overtime to meet the demand the ads generated. The division had twenty-five computers, and they had not been coordinated into an efficient system. When a new car was designed, its specifications had to be taken from the engineering department's computer and reprogrammed into the manufacturing department's computer. Things broke down altogether when the 1969 models were introduced; the computers failed to invoice hundreds of new cars.

All in all, DeLorean faced a staggering assignment: he was being asked to turn around what amounted to the world's fifth-biggest industrial company. By FORTUNE's estimate, the annual sales of Chevrolet total some $10 billion, about the same as the sales of General Electric.

The tyranny of the perfectionist
DeLorean visited plants and talked to supervisors and workers as he searched for the trouble spots. He met with the dealers, whose low morale had been driven even lower when the division's sales manager told *Automotive News,* the industry's trade paper, that part of Chevy's problem was too many fat-cat dealers.

• • • •

DeLorean fashioned his staff into a dedicated team. He would sit in his office, his feet on the desk, while questioning each new visitor incisively and answering an incessant barrage of telephone calls. He grasped one complex issue after another, as if he were performing a cerebral juggling act. "He wasn't hanging over anybody's shoulder to keep an eye on them," says Gerstenberg. He didn't have to, for he cultivated his people, delegating authority and persuading them that his demands were really their own ideas. But he would brutally tyrannize anyone who didn't measure up to his standards.

• • • •

The division's slide stopped, and its market share leveled off at about 22 percent. Chevy's profits continued to decline during 1969 and 1970, the latter year because of the long United Auto Workers strike. But they turned up in 1971 and have been growing ever since. Dealers' profits before taxes have doubled since 1969 to more than $400 million in 1972.

• • • •

While absorbed in trying to bring Chevrolet under control, DeLorean was beginning to have problems at home. He was on the road much of the time and worked long hours when he was back in Detroit.

• • • •

To be sure, DeLorean earned more in a year than many people do in their lifetimes. But he was discovering that neither the money nor the position could guarantee happiness. Some dealers he knew, including one of his three brothers, were making as much as he and giving a lot less of themselves to the job. "I make $600,000 a year," he once told a Chevrolet dealer in Illinois. "But I can't play golf next Thursday and you can."

Toward the end of 1970, DeLorean heard that a franchise for a new Cadillac dealership might soon become available in California.

• • • •

DeLorean was promoted to corporate vice president for the car-and-truck group, which accounts for about a quarter of G.M.'s operations. He moved onto the fourteenth floor, where he worked with other senior officials, attending meetings of the many committees that made the decisions at the top. Such a post might be viewed as the place where G.M. puts the final trim on its future presidents. But the change was too much for DeLorean.

• • • •

He found that a group executive, who oversees the division managers, is cut off from sources of information. The committee system so annoyed him that, if a particular meeting seemed to him unimportant, he deliberately stayed away, to the irritation of his superiors.

"You were getting all your input from lower-level specialists," he says. "They provided information in such a way that they would get the answer they wanted. I know, I used to be down below and do it. The feeling I started to get, being suddenly put on the fourteenth floor, was that now I was being presented with information that had limited alternatives. This is totally inconsistent with any thoughtful and creative originality. You never could reflect on and modify a proposal. You couldn't be a planner. You were too harassed and oppressed by committee meetings and paperwork— you just had tons of it. You were cut off from the outside world. You saw only the men on the fourteenth floor. The corporate hierarchy was just reacting to the demands of the organization and responding to some degree to the government and the public. It was like standing in the boiler room and tending a machine and you were just watching it instead of running it."

As high up in the corporation as he was, DeLorean continued to have trouble getting his views across. About three months after his arrival on the fourteenth floor, he proposed that General Motors save what he claimed would amount to $1 billion annually by making a number of changes.

• • • •

But DeLorean's seniors decided that his proposals would not save any money. . . .

"A guy who is giving his life's blood"
Perhaps the most controversial issue DeLorean got embroiled in was what position G.M. should take on federal emission standards, and whether it should request a year's extension of the 1975 deadline set by Congress.

• • • •

According to sources within the company, what bothered DeLorean was that General Motors . . . was arguing for the year's delay because it did not know for sure that [its] converters would meet the standards completely. DeLorean contended that instead of asking for the delay, the company should take a more positive and realistic stand and announce that it was willing to *try* to meet the existing standards—even if it could not guarantee 100 percent success —by equipping the 1975 cars with the new converters. Because he was getting nowhere with a lot of his arguments, he became dejected: "When this happens to a guy who recognizes what ought to be done, and who is giving his life's blood and can't get it done, then hell, he ought to go on and do something else."

The longer he inhabited the fourteenth floor, the more DeLorean realized that the rewards he had believed would lie at the top, the immense power and sense of fulfillment, simply were not there. Suppose he did one day become president, what would it mean? Cole was a man who knew the product and its market, yet as president, Cole often seemed to be powerless. Cole had also urged that G.M. be more aggressive in small cars, but lost. DeLorean finally concluded that what he regarded as Cole's predicament would be his own.

In March he told Murphy he wanted a Cadillac franchise that was opening in Florida. Murphy, Gerstenberg, and others tried to dissuade him, but this time they did not push very hard. "After awhile you begin to wonder whether you're wasting his time and ours," says Gerstenberg.—Rush Loving, Jr.

Fortune, Sept. 1973 Reprinted with permission. Copyright 1973 Time, Inc.

Professionals are likely to be particularly disturbed when they believe they are in a situation where they are unable to most effectively utilize all their skills. In such a situation, the professional feels underutilized. Most importantly, his self-esteem may be threatened because he does not have the opportunity to do the things which he has been trained to do best.

Often professionals refuse to play the organizational status game, looking outward to other professional colleagues for approval. The professional would rather not be in the organization. He would rather be operating independently. Yet an organization is necessary to him, since it is imperative that he have a place to work, a base of operations and an economic base for his work. The professor who does not purport to have a high degree of loyalty to his university must still be in some university to do what he wants to do. Otherwise he cannot teach, do research, or engage in those other scholarly activities which the profession requires. The professional must adapt in some way to these supportive needs, and often these accommodation patterns are highly conflictful.

The Socialization of the Professional.   Presthus (1965) states that the professionally-oriented person comes from the middle class and has become successful through higher level of education, or by his own efforts to increase his skill. He is likely to have a strong "ideological" orientation and to be extremely concerned that he does well in his chosen field. Success for the professional is usually defined in terms of personal achievement. More than likely it is measured by recognition from external colleagues, rather than by the rewards received internally in the organization. Organizational rewards are not valueless however, since they do represent a way that the professional may estimate the importance of his professional contribution relative to others in the system. His specialty may be extremely fulfilling for him if he is able to operate in an organization where, due to the importance of his professional skills, he is accorded higher status and pay than those in other work groups.

Organization Socialization—The Psychological Contract

To a large degree, the character of a person is fairly well shaped by the time he begins his work life. Early socialization experiences have caused the person to develop some ideas about how he should interact with an organizational system. His early socialization experiences are the basis for his values, expectations, and beliefs about what he should do at work. By the same token, there are expectations by the members of the organization about what employees should do. The *psychological contract* refers to the mutual expectation between an organization and its members about what is expected of each (Schein, 1970). An industrial organization and its employees, whether managers, specialists, or operative workers, have expectations about how much work is to be performed for the pay received. Students and professors have a set of expectations about what is appropriate performance for the other in a course when a grade is to be given. These expectations, however, are not limited to compensation only. They may focus on demands such as loyalty to the firm or the special rights of long-term workers.

Norms are ideas about what kind of behavior patterns and values are acceptable in a group or organization. They are expressed in terms of acceptable performances expected of others. Naturally, there are many norms that apply in any organization. For instance, there are accepted ways of dealing with a superior. In some organizations, certain kinds of dress patterns are appropriate, while others are frowned upon. Dark suits and subdued shirts and ties may be "right." Flowery shirts, open at the neck, and sandals may be "wrong." Some norms are more important than others. Schein calls the most important norms—those which must be accepted by organizational members—*pivotal* norms. The *peripheral* norms are less important. They may be desired in a member but it is not essential that the person accept them. Schein says there are three models of individual adjustment to an organization: *active rebellion*, when both pivotal and peripheral norms are rejected; *conformity*, when both are accepted;

and *creative individualism,* when the pivotal norms are accepted and the peripheral ones rejected. It is more possible for an organization to grow and change itself in a productive way in the creative individualism mode than if the first two adjustment modes prevail.

Schein (1970) points out that the psychological contract between an organization and an individual is informally negotiated over time—at least partly—through the *organization socialization process.* New members learn performance expectations of their superiors, as well as the organizationally-preferred values and ways of doing things. This occurs in a variety of ways, as in the case of early socialization experiences of life. The teaching may be direct, as when a new employee is told about performance standards and rules, or it may be learned through "behavioral modeling," in which the employee imitates others in the organization. Most behaviors, however, are probably learned through reinforcement. Of course, the consequences of certain responses may be mixed—approval for some, disapproval for others—but the individual's future behavior is going to be influenced importantly by reinforcements from his dominant reference group. A new production employee, for example, may be far more concerned with approval from his fellow workers than from his foreman. A student's fraternity brothers or sorority sisters are likely to have more influence on the development of his or her values than will the college dean.

The new organizational member, then, comes to the job with a set of work expectations. He expects certain things about his working conditions, the mode of supervision, type of work assignments, and organization expectations of him. As the individual is socialized to organizational life, he may learn that there is a divergence between what he expected and what the organization expects. In one study of college graduates hired by one of the large automotive companies, typical graduates found most of the job characteristics were worse than expected (Dunnette, Arvey, and Banas, 1973). In this study, it was also found that there was a wider divergence between what the graduate expected and what was present in the job situation for those who terminated as compared to those who stayed. Thus, more often than not, the typical new organizational member has a set of expectations about his job which are somewhat unrealistic in terms of the organization's expectations. A period of adjustment and change takes place, and gradually the organization's expectations become better known to the individual, and management becomes more aware of the individual's expectations. Thus, the stereotyped idea of an individual being simply a pawn molded by an organization is not an appropriate way to view reality. It is certainly true that individuals are shaped by their organizational environments. However, organizations must, of necessity, adapt to the needs and values of various individuals or their very existence is threatened. Unless an organization can continue to secure the services of new members, it will atrophy and die.

When a person changes organizations, he must be "resocialized." Schein (1968) has followed business school graduates through various stages of their careers. He has found, as expected, that the values learned by students in the university setting change once they take jobs elsewhere. When they are in school, the values of the students reflect those of their professors. After a time in an organization, the students' values become significantly less like those of faculty members and more like those of top management personnel in the organizations where they work.

This chapter has discussed how individuals develop attitudes, values, and needs in their early experiences that are important in their affiliations with work organizations later. Three organizational orientations that result from socialization experiences were defined, and we have also discussed briefly the effect of organizational influences on individuals. Later in this book we will suggest how different organizations may, among their personnel, find different compositions of these individual personality patterns. In later chapters, also, many of the concepts sketched in this chapter will be reintroduced and expanded.

In the next chapter, we move to another problem—interaction in groups. Maslow's need hierarchy places social needs in an important position; therefore, group processes must play an important role in individual behavior in an organization and must be understood so that the managerial process can be effectively carried out.

Discussion Questions

1. Can you recall, from your own experience, a situation when you misinterpreted a cue, or stimulus, from another person? Did it get you in trouble? How?

2. Have you ever given someone a compliment (a positive reinforcement) and had that person react differently than you had anticipated?

3. Look around you right now. Select a part of your environment that you weren't aware of when you started reading. Why didn't you see it?

4. Close your eyes and listen to the sounds around you. What is happening? Is anything going on that shouldn't be? Pick up the differences by listening.

5. Parents, teachers, scoutmasters are authority figures. Do you react to your boss at work in the same way you reacted to them?

6. Was there ever an instance in your school days when the teacher disciplined you yet you were a hero to your friends? How did you feel? Would you do again the thing that got you into the predicament?

7. Consider Maslow's "ego" needs. How can yours best be satisfied? How about those of your best friend? Your mother? Father? Boss? Husband? Wife? Other friends?

8. In this chapter, we describe three stereotyped ways of reacting to organizations. Think of two people who fit in each category. Think of an *executive* that you know who would fit in each category. Think of a *professor* for each. Can you think of an "operative employee" or worker for each?

9. What is   your reaction to John DeLorean? Did he make a good decision? How would you characterize it? Would you do what he did? What makes you the same? Different?

Chapter 4

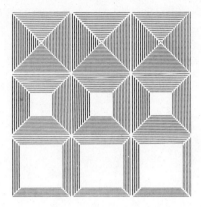

The formal structure of an organization is nothing more than the creation and specification of groups, along with the description of how they should relate to each other, and thus groups of all kinds and sizes abound in work organizations. Departments, committees, integrated task teams and the like are all formally designated groups. Within these units, members may go on to act in ways not specified in their job descriptions. No job description, for example, defines the individuals with whom an employee has lunch or travels to and from work. Yet from these activities may develop lasting relationships which can affect job performance.

Many problems in organizations can only be understood when the group is the unit of reference. Conflict between labor and management, for example, or between production and sales units, or between line and staff may be considered as special cases of group conflict. For these reasons it is important for managers to know something about group characteristics, phenomena, and processes.

All groups start from a collection of individuals assembled for some purpose. The purpose may be to accomplish together some common personal objective of the individuals or to accomplish some temporary or more enduring objective of the organization or of a manager with authority over the individuals that make up the group. For example, a group of workers or managers may voluntarily get together to form a car pool or to discuss possible approaches for obtaining a change in a disliked organizational policy. Or a department head may form a committee of six subordinates to produce a set of recommendations for reducing customer complaints. Or a collection of general lathe operators may be put together in a particular section of a new plant to perform various assigned tasks. These permanent or temporary collec-

Group Behavior

tions of individuals then develop norms, values, roles, a status hierarchy, and other group characteristics. Then, depending on the degree of attraction the members develop for the group, and the group's success in achieving its objectives and the objectives of its members, the group becomes more or less cohesive over time.

Groups—Primary and Secondary

A group may be defined as a collection of individuals who regularly interact with each other, who are psychologically aware of each other, and who perceive themselves to be a group. There are two kinds of groups: primary and secondary.

Primary Groups

When people interact together on a face-to-face basis and where the relationships between members are personal, the group is called "primary." Primary groups have no formal written rules and procedures. Family and friendship groups are examples of primary groups.

In the work setting, primary groups are usually made up of individuals who feel they have something in common. Perhaps they all come from the same part of town. Primary groups at work might be based on similar racial or ethnic backgrounds. Or the cribbage players, bowlers, or classical music fans may spend time together at work, forming a primary group. Among managerial groups, in some organizations, primary groups may be based on the "old school tie," that is, a common educational and class background.

Secondary Groups

Secondary groups are usually larger and more impersonal than primary groups. They are governed by formal rules, procedures, and policies. The work organization is a secondary group, as are professional associations and unions. Most secondary work groups are fairly stable over time (departments, for example). Others are more temporary (committees, for example).

Departments or Permanent Functional Assignments

The formal work assignment of an individual is likely to be related to the manner in which he perceives problems and his perception of his unit's status. For example, Browne and Goliembiewski (1974) found that members of staff or support units saw their "organizational unit as unimportant, impotent, as having an inward orientation. . . ." Operating unit personnel, however, saw their units as "important powerful, having an outward orientation." Dearbon and Simon (1958) found that executives from different functional areas such as production, marketing, and accounting defined problems in terms of activities and goals of their work assignments.

These studies point up the fact that the nature of the work group, together with the job requirements, can have significant effects on the attitudes and perceptions of individuals. In addition, individuals operating in groups are often strongly influenced by group norms. This is true whether or not the group forms itself or is an organizationally-defined unit.

Committees

Committees are common to all organizations. They are contrived groups, meet only periodically, and are established for a variety of purposes. Committees may investigate problems and report the results of their investigation. They may be used to obtain new ideas: to make decisions; or be created to coordinate the activities of various groups in the organization. A committee is usually a temporary work assignment. Its members meet together to discuss the issues before it.

The effectiveness of a committee in reaching its objectives depends upon a number of factors. For instance, both the structure and composition of the committee and the process of communication and deliberation are important. For greatest effectiveness, committees should not be so large as to preclude involvement of all members; should contain individuals with the necessary authority to implement decisions that are reached by the group; should be motivated to achieve the group task; and should not be made up of members with personal characteristics (such as quite unequal statuses) which might hinder full participation of all members.

Many studies have been made of how differences in the way committee meetings are conducted can influence the results obtained (Maier, 1963). It has been found that in addition to the formal agenda or official task before the group, many meetings have a hidden agenda which involves the personal objectives of the individuals at the meeting. These personal objectives may be to increase one's prestige, to humiliate others, to gain control over an activity, or to sabotage a new policy or precedure. These hidden agendas of course may prevent the attainment of the committee's task.

Certain behaviors on the part of the group leader may contribute to the effectiveness of the meeting. For example, separating the obtaining of ideas from the evaluation of ideas or bringing out into the open any hostility to proposals may facilitate the accomplishment of a group's task objectives (Maier, 1963).

Considerable attention has been directed toward decision making in groups or committees and whether such groups are effective for this purpose. Obviously, committee or group meetings consume time that could be used for other productive purposes; the larger the groups or committee, the more costly the meeting becomes. Some research shows that committee members working on a problem individually are more effective at reaching certain solutions than the members working together collectively (Bunker and Dalton, 1965).

Required and Emergent Behavior in Groups

Organizational units such as departments and committees are established on the basis of task requirements, or the job to be done. They are set up as a result of a rational decision-making process or they may in part simply evolve as a response to some organization need. *Required behavior* refers to that which is established for, and expected of, the members. It is an organizational requirement. *Emergent behavior* is that behavior which actually occurs in the group. It is a result, not only of job requirements, but of a wide range of individual and group characteristics which we will discuss later in this chapter.

As Homans (1951) points out, emergent behavior is likely to be different from, and more complex than, required behavior, because required behavior only considers the needs of the organization, not the needs of individuals and of the group itself. On the other hand, emergent behavior—the behavior you actually see in a group—is the result of an accommodation between organizational demands and the interests of group members.

Most emergent behavior is probably functional for the group. It helps the group to cope with the stresses arising from the nature of the work and the interaction between individuals in the group. For instance, where workers have a monotonous job, the monotony may lead the workers to trade jobs, gamble, or engage in horseplay and other social activities—all diversions which enable them as a group to cope with the demands placed upon them by boring and repetitive work.

Some emergent behavior of course may be highly undesirable from the organizational point of view. Restriction of production, for example, is organizationally undesirable, but it may also be a way by which workers adjust to managerial pressures which conflict with individual or group needs, a way to avoid threatening comparisons between group members, for instance. Or, since the restriction of production is a group activity, it may provide the excuse for social interaction which gives the group a sense of purpose and a reason for existence. Production may also obviously be restricted in order to protect the jobs and income of group members.

The Effects of Groups at Work—Two Studies

The importance of groups in the work setting is highlighted in the two studies that we discuss here. The first, the Bank Wiring Observation Room study, is part of the Hawthorne studies mentioned in chapter 2. It shows how required and emergent behavior exist in the work place. The second, a study of coal-mining methods in England, illustrates how re-forming groups (or departments) can have positive effects on productivity.

The Bank Wiring Observation Room.   As part of the Hawthorne studies, the researchers wanted to examine a stable and experienced group of workers which had control over its own output and where it was easy to measure individual output quite precisely (Roethlisberger and Dixon, 1939). The men chosen—nine wiremen, three soldermen, and two inspectors—attached wires to banks of terminals used as parts of switches for central office telephone equipment. To perform this job, each wireman first attached wire by hand to terminals on a plastic bank which was stabilized in a holder. Next, a solderman soldered the wire in place. Then the inspector, using an electrical test set, tested the work.

Before the study began, output records from the department from which the men were chosen were obtained for 18 weeks. In addition, all 32 workers in the department from which the men were chosen were interviewed prior to the study period. During these interviews, the men expressed their attitudes toward their jobs, supervisors, and working conditions. The 14 men chosen were told by their foreman that they were to be studied and were asked to cooperate. The experimental subjects were then introduced to the man who would observe them in the observation room. They were assured that no information obtained by the observer would be used to their disadvantage. All but one of the men studied were between 20 and 26 years of age, and only one had any college education.

The Bank Wiring Observation Room was separated from the main department by high partitions. In it, in addition to the 14 subjects, there was the observer and, for a good part of the time, a trucker who brought in materials and removed completed work, and a group chief, the lowest grade of supervisor. As in the main department, the wiremen who wired "connectors" were placed in the front of the room and the wiremen who wired "selectors" were placed in the back of the room.

Group piecework was the system of wage payment for the department. Each piece of equipment completed by the department as a whole was credited to the department as a fixed sum. Each worker was paid an hourly rate of pay, depending upon his efficiency rating, plus a bonus.

Observation of the group at work showed that the actual behavior of the workers was different from, and more elaborate than, the work behavior described in the official descriptions of the jobs. For example, the men helped each other when someone fell behind in his work, though not all workers were helped and not all workers helped. In addition, the wiremen and the soldermen traded jobs (with the offer to trade being made by the wiremen).

The men also formed two friendship cliques within the Bank Wiring Observation Room. Each clique participated in its own games and other social activities. In addition to conversations, there was kidding and horseplay within the groups. The men gambled in a number of different ways. They organized pools and together would choose and place bets on horse races. They also matched coins, shot craps, and played cards. The men brought candy together and shared it, and they ate lunch with each other.

The researchers soon realized that the men in the Bank Wiring Observation Room, as a group, were controlling the rate of production. They had a definite idea of what constituted "too much" and "too little" work. At times, slower workers were bawled out for not working fast enough.

In addition to setting production norms, the group felt that no worker should "squeal" to higher management about another group member and no group member should attempt to put himself in a superior position in relation to the other workers in the room. One of the inspectors, the oldest man in the room and the only worker with some college education, was teased by the men. They adjusted his test set so that it did not work and reported to their supervisor that he delayed them. He retaliated by reporting the men to a higher level, an act that created so much hostility toward him that he had to be transferred out of the room.

The Bank Wiring Observation Room study ended in May, 1932, after 6½ months. During this time, the researchers observed that the men had created an informal social organization which developed an unwritten but understood set of rules governing the behavior of the men in the group and specifying the nature of the relationships among them. The Bank Wiring Observation Room group illustrates many important characteristics of all groups, characteristics which will be discussed later in this chapter.

Integrated Task Teams. Naturally efforts have been made to more carefully construct work groups and assign work to them to improve performance as well as the satisfaction of members. One such effort is the "integrated task team." It is based on several assumptions (Rice, 1953). The first is that a work group should have just the right number of workers to complete the task efficiently, but be small enough to enable individual members to identify with the group's output, thus allowing them to experience a sense of task completion, of accomplishment, of success, and of satisfaction. To accomplish this means that the tasks assigned to a group must be extensive enough for the group members collectively to feel they have accomplished something worth-while, such as producing an identifiable result.

The second assumption is that work groups will be more cohesive and stable if they can identify with a territory or area different from that occupied by any other workers. This could be accomplished through the use of walls, partitions, special marking on the floor or on the equipment, or by some other means.

The third assumption is that cohesiveness, stability, and satisfaction will be higher in groups with satisfactory interpersonal relationships, with control over their own day-to-day work and organization, and with a fairly narrow range of skill levels and pay differentials within the group.

An investigation was made in the British coal mining industry of the consequences of assigning work to integrated task teams instead of on an individual basis (Trist and Banforth, 1951). Prior to World War I, mining companies in Great Britain obtained coal with the use of small work teams—often consisting of three persons—which worked on a contract basis. Paid according to how much coal they brought to the surface, the teams were very cohesive. This system was replaced by the longwall system under which coal was obtained through specialization. Under the longwall method, each miner was a specialist and each shift did specialized tasks.

TABLE 4.1

	Conventional Longwall (specialization)	Composite Longwall (integrated task team)
Percentage of time spent reworking tasks done poorly by other shifts	25	5
Absence rate percentage	20	8.2
Productivity as percentage of ideal productivity (perfect efficiency in getting out all coal)	78	95

Source: E. L. Trist and K. Banforth, "Some Social and Psychological Consequences of the Long Wall Method of Coal Getting, *Human Relations* 4 (1951).

In the conventional longwall method, the first shift in each new location bores holes in which to place explosives in the coal face, undercuts the coal face so the coal will drop when the explosives are set off, and takes down the conveyer equipment at the previous location. The second shift reassembles the conveyer at the new location, makes passageways, and props the roof. The third shift takes out the coal and brings it to the surface.

In one mine a new system was developed and used which has been called the "composite longwall system." In this system, miners with various job specialties are placed in teams which have the skills to perform all of the necessary tasks in mining the coal. Each team works in the mine as a shift and does whatever tasks are necessary to carry forward the work done by the previous shift. This means that one shift does not have to complete certain tasks before the work of the next shift can commence. In addition, each work team is given autonomy and the right to control its own activities. Each team was also put on a group incentive plan in which all members of the team shared. Table 4.1 presents a comparison of some results achieved under the two systems. Clearly the quality and quantity of work improved significantly and the absence rate decreased when the group was re-formed to use the integrated task team approach.

Some Properties of Groups

Groups, like individuals, can be characterized or described along certain dimensions which are characteristics of the group, not of any single member, characteristics such as group *values, norms, roles,* and *cohesiveness.*

Group Values

Individuals bring values and attitudes to a group and also learn them from the group itself. A group's values refer to what is important or unimportant to, or what is good or bad for, most members of the group. Activities of other groups, the organization, and of its own members are evaluated against the value structure of the group. Some groups place a high value on education, for example, some on money, others on experience. Others place a high value on the establishment of strong personal friendships.

Norms

Group norms refer to the unwritten set of behavioral expectations—what members "ought to do." Norms are rules and standards that govern the conduct of group members. Norms will obviously be congruent with the values of the group, and are a means of social control, a means of evaluating the behavior of others. Norms tell an individual what to do and what not to do.

Learning of Norms. Norms are learned in a variety of ways. They may be learned by simple observation of other group members, by being directly taught, or by conditioning, (as discussed in chap. 3). Conditioning occurs as a result of reinforcement from other group members. When, for instance, a new member works at too fast a pace the first day on the job, he may be subjected to derogatory comments such as "Look at old speed king there," "Look who's trying to make us look bad," "Look who's trying to impress the foreman," "Look at who's trying to make us lose our jobs," and so on. A little of this goes a long way in obtaining compliance with group norms.

Norms of a group are enforced, then, by sanctioning violators. Sanctions may range from communications of disapproval, such as those cited above, to social ostracism, threats, and actual physical attacks, pranks, and the direct sabotage of another's equipment, raw materials, or finished goods. For example, in a steel mill a work team found that the previous shift filled the furnace with grit each morning until they reduced their level of production to the norm of the other furnace teams. A worker in a sweater factory found that other workers cut his yarn and damaged his machine when he worked at a pace which they considered too fast.

Factors Affecting the Level of Compliance.   There are usually varying degrees of compliance to group norms. Some individual members are quite conformist, while others are not. A number of personal characteristics seem to be related to susceptibility to group influence. One such personal characteristic is the degree of identification with the group. Some individuals identify strongly with a group, while others do not. A higher level of education, or being of higher social class than most other workers may generate negative identification with the group. In the Bank Wiring Observation Room study, the individual who violated the group norms had a higher level of education and was older than the other group members. Also, most organizational members are the members of several groups. If the norms and values of the other groups conflict with those of organizational groups, a problem is created. This problem often becomes a matter of which group the organizational member primarily identifies with. The group with which an individual identifies most strongly is a primary reference group—the one to which he looks for guidance in his behavior and attitudes. Some research has indicated that the professionals in an organization, such as scientists, engineers, and economists, are more likely to identify with an outside group than are managers. If they identify strongly with their professional colleagues outside the firm, they may, of course, be less loyal to the firm than are managers.

Conforming behavior has also been found to be associated with certain personality characteristics. Individuals with low levels of self-confidence, with high levels of insecurity, or with a fear of being different are likely to be more responsive to group influence than their opposites.

One's position in the group also influences norm conformity. The lower a person's status in the group, the less the other group members expect of him. In general, individuals in high-status positions are expected to be models of conformity to group norms.

The level of norm compliance also depends on factors peculiar to the group itself. All norms are not of equal importance to the group, and all deviations from norms are not equally visible to other group members.

Role and Position

Norms define the kind of behavior another person *should* exhibit. The behavior sequences of an individual's interaction with others is called a "role." ("Role prescription" is another way to define norm.) In a group, formal or nonformal, an individual may interact with several others. For instance, at work a manager may interact with subordinates, fellow managers, and his secretary. The manager's relationship with his subordinates is one role. His relationship with fellow managers is another role. Each of these different role partners have expectations (or norms) about how the manager should act.

All of an individual's group roles, as a cluster, define that individual's *position*. The position, a cluster of related roles performed by an individual in a group, locates him in relation to others "with respect to the job to be done, and the giving and taking of orders" (Katz and Kahn, 1964).

Since different individuals may occupy the same position at different points in time, it is expected that there would be some differences in role behavior between individuals in the same position, but also much similarity. Role behavior would depend upon the role incumbent's own personal characteristics and his perceptions of what others expect in the behavior of a person in his position, as well as the demands of others. Behavior of different individuals in the same position would be similar in many ways because of the expectations of others, and would be different in many ways because of differences in abilities and personality. In the Bank Wiring Observation Room, there were two inspectors, and they perceived their roles quite differently, one ingratiating himself with the group and not carrying out his officially assigned duties; the other acting quite officiously and informing on the men.

An individual may have many roles simultaneously, but in any particular instant of time only one role may be activated. Which one it is depends upon which group an individual is acting with at the time and with which individuals he is interacting.

The roles that an individual may have vary from one group to another and from one group member to another. At times an individual is the superior and at times he is a subordinate. At times he is expected to provide information and at times to receive information. At times he must make a decision and at times he must carry out another person's decision. And at other times, of course, he may be a parent, a Little League umpire, or the secretary of the local bridge club.

The *role set* consists of all those other individuals in the group with which a person has contact and who have expectations about his behavior. He himself is included in his role set. Of course, there may be misunderstanding by a group member of what behavior is expected of him by others in his role set. His role perceptions may differ from what is sent or communicated by members of his role set. Or the group member may understand clearly what the expectations of members of his role set are, but he cannot comply for a number of reasons. One reason may be role conflict. For example, a foreman's subordinates may expect him to ease up on them after an especially difficult day, while his superiors may expect him to increase pressure on his men to get out a particular order.

Status

Role relationships are defined in terms of interaction between incumbents of positions. Roles may also be different in terms of *status* within the group. Status refers to the hierarchical ranking of roles in a group so that some roles may be said to be "higher" than or "superior" to others. Newcomb and his colleagues (1965) note that such distinctions may be functions of "skill, wealth, power, popularity."

Individuals in roles may have high or low status because they belong to particular professions (such as the medical), have a particular formal position (say as the vice-president), have a particularly important skill for the group (say as a computer programmer), or have achieved recognition in another area (such as a professional ballplayer). Having high status gives one a set of rights and obligations. For example, individuals in a high-status position have the right to make suggestions to individuals occupying lower positions. At the same time they may have an obligation to provide certain types of advice and help incumbents of lower-status position. In the Bank

Wiring Observation Room, the higher-status wiremen always initiated
the request to change jobs with the lower-status soldermen. For a
solderman to initiate such a request would be considered inappropriate behavior for a person in the low-status position.

Group Cohesiveness

Both primary and secondary groups differ in their solidarity or cohesiveness. *Cohesiveness* is the ability of the group to maintain itself, or
continue to exist, when it is subjected to pressures and stress (Stogdill, 1959). Some groups are closely knit, while others are much less
so. A number of factors have been found to be associated with group
cohesiveness. Size is an obvious factor; other factors being equal,
smaller groups are generally more cohesive than larger. Interaction
opportunities contribute to cohesiveness. In many organizations, it
may be quite difficult for members to talk to each other or be in close
contact. Noise, physical separation by machinery, and other factors
may limit interaction.

Cohesiveness generally increases as a group experiences success in
its collective activities. Repeated failure often creates internal dissension and bickering within a group, but if a group is successful in
meeting its objectives, pride in being a member may increase, and
members may increase their commitment to the group. External
attacks and pressure may also greatly increase group cohesiveness. To
meet a common threat, the members will pull together.

Personal characteristics of members may also influence group
cohesiveness. Individuals with similar backgrounds are likely to have
common values and are therefore less likely to disagree. A common
background may contribute to patterns of similar interests, making
communication easier. Similar backgrounds may make individuals
more comfortable in one another's presence.

Status factors are also important. If one believes his professional,
ethnic, or racial group is superior to those of others, he may not want
to associate with those believed to be of lower status. Also, persons
may not want to associate with others whose status is ambiguous,
because the uncertainty makes them uncomfortable. *Status congruence* means the degree to which the factors associated with group
status line up with respect to each other for a particular individual.
(Zaleznik et al., 1958). A person has high status congruence if his
personal characteristics are consistent in placing him at a high-, a
middle-, or at a low-status position in the status hierarchy. Low-status
congruence means there are inconsistencies with respect to such

factors. The important factor is consistency. For example, assuming
that a particular group values individuals with high levels of education, who are older, experienced, can tell funny jokes and have a
native American background, a young immigrant with little education
or experience, who is not funny, would still have high-status congruence because he is consistently low in all his status factors. On the
other hand, another person, well-educated, funny, but young with
only a moderate amount of experience would have low-status congruence. It is likely that the first young person would be accepted by the
group. Members would find it easy to interact with him because his
status position in the group is clear, and one's expected behavior
toward him is also unambiguous. The other young person might find
only limited acceptance, however, because his status position in the
group is unclear and there is uncertainty about how others should
behave toward him. The uncertainty is likely to lead to avoidance,
since uncertainty contributes to interpersonal anxiety and most individuals attempt to avoid anxiety-producing relationships.

Some Effects of Membership in Groups

Membership in groups has an impact, both positive and negative, on
the attitudes and behaviors of members. Groups can be highly satisfying, providing sources of social support, while at the same time be the
source of problems for an individual.

Individual Support.   An individual becomes a group member to gain
the advantages of such membership. The advantages may be many. In
the previous chapter we discussed basic human needs. Some of these
needs are satisfied in the group. For example, the group provides
opportunities for social interaction, which in itself may be satisfying.
The individual may find others who care about him and his problems.
The group also provides help and assistance to its members. Though
the group, the new employee may find out which rules have to be
followed and which do not. He is told how to get on the best side of
his superior. He gets advice and help with his work.

The group also protects the individual. In unity there is strength. A
group can often stand up to a foreman, or to organization pressures,
when an individual cannot. The opportunities to exercise leadership
and other skills may also exist in a group. A group may be a means of
achieving a high individual status, if the group is highly regarded by
others. Individuals may grow and develop in groups, and group
members may learn from each other.

Secondary groups, as well as primary, are of value to the individual. Obviously, membership in some secondary groups is the means by which one makes a living. Secondary groups may authenticate one's professionalism, and also—along with primary groups—may provide many off-the-job satisfactions.

Effects on Performance and Attitudes.   Group members are influenced in their performance by what they perceive others expect and want of them. A cohesive group may perform at a consistently high level as well as at a low level. Seashore (1957) found in a study of 228 groups in a machinery company that attitude toward management was an important determinant of whether performance norms for a group were at a high or low level. It is not known, however, whether the effect of *most* groups is negative or positive with respect to performance level.

Job Satisfaction.   The evidence seems clear that workers who are accepted members of industrial work groups have higher job satisfaction (Vroom, 1964; Helmreich, Bakeman, and Schenwitz, 1973). Several studies have shown that as opportunities to interact with other workers are diminished, job satisfaction goes down (Jasinsi, 1956).

Turnover-absenteeism.   There is a demonstrably constant and close relationship between satisfaction and turnover and absenteeism. As job satisfaction decreases, absenteeism and turnover increase (Vroom, 1964). Therefore, it is not surprising that a number of studies show that workers who are accepted group members or who have an opportunity for conversation and interaction with other workers have lower absenteeism and turnover rates than those who do not (Porter and Steers, 1973).

Helping Behavior.   Helping others seems to be a fairly universal activity in groups. This phenomenon is found in all groups—family groups, college fraternities, military units, industrial work groups, primitive tribes, and so on. Such helping behavior may be of considerable value in improving production. For example, where the work in interdependent, better coordination and team effort can help the job. On the other hand, of course, it is also possible that members may help each other sabotage work.

Tension and Anxiety.   Seashore (1954), in his study of 228 industrial work groups in a machinery company, found there was less anxiety among workers in the highly cohesive groups. There is other evidence also that individuals associate being with other people with a reduction in tension and anxiety (Schacter, 1964). Thus, positive mental health benefits may result from the individual employee's acceptance in his work group.

Individual Growth and Development.   There is increasing concern today with providing opportunities for personal growth and development in work and social situations. But while individuals may become more competent as a result of group membership, such membership may prove a barrier to self-development efforts. Zaleznik, Christensen, and Roethlisberger (1958) made an intensive study of 50 workers in a manufacturing plant and found that there was a certain amount of suppression of the individual by the group. In some groups, individual members were not allowed to learn new modes of behavior or to adopt new ideas and perspectives.

There is a cost to conformity, and some part of it is a loss of individual freedom in growth and development. The Volvo plant in Sweden, for example, has used a form of job enrichment (see chap. 5) to change its assembly procedures. Rather than a typical assembly line, as found in U.S. auto manufacturing, teams of three of four Volvo workers decide among themselves who will work on the various parts of the engine. A group of visiting U.S. auto assemblers worked in the plant. Some liked the quite different atmosphere, but some felt that "working with a team . . . required accommodating to the habits of others; they preferred to be responsible to themselves."

Problems of Groups

In groups, individuals, as we have noted, do not always find the going easy. Groups can impose many pressures and sanctions on individual members, and thus contribute to individual stress. Also, groups can be a cause of many problems in organizations because they are in conflict with each other. In this section, we will examine two sets of problems. One set deals with stresses on the individual—those of role conflict and role ambiguity. The second set deals with intergroup problems.

Role Conflict and Ambiguity

Katz and Kahn (1964) have treated the problem of role conflict and ambiguity extensively. These stresses to which an individual is exposed in groups, whether a work group or formal departmental assignment, can affect the way group members perform and feel.

Role conflict occurs when a person is subjected to inconsistent demands with respect to his behavior. *Intersender role conflict* occurs when the inconsistent demands come from different individuals in the role set. The salesman, for instance, is under pressure from his superior to get the highest possible price, while the customer presses for a low price. *Intrasender role conflict* occurs when the inconsistent demands come from the same source, as when a manager expects a subordinate to complete a project which requires more personnel to do it, but at the same time refuses to assign added staff to the subordinate's unit. *Interrole conflict* develops when a person outside the role set imposes demands which cause problems within it. The family of a manager may expect the manager to spend time with them, rather than at the office, thus inducing role conflict. *Person-role conflict* occurs when the demands in the role are inconsistent with the individual's own value system. This problem could occur, for example, in cases where a work assignment calls for a legal but perhaps unethical activity which the person feels is wrong.

Role conflicts exist in all organizations, and people learn to adapt to some moderate levels. Organization structures which define jobs and accountability are efforts to minimize this condition.

The condition in which individuals may not be clear as to what the role requirements are—that is, they may not know precisely what to do—is called *role ambiguity*. Two types of role ambiguity may exist. Ambiguity with regard to what behavior, or task, is expected is called *task ambiguity*. Or a person may be unclear about what others think of him. This may be related to how his supervisor rates him, or what his status in a group is. This type of role ambiguity is sometimes called *social-emotional ambiguity*.

Sources of Role Conflict and Ambiguity. Role problems may occur for a number of reasons. Perhaps an individual is a new group member. It will take him some time to "learn the ropes." Or role relationships may be unclear due to rapidly changing membership in a group. In formal organization structures, we would expect higher levels of role ambiguity when there is rapid growth or change. Role conflict may be high, for example, when the organization structure must be constantly changed to accommodate developing markets or changing technology.

In subsequent chapters we will be more specific about the particular types of role conflict and ambiguity in differend kinds of organizations, along with their effects.

Intergroup Conflict

An organization is made up of many different groups. Some of these groups have work which is relatively independent of other groups, while others may be interdependent due to the nature of their work. When the work of different groups is interdependent, the relationships between or among the groups is of critical importance organizationally. Such relationships may be characterized as being cooperative, helpful, synergistic, or uncooperative, antagonistic, mutually destructive, and so on.

This does not mean that intergroup cooperation is good and intergroup conflict is bad for an organization. Some conflict is productive if it results in two conflicting objectives being satisfied. For example, there may be substantial disagreement in an organization between the engineering group and the sales group as to whether a product should be designed with an emphasis on quality or on price. Both quality and price must be considered and the disagreement between the two groups may insure that both factors are considered in the design and production of the product.

On the other hand, two groups may cooperate to the detriment of the organization by jointly opposing needed changes. Or two groups may place such a high value on avoiding disagreement that problems that should be surfaced and discussed are not.

Some Determinants of Group Conflict.   A number of different factors can contribute to intergroup hostility, leading to unproductive results such as confrontation, maneuvering and marshaling strength to overcome the other.

1. *Competition over Resources.* Groups will find it easier to function and group goals will be easier to achieve when resources, money, people, or physical assets are plentiful. When a number of groups are dependent upon a single or otherwise limited resource base, however, there is likely to be a great deal of competition for resources. This gives rise to hostility and conflict. In addition, groups will want representation in decision making about resource allocation to insure that they are equitably treated.

2. *Status Differences and Work Flow.* Group conflict can develop because of the work-flow sequence in an organization. If work relationships are such that individuals from a low-status group appear to be telling individuals in a high-status organizational group what to do, considerable resistance may develop. The higher-status group may attempt to show its independence and power by doing the opposite of what is requested, by anger, by ridiculing members of the lower-status

group, or by avoiding contact with representatives of the lower-status group. If a waitress gives a cook an order from a customer, he may swear at her just to let her know who is boss. When draftsmen give suggestions to engineers, when technicians criticize the work of production experts, or when students criticize faculty members, there may be negative, hostile feelings generated in the higher-status group member because of what appears to be inappropriate behavior on the part of the lower-status group.

3. *Conflicting Objectives.* Different groups often have different objectives. These may be contradictory, leading to considerable disagreement between two groups which must coordinate their efforts. For example, a production group responsible for minimizing production costs may disagree with a sales group trying to maximize sales revenue by processing customer orders at a faster but more costly rate. Disagreement is especially likely when the two different groups are rewarded or punished for meeting or not meeting their assigned objectives. Such conflict is inevitable because an organization pursues many objectives simultaneously and many of these objectives are contradictory.

Different executives may not agree on the relative importance of different company objectives. Some may stress short-run objectives of the organization, while others may be more concerned with long-run objectives. Such differences in objectives are related to differences in group memberships in the organization, as we have noted earlier. These, in turn, are related to differences in the problems facing different groups and differences in their values.

4. *Different Perceptions.* Even though different groups may interact regularly, members of one group may perceive things differently than members of another. One frequent source of disagreement is the tendency of any group to value its own ideas, proposals, and creations more highly than those of other groups. Each of two groups making a proposal tends to overvalue its own work and to undervalue the work of the other group.

Perceptual differences arise from the tendency of an individual to evaluate things in terms of his own experiences. Since organizational members have had different experiences, training, and education, they tend to perceive problems and their causes differently (Simon and Dearborn, 1958). This is especially likely to occur when the problems or possible causes of a problem are ambiguous.

5. *Ambiguous Authority and Work Assignments.* Many tasks require the work of two or more groups. In such cases it may be difficult to pinpoint responsibility or to correctly allocate credit or blame

for good or bad performance. For this reason, members of some groups may not wish to undertake joint assignments. A group may attempt to get another to assume responsibility for the unpleasant, difficult, or unfairly rewarded tasks, while it tries to gain control over the more pleasant, easy, or fairly rewarded tasks. Actions such as these lead to conflict between groups.

6. *Reciprocity.* Gouldner (1960) has noted the importance of reciprocity in and between groups. Group members feel that they should receive a just return for their services. If the relations between groups are such that one group seems to be always doing something for another group without receiving benefits in return, this gives rise to a feeling of being exploited and the first group will be motivated to terminate the relationship.

Relationships Between Competing Groups. Some research in both organizational and nonorganizational settings shows that competition among groups affects what happens *within* groups and between them (Schein, 1970).

What happens *within* each competing group? Each group becomes more closely knit and elicits greater loyalty from its members. Members close ranks and bury some of their internal differences. The group climate changes from informal, casual, and playful to work- and task-oriented, and concern for members' psychological needs declines, while concern for task accomplishment increases. Leadership patterns tend to change from democratic toward autocratic and the group becomes more willing to tolerate this. Each group becomes more highly structured and organized. More loyalty and conformity are demanded from members in order to be able to present a solid front.

What happens *between* the competing groups? Each group begins to see the other groups as the enemy, rather than merely as a neutral object. The group begins to experience distortions of perception—it tends to perceive only the best parts of itself, denying its weaknesses, and tends to perceive only the worst parts of the other group, denying its strengths. Each group is likely to develop a negative stereotype of the other ("They don't play fair like we do"). Hostility toward the other group increases, while interaction and communication with the other group decreases, making it easier to maintain negative stereotypes and more difficult to correct perceptual distortions. If the groups are forced into interaction—for example, if they are forced to listen to representatives plead their own and the others' cause in reference to some task—each group is likely to listen more closely to their own representative than the representative of the other group, and to find fault with the latter's presentation. In other words, group members tend to hear only that which supports their own position and stereotype. As mentioned earlier, the group that wins in the competitive situation is likely to become more cohesive. The losing group tends toward internal dissension and finding fault with certain of its members.

These concepts about groups and group problems are underlying explanations for many coordinating problems which managers must face. (In chap. 16, for example, we discuss how a manager can approach the job of bringing together, for the purpose of achieving organizational goals, groups with very divergent points of view.) To be an effective manager, it is essential not only to understand a great deal about the nature of individuals, but also a great deal about the nature of groups.

Discussion Questions

1. Are the experiences described in the Bank Wiring Observation Room Study similar to or different from those you have encountered in work groups? Other groups?

2. Think about your experience in observing an ethnic group from a distance. Were the characteristics which you associate with individuals from that ethnic background prominent to you? Did you have positive or negative feelings about the group? Think of how they felt, good or bad, while they were together. When you meet individually with your close friends from that same ethnic background, are they like the "group" you observed?

3. What do your answers to the questions in no. 2 above tell you about

   a) group norms and values?
   b) group pressures?
   c) differences in behavior when alone or in a group?

4. Have you ever experienced *role conflict*? How did you resolve it? Have you ever experienced a role conflict situation in which resolution to the satisfaction of all involved was impossible? How did you decide with whom you would comply?

Chapter 5

Now that we have considered the questions of how individuals get to be what they are—and how they are—and how groups work together (or don't), we can more closely address the practical consequences of some of these ideas.

Ask a manager what his most common problem is, and he will probably respond, "People. How to get those who work for me to carry out their tasks satisfactorily—how to 'motivate' them to perform well." The ability to motivate subordinates is generally considered an essential management skill. Perhaps not surprisingly, those in top management positions in most organizations tend to feel that *people* seldom perform up to their capacity, the implication being that either people are not working well, or that they are not being managed effectively by lower-level executives. For example, two top managers said this about their work groups:

> "I'll tell you my honest opinion. About 5 percent of the people work, 10 percent of the people think they work, and the other 85 percent would rather die than work!"

> "There are lots of workers in this plant, hundreds of them, who don't have the capacity to do things other than what they're doing. And they're lazy! They might be able to develop some capacities, although I think there are a lot of them who couldn't even if they wanted to. But *they don't even have the desire*" (Argyris, 1953).

Motivation, then, is a prime concern of today's managers. Managers at all levels believe that if they can only "motivate" their subordinates, those subordinates *will* perform to capactiy, and life for everyone will be simpler and better.

Motivation
and Performance

This concern with motivation is due, in large part, to the fact that measureable differences in performance between companies, government agencies, departments, and other types of organizational units are more often than not attributed to human factors. If, for example, you were to enter an automobile plant in which all signs and symbols designating the company had been removed, you probably could not differentiate it from the plant of any other auto company. The assembly line at a Chevrolet plant looks very much like that at a Ford plant. Therefore, given this similarity between hardware and technology, it is easy to attribute differences in productivity and performance between a Ford plant and a Chevy plant to human factors—a problem of differences which can be solved, it is commonly thought, by proper motivation of the workers.

Motivation is also a concern in our contemporary culture because of our historic stress on the "work ethic"—the belief that to work is good and that everyone should *want* to work. The socialization experiences of large segments of our society have led them to believe that they should be involved and committed to their work. (This causes some psychological problems for people when they are out of work. At the 1975 convention of the American Psychological Association, for example, Dr. Hannah Levin reported that after interviewing 45 unemployed men and their wives and children in Brooklyn and Staten Island, her finding was that many unemployed look upon themselves as "nonpersons." She said that "lack of work, especially for a male, puts him in a psychological no-man's land. He doesn't feel legitimate anymore, nor adult," and that 90 percent of the 45 unemployed she interviewed felt responsible for their predicament. "'I should have gone to college,' said one. 'Maybe I lacked initiative,' said

another. 'I didn't try hard enough,' said a third." This is the work
ethic functioning when there is no work.)

Many managers subscribe to the work ethic, and it upsets them to
discover that many who work for them do not—may, in fact, be alienated from their work. The most common tactic used (or tried) to
counter this alienation is "motivation," because it it widely believed,
especially among those who subscribe to the work ethic, that if one is
committed to and generally satisfied with his work, he will perform
better. If he *thinks* well of his job, he will *do* well at it. This is one
concept of motivation frequently held by managers who wish to "motivate" their subordinates. The question is, is it a sound concept?

An oft-cited story whose moral is intended to stress the importance
of work involvement has three stonemasons of the Middle Ages
working on a cathedral. An onlooker approaches the three and asks
the nearest, "What are you doing?"

"I am earning a living," is the reply.

The observer turns to the second and asks the same question.

"I am practicing my craft."

The observer turns to the third mason and again asks the same
question.

The third stonemason's reply is: "I am building a cathedral."

The *intended* moral of this anecdote is that the third stonemason
has been doing the best job because his work is the most meaningful
to him—he is "motivated." It is our guess, however, that if we could
find that cathedral, and the three locations where the stonemasons
were working, there would be no differences between quality of any of
the stone placement. If the anecdote's moral were true, buildings all
around us would have bricks falling out of them where the least
motivated brick layers toiled. When motivation is defined this way (as
job involvement, job satisfaction, or work commitment) it may—or
may not—be related to performance. The attitude of an individual
worker toward his job, how he thinks about it, may be substantially
less important in determining how well or poorly he performs than
are a good many other factors.

Motivation—Two Definitions

Perhaps some of the difficulties of understanding the relationship of
motivation to work occur because there are several ways this term is
used and, often, there is confusion. One way to define motivation is as
a *management activity,* or something that a manager does to induce
others to act in a way to produce the results required organizationally.

In this context we might say, "The teacher tries to motivate the student," or "The role of a manager is to motivate the worker." We use the term in this way when, later in this chapter, we describe several managerial motivation strategies.

We also use it another way. Motivation can also be defined as an internal mental state of an individual which causes him to behave. This is a *psychological* definition of motivation, some facets of which were examined in chapters 3 and 4. Some of these facets will be expanded upon later in this chapter in our discussion of different theories of motivation.

Job Satisfaction, Motivation, and Performance

Job satisfaction may well be the most studied human factor in organizations, with much of the work resulting from the interest generated by the Hawthorne studies and the point of view known as "human relations." The logic underlying the human relations point of view was the assumption that if a worker is committed to his job, he will be more productive. Such a commitment is likely to be made because of, and reflected by, the level of job satisfaction. By increasing job satisfaction, goes the assumption, we will improve performance.

But why *should* satisfaction cause a worker to perform at a higher level? A worker may be perfectly happy in his job while at the same time be wholly uninterested in exerting much effort at it. Or a worker may perform at a very high level even though dissatisfied, because he fears losing his job. Or he may perform well because he believes it is his duty as a responsible person to do the best he can. (Professionals, especially, often feel this way.) He also may work hard because he needs the money to pay his bills.

That satisfaction causes high performance is an intriguing assumption and would be very useful if it were consistent with reality. Victor Vroom (1964) has examined 20 studies in which various measures of job satisfaction (or employee attitudes toward work) were correlated with different measures of performance. He found that the average correlation in these studies between satisfaction and performance was very low, leading him to conclude that:

> There is no simple relationship between job satisfaction and job performance. . . . We do not know yet the conditions which affect the magnitude and direction of relationships between satisfaction and performance.
>
> . . . The absence of a marked or consistent correlation between job

satisfaction and performance casts some doubt on the generality or intensity of either effects of satisfaction on performance or performance on satisfaction. It also suggests that the conditions which determine a person's level of job satisfaction and his level of job performance are not identical.

Thus, it would seem, as we have stated, that improving job satisfaction may not in itself necessarily improve job performance. On the other hand, there is some evidence that higher job satisfaction may *follow* better job performance (Greene, 1973). This is likely to happen when the higher performance is followed by receiving rewards important to the employee, such as a promotion when a job is done well by the organizationalist type of employee. In chapter 3 we discussed learning theory and stated that for a reward to be positively reinforcing it must be *associated* with the event by the individual. Thus, the externally-oriented employee who performs well and is promoted may not be as satisfied as the organizationalist, because, as we said, his values lie outside the organization.

At the same time, research has shown a definite and consistent relationship between job satisfaction and the turnover and absenteeism rate among workers (Vroom, 1964). Absenteeism and turnover can both, of course, affect both costs and productivity. If a worker is absent from his job, for example, others may have difficulty performing their jobs because of that absence. If a worker quits, his equipment and machinery stand idle until he is replaced (perhaps by a less experienced worker).

High turnover and absenteeism can be very expensive. Consider, for example, a plant employing 1,000 workers at an average wage (salary and fringe benefits) of $15,000 per employee. If the absentee rate is 5 percent, this means that the plant must hire 50 additional employees at a cost of $750,000 to offset the absenteeism. Conversely, cutting absenteeism by one-fifth (20 percent) would result in a savings of $150,000 a year.

Jeswald (1974) describes some of the costs incurred by organizations due to turnover. Fringe benefits, severance pay, overtime costs, under-utilization of facilities, administrative expenses, training cost, and productivity losses are substantial. Nash and Carroll (1975) estimate that a rank-and-file employee who quits can cost a company at least $3,000. The costs are significantly greater for managers and professional employees. If 10 percent of a rank-and-file work force of 1,000 workers quits each year, then turnover costs will amount to at least $300,000.

So, while it is very difficult to associate job satisfaction with productivity levels, if we accept the idea that it is related to absenteeism and turnover, then it is clear that some substantial costs may be reduced if satisfaction can be increased. We can see that because of high cost associated with job dissatisfaction, leading as it does to turnover and absenteeism, it is necessary to try to determine what factors may increase job satisfaction.

Factors Affecting Job Satisfaction

A person's satisfaction with a job is determined by the difference between the characteristics of the job, what he wants from it, and what he feels he receives from it.

What an employee *wants* is determined by his values, and is related to his economic and psychological needs. What he *feels he receives* is determined by a personal sense of equity—by his perceptions of what other individuals are receiving for what they do compared to what he believes he does. Thus, if an employee finds out that another worker is earning more than he is, but is not exerting more effort, putting in more hours, or does not have more seniority or education, then he will feel a sense of inequity or injustice and will be dissatisfied. On the other hand, an employee may be satisfied with his pay even if he finds out that other workers doing work similar to his are getting more pay than he is, *if* he perceives that they work harder than he does or have more seniority, education, or ability.

It is also true that in certain circumstances, pay satisfaction or dissatisfaction is not highly related to *overall* job satisfaction. If a worker places relatively little value on pay, as compared to the value he places on other job factors, pay dissatisfaction may not significantly reduce his total job satisfaction. And even when workers on similar jobs receive exactly the same benefits, we would still expect differences in job satisfaction among them because they will have different job values. As mentioned in previous chapters, some individuals place a high value on pay, while others place a lower value on it. Some employees place a high value on using their abilities; some do not. A variety of job satisfaction and dissatisfaction factors, then, and their relationship to one another, must be weighed and reckoned with when devising motivational programs.

All this is to say that if the manager expects to increase satisfaction, *he must work on those factors which make a difference to employees*. In one organization which was experiencing high dissatisfaction, the management believed a "communications" gap existed. They began bombarding the employees with "newsletters" and other informational devices. The general dissatisfaction remained. A more objective assessment by an outside consultant found that the problem came, not from lack of information, but from several policies the workers thought unfair. One cause of discontent was the "parking policy." Certain parking places were *always* restricted, even after working hours. Some employees who worked a later shift thought this unfair, especially since the spaces were generally unused after 5:00 o'clock. A reconsideration of the policy led to a change, removing a cause of dissatisfaction.

Herzberg's Two-factor Theory

Herzberg (1959) argues that satisfaction and dissatisfaction may not be opposites, that the provision of certain job benefits may only serve to minimize dissatisfaction and will not increase satisfaction. For example, making satisfactory parking available to workers may not cause them to be unusually happy, but the lack of satisfactory parking *will* create dissatisfactions. Herzberg maintains that providing fringe benefits, nice offices, and good vacation plans serves primarily to minimize dissatisfaction and to keep people in the organization; it does not lead to more work or better performance.

According to Herzberg, job characteristics can be classified as either "Satisfiers" or "Dissatisfiers," depending on whether they affect satisfaction or dissatisfaction. Dissatisfiers, also called "hygiene" factors, create dissatisfaction. Some of these hygiene factors are:

1. Technical supervision
2. Interpersonal relationships with peers
3. Salary
4. Working conditions
5. Status
6. Company Policy
7. Job security
8. Interpersonal relations with the superior

According to Herzberg, the absence of a certain job factor in this category—such as good relations with peers—creates dissatisfaction; but if there are good peer relations, that does not generate satisfaction.

Satisfiers are also called "motivators," because they are related to high satisfaction and willingness to work harder. These job factors may induce more effort, but if they are absent, will not produce dissatisfaction in most people. The following characteristics of the work situation are "motivational" in nature.

1. Responsibility
2. Achievement

3. Advancement   5. Recognition
4. The work itself   6. The possibility of growth

If, then, a person is in a challenging job, he is likely to be satisfied and motivated to perform better. The lack of challenging work does *not* cause dissatisfaction, but merely the absence of satisfaction.

The attractiveness of such an approach for a manager is obvious. It is very helpful in deciding what to do. For instance, if a high level of worker dissatisfaction is seen as the major problem, then it is clear that attention must be given to the *hygiene* factors. But the manager knows that this will not be enough to improve performance. To do this the manager must work on the *motivators,* and this means changing the character of the work to make it more challenging and intrinsically rewarding.

While there is research to support some of Herzberg's claims, most does not, at least not completely. Those studies that do not support Herzberg's theory show that certain job characteristics can produce either satisfaction or dissatisfaction, depending upon their presence or absence, though some factors are more likely to influence dissatisfaction than satisfaction, and vice versa. Table 5.1 summarizes the results of several studies carried out by Locke who used Herzberg's research technique which asks employees to think of days when they felt unusually good or unusually bad about their job. As table 5.1 shows, being given an interesting task activity is associated with satisfaction,

---

TABLE 5.1   Frequency of Motivator and Hygiene Events as Satisfiers and Dissatisfiers for Five Samples

Event Category	Frequency as: Satisfier	Dissatisfier
1. Task Activity	40	39
2. Amount of Work	9	27
3. Smoothness of Work	11	32
4. Achievement/Failure	114	64
5. Promotion	20	13
6. Responsibility	33	8
7. Recognition	81	93
8. Money	35	20
9. Interpersonal Relations	17	40
10. Working Conditions	7	26
All Motivators (1-7)	308	276
All Hygienes (8-10)	59	86

Source: Locke, E. A., "The Nature and Consequences of Job Satisfaction." In M. D. Bunnette (ed.), *Handbook of Industrial and Organizational Psychology* (Chicago: Rand McNally, in press).

as one would suspect. Being assigned an unpleasant task is related to dissatisfaction. Similarly, successfully completing an assignment is related to happy feelings, and failing to complete a task successfully is associated with unhappy feelings. Locke's research (1975; in press), and that of others, indicates that for most employees, the task is mentioned more often as a source of unusually high or low levels of satisfaction than are other job factors, even pay. This is probably because on most jobs pay does not vary as much as does the nature of the task. Most employees receive a pay increase at regular intervals of time, annually, let us say, and the amount of the increase is antici- pated in advance.

The employee's answer when he is asked to think of a time when he felt unusually good or unusually bad about his job is influenced by the employee's memory, what has actually occurred, and his tendency toward selective perception. This leads, using such a research method, to attributing successful events to himself and unsuccessful events to others.

In general, the research suggests that the following job factors are associated with "good" days:

1. Being given an interesting work assignment.
2. A feeling of achievement from success in doing a task well.
3. Recognition from others for good work.
4. An advancement, an unexpected salary increase, or an increase in resposibility.

In general, then, something that the person *himself* can take credit for produces reported satisfaction.

The following tend to be associated with "bad" days:

1. Being assigned unpleasant work.
2. Inability to complete an assignment successfully.
3. Criticism from employer or associates.
4. Failure to receive rewards that are expected.
5. Unfair treatment, unfair distribution of work, etc.

In general, then, bad days are blamed on others.

In reviewing these finding, Locke concluded that a person wants the following from his job:

1. Challenging work he can cope with successfully.
2. Just rewards for performance which are in line with his aspira- tions.
3. An understanding of what is expected by others.

4. Appreciation and acceptance by supervisor and co-workers.
5. Working facilities and resources which facilitate task performance.

Locke's study shows that the factors listed by Herzberg as satisfiers and dissatisfiers are not as clear-cut and obvious as they may seem on the surface. For example, a person wants "challenging work he can cope with successfully." Self-confidence, as well as skill, will be a determinant here. For instance, one person may find it challenging to repair an automobile engine. The highly-skilled mechanic who views an engine as a problem to be solved will be motivated to work on it. That same engine, broken down, would be avoided by a person who has no knowledge of internal combustion engines, for he knows that if he works on it, the problem will probably become worse.

Motivation and Performance—A Complex Relationship

Pragmatically, the manager must get results from other people. He must structure the work situation, with a mix of people and equipment, to yield some outcome—a product or service—to be used by others. This can happen only when someone works, either physically or mentally.

These results are what we mean when we use the term *performance*. Performance is the result of the application of effort, mental or physical. It is usually evaluated against some standard which may reflect earlier achievement by others, the person himself, or a standard developed from a time study. Performance levels may be stated in terms of quantity or quality, and may reflect some subjective judgment by a manager. A particular level of performance may be considered "high" for one person, but the same level may be only "satisfactory," or perhaps "unsatisfactory," for another. Finally, although performance is the result of effort, it is not correct to think that the level of performance can be raised by more effort. Sometimes a student, for example, receives an A in a course with little work and a D in another in spite of more work on the latter. The level of performance, relative to some standard, is called "productivity."

As mentioned, when the performance of an organization or a subunit is at a lower level than desired, the blame is usually placed on the people who work in it. The manager will want to get "better people," "more motivated personnel." Before a manager concerns himself with "motivation" however, he should attempt to determine what other factors cause poor performance.

If it is truly due to lack of motivation, he should of course, attempt to induce his subordinates to exert more effort, but other factors— such as an individual's ability, the amount of help received from the supervisor, and technological considerations—also affect performance and should be considered when evaluating it. The way we view motivation and performance in this book is shown in figure 5.1. Basically, results at work (performance) are dependent upon the characteristics of the *people* (IA) and the nature of the *technology* required to produce (IB). These are the raw materials with which a

---

FIGURE 5.1 A Motivational Model of Performance

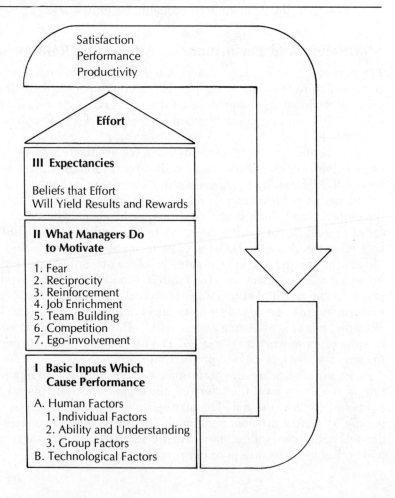

Satisfaction
Performance
Productivity

Effort

III Expectancies

Beliefs that Effort
Will Yield Results and Rewards

**II What Managers Do
to Motivate**

1. Fear
2. Reciprocity
3. Reinforcement
4. Job Enrichment
5. Team Building
6. Competition
7. Ego-involvement

**I Basic Inputs Which
Cause Performance**

A. Human Factors
    1. Individual Factors
    2. Ability and Understanding
    3. Group Factors
B. Technological Factors

manager must work. The manager may do a number of different things in trying to achieve the most effective blending of people and equipment. These are *managerial motivation strategies* (II). What the manager does affects the individual's beliefs about what the work will yield, both for the organization and for himself. These beliefs are called *expectancies* (III) and, according to some research, they seem to be related to levels of performance (Lawler and Suttle, 1973).

Finally, the result of the effort put forth is *performance*, which has no less than two aspects. The first is *productivity*. Productivity simply means how the results obtained from this effort compares to some standard. Productivity is a measure of the efficiency of resource utilization. Performance also has a *satisfaction* dimension. When we accomplish any task, we have some feelings about it. If we like what we do or how we did it, we feel good. If we expect to be rewarded somehow with pay or recognition, we feel good. If we get these payoffs, we are *reinforced* and that has an effect on whether or not we will want to put forth the same effort later.

The rest of this chapter discusses the basic components of this motivation-performance model. First, however we must discuss in more detail what we mean by performance and how it ties in with the other factors. Then we consider the inputs (I), managerial strategies (II) and expectancy theory (III).

Performance—A Multidimensional View

What do we mean when we say someone is a good performer? A weak performer? A "star"? Think about *any* person's job. There are many parts to it. A quarterback of a football team must be able to pass, understand defenses, and run. A professor teaches and carries out research. The manager of an auditing unit must deal with his staff, run meetings, and understand the financial structure of the organization.

The point is that *several* components exist on most jobs. When we speak of performance, we must understand this, because a person may be highly competent in one dimension, not so in another. He may be more motivated (interested) in one than another. A quarterback may be most interested in throwing passes, either because this is the activity in which he is most skilled—or the one that gets the most attention. And there is another point. A superior may view some facets of performance as more important than others. Superiors may focus on, and reinforce, only one aspect of a job. For example, a production foreman's job is complex (see fig. 5.2). Suppose we conceptualize it as being composed of the following activities:

1. Preparing work schedules
2. Ordering raw materials
3. Dealing with subordinates
4. Running departmental meetings

It is possible that top management, being concerned with cost reduction, emphasizes raw materials' costs. Consequently, they create an incentive system which rewards cost reduction. This may cause the foreman to emphasize this aspect of his job, perhaps to the neglect of the other aspects.

FIGURE 5.2 A Hypothetical Production Foreman's Job

---

1. Preparing Work Schedules	Ability: Know Skills of Workers Expectancy: That a Good Schedule Will Result Expectancy: That This Is Important to Superior Superior's Behavior: Very Little Interference
2. Ordering Raw Materials	Ability: Technical Knowledge of Product Specifications Expectancy: This Activity is Critical to Cost Reduction Superior's Behavior: Constant Monitoring of Reports of Raw Materials' Cost
3. Dealing with Subordinates	Ability: Human Skill at Interaction Expectancy: Harmony in Workplace Will Result in Productivity Superior's Behavior: Stresses Need for Better Human Relations
4. Running Departmental Meetings	Ability: Skill in Defining Problems, Handling Participation Expectancy: That Solutions Will Emerge from Meetings Superior's Behavior: Frequently Attends Meetings to Show Belief in their Importance

From figure 5.2 we can also see that different abilities are required for each of the job components, and these may have a different technological/human mix (as we discussed earlier). For example, running departmental meetings will require more human skills than ordering raw materials. However, ordering raw materials may require the use of computers and the ability to understand materials flow.

There are clearly different skills required for the two job components, but the same person is expected to have them.

Similarly, the foreman will have different expectancies about each component of his job. He may feel that if he increases his effort at work scheduling, he will get a smoother flow of work. And if he does, then he may receive a pay increase, which he values. The foreman may thus spend more time on this activity than on the others. He may not have the same feelings about the other task components. He may have low expectations of the payoffs for ordering raw materials. He may know that this area is of great importance to top management, but he may have little control over the activity if he must clear his requests with, say, a purchasing department. The manager of this foreman must, therefore, not look at "performance" in a global sense, but in a specific way, trying to understand the strengths and weaknesses of the individual for each task component. This may mean, for instance, providing help and coaching if the foreman is weak in the use of the computer. At the same time, if he can run meetings well, the foreman may need no help in this area.

Basic Input Factors

For figure 5.1, we show the basic inputs which yield results as *human* and *technological* factors. In chapters 3 and 4, we dealt extensively with factors that affect human inputs. We will be more detailed about technological factors in chapters 6 and 7. Here, however, we can present enough material to indicate how these human and technological factors affect motivation and performance.

Human Factor Inputs

Human factors that affect performance are individual skill and ability, values, attitudes, and the effect of work groups.

Needs and Values. Individual needs, attitudes, and values interact with other factors in the work place to condition the results. First, they affect the reaction to the strategies used by managers to motivate workers. In addition, work experiences contribute in many ways to the satisfaction of individual needs, often providing an opportunity to fulfill unsatisfied needs. (See the discussion of Maslow's hierarchy of needs in chap. 3). The level of personal satisfaction also follows the attainment of a particular performance level. For example, doing well in a job may make an employee feel more secure, while performing

below a certain level may be associated with a fear of job loss or negative reaction from the supervisor.

The relationship of individual needs to job characteristics has been
shown in two studies. In one study of 200 employees of a telephone
company, it was found that more complex jobs were associated with
higher motivation, satisfaction, and quality of performance for those
employees who were concerned with higher-order needs (Hackman
and Lawler, 1971). In another study (Carroll, 1974) it was found that
dental assistants with high accomplishment needs had low job
involvement in a clinic where the jobs were well-structured and
simple, but high job involvement in a clinic where many of the jobs
were expanded to make the tasks more varied and complex. Those
who were primarily concerned with security needs were more
involved with their work than were the dental assistants who were
primarily concerned with achievement needs.

Achievement needs are of particular importance in managerial
effectiveness in increasing performance. McClelland (1965) has
demonstrated the relationship of high achievement needs to entrepreneurial behavior. He has extensively studied this particular individual
characteristic. Research shows it to be an important factor in organizational effectiveness (Wild and Kempner, 1973).

Individuals high in achievement needs derive a deep feeling of
satisfaction from competing against some standard of excellence
(McClelland et al., 1953). They seek success for the sense of accomplishment that it gives them and they may perform at high levels even
in the absence of material rewards for achievement. The standard of
excellence to be obtained may involve an attempt to do better than
others, or it may be an attempt to improve on earlier performance.

The need for achievement is an internal drive state of the individual
—the extent to which he believes success is important and he values
it. The level of the individual's need for achievement is related to
early socialization experiences (Heckhausen, 1967). One's early
success experiences, in frequency and in terms of where they were
experienced, determine the level of need achievement. All individuals
have some level of achievement need, but this level varies from individual to individual. It may also be directed toward different sources
of need satisfaction. For instance, the "organizationalist" may find his
achievement needs satisfied by becoming successful within the firm,
while the "professional" may seek recognition and achievement
within a group of colleagues who are also specialists, as he is. The
"externalist" may find his achievement needs satisfied in social
organizations outside the work setting.

Some persons have a need to avoid failure, rather than a need for achievement (Atkinson, 1957). Rather than obtaining need satisfaction by seeking to be successful in situations, they do so by attempting to avoid circumstances in which they might fail. Failure avoidance rather than achievement is their main driving motive. These individuals, setting performance goals for themselves, tend to set them at either such a low level that they cannot fail, or at such an impossibly high level that no one expects them to achieve them.

Individuals oriented toward achievement value success and want to do well in competitive situations. They want to win, and they usually exhibit a great deal of drive, initiative, and aggressiveness in their work. They find a situation in which they cannot be successful discomforting. If placed in such a situation, they will either be frustrated, or will leave. By the same token, those high in need to avoid failure will try to stay away from challenging and difficult assignments. Thus, for the manager there should always be careful consideration of matching the characteristics of a particular situation with the needs of the individual. This is not always possible, nor is it easy. The conflicting demands between organizational requirements and the needs of people may not be highly congruent.

Group Factors.   As discussed in chapter 4, groups often develop production norms—that is, what members consider appropriate performance levels—and they take actions to insure that members conform to these norms. In addition, groups can affect perceptions and attitudes as well as behavior. Individuals, however, differ in their susceptibility to group pressures. Research indicates that compliance is greatest when a group's member's previous values and attitudes are congruent with the compliance attempt and when the individual places a high value on group acceptance (Helmreich, Bakeman, and Scherwitz, 1973). The individual then internalizes the group norm, and it governs his behavior.

Ability and Understanding.   A person must have the ability to perform and must understand when those abilities are to be used. *Ability* is the capacity to carry out a set of interrelated behavioral, or mental, sequences to produce a result. One has the ability to play the piano when he can read music, understand chord structures, and has the manual dexterity to finger the keyboard appropriately. One has the ability to operate a computer when he is capable of preparing data, programming it, and processing it. Ability levels differ among and within individuals. It is important to be aware of this individual difference, since most jobs have several different characteristics which require different abilities. For example, the production foreman's job (fig. 5.2) included the scheduling of work, ordering raw materials, dealing with subordinates (handling grievances, supervising his crew), and running departmental meetings. Each of these separate activities requires different skills, and a person may be high in some and low in others. There may also be a wide range of performance among individuals who perform similar jobs. Some personnel managers are better than others. Some carpenters are more skillful than others. Some musicians perform better than others. Like needs, individual differences in ability must be taken into account when a manager makes a job assignment.

Understanding what to do, when something must be done, is also important. The organizational member must know what he is supposed to do, when and how he is supposed to do it, and also must know how well he is doing. The problem of misunderstanding what is to be done is highlighted by some research which indicates that a good deal of disagreement exists between superiors and subordinates with respect to performance expectations (Maier et al., 1961). Many subordinates do not seem to know what their superiors expect of them, and this misunderstanding itself can contribute to poor performance. A number of studies have indicated that when individuals are given specific performance goals rather than being given the more generalized goal of "do your best," performance significantly increases (Locke, 1975). Certainly part of this performance increase is due to the fact that the individual's efforts and energies are directed in specific directions rather than being diffused wastefully over a number of activities. Some of the performance increase can also be attributed to the individual's knowing specifically what will constitute good performance.

One way to increase understanding about work requirements is by providing a person with feedback about previous results. Feedback is necessary since it is sometimes difficult for an organizational member to determine how well he is doing or has done without being told by a superior. Studies have indicated that providing feedback on progress toward goals can improve performance (Carroll and Tosi, 1973; Ronan, Latham, and Kinne, 1973). One reason why feedback helps is because the performance of individuals is selectively perceived by themselves. Individuals tend to rate their own performance higher than do their supervisors. They often tend to assume their performance is adequate when it is not. In addition, if they are having difficulties, they tend to attribute them to outside forces rather than to themselves (Locke, 1975), and thus they are not inclined to take actions themselves to correct such difficulties. In general, then, management can improve performance by taking actions to communicate performance expectations clearly and then by providing appropriate feedback on such performance.

Technological Inputs

The term "technological factors" refers to the tools, machines, facilities, and equipment a person uses in performing a task. Cooks use pots, stoves, and recipes to produce a meal. Auto workers "use" a complex assembly line with highly interdependent activities to manufacture a car. An artist uses, perhaps, a drawing board, paint, and a brush. Obviously the technological structure varies tremendously from one organization to another—as, say, between a steel mill and an advertising agency—as well as within organizations—as, say, where one group of employees must use giant computers and another group simply pencils and paper.

The Dynamics of Technological and Human Inputs.   The manager must determine which of the two factors—human or technological— are most important in affecting the level of performance, because efforts to improve performance must be focused correctly.

In some tasks, the individual skill component is the most important factor. In others, technology may be the most important factor. Consider, for example, the design engineer. His performance is not likely to be a function of the kind of equipment he has, but rather it will depend on his personal skill. Giving him better equipment is likely to have only a marginal effect on his performance.

Contrast this with the assembly-line worker. Perhaps only limited skills are required in his job. One advantage of an assembly-line technology is that high levels of training and skill are not required. The most effective method of improving performance here would be to make substantial improvements in the manner in which the technology is used. Investment in new machines and equipment may be most appropriate under these sorts of technological constraints.

The manager must analyze the work situation of his subordinates along these lines. To expect performance to increase simply because we obtain competent people may result in disappointment when technology is the controlling variable.

TABLE 5.2 Supervisory Ratings of Alternative Managerial Strategies

Motivational Approaches	Not Effective	Somewhat Effective	Effective	Very Effective
1. Fear (threat of sanctions)	Police			
	Factory			
	Government			
	Engineering			
	Bank			
2. Reciprocity (exchange favors for performance)	Police			
	Factory			
	Government			
	Engineering			
	Bank			
3. Reinforcement (make performance path to personal goals)	Police			
	Factory			
	Government			
	Engineering			
	Bank			
4. Job Enrichment (motivation through work itself)	Police			
	Factory			
	Government			
	Engineering			
	Bank			
5. Team Building (build team spirit)	Police			
	Factory			
	Government			
	Engineering			
	Bank			
6. Competition (compete for rewards)	Police			
	Factory			
	Government			
	Engineering			
	Bank			
7. Ego-involvement (tie in performance with self-concept)	Police			
	Factory			
	Government			
	Engineering			
	Bank			

Police N=39, Factory N=19, Government N=19, Government N=51, Engineering N=39

Motivation—The Managerial Function

Virtually all writers on management stress that motivation is a function of management, that it is something a manager must do to get things done through people. This view is appropriate so long as we remember that managerial motivation strategies are manipulative in nature. This means simply that a manager is trying to get someone to do what he, the manager, wants them to do. These manipulative, or motivational strategies, in and of themselves, cannot be regarded as either good or bad. Goodness or badness depends upon whether or not an individual, so motivated by another, is ultimately placed is a position he might not have chosen freely, or is injured. To be "motivated" by an attractive woman to ask her to dinner may be fully consistent with the desires of a man. To be "motivated" by a superior to do something illegal is entirely another matter. Both the woman and the superior may use similar manipulative strategies. It is the outcome which is the cause of concern.

When a manager attempts to motivate others, he is trying to act primarily on the human input factor within the technological constraints of the situation. Essentially he attempts to increase the individual's drive to perform better. A number of different motivational strategies have been used by managers. Each has its advantages and disadvantages, and each varies in effectiveness from one situation to another. Some of the strategies have been evaluated by Carroll (1973), who surveyed a number of different supervisory groups to assess which of these strategies they believed to be most useful in their work. The ratings given to some of these motivational strategies by several groups are shown in table 5.2.

Fear or Threat.   With the fear strategy, an individual is threatened with undesirable consequences unless he complies. "If you're late for work, you will be given a three-day layoff," or "You will be fired if you are insubordinate." The threat may be, then, something very specific, such as the loss of one's job, or it may be unspecified, as when an organizational member complies simply to avoid displeasing a higher level of authority. This approach seems to be fairly widely used, perhaps because it is easy. One study showed that this approach is effective in motivating organizational members to perform at a high level if they have limited alternative employment opportunities (Goode and Fowler, 1949). The approach is not perceived to be effective by supervisors, however, in the typical situations they encounter, as table 5.2 shows.

The use of threats, or fear, is limited. First, it only works in the short run. In the long run, most individuals can find alternative employment opportunities where there is less reliance upon fear as a managerial strategy. Second, it creates anxiety, which may disrupt rather than facilitate performance. (A number of studies indicate that performance is lower under conditions of high anxiety; see Vroom, 1964). Also, threats directed at some employees may increase anxiety in others. Third, to work, the threats must have credibility. This is difficult to achieve where employees are protected by a strong union, by tenure rights, or by other safeguards. In addition, threats induce hostile feelings toward the supervisors who make them, feelings which may be manifested in aggressive acts against either the supervisor or the organization.

Another problem with the fear strategy is that it creates a punitive climate in which individuals are afraid of being different from or of offending others. This diminishes creativity and can lead to intellectual stagnation.

Reciprocity.   The expression "If you scratch my back, I'll scratch yours," describes reciprocity. The "norm of reciprocity" states that what one is given, he will repay in approximate equivalence (Gould- ner, 1960). Individuals who receive benefits from others feel guilty if they have a chance to reciprocate and do not do so. In fact, they feel a sense of relief at repaying an obligation when they can.

Using reciprocity, a supervisor may attempt to trade certain things of value to subordinates in exchange for satisfactory levels of performance. The commodities traded may include special privileges, special concern for the individual, and the acceptance of rule violations, in addition to more obvious favors.

Reciprocity is widely used and generally seen as effective (see table 5.2). To some degree, the popularity of this approach can be accounted for by its ease of use. But it presents problems. First, there can be disagreement about the value of the things exchanged. For example, a group of workers may feel their supervisor is asking them to do a "big" favor for him when he has done only "little" favors for them. Second, certain favors may become so common that the recipients no longer consider them to be favors. For example, in a case, say, where employees can leave early when their work is done, they may begin to plan on it and not see early departure as a "favor" anymore. The workers may become extremely upset when the supervisor attempts to withhold the favor. Finally, there may be resentment created when a recipient of a favor does not have the ability to repay

—a person may feel he is getting more and more committed to do something special for his boss.

The psychological contract, discussed in an earlier chapter, includes the concept of reciprocity. The employee agrees informally to meet some of the organization's performance expectations in return for the benefits the organization provides him. But, as they do with the individual supervisor, organizational members often disagree with the organization as to the value of the benefits exchanged between them.

Reinforcement. With this strategy, the manager attempts to reward workers who perform well, and either not reward or impose sanctions on workers who perform poorly. Behaviors followed by desired rewards are repeated, while behaviors followed by nonreward are extinguished, or not repeated, as noted in chapter 3. Thus, if an individual sees a clear relationship between good work and the attainment of a desired reward, he has a tendency to perform at a high level.

A number of studies have found that people perform at a higher level when they perceive a relationship between high performance and the obtaining of desired rewards, such as pay increases and promotions (Lawler and Suttle, 1973). Experimental studies conducted in the laboratory situation, in the military, in educational organizations, and in industrial organizations demonstrate that using money, tokens, signs of social approval, or surrogate rewards can increase the frequency with which certain desired behaviors occur (Krasner, 1971). Nash and Carroll (1975), after reviewing studies on the effectiveness of incentive wage plans in industry, conclude that, on the average, there is an increase in production when workers are paid by the piece rather than on the basis of the amount of time they work. Item 5.1 describes some recent attempts by industrial firms to tie executive performance to pay incentives. It is, as noted, no easy task, but it has a great deal of appeal.

In general, managers view the reinforcement approach as effective (see table 5.2), but it too has its problems. First, it is only effective if the rewards used are those desired by the organizational members. Pay increases, promotions, social status symbols (such as office rugs), all may be regarded as different kinds of rewards, but there are substantial individual differences in preferences for payoffs. Some people prefer pay increases. Others seek promotion. Still others may desire new rugs on their office floors. Some may regard compensatory time off as a reward. Individual differences in preferences for rewards make it very difficult for a manager to effectively utilize organizational factors as incentives. The value a person places on different incentives is internal.

Second, linking rewards with performance is especially difficult. This is most likely to be the case for those whose jobs are extremely interdependent. How do you determine the contribution of one worker on an assembly line to the final product? How do you assess the contribution of one research scientist in a team working on environmental pollution controls? It is also extremely difficult to measure individual performance for staff personnel, higher-level managers and many professionals, since there are problems with quantifying results and isolating outcomes that can be associated with an individual.

Most pay systems in organizations violate the principles derived from the theory and research on reinforcement. In the typical organization, pay increases are given at predictable times, without much differentiation between good and bad performers. The research on reinforcement shows that awarding increases at unpredictable times is more effective than giving them at predictable intervals (Nord, 1969). Organizations which reward performers relatively equally, without regard to their performance, are in effect reinforcing the poor performers to maintain their present levels of performance while discouraging the better performers. When a group of employees receives an across-the-board pay increase of, say, 10 percent, the poorer employees are treated in the same way as the good ones.

ITEM 5.1   Incentive Plans

Payoff in "Performance" Bonuses

The Age-old Executive Bonus has a New Look   Meeting in the richly appointed Empire Room of New York's Waldorf Astoria Hotel last month, the stockholders of Manufacturers Hanover Corp., holding company for the nation's fifth-largest bank, quickly dispatched their business. Cheered by Chairman Gabriel Hauge's announcement that the corporation had just completed its best quarter in history, they responded by electing management's slate of directors, ratifying its selection of auditors and voting down two proposals from individual shareholders.

Then the company's owners did something more important for the future: They approved a spanking-new bonus plan that will for the first time relate the compensation of its top executives both to corporate performance and to their own performance on the job.

On the face of it, performance-based bonuses would hardly seem worth mentioning in the esoteric world of executive compensation. Nevertheless, they are the hottest thing around right now—not only for banks, which have traditionally lagged behind in awarding incentive extras, but for many industrial companies as well. Just within the past year, performance bonus plans have been installed or improved at such major companies as IBM, Exxon, Bendix, LTV, Gulf & Western, McGraw-Edison, Kennecott Copper, U.S. Steel and Lone Star Industries. "This," declares partner Donald Simpson of Philadelphia consulting firm Hay Associates, "is the year for incentive plans based on performance."

Theoretically, of course, bonuses have always been related to performance. In practice, however, most companies have used them as little more than a way of dividing up the pie at the end of a good year. Soon taken for granted by everybody, they have largely lost all value as an incentive. "A lot of companies," says partner Jack Salwen of consulting firm Rothschild & Salwen, "got into the bad habit of paying a man a bonus just for showing up in the morning. That, after all, is what you give him a salary for."

Amid today's pressures, however, all that is changing. In a time of mounting cost-consciousness, top management is eager to get the greatest possible impact from every compensation dollar. Moreover, with the competition for top-notch executives more avid than ever, it is equally eager to attract and retain the best man. For both reasons, companies are now trying to make bonuses more meaningful by using them more selectively than in the past. "Many companies," observes Frederick Teague, compensation specialist for Booz, Allen, Hamilton & Co., "have decided to make no special effort from now on to retain the executive whose performance is merely average. Instead, they intend to single out for monetary rewards the few who really make the mare go."

As a result, this season one proxy statement after another is setting forth a new performance-oriented bonus plan for share-holder approval. But that is only part of the story. For one of the quiet attractions of a bonus plan from management's viewpoint is that unlike an option plan, for example, it need not be voted on by the stockholders. The company may choose to submit it to them to get their moral support, but in most cases the step is strictly optional. Consequently, as Donald Simpson puts it, "The plans you see in this year's proxy statements are only the tip of the iceberg."

Bonuses, of course, can be based on either long-term or short-term performance. A company might want to motivate some executives to optimize each year's results, while giving the top people longer-range incentives to make sure that the company does not sacrifice its long-run interests for the sake of one spectacular year. Most of the new bonus plans, though, are being formulated for the short-term, paying off in cash on the barrelhead soon after the end of the year. "A lot of boards," explains President Robert Sibson of consulting firm Sibson & Co., "have become disenchanted in recent years with long-term incentives because so many things can go wrong along the way."

Strengthening the push for performance bonus plans right now is the winding down of federal controls on compensation. No one knows for sure whether anything will be left of the Administration's wage and price program after May 1. But clearly the impetus at both ends of Pennsylvania Avenue is to free companies from the rigid controls of the past three years. The recent emphatic vote for decontrol by two committees of Congress suggests that the Cost of Living Council may be totally dismantled. In any case, particularly eager to make up for lost time are the companies that got caught with their plans down when controls were slammed on. "Ordinarily," notes one compensation man, "a company should change its incentive plan every three years or so—not only because tax laws and accounting rules change, but because as people get used to any plan, it no longer motivates. So a lot of companies will be playing catch up."

• • • •

Reaching Down While financial-oriented companies are eager newcomers to the bonus lists, manufacturing corporations have of course been at the game for some years. But now there is a new flurry of activity as managements try to make their bonus plans more performance-oriented.

Some companies that have long paid bonuses at the corporate level, like those in the oil, steel and food industries, are now seeking to devise comparable cash incentives for executives who head their best-performing divisions. Others are trying to fine-tune their compensation programs so that they can reward deserving individuals at any level in the corporate hierarchy. As Richard Jamison, compensation director of General Mills, notes: "There is hardly a compensation man today who is not aware of the need to develop rewards more closely related to individual performance."

Among the companies that now reach down two or three echelons to reward a man for a job well done are McGraw-Edison, Colt Industries, J. C. Penney, Bendix, Owens-Illinois, Indian Head, Lone Star Industries, G. D. Searle, du Pont and Thiokol Chemical. Others are clearly moving in that direction. IBM, long a believer in the value of incentives, last year introduced a new plan of this sort. "The corporation," the proxy statement explained, "has decided that the measure of an executive's performance should be more closely related to that part of the corporation's activities for which he is directly responsible." About sixty executives will be eligible for such awards.

Beyond that, the company plans to grant "special supplemental awards to a limited number of executives for extraordinary achievement." Last year was a good one—financially, at least—for the computer giant. And both Chairman Frank T. Cary and Senior Vice President Gilbert E. Jones were awarded bonuses larger than their six-figure salaries.

One unsung company that has been using incentive compensation most effectively at the divisional level is Scovill Manufacturing Co. The Waterbury, Connecticut-based brass manufacturer has had such a plan in use, in one form or another, for about ten years. Scovill has set up its incentives in such a way that the chairman, the president and the other top corporate officers cannot get a bonus equal to more than 25% of their salary, no matter how prosperous a year the company reports. Division managers, in contrast, can earn bonuses of as much as 50% of salary if their divisions top specific goals in pretax profits.

An "Exacting Discipline" As companies generally become more sophisticated about their incentive plans, they are giving increased attention to the process of goal-setting that lies at the heart of it all. For any plan is only as realistic as its goals. Too high, they become a constant discouragement; too low, they simply fail to motivate. "Goal setting is becoming a very exacting discipline," says Robert Sibson. "Goals have to be set shrewdly, be widely known and result in payoff for performance—or else you wind up with a simple profit-sharing scheme, which isn't a motivator at all."

• • • •

The happy thing about the true performance bonus is that it marries so well the interests of the recipient and of the shareholders. For if the bonus plan is skilfully designed, no executive will get any extra pay unless the shareholders, too, have a much better-than-average year. And if the company rings up a truly superlative year, the stockholders should hardly begrudge a bonus—even one in six figures—to the executive chiefly responsible. The man who performs has a right to the payoff.—John C. Perham

Dun's Review, May 1975

Job Enrichment. With job enrichment, emphasis is placed on motivating the worker through the task, or job itself. The assumption is that if the work is challenging, then no outside motivational efforts are necessary. This is especially true where the work is routine and/or broken down into such small components that the person cannot see how his work is related to that of others, or to the end product. Job enrichment involves assigning work to individuals in such a way that they have the opportunity to complete an identifiable task from beginning to end. They are then held responsible for successful completion of the task. Basically, the motivational effect of job enrichment flows from the opportunity for personal achievement, challenge, and recognition.

The experiment in job enrichment underway at the Saab-Volvo automobile manufacturers in Sweden (see item 5.2) illustrates rather nicely how job enrichment works. Rather than the monotonous production system which characterizes auto manufacturing in the U.S., at Saab-Volvo they use a team-assembly concept in which workers rotate the tasks required for building an auto. Basically, the entire group is responsible for assembling the entire auto.

Such an approach is being widely experimented with in industry. Companies which have undertaken job enrichment programs are AT&T and Texas Instruments, among others. But these programs have not always met with success (Miner and Dachler, 1973). Research to date suggests that these efforts may improve morale and the quality of work more than the quantity (Miner, 1973).

Job enrichment is generally seen as effective by managers, but is not without its problems, some of which were noted in chapter 4. When workers are given a more complex job, they realistically expect commensurate increases in compensation; otherwise they feel inequitably treated, and some work—such as large-scale assembly operations —may not lend itself to job enrichment.

Team-building. Team-building is an effort to foster the formation of cohesive work groups which adopt a high level of performance as a "norm." The idea is that groups with a high standard of performance will pressure individual members to perform at a high level. This means that the individual is subjected to performance pressures from his peers, as well as from his superiors, and will perform at a high level in order to live up to the desires and expectations of his fellows.

The supervisor can contribute to group cohesiveness and to high performance by isolating the group from others; by assigning the group tasks which require collective effort; by putting individuals together in a group who can work well with each other; by assigning tasks of an appropriate difficulty level so that the group can experience success; by rewarding the group collectively for their high performance; and by fostering the formation of positive attitudes toward the organization. In general, supervisors seem to rate this motivational strategy as quite effective (see table 5.2). They stated in discussions that many could be pressured into high performance *only* by their peers and not by higher management.

Some problems in using the approach, however, must be taken into account. Some groups become cohesive, but adopt a low, rather than a high, standard of performance. In addition, in many work situations, it may be difficult to get the workers together in group activities, since their work is not interdependent, or because they are physically separated from each other.

ITEM 5.2   Job Enrichment

Volvo's Valhalla

To Henry Ford, patron saint of mass production, the new Volvo plant in Kalmar, Sweden, would seem curious indeed. It looks more like a giant repair shop than an auto factory. The working space is airy, uncluttered by stacks of spare parts. The plant is so quiet that workers can chat in normal tones, or hum along with the pop tunes playing on their cassette tape recorders. Troubleshooters on lightweight bicycles ensure a steady flow of spare parts. Sunlight plays against bright-colored walls through huge picture windows looking out on the landscape. But the most puzzling question in Ford's mind would be: What happened to the assembly line?

Busy Interest.   The answer is that it has been changed beyond recognition as part of an attack on an international labor problem: the growing dislike that today's young, comparatively well-educated workers have shown for tedious, repetitive factory jobs. In the U.S. and other countries, that attitude is reflected in heavy absenteeism and high turnover among factory work forces, poor-quality production and occasional strikes by workers desperate to get away from the line for a while. Volvo's system at Kalmar is attracting worldwide attention as an imaginative effort to set up a factory that will keep workers interested while busy.

Instead of a clanking, high-speed conveyor line, the Kalmar plant uses 250 "carriers"—18-ft.-long computer-guided platforms that glide silently over the concrete floor. Each carrier delivers the frame for a single Volvo 264 to each of the plant's 25 work teams. The teams consist of 15 to 25 workers who are responsible for a certain aspect of assembly; one team, for example, will install the car's electrical system and another will work on the interior finish.

The teams organize themselves as they wish and work at the speed they choose. While a worker on a conventional assembly line might spend his entire shift mounting one-license-plate lamp after another, every member of a Kalmar work team may work at one time or another on all parts of the electrical system—from taillights to turn signals, head lamps, horn, fuse box and part of the electronically controlled fuel-injection system. The only requirement is that every team meet its production goal for a shift. As long as cars roll out on schedule, workers are free to take coffee breaks when they please or to refresh themselves in comfortable lounges equipped with kitchens and saunas.

The Kalmar system was worked out by Pehr Gyllenhammar, Volvo's managing director. Three years ago, when he stepped in as chief executive, he had to cope with an incredibly high labor turnover rate. At Volvo's main assembly plant near Göteborg, turnover reached an annual rate of 41% in 1971, even though the company pays some of the highest wages in Swedish industry. The company had to spend heavily to train replacements, and the rapid turnover contributed to declines in quality that have marred Volvo's reputation for durability. Gyllenhammar was convinced that the workers simply did not like their monotonous assembly-line jobs. "As people became more educated—and Sweden spends perhaps more money per capita for education than any other country—their jobs have become less complex," he says. "That does not make sense."

Gyllenhammar assigned a task force of young executives (all under 30) to design a new plant where "machines would be the product of people and not vice versa." After two months of intensive work and study the group presented its plan. Kalmar (pop. 53,000) was chosen as a site in large part because of its high unemployment rate. Ground was broken in 1972, and 19 months later the first team-made model Volvo rolled out of the workshops.

The new plant cost $23 million, about 10% more than a conventional factory of the same capacity. It includes the most up-to-date devices to monitor production and promote quality control. At each team's work station, for example, a computer-connected television screen projects figures comparing the team's production goal with the number of assemblies it has actually completed. On top of the screen a yellow light flashes if the team is behind schedule; a green light comes on when it is ahead. So far, the plant is only turning out 56 cars a day, but by 1975 the company hopes to achieve annual production of 30,000 cars.

Many Skeptics. A steady stream of auto executives, from Henry Ford II to Fiat Managing Director Umberto Agnelli, has visited the Kalmar plant. Some have incorporated similar ideas in their own factories. In June, for example, Fiat introduced an entirely new system of engine assembly at its plant in Termoli on the Adriatic coast; work is now performed in fixed position "islands." There are many skeptics though. Most U.S. auto executives insist that the Kalmar system would not work in American assembly plants. which serve a vastly larger market and so must turn out many more cars per day than Kalmar.

Some workers and union leaders consider the Kalmar plant less than Valhalla. "The environment is better," says Göran Nillson, 38, who worked on Volvo's conventional assembly line near Göteborg, "but you should not forget that we have the same productivity objectives as any other plant. It looks like a paradise, but we work hard." Adds Kjell Anderson, an official of the militant Swedish metal workers' union, "They haven't really changed the system and they haven't changed the hierarchy. For example, we don't think it's necessary to have a foreman when you have groups."

Gyllenhammer remains convinced that Kalmar will work. "We think the extra capital involved will be offset by increased productivity," he says. Still, Gyllenhammar is a prudent manager, and Volvo is prepared to adapt if the Kalmar experiment fails. The plant was

designed in such a way that it can be
reconverted into a conventional assembly line at a minimal cost.

TIME, Sept. 16, 1974

Competition.   Using the competition strategy, individuals or groups
compete against each other for a reward. This approach is especially
common in sales work, where employees participate in contests for a
variety of rewards, including bonuses, vacation trips, automobiles,
and so on. Competition has been used also, however, for motivating
other types of employees. In an early study, it was found that a pay
system which gave a bonus to only the five highest-achieving blue-
collar workers was more effective than a traditional incentive wage
system in which everybody received a bonus who surpassed a certain
standard (Mariott, 1968).

   Several case studies by Carroll (1975) indicate that competition is
effective only when the reward offered is desired by all the participants and when competing individuals or groups feel they have a
good possibility of winning. When the reward is not considered desirable, or when the same individuals or groups seem to win most of the
time, competition strategies do not have any good effect. Competition
can also lead to blocking the performance of others (Miller and
Hamblin, 1963). Problems occur with this strategy when work is
interdependent and competition would decrease cooperation. Sherif
(1958) has shown that competition can also lead to a great deal of
hostility toward one group by another.

Ego-involvement.   One strategy used to obtain high performance is
allowing organizational members to participate in the establishment
of performance goals for themselves. It is felt that a person is likely to
try to achieve a performance goal that he has himself established,
since the person's self-concept or self-perception will be involved.
Since most individuals think positively about themselves, they should
feel positively about performance goals established by themselves.
There is also evidence that individuals and groups are most likely to
attain goals when they make a public commitment to do so (Hilgard et
al., 1971). This may be because such commitments are promises and
most people view themselves as persons who keep their word.

   Korman (1966) and Vroom (1964) have described research which
indicates that individuals attempt to behave in accordance with their

self-concepts. They try to make their behavior consistent with such self-perceptions. Thus, individuals who promise to achieve a certain result can be expected to be strongly motivated to be successful in carrying out their promise. Vroom (1964) also reports research which indicates that individuals apply high effort to tasks which are perceived to require abilities they take pride in. Conversely, there is less effort expended on tasks which have ability requirements which do not rate high in a person's self-perceptions. Thus, we would expect people who view themselves as being high on creativity to expend a good deal of effort on tasks which they believe require creativity for success in order to validate their self-perceptions. The implications of this for motivation are obvious. An organization should be able to obtain higher performance if it can assign tasks to individuals which require the abilities the individuals take pride in. Of course, such an approach would require a personnel appraisal system that would identify each organizational member's strengths.

Ethical Considerations.   Most managers evaluate the effectiveness of alternative motivational approaches in terms of the achievement of the organizational goals of higher performance. Another consideration in choosing from among alternative motivational approaches, however, might be their relative impact on individuals. In no way would the use of fear meet individual needs unless the subordinate is a masochist. Competition may break down cooperativeness, leading to a lessened satisfaction of social needs. Reciprocity, though widely used, probably contributes little to individual growth and satisfaction and can be quite Machiavellian, depending upon how it is used. The use of ego-involvement through participation in goal setting and decision making is difficult. Managers must be willing to allow subordinates to influence decisions, guarding against pseudo-partici-pation which can have disastrous affects on morale. The team-building approach may provide social need satisfaction as well as the opportunity to experience achievement in situations where individual achievement is not possible, but the group may end up stifling the individual. The job-enrichment strategy would appear to be the approach most in line with individual needs, including growth needs, although care must be taken not to force individuals to accept more responsibility than they are capable of handling. Reinforcement methods, used appropriately, offer individuals a fair opportunity to achieve their personal monetary or advancement goals, depending upon their ability and competence.

Motivation by Lower-level Personnel

The various motivational strategies are not only used by higher organizational levels on lower levels; the lower levels attempt to motivate superiors to behave in certain ways also. For example, reciprocity is used by lower-level personnel to gain future benefits for themselves. The team-building approach can be used by a group of employees to get their supervisor, or other employees, to behave in certain ways. Subordinates often attempt to obtain commitment to a certain idea from their superior by making him believe that he originated it. Even the fear approach can be used effectively by lower-level employees. By selective slowdowns, employees can create anxiety for higher-level managers who are being held accountable for meeting a schedule.

The Development of Expectancies

Motivation in psychological terms, rather than as a management function, is an internal state of the individual that drives a person to behave in a certain way. A person may do something because he believes the effort he puts forth will yield the results he wants. These beliefs are called *expectancies,* and are basic elements in a theory of motivation called "expectancy theory." An *expectancy* is an individual's estimate, or judgment, of the likelihood that some event, or outcome will occur. These outcomes may be performance levels resulting from effort, or they may be rewards resulting from performance. Any specific act may have several outcomes. For example, working hard on a project may result in (1) high performance, (2) high satisfaction, and (3) problems at home because the person had to work late several nights.

Not all outcomes are equally desired by a person, of course. Different outcomes may have different *valences.* Valences are *anticipated* satisfactions that result from outcomes. They are the individual's estimates of the future pleasantness—or unpleasantness— of an outcome.

One way to conceive of motivation, in the psychological sense, is as a result of *expectancies* and *valences.* The force (or motivation) to behave can be stated as follows:

$$\text{Force (Motivation)} = \Sigma \text{ (Expectancy} \times \text{Valence)}$$

where all expectancies and valences a person associates with a particular act are considered.

Certain expectancies have been found to be related to performance (Porter and Lawler, 1968). The first of these, sometimes called the "effort-performance" expectancy (E→P), refers to the person's expectations about the relationship of his effort expenditures to the attainment of certain performance levels. This expectancy can be related to self-esteem. In a study of managers, it was found that managers low in self-esteem expended less effort than in previous years when given goals that were perceived to be more difficult to attain than in previous years (Carroll and Tosi, 1973). On the other hand, managers high in self-esteem expended more effort than in previous years when given more difficult goals. Another study found that foremen did not try to achieve goals they viewed as impossible (Stedry and Kay, 1966). Thus, individuals low in self-esteem will not try to achieve performance goals they feel they have little likelihood of reaching, even if they desire the rewards associated with reaching those goals, and vice versa. A student with little self-confidence in his mathematical skills, for example, will probably not try to obtain an A in a statistics or mathematics course.

Other factors may influence the effort-performance (E→P) expectancy as well. For example, even an individual high in self-esteem may not believe that efforts on his part will result in the attainment of a certain level of performance because of a lack of resources or other technological deficiencies.

Another type of expectancy is the "performance-outcome" expectancy (P→O). This refers to an individual's expectations about the relationship between achieving a particular performance level and the attaining of certain outcomes. For example, an employee may feel that if he consistently attains a particular high performance level there is a moderate probability he will become fatigued, a high probability that his co-workers will be angry with him, a high probability that he will get a pay increase, and a moderate probability that the foreman will give him a compliment.

It is obvious that some of these outcomes are positive and some are considered negative. In addition, while these outcomes are anticipated by the employee, a different set of outcomes may actually occur if the particular performance level is achieved. The degree to which a particular anticipated outcome is positive or negative depends upon the person's anticipations and expectations of the outcomes. For example, an employee may expect that there is a high probability of receiving a pay increase if he achieves a particular performance level. How positive the pay increase will be to him will depend on his perception of the consequences of his getting a pay increase. If he can use the extra pay to buy something he has long desired, then he will probably put a high positive value on the pay increase. On the other hand, he may anticipate that the pay increase will be spent by others in his family or by somebody he owes money to, and he may therefore put only a slight positive value on the pay increase.

If we subscribe to expectancy theory, we would assume that individuals tend to choose performance levels they are likely to be able to achieve and which are also anticipated to result in a set of outcomes with more positive than negative values to the individual, given his needs and his situation (Mobley, 1971). Research also indicates that the behavior of a superior can influence employee expectations. One study, for example, found that when supervisors increased the use of specific performance goals for subordinates and also reviewed their performance more frequently, employees increasingly felt high performance would result in pay increases and promotions for them (Tosi, Chesser, and Carroll, 1972). When management switches to an incentive pay plan, employees perceive a stronger relationship between high performance and the receiving of economic rewards than they did before (Cummings and Schwab, 1973).

Satisfaction—The Result of Performance

Not only does task-oriented effort produce products, but feelings of satisfaction or dissatisfaction may also develop as a result of it. The latter have been called "intrinsic reward." A person may feel good after performing a task. Work may be enjoyable, especially if the person is interested in it. His feelings of self-esteem may be enhanced when he is doing something he believes worthwhile. "Extrinsic rewards" are rewards that are controlled by others, such as pay, promotion, recognition, and so forth. Work activity may also of course lead to rewards such as these. These rewards are the incentives that are available if reinforcement motivational strategies are used.

When the individual finds work intrinsically and/or extrinsically rewarding, job satisfaction may increase. Conversely, if work is drudgery, with no rewards, dissatisfaction may increase. In general it is now believed that satisfaction follows performance when the performance results in outcomes valued by the person. Therefore, in our model in figure 5.2, we show satisfaction resulting from work, influencing the human input factor, especially the individual-need dimension. For example, if a worker high in achievement needs is successful, he is likely not only to be satisfied but also to raise his level of achievement orientation. The converse may also be true.

The Management of Performance

Our analysis shows that performance is the result of a number of factors. Motivation to perform at a high level is the result of individual ability and needs and the particular motivational strategy being used by management, along with the resources necessary to attain the desired performance level. Technological factors, and the absence or presence of certain inhibiting or facilitating forces such as those found in group norms, also play a significant role in performance.

In analyzing the causes of poor performance, management would be wise to take a systems point of view, evaluating the relative importance of human versus technological inputs on performance, and the most effective motivational strategy to obtain the performance level desired. The perspective to be taken is the management of performance rather than the usual management conception of motivation—how a person *thinks* about his job, which involves a much narrower focus.

Management should be aware of the expectancies that organizational members have and the reasons for such expectancies. House (1971) has drawn a useful link between managerial behavior (or motivational strategies, as we have called them) and motivation. He has pointed out that the supervisor can influence subordinate expectancies (E→P and P→O) by his behavior. He can clarify what he expects of the subordinates when role ambiguity exists. He can attempt to increase the payoffs to subordinates for achieving high performance levels by rewarding high performance. He may be able to build up a subordinate's self-esteem and abilities by appropriate training, support, and work assignments. He can provide facilitation of performance by insuring that supplies and other resources are available at the time and in the form needed, and he can increase the amount of productive time available to an employee through delegation or some other means of more effectively utilizing time. This linking process by the superior will be examined more extensively later, in chapter 8.

Discussion Questions

1. Think of the most highly motivated person you know. What is it about them that makes you arrive at this judgment?

2. Do you agree with the statement "Job satisfaction is *not* related to the level of performance." Why? Why not?

3. Think about a specific time you were very satisfied with your work—motivated to do more. Write down on a piece of paper what happened. What about a time when you were dissatisfied? Write that down. Go back in this chapter and read the difference between Herzberg's concepts of satisfiers and dissatisfiers. How do your answers fit with his results?

4. How does the type of technology interact with human skills to affect performance? Describe three jobs in which skill is most important. Three types in which ability is very important.

5. Which of the managerial motivation strategies do *you* believe would be most successful in dealing with subordinates? Which would you respond to most? Is there a difference between the way you would manage and the way you want to be managed?

6. Have you ever been involved in a "team project" for which a grade was given? What problems did the grader have if each team member were to be graded on the value of (1) their work; (2) their contribution? How did you feel about the grade received by those who did not work hard? About the grade received by those who did not contribute as much?

7. Why do you believe that managers are so concerned with "motivation"?

8. What are "expectancies"? How can they affect performance levels? How does personal skill fit in? How about technology?

Part III

The Organization

Just as individuals are different from one another, so are organizations. They differ not only in what they produce (such as military security, automobiles, advertising) but also in terms of their structure. Differences in how much discretion a person has in making decisions, how broadly jobs are defined, how organization mechanisms are designed—or emerge—to react to the external environment—all affect how an organization must be managed.

A critical determinant of an organization's structure is the degree of uncertainty about other segments of society with which it must interact (government, competitors, or labor unions, for example). Chapter 6 examines this environment, especially the market and technological sectors, while chapter 7 describes four forms of organizational adaptation to environments. The hierarchical form interacts effectively with a stable environment, the flexible form with a volatile environment, and the mixed organization with both a stable and a volatile environment.

These different forms of organization attract different types of individuals to work in them. The differences in people interact with the differences in structure such that the way a manager performs the managerial processes must differ if an effective level of performance is to be reached.

Chapter 6

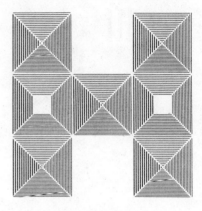

We all know that differences exist between organizations. They differ in what they do, how they are structured, and the manner in which decisions are made. Managers, and students of management, must understand what these differences are, what conditions give rise to them, and how they should be dealt with.

In this chapter, two major sets of ideas which deal with these differences are presented. The first has to do with a way of categorizing the various activities of an organization. The second focuses on the external environment within which an organization operates, and some conditions of this environment which affect the shape and form of the organizational components and mechanisms which operate to adapt to the environment.

The Open and Closed Systems Perspective

All organizations are in an active relationship with their environment. Just as any organism, such as man, must learn to adapt to its environment or perish, so too must organizations. The form, or structure, of an organization must be functional: that is, keyed for survival. The functional point of view assumes that if something survives, it does so because it contributes in some way to the survival or maintenance of a larger system. Organizations must evolve or in some other way shape a form that is functional for the environmental demands placed upon them. Thompson (1967) presents this *open systems* point of view in this way:

> . . . The complex organization is a set of interdependent parts which together make up the whole because each contributes something

The Environment
and the Organization

and receives something from the whole, which in turn is interdependent with the larger environment. *Survival of the systems is taken to be the goal, and the parts and their relationships presumably are determined through evolutionary processes* [our emphasis]. Dysfunctions are conceivable, but is is assumed that an offending part will produce a net positive contribution or be disengaged, or the system will degenerate.

The *closed systems,* or rational systems, approach takes a different view of organizations. It is one often taken by management scholars and practitioners. In the closed systems approach, there is an emphasis only on what is considered controllable—the internal systems of the organization. The environment of the organization, being more unpredictable, is ignored, assumed to be given, or neglected in favor of concentrating on making the internal operations of the organization as efficient as possible.

There is, of course, nothing incompatible between these two approaches, and certainly today a sophisticated management considers both the external environment and the efficiency of internal operations when making decisions. For an individual inside the organization, however, the environment must sometimes be closed off by definite decisions made by another, because unless this is done there can be no basis for formulating internal plans. There is no other way a manager can develop a strategy to achieve the objectives of his unit and the organization. On the other hand, recognition of the variations of the environment becomes extremely important from a policy-making point of view, especially for decisions of corporate strategy. Managerial strategy is used to change the general direction of an organization in response to changing external pressures or conditions. There are important accommodations that organizations must make with the environment, and these show up as different forms and functioning of the organization subsystems.

Organization Subsystems

The standard treatment of organizational components usually defines different departmental structures with the concepts of "line" and "staff." Rather than taking this view, Katz and Kahn (1966) consider a more general form of subsystems, which we use here because it provides a way to conceptualize a wide range of different organizations, from advertising agencies to manufacturing firms. To understand this more general form, we must first define a "system."

A system is a set of interrelated components surrounded by a boundary which absorbs inputs from other systems and transforms them into outputs that serve a function in other systems. Complex organizations are open systems, interacting with an outside environment and adjusting to it. A business organization must react to changes in the environments from which it takes its inputs or resources (e.g., suppliers of raw materials), and to changes in the environments in which it delivers outputs or goods and services (i.e., to clients or customers).

This, of course, is not to say that an organization does not try to influence or exert control over its environments to some extent. For example, a firm may decide to buy another which is a supplier in order to insure that it has a guaranteed source of raw materials. But no organization has complete power over its environments, and all are influenced by their environments in a number of ways. As discussed in chapter 1, the view in this book is that the structure of the organization, the type of human resources required, and the appropriate way to manage are significantly influenced by the problems of dealing with the environment.

An organization transforms inputs (or resources) into outputs (or goods and services) by means of a technological process—a complex of physical objects, procedures, and knowledges by which a certain result is obtained. Some technologies are composed primarily of physical objects, as when steel, component parts, and other materials are transformed into automobiles by an assembly line in the automobile industry, or as when gasoline is produced by the sophisticated and complex equipment used in a refinery. In other technologies, the physical objects may be quite simple but the procedures and the knowledges quite sophisticated, as when a surgeon performs a delicate operation using simple instruments. Thus technologies consist of a number of mental and physical tasks, some of which may be performed by human beings and some by machines (including computers). The mental or physical tasks may be few or many in number. They may differ widely in their complexity. Some technologies require the services of many human beings or machines and some require the services of only a few human beings. These activities are called *production* subsystems.

There are also processes (activities) which handle the transfer of inputs both into and out of an organization. The technology needs raw materials to operate. Its products must be sold, or otherwise distributed. These functions are called *boundary-spanning* activities.

It is necessary to adapt to the environment, and for this purpose some parts of the organization try to monitor the environment. For example, market research attempts to figure out what changes are likely to take place in consumer demands. These *adaptive* activities are necessary to any organization.

There are also coordination and control problems. Data must be collected, to be used for decision making. Conflict between different units must be resolved. These things are done by *maintenance* and *managerial* subsystems.

Subsystems are related groups of activities which various units perform to meet the objectives of the organization. These related activities, which absorb inputs, transform them into outputs, transfer them to users, and coordinate all of these activities are (1) production subsystems, (2) adaptive subsystems, (3) boundary-spanning subsystems, (4) maintenance subsystems, and (5) managerial subsystems.

Primary and Collateral Subsystems

All subsystems must function with some degree of effectiveness in order for the organization to survive, but some are more actively involved in the process of resource acquisition, production, and distribution than others. Those subsystems which either produce a salable or usable value for clients, or operate in the external environment to obtain information and inputs or exchange outputs, are called *primary* subsystems. They make the organization go—producing, selling, and so on. These primary subsystems are similar to the concept of "line" in an organization, as discussed by classical management theorists (Davis 1951). They are the primary functions and, according to Barnard (1938), are "fundamental requirements."

Primary subsystems are the *production, boundary-spanning,* and *adaptive* subsystems.

The carrying out of support and coordinating activities is done by *collateral subsystems.* Their chief purpose is to insure smooth relationships between other subsystems. The collateral subsystems are the *maintenance* and *managerial* subsystems. The maintenance subsystem is similar to the concept of "staff," and carries out support activities. Managerial subsystems are "administrative" in nature.

These two types of subsystems are common to all organizations— business, government, health, educational, or military. In different organizations, jobs and organizational units with quite different titles from their counterparts elsewhere actually perform the same kind of work, and if we think in terms of subsystems, there is less danger of becoming confused by inconsistent terminology. The descriptions of the organizational subcomponents and individual jobs may otherwise obscure the nature of the essential functions being performed for the organizational system as a whole.

While the primary subsystems might possibly maintain the life of an organization even with ineffective performance from the collateral subsystems, in the long run this would lower the organization's effectiveness. When in economic difficulty, many organizations cut back on maintenance activities, such as training and morale improvement. They later pay for this neglect with significant losses of valuable human resources and diminished long-run performance.

The individual primary and collateral subsystems describe activities, not necessarily formally designated departments. One individual or unit may perform several functions, or be involved in more than one subsystem. A professor is part of the production subsystem of a college when he is teaching, but he participates in the maintenance subsystem when he serves as a member of a committee to establish individual faculty pay increases. He may also perform managerial subsystem activities such as resolving conflicts among research assistants assigned to him. Typically, individuals with the title of "manager" participate in several subsystems.

Production Subsystems

The production subsystem is the technical core of the organization (Thompson, 1967), producing the product, service, or ideas which are bought, or otherwise consumed, by the public. Organizations are often categorized by their production subsystems. Automotive firms, hospitals, educational institutions are designated as such specifically because of what they do, and how they do it.

Every organization has a production subsystem, whether it is a top 500 company, a hospital, a department store, or a public service agency. Too frequently the tendency is to equate production with manufacturing. This is too narrow a view. In a business firm, the production system is the task-oriented work which created the product or service—for example, an assembly line, a transaction system for tellers in a bank, or those activities in a retailing outlet which take place after goods are bought but before they are sold. In hospitals, the care facilities, operating rooms, and emergency operations are different parts of the total production subsystem. The production subsystem is important, largely because it is the "technical core" of the organization and as such it is likely to be a high-cost subsystem; that is, large sums will be required to build, create, or otherwise develop it. This large investment produces pressures for effective and efficient utilization designed to protect it from unpre-

FIGURE 6.1 The Production Subsystem—Task-oriented Activities

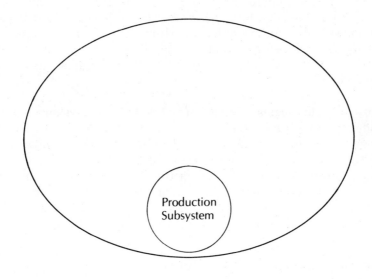

Production
Subsystem

dictable fluctuations in the environment. (Some of these mechanisms, such as buffering and smoothing, are discussed later in this chapter.) Thompson (1967) has proposed a general classification of production technologies: long-linked, mediating, and intensive.

Long-linked Technologies.   Long-linked technologies involve serial interdependence, such as task B which can be performed only after task A is completed, while task C requires both to be finished. An assembly line is a good example of long-linked technology. For instance, in a food processing plant each step must follow sequentially to obtain the correct quality of product. To process tomato juice, the tomatoes must be cleaned, mashed, strained, cooked and the juice sealed in cans, in that sequence.

Mediating Technologies.   Mediating technologies carry out production activities which have as their primary function the linking of clients or customers who are or who wish to be interdependent. The phone company links callers with those called; banks link depositors with borrowers. A problem with a mediating technology is that though it may be standardized, fluctuations in demand may be very extreme and not subject to much influence from the organization. This variability in demand often requires a substantial investment in the production subsystem to handle peak loads, which means that it is underused in one period, but has high demand later. Long-distance telephone circuits, for example, are extremely busy on Christmas and Mothers' day, while it is virtually certain there will be open lines any weekday at 1:00 A.M., a time of day when there is underutilization of equipment.

Intensive Technologies.   Intensive technologies are systems in which a wide range of different techniques can be used, says Thompson, to change a "specific object, but the selection, combination and order of application are determined by feedback from the object itself" (Thompson, 1967). Job-shop manufacturing (where general-purpose equipment is used to manufacture different products), construction firms, and hospitals are all examples of organizations in which the specific tools used depend on the nature of the problem or project.

Boundary-spanning Subsystems

Boundary-spanning subsystems carry on the environmental transactions in procuring the input, disposing of the output, or assisting in these functions. They are called "boundary-spanning" because while the activities themselves are performed *within* the organization, they connect it with external points of contact. They are systems which link the organization with the relevant world outside.

The sales unit of a firm, for example, is engaged in boundary-spanning. Exchanging a refrigerator for the customer's dollars, for instance, is a boundary-spanning transaction conducted by a salesman. The purchasing department of a steel company, when buying iron ore, secures the raw materials needed to produce the final product. The function of recruiting, where the personnel department seeks human inputs, can be classified as a boundary-spanning function.

FIGURE 6.2 Boundary-spanning functions connect the inside of the system with organizations beyond the boundary.

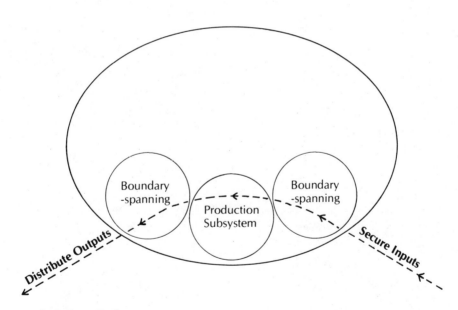

Adaptive Subsystems

Adaptive subsystems perform those activities within an organization which are designed to monitor or sense the nature of the world in which the organization operates. Since the major objective of an organization is survival, and it does so—if it does—in some environmental context, when that context changes, the organization must change. Therefore, the environment is monitored. Research and development are one kind of adaptive subsystem activities. Efforts to keep abreast of current technology and to provide products which are being demanded by the market are organization attempts to adapt to the world.

Lobbying to influence government policy in areas which might affect the organization are also adaptive activities. Major changes in government requirements on pollution control, for example, could have a serious effect on the level of an organization's survival. Therefore, any internal activities designed to monitor the government are adaptive.

Financial and other control activities to monitor and control the level of efficiency and performance of a firm to insure that it is profitable enough to save capital for future investment are also adaptive.

FIGURE 6.3 The adaptive activities complete the set of primary systems.

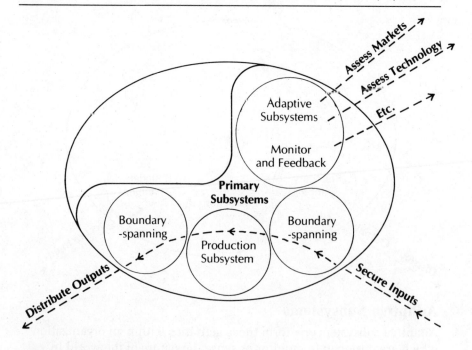

Maintenance Subsystems

Maintenance subsystem activities seek to smooth out the problems of operating the other subsystems, and to monitor their internal operation. One important function of the maintenance subsystem is to maintain morale. Maintenance activities include indoctrination, socialization, rewarding, and punishing of organization members, training activities, and overseeing the compensation system, the performance appraisal system, and other systems in which all supervisory personnel are coordinated by personnel administration professionals.

Maintenance activities also focus on setting performance standards for tasks, raw materials standards, and product or service quality standards. Surveillance or evaluation activities are carried out to insure that such standards are met. The maintenance subsystem devises and monitors adherence to preestablished rules and norms. Specialized groups using the titles of industrial engineering or quality control may have responsibility in these activities.

The general concern of the maintenance subsystem is that of insuring predictability and the smooth operation of the rest of the organization. Its efforts to insure the effective operation of the entire system involve increasing the level of predictability. Equipment and machinery require standardized raw material inputs, and thus there must be certain minimum quality standards for such materials. Machinery must be operated in certain ways to protect it and to insure proper coorination with other machinery or the production system will break down or, at best, will operate inefficiently.

Individuals are hired to make certain kinds of contributions to the organization. Their values, motivations, attitudes, knowledges, abilities, and interpersonal orientations affect these contributions. The maintenance subsystem trains, lectures, motivates, punishes, evaluates, and negotiates with organizational members in order to insure that the system works as planned.

This is not to say that there is no attention paid to individual needs and personal objectives. The effective operation of the system—an integration of human resources with equipment, procedures, and other resources—often requires an organizational accommodation to such personal objectives. The organization must pay the price necessary to obtain the degree of quality and performance required from both human and material resources for the effective operation of the primary subsystems.

Managerial Subsystems

"[Managerial] subsystems," say Katz and Kahn (1966), "comprise the organized activities for controlling, coordinating, and directing the many subsystems of the structure. They represent another slice of the organizational pattern and . . . deal with coordination of subsystems and adjustment of the total system to its environment." The managerial subsystem is concerned with general policy questions. Determining general policy and strategy to interact with the environment with the intent of insuring long-term survival is a function of the managerial subsystem. The resolution of internal conflict between departments is also one of its functions, as is the use of the authority structure to disseminate directives and to resolve conflict. The total system is shown in figure 6.5.

FIGURE 6.4 The maintenance subsystem increases system predictability.

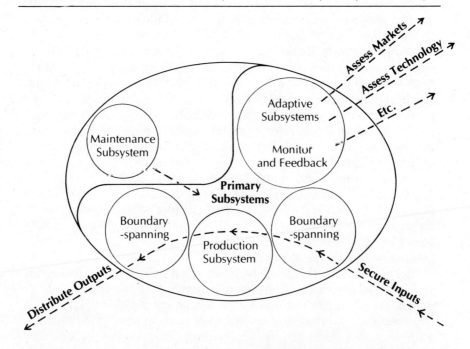

Some Concluding Ideas about Organization Subsystems

Specific forms of an organization's subsystems vary from organization to organization. The production subsystem of a hospital is different from that in a department store, for example, or in a manufacturing plant.

There is also great variation in how these subsystems are related to each other to form an organization's structure. Some organizations

FIGURE 6.5 The Total System

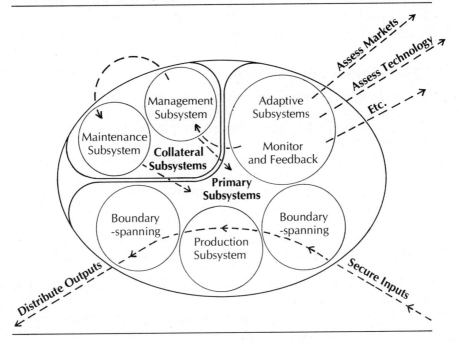

have extremely rigid, bureaucratic structures. Others have more flexible, colleague-oriented systems. Research and development activity,
for example, may be performed very differently: people with similar
backgrounds in engineering may be doing applied research in one
organization, pure research in another.

What are the factors which bring about these differences? Our view
is that it is the environment within which an organization tries to
survive that influences the specific form its subsystems take. In the
remainder of this chapter we will describe more fully the environment
and its characteristics. In the next chapter, we will describe alternative forms of organization structure.

The Relevant Environment of the Organization

Organizations interact with other organizations which provide inputs,
make use of outputs, exert pressures for certain kinds of decisions,
and in general deal in some important fashion with the organization

with which we should be concerned. This is the concept called "organization set" (Evan, 1966) and refers to the sectors of a society, institutions, or processes which have a direct bearing on what an organization does, and how it does it.

The Relevant Environment

There are many pressures outside an organization and they affect it in different ways. Its *relevant environment* is made up of groups, or institutions, beyond its boundaries which provide *immediate* inputs, exert significant pressure on decisions, or make use of the organization's output. This means that at any one point in time there are some external organizations which are closer and have a more significant effect on what goes on in a firm than do others. For instance, customers and suppliers are in immediate juncture with a business organization. They comprise the relevant environment. A sudden shift in the level of consumer demand, for example, can force internal changes, as when a slump in auto sales causes auto firms to lay off workers.

Other conditions could bring other institutions or organizations into the relevant environment. When other sectors in the organization set impose pressures, they may threaten the existence of the organization. Any outside force which is able to generate sufficient pressure to create pressures within organizations, either in the managerial structure, the production structure, or the boundary-spanning structures, must of necessity be defined as part of the relevant environment because the organization must adapt to it. When equal opportunity laws were passed, for instance, many firms had to change their hiring procedures as well as the criteria used for promotion. Laws passed to control the quality of air caused shifts in types of fuel used as well as product design of devices using fuel.

Can we be more illuminating than simply to say that the organization reacts to the relevant environment? Perhaps we can by defining certain subsectors of the environment. At the outset, let us make clear that the relevant external environment of an organization may be composed, at least, of

1. customers;   4. public pressure groups;
2. suppliers;   5. government agencies;
3. unions;   6. investors.

Here we will focus on the two sectors of the environment which are of most use in analyzing problems in the management of business organizations. These are the *market* and *technological* environmental sectors. Again, it should be noted that other sectors may be more critical in different organizations. They would, however, have similar effects, though on different subsystems from those we will outline in this and the next chapter.

The Market Environment.   Organizations produce some sort of commodity, product, value, or service for a particular set of individuals, the consumers of the output. The output can obviously take many forms—automobiles, steel, television sets, bread, pencils, books—the list of products consumed by people is virtually endless. The same holds true of services. Advertising agencies sell ideas and services to clients. Welfare agencies provide services or information to clients. Hospitals provide services to patients by having available a wide variety of health care facilities in one location convenient for both patients and doctors.

For some organizations, the users of the output may be the members themselves. Interest groups form the nucleus of many clubs. Fraternal organizations such as the Elks, Masons, or Knights of Columbus essentially provide greater values to their members than to others in the usual sense of clients or customers. Even these organizations, however, frequently provide a charitable service to other parts of the community.

On a more microcosmic level, we might also consider the "market" for units (or departments) within a complex organization. The notion of organization subsystems suggests that the output of the production subsystem becomes an input for the boundary-spanning market subsystem. Departments in organizations provide some sort of product or service to other units. Indeed, demands of these users may range from specific tangible products such as subassemblies, completed units, memoranda or reports, to services, ideas, or other, more abstract values. For example, the marketing division may be viewed as the "market," or user, of the product of the manufacturing division. The shop foreman is a user of reports produced by the production control department. The marketing department may be a user of ideas generated by the advertising group; the accounting unit, when adding new employees, is a client for the services of the personnel department.

Markets may vary along several dimensions. These dimensions include time, shape, or size. The market for a particular product may exist only for a specific period of time, then dissipate until that time reoccurs. Certain food products are consumed seasonally, such as pumpkin and turkey. Toy sales soar before Christmas. Other markets vary by size. There is a vast market for automobiles, a much smaller market for cross-country skiis. The shape of the market can vary also. If we consider population age segments, we would find that some products—for example, home furnishings—are sold principally to adults in age ranges over 25. Other products—such as rock music records—may have their highest demand among younger consumers.

The Technological Environment.   The technological sector of the environment has two components. The first is the availability of techniques and processes which the organization can obtain to form the production system. In this sense, technology refers to available hardware. How this is absorbed, organized, and set up internally defines the production subsystem described earlier—which means that internal production systems cannot be any farther advanced than the technology available, although it is also quite possible that production systems may not come close to using all available technology advances. (For example, customer credit accounts in a large department store might be handled by computers, while the same function in a small specialty store might be performed manually.)

Technology also refers to the ideas or knowledge underlying the processing or the distribution of the service; that is, the translation of science to useful application. Research and development, as well as applications engineering, are functions that would fall into this category. Every organization makes use of some knowledge base, some science in its subsystems.

Characteristics of the Environment

We have defined two major environmental sectors which will form the basic framework for much of the material presented later in this book: the market sector and the technological sector. We do not of course discount the possibility of other environmental sectors impinging on the organization, but if they do, the concepts in this chapter will still accommodate them.

Defining the elements of the environment only tells where an organization operates—what affects it. What causes the organization to take the form—structure—that it does is the degree of change in the environment. Our conceptual scheme is based on the idea that environmental variability and its potential impact on the organization must be understood before a manager can manage well.

Research has shown that degree of change is a very important aspect of the environment as it affects an organization's structure (Lawrence and Lorsch, 1967; Harvey, 1968). Degree of change may be conceived of as a continuum, at the opposite ends of which are (1) stability, and (2) volatility. These two states of the environment have substantial implications for the internal structure of the organization, the type of individual who is likely to join a particular operation, and the shaping of perceptions, attitudes, and values in the organization. Most important, however, the environment has a significant effect on the degree to which internal subsystems of the organization take on highly routine or stable characteristics. For example, when there is a large steady market for a product and a well-developed technology, a firm may invest large sums in plant and equipment to serve it. Advanced forms of mechanization can keep costs very low so that the market can be expanded, but this comes at the cost of increased mechanization, and this process in turn lowers the skill level of employees needed to run the plant, influences who will join the organization, and affects how they will adapt to it once they are members.

The Stable Environment. The stable environment is one in which changes are relatively small, occurring in small increments, with a minimal impact on the structure, processes, and output of the organization. Changes are likely to be in size (e.g., the amount of beer consumed or insurance sold) rather than in kind. For the organization, the impact of changes in the stable environment will largely be on the size of the membership of the organization. The product is unlikely to change significantly and there will be little need to alter the production subsystem of the organization with change in the environment. With this high level of stability, it is likely that there will be extensive investment in plant, equipment, and distribution methods, and when there are increases or decreases in the market, the method of adaptation can be a short-term one, consisting of reducing or increasing the work force, rather than making changes in the product or the method of production. For example, large commercial bakeries use a fairly high-cost system of production, but the final product is still bread. Alterations in this production system come rather slowly, but steadily. If there is a shift in demand, say a drop, then the mode of accommodation is not to seek new products, but rather to lay off personnel until demand increases, or perhaps to permanently adjust to lower sales levels.

The stable environment is characterized by high levels of predictability. It is very likely that we will be able to make fairly accurate predictions of the level of the market based on some fairly common set of change measures, or indexes. For instance, the level of automobile sales may be predicted reasonably well if there are reasonably accurate data available on changes in population and income. The demand for telephone services in use may similarly be predicted rather well.

The Volatile Environment. When we say an environment is volatile, we mean that it is likely to be turbulent, with more intense changes than in the stable environment. Changes are also more rapid and random, and prediction is difficult.

When the market is volatile, it is—by definition—unstable. The customers may change. The level of demand may vary widely. The women's fashion market, for instance, may be considered in most senses as volatile. Product decisions of designers and manufacturers are based on consumer tastes and preferences, and these are highly changeable and difficult to predict. (Item 6.1 gives another example of market volatility.)

When the technology is volatile, new concepts and ideas are being rapidly generated, and these new ideas affect either the manner in which the production processes are carried out, or the nature of the processes themselves. The electronics industry, with breakthroughs in integrated circuits, transistors, and general miniaturization, presents an example of technology changes which affect the nature of the product. If these technological developments reduce the selling price of the product, marketing strategies may be affected as well. Item 6.2 tells about the problems of digital watch manufacturers. As technology changes, and prices drop, the manufacturers find themselves in a quandary, not knowing what will happen to their costs of production and uncertain about the buying strategies of the retail outlets which are their customers.

ITEM 6.1   Market Volatility

Semiconductors Take a Sudden Plunge

Enthusiastic employee-stockholders at Advanced Micro Devices, Inc. are fond of charting the integrated circuit maker's over-the-counter stock performance. Last year, as the Sunnyvale (Calif.) company basked in the glow of unprecedented growth and profitability, the price scale on the chart began at $10. But recently, the chart has been revised. "The new bottom line doesn't say 'zero,'" jokes W. J. "Jerry" Sanders, AMD president, "it says 'free.'"

AMD stock is not yet being given away, but this week's bid price of around $3.50 reflects a sudden reversal of fortunes not just for Sanders' little company but for the entire semiconductor industry. Six months ago, the producers of ICs, transistors, and other solid-state electronic components could not keep up with demand. Order backlogs had soared, and delivery times stretched out more than a year on major product lines. Big new plants were springing up in such unlikely locations as Beaverton, Ore., and Orem, Utah.

But the picture has suddenly and dramatically changed. Many of the new plants are being left half-finished or unoccupied, company after company is slashing its work force, and the first signs of red ink are showing up. During the third quarter, shipments dropped for the first time since the disastrous industry recession of 1970.

A big surprise. The rapidly deteriorating marketplace caught nearly everyone by surprise. In a few months, the industry's big order backlog was cut in half. Order cancellations and returns have reduced backlogs by $620-million since May, estimates Jon D. Gruber of Robertson, Colman, Siebel & Weisel, a San Francisco investment banker.

• • • •

Now the industry is wondering whether it faces a repeat of the 1970 debacle, in which sales of some product lines fell off more than 50% in less than a year, over-all shipments declined about 25%, and all but a few companies lost money. "This is as uncertain a business environment as I've ever seen," says Charles C. Harwood, president of Signetics Corp.

Business Week, Nov. 16, 1974

Strategies for Adapting to the Environment

Perhaps the most important assumption underlying management process contingency theory is that an organization must operate its most costly subsystem as efficiently as possible. Generally, the production subsystem (the technical core) will be the most costly, whether it is made up of expensive equipment or highly-trained professionals.

James Thompson describes ways in which the technical core can be protected against environmental variations—protective devices of *buffering* and *smoothing*, for example. The need for use of these devices is of course greatest when there is a substantial degree of volatility in the environment. When the environment is smooth (e.g., when demand is reasonably uniform over time), the internal systems which deal with it can be relatively simple.

Buffering attempts to protect internal operations by sealing off the production system from external variables. For example, say that a plant has a continuous-assembly operation and therefore needs a steady flow of raw materials, but the supply of raw materials is variable, uncertain, or otherwise not in synchronization with use. The solution, then, is to create an inventory of raw materials which will permit steady production even with varied inputs. The same holds true when there is smooth steady production, but variable demand. The firm simply produces to inventory.

Smoothing attempts to minimize severe fluctuations of the environment by "offering inducements to those who use . . . services during 'trough' periods, or [charging] premiums to those who contribute to 'peaking'" (Thompson, 1967). Offering discount rates to early-morning callers is a smoothing strategy used by the telephone company. Discounts offered to buyers during off-seasons is another such strategy (e.g., lower tourist rates in Florida during the summer months).

Another way to adapt to a volatile environment is to have an extremely flexible organization. The most extreme form of adaptation is to have an organization structure which has enough resiliency to cope with unpredictable demands. The "intensive technology" production system is an example. Not knowing what the demand of a customer may be, general-purpose resources are used in various ways. The emergency room of a hospital has equipment which may be used to treat heart attacks, broken legs, burns, and virtually every other possible medical emergency. For each emergency the particular configuration of equipment varies. The role of the doctor (a professional) is to know how to arrange this general-purpose equipment to be most effective in a particular situation.

ITEM 6.2   The Technological Environment

Prices of Electronic Digital Watches Fall As Makers Compete for a Share of Market

If you think prices of portable electronic calculators fell fast, keep an eye on electronic digital watches.

Watches that use light-emitting diodes (LED) and liquid crystal display (LCD) have been fighting each other and traditional, mechanical watches for a share of the market. Prices have begun to plummet and there is much talk of "dumping," or selling in quantity at very low prices.

"There's been a fantastic erosion in prices in the past four months," said Ar-dith Rivel, Benrus Corp.'s vice president for quartz watches.

• • • •

He said that electronic digital watches that had been selling for $125 to $150 are selling currently at about $30.

Trade observers note that early electronic calculators that sold for $300 or more currently can be bought for $20 and less.

Both the LED and LCD watches use as their timers the extremely high-frequency vibrations (32,768 a second) of their battery-electrified quartz crystals. The vibrations are translated into lighted digits by circuitry.

Must Push Buttons. With an LED watch, the wearer must push one or two buttons to see the time; on an LCD watch, the time is displayed constantly.

The first brand-name electronic digital watch on the market was Pulsar, by the Time Computer Inc. division of HMW Industries Inc. It sold for $2,000 in an 18-caret gold case in 1971. HMW later introduced a $250 model in a stainless-steel case.

Other major watch makers gradually began producing electronic digital watches, followed by some calculator and semiconductor producers. As more companies became involved, the tech-nology changed and prices dropped rap-idly.

At a panel discussion by retailers, sponsored by Burgess & Leith, brokers, Alice Klein, merchandise manager of Alexander's Inc., a department-store company, compared the electronic digi-tal watch situation to what happened with calculators. Retailers are holding back orders because so many changes were made when the device caught on, she said, adding, "We have to keep our inventory low because of the changing technology." . . .

The Wall Street Journal, April 16, 1975

Reprinted with permission of *The Wall Street Journal,* © Dow Jones & Compa-ny, Inc., 1975. All Rights Reserved.

Adaptation—Active and Passive. The preceding discussion could lead to the assumption that organizations are passive, subject to the buffeting of the environment, adapting to it or perishing. It is possible, however, for an organization to do many things which might influ-ence the nature of its environment. For example, lobbying to change government regulations or laws can help insure relatively moderate to low government intervention. Or, where a stable technology exists, spending large amounts of time and money on research may produce a breakthrough, thus increasing technological volatility. In chapter 17 we will discuss in detail how an organization can influence its envi-ronment.

The Environment-Organization Linkage

In this chapter we have emphasized the idea that organization struc-tures will differ according to the conditions of the environment. That is, the organization's subsystems (production, adaptive, etc.) will differ, depending on whether the market and/or technology is stable or volatile. From these ideas about subsystems, their interface with the environment, and the character of the environment, we can begin to form some ideas about types of organizations. One axis of figure 6.6 is the technological dimension of environments; the other axis is the market dimension. Both dimensions are divided into two levels of uncertainty—stable and volatile. These two levels are used only for analytical purposes. No environment can be characterized by only two discrete categories, but the categories shown will be adequate for our analysis and discussion. Figure 6.6 shows four different types of organizations. We will describe them briefly here, and in chapter 7 will describe how the different organization subsystems look in each type. In chapters 12, 13, 14, 15, and 16, we will suggest different approaches to managing in these four types of organizations.

Hierarchical, Bureaucratic Type.   The hierarchical organization develops in response to a stable market and a stable technology. It uses standard production methods and has well-defined and fixed channels of distribution. Tasks in it change slowly. Authority/responsibility relationships are specified. The hierarchical form is the appropriate adjustment to the stable environment.

Flexible, Dynamic Type.   The important characteristic of a dynamic organization—which must adapt to a volatile environment—is its ability to change. There is not an intensive investment in plant and equipment, and high skill levels are required of employees. They may be moved from one part of the organization to another as demands change. There is little centralized decision making, and authority is often not well-defined.

FIGURE 6.6

		Technology	
		Stable	Volatile
Market	Stable	Hierarchical, Bureaucratic	Technology-dominated Mixed (TD Mixed)
	Volatile	Market-dominated Mixed (MD Mixed)	Flexible, Dynamic

Market-dominated Mixed Type.   In the market-dominated mixed (MD-mixed) type of organization, the technology is relatively unchanging, but the markets are in constant flux. Under such conditions, their marketing units are their most influential subsystems. An example of a market-dominated mixed organization would be a women's apparel manufacturer. The technology for making the product has been stable for a long period of time, but the market is extremely volatile because competitors go into and out of business constantly due to price competition, because there are several distinct selling seasons, and because of unpredictable style preferences of customers.

Technology-dominated Mixed Type. When the market is stable, but the technology is constantly changing, then the research and development (R & D) group—the scientists who deal with that technology—will be the dominant force in the organization. This is the technology-dominated mixed organization (TD-mixed). The marketing group will be much like that in a hierarchical organization, but the R & D group will be relatively flexible.

ITEM 6.3   Changing Structure

Westinghouse Opts for a GE Pattern

Westinghouse Electric Corp. has never admitted that it is excelled by its larger rival, General Electric Corp., in anything but size and profits. But when Robert E. Kirby assumes command of Westinghouse next week as chief executive officer, he will preside over a trimmed-down corporate structure that is modeled in part on a GE management concept.

Fighting a severe profits slump, Westinghouse has recently lopped off losing businesses that account for about $700-million in annual sales. It has been preparing for the time when Donald C. Burnham, chief executive since 1963, steps down under a pre-retirement program for top officers that he himself devised. When he reaches 60 next week, Burnham will become an "officer-director" at two-thirds of his former pay. Last week, the 56-year-old Kirby, former head of Westinghouse's profitable industry and defense group, told 200 line and staff managers at a Lancaster (Pa.) meeting how the corporation will reshape itself when he takes over as chairman on Feb. 1.

Shrinkage. Instead of doing business through five operating companies, Westinghouse is shrinking back to three, each headed by a president who serves on a top, five-man management committee. The change eliminates the Consumer Products Co., already decimated by the pending sale of Westinghouse's $600-million-a-year major appliances business to White Consolidated Industries. Other consumer lines are being absorbed by two of the remaining companies—Industry Products under Douglas D. Danforth, 52, and Public Systems, headed by Thomas J. Murrin, 45. Public Systems also gets five business chunks from the old Broadcasting, Learning & Leisure Time Co., which is reduced to subsidiary status under Chairman Donald H. McGannon and contains only the money-making Group W television and radio stations. The third company, Power Systems, headed by Gordon C. Hurlbert, 50, continues as at present.

Replacing an old, seven-man policy committee, the five-man management committee will meet more often and make "more coordinated" corporate decisions. The fifth member, along with Kirby, Hurlbert, Danforth, and Murrin, is Marshall K. Evans, 57, vice-chairman and chief of staff. Faster decision-making at the top supposedly will be aided by the most interesting facet of the reorganization: the grouping of Westinghouse's 120 divisions into 37 "basic business units," each headed by a general manager. The divisions will remain profit centers, but "strategic planning" decisions on market growth and capital expansion will be coordinated at the business unit level instead of in the divisions. "We had gone too far in the decentralization to divisional profit centers and had fragmented several businesses that weren't fragmentable," says Evans.

The model for this approach is the "strategic business unit" plan adopted in 1970 by GE, which is divided into 42 SBUs. Westinghouse had been grouping its divisions by markets for some years, but now it has taken the final step to the unit concept. "We learned a helluva lot from GE," says Evans. "We struggled like mad to find something better than

GE has, but theirs is as good as there is. Ours is not a copy of GE's, but we're coming out at the same place."

Other changes. In a further effort to make the new units cost-accountable, Westinghouse is reassigning corporate technical staff to the unit level. This will result in a "significant reduction" in corporate staff, Evans says.

Whether these and other changes will reverse the erosion of profits that had taken place over the last two years remains to be seen. The decline occurred in large part because the company moved too fast into service businesses unrelated to electrical equipment manufacturing and nuclear power. In recent months, in addition to the huge appliance business sale—which awaits Justice Dept. approval—Westinghouse has disposed of $100-million worth of business that had lost a total of $59-million in 1973. Included are a mail order company, water pollution control equipment operations, military and low-income housing, and a French elevator company. The divestiture program, now completed, will require write-offs of $66-million on 1974 income. But, says Evans, "we've managed to shoot all the dogs."

Business Week, Feb. 3, 1975

There is, of course, no such thing as a pure organizational type. But by understanding the four theoretical types we can apply their basics to any size unit (department, groups, firms) for analysis and prescription of strategy.

More than one organizational type will probably exist in the same company. Certain very large companies—such as Westinghouse, General Electric, General Motors—are actually composed of many separate organizations, some of which have relationships with each other and some of which are quite independent of each other. These organizations must carefully *differentiate* (segregate) their individual units from each other while at the same time providing some sort of *integrating* mechanism to coordinate them. Item 6.3 describes how this is done at Westinghouse.

The market and the technology are not the only environmental sectors influencing organizational structure and the managerial process. Considering these two sectors illustrates, however, how organizational types can vary. There are obviously many other influences as well. In this book we want to acquaint the student with the most important factors contributing to organizational structure and the process of management.

In chapter 7 we will review the organizational subsystems and their interactions with environmental forces. We will also discuss in detail each of the four basic organizational types—the bureaucratic organization, the dynamic organization, the market-dominated mixed organization, and the technologically-dominated mixed organization.

Discussion Questions

1. What is the production subsystem in a restaurant? The boundary-spanning subsystem?

2. How can the different levels of technological environmental volatility affect the reactions of two people similarly trained, but in different conditions—for example, an electrical engineer in a stable technology firm and one in a volatile technology.

3. What particular organizational environment is currently volatile for the automotive industry? Fast-food franchisers? Hospitals?

4. Is it easy for you to visualize how a unit may perform boundary-spanning functions at one time, production another, and maintenance functions another time?

5. What is the relevant environment of an organization in which you have worked? Is it stable? Volatile?

Chapter 7

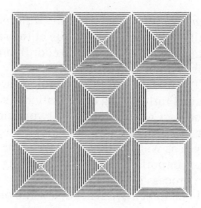

In chapter 6 we stated that an organization can be viewed as a system composed of interrelated subsystems, (production, boundary-spanning, adaptive, maintenance, and managerial). The structure of an organization (the relationship between subsystems) is influenced by the demands placed on it by its relevant environment. An organization's market and technology are especially influential environmental factors in the shaping of its structure.

Market and technological factors may take on characteristics ranging from a high degree of stability (infrequent change and thus high predictability) to high levels of volatility (frequent change and thus high unpredictability or uncertainty). Figure 7.1 summarizes the environmental/organization relationship described in chapter 6 (and shown in fig. 6.6). The subsystems which are in all four organizational types will take on different characteristics and relate to each other differently in each of the types of organization. The variations are largely determined by the external environment.

In this chapter we will describe how the five subsystems can be expected to vary within each organizational type. Of course these variances can only be expressed as theoretical, general tendencies, not as hard-and-fast rules. Nevertheless, organizations of all types do exhibit certain general structures and characteristics, depending upon their environment. Similarities and differences in structure and characteristics from organization to organization reflect adaptation to the forces and problems presented by their environments.

The hierarchical and flexible organizations represent extreme ends of a continuum of types. For both of these organizations, the different environments are relatively fixed. For the former, the market and technological sectors are stable; for the latter, they are both volatile.

Organization Structural Alternatives: Adapting to the Environment

Many organizations interact with environments which have both stable and volatile characteristics. We call organizations which have at least one major subsystem interacting with a stable environment and another interacting with a volatile environment "mixed-form" organizations. The mixed-form type of organization is probably more prevalent than either the hierarchical or flexible types.

There are two mixed types in our analytical framework. The first, called *technology-dominated mixed* (TD-mixed), has a relatively stable market and a volatile technology. The second, the *market-dominated mixed* (MD-mixed), has a stable technology and a volatile market.

FIGURE 7.1 Environment Characteristics And Organization Types

Characteristics of		
Market	**Technology**	**Organization Form**
Stable	Stable	Hierarchical, Bureaucratic
Stable	Volatile	Technologically-dominated (TD) Mixed
Volatile	Stable	Market-dominated (MD) Mixed
Volatile	Volatile	Flexible, Dynamic

There are two points that are important in considering these two types of mixed organizations. The first has to do with a major managerial problem: How can you develop a strategy for integrating the operations of two organizational components which take on very different structural characteristics because they interact with different environments? This particular problem is illustrated in item 7.1, which describes the managerial problems of Gulf & Western Industries.

The second has to do with power and influence over policy and strategy. As a general rule, the organizational sector which interacts with the most volatile, or uncertain, sector of the environment will exert the greatest influence in determining what the policy, strategy, and general direction of the total organization will be. It is for that reason that we have classified organizations as market-dominated or technology-dominated according to which subsystem of the organization faces a volatile environment.

The Hierarchical, Bureaucratic Organization

The hierarchical form of organization is often called a "bureaucracy," a label that immediately conjures up a vision of a vast, impersonal organization with an overriding emphasis on standardized procedures and consequent "red tape" and very little if any responsiveness to the problems of its staff and customers. Those who have studied bureaucracies agree that this is a valid criticism (Merton, 1957). On the other hand, many management researchers have found through their studies that the hierarchical form of organization is the most appropriate form of organizational adaptation when the environment is highly stable (Burns and Stalker, 1961). We can thus expect the hierarchical form to emerge whenever the market and the technology are stable and predictable. This is the case, for example, for many government agencies. The changes in technology for them are few, the markets served are fairly well-defined, and there is an absence of competition in the provision of services. The same is true for similar organizations, such as banks and insurance companies, or for, say, companies in the container industry which produce bottles and cans and which have had a very stable technology and market for a number of years. These organizations tend to be structured in the bureaucratic—that is, hierarchical—form.

Production Subsystems

Tasks in the hierarchical organization's production subsystem (the subsystem whose activities are primarily directed at creating the output of the organization) are characterized by a relatively high degree of repetitiveness. That is, a standard way of performing tasks is established and routinized and all organizational members assigned those tasks must perform them the prescribed way. Tasks are repetitive in that organizational members are usually assigned only a few tasks and they perform these over and over again during the work day. The assembly-line worker is, of course, a good example of one who has such tasks, but white-collar workers in banks, insurance companies, and government agencies similarly follow a routine. This is so because most customers require basically the same kind of service and it is easy to standardize procedures for providing it.

ITEM 7.1   A Mixed Organization

Bluhdorn the Raider as Elder Statesman

Charles G. Bluhdorn, the 48-year-old chairman and chief executive officer of Gulf & Western Industries, Inc., is no longer the brash corporate raider of the 1960s who took over more than 100 companies in building G&W. The company's acquisitions phase is pretty much over and Bluhdorn's role today is almost that of elder statesman, watching over the management of his $2.3-billion conglomerate.

Moreover, G&W seems to be vindicating the conglomerate theory that diversification would smooth out cyclical swings in earnings. The movies *Love Story* and *The Godfather,* produced by G&W's subsidiary Paramount Pictures, pumped up earnings in 1972 and 1973. Last year, income from films and financial services trailed off, but soaring prices for sugar (South Puerto Rico Sugar Co.), zinc (New Jersey Zinc Co.) and paper (Brown Co.) saved the day. G&W earned $100-million in its fiscal 1974, ended last July 31, a 13% increase over 1973, the third consective year of record profits.

It is not clear that the Vienna-born Bluhdorn has a winner even now. With the gloomy economic outlook for the year ahead, and with G&W's high leverage ($1.95 in debt per $1 of equity) and

its massive interest costs, the company will require superior management as well as diversification to produce a fourth record year. Bluhdorn, for one, believes G&W is in good shape to accomplish this because of the emphasis the company has been giving to operating management. But few on Wall Street share Bluhdorn's optimism. . . . Most of all, they wonder if Bluhdorn the raider has really become Bluhdorn the skillful corporate manager.

Big as G&W has become, it is still very much a creature of the man who put the pieces together. Although Bluhdorn has given up trying to run the various operations himself, he remains the ultimate arbiter. "Bluhdorn is the imagination and the energy of the company," says John Duncan, former president and current chairman of the executive committee. "He is very much the player-coach. He penetrates deeply into that organization."

The coach.   From his office on the 42nd floor of the G&W building in Manhattan, Bluhdorn filters his plays through three key aides. David N. Judelson, 45, president and chief operating officer, supposedly supervises the company's eight operating groups and actually does keep up with at least five of them. Don F. Gaston, 39, a certified public accountant from Nacogdoches, Tex., is executive vice-president and Bluhdorn's chief financial man. He also oversees the financial services group, which is involved in making direct installment and commercial loans and underwriting insurance. And because of his Texas background, Gaston keeps tabs on G&W's Automotive Replacement Parts Group in Houston. Martin S. Davis, 47, also executive vice-president, is a former theatrical press agent at Paramount who handles the administrative staff, some of which also reports to Gaston and Judelson.

Indeed, it is a loose management structure that could only work among long-time friends. Judelson, an engineer, has been with G&W for 16 of its 18 years. Gaston has been there for 12. It is also a harsh system, and the manager who does not produce can find himself out in a hurry. For all that, it is a more formal system, with greater stress on corporate staff work, than might have been expected.

The empire. The test in 1975 will be whether the structure can keep so many diverse elements working together in a difficult economic climate. The list of G&W subsidiaries runs nine full pages in its 10K report, in businesses as remote from one another as sugar, zinc, auto equipment, consumer finance, and motion pictures. All these units are lumped into the eight semi-autonomous operating groups: manufacturing, leisure-time, natural resources, food and agricultural products, paper and building products, and consumer products, plus financial services, and automotive replacement parts.

Top management, says Judelson, tries to strike a balance "between corporate autocracy and corporate surrender." Each unit has to compete for funds against the others, as well as against Bluhdorn's investment of G&W's cash in the stock market. The corporate staff

evaluates each group's budget, Bluhdorn and his chief aides determine who gets the money for capital expenditures and acquisitions, and the operating group executives run their businesses.

G&W's corporate staff of approximately 225 not only helps the subsidiaries prepare their annual business plan, which it then monitors, but also acts as internal consultant on marketing, data processing, and cost control.

The company, in addition, has developed other controls. Each of the eight group executives must give Judelson a "flash forecast" at the middle of each month on how closely he is meeting his business goals for that month, and the company does unannounced internal audits on about half of G&W's units each year. Also, the company has a dual system of financial reporting, which means that each group controller reports to the corporate controller as well as to his own chief executive.

With this arrangement, Bluhdorn and his key executives feel confident in their ability to decide where to invest the corporate cash. The bulk of $120-million capital budget in each of the last two years has gone to New Jersey Zinc, Brown, and South Puerto Rico Sugar, all riding the crest of the high prices in commodities, and the manufacturing group, benefitting from the boom in capital goods.

Flops and egos. Bluhdorn's style is to manage by letting others run things as long as they produce. The six groups with record earnings last year were given considerable autonomy. But there were management shakeups in both the leisure-time movie group, where pretax income dropped from $38.7-million in fiscal 1973 to $18.7-million in 1974, and financial services, where the drop was from $48-million to $20-million.

Bluhdorn's methods are plainly not to everyone's liking at G&W, and he has lost some of the management talent that came with companies he acquired.

Some did not like G&W's corporate staff. "The staff used to interfere with my operating people," a former Brown Co. executive explains. "Why, I had to throw a couple of them out of my office one time so I could get to work." Another manager, who left the E. W. Bliss Co. in the manufacturing group, complains: "The staff people used to come in and try to change things they knew nothing about just so they could look like heros in New York." Both men now have top jobs at other companies.

Business Week, Jan. 20, 1975

Reprinted from the Jan. 20, 1975, *Business Week* by special permission. Copyright © 1975 by McGraw-Hill, Inc.

Another aspect of bureaucracy is the extreme division of labor in many such organizations. Since the work activities can be standardized, they can be reduced to relatively small work units. This condition often leads to the case where each employee has only limited knowledge of the total situation.

The low level of worker skill required in the hierarchical form can lead to a high level of dependence of the individual on the organization. It is easy to replace workers, since low skill levels mean that probably a large number of people are available who can perform the work, and the individual who does the work has little control over how he produces or what he does. This lack of job security may give rise to a need for some protective mechanism. In bureaucratic organizations there is a need for some sort of external agent—such as a union or the civil service system—to provide a degree of job security against arbitrary actions of managers.

Boundary-spanning Subsystems

The two major boundary-spanning activities are, first, a mechanism which distributes the product and/or service and, second, the procurement mechanisms that secure the raw materials or the resources required to produce the product or service.

Marketing and Distribution. Because the market for the hierarchical organization is relatively unchanging, it is likely that the channels of distribution—those organizations through which the product or service flows to the final user—will be fairly well defined and standardized. New distribution channels will arise only if current methods of distribution become extremely inefficient. It is also likely that the organization will have a great deal of influence over the distribution mechanism. The automobile industry, for instance, strongly controls its dealers, as do steel manufacturers and petroleum firms.

In some organizations, such as banks and certain government agencies (such as employment services), the distribution system is simple because the customers come to the production system. The marketing approach of a firm of this type will base its efforts primarily on pricing strategies and attempts to increase the effectiveness of distribution. It is likely that the products manufactured or the services of organizations in an industry characterized by hierarchical organizations will be fairly similar in terms of function and use. Therefore, a consumer may use any one of a large number of products from different firms to obtain the kind of satisfaction he needs. This means that a marketing strategy might be based on pricing. That is, the firm which can give the best price can obtain a competitive advantage.

Product differentiation in such firms will be largely through advertising. Witness the automobile industry. A General Motors' product performs the same functions and has the same use as a Chrysler product. It is the "image" of the car that is important. The "better" car is better not because it is a substantially different product, but because it is perceived by the consumer as a different product.

The Procurement Function.   In a stable environment there are likely to be well-developed and well-defined sources for inputs. In large industries, such as the auto industry, firms may have captive suppliers. A captive supplier is a firm which sells a large portion of its product to just one other firm. It depends primarily upon one customer for the bulk of its business. This gives the customer the capacity to influence such things as price and production techniques to such an extent that the supplier may well be considered as a subsidiary.

When there is a highly repetitive production subsystem with well-defined sources of supply, it is possible to deal with the boundary-spanning activities so as to minimize the production cost. Repetitive production subsystems operate most efficiently when they can function at a fairly level rate. Since even in a stable market and with a stable technology there are minor fluctuations, a level rate of production activities may be sustained by maintaining inventories of both raw materials and finished goods (the buffering that cushions variations in demand). Thompson (1967) points out that:

Buffering of an unsteady environment obviously brings considerable advantages to the technical core, but it does so with costs to the organization. A classic problem in connection with the buffering is how to maintain inventories, input or output, sufficient to meet all needs without incurring obsolesence as needs change . . . .

Thus while a fully buffered technological core would enjoy the conditions for maximum technical rationality, organizational rationality may call for compromises between conditions for maximum technical efficiency and the energy required for buffering operations.

Other Boundary-spanning Functions.   Other activities can also bring resources into the organization. Recruiting by the personnel department, for example, is a boundary-spanning activity. The personnel department must go beyond its boundaries to acquire the human inputs required to maintain a viable organization over time —it must find workers. The recruiting process may legitimately be regarded as a boundary-spanning activity, but the other responsibilities of the personnel department, such as the implementation of performance evaluation and compensation (programs designed to stabilize or obtain desired performance), belong in the maintenance subsystem.

Adaptive Subsystems

The adaptive subsystems sense the nature of the environment in which the organization operates. When operating in a stable environment, they will be relatively simple in structure, since interpreting the environment is relatively easy; that is, there will be set rules for interpreting changes in the environment because the experience of the organization will be such that it has learned what parts of the environment it should monitor. It will have a fairly good information base to be used in making decisions. An organization operating in a stable environment may be able to use standard census data, for example, or other similar market research information as a basis for deciding how to adjust internally. If this information is generally available, and if we know what it is, then collecting it can be done fairly easily. There will be no need to design elaborate research studies to examine otherwise incomprehensible market events (since there will be none), or for individuals to make subjective judgments about what is happening in the external environment (since what is happening is objectively known).

In hierarchical organizations, then, fairly simple ways of adapting to changes in the environment will emerge. For instance, management might decide on the basis of experience, as well as because of cost studies, that a sales reduction of 3 percent requires a work force reduction in Plant X of 10 percent, 3 percent in Plant Y, and the elimination of all overtime in other plants. In short, it is possible to develop a fairly systematic procedure which can be implemented in a simple way to deal with changes in the environment.

The stability of the environment, with its generally attendant high predictive accuracy, facilitates long-range planning. Long-term commitments of resources may be made with a great deal more certainty than in less stable environments, in turn facilitating the acquisition of the required capital at costs lower than where more risk is involved. The more stable the environment, the more likely that the firm will be able to make use of borrowed sources of capital rather than equity (internal) capital. There will be less need for investors to assume high levels of risk, and the organization can make long-term commitments to pay for the use of the borrowed capital.

Research and development and engineering is an important adaptive subsystem usually concerned with attempting to assess changes in technology which may alter the production subsystem of the organization. However, since by definition technological changes are relatively minimal in an organization that is in a stable environment, engineering and research and development activities in such a situation are more likely to focus on applications engineering than on advancing the science or state of the art. Thus, the job of the engineer in the stable organization will be more concerned with product improvement within the existing technology than with trying to develop a new product. The engineer will be concerned primarily with internal cost reductions to increase production efficiencies. One of the few ways to obtain increased return on investment in such an organization will be through cost reduction, because market potential is relatively limited, precluding substantial sales increases.

Maintenance Subsystems

Maintenance subsystems in a hierarchical organization will be fairly stable. For control purposes they will chiefly use historically-developed information that has achieved organizational credibility. For instance, fairly standardized auditing and budgeting procedures will collect and examine information which has come to be regarded, within the organization, as an acceptable performance measurement. Even in organizations in which no measures of profitability are available, costs which have been historically associated with sets of activities will come to be regarded as acceptable measures.

The focus of the maintenance subsystems will be on measuring performance, and employees in these activities will become extremely involved with performing their function, perhaps at the expense of not placing proper emphasis on the achievement of objectives. This is called "the inversion of means and ends." The purpose of the maintenance subsystem is to increase internal effectiveness, which means they are support systems; they should provide benefits to the organization, not cause problems. This, however, is not generally the situation when the auditor, the personnel executive, or the quality control manager argues insistently that his field of specialization must be performed at a high level of proficiency. Thus, auditors who sometimes audit for auditing's sake, or personnel executives who collect data for no other reason than that it is a "common" personnel practice, are not aiding anything other than their own status.

In a hierarchical organization, employees in maintenance activities will be extensively involved in performance evaluation, especially of managers. Since there will be a great deal of cost and other performance information available, it will be easy for someone to sit in judgment on the "numbers" which are used as performance measures. Having this kind of information gives a department—say personnel—a great deal of power, and its power can have a significant effect on decisions made in other parts of the firm. Auditing and budgeting units have the same potential power. When information is centralized and controlled, those who have it are extremely influential. Since information is localized in maintenance subsystems, these subsystems have a great deal of organization influence.

Since the production subsystem is highly repetitive and the work is divided into small activity units, it is likely that personnel testing may be a very effective means of selection. That is, as mentioned earlier, in a stable organization with jobs having lower skill requirements than in other types of organizations, a larger labor pool is available. Thus, from a large number of workers it may be a great deal more effective to screen them with some sort of performance test than attempt to make subjective evaluations of their abilities, or to test them later when they get on the job.

High morale and motivation are especially difficult to maintain when the work is routine, repetitive, or programmed. Most of the research on this topic indicates that job satisfaction and job involvement decrease as job complexity and job autonomy decrease. At the level of rank-and-file workers in the hierarchical or bureaucratic organization, boredom and alienation have been found to be higher for assembly-line workers than for workers with less structured jobs

(Blauner, 1964). Boredom, of course, means the person wants a change in activity. Work alienation is a feeling that work is meaningless, or lacks significance. In addition, workers may have a feeling of isolation, of not feeling a sense of identity with the organization and what it does, and a feeling of powerlessness—helpless and controlled by various forces in the organization. Such feelings of boredom and alienation are associated with high rates of absenteeism and turnover, as well as with grievances and work stoppages. It is a fact, however, that the majority of workers on highly routined and repetitive jobs do not say they are bored or dissatisfied with their jobs (Kornhauser, 1965; Sheppard and Herrick, 1972; Wyatt and Marriot, 1956).

It is true, however, that a greater percentage of them are less satisfied and more bored than workers in other industries where the work is less routine and repetitive (Kornhauser, 1965; Wyatt and Marriott, 1956). Thus, at least most individuals in the bureaucratic organization seem to adjust to the organization's work demands. Those who cannot adjust, leave. Furthermore, some studies show that most employees in repetitive programmed jobs will not choose more complex jobs when given the opportunity to do so (Kilbridge, 1960). It is quite possible that work which demands little of the job holder attracts individuals who, because of low self-esteem or some other factor, prefer jobs of this type.

Managerial Subsystems

In a hierarchical organization, the managerial subsystem will be characterized by a high degree of centralized control at the top administrative level. The nature of the information, in organizations of this type, is such that it can be quickly collected and transmitted to the higher levels, so that decisions can be made there to change operations at lower levels without requiring a great deal of involvement of managers at those levels. Thus, decisions are made in large part by administrative management.

There will be a high degree of fairly close control and monitoring of operations, and this control will be centralized in the hands of a relatively small number of people. The amount of discretion that lower-level managers have is likely to be relatively small.

The bureaucratic organization is characterized by a fairly rigid hierarchy. Lines of authority and responsibility will be clear. Jobs will be very well-defined. Often problems will be solved by appealing to executives at higher levels, or using the formal hierarchical system as a problem-resolution mechanism.

One of the major problems with which the managerial subsystem must deal is conflict between the "management" group and employees. In industrial organizations this will take the form of union-management bargaining, and in public organizations by the relationship between the administrative staffs and civil service agencies.

People will move to top-level managerial positions in a hierarchical organization after fairly long careers. It is very likely that there will be a relatively small proportion of managers relative to the number of workers, and that the number of positions at higher levels will be relatively small. If this is true, and since the managers at the higher levels make promotion decisions, it is likely that there will be a high degree of similarity in point of view, or homogeneity of attitude, among high-level executives. Promotions will come not only for what one can do, but also because one has the "right" point of view. This can create a special problem when individuals employed by such a firm have high needs for achievement, because they will find promotion opportunities limited, leading them to go elsewhere to satisfy their advancement needs.

In the hierarchical organization, managerial control will be based on power that is a function of the particular position. Generally, there will be fairly well-defined goals. It is unlikely that the organization will be seeking to provide products or services different from its current capability. The major decision about goals in an organization of this type will be *how much* and *when* the product or service is to be provided. This will be relatively easy to forecast, since—by definition —the market is stable.

This kind of organization structure has been criticized because of its failure to adapt and cope, but in fact the hierarchical form of organization is precisely the kind which does cope effectively with a stable environment. To have a different organization form would very likely endanger survival. Those who hope for the death of bureaucracy because of its demands on its human resources must consider these points.

The Flexible, Dynamic Organization

The flexible, dynamic organization is found where the market and technological sectors are highly volatile. We call this form of organization "flexible"; it has been called "organic" by Burns and Stalker (1961). Generally, it is one in which the structure, relationships, and jobs are loosely defined, so that the process of adapting to change is relatively easy. What, then, are the characteristics of the flexible organization's subsystems?

Production Subsystems

The production sybsystem of the flexible organization is composed primarily of general-purpose equipment or technology. Essentially, it is job-shop oriented. The various production elements will be rearranged, when necessary, in order to perform the particular kinds of activities necessary to provide the required outputs as the market or the technology changes, and thus the production subsystem itself will be in a fairly constant state of change. The sequencing of operations will vary from project to project so that the development of routine, repetitive production procedures is relatively difficult, if not impossible. Thompson (1967) describes this as intensive technology, one where a variety of

> techniques is drawn upon in order to achieve a change in some specific object; but the selection, combination, and order of application are determined by feedback from the object itself. When the object is human, this intensive technology is regarded as "therapeutic," but the same technical logic is found also in the construction industry . . . and in research where the objects of concern are nonhuman. . . .
>
> The intensive technology is a custom technology. Its successful employment rests in part on the availability of all the capacities potentially needed, but equally on the appropriate custom combination of selected capacities as required by the individual case or project.

Boundary-spanning Subsystems

The method of getting the product to customers will vary from customer to customer, and channels of distribution will be relatively unstructured and will change from time to time. This means, essentially, that the organization will probably have to handle its marketing by itself. It cannot transfer this function easily to other jobbers, or develop a channel of distribution similar to that which distributes, say, automobiles or groceries. Since the distribution function cannot be routinized, highly skilled individuals in both the technical and marketing functions will be needed.
Those involved with the procurement function will also need to be

highly skilled in finding different types of raw materials and resources, because both the level and type of raw material inputs will change from time to time. This means that those concerned with resource acquisition will need to keep in close touch with suppliers, and they will have to have knowledge of methods of financing purchases.

Adaptive Subsystems

Adaptive subsystem activities in the flexible organization are extremely important. They will be performed by individuals in marketing and distribution functions and procurement, as well as in engineering and research development. Individuals in the adaptive subsystems must be highly skilled at interpreting the environment. Whereas in the hierarchical form there are fairly well-defined cues which trigger internal organizational adjustments, in the flexible organization the information which might cue an internal change in the subsystem will vary from time to time and will probably occur in a random fashion. Thus, individual skill becomes essential in making some assessment as to the nature of the organization change, since it is practically impossible to specify in advance what specific aspect of the environment must be monitored. The relevant aspect may change from time to time, making the ability to read it a very individualized skill. Item 7.2 describes the nature of change in the role of purchasing agent. He is performing both an adaptive and a boundary-spanning activity. As raw material costs increase and the sources of supply become more limited, his role must take on more significance in the survival of the organization.

This same kind of clinical, analytical skill is required of those who must determine how to restructure the organization in response to external changes. In the hierarchical form of organization, a minor change in one of the external indicators may trigger a specific type of internal change. In the flexible organization, however, the process of adjustment and the resulting set of relationships will nearly always vary. This variation will be a function of different sets of circumstances and, thus, it will differ according to the circumstances. This means that the individuals in the adaptive subsystem in a flexible organization will be very influential in decision making.

Marketing activities will usually take the form of both extensive market research and a clinical subjective assessment of what the data mean. In research and development, the adaptive processes will likely be more toward the side of pure, rather than applied research.

Members performing adaptive activities must, of necessity, continually update their skills and abilities to maintain them at a high level. In order to maintain high individual skills in these critical areas, the organization may revert to a strategy of hiring individuals with the required capability, rather than engage itself in a training function. And since, by definition, these skills may be rapidly changing, there may be a fairly high level of turnover among those involved in the adaptive processes.

ITEM 7.2 Boundary-spanning and Adaptive Activities

The Purchasing Agent Gains More Clout

After years of corporate obscurity, the purchasing agent suddenly is moving into management's top ranks. First it was shortages that propelled him into the spotlight. Now it may be excessive inventories. Either way, the purchasing man today is likely to be juggling a lot of new duties under the catch-all title of "materials manager" and to be poking into practically every aspect of business operations, from new products to capital spending.

"In this suddenly mad world," says David K. Barnes, vice-president and general manager of Du Pont's new Energy & Materials Dept., "corporate management quickly rediscovered the purchasing function and—at least in our case—came to the conclusion that planning to achieve furture supply needs and executing those plans well was going to be a major factor in determining future earnings."

Until about two years ago, purchasing was being steadily decentralized along with other corporate operations. Then the acute shortages suddenly began showing up, and companies discovered they needed all the buying clout they could muster. "Companies are realizing they've lost leverage through decentralized purchasing," says William A. Bales,

director of corporate purchasing at Quaker Oats Co. in Chicago.

Evolving strategy. Now purchasing functions are being pulled together again, but for many corporations, the change has been evolutionary. Norris Industries, Inc., in Los Angeles, for example, began by buying fuel centrally during the crunch and then started purchasing steel and other commodities the same way. At Dymo Industries, Inc., a San Francisco-based manufacturer of embossing and coding equipment, all 18 decentralized purchasing managers—even those overseas—were enlisted into a multinational mutual assistance pact. "We found some smaller divisions didn't have purchasing clout," admits Claude L. Ganz, president and chief executive officer.

Broader role. Centralized purchasing has led to broader responsibility for procurement managers. Not only are they looking for the best buy today, they increasingly are making sure there are supplies for the future. That means they participate in top-level discussions about acquisitions, development of raw materials sources, research on substitute materials, and capital expenditures.

Du Pont, for example, has had centralized purchasing since 1944, but the Energy & Materials Dept., formed this year, not only buys all raw materials, supplies, and equipment for the company worldwide, but also plans for long-term procurement of energy, conducts exploration for minerals and petroleum, plans development of alternate energy sources, and recommends investments in mineral resources, where necessary, to assure supplies.

New status. Such innovative methods are requiring more and more of purchasing or materials managers, and their status is shooting up. At Xerox, where 75% of the manufactured cost of the typical product is in materials, the job of Gaylord Powell, director of materials, did not even exist prior to last year. Now he reports directly to Robert M. Pippitt, senion vice-president. At Gillette, Jenal re-

ports directly to William Salatich, president of Gillette North America. Purchasing jobs have been elevated to the vice-presidential level at dozens of major corporations.

Increasingly, top management recognizes that a job that affects more than half of the sales dollar should command a higher level of training and compensation. As a result, more and more companies are recruiting talent from business schools for purchasing jobs. Two years ago Rockwell began hiring two to four MBAs each year for purchasing, and Xerox is bringing MBAs directly into its buying ranks for 1975.

Business Week, Jan. 13, 1975

Since the cost of developing adaptive skills is usually too high for an organization to bear, individuals who have acquired these skills on their own will be recruited. This means that those who come to an organization and function in an adaptive capacity are likely to be more highly trained or more highly skilled than those performing other functions. This will have important implications for the levels of compensation in organizations. In the flexible organization, individuals are as likely to be paid for the level of education and training they bring to the job as for the level of importance of their job within the organization.

Capital acquisition in a firm of this sort is difficult, since there is high risk involved. With a great degree of fluctuation in an environment that is highly unpredictable, investors are less willing to take the long-term risk of lending capital for a fixed return. With the high risk that might go along with the flexible organization, the capital structure will be weighted toward equity or self-generated investments, which would provide great potential gain attendant with the high risk.

Maintenance Subsystems

In flexible organizations, the utility of historical data for control purposes is minimal, since there may be little history to go by. Therefore, cost standards used to evaluate projects will come from projected estimates. This means that control and evaluation of performance will be much more likely to be subjective than to be based on "objective" performance measures. In flexible organizations it is likely that "end results" will be less frequently used for assessment than in bureaucratic organizations, and there will be stronger focus on the manner in which individuals go about performing their work.

The control function will reside in either the person with expertise in a particular area or the person with the greatest financial interest. The expert will have great influence simply because of his capabilities. He is the one who knows the most about a particular activity. If expertise is the predominant power base, the influence pattern will shift from time to time, depending upon the nature of the project or activity and who is the house expert at a particular point in time. When influence derives from the level of financial interest, this simply means that the owner, or the major stockholder, makes the decisions. In this case, the organization will be an extension of that person's interests.

Personnel in flexible organizations are likely to have a short-range commitment to the organization. Their focus will be on their area of professional expertise or on their self-interest in promotion and advancement, since in a flexible organization there may be relatively few long-term activities to provide a basis for lengthy tenure. Individuals will be brought into the organization when they are required. When their services are no longer needed they may be relieved of responsibility, or they may move on voluntarily. This may make it undesirable and, from an individual point of view, unwise to be highly committed to the organization as a place to work.

This uncertainty may not pose a particular problem for the individual or for the organization. It is likely that people who accept employment in flexible organizations have learned that relatively rapid movement is part of the game. As in the case of the aerospace industry, engineers typically move from firm to firm as the major contracts move. Professionals who work in organizations may be willing to exercise their skills in any number of organizations so long as they are able to do what they have been trained to do and what they believe to be important.

Managerial Subsystems

The managerial subsystem in a flexible organization will be relatively less structured than in other forms of organizations. Essentially, there will be few policy guidelines to use in the decision-making process, because the variability of the environment will preclude well-defined, set policies, over time. Guidelines must be consistently changed to meet the changing requirements.

The organization structure will be flexible, one where individuals move from project to project as the need for their skills arise, with the authority structure different for each project. Individuals will move from superior to superior, depending upon what needs to be done. Teams will be composed of individuals who will work on particular projects. When the project is completed, the individuals on a team may move to different teams. If their skills are no longer required in the organization, they may be terminated either willingly or unwillingly. This mobility can cause problems unless the individual has a capacity to tolerate uncertainty, ambiguity, and role conflict.

In a flexible organization, the individual may not have the luxury of reporting to one superior. Over a period of time, he may report to several, and he will probably be placed in situations where he is faced with conflicting demands, and certainly with different leadership styles. This may be good or bad for the individual. On the one hand, it allows him to learn and grow from varied experience. On the other hand, it precludes the opportunity to build long-term relationships with a superior, which may be important for some individuals both from a personal viewpoint as well as from the standpoint of organizational advancement.

Flexible organizations, then, operate in a highly dynamic environment. It is likely that they will be relatively small compared with the size of hierarchical forms. This smallness, in and of itself, facilitates adaptability to the environment. As an organization grows, however, it begins to build-in some degree of procedural rigidity and hierarchy. This may mitigate against effective adaptation to a changing environment.

It is likely that flexible organizations will, when possible, move to a more stable sector. That is, if at all possible, they will try to increase the degree of certainty in which they operate. This is desirable in that it facilitates and eases the processes of planning and control. If it can make such a move, the organization will be able to make long-term commitments to its members, perhaps facilitating recruitment, since persons will be willing to join an organization where they can make a "career."

This last point may be an important one, especially when individuals have a high degree of anxiety about their careers. While a person might have a great deal of confidence in his own skills and abilities as a professional, the uncertainty of where he will be working can pose a problem. This uncertainty is probably related to lower levels of commitment to the organization, which in turn would make the problem of obtaining high levels of compliance from individuals extremely difficult.

Project Management.   The kind of managerial subsystem in the flexible organization, the one we have just described, is called *project management*. Project management is an important organization tool, and widely used, warranting some added discussion. When a job can be broken down into a number of fairly small segments, and when the activity will be required for a fairly long time period, then the organization can hire people to do these more narrow jobs. These jobs stay the same; they are repetitive. A manager may supervise, say, a production unit where such a situation exists. However, in the flexible organization, the nature of the work changes when the environment changes. Therefore, we can expect to see "projects" change. A project is a series of related activities required to achieve a work outcome, but one characteristic is that it may have a discrete completion time. For example, the lunar landing of U.S. astronauts was the end of a particular space project. Once the astronauts returned and the data was analyzed, space workers were shifted to another project.

Project management recognizes this need to shift both physical and human resources. Individuals are assigned to temporary, ad hoc, work teams, though they may exist for extended time periods. Still, there is a planned termination date to which planning and control are keyed in this type of organization. An important determinant of the composition of a project group is the particular configuration of skills required on the project. As skill configurations change for each project, so will the composition of the team members. (Techniques for managing such groups are described in chaps. 14 and 15, while chap. 16 discusses several methods for integrating project team activities.)

Technology-Dominated Mixed Organizations
In technology-dominated mixed organizations, the major threat to survival and effectiveness stems from uncertainty in the technological environment. The market sector of the environment of these organizations is relatively stable. Scientific breakthroughs, new production technology, or other new concepts can provide their creator or early adopter with a significant competitive advantage. Therefore, it is

important to monitor the technological sector of the environment carefully and make changes in the system when necessary.

The technology-dominated mixed organization, like its market-dominated counterpart, will have one major part of its structure which will take on hierarchical characteristics, with some degree of rigidity, and another part which will be less tightly structured. This combination presents the problem of achieving good relationships between these two parts of the organization. Attempting to resolve conflicts between them by using the position authority of higher management levels is likely to be ineffective, since it is improbable that individuals in the managerial hierarchy or the marketing sector will have a level of technical expertise as high as those in the technical sector or that is acceptable to the latter. The professionals, that is, are likely to react negatively to administrative decisions. (These integration problems are examined extensively in chap. 16.)

Organizational members in the stable market sector are likely to be either externally-oriented (seek satisfactions away from work and the job) or organizationally-oriented (highly committed to the organization and its values), as opposed to the professional orientation (extremely committed to the work that one does) of those in the volatile, technical sectors. This difference will result in different reactions to pressures from the maintenance system seeking to impose regularity through standardized procedures and methods. Item 7.3 describes some of problems of this type faced by Polaroid, a company that has many of the characteristics of the TD-mixed firm.

Production Subsystems

The production subsystem in a TD-mixed organization will likely use an intensive type of technology in which human beings choose from a variety of possible procedures that one which is most appropriate in a given situation. It is unlikely that we would find assembly-line technology in this type of environmental setting. Equipment would have unpredictable life, making investment in special-purpose technology or machinery highly risky. The tendency would be to use, where possible, general-purpose processes to increase the productive life expectancy.

Personnel who work in the production subsystem are likely to be highly-skilled craftsmen who have spent relatively long times developing skills on particular types of equipment. They might have done this in apprenticeship programs, or through vocational training. It is also likely that their work requires much attention to detail.

Boundary-spanning Subsystems

In the TD-mixed organization, the channels of distribution will be
fairly well fixed, or set in place. Products will perhaps change technologically, but they will be sold as they had been before any new
developments. For example, item 7.3 describes Polaroid's development of the SX-70 camera. This remarkable new product is sold
through camera shops, department stores, and discount stores—as
were earlier Land cameras.

If a boundary-spanning unit must be in contact with an outside firm
in the technological environment, however, it must be able to change
with technology. New sources of supply will be needed as raw material requirements change.

In the early stages of technological change, product pricing will take
advantage of the innovation and price will be high. However, if
competitors enter the market with similar but lower-priced products,
there will be some problems in the rigid marketing section. Customers
may be reluctant to buy until there is more price stability. The
example of digital watches in item 6.2 describes how retailers are
unwilling to purchase and inventory the product until the technology
stabilizes.

Adaptive Subsystems

Major policy and strategy influence in a technology-dominated organization comes from those in the technological sectors. In this group, a
great reliance will be found on individual skill and ability of a subjective nature in assessing the environment. Research and development
activities will be more extensive than applications engineering, thus
placing more emphasis on advanced knowledge and skills than on
pragmatic application of design.

Market research activities will be fairly simple. They will most
probably focus on existing, or easily collectible, data which have
become fairly widely accepted indicators to be used in decision
making. In this adaptive activity, there will be a need for individuals
not necessarily with experience in the firm or industry, but who know
how to apply standard research techniques.

Maintenance Subsystems

Maintenance subsystems in TD-mixed organizations face a paradox-
ical problem. Since pressures are exerted from them for stability and

ITEM 7.3   Volatile Technology, Stable Market

The SX-70 Camera and Polaroid

"This was no Boy Scout outing, but an expedition over the Pole," sighs Edwin H. Land, founder and chief executive of Polaroid Corp. That is how he describes the $350-million industrial gamble his company has taken to manufacture and sell its much-publicized SX-70 instant camera. In essence, Polaroid has been transformed on a crash basis from a company basically oriented to research and product assembly into a largely self-sufficient manufacturer of very complex products.

One aim was to reap the higher profits of a fully integrated producer by reducing its dependence on the outside sources. Another was to protect the new technology represented by the SX-70, since Eastman Kodak, a major Polaroid supplier, threatens to become a big competitor in the instant photography market.

Polaroid's corporate transformation has been dogged by costly production problems that have sapped the company's profits and destroyed its glamour as a Wall Street favorite. The production problems have been essentially solved, Polaroid claims. But now the company faces the basic test of generating sufficient sales volume to exploit its costly new manufacturing capacity. As the vital Christmas retail sales season begins, Polaroid's test reaches a critical stage.

Inflated expectations. "What we need now is volume," says I. M. Booth, manager of the company's New Bedford (Mass.) plant that makes negatives for the SX-70. "We have all that capacity staring us in the face." Booth's plea is echoed at other Polaroid plants, some of which now run at less than 50% of capacity. Under Polaroid's "razor-and-blades" philosophy, top priority now is to sell enough cameras to generate steady, long-term demand for film.

Producing the camera and its film involves a complex blend of optics, electronics, and chemistry. The camera automatically produces a finished color photo—the user has only to press the shutter. There is no litter, as with the earlier Polaroid peel-apart film cameras. For Polaroid the SX-70 is the key to future growth. "They're too much tied to one product and one market, like we used to be," warns the president of a Boston technology company that has recently diversified. Retorts Edwin Land: "At Polaroid, we deliberately choose to have very few products, that only we can make, and to make them very important."

Now 65 and the 15% owner of Polaroid's stock, Land continues to make the fundamental product decisions for the company as chairman and president. Pacing about his book-lined office-laboratory in Cambridge, Mass., cluttered with at least a half-dozen telephones, Land notes that he has vetoed ventures such as 35-mm photography urged on him by other executives, because they were "ordinary, not the extraordinary that we choose." Bill McCune says Land's "essential impatience" and his refusal to heed doomsayers are major reasons for breakthrough projects.

Despite his dominance of new product development, Land insists that there is less of a one-man rule flavor at Polaroid than at most companies, and that Polaroid has managers who will instinctively follow his tradition when he leaves. Says he: "I represent a framework of ideas. The men who have come with us know this framework and have chosen to live with it." As a firm believer in corporate informality, Land scornfully says that "institutionalization is an aspect of a corporate death wish . . . a mausoleum drive."

No Cash Bind. But as Polaroid grows bigger, management responsibility is inevitably falling more heavily on others. Day-to-day operations are now handled by a triumvirate, consisting of McCune, 57, Wyman, 44, and Wensberg, 44. Below them, another cadre of managers, many of them in their 30s, but nearly all at least 10-year Polaroid veterans, have

taken over more authority at the division level.

One reason for delegating more authority could be that Land underestimated the size and complexity of the SX-70 project. Land demanded too much perfection and too much speed in the development of the new camera.

Business Week, Nov. 30, 1974

predictability, the market sector will attempt to develop systematic marketing and distribution processes. If they can do so, this will result in a somewhat "bureaucratic" marketing unit. For the organization's technological activities, however, this development of a rigidly structured system may cause problems, since freedom to adjust and react to the changing environment requires that individual discretionary limits must be relatively broad. By their nature, procedures and rules that accompany the bureaucratic structure limit discretion.

For control and evaluation purposes, other problems exist for the maintenance subsystems. For example, because of the stable market, it may be easy to develop a good set of distribution cost estimates. This could result in quantified, objective "cost" estimates against which actual costs can be compared. A manager will therefore be able to measure marketing efficiency with some accuracy. When "objective" data such as these are available, they become the basis for performance evaluations.

Now consider the same performance evaluation problem in the technological sector. At the volatile boundary, the individual has little control over what outside people and organizations do. In addition, since the determination of a need for change, the internal implementation of the change, and the resulting effect on the performance level of the organization may cover a long period of time, it is difficult to develop performance criteria quite as objective as we can for, say, marketing or production costs. Therefore, there will be two obviously different types of criteria used in performance evaluation, one subjective and one objective. This is likely to lead to perceived inequities among organizational members, because no matter which criteria are used in a part of the organization, members may feel that the other type is better.

In personnel selection, emphasis will be on acquiring highly skilled and trained professionals for the technological sector. The level of *organization* commitment of this group will probably be lower than that of those in the more stable sections of the organization, since they will identify to some extent with their professional group. This identification with other professionals outside the company should be of value to the organization, however, since such contacts are a valuable source of ideas.

Managerial Subsystems

The authority structure of the TD-mixed organization will present a varied appearance. For instance, in the marketing sector we would expect to find fairly well-defined job responsibilities, accountability to specific superiors for work, and limited discretion for decisions. Those in this unit will find themselves subjected to standardized rules, policies, and procedures. On the other hand, in the technological sector, there will be more latitude of action. The production subsystem is likely to be caught in the middle, between pressures from research and engineering to adopt newer production methods and the marketing unit's desire to maintain the product relatively as is.

Market-dominated Mixed Organizations

In the market-dominated mixed form organization, the significant policy-influencing group will be from the marketing sector because of the need to stay in close touch with a constantly changing, unpredictable environmental consumer or client group.

Production Subsystems

The type of environment confronting MD-mixed organizations leads to programmed production tasks performed within a stable technology. Skill requirements for those in this system will be moderately low, and job security will probably result from union protection. The performance of the production system will be measured by relatively objective measures of cost. There will be considerable pressure from the marketing segment to change the product to meet changing consumer preferences.

Adaptive Subsystems

The relatively placid condition of the technological external environment calls for little scientific research or development in the MD-mixed organization. Where there are technical functions to perform, they will probably be of an applied nature. Engineers, for instance, though highly trained, will probably not be engaged in research on new projects but rather will spend their time trying, say, to find sources for less costly raw materials.

In the marketing sector, there will be extensive market research devoted to uncovering new markets. More than likely, those performing this function will rely on a clinical assessment, or judgment, of markets. Experience, intuition, and judgment will be more useful in determining what and where markets will be than extensive research efforts using standard market data sets such as population data, income estimates, or traditional buying patterns.

Boundary-spanning Subsystems

In general, changes in a product of an MD-mixed firm will be style or design changes, rather than changes in what the product will do. Therefore, in MD-mixed organization the acquisition of inputs will only be significant when they may directly change the character of the output, or if the market requires a product with different raw material requirements. That is, if market changes require a different type of raw material, then purchasing must seek new sources of supply. For instance, when a dress manufacturer finds that new materials are selling in the market and he must use them in his manufacturing, his purchasing staff will have to seek out various new sources of supply.

Product pricing will be controlled by the marketing subsystem, since it will need latitude and discretion in price setting to market effectively. There will be catering to customer orientations, and those in the marketing staff can be characterized as "promoters" rather than as sales managers.

Maintenance Subsystems

Primary organizational control problems will be found in the marketing segment of the MD-mixed firm and consequently it is difficult to develop internal controls satisfactory to those who perform maintenance functions. The flexible and varied nature of the marketing and distribution system will make collection of historical and relevant cost data difficult, since distribution systems may be changing, and some difficulties are likely to occur as a result of the applied nature of the required technical activities. While engineers and scientists may have been socialized through an education which has taught them to value research activities, their jobs may be concerned more with mundane applications problems. This can lead to disillusionment, dissatisfaction, and attendant problems of keeping staffed adequately. This may be an especially acute problem because of the higher status of the marketing group in the organization.

Managerial Subsystems

A hierarchical type authority structure will prevail in the technical sectors of the market-dominated firm, a more loose authority structure in the marketing and distribution sectors, which will have more individual discretion and freedom in decision making. Control systems to monitor changes in and adapt to the environment will be developed in such a way as to be triggered by decisions made in the marketing sector. It is highly likely that this type of mixed organization will be headed by someone with marketing or sales background.

As in a technologically-dominated firm, there will be problems in relating the stable and dynamic segments of the organization to each other. The well-defined structure of the technical sector may not only pose adjustment problems for the professionals who work in it, but also may present difficulties when it is interrelated to the more flexible organization structure in the marketing sector. Remedies for coping with this integration problem are given in chapter 16.

The Structure-Environment (SE) Model

We have proposed a conceptual scheme for determining what the structure of an organization will look like, given certain environmental factors. The scheme presupposes that the organization type and the way in which its subsystems function will vary with variations in the organization's market and technology situation, but there are other factors which must also be taken into consideration.

First, large organizations, especially conglomerates or multidivisioned companies, may have major divisions in different environments with different uncertainty characteristics. For example, one division of a multidivisioned firm may be in a stable industry, such as steel, while another division may be in the aerospace sector. This disparity creates problems for the parent company. Great care must be taken not to impose a managerial system inconsistent with the characteristics of the environment of the subsidiary units. For example, suppose a group of successful managers of an electronics firm acquires a clothing firm and attempts to impose a managerial structure on it that has worked in electronics. What happens? The system fails miserably in the clothing firm, because managerial strategies are imposed which work in the electronics segment but do not in the clothing segment.

A second consideration is that there is always a tendency for an organization to move toward more stable conditions, just as within most human beings there is a drive toward achieving predictability and regularity. Organizations attempt to structure themselves according to rational principles (Thompson, 1967). As this happens, the organization's growth rate inevitably begins to slow down. And when growth achieves a more deliberate rate, it may be in an organization's interest to change its environmental setting to return to a rapid growth stage. Major increases in sales, for instance, are more likely to occur in a volatile than in a stable environment because of the increased markets for, perhaps, innovation. This problem is extensively examined in chapter 17, where we deal with the *changing* character of the environment and the organization structure. Some of the strategies are briefly noted here, however.

A change in environmental setting can be brought about if an organization takes certain actions. By engaging in heavy research and development activities, for example, a firm in a stable environment may be able to generate a technological breakthrough which suddenly creates a technologically *volatile* environment. Or marketing and advertising efforts can conceivably cause enough of a shift in usage for a product so that the market changes in nature and size.

Another possibility, and perhaps a more feasible alternative, would be for a stable firm to engage in acquisitions or mergers. Thus, an automobile manufacturer might acquire an electronics firm. Or, if a particular subunit in an organization has a particular skill not suitable to the general market and technological structure, it may spin off a "division," creating an autonomous unit. Publishing firms, for instance, which produce and market textbooks may spin off a unit to create and market alternative learning devices such as tape cassettes, fim strips, computer-assisted learning systems, and so on.

There are, of course, different ways that these four types of organizations should be managed. In chapters 3, 4, and 5 we discussed how individuals develop particular orientations to work, as well as some sociological (groups) and psychological (attitudes, motivations, and needs) factors. In chapter 6 and this chapter we showed how organizations get to be what they are. When we have explained managerial processes in chapters 8, 9, 10, and 11, we will be in a position to suggest ways to manage the different types of organizations.

Managing the bureaucratic organization is discussed in chapters 12 and 13, managing the flexible in chapters 14 and 15. In chapter 16 we examine methods for the management of the mixed type organizations.

From this point on, then, we will consider structure as it relates to strategy—always keeping in mind that what we are discussing are theoretical constructs. While few everyday situations fit the strategies *exactly*, if a manager approaches his problems from a contingency stance, he can develop more effective solutions than if he does not.

Discussion Questions

1. If it is true that bureaucratic organizations are the most appropriate way of adapting to a stable environment, why is there so much criticism of this form?

2. Can two organizations be producing essentially the same product— say food products—and have basically different distribution methods? Why? Why not? Under what conditions would this prevail?

3. "Power is greatest at the volatile boundary of an organization." Why? Comment.

4. What are the reasons for different kinds of power in the bureaucratic and the dynamic organization?

5. Mixed type organizations have units in environments with different volatility characteristics. What type of organization is a pharmaceutical firm? A corner grocery store? A firm which manufactures electronic calculators?

Part IV

The Management Process

Getting things done through people, planning and allocating resources, making decisions and implementing them—these are what managers do. There are some fundamental ways that each of these things can be done, ways that can help a manager manage better. According to management process contingency theory, these functions are performed differently depending on the kind of organization. (We shall have more to say about that in part V.)

Leadership (chap. 8) is influence, and influence comes from power. The basic concepts of leadership practice and theory are examined, beginning with work in the late 1930s to the recent situational approaches which are consistent with management process contingency theory.

Managers are decision makers, and decision making is selecting from alternatives to solve problems. In chapter 9 the aspects of decision making emphasized are (1) problem definition and (2) approaches to selecting alternatives.

When decisions have been made, they must be translated into plans and controls used in managing. In chapter 10 we show how several types of budgets can be developed to provide important bases for managerial control. Both long- and short-range planning are also discussed.

Finally, the plans must be implemented. The manager must eventually translate general objectives into specific activities for each particular member of the organization. Chapter 11 shows how this can be done.

Chapter 8

Leadership is the process of influencing others to do what you want them to do. Such a concept may seem simple enough on the surface, but in reality it is often complex. Suppose a foreman asks an employee to work past normal quitting time. The worker agrees. Has the foreman exercised "leadership"? Perhaps, and perhaps not. Maybe the employee needs the extra pay, or perhaps he stays because he knows he is needed, or because he is afraid he will lose his job if he doesn't.

Many things that people do at work—such as following orders, doing what is required of them, working harder than is necessary—cannot be explained in terms of leadership alone. Perhaps, then, we should start a discussion of leadership not by asking, "How does one person influence others?" but by asking, "Why do people comply?"

Why Do People Comply?

A powerful, yet relatively simple concept which can account for a great deal of compliance in organizations is the *psychological contract.* Schein (1970), states the concept of the psychological contract in this way: "The individual has a variety of expectations of the organization and the organization a variety of expectations of him. These expectations not only cover how much work is to be performed for how much pay, but also involve the whole pattern of rights, privileges, and obligation between the worker and organization."

Basically this implies that people in any situation—including that at work—will do many things *because they believe they should.* And for what they do, they expect reciprocation in the form of pay, benefits, and favors.

Leadership

The terms of the psychological contract are affected by what one has learned and experienced before he arrives in an organization and by what the organization needs. The professional, the organizationalist, and the externalist all, because of their particular values, strike different "bargains" with their work organization (or more specifically, its management). These different organizational types, how they view authority, and why their particular view develops was the theme of chapter 3. As noted there, individuals learn to respond to higher authority throughout their lives as a result of dealing with parents, teachers, and other authority figures. They are not only taught directly, but through films, books, TV shows, and other means which illustrate acquiescence to authority. These socialization experiences contribute to the development of personal values which usually cause the individual to feel that it is "right," under certain circumstances, for those in higher authority to tell him and others what to do. When the individual feels this direction to be right, the authority is said to have "legitimate" power.

In other words, legitimacy of power refers to whether or not the subject of influence believes it is proper for another person to influence him, and thus, legitimacy stems from the internalized values of a person. The organizationalist, for example, believes that many directives from his superior are legitimate. The professional may respond more readily to influences from colleagues. The externalist responds primarily to organization demands so long as they are made during job hours.

The legitimate power of authority figures is not unlimited. As Barnard (1938) has pointed out, organizational members believe that some directives from a leader are legitimate and some are not. Barnard uses the term "zone of indifference," similar to the concept of psychological contract, to define that collection of directives which will be followed without question, since they are clearly legitimate for a superior to make. Directives which fall outside this zone of indifference are considered nonlegitimate by those to whom they are given.

The Boundaries of the Psychological Contract.   The psychological contract is not static. It often changes by mutual consent, as when a person is promoted with expectations of more effort for the increased pay, status, and privileges that come with his new position. Sometimes it is changed by pressures from one or the other of the parties, as when a union is able to obtain increased hourly wage rates from management.

So long as the request, commands, directives, and suggestions fall within the boundaries of the psychological contract, however, there will be a response to them. Take, for example, the salesman whose psychological contract is shown in figure 8.1. In general, he will do without question anything that falls within the *public* boundaries of his contract. The public boundaries encompass those things which he leads others, especially his superior, to believe he will do as part of his job. They are generally-agreed-upon work activities. But they do

FIGURE 8.1   Hypothetical Psychological Contract for a Salesman

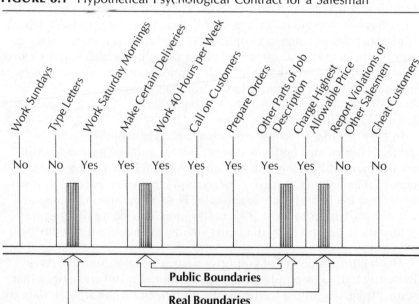

not represent the effective limits of his bargain. The *real* boundaries
for the salesman are broader. He will do *more* than is represented by
the "public" zone. The *real* boundaries do, however, define the limits
beyond which he will not go.

For tactical reasons, the salesman may wish to have his superior
believe that the public boundaries of his psychological contract represent his actual limits. Then when he complies with requests that fall
between his public and real boundaries, he will appear to be giving up
something. He may do this in order to extract a "favor" at some future
date. He has made it appear that he has gone beyond the normal call
of duty and thus expects a quid pro quo—a favor—in return for
exceeding the normal requirements of his job. Suppose, for example,
that in the past he has created the impression that he believes it is his
job to give customers the lowest possible price. When his superior
asks him to charge the highest possible price and the salesman
complies, he may feel that his superior now owes him a concession of
some kind in return.

It is when an individual receives orders which fall outside the real
boundaries that problems begin to occur. Any request beyond these
real limits is excluded from the range of things the salesman will
normally do. Thus, for example, if asked to work on Sundays or to
cheat customers, he may resign. However, as we have said earlier, the
boundaries of the psychological contract are not static. When faced
with a request to act outside these real boundaries, the person may
decide to comply, especially if he has no other job alternatives available. Thus, a person who is pressured by his superiors to act unethi-
cally, or in a way he doesn't want to, may do so, at great personal and
psychological cost, if he cannot find a job elsewhere, or must stay in
the organization for some other reason.

Leadership and Administration in Management

Accomplishing goals through others is done through administration as
well as leadership, and there is a significant difference between these
two concepts. By administration we mean the use of the prerogatives
and rights associated with one's position in an organization, such as
making decisions and giving directions. Managerial tools such as
budgets, standard operating procedures, compensation systems, plans
and other control mechanisms are the devices used in the administrative process. Their use to obtain compliance from subordinates,
within the real boundaries of the psychological contract, is administration.

This is an important concept, for it means that a very significant part of what a manager does can be taught. The way to design these administrative tools, as well as their effective use, can be imparted to others by commonly used teaching methods. For instance, a person can learn how to prepare a budget, design a procedure, develop a compensation program, and prepare plans. Understanding the boundaries of the psychological contract and requiring subordinates to perform within the real boundaries rather than the more narrow public boundaries is part of this process. Generally, reasonable requests from a superior, although they may be outside the public boundaries of the psychological contract, are within the real boundaries, and subordinates, typically, will do more things if they are asked to do them. Generally, reasonable requests from a superior, although they may be outside the public boundaries, are within the real boundaries. Often, however, there is a need to go beyond even the real boundaries.

To obtain compliance to requests beyond the real boundaries of the psychological contract is leadership. Katz and Kahn (1965) "consider the essence of organizational leadership to be the influential increment over and above mechanical compliance with a routine directive of the organization." When a person is able to broaden or expand the real boundaries of another's zone of indifference, either permanently or temporarily, it is an act of leadership. Some of the ways in which one might alter the boundaries of the psychological contract are: (1) fear or threat, (2) reciprocity, (3) reinforcement, (4) job design, (5) team building, (6) competition, and (7) ego involvement. These strategies are discussed in chapters 5 12, and 14.

Power—The Basis of Compliance

Influence is a process, a series of actions that one initiates intended to get another person to do something. When one is successful at influencing another—either because the influence attempt falls within the boundaries of the psychological contract or the boundaries are moved—it is because power has been exercised. Power is a force which one can use to obtain compliance. Power, the force, is activated in the influence process. The use of power is leadership. People act and decisions get made. Things happen when power is exercised.

Power comes from several different bases: (1) organizational factors; (2) skill and/or expertise; and (3) the personal qualities of the leader. These relationships are shown in figure 8.2.

Organizational Factors

A person's position in an organization gives him power. Each position, or job, has certain activities formally specified for it which the incumbent must perform. There are certain decisions which he is allowed to make. It is also possible that a position enables its incumbent to act as a gatekeeper for critical information, or access to important other people. These organizational factors—formal authority and organizational location—are two important determinants of power inherent in a position. Organizationally-based power resides in the position, not the person in it. He may only use it. When he leaves the position, he loses this power base.

FIGURE 8.2 Bases of Power Related to Influence and Leadership

---

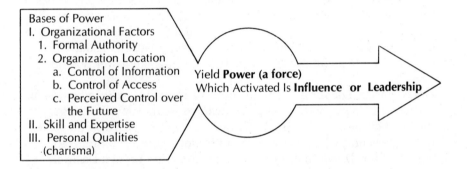

Bases of Power
I. Organizational Factors
  1. Formal Authority
  2. Organization Location
    a. Control of Information
    b. Control of Access
    c. Perceived Control over
      the Future
II. Skill and Expertise
III. Personal Qualities
  (charisma)

Yield **Power (a force)**
Which Activated Is **Influence or Leadership**

Formal Authority.   Formal authority is the right of decision and command a person has derived from the position held. These decision-making rights are delegated from higher organizational levels. In a managerial position, one has the right to allocate resources, make decisions, and distribute rewards in certain amounts and under certain conditions which are typically specified in the job description. The attendant responsibility of a person in a position is the obligation to perform well. Basically, *formal authority is the amount of designated discretion that an individual has in determining who gets what.* In most instances, the higher the position, the greater the discretion. When a decision is made in a discretionary area, it usually can be overturned only through appeals to even higher management.

Consider the case of a manufacturing vice-president. His position may give him discretionary power over how to expend funds for capital investments, who at lower levels in manufacturing should be promoted, and so forth. These will be the rights of anyone in the position of manufacturing vice-president. At lower organizational levels in manufacturing, the amount of discretion will be less than that at the vice-president's level.

There are other ways than through decision making that a manager can exercise influence. A person in a high-status position in an organization, whether deriving from its importance or its level, can exercise a great deal of control over who interacts with him, and when. For example, a subordinate generally sees his superior at the superior's convenience, not his own. And, typically, the superior will determine how long the meeting lasts. Through socialization, individuals learn that they should defer to higher-status individuals:

The very title of a position—"chairman," "chief," "planning coordinator"—may be perceived by others to represent a power base. The higher the position, the more likely it is that the incumbent will be able to determine either who gets promoted, or the criteria used to determine promotions. Thus, those in higher positions usually have significant effects on the career patterns of those in lower positions.

Organization Location.   The location of a position within an organizational setting may be a base of power, sometimes without regard to the level of the position in the hierarchical structure. In some positions, for example, a great amount of important information is collected for dissemination to other organization points. Desired information, when controlled, gives power to the person who has it. The finance group may have information about future spending plans and plant site locations, for instance. If there is internal competition among managers for, say, the positions of plant manager at these new plants, having advance information that others do not have can give those who have it an advantage in making the strongest possible personal case for a plant managership. The finance group, with the information, has power.

Control over access to key people is another source of organizational power. In order to see the president, we may have to clear an appointment with his administrative assistant. When attempting to speak by phone with the director of personnel, we may find a secretary making the decision whether or not we initially see him—or an assistant. In both these instances, lower-level personnel have a great deal of influence over others in the organization at higher levels. This kind of power base is clearly illustrated in item 8.1, describing the role of the White House Staff of ex-President Nixon, which often stood between the President and those who wanted to communicate to him.

Perceived control over the future is another important source of lower-level influence. The personnel unit is a classic example of this case. Often managers, rightly or wrongly, feel that lower-level personnel staff members have a great deal of influence over who gets future assignments. So, in their efforts to insure favorable consideration, they often comply with requests from personnel staffers in order to stay on their "good side."

ITEM 8.1   A Power Base

Nixon's White House

Surrounding the outwardly calm White House Oval Office that is the President's citadel is a symbolic battleground pocked with shell holes and scarred with trenches. The tactical objective of the attackers is the President's attention. The besiegers include great institutions and the meekest citizen. There are the representatives of the Federal Government itself: the Cabinet en bloc and as individuals, Senators and Congressmen, military chiefs, economic advisers, satraps of the independent and quasi-independent agencies.

Those are the front-line supplicants, but many others constantly seek to infiltrate the presidential stronghold. They include state governors and city mayors, and the senior national and state political leaders of the President's party. After them comes a helter-skelter militia of citizens, often sniping at one another, enemies of the President as well as friends: banker, lawyer, merchant, chief, cleric, doctor, scholar, journalist, student, housewife. Some advance to plead a cause, others to criticize and fix blame.

Patrolling the battlefield, defending the fortress against unwanted infiltrators, is the President's personal staff. It is his own creation. Each of the staff members is ultimately answerable to a constituency of only one man: Richard Milhous Nixon. Theirs is a hazardous occu-

pation; often criticism aimed at the President falls short and bursts directly on them.

Throughout his first year in office, Richard Nixon's elaborately organized network of assistants, counselors, advisers and lesser factotums went largely unscathed. Any concern that it might insulate him from reality came only in sporadic muttering from Congressmen and disgruntled favor-seekers. No longer. When Nixon decided to move U.S. forces into Cambodia, evidently without realizing the outcry of protest that this would provoke, he set off angry charges that he is too isolated from many sections of American opinion. Interior Secretary Walter Hickel pleaded that Nixon pay more attention to the young, complained that he got a swift brush-off from the President's staff—and reported that he had been able to see Nixon alone exactly twice since taking office 16 months before.

Suddenly it is fashionable in Washington to fret and fulminate that a palace guard has separated Nixon from realities. In the White House, the key figures around the President are Staff Chief H. R. (Bob) Haldeman, Domestic Affairs Aide John Ehrlichman and National Security Adviser Henry Kissinger. Because of their ancestry—and their closemouthed habits—the Teutonic trio is now known as "the Berlin Wall" in the White House pressroom.

• • • •

Criticism and anger directed at the men who guard the President's doors and carry out his orders are no novelty. "This is a problem that must have started with George Washington," says one Nixon man. "If everybody went in immediately whenever he needed something, the White House wouldn't work." Harry Truman kept on his desk a sign that read THE BUCK STOPS HERE. It was a nice, punchy slogan, but the buck got to him only after it had filtered through his personal staff. Nor is it a new idea that the men who do the winnowing can exercise extraordinary power. Clark Clifford, a perennial adviser to postwar Democratic administrations, remembers an Eisenhower aide telling him that Ike was spared night work because his staff boiled 150-page memoranda down to two pages. Clifford replied: "There is only one trouble. If I could be the fellow who prepares the two-page memo, I'd be President instead of Ike."

• • • •

Observes a White House staffer: "Everything is funneled through these two guys [Haldeman and Erlichman]. Haldeman is not at all interested in policy, and Ehrlichman is. This explains how they manage to get along. Ehrlichman views himself as a broker, a sifter of ideas, rather than an advocate." But he has taken substantive positions: in favor of Presidential Counselor Daniel Patrick Moynihan's plan for a minimum annual welfare income, in favor of the conservationists who successfully blocked a Miami jetport in the Florida Everglades. He is as critical of the liberal press as Spiro Agnew, and once told a reporter who said that a Nixon decision would not go down well in the East: "It'll play in Peoria." His staff meetings are less bang-bang-bang than Haldeman's; he

moves briskly, but everyone has his say. One joke has it that Ehrlichman eats breakfast the night before.

• • • •

California Representative Paul McCloskey Jr., a liberal Republican and a college friend of Ehrlichman's, thinks that the Nixon staff has wrapped the President in a cocoon. Says McCloskey: "For the President to isolate himself from all criticism, from differing opinion is a dangerous thing. Hell, every time I see the President the band has been playing *Hail to the Chief* and everyone has been bowing and scraping. That's not the real world. I see no one who has the guts to stand up to the President down there and say 'You're wrong.' He needs that, just as a Congressman does."

That sums up the principal complaint against the entire palace guard that surrounds Nixon. It is true enough that the loudest complainers are those whom Nixon does not see, but it can well be argued that their differing views are precisely what he needs to hear in order to grasp reality firsthand. What some have called "the triumph of the advance men" has left many open wounds all over town. Says one Nixon aide: "When you come into the White House after eight years on the other side, you bring in people who are bright but not experienced in Government—especially in protocol, the proprieties of dealing with the Hill and other parts of Government, which can matter more than substance. They think they're bright—that's part of the problem—and experts in politics because they worked in a campaign. Actually, they know very little, especially about the politics of dealing with politicians."

The advance man lives for tomorrow's headlines, worries about deadlines on his flow charts, and reckons achievement by the number of specific tasks he manages to get done. These men, says a high official in one Government department, are "consumed with running the

Government, but in the process they've lost sight of the fact that they ought to be running the country."

TIME, June 8, 1970

Skill and Expertise

Often we respond to influence attempts of others because they presumably have a greater amount of skill or knowledge in a particular area than we do. It is common practice to rely on expert opinion in our personal life, accepting the advice of accountants, lawyers, and doctors because, we believe, their training and knowledge can solve a problem. At work, the same thing happens. In designing and implementing a computer-based management information system, we rely on computer experts to define the capacity of the equipment and what it can provide. When a customer threatens legal action, the president or chief executive goes to the company's attorney for advice. When the director of engineering wants to know company policy on travel expenses, he will call the administrative assistant in personnel.

An important aspect of expert power is that it is very specific to the type of problem and to the person with the skill. We are unlikely to ask the company attorney for marketing advice, or the computer programmer for legal advice. Expert power is task-specific, but—more important for this discussion—it is generally associated with a particular person. It is not easily transferred to another person, as is the case with organizationally-based power. When a person becomes a plant manager, he generally has the same formal authority as the previous manager, but a person gets expert power only through demonstrating competence or by having it "given" to him because he has the appropriate education, experience, and appearance. When an individual with expert power leaves the organization, his replacement will probably not have the same amount of influence, even though he may have the same organizational title.

Personal Characteristics of the Leader

In some cases, individuals are susceptible to influence because they identify with another person. French and Raven (1959) call this "referent power" and say that it has its base in the "feeling of oneness" that a person has for another, or the desire for such a feeling. Referent power is based largely on the attraction exerted by an individual on another person, or on a group. The stronger the attraction, the stronger the power.

Identification with another may come about because he possesses personal characteristics and qualities highly valued by the group, such as family background, appearance, athletic ability, and so on. Or the identification may come about because of the leader's ability to articulate the values and concerns of the followers. Persons who exert this kind of influence are called "charismatic" leaders. They have the loyalty and commitment of their followers, not because they have a particular skill or are in a particular position, but because their followers respond to them as individuals. Like the skill and expertise power base, this power base is unique to the individual and the situation. Charismatic influence cannot be transferred to another person.

Leadership, Power, and Dependence

One way to view leadership is in terms of dependence. If a leader can influence others, it is because the others are dependent upon him. This can arise because of psychological identification, as discussed above, or because someone has the power to allocate rewards or impose sanctions, either objective or subjective. Objective rewards are such things as pay increases, promotions, or the bestowal of prestige and status symbols. Objective sanctions take the form of disciplinary actions, demotions, removal of rights, and so on.

Subjective rewards and sanctions are less tangible. They exist in the minds of the individual. Recognition or disapproval from a supervisor may or may not be viewed as a reward or a sanction by subordinates; it depends upon their esteem for him. A way to think about how to increase leadership effectiveness is to increase the dependency of the subordinate on either the manager or the organization. In fact, the managerial motivation strategies described in chapter 5 should be viewed in this light. In order to use reinforcement, for example, the manager must have a subordinate who desires (or wants) the reward. Reciprocity is only effective when the manager can provide "desired" favors.

Different Perspectives on Leadership

It is possible to learn and to improve administrative skills in schools and by experience, but the elusive dimension of the manager's job is the leadership process. While we can conceptualize with some ease why people comply (the psychological contract) and the bases of power (organizational, skill, and personal), it is more difficult to characterize the qualities, or behavior, of individuals who exert influence and are capable of managing in a way to achieve organizational goals. (We do not believe it is correct to consider management synonymous with leadership. We have not done so in the preceding section of this chapter, but so much of the leadership theory and research uses the terms interchangeably that we will abide by the convention in what follows.)

Leadership has long been the subject of speculation, theorizing, and research, the ultimate purpose being to select individuals likely to be able to influence others to achieve organizational goals, and to place them in a position which enhances this capacity. Early research in this century studied leadership as if it were a collection of personal traits or characteristics of those identified as leaders, and tried to identify the traits and characteristics. Subsequently, research emphasized a behavioral approach which looked upon leadership as a series of acts, or a behavioral repertoire, designed to help a group achieve its objectives. Viewed from this perspective, leadership was seen as acting out a set of behaviors which would vary, depending upon the group's need for greater task effectiveness, member satisfaction, and cohesiveness. More recently, attention has been directed toward developing "contingency" theories of leadership. This view recognizes the fact that effective leadership is a function of the situation in which leader and followers interact. These themes, then (1) the trait approach, (2) the behavioral approach, and (3) situational theories, are the main thrusts of leadership theory and research.

The Trait Approach

The underlying premise of the trait approach to leadership is that leadership is an attribute of personality, that a certain identifiable trait or collection of traits makes a person effective as a leader, and that better organizational results can be obtained by selecting as leaders those who have these identifiable qualities.

Many researchers and theorists feel that there are no readily identifiable traits related to possession of leadership status, or to effectiveness as a leader, in all situations. This may, however, be principally because the research on leaders has been done with leaders in a wide variety of situations and jobs. When studies are more situation-specific—for example, relating various personal characteristics to managerial (a special kind of leadership as we noted earlier) success —consistencies are found. Dunnette (1970), for instance, reviewing research on traits associated with executive success, states that successful executives tend to be *dominant, self-confident,* and *assertive,* and tend to *have a high aspiration level as well as a general success pattern throughout life.* Ghiselli (1973) found self-perceived *intelligence, initiative, supervisory ability, self-assurance,* and *occupational level* to be positively related to general management success in terms of upward mobility and rated job success. These findings are consistent with Stogdill's (1974) summary of a large number of leadership studies.

One reason for some of the difficulty in finding traits differentiating leaders from nonleaders and effective from less effective leaders is that mere possession of a characteristic is not, in itself, a sufficient condition for assuming a leadership (or management) position and then being successful in it. The individual must *want* the position and must *want* to be effective. In addition, the characteristics related to leadership do not operate singly, but in combination. Thus, individuals who seek the responsibilities of leadership and who possess the combination of traits commonly associated with success as a leader— such as initiative, self-confidence, and persistence—have an advantage over those individuals without these characteristics or those who have them but lack the interest (Stogdill, 1974; many of the references in this chapter can be found in this extensive review of research and theory on leadership by Stogdill.)

Some early leadership scholars concluded that situational factors determined who would emerge as the leader (Gibb, 1954). Today it is recognized that individual characteristics and situational factors are important. As Stogdill (1974) points out: "Most recent theorists maintain that leader characteristics and situational demands interact to determine the extent to which a given leader will prove successful in a group."

Behavioral Approach

Much research on leadership has focused on leadership *behaviors.* Instead of looking at what a leader *is* (a trait), these studies aimed at finding out what he *does.* Many studies sought to relate specific behaviors of individuals in managerial, supervisory, or leadership positions to group effectiveness—that is, the productivity and satisfaction of group members. Of course, it was recognized that many leaders were only designated. Perhaps they were not individuals accepted as leaders by the group but they were in managerial positions. (This situation, however, may make it easier to study leadership, since among appointed leaders it is likely there will be a set of "bad" or ineffective leaders, necessary for comparison purposes.) Some of the earliest studies focused on very specific behavior. The different supervisors of groups with high and low performance, or with high or low satisfaction levels, were compared with respect to the amount of time they spent planning, how they disciplined employees, communication patterns, the amount of recognition given to subordinates, the amount of pressure exerted for higher production, and other supervisory behaviors.

Many studies have been conducted on how much influence the leader allowed subordinates in the decision-making process (Stogdill, 1974). From these studies, a particular classification system for describing leader and managerial behavior became popular. In these studies, flowing from the early work by Lewin, Lippitt, and White (1939), leaders were described in one or more of the following terms:

1. *Autocratic or Dictatorial.* The leader makes all decisions and allows the subordinates no influence in the decision-making process. These supervisors are often indifferent to the personal needs of subordinates.

2. *Participative or Democratic.* These supervisors consult with their subordinates on appropriate matters. They allow their subordinates some influence in the decision-making process. In addition, this type of supervisor is not punitive and treats his subordinates with dignity and kindness.

3. *Laissez Faire—or Free Reign.* Supervisors in this group allow their group to have complete autonomy. They rarely supervise directly, so the group makes many of their on-the-job decisions themselves.

Thus, the amount of influence of either the superior or the subordinate can be viewed on a continuum, as in figure 8.3.

Many research studies have directly compared the autocratic and democratic styles of leadership. Such studies usually show that the democratic, or participative, leadership style is associated with higher subordinate satisfaction. High performance is also often present under democratic leadership, but there are no consistent performance differences between democratic and autocratic styles—in some studies there were no performance differences between groups even though different leaders used different approaches. However, the participative style is more often associated with greater acceptance of change and more organization identification than is the autocratic (Stogdill, 1974).

The relationship of the laissez-faire supervisory style to satisfaction and performance has not been studied as extensively as the autocratic and democratic leadership styles. What little research has been done seems to indicate that subordinate satisfaction and performance under laissez-faire is less than under the democratic approach but higher than that under the autocratic approach (Lippitt and White, 1958).

FIGURE 8.3 Continuum of Influence in the Leadership Process

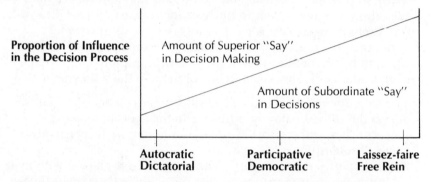

| Proportion of Influence in the Decision Process | Autocratic Dictatorial | Participative Democratic | Laissez-faire Free Rein |

The Ohio State Studies. Beginning in the late 1940s and continuing through the 1950s, a group of researchers at Ohio State conducted extensive studies of leadership effectiveness in industrial, military, and educational institutions. The research ranged from the development of instruments to measure leadership to the evaluation of factors which might determine group effectiveness. From these studies emerged two leader behavior characteristics often associated with group effectiveness:

1. *Consideration:* The extent to which the individual is likely to have job relationships characterized by mutual trust, respect for subordinates' ideas, and consideration of their feelings. High scorers tend to have good rapport and two-way communication with subordinates.

2. *Initiating Structure:* The extent to which an individual is likely to define and structure his role and those of his subordinates toward goal attainment. High scorers are those who play an active role in directing group activities and communicating information, scheduling, and trying out new ideas.

Effective leaders, according to the Ohio State Studies, were high on *both* these measures. That is, the leader had to show both a concern for those who worked in the group (high consideration) and an ability to plan, organize, and control (or otherwise administer) its activities (high initiating structure). The two factors are measured with a scale called the "Leader Behavior Description Questionnaire" (LBDQ), the widespread use of which facilitates comparison of results from different research efforts.

Most studies show that consideration is generally related to high employee satisfaction; it is related much less often to high performance, although occasionally it is so related (Stogdill, 1974). In a number of studies, initiating structure has been found to be related to high job satisfaction, less often to high productivity, low absenteeism, and low turnover (Stogdill, 1974). However, in other studies no relationship of any kind was found between initiating structure and subordinate behavior.

The relationship of consideration and initiating structure to performance and satisfaction varies from one study to another. Some of the inconsistencies are due to the fact that there are very different organization settings where these studies have been done. Other discrepancies may arise because researchers use slightly different versions of the LBDQ, and thus arrive at different conclusions (Schreisheim, House, and Kerr, 1975).

The Michigan Studies.   The Institute for Social Research at the University of Michigan was formed after World War II. This group has made significant empirical, theoretical, and practical contributions to the study of organizational effectiveness. They conducted, for example, a number of leadership studies in offices, railroad settings, and in service industries. From the early studies, they concluded that leadership behavior could be described in terms of two dimensions similar to those used by the Ohio State group. But there was an important difference. In the early stages of the Michigan Studies, leaders were described as engaging in behavior which was *either* production-centered *or* employee-centered (Stogdill, 1974), thus differentiating the Michigan from the Ohio studies, since the Ohio Studies attempted to characterize an individual on both dimensions. The *production-centered* supervisor was defined as primarily concerned with achieving high levels of production and viewing subordinates merely as instruments for doing this. The *employee-centered* supervisor, on the other hand, was defined as concerned about subordinates' feelings and attempting to create an atmosphere of mutual trust and respect. Some early interpretations of the Michigan research concluded that the most effective leadership style was employee-centered, that employee-centered supervisors were more likely to have highly productive work groups than production-centered. Other studies, however, showed that effective supervisors engaged in *both* employee-centered and production-centered behavior at the same time (Stogdill, 1974).

A later study at Michigan by Bowers and Seashore (1966) expanded the number of leader behaviors to a repertoire of four. They found four supervisory behaviors associated with satisfaction and performance in a study of 40 agencies of an insurance company. These four basic supervisory behavior dimensions are:

1. *Support:* Behavior that enhances someone else's feelings of personal worth and importance.
2. *Interaction Facilitation:* Behavior that encourages members of the group to develop close, mutually satisfying relationships.
3. *Goal Emphasis:* Behavior that stimulates an enthusiasm for meeting the group's goals or achieving excellent performance.
4. *Work Facilitation:* Behavior that helps achieve goal attainment by such activities as scheduling, coordinating, planning, and by providing resources such as tools, materials, and technical knowledge.

The work at Michigan strengthened the case for conceiving of leadership as a complex activity. It has been instrumental in shaping much of the work of the situational theories of leadership.

The Managerial Grid.   Blake and Mouton (1964), seeking to develop a more integrated concept of leadership while the research was pointing in several directions, devised the Managerial Grid. The Grid puts the two dimensions, *people orientation* and *task orientation* together. Blake and Mouton describe five basic styles, according to these two basic supervisory dimensions. These styles are located at different Grid positions, as shown in figure 8.4. The 1.1 supervisory style shows little concern for either production or employees; it is the equivalent of the laissez-faire supervisory style described earlier. The 1.9 supervisor has high employee concern but little concern for performance, while the 9.1 supervisor has little concern for employees but places strong emphasis on performance. The 5.5 supervisor is a compromiser; he places only moderate emphasis on satisfying employee needs and on achieving satisfactory levels of performance. (Blake and Mouton feel this is the most common supervisory style.) Finally, there is the 9.9, or ideal, supervisory pattern, in which there is high emphasis on achieving both employee needs and high levels of

performance. The 9.9 supervisor is able to integrate employee needs
and organizational needs with a team-building approach (explained in
chap. 5 as a managerial motivational strategy). Though research on the
effectiveness of these approaches is limited, one study shows
improvement in both individual satisfaction and organization performance after managers participated in a change program designed to
teach them the 9.9 supervisory approach (Blake, Mouton, Barnes, and
Greiner, 1964).

FIGURE 8.4   The Managerial Grid

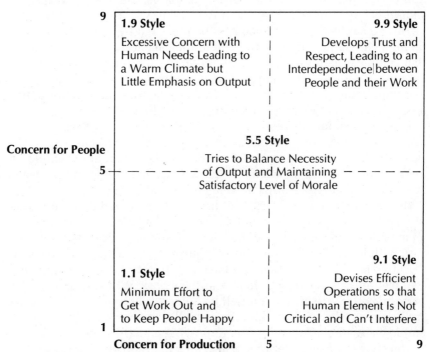

Source: From *The Managerial Grid*®, by Robert R. Blake and Jane Srygley Mouton. Houston: Gulf
Publishing Co., copyright © 1964, p. 10. Reproduced with permission.

Situational Theories

It has long been known that situational factors affect a leader's style
and effectiveness in using a particular approach. The context within
which a human being operates makes a difference, but until recently,
these ideas were not part of the leadership research literature. Situational factors were not prominent facets of either the Ohio State
Studies or the Michigan Studies, though the researchers were aware of

their importance. Some of the factors which seem to be especially important to the effectiveness of a leadership style are (1) the characteristics of subordinates, (2) the organizational situation, and (3) the style of one's superior in an organization.

Subordinate characteristics are related to effectiveness. For example, *the participative management style was found to be ineffective when subordinates were not used to influencing decisions of their superior.* Leadership style which varies from what a subordinate expects may meet with negative reaction (Carroll and Tosi, 1973). Subordinates seem to have a better response to the participative approach when they feel it is legitimate; that is, the way a manager *should* behave (French, Israel, and Aas, 1960; Vroom and Yetton, 1974). The autocratic approach may be preferred by individuals who do not feel competent to participate in the decision-making process; that is, in a situation where, for example, the subordinate feels his superior is more expert than he, the subordinate is not likely to try to exert much influence, and he will find an attempt by a superior to use a participative style quite uncomfortable (Mulder, 1971).

The organizational situation also influences the supervisory approach. The degree of crisis and the type of work are but two possible situational factors which could be important. For example, in an emergency where a decision is quickly needed, it may be unwise to use a "participative" approach, since this would take undue time.

House (1971) and Fiedler (1967) have both theorized that the degree of task structure is an important determinant of leader effectiveness. If a person's job is well-defined, narrow, and highly routine (often the case with lower-level employees in a bureaucratic organization), then directive leadership styles might have negative effects. The employee will feel pressure from both his job and his boss. While he may perform better, dissatisfaction will be higher. When the task is less well-structured, however, directive behavior may provide the employee with needed guidance, improving effectiveness.

The style of one's superior can also affect one's own supervisory approach. Fleishman (1953) found that a manager's style was more related to the way his superior managed than whether or not he had been in a training program. Carroll and Tosi (1973) found that a subordinate models his behavior after that of his superior, especially when the subordinate finds himself in situations where he is unsure of what to do. For example, an assistant manager of a department store may be given the assignment of presenting an advertising program to the board of directors. If he has never done this before, he may pattern his approach after what he has seen his boss do. Likewise, in dealing with subordinates, a manager may handle a troublesome employee as he has seen his boss do it. The way many people learn to manage is by modeling their behavior after those who are already in management jobs.

Perhaps the two most prominent situational theories at present are (1) a contingency theory of leadership (Fiedler, 1967), and (2) path-goal theory (Evans, 1968; House, 1971). In both of these, an attempt is made to specify how a leader's or a manager's behavior is related to effectiveness in different situational circumstances. This, of course is quite consistent with managerial process contingency theory. Such work on leadership provides us with more specific prescriptions about how a manager should function in different types of organizations, and we will consider these prescriptions in chapters 12 and 14.

Fiedler's Contingency Model of Leadership.   Fiedler (1967) has developed a formulation about how leadership style, the group, and the situation interact to affect group performance and satisfaction. The style of a leader is, in part, a function of his own needs and personality. Therefore like personality, Fiedler suggests leadership style is relatively well-fixed and established. The style is measured by the "Least Preferred Co-worker" scale (LPC). On the LPC, a manager is asked to describe the co-worker with whom *he least likes to work*. From this description, two classifications of leadership style are developed:

1. *People-centered* (Hi LPC). This style is one in which the leader is oriented toward the feelings and relationships in the work group, with a tendency to be permissive.
2. *Task-centered* (Lo LPC). This style focuses on the task, with a tendency to be directive and controlling.

Obviously, these two dimensions are much like those used in the Ohio State and Michigan studies. Fiedler, however, extends both those approaches by defining what characteristics of the situation are important in determining which style is more effective. The important situational characteristics are:

1. *Leader-member relations*, which refer to the amount of trust and how well-liked the leader is.
2. *Task-structure*, which refers to the extent to which the job is defined. High task structure refers to well-defined jobs in which each aspect is spelled out. Low task structure is present where job requirements are unclear and ambiguous.

3. *Position power,* which is a function of the formal authority structure; that is, whether or not an individual has the right to reward,
sanction, evaluate, or promote those who work for him.

Figure 8.5 shows the eight possible combinations of these three
factors and which supervisory style is predicted to be more effective
in each. Fiedler reports that the task orientation is generally best in
situations where leader-member relations are *either very good or very
bad.* When relations are good, the group may be quite willing to
accept a task orientation. Where all situational factors are bad for the
supervisor, the group will fall apart unless the leader takes charge and
controls their behavior. Under some of the moderately unfavorable
conditions the leader must use a people-orientation approach, either
to motivate group members to become involved in attempts to deal
with an ambiguous task or to win their support.

FIGURE 8.5 Classification of Group Task Situations and the Predicted
Relationship of Group Performance and Leadership Style

Task Structure	Leader-Member Relations	Position Power	Suggested Leader Orientation
High	Good	Strong	Task
	Good	Weak	Task
	Poor	Weak	People
	Poor	Strong	People
Low	Good	Strong	Task
	Good	Weak	People
	Poor	Weak	Task
	Poor	Strong	People

Source: F. Fiedler *A Theory of Leadership Effectiveness* (McGraw-Hill, 1967, p. 37).

Fiedler's work has some important implications. One is that if
leadership style is not flexible, then when an organization is not
performing well, the situation should be restructured to make it more
favorable to the style of the person leading—or the leader should be
replaced. In chapters 12 and 14, from a similar premise, we describe
the way a leader should function to achieve best results in a bureaucratic and in a dynamic organization.

The research evidence supports some, but not all, of Fiedler's
predictions as to the most effective supervisory approach for each of
his eight conditions (Graen et al., 1970). Obviously, there could be

other situational factors not considered by Fiedler which could also have an effect on performance.

Path-Goal Theory. The research on path-goal theory also supports a contingency approach to leadership. As discussed in chapter 5, House (1971) asserts that the leader obtains good performance from his work unit by making sure that subordinates know what they have to do to be rewarded for good performance *and* also by reducing barriers to effective performance. In addition, the supervisor must behave in such a way as to help his subordinates satisfy their needs through high performance. Since different groups of employees have different needs and different types of work problems, the most appropriate leadership approach depends on the types of individuals involved and the characteristics of their work situation. For example, House (1971) has cited research which indicates that a leader's attempts to clarify what subordinates are supposed to do contributes to high satisfaction where the task requirements are ambiguous but may reduce satisfaction when the task requirements are quite clear. In the latter case, the supervisor's efforts to explain already clear task requirements are viewed by subordinates as unnecessary and perhaps, also, insulting. House has cited a number of other studies which indicate that a manager's emphasis on either *consideration* or on *initiating structure* can be effective, depending upon the needs of the individuals in the situation at the time.

One important aspect of House's work is that he has drawn four general propositions that link performance and leader behavior through motivation (see chap. 5). These propositions are:

1. The leader's role in motivation is to increase to the subordinate the utility (positive value) both of achieving work goals *and* of the work itself. Where there is uncertainty, he should also clarify the path (the things that have to be done) to achieve work goals.

2. With clear paths to work goals, the subordinate will be motivated because he can be more certain of how to achieve goals (or his role ambiguity will be reduced). When, for example, an employee is given a new assignment, if he does not know how to do it, then he should receive some help or coaching from his superior. Clarification of the task assignment also permits the manager to reinforce desired behavior because it may then be easier for the individual to perceive the link between performance and rewards (or sanctions), since they are now specified.

3. If the path to the work goal is already clear because of the nature of the work or the rigidity of the structure, then the leader who is

directive (exercises high initiating structure) may increase performance through added pressure, but will decrease satisfaction. Close supervision of a skilled worker may upset him greatly, though he may produce more because of it.

4. If the leader acts to satisfy subordinate needs, better results will occur *only when increased satisfaction results in the individual placing greater value on the work, or goal-directed effort.* This means that if a manager provides, say, favors to a group and they are happier but don't like their work assignment, performance will not increase.

Leader Behavior—Cause or Result of Effectiveness?

One question which arises out of much of the research cited in this chapter is whether group effectiveness is caused by how the leader behaves or whether the leader behaves as he does because of the group's performance. Put another way, "If I am a manager of an effective group, will I exert less pressure, and be more concerned about their needs and more considerate because they are a goal effective group? Or if I am head of a less effective group, will I push them, be directive, and exercise high initiating structure in an effort to improve performance?" Which comes first, chicken or egg?

The research on this subject leads to the conclusion that supervisory behavior operates in a dynamic way with performance. In some studies, it has been shown that the behavior of the supervisor caused group performance. Rosen (1969) found that when supervisors were given new assignments, group performance influenced leadership style and leader behavior also influenced group behavior. Lowin and Craig (1968) found that high-performing groups tended to cause the leader to act in a considerate way, while low-performing groups tended to cause high initiating structure behavior.

Two studies (Tosi et al., 1975; Greene 1973) indicate that some aspects of leader behavior may cause performance, while other aspects may be affected by performance. Greene (1973) concluded that the level of subordinate performance causes the leader to exhibit different degrees of initiating structure. The manager of a less effective department will be more directive than one of a more productive unit. It is the level of consideration, however, that causes the degree of subordinate satisfaction.

Can Leadership Style Be Flexible?

A number of writers have said that supervisors should be flexible with respect to the supervisory approach they use (for example, Reddin,

1970). The leader, they argue, must first evaluate the situation and then decide on the appropriate supervisory style. There is, however, a question of the extent to which supervisors can do this. Fiedler (1967), for example, considers his dimensions of supervisory style as relatively fixed, since they are aspects of individual personality. He proposes that since a particular supervisory approach is optimum for a situation, if a person with a different style is in the supervisory position, then the situation should be changed to fit the supervisory style rather than trying to get the supervisor to change his style to fit the situation. Blake and Mouton (1964), however, believe that leadership-style flexibility is a characteristic that varies among leaders; that is, they believe that some individuals can change their supervisory style and some have only a very limited ability to do this. It is our belief that it is not possible for a person, in the short run, to drastically change his behavioral style. It is possible however, to improve certain administrative skills, as we have discussed. But to the extent that behavior is reflective of personality, changes are likely to take some time to occur. It is probably more productive, then, to be concerned with effective matching of situational factors and a person's behavioral style than to try to change either.

How Leader Behavior Affects Performance

Until recently, there has been little attention paid to the specific mechanisms by which a particular behavior affects performance. We touched on this issue briefly in chapter 5, but will note here again some of the mechanisms. A manager *can* affect individual and group motivation, and in these ways:

1. *He can affect expectancies.* This can be done by spelling out relationships between efforts and performance levels and between performance levels and various outcomes such as rewards or punishments. This, of course, assumes that the supervisor has some influence over rewards or punishments (salary increases , promotions or demotions). When he does, he may be able to use this power to affect performance. When he doesn't, he still has the capacity to use social rewards, such as recognition or approval, but for these rewards to be effective, the subordinates must see this social recognition as important. Kahn (1951) found that productivity of work groups was related to beliefs by group members that high performance would lead to the receiving of the reward of supervisory approval. Such supervisory recognition must be given

only for high performance. If it is also given for average performance, then subordinates assume that average performance is
perfectly satisfactory.

2. *He can set goals.* Motivation may also be affected by the difficulty of work goals which the supervisor establishes for individuals
or groups. In one study, it was found that when work goals set for
foremen were viewed as impossible, very poor performance resulted
(Stedry and Kay, 1966). On the other hand, when goals were
perceived to be difficult but challenging, performance increased. In
another study it was found that there was more enjoyment with
goals of intermediate difficulty than there was with quite easy or
quite difficult goals (Locke, 1973). It should be kept in mind,
however, that personal characteristics affect the perception of the
relative difficulty of goals and of the response to this perception. In
one study, for example, managers low in self-esteem reported
diminished effort expenditures when given goals that were
perceived to be difficult, while managers high in self-esteem
reported increased effort expenditures when given what they
perceived to be difficult goals (Carroll and Tosi, 1973).

3. *He can clarify how to achieve work goals.* The clarification of
work goals is another way that performance can be affected. As
House (1973) points out in path-goal theory, a leader's high initiating structure can reduce role ambiguity, which can increase
motivation by making it more probable that effort will result in goal
attainment. On the other hand, confusion among subordinates as to
what, when, and how something should be done wastes time and
energy and contributes to personal frustrations, which in turn leads
to diminished motivation.

In spite of the differences in terminology used, out of the research
on leadership two basic and important dimensions of supervisory
behavior emerge; one emphasizes task performance, one emphasizes
satisfying individual employee needs. Figure 8.6 shows the similarity
between the different approaches to leadership behavior described in
this chapter. The relationship of these factors to employee needs and
performance is definitely associated with the situation. Especially
important situational factors are (1) the structure and nature of tasks,
(2) the needs and abilities of the group members, and (3) the superior.

Of course, the administrative aspect of the manager's job cannot be
overlooked. Planning, budgeting, development, and training are
important functions that can be done to affect performance. The
manager must be both a leader and an administrator.

FIGURE 8.6 Similarity Between Selected Concepts of Leadership

Ohio State Studies	Michigan Studies	Blake and Mouton	Bowers and Seashore	Fiedler's Contingency Theory	House Path-Goal
Consideration	Employee -centered	Concern with People	Support	People -centered (High LPC)	Consideration
			Interaction Facilitation	**Situational Factors**	
				Position Power	
				Task Structure	Clarity of Path-Goal Relationships
			Goal Emphasis	Leader -Member Relations	
Initiating Structure	Production -Centered	Concern with Production	Work Facilitation		
				Production -centered (Low LPC)	Initiating Structure

Discussion Questions

1. Do you agree with the concepts of leadership and administration, as presented in this chapter?

2. Think of a charismatic leader. Has this person been able to transfer his influence to another leader? Why?

3. Close your eyes and visualize a "leader"—his or her clothes, appearance, height. Is there a specific person that you have in mind? Who?

4. Close your eyes again. Visualize the chairman of the board for a large company. What does this person look like? Was it a male? Describe his clothes, height, and general appearance to your colleagues after they have done the same thing.

5. What are the problems in prescribing how one should manage using the leadership models derived from the Ohio State and Michigan, studies? How are situational theories more prescriptive in helping to manage effectively?

Chapter 9

Decision making is the act of choosing from among alternatives—coming to a conclusion as to what should be done in a particular situation. Every human being makes decisions. On a daily basis you must decide when to get up, what to wear, what to eat, when to go to bed, and so on. During your lifetime you will decide who to marry—if you decide to marry—and what occupation you will follow—as well as how much to smoke, to eat, to drink, to sleep, and so on and so on.

Managers not only make decisions about their personal lives, but also about and for the organization in which they are employed. Decision making is an essential aspect of any manager's job. A manager is employed to make organizational decisions, and is evaluated on the ability to make effective decisions, "effective" from a superior's point of view. Indeed, some feel that decision making is synonomous with management (Simon, 1960)—that it is the essence of management.

At different levels in an organization the scope and importance of the decisions managers make varies. For example, first-level supervisors may make decisions about work schedules, but not about large capital expenditures, while higher-level managers often make decisions that involve the expenditure of millions of dollars (but not, perhaps, about work schedules).

Although decision making ultimately refers to arriving at a conclusion through the choice of one alternative from many, there are obviously other stages of the decision-making process which precede the decision itself. Simon (1960), one of the leading investigators in the area of decision making, characterizes stages in the decision-making process as: (1) *intelligence*—finding occasions for making a decision; (2) *design*—finding, inventing, developing, and analyzing

Decision Making

alternative courses of action; and (3) *choice*—selecting a particular course of action from those available.

Of course one individual may not be involved in all three stages of decision making. Different individuals and different groups may be involved at different stages. A higher-level manager, for example, may present a lower-level manager with a problem about which a decision has to be made. Staff members may then develop and present the possible feasible alternative courses of action to the decision maker, who then makes a choice after evaluating the alternatives against a set of objectives, or decision criteria. Or the decision maker may carry out all stages in the decision-making process himself. He may first identify an event as a problem or a decision-making situation (such a situation is generally one in which there is a *gap* between a present state of the person or organization and a desired state), and then generalize alternatives and choose from among them on the basis of a set of objectives.

Problem Solving —The Context of Decision Making

A decision must be made when a person wants things to be different in the future. Decision making, then, is one aspect of a broader area— problem solving. A problem exists when something is not as it should be. For example, a manager may learn that a department is producing a very high number of substandard units. He will want to change this situation. Since problems usually don't go away if ignored, there is a need to do something, or several different things, to reduce the rejection rate. New equipment may be obtained; workers may be retrained; machines may be adjusted. Selecting one or more of these alternatives is decision making. It is done to solve a problem.

Problem Solving and Decision Making

Suppose a student desires an A in a course. In his first exam he receives a C. He knows that if he continues as is, he will receive a C in the course. If the C grade is unacceptable, some action must be taken. He must change what he is doing.

When the student generates alternatives, they reflect his perception of the *cause* of the problem. Consider some possible alternative actions and how they are associated with *causes*.

1. *Spend more time studying.* This assumes that the cause is simply not knowing enough and that the student is capable of learning the material at the desired level.
2. *Do additional reading.* This assumes that the student may not understand the concepts, and that by studying additional material can become capable of learning the material at the desired level by providing the appropriate foundation.
3. *Change course sections.* This assumes that the cause of the problem is the instructor, his standards, the time of the class, or perhaps the size of the class.

What is the best alternative? It depends upon the *cause* of the problem. If the student has a night job and the class meets at 8:00 A.M., the best alternative may be to change sections to one that meets later in the day. If the student is in an advanced course and doesn't have the necessary background, the best alternative may be to do additional reading. If the student hasn't read the assignments, the best alternative is to spend more studying.

What happens if the student is in an advanced course without the necessary background and changes sections? The discrepancy is very likely to continue to exist. Or suppose the standards of the instructor are so high that the student's potential in the course with his present instructor is only a C grade. Or assume that the student may not have the time to devote to more work. In both cases, the discrepancy may be reduced by changing from the present course section to one with an instructor with lower standards.

The Steps in Problem Solving

There are four basic steps in problem solving: (1) recognizing that a problem exists; (2) identifying possible causes of the problem; (3) generating alternative solutions; and (4) selecting and implementing the chosen alternative.

We will describe the important aspects of each of these steps in this chapter. (Part of step 4, implementing decisions, is such an important part of the manager's job that we will discuss it again in chapter 10).

Step 1—Problem Recognition

Kepner and Tregoe (1965) argue that an essential part of the manager's role is problem solving. This means a manager must be competent in both the definition *and* the solution of problems. The need for a decision arises when a problem exists. A problem exists when something is not as it should be. Problem solving is a process in which a change is consciously made to bring about a desired, or acceptable, state of affairs. This implies that the manager is able to describe two conditions: (1) *what should be* and (2) *what is (or will be)*.

What should be can be thought of as a standard, an objective, or a criterion against which alternatives can be evaluated. *What is (or will be)* is the state of the world as it is, or as it is predicted it will be, in the future.

When the discrepancy between the two states is unacceptably large, action is taken to reduce it, usually by trying to change *what is*. To do this effectively requires that the cause of the problem be properly identified (step 2), for if alternative solutions fail to attack the cause of the problem, the size of the discrepancy will not be reduced.

The definition of a problem we are using *always* implies a performance standard against which what is actually occurring is compared. The performance standard may not be explicit. It may be objective or subjective. It may be a feeling—what the manager considers to be a desirable state of affairs. Subjective performance standards vary among managers depending upon their previous experience, motives, and personality. When such differences among managers about subjective performance standards exist, it leads to differences of opinion about the existence and severity of problems. A superior may feel a problem exists, while his subordinate does not, and vice versa. Similarly, those from different specialized areas in an organization may also disagree as to the existence and severity of problems. The greater the use of objective performance standards, the easier it will be to recognize that a problem exists, since a problem by definition is a deviation from what "should be."

Types of Problems.   In a very important way, the *type of problem* has an impact on the type of approach that should be taken in solving it. Problems may be *structured* or *ill-structured*. According to Simon (1960), *structured problems* can be described in numbers, or can be specified in terms of a numerical objective, such as "to minimize costs." In structured problems, specific computational techniques or routines (sometimes called "algorithms") may be available which permit a solution to be found. With an algorithm, a solution is guaranteed. For example, suppose that a firm wants to minimize its cost of shipping tomato juice from six different manufacturing plants to seven different central warehouses. Since it knows the shipping rates from each plant to each warehouse, it can use a linear programming approach to solving the problem. (We will discuss this method in chap. 13). A specific solution exists and can be found.

Many of the problem-solving situations which develop, especially at lower levels of bureaucratic organizations (see chap. 6), are structured problems. In dynamic organizations, however, managers are more likely to be faced with ill-structured problems, since dynamic organizations exist in volatile environments.

In the *ill-structured problem*, the objectives may not be capable of quantitative definition and the alternatives available may not be susceptible to mathematical analysis. Ill-structured problems require more judgment and creativity to solve than do structured problems. An aid in making decisions about ill-structured problems is the "heuristic," a suggested procedure that requires the carrying out of a number of specified steps to achieve the objective. Heuristics are very useful to managers, since more managerial problems are ill-structured than structured, even in bureaucratic organizations. One heuristic suggested by Kepner and Tregoe (1965) is discussed later in this chapter (see "Step 4—The Evaluation of Alternatives").

Another way to classify problems—and thus to decide how to go about solving them—is according to whether *acceptability* or *quality* is the most critical aspect of the decision. This distinction was developed by Maier (1963) and expanded on by Vroom and Yetton (1973). When a problem is *acceptance-dominated*, it means that the alternative selected for solution must be accepted by those who are to implement it. They must be willing to follow through on the chosen alternative, or nothing will happen. The most effective way to get them solved and have the solution implemented is to involve those who will carry out the solution—or use a participative management strategy. Of course, the alternative selected must be adequate to solve the problem; that is, it must reduce the discrepancy between *is* and *should be*.

Quality-dominated decisions require that the "right" alternative be chosen. Generally these are problems that have technical, objective alternatives. For example, deciding on which of several computers to install is a quality-dominated decision, since it is possible to objectively assess computer characteristics such as speed, flexibility, and cost. The decision-making techniques we discuss in the remainder of this chapter are more appropriate for quality-dominated problems than they are for acceptance-dominated problems. (In the next chapter we will discuss techniques for gaining acceptance.)

Who Defines Problems.   The recognition of a problem is not always within the province of the person who carries out later steps in the problem-solving process. It is possible that one manager may go through all the problem-solving steps, but it is also possible that one manager may define a problem (step 1), and then leave the solution to others. For example, the plant manager may say, "Scrap rates are 10 percent too high." Next, the quality control department may seek the causes of the excessive scrap rate and develop alternatives for scrap reduction, and finally the plant engineer in conjunction with the cost accounting department may decide what to do.

But before alternatives are generated, the decision maker typically attempts to obtain information about the problem. This is especially important where the true cause of the problem is unknown.

Step 2—Identifying Probable Causes of the Problem

Kepner and Tregoe (1965) believe that managerial ineffectiveness in problem solving is usually the result of failure to correctly identify the cause of the problem, and that this is caused by a failure to obtain, to use, and to process systematically the necessary information. Such a situation is described in item 9.1. It shows how failure to process information may lead to an incorrect assessment of the cause. Very often managers fail to distinguish between the problem itself and possible causes of the problem. This causes them to leap to incorrect conclusions about the cause of the problem, resulting in decisions which do not solve the problem since they do not address the actual causes. Item 9.1 demonstrates clearly how a systematic approach to a situation can lead to the most likely cause of the problem.

Kepner and Tregoe's suggested heuristic for solving problems is given below. According to Kepner and Tregoe, the problem-solving process starts with the identification of the problem, moves to an analysis to find the cause of the problem, and ends with decision making or choosing specific corrective action. The steps are:

1. Select deviations to work upon. In the typical managerial situation many things are not what they "should be." Since the

manager has limited time, resources, and energy, he must choose to work on some problems and to ignore at least for the moment other problems. Some considerations in choosing which of several problems to work on are: the problem's potential for growth, time pressures, seriousness, and the manager's best use of his time.

2. Apply decision-making process if cause of problem is known. Many managers, however, like all of us, tend to assume they know the true cause of a problem when they do not. Organizational members often leap to a conclusion about the cause rather than systematically evaluating the information available.

3. If the cause of the problem is unknown, then one must systematically gather and evaluate the information necessary to identify the cause of the problem. This will involve:

   a) Describing the deviation precisely by answering the questions of: What is it? What is it not? Where is it? Where is it not? When is it? When is it not? And the extent of deviation is _____? And is not _____?

   b) Look for distinctions between the *is* and the *is not*. For example, if a problem is an unsatisfactory part from a machine, it is important to identify the time when the problem occurred as compared to when it was not occurring, the machines involved and those not involved in the problem, the nature of the defects as compared to the parts of the piece that are satisfactory and so on.

   c) Focus on changes in developing possible causes. If the machine was producing satisfactory parts at one point in time and was not at a later period of time, then some change must have occurred to cause the change in the quality of the part.

   d) Test for cause. Here the problem solver must evaluate each possible cause against the information collected and summarized in step *a*. The true cause of the problem will provide an explanation of the *is* and the *is not* for each question.

The decision maker knows at this point what he believes to be the most likely cause of the problem. He must now move to the next step, generating alternatives. (See step 3 below, "The Generation and Identification of Alternatives.")

Kepner and Tregoe (1965) suggest three kinds of action that a decision maker may take in correcting a problem. The first is *interim action*. This is usually a stopgap effort, and is the first thing done before the *cause* of a problem is identified. It may be a decision to shut down an assembly line, to stop delivery of a product, or to suspend an employee. It is a temporary action designed to give the decision maker time to determine the problem's cause.

Next comes *corrective action* to eliminate the cause of the problem. Appropriate corrective action can only be taken, of course, if the decision maker finds the real cause of the problem.

Finally, there is *adaptive action*. After a decision maker has identified a problem's cause, the decision may be to live with the problem rather than to try to correct it. Such adaptive action may be taken because the problem's cause is too expensive, or difficult, or impossible to correct. A physician, for example, may decide to treat a patient who has an excess of some chemical in the body by administering a drug which compensates for rather than reduces the excess, or a production manager may compensate for extra hard material by increasing machine speed, rather than by replacing the material.

ITEM 9.1   How to Analyze a Problem

The Burred Panels

The problems to be solved are presented in the form of dialogues between various managers in a plant which manufactures quarter panels—the body parts that cover the front quarters of the car, including the wheels. The quarter panel is the successor to the fender, and is the part most often damaged in collisions in traffic accidents. This plant has 3,000 employees and makes not only quarter panels but many other smaller parts and components for two of the models sold by one of the Big Three auto companies.

The panels are made on four separate production lines, each line headed by a huge hydraulic press that stamps the panels out of sheet-steel blanks. When the flat steel arrives at the plant from various suppliers by rail, it is unloaded and carried to a machine which cuts identical-size blanks for all four hydraulic presses. Blanks go to the presses by forklift trucks in pallet stacks of 40 each, and the schedule is so arranged that there is always a supply on hand when

the presses are started up on the morning shift.

The Principals
- Oscar Burger, Plant Manager
- Robert Polk, Production Chief
- Ben Peters, Quality Control Manager
- Ralph Coggin, Industrial Relations Manager
- Andy Patella, Shop Steward
- George Adams, Supervisor on Line #1
- James Farrell, Supervisor on Line #2
- Henry Dawson, Supervisor on Line #3
- Otto Henschel, Supervisor on Line #4
- Tom Luane, Scheduling Supervisor

Morning Emergency *The situation opens at 11:00 A.M. on a Wednesday in the office of Plant Manager Oscar Burger, who has called an emergency meeting. Fifty minutes ago he learned from Production Chief Bob Polk that nearly 10* percent of the panels coming off lines #1 and #2 were being rejected by Quality Control because of burrs and other rough spots.

Burger: I've called you in here because we're in real trouble if we can't lick this reject problem fast. The company needs all the panels we can ship, and more, if it's going to catch up with this new-model market. Both new models of the Panther and the Cheetah are going over big, and if we slow down on panels, the old man in Detroit will be on my neck fast. So let's get all the facts out on the table and run the thing down before lunch. Bob here tells me Line #1 started putting out rejects about three minutes after the end of the 10 o'clock relief break and Line #2 went wild about 9:30. Bob, suppose you tell us just what you've found out so far.

Polk: You've about covered it, Oscar. Farrell, the supervisor now on Line #2, says he's checked several times to see if these burrs in the panels are being caused by something in the sheets, but he hasn't found anything suspicious. Sheets all look nice and clean going into the press, but many come out rough as hell. He says the inspectors report that rejects rose from the normal one or two an hour to eight or nine in the last hour. On Line #1, George Adams says it's about the same story, and he can't figure it out—it just started up suddenly after the relief break.

Burger: Doesn't Farrell or Adams have *any* idea why it started?

Polk: Well, Farrell is sure it's deliberate sabotage by the drawpress operators, but he can't catch them at it. He says it's not hard to produce burrs and rough spots if a man positions a sheet just slightly wrong. He says the men on his line are mad as hell over his suspending Joe Valenti yesterday, and he had another argument when Valenti came in this morning against orders and tried to take back his press job. Farrell called the guard and had Valenti escorted to the gate.

• • • •

Burger (turning to Quality Control Manager Ben Peters): Ben, what is your idea about this?

Peters: It's hard to say what might be causing it. We've been checking the sheets from Zenith Metals we started using this morning, and they looked perfect going through the blanker.

Besides, it's only on lines #1 and #2 that we're getting burrs, so maybe we've got trouble with those presses.

Polk: I'll check it with Engineering, but I'm willing to bet my last dollar the presses are OK.

Burger: Yes, I think you can forget about trouble in the presses, Ben. And the blanker's never given us a hard time, ever. Still, you'd better have Engineering check that too, Bob, just in case. Meanwhile, I'd like to . . . . (*He pauses while the door opens and Burger's secretary slips in and hands Peters a note.*)

Peters: I'll be damned! My assistant, Jerry, tells me that Line #4 has just begun turning out a mess of burred rejects. I wouldn't have thought that slow old line could go haywire like that —those high-speed presses on the other lines, maybe, but not on Henschel's steady old #4 rocking along at 50 panels an hour.

Polk: Well, that seems to knock out a theory I was getting ready to offer. With #4 acting up, too, it looks like the press speeds aren't to blame. Now I guess we won't have long to wait before Dawson's line also starts bugging up the blanks.

Coggin: Maybe #3 won't go sour if what Patella says about Dawson is true. He says Dawson's men would go all out for him if he asked them, and I gather Patella hasn't had much success selling them on his anticompany tactics.

Burger: What's he peddling now?

• • • •

Informal Get-Together *The meeting breaks up, and Polk goes to the shop floor to check on the presses and the blanker. Peters goes to his quality-*

control records to see when the reject rate last hit its current level. *Industrial Relations Manager Coggin seeks out Patella to check on Farrell's handling of Valenti and the other men on his line. During the lunch hour in the cafeteria, an informal meeting of the four supervisors and Production Chief Bob Polk takes place.*

Farrell, Line #2 Supervisor: I suppose you got the boss all straightened out on those rejects, Bob. That Valenti has a lot of buddies, and we'll need to keep our eyes peeled to actually catch them fouling up the stampings.

Henschel, Line #4 Supervisor: You can say that again! I've got a couple of Valenti's old buddies on my line, and ever since the burrs started showing up about 11:20, they've been extra careful. I've traced at least three rejects that I think I can attribute to him.

Polk: Keep a count on who makes the most rejects, and maybe we can pin this down to a few soreheads.

Adams, Line #1 Supervisor: You fellas sound like you're on a man-hunt. As for me, I think Engineering will come up with the answer. The press on my line has been making more noise than usual today, and I think there's something fishy there. Right now, Bob, I'd like your help in getting the night shift to cut down on the number of stacks of blanks they leave us for the morning runs. It'd help a lot if they'd keep it down to two stacks of 40 each. Again this morning I had four stacks cluttering up my area.

Polk: I'll see what we can do with Scheduling.

Henschel: I'm with you there, Adams. I've been loaded with four stacks for the last five days running. With my slow-speed old equipment, I could manage nicely with only one stack to start off. I noticed that Farrell had two stacks and Dawson had only one to start his line today, and why should they be getting favors?

Dawson, Line #3 Supervisor: Now, Otto, you're just jealous of my new high-speed press. You got an old clunker, and you know it. What you need is to get off that diet of Panther panels and join me banging out those shallow-draw panels for the Cheetah. Also, it might help you to smile now and then when one of your men cracks a joke. Remember that old proverb, "He that despiseth small things shall fall by little and little."

Farrell: I can think of another proverb that you might consider, Dawson. "Spare the rod and spoil the child." Is it true that your crew is going to win a trip to Bermuda it they're all good boys and make nothing but good panels?

Adams: Aw, cut it, Farrell. We can't all be tough guys.

Farrell: Well anyway, I'm glad Dawson didn't have to cope with Valenti today. That boozer is finally out of my hair. I can't forget last year when he helped Patella spread the word that if the men would burr a lot of the stampings, they could pressure management into a better contract. I wouldn't be surprised if Valenti and Patella were in cahoots now, trying the same angle before negotiations start.

Adams: Relax, Farrell. You can't prove that's so. The men aren't as dumb as all that, as last year proved when they refused to believe Patella. What bugs me is those rejects this morning. Never saw so many bad burrs show up so fast.

Henschel: They sure surprised me, too, but you know I think Quality Control may be a little bit overexcited about the burrs. I figure all of them could be reamed and filed out with a little handwork. Put two extra men on the line, and it would be all taken care of.

Farrell: Maybe so, but you know how Burger would feel about the extra costs on top of the lower output. And don't forget, Henschel, our high-speed presses are banging out 30 more an hour than yours. Well, I gotta get back and see what's with Valenti's buddies on my line.

• • • •

Afternoon Meeting. *Three hours later, Plant Manager Burger is again in a meeting with Production Chief Polk, Quality Control Manager Peters, and Industrial Relations Manager Coggin.*

• • • •

Burger: . . . By the way, Ben, are the rejects still running as high this afternoon?

Peters: Higher. Line #1 is lousing up nine or ten an hour, Line #2 is ruining about a dozen, and Line #4 is burring about seven an hour.

Burger: What about Line #3?

Peters: Nothing so far. Dawson's line has been clean as a whistle. But, with Valenti's brother on the line, we can expect trouble any time.

Peters: By the way, Bob, have you heard that some of the men on the other crews are calling his men "Dawson's Darlings"? The rumor is that those shallow Cheetah panels are easier to make, and someone played favorites when they gave that production run to Dawson's crew.

Polk: That's crazy. We gave those panels to Dawson's line because this makes it easier for the Shipping Department, and they just aren't any easier to make; you know that.

• • • •

Burger's Dilemma *The meeting breaks up and the managers go back to their respective jobs. Plant Manager Burger spends some time by himself trying to resolve the dilemma. He sees two choices facing him: (1) back up Farrell and risk a strike that might be stopped by injunction, or (2) avoid a strike by undercutting Farrell, reinstating Valenti, and asking the men to cooperate in eliminating excess rejects. He does not like either of the alternatives, and hopes he can think of some better way to get out of this jam. At least, he tells himself, he has a night to sleep on it.*

Problem Analysis

The situation for Part II of this case opens

at 9:30 A.M. on Thursday in the office of Plant Manager Burger (the next-morning meeting).

Burger: Before we begin this morning, you notice I've asked Tom Luane, our Scheduling Supervisor, to sit in with us. He's just returned from taking a five-day course in problem solving and decision making, and I thought this would be a good chance to see if he's really learned anything. Now then, Ben, let's hear about those reject rates on the panels. How do they look this morning?

(Now begins a discussion in which each of the participants state what they believe to be the cause of the problem. After a short period, Luane speaks. [ed.])

• • • •

Luane: Let's see . . . that makes six problems you have mentioned—rejects, union antagonism, shop discipline, lack of supervisory training, low morale, and poor communications.

• • • •

Defining the Problem. *Let us pause here for a moment and see what these managers have been doing. First, Plant Manager Burger checked on the points of information he'd asked for at the previous meeting, and these satisfied him that he was right in assuming sabotage to be the cause of the high reject rates on the panels.*

He then made several decisions which he judged capable of taking care of both the reject problem and the labor difficulties.

Some of Burger's decisions seem right to Production Chief Polk, who only disputes Burger's handling of Farrell and Valenti; and all seem right to Industrial Relations Manager Coggin, who accepts Burger's reasoning completely.

Then Scheduling Supervisor Tom Luane begins to ask some pertinent questions and finds that each manager is using the word "problem" in a different sense, without realizing it. And they have been repeatedly committing the major error in problem solving—namely, jumping to conclusions about the cause of a problem. For example, Polk says the "basic problem" is lack of discipline in the shop, and he assumes that this problem is the cause of the excessive rejects. On the other hand, Coggin sees one problem as the need for training, which he says is the cause for low morale, and he sees another problem as lack of communications, which he assumes caused Farrell's blunder; while Burger views all these failings and assumed causes as part of one big "problem of managing this entire plant."

These confusions in meaning are apparent to Luane because he has learned to distinguish problems from decisions. He sees any problem as a deviation from some standard or norm of desired performance. And to him a decision is now always a choice among various ways of getting a particular thing done or accomplished. Thus he recognizes that Coggin is really talking about a decision when he says that "our real problem is the need to train supervisors." Similarly, Luane realizes that Burger's "whole problem" is not a mere collection of failures and causes, but a statement describing his responsibility for making decisions as head of the plant. So Luane tries to clarify some of this confusion.

Luane: I suggest we agree on what we mean by a problem so we can concentrate on that, and not worry right now about any decisions or any causes. The simplest way to solve a problem is to think of it as something that's wrong, that's out of kilter, something we want to fix. If we identify that for sure, then we can begin to look for what caused it; and when we've found the cause, then we can get into decision making, which is choosing the best way to correct the cause. . . . I think you'll find that the key problem is almost always at the end of a chain of other problems and causes. That is, the cause of one problem is itself a problem, and it's cause is another problem, and the cause of that other problem is still another problem to be solved, and so on. It's kind of a stair-stepping sequence. Usually, if you correct the cause of the basic problem in such a sequence, the other problems and their causes will automatically disappear.

• • • •

Outlining the Specification. Again let us see what these managers have been accomplishing. Luane has stated three basic concepts: a problem is a deviation from some standard of desired performance; a decision is a choice of the best way to correct the cause of a problem; and every problem has only one cause. He also has pointed out the stair-stepping process of going from one problem to its cause, which, in turn, may be a problem to be solved.

But the managers don't pay much attention to these ideas, and Polk clearly misunderstands stair-stepping, for he clings to the conclusion he earlier jumped to—that lax discipline is the cause of several problems. Industrial Relations Manager Coggin thinks "people problems" are fundamentally more important, but he accepts the priority his superiors give to the reject problem. At this point, Luane has tried to get the managers to think in terms of the urgency, seriousness, and growth trend of the problem. Having settled on the reject rate as the most important problem, they now are ready to start analyzing it.

Luane: How would you describe this reject problem, Bob?

Polk: Why, I'd say the problem is that the reject rates are way out of line.

Luane: We'll have to get more specific. We're trying to describe this exactly. As an overall description, how about "Excessive rejects from burring on quarter panels"? Anyway, let's write that down for a starter. (He goes to an easel blackboard and writes these words out.) Now we have to dissect this problem in detail, getting specific facts about it in four different dimensions—What, Where, When, and Extent. (He writes these four words down on the left side of the blackboard.) What's more, we want to get two sets of facts opposite each of these dimensions—those that describe precisely what the problem Is and those that describe precisely what the problem Is Not. *(He writes* Is *and* Is Not *at the top of two columns of blank space.)*

....This is the specification work-sheet, and the point is to fill the *is* column with only those things directly affected by the problem. In the *Is Not* column we will put the things that are closely related to the problem but not affected by it. You'll see why we do this in a few minutes.

Burger: OK, but I hope this doesn't take too long. Sounds kind of detailed to me.

Luane: It's pretty simple, actually. Under *What,* we can first put down "burrs" as the deviation in this *Is* column, and "any other complaint" in the *Is Not* column, since, as I understand it, there are no other complaints reported on these panels. But we can be more specific here, too. For instance, what did this deviation, "burrs," appear on? Were they on all kinds of panels?

Polk: No, Tom, just on the Panther panels, not the Cheetah panels.

Luane: So we can put down, under *What,* the words "Panther panels" in the *Is* column, and "Cheetah panels" in the *Is Not* column. Got the idea?

• • • •

Luane: Now we do the same thing for this *Where* section of the specification. Where was the deviation seen on the objects affected? Obviously, the burrs appeared on the Panther panels, so we put this down under *Is.* Also, where in the plant were the burrs observed?

Burger: So far, only on lines #1, #2, and #4, but with Line #3 expected to go bad any minute.

Luane: So under *Is* of this *Where* section we can put "Lines #1, #2, and #4," and under *Is Not,* we can put "Line#3." Also, we have to fill in the *Is Not* opposite the words "Panther panels." Where didn't the burrs appear?...We can put down "other

parts" under *Is Not,* since we know no other parts were affected. ... Now we come to the *When* part of this specification. Here we ought to be extra careful and get exact times, if possible. Ben, what times did those reject rates start going up yesterday morning?

Peters: You mean exactly? *(He consults his papers.)* On Line #2, the first excessive rejects showed up at 9:33 A.M.; on Line #1, they appeared at 10:18; and on Line #4, at 11:23A.M. From those times on, each of these lines turned out rejects that were far above our tolerance of 2%.

Luane: That's nice and precise. Can't tell, it may be important, so we'll put the exact times down. Now, how about the *Is Not* here? There were no burrs at all on lines #1, #2, and #4 before these times, and none at all on Line #3 at any time.

Burger: I think I begin to see why you use those *Is* and *Is Not* columns. It's to put off to one side all the facts you aren't going to think about in solving this problem.

Luane: No, that's not exactly why, but it will be clear as soon as we finish this specification. This last section, called *Extent,* covers the size of the problem—how big or serious it is, how many times are involved. We can put down "bad burring" and list the percentage of rejects on each line. Now what were those percentages, Ben?

Peters (consulting his papers again): On Line #2, 11% rejects. On Line #1, 17.5%, and on Line #4, 15%. That's according to final counts last night.

Luane: That leaves us only the *Is Not* column to fill in here, and this would cover the rejects on Line #3. We can say "Line #3 rejects" here, since they have stayed within the 2% tolerance. Now we've got the specification all filled in.

• • • •

Spotting the Distinction. *Here we can briefly review what Luane has done in drawing up this specification. He followed a systematic outline to describe precisely both the problem and what lies* *outside the problem but is closely related to it. (See Exhibit 9.1 for Luane's specification worksheet). The contrast between the Is and Is Not not only draws a boundary around the problem, but strictly limits the amount of information needed for its solution. There is no need to "get all the facts"—only the relevant facts.*

Note that Burger, Polk, and Peters all had different ways of describing the reject problem at first. Also, Burger thinks the specification looks too "detailed," while to Polk it sounds "too simple at one point. The separation of the Is and the Is Not sounds strange to these managers because, like everyone else, they have learned to think in terms of similarities, not differences. This habit will bother them again a little further on in this problem analysis. Both Burger and Polk are impatient with this specification stage because they haven't yet seen the reasoning behind it.

A precise specification makes possible two logical steps toward finding possible causes of the problem, and after that, as Luane pointed out, it serves as a testing sheet to identify the most likely cause. Luane now turns to the specification on the board and introduces the managers to the most demanding part of this analytical process.

Luane: We're ready now to use those contrasts between the Is and the Is Not of this specification. Whatever caused this problem produced *only* those effects we have described on the Is side; so if one thing is affected and another related thing is not, then there must be something distinctive or unique about the thing affected to set it apart from the other. If we know what is distinctive. . . .

Burger (interrupting): I don't see any contrast between "burrs" and "any other complaint" in this specification, but I do see one between "Panther panels" and "Cheetah panels." I begin to get what you're driving at. The Panther panels are affected by the cause; the Cheetah ones aren't. We want to find

out what sets the Panther panels apart from the Cheetahs, isn't that it?

Luane: Yes, you look first for a sharp contrast between the Is and the Is Not, like the one you've spotted. Then we know there must be something distinctive about those Panther panels.

Burger: Both panels are made from the same steel sheets, so the only way you could distinguish one from the other would be by its shape. The Panther panels are a deeper draw than the Cheetah panels.

Luane: That's a distinction all right. We'll put down "deep draw" as a distinction in this What section of the specification. *(He writes the distinction off to one side of the blackboard.)* Now can you see any distinction in the Where section?

Burger: I don't see any distinction there, like in the first case. Nothing distinctive of "Panther panels" as opposed to "other parts" that I can think of. Then you've got lines #1, #2, and #4 on the Is side and Line #3 on the Is Not side, and these lines are damned sir. ilar, except that Line #4 is a slow, old-time press. But that would only distinguish Line #4 from lines #1 and #2, which isn't what you're asking for.

Luane: No, we don't want a distinction like that, between things that are together on the Is side. We're looking for what sets the Is apart from the Is Not.

Polk: How about saying that Panther panels are distinctive of those three lines on the Is side? Line #3 makes only Cheetah panels, as we said a moment ago.

Luane: We can put it down if we want to, but it's really a contrast we already have in our specification, and not a distinction. It's the same contrast we have here in the What section between Is and Is Not. What we want is something that really sets lines #1, #2, and #4 apart from Line #3.

Polk: Then the only distinction you have there is that same "deep draw," as we said before.

Luane: I agree. We'll put it down again in this *Where* section. Let's go and see what distinction we can find in the *When* section, where we put down the different times that the burrs showed up on lines #1, #2, and #4.

Polk: How about saying those times are all distinctly in the morning, not the afternoon?

Luane: But how does that make them distinct from Line #3, where there are no times given at all? We're looking for something distinctive associated with those times.

Peters: Wait a minute! I've got a hunch those times have something to do with the stacks of blanks delivered to the presses. I remember Adams on Line #1 told me late yesterday that the bad burrs begin on his line just after using up the four stacks of blanks his area had been loaded with in the morning. And another thing—maybe those high-speed presses are just right for the shallow-draw panel that Dawson's line is stamping, but not quite right for the deep-draw Panther panels.

Polk: Come on, Ben, slow down! You know Henschel's Line #4 has an old, slow press, and he's getting a lot of burrs, so the speed can't be causing the rejects.

Peters: Not just the speed, Bob, but the speed in combination with the deep-draw panels.

Luane: Let's stick to this specification job and not jump to conclusion. I'm not knocking your hunches, Ben, for I've found they can often be useful, providing you hold them aside until you start looking for possible causes. We can make a note of them so we won't forget them later. *(He writes off to one side of the specification, "Burring times connected with using up the stacks of blanks," and "Press speed and deep-draw combine to make burrs.")*

Polk: I don't think Ben's hunch on press speeds and draws is any good, in any case. Engineering told me a while ago that they spent a lot of time examining the presses at various speeds and never found any stamping defects traceable either to press speeds or to the depth of draw.

Peters: But how about the combination of speeds and different draws? Bob, I think you've got too much confidence in Engineering.

Luane: Can we get back to this specification? Does anyone see any distinction in this *When* section?

Burger: I think Ben has a point there about the stacks of blanks on Line #1 being used up just before the bad burring started. How about the other lines?

Peters: I don't know, but we can find out.

Luane: Will it take long?

Peters: No, just a phone call. *(He reaches for the phone, gets his assistant on the line, and asks him to check the times when lines #2 and #4 used up the stacks of blanks they started out with the morning before.)*

Luane: While we're waiting, let's look for distinctions in this last section of *Extent.*

Polk: don't see any, unless it's that "deep-draw" distinction again.

Luane. As I see it, the distinction would have to be in those rates of burring we put down here, not in the panels or the presses.

Burger: Well, you could say that the rates of burring on lines #1, #2, and #4 don't correspond very well with the ways those lines were involved with that Farrell-Valenti quarrel. I mean, Farrell's Line #2 ought to show the most burrs, and actually it shows less than the other two lines.

Coggin: Maybe the reason is that the men on lines #1 and #4 are really sorer than the men on Farrell's line. Maybe Valenti has more friends on the other two lines. You can't distribute and measure feelings with percentage points, like you can with those reject figures.

Luane: Sorry to have to remind you again, Ralph, but that's jumping to a conclusion about the cause. We'd better not do this until we've finished with this specification.

Coggin: Well, I can't just sit here and let the rest of you ignore the human side of this problem. When are we going to get to that, anyway?

Luane: We'll take it up if this analysis leads us in that direction. It hasn't yet. So let's put down that distinction connected with the different rates of rejects and the different degrees of involvement with the Valenti affair. We can call this distinction, "Reject rates not proportional to involvement in Valenti conflict."

Peters (reading a note his assistant has just brought in to him): Here are those times we asked for. Line #2 used up its stacks of Tuesday blanks at 9:30 a.m. yesterday, and Line #4 at 11:20 a.m. That checks out, as I thought. The bad burrs started on all these lines just after they started using stacks of blanks delivered to the floor Wednesday morning.

Luane: Looks like that gives us a distinction for the *When* section. We can call it, "Stacks of Tuesday's blanks used up at these times."

Polk: But how about Line #3? Ben, did your man get the time that Dawson's line finished using its supply of Tuesday's blanks?

Peters: Yes. At 8:30 yesterday morning.

Polk: And no bad burring started on Line #3, so what's the importance of this distinction?

Luane: We can't tell yet, Bob, but we'll just put it down for now. That seems to complete our distinctions, unless anyone sees any more in this specification. If not, we can proceed to look for the possible causes of this problem.

Seeking the Cause. *At this point these managers have presumably collected all the relevant information that describes their problem precisely and have dug out those distinctive things in the Is facts that are characteristic marks of the problem. But they had trouble spotting the distinctions, as Luane expected. Also, one of them, Peters, introduced a couple*

of hunches into the discussion, exhibiting a tendency to "feel" that things are connected somehow or are important.

Note that Luane does not completely discourage such hunches, only recommends they be set aside until later. But note, too, that Peters' reasoning about his first hunch is faulty, as Polk quickly points out, while his second hunch is simply another example of jumping to a conclusion about the cause, as Luane points out. It is Burger who seems to be the sharpest here in spotting a distinction, after stumbling at first. By this time apparently only Industrial Relations Manager Coggin is still interested in the "human side of the problem," as he puts it, but his job is, of course, most directly concerned with this angle.

Luane, by keeping the discussion on the specification, prevents a time-wasting disgression. He also warns Polk against prematurely judging the last distinction (about using up Tuesday's blanks) as useless just because it doesn't seem to fit in with another fact in the specification–that is, the absence of serious burrs on Line #3.

Now Luane introduces the managers to a concept that lies at the heart of problem analysis, the concept that the cause of every problem is a change of one kind or another.

Luane: The distinctions we've gotten out of the specification give us the areas where we can look for possible causes of these burred panels. Let's look for any changes we can find in any of the distinctions. What's new or different in these distinctions? We probably won't find many. Maybe only one.

Burger: Do you mean any kind of change?

Luane: No, only those changes which have occurred within one of these areas of distinction, or have had an effect on one of them. We can start with that distinction of "deep-draw."

Polk: I can't believe that a change is always the cause of a problem. It can be any little thing, or some goof-off, or bonehead action.

Luane: Maybe those things go along with the cause, but I think we'll find here that these burred panels are being caused by some change. Also, Mr. Burger, I meant to point out that we don't want to go looking for everything that's changed, or we'll be here all day. There are things changing all over the plant all the time. But what we want to find is any change that's in one of these areas of distinction.

Polk: I'm not convinced, and what's more I don't see anything changed in that "deep-draw" distinction. The deep-draw is standardized on all three presses making it, and has been for months.

Luane: OK, so there's no change there. But what about that distinction we were going to check out in the *When* section? What's changed about those "stacks of Tuesday's blanks used up at these times"? Anything new or different about these stacks?

Peters: Well, the shift from Tuesday's blanks to Wednesday morning's blanks would be a change.

Luane: That sounds like a real change to me. Wednesday's stacks are the new blanks the lines started to work on just before the burring started.

Burger: If that's the cause of these rejects, how do you figure it? I can see that if Wednesday's blanks were different in some way from Tuesday's, that might make them the cause of the rejects.

Luane: Let's hold off on possible causes until we're sure there aren't some more changes in these distinctions.

Polk: I can't see any more changes. I say let's get on with it and start looking for possible causes.

Luane: OK, if you want to, but are we sure there's not some change connected with that other distinction in the *Extent* section, which we put down as "rates not proportional to involvement in Valenti conflict"?

Burger: I don't see anything new or different there, unless it's the differences between those rates themselves.

Luane: I can't either, so let's go ahead and check that possible cause you suggested a moment ago, when you said yesterday's blanks might be the cause of the excessive burrs. But we should test this possible cause, not just rationalize ourselves into accepting it. If this possible cause fails to explain all the facts in this specification—that is, both the facts on the *Is* side and those on the *Is Not* side—then we can be sure it's not the actual cause. Because the actual cause would have produced exactly all those things that we put down as *Is* in the specification, and also would explain those things we put down as *Is Not*.

Burger: I assume this is what you meant when you said earlier that the specification would be used in testing the possible causes?

Luane: That's right. We can start testing against the *What* of the specification by asking, "Does the use of yesterday's blanks explain the fact that the excessive burrs appear on the Panther panels and not on the Cheetah panels?"

Polk: No, of course it doesn't. Line #3 started using Wednesday's blanks even before the other lines did, and it still hasn't produced excessive burrs on the Cheetah panels.

Luane: Well then, there goes your possible cause. It doesn't fit the first facts in our specification's *Is* and *Is Not*. We'll have to toss it out.

Burger: You mean we've got to find a possible cause that accounts for every fact in this specification?

Polk: That's what the man said, Oscar. But now where does this leave us? We've run out of the only change we could find.

Luane: What this means is that our specification isn't really complete. We must have missed something somewhere. We'll have to go back and sharpen up our facts if we can.

Respecifying the Problem. *We can*

pause briefly here to point out that Luane himself was responsible for the unsatisfactory results of this first search for the cause of the problem. When he accepted the change that Burger suggested—that is, the change to Wednesday's blanks just before the bad burring started—Luane didn't think to ask about the difference between Tuesday's and Wednesday's blanks. A shift from one day's blanks to another's is not a change if the blanks are identical. Polk saw this at once, of course, and torpedoed this possible cause, as he should have. But this error of Luane's might not have occurred if he had been more careful earlier, as we shall now see.

Luane: We can get back and look over our *Is* and *Is Not* facts in the specification, but these look pretty accurate and precise to me. I think we probably missed a distinction or change.

Peters: What about those hunches of mine? You said we might come back to them.

Luane: That's an idea. What was it you said? We wrote them down over here somewhere. Here's one, "Press speed and deep-draw combine to make burrs."

Polk: That's no good, as I said before. Engineering checked that thoroughly.

Luane: Well, here's Ben's other hunch, "Burring times connected with using up the stacks of blanks."

Burger: We just tested that one out and got nowhere.

Peters: Hold everything! I think we skipped a point. We talked about yesterday's blanks, but those aren't just yesterday's blanks—they're also blanks from a new supplier, Zenith. I missed this point because we'd made some parts with the Zenith metal before we ever put it in production, and it worked fine. Besides, Zenith's metal met all our specifications. We checked the blanks again when the excessive burring first occurred yesterday, and they looked perfect going through the blanker. So we dropped this as a possibility, especially when the labor trouble looked so hot.

Luane: Then that means we should change that distinction in the *When* section of our specification to "Stacks of Zenith's blanks began to be used at these times."

Polk: How will that help? Dawson's Line #3 is also using Zenith blanks, and there's no burring there.

Luane: That's jumping to a conclusion about the cause. Let's look for a change in this revised distinction. Is there anything new or different about Zenith's sheet steel? How long have we been using it?

Polk: We signed the contract a month ago.

Peters: Yes, but we didn't get delivery right off. The first shipment didn't actually get here until two days ago.

Coggin: Matter of fact, Ben, we didn't get those Zenith sheets until late Tuesday. I know, because one of the men got hurt unloading them that evening. He wasn't familiar with the way Zenith blocks the sheets for shipment.

Luane: Let's concentrate on what's new or different in Zenith's sheets.

Peters: I think they're just the same as we got from our other sheet-steel suppliers.

Luane: Are you sure?

Peters: Pretty sure. We specified a slightly different alloy for Zenith's sheets, but not enough different to matter.

Luane: Well, anyway, the new alloy is a change in an area of distinction. What is distinctive about those burring times is that stacks of new metal began being used then, and the change here is that a slightly different metal is going into the presses. We can state the possible cause this way—"A new alloy in Zenith's sheet steel is causing the excessive burring in the presses."

Burger: Ben just said he thinks the alloy change wasn't enough to matter.

Luane: I know he did, but it was a change in an area of distinction, so it's a possible cause. We can test it against the facts in the specification. Could this change—the slightly different alloy—

EXHIBIT 9.1 Problem Specification

Deviation: Excessive rejects from burring on quarter panels				
	Is	**Is Not**	**What is Distinctive of the IS!**	**Any Change in This?**
What Deviation Object	Burrs Panther panels	Any other complaint Cheetah panels	Deep draw	
Where On object observed	Panther panels Lines #1, #2, & #4	Other parts Line #3	Deep draw	
When On object observed	Line #2 —9:33 a.m. Line #1 —10:18 a.m. Line #4 —11:23 a.m.	Any burrs before these times on Lines #2, #1, & #4 Line #3 at any time	Stacks of Zenith's blanks began to be used at these times	New alloy in Zenith steel
Extent How much How many	Line #3 rejects Bad burring Line #2—11% rejects Line #1—17.5% rejects Line #4—15% rejects		Reject rates not proportional to involvement in Farrell-Valenti conflict	
Possible Causes for Test	A new alloy in Zenith's sheet steel is causing the excessive burring in the presses.			

explain the appearance of excessive burrs in the Panther panels, but not in the Cheetah panels?

Coggin: No, it couldn't, because the Cheetah panels aren't having trouble with excessive burrs.

Polk: Hold it a moment! Maybe the alloy could explain it. It just dawned on me that Engineering did say something about those Cheetah panels a couple of months back. Something about how their shallow draw would make it easier to use a tougher alloy in the blanks. That could mean the Panther panels are fouling up on these Zenith blanks with the new alloy! Let's check it! *(He picks up the phone and calls Engineering, which immediately confirms his hypothesis.)* Engineering says the new alloy in the Zenith sheets makes the Panther panels much more likely to burr than the Cheetah panels.

Luane: Looks like you've found it, Bob. We could go on and test this out against the rest of the specification, but I'd say you've probably discovered the most likely cause of the excessive burrs. I suggest you have Engineering verify this.

• • • •

Conclusion

In these concluding exchanges we see that the analysis has clearly uncovered a cause which none of the managers were thinking of when they began, and which was actually verified as the cause. Note that the clue to the change that caused the trouble did not appear until Luane went back to the specification and sharpened up one of the distinctions. It was the point about Zenith's steel sheets that finally jogged Polk into recalling the possible effects of a deep-draw on blanks made of the new alloy.—Perrin Stryker

Harvard Business Review, July–Aug., 1965

Step 3—The Generation and Identification of Alternatives

There is disagreement among decision theorists about how people generate and evaluate alternatives. A rational decision is the selection of the *best* alternative, the implication being that all possible alternatives are evaluated. In most decision-making situations, however, all of the possible alternatives are not known, and even if they were, a human being would generally find it impossible to consider all alternatives. Herbert Simon (1957) therefore argues that a person cannot "maximize" in decision making because of this human limitation.

Simon draws a distinction between "economic" man and "administrative" man. Economic theory assumes that in a particular decision-making situation, a manager knows all of the alternatives and their outcomes. It is further assumed that the choice among alternatives will be according to a system of values which involves the maximization of an economic referent, such as profits. This "economic man" is contrasted by Simon with "administrative man." He points out that in real life "administrative man" is *not* aware of all of the alternatives available, and cannot possibly know all the consequences of choosing one alternative over another. So "administrative man" reduces the complexity of a problem to the point at which his knowledge and judgment limitations can make the decision. The typical decision maker, then, is subject to "bounded rationality," since his capacity for solving complex problems is limited to the alternatives of which he is aware. In addition, the manager makes decisions on the basis of his perception of the situation, and this may or may not be what the situation actually is. Subjective, idiosyncratic, and individualistic elements play highly significant roles in the making of decisions.

"Economic man," then, is assumed to have full knowledge of all alternatives, of the consequences of each alternative, and of the probability of occurrence of various conditions affecting the decision. "Administrative man," on the other hand, has limited knowledge of alternatives and consequences, and he makes guesses about the likelihood of certain events occurring in the future.

Simon argues that administrative man has the goal of "satisficing" instead of optimizing or maximizing, as does economic man. *Satisficing is a decision strategy in which one searches for an alternative that achieves some minimum level of satisfaction for the desired objectives.* This is the alternative usually selected. In other words, the decision maker will not identify *all* possible alternatives in order to choose the best from among them, but rather will stop his search for alternatives when he finds one or two that seem to be adequate, given his objectives or expectations. Of course standards may change from one situation to another, depending upon personal experience. If the decision maker has great difficulty in finding an alternative which meets his standards, he may lower those standards in the future. On the other hand, if he easily achieves his objectives, he may raise his level of expectations the next time he is making a similar decision. Doing this would clearly suggest that better alternatives were available in the past.

Considerable time and energy must often be expended to discover feasible alternatives, especially when one is faced with a new problem. If the problem is a recurring and routine one, it is likely that a set of alternatives has been generated previously, and it will be possible to identify and then implement the standard solution, but if the problem does not have a set of standard responses or alternatives, alternatives can be generated in several ways: (1) from experience; (2) by using decision models; (3) by research; and (4) through creativity.

1. Experience.   Here the decision maker may attempt to find out how others in his own, or in other organizations, have attempted to solve a similar problem. External consultants or other resource individuals or groups may have considered this type of problem and may have suggestions. Managers may seek solutions of this type by personal contact, or they may find suggestions in books or articles dealing with the subject.

2. The Use of Models.   A model is an abstraction of reality. It is an attempt to portray, in some miniature fashion, a particular state. Models can be useful in generating alternatives. For example, suppose you want to build a bookcase for a room. You take some measurements of the space where it is to fit, draw a rough diagram, evaluate its appearance, change the design, check the measurements, and build it.

There are different kinds of models, ranging from very simple to complex, and from real to abstract. A *physical model,* for example, often is a miniature version of the real thing. For instance, aircraft designers test alternative "scale models" of planes in a wind tunnel and make changes which improve the final product. *Qualitative models* explain a phenomena with everyday language or sometimes symbols. For example you explain to a friend why costs increase as the size of the firm grows.

In management today there is an increasing use of *mathematical models* (see item 9.2). Relationships between the features or characteristics of the subject of interest are represented by numbers. For example, the relationship between the amount of investments and the interest rate may be represented by an equation. Mathematical models are more precise and less ambiguous than qualitative models and are therefore of greater value in obtaining specific answers to certain managerial questions. Item 9.3 explains how models have been used to study the alternatives facing humanity, given increasing population and limited resources. Since the mathematical model describes how various critical factors in a situation relate to each other, it is possible to use the model to generate alternatives. In a mathematical model, the objective is referred to as a "dependent variable." The factors in the situation which affect the attainment of the objective are referred to as "independent variables." For example, a model might describe the relationship between the objective—profit—and an independent variable—amount of output. The model might show that profits steadily rise up to a certain point as quantity of output rises, but that after that point, profits decrease because costs rise when any given facility is used to excess capacity. Such a model would show what the

profits will be at alternative levels of output and the decision maker
can select the optimum output for the profit objective. A mathematical
model might also be developed which describes the relationship
between machine speed, material strength, and the number of rejected
pieces. In this model, the number of rejected pieces is the dependent
variable and machine speed and strength of raw material are the
independent variables. The varying combinations of machine speed
and material strength are alternatives which a decision maker will
consider.

ITEM 9.2   Decision Making

Using a Computer for Decision Making

Some imponderables outside the business but directly relating to it can be evaluated in a computer model. SRI and Gulf Oil Corp. recently developed a sophisticated U.S. energy model for an analysis of synthetic fuels strategy. It covers all major energy forms, conversion technologies, transportation modes, and demand. It also projects investment, financing, and resource depletion aspects to the year 2025 and computes price by balancing supply and demand.

Still, the inability of computer model builders to spot unexpected events on the horizon has inevitably provoked wide-spread disillusionment among planners with econometric models. "Econometric models have gone to pot because of the inability to quantify variables going into a model," says A. J. Ashe, vice-president for planning and development at B. F. Goodrich Co. "If you are forecasting the replacement tire market, you have to go back and decide how many miles will be driven, driving patterns, etc. My problem is that relationships never stay the same."

Many large companies scoff at the models but use them anyway. "When you're in an era of profound change you grab at what you can," says Exxon's Sachs. "They're a framework for analysis even if you can't put much faith in them. If anything, we use them more, though we may rely on them less."

More than half of the corporations reporting the use of computer modeling techniques in Social Systems' survey also subscribe to at least one national econometric forecasting service, such as Wharton, Chase, or Data Resources, Inc. (DRI). Many companies subscribe to several. John Doyle, director of corporate development at Hewlett-Packard, says none of the outside econometric models the company uses is particularly helpful by itself, but together they are useful.

Business Week, April 28, 1975

---

3. Research.   Preferably, the form of the mathematical model should
be determined through research. Research involves the use of system-

atic observation in order to find the answers to problems. As mentioned in chapter 2, Frederick Taylor, the father of scientific management, emphasized research as a means of managerial problem solving. In his famous metal-cutting experiments conducted over a period of 26 years, locomotive wheels were cut up in order to identify the factors affecting the cutting of metal. Taylor found that 18 factors were important. The interrelationships between these were specified in a series of equations and converted to notations on a slide rule which could then identify the various alternatives for a situation in which metal was to be cut. For example, the decision maker could choose between increasing machine speed or changing the composition of the metal to be cut. Thus, through careful research, a mathematical model was developed which identified the various feasible alternatives available.

4. Creativity.   In many situations, it is not possible to use previous experience, standard responses, research, or models in order to generate alternatives. Item 9.4 makes this clear. New or novel alternatives must be generated. In some organizations, the creation of new or novel alternatives is considered so important that much effort and energy is expended in an attempt to increase creativity.

Selection of creative individuals is not easy. Many research studies have attempted to identify the personal characteristics related to creativity. Intelligence and certain personality factors such as dominance, resourcefulness, and self-sufficiency have been associated with creative persons (Taylor, 1964; Torrance, 1967). While this would seem to indicate the feasibility of the selection approach, other research shows creativity is specific to the situation (Miner, 1973). Thus an individual may be creative in one situation and not in another, limiting the utility of the selection approach.

Establishment of a creative climate can facilitate the generation of alternatives. Some research indicates that personal stress and frustration is associated with low creativity (Miner, 1973). Organizations might therefore try to minimize job stress and frustration and thus encourage creativity. Other research shows that creativity is high in environments in which individuals have the freedom to express novel ideas and where these ideas are recognized and valued by supervision or by the organization (Miner, 1973).

Procedures have been suggested for generating creative solutions, especially from groups. One of the earlier methods, brainstorming (Osborn, 1957), requires individuals to gather in a group setting and to generate as many ideas as possible without criticizing anybody else's ideas. Some studies of this process, however, have shown that the individuals working alone may generate more and better ideas than in the group setting (Dunnette, et. al., 1963). The synectics approach (Gordon, 1961) requires the decision maker to make analogies from nature to the problem at hand (ability of some species to change color), use fantasy, or to place himself in the role of some element in the problem ("Assume you are the machine").

ITEM 9.3   Mathematical Models

Model Makers Keep Trying to See the Future

Between now and the year 2025, according to computer printouts from the latest large mathematical model designed to predict future world development, these ponderables are in the cards:

• If the oil-producing nations price their products optimally, the nations of the Middle East could assume control of up to 14% of the total capital wealth of the developed countries.

• By applying an effective population-control policy next year instead of in 1990, South Asian countries could avoid starving 500-million children to death. With no population control, despite help from developed countries, famine conditions will be "apocalyptic."

• To replace fossil fuels with nuclear power, an average of four nuclear power plants will have to be added each week to the world's network. If nuclear power remains the primary source of energy 100 years from now, it would take two huge nuclear power plants per day just to replace obsolete units.

These projections are from computer-generated "scenarios" collected in *Mankind at the Turning Point,* a small chart-packed volume produced by two systems analysis groups—one at Case Western Reserve University in Cleveland and the other at Hannover Technical University in Germany. Like an earlier work, *The Limits to Growth,* published in 1972, the new analysis is an expensive effort in large-scale systems analysis sponsored by the Club of Rome. A controversial technique that has its roots in war gaming, operations research, and econometric analysis, computer-based mathematical model building has nevertheless become one of the fastest growing new research activities.

Scepticism. The accuracy of long-term forecasting is still very much in doubt, and even practitioners admit that there is as much art as hard science involved. Critics complain and systems analysts worry, justifiably, that the computer's hard numbers add a degree of precision and credibility that is totally undeserved. Unexpected events—wars, technical discoveries, and unpredictable political changes—can invalidate any forecast. Yet the work goes on, not so much to provide an infallible crystal ball that will spell out every detail of the 21st Century, but in the hope of gaining better insight into the complex interrelationships between such basics as energy, food, and population that in themselves could bring unexpected surprises.

Since *Limits to Growth* appeared, with its pessimistic predictions of the probable collapse of world civilization within

50 to 100 years, dozens of governments and private institutions have begun major efforts to build up data bases and mathematical techniques that they hope will turn the computer into a more useful aid in social and economic planning.

But such cosmic crystal-ball gazing is still suspect. Certainly in the 1960s, the bright star of large mathematical model building dimmed—first in the Pentagon with the demise of the computerized whiz kids, then in business, where disappointment over the lack of results and the high costs of flashy operations-research projects further clouded its image.

A big pull. Still, models of the future of the world are heady stuff, and the field consistently attracts brilliant researchers eager to branch out from constraining specialties and work in interdisciplinary teams. Moreover, the data on which the national and global models depend are improving. Better information is pouring in from sources as diverse as satellite surveys of arable land, improved census and resource data submitted to the United Nations, and even from the improving quality of communications in the less developed countries. With good data, modelers insist, building a computerized system capable of predicting the interaction of major trends, such as capital flows, food availability, and population growth, is hardly black magic.

A clearer view. We are getting better models," says Jay W. Forrester, whose pioneering work in systems dynamics at MIT's Sloan School of Management is the direct antecedent of the Club of Rome studies completed so far. A greying, soft-spoken man of philosophical mien, Forrester has pushed the use of mathematical analysis to its limits. Resentful of criticism that he considers nitpicking or shortsighted, he points out that the technique of building and working with large complex models of corporate, national, or global systems is very much in its infancy. "People are working on projects that will take years and will perhaps never be completed in the ultimate sense," he says. "Much of the criticism stems from comparing early work to a nonexistent perfection."

Much of Forrester's early work involved creating "systems dynamics" models of corporations. Adopted into the curriculum of the Sloan School, many of his techniques have been carried to industry by MIT graduates. The models can be used to simulate corporate reaction to external events or to test the effects of changes in company policy, pricing, or marketing.

Success with corporate systems dynamics led Forrester to take on even larger problems, and in 1970 the group built an elementary world model known among analysts of global systems as "World II." World II produced some of the first "doomsday" charts indicating that pollution, overcrowding, and resource shortages could lead to disasters by the end of the century.

Business Week, Nov. 23, 1974

Step 4—The Evaluation and Selection of Alternatives

Having generated, in whatever fashion, alternative solutions to a problem, the decision maker now proceeds to the next step—the evaluation and selection of alternatives.

A decision is the selection of an alternative in order to solve a problem. A bad decision obviously will not solve the problem. Not all problems, however, give rise to problem-solving situations in which the manager can make a decision. In many cases the manager simply takes a predetermined action when a problem arises. For example, when a worker is late for work, there may be a specified action that a manager is required to take, such as to give the worker a written warning. When the worker is late a second time, the manager might be required to give the worker a two-day disciplinary layoff. Problems solved this way are called "programmed decisions." Often such decisions take the form of procedures and policies. *Procedures* specify the steps required for a given situation; for example, how to handle customer complaints. They tend to focus on specific, narrow problems. *Policies* tend to be general guides to action and often give only a broad context within which a manager should make a decision. A company policy may be, "to operate within the legal constraints applicable to the firm and industry." The manager must use his judgment in selecting alternatives which fall *within* these guides.

ITEM 9.4   Decision Making

The Scramble for New Techniques

The inability to project ahead with any certainty also lies behind the scramble for new techniques that allow plans to be "rolled over" more often. Companies increasingly are turning to the computer for help in assessing the impact of dozens of constantly changing variables on their businesses. While corporations can trace some effect from hundreds of factors, most concentrate their attention on the eight to twelve most crucial to their industry—rate of inflation, consumer spending on nondurables, interest rates, for example. At Tyler, managers have a list of 8 to 10 "key influencing factors" which they suggest their board members keep an eye on all year. The price of ammonium nitrate, an important ingredient for its newly acquired explosives business, currently is at the top of the list.

Even monitoring a dozen variables on a timely basis, though, and evaluating their cumulative effects, can tax a planning department. With a computer, suggests Planmetric's Neale, not only can long-range and short-range plans be updated continuously, so whenever managers refer to them they are current, but any number of what-if questions can be asked. The probable effect of a change to LIFO from FIFO accounting can be gauged, for example, or the actual effect of a rise in the cost of a critical component can be factored in. At Dow Chemical Co., 140 separate cost inputs —constantly revised—are fed into the corporate model. Such factors as major raw materials costs and prices by country and region are monitored weekly.

Hewlett-Packard Co., using its own H-P 2000 computer, runs as many as 50 different scenarios on four different models—economic statement, intermediate range plan, econometric, and aggregate sales. One major issue last year —whether to sell $100-million of long-term debt—involved some 100 different scenarios on the computer. The models helped the company finally decide to stay with in-house financing.

But planners today are also increasingly concerned about the kind of information that cannot be analyzed by a computer. They worry about the tendency of executives to extrapolate from the statistics of the past. "People tend to project from where they are today," says Mead's Wommack. "The truth of the situation is that the 1973 and 1974 period was an upward blip. On the other hand, 1975 will be way below the trend, and people may project off that."

Business Week, April 28, 1975

Programmed versus Nonprogrammed Decisions. In the programmed type of decision, the alternatives are presented to the decision maker. He simply chooses from a pre-established set of alternatives that one which is most appropriate given the specific dimensions of the problem. The possibilities and their consequences are worked out in advance. Programmed decision making is widely used where the tasks and/or problems are routine and stable—as, for example, in a factory assembly-line operation. In such an operation, if the equipment stops working, for instance, the manager immediately chooses a pre-established strategy based on the nature of the stoppage. Similarly, a dentist or physician often applies a standard procedure whenever he encounters a dental or medical problem of a particular type. (The available procedure may be memorized by the decision maker in advance or may be available to him in the form of written instructions.) All of us make many programmed types of decisions every day: for example, with respect to eating, the time to eat, the sequencing of food to be eaten, and the choice of eating utensils may all be highly programmed. For a wide variety of situations, our culture has provided specific alternatives that are available, along with the criteria necessary to guide us in our choice among them. Programmed decisions are most applicable to situations where the decision-making problem is quite common or frequent so that solutions can be specified in advance. They are also most useful when a decision must be made very rapidly or where the qualifications of the decision maker are low.

The manager in a bureaucratic organization (see chap. 7) will have a very high proportion of "programmed decisions." In fact, one of the problems often cited by people who work in bureaucratic organizations is that creativity is stifled, that they aren't permitted to make

decisions. This is certainly true, but the nature of these organizations
lends itself to such programmed guidelines.

In the dynamic organization, the decision maker faces a high
proportion of unprogrammed decisions and must exercise a high level
of judgment (or creativity), since the alternatives are not pre-established. Research (Friedlander, 1970) indicates that the ratio of unprogrammed decisions to programmed decisions is higher in organizations in which there are many product changes and where the tasks
tend to be nonroutine and complex—as, for example, in an organization involved in research and development work. In such organizations unprogrammed decisions have to be made for unfamiliar types
of problems. Obviously, unprogrammed decisions require more
competence and experience on the part of the decision maker than do
programmed decisions. Thus, in organizations characterized by rapid
product changes or complex tasks, and employing highly trained and
experienced personnel, there will be found a greater frequency of
unprogrammed decisions than in organizations with the opposite
characteristics. Often unprogrammed decisions require the help of
experts, or the use of group decision-making methods to improve the
quantity and quality of alternatives to be evaluated, as well as the
evaluation itself.

The formulation of procedures and policies for programmed decisions is an important organizational task, since they have a significant
effect on how efficiently an organization operates. All too often,
however, these decision rules are designed without fully considering
their implications for the overall effectiveness of a unit. In one major
company, for example, it was concluded that absenteeism was high
enough to be a problem that required the attention of top management. It was then discovered that one of the major reasons for the
large number of absent days was that when a worker's wages were
garnished by outside creditors, the employee automatically received a
three-day suspension. This programmed decision made the application of disipline uniform, but because of a large number of garnish-
ments it generated a large number of three-day absences. It also added
to the initial problem, since it created further financial difficulty for
workers.

In any case, managers must live with programmed decision rules.
They generally have to implement alternatives required by such rules,
and if they want to change them, they must seek higher-level
approval. In effect, managers do not *make* decisions in programmed
situations. It is in the unprogrammed area where managers need a
decision-making strategy. Two approaches to selecting alternatives in

the unprogrammed area will be discussed here: (1) The Kepner-Tregoe (KT) approach, and (2) decision theory.

KT Approach to Selecting Alternatives

The Kepner and Tregoe problem definition method was described earlier in this chapter. Their approach to decision making or selecting alternatives basically involves the comparison of alternatives against different classes of objectives and the evaluation of alternatives in terms of their likelihood of eliminating the cause of the problem and/or generating new problems.

Suppose a manager for the LAG Company wants to locate another plant that must have, at a minimum, 200,000 square feet of operating space. Four locations are available that meet this requirement: Atlanta, Annapolis, Chicago, or Boston. Before selecting, the manager must know more precisely what the objectives of the decision are; that is, what end states he would like to exist when the plant is in operation. Kepner-Tregoe suggest he can approach this decision through the following steps:

1. Set Objectives Against Which to Choose.   Objectives are derived from the results desired and the resources available. Since every decision involves a manager using resources to accomplish some desired end result, alternatives should be assessed against these end results. Basically, setting problem-solving objectives means that the decision maker should list what he expects to obtain when the alternative is selected. This may include several desired outcomes. For example, a decision maker might want an alternative to yield (1) 200,000 square feet of space, (2) $2.50 unit cost, (3) $1.00 unit shipping cost, (4) be near a major port, (5) close to the home office, (6) have warm winters, and (7) be in a rural area.

2. Classify Objectives According to Importance.   Problem-solving objectives are classified into two categories: *musts* and *wants*. "Must" objectives specify the outcomes that have to be achieved. Unless these are attained by an alternative, the problem will not be considered solved. For example, given the list of objectives stated above, the decision maker might consider (1) the space requirement, (2) unit costs, and (3) shipping costs as "must" objectives. Figure 9.1 shows how this manager distinguished between those requirements.

"Must" objectives also frequently contain resource limits. Problems are solved with resources which are usually in limited supply in any

situation. Any alternative which does not meet *all* the "must" objectives is eliminated from further consideration. Those which do are
then assessed against the "wants."

"Want" objectives are outcomes which are not necessarily critical,
but are desirable. They are, in a sense, extras that may be obtained
when an alternative is selected. Naturally the decision maker will
select the alternative which, after meeting the "must" objectives, satisfies the most "wants." These "want" objectives should then be
weighed or ranked in order of importance to the decision maker. In
our example he may rank the remaining decision objectives as
follows:

a). Near a major port
b). Near home office
c). Warm winters
d). Rural—not urban

Numerical weights can be assigned to these "wants." Here we have
concluded that locating near a major port is more important than
being near the home office, and given it a weight of 4.

FIGURE 9.1 Evaluating the Location Alternatives for LAG Company

		Atlanta	Annapolis	Boston	Chicago
	Must Objectives				
	200,000 sq. ft.	Yes	Yes	Yes	Yes
	$2.50 Unit Cost	Yes	Yes	Yes	No
	$1.00 Unit Shipping Costs	No	Yes	Yes	Yes

Rank	Want Objectives	Score x Rank	Score x Rank
4	Near Major Port	5 × 4 = 20	5 × 4 = 20
3	Near Home Office	3 × 3 = 9	4 × 3 = 12
2	Warm Winter	3 × 2 = 6	2 × 2 = 4
1	Rural—Not Urban	4 × 1 = 4	1 × 1 = 1
	Total Score	39	37

---

3. Evaluate Alternatives against Objectives and Choose.   Each alternative is compared against each "must" objective first, since the
"must" objectives set maximum and minimum limits. Any alternative
which stays in contention must meet all the "musts." Since Atlanta's
shipping costs are too high, as are the unit costs in Chicago, both of
these cities are eliminated from further consideration (see fig. 9.1).

The remaining alternatives are then evaluated against the "wants." A 1-to-5 scale can be used, with 5 representing meeting a "want" to the highest degree and 1 the lowest degree. The scores assigned to how well both the remaining alternatives satisfy each "want" are shown in figure 9.1. These scores are the best judgment the decision maker can apply based on his knowledge of the facts.

4. Choose Best Alternative as a Tentative Decision. The best tentative alternative will be one that meets all the "must" objectives and satisfies the *most* "want" objectives to a significant degree. This can be determined by simply multiplying the weight assigned to a particular "want" times the score that each alternative gets for meeting that "want." For instance, the weight for the objective of being near the home office is 3. If the home office is in Hartford, Connecticut, then since Boston is closer to Hartford than Annapolis, it would be given a value of 4. Since Annapolis is not too distant, it is given a score, still high, of 3—but not as high as Boston. The weighted score on this dimension is Boston 12, Annapolis 9. The alternative with the highest total score is probably the best alternative. From figure 9.1 it can be determined that the best alternative is to locate in Annapolis.

5. Assess Adverse Consequences of Tentative Decision. It is not enough that an alternative meet the "must" and "want" objectives, however, since its implementation may generate other problems, and an alternative that creates a problem worse than the one it solves is not a feasible alternative. Decisions often involve change, and change itself can create problems. Therefore, it is important to identify possible future problems that may be created if the alternative is chosen and implemented, together with the possible seriousness of those problems and the probability of their occurrence. Such an evaluation may lead to the rejection of what initially appears to be a highly desirable alternative. If it does, the manager goes back and evaluates the next most desirable alternative. Under the KT approach, alternatives should maximize the satisfaction of objectives and minimize the creation of future serious problems.

Implementing the Decision. Even though a decision is made by a manager, he may still be faced with the problem of getting others to carry it out. If the decision falls within the *real* boundaries of the psychological contract (see chap. 8, "Leadership") there will be little problem. Otherwise, the manager may have to resort to other methods. There are discussed in chapter 11, "Implementation of Decisions."

Decision Theory Approaches to Selecting Alternatives

A substantial body of literature exists on the subject of decision theory. Decision theory is a set of concepts generally mathematically based which describes what decision should be made in order to achieve some *objective*. A decision maker has a *number* of alternatives from which he must select *one*. Therein lies a difficulty, perhaps the major difficulty facing any managerial decision maker: that of coping with uncertainty. There is uncertainty everywhere in the decision-making situation: uncertainty about the causes of the problem, the alternatives, the resources available, and about the future events that may affect the consequences of choosing one alternative and not another. Among the uncertain environmental events that may influence the success or failure of a decision could be the actions of competitors, government policies, economic forces, and shifts in demand for the organization's output.

Individuals cope with uncertainty in a variety of ways. Many simply ignore the uncertainty arising from their decisions. This coping by avoidance is usually a type of defensive behavior. Those who cannot handle uncertainty may operate as if it is not present. Another coping technique is for the decision maker to assume that the outside forces which may influence the success of his decision will be the same in the future as in the past, or to assume that outside forces will operate in his favor. Decision makers at higher organization levels may reduce uncertainty from the outside environment for lower levels by establishing inventories of inputs or outputs to serve as a buffer between the organization and its environment. Or they may contract with various outside organizations for goods and services at certain fixed prices for a given time period. They also may attempt to reduce uncertainty by collusion with competitors; this of course is illegal, but it happens. Uncertainty may also be reduced by vertical integration, or by acquiring control of sources of supply and channels of distribution, or by diversification.

Finally, uncertainty arising from incompetence in one's own organization can be minimized by stressing the use of standard operating procedures. This, of course, also has the effect of reducing uncertainty for the subordinates as well as for top management, since subordinates when faced with a particular decision need only decide which of several alternatives to choose.

In decision theory, the decision maker must know, or make some assumptions about the conditions or situation in which the selected alternative will be implemented. This environment is called the "state of nature" and it will determine the success or failure of the decision.

"States of nature" are "factors that are outside the control of the decision maker" (Miller and Starr, 1967). Generally they refer to the possible conditions in which a strategy or decision will be implemented—that is, what the decision environment may be. For example, a manufacturer of fighter aircraft may consider the possible states of nature as different types and degrees of hostility between countries: (1) an all-out war, (2) limited-action wars, (3) cold war, or (4) peace. A tomato juice processor, on the other hand, may define states of nature in terms of weather conditions, such as: (1) perfect growing conditions, (2) average conditions, (3) poor conditions. For both firms, the "bestness" of a decision will depend upon what state of nature occurs at the time the decision is implemented, and this is often not known in advance. *When it is, the decision maker operates under conditions of certainty. When it is not, he makes decisions under uncertainty. Often it is possible to estimate the likelihood of various states of nature, in which case the manager is making decisions under risk.*

It is for decisions under uncertainty or risk that the concepts of probability are useful. The use of probability estimates in decision making will be described later in this chapter and in chapter 15. As we have said, the decision maker in the dynamic organization is much more often faced with conditions of risk and uncertainty than the decision maker in the bureaucratic organization.

A manager can assess probabilities in several ways. Probability simply refers to the frequency of occurrence of a particular outcome— the percentage of times that an outcome occurs if an event occurs a large number of times. We can be certain, for example, that if we flip a coin 1,000 times, very nearly 500 heads and 500 tails will occur. If an event is certain to happen, it has a probability of 1. If it occurs 1 time in 5, the probability is .2 or 1/5.

There are three types of probability: *a priori*, *empirical*, and *subjective*. An a priori probability is known because something is known about the possible outcomes as a function of the situation itself. For example, if a coin is evenly balanced, then a priori it can be said that the odds of a head when it falls are 1 in 2. The same is true of a tail, while the probability of a head *or* a tail is 1.

An empirical probability is one that has been derived from experience with an event. For example, it may be the experience of a university that only 75 of 100 incoming freshmen continue to graduation. The empirical probability of graduating then is ¾ or .75. Both a priori and empirical probabilities are called *objective* probabilities.

Subjective probabilities can be defined as one's best estimate of the probability. Subjective probabilities are educated guesses based on one's experience, intuition, and feelings.

Evaluating probabilities of states of nature allows the decision maker to compute *expected values* for strategies, or alternatives. An expected value is calculated by multiplying the payoff (what we would win or lose) if an event occurs by the probability.

$$EV = \text{Probability} \times \text{Payoff}$$

Expected values may be thought of as the average value (or loss) one would receive by making a particular decision a large number of times. If you, for instance, can win $5.00 if you flip a coin and heads comes up, the expected value is $2.50

$$\$2.50 = p(.5) \times (\$5.00) \text{ payoff.}$$

If you have to pay $3.00 to get in the game (i.e., to flip the coin), then getting in the game is a bad decision, since the cost is greater than the expected value. If the game costs $2.00, getting in the game is a good decision.

Decisions Under Conditions of Certainty

In situations of certainty, the decision maker knows the environment of the decision before the decision is made. Therefore, he can calculate, in terms of his objective, the consequences (or payoff) for each alternative. A situation such as this sometimes exists for problems involving internal operations of an organization. For example, in making a decision about alternative work assignments among various machines in a shop, the capacity and availability of each machine is known. Or, the manager may have to decide which of several engineers should be given a problem to solve. If only one engineer possesses the skill to solve the problem, the decision is easy to make.

In decisions under certainty, the decision maker chooses the alternative which has the largest payoff in terms of his objective. The primary problem may be calculating the payoff for all possible alternatives. For example, if you have 20 production jobs to perform and 20 machines which can perform them, several million alternatives would not cover all possible alternatives. Various techniques such as linear programming (see chap. 13), have been developed to solve these kinds of problems.

Decisions under Risk

The decision environment is one of risk whenever the decision maker does not know for certain which state of nature will occur but is willing to assign a probability to each of the states of nature which may occur. The probability is an estimate of the likelihood that a certain event will occur and states the proportion of times that a decision maker believes a certain state of nature is going to happen. We may know from past experience, for example, that a worker obtaining a certain score on a finger dexterity test has a 25 percent chance of failure at a certain task. Thus, if we hire a worker for that task who obtains this score on the test, he would have a .25 probability of failure and a .75 probability of reaching an acceptable level of performance by the end of the probationary period of employment. Of course probability derived from past experience will not be accurate in the present unless present conditions are quite similar to those in the past. For example, if the production worker's job was changed so that finger dexterity is no longer as important as it was, employees obtaining that certain score on the test would not fail at the same rate as in the past.

The payoff matrix is a useful way of presenting the alternatives in a particular decision-making situation. In a payoff matrix, various payoffs for different strategies for each state of nature are placed in a matrix. This facilitates the computation of expected values for each alternative. Figure 9.2 presents an example of this approach in calculating the expected cost of two alternatives. It describes a common decision-making situation for the average person. In making a long-distance telephone call, one must choose between making a person-to-person call or a station-to-station call. The person-to-person call is more expensive if the other party is able to answer the phone, but is cheaper than the station-to-station call if the other party is not able to answer. The probability of a person being in his office varies by time of day. At lunch time, the probability is low that the target person would be in his office. At other times during regularly scheduled office hours, the probability is higher. Thus, there would be different probability figures at different times during the day, and perhaps also for different days of the week. If we assume that the probability of the target person being in his office is .60, then the probability he is not in his office is .40. If the cost of a person-to-person call is 70 cents and that of a station-to-station call is 35 cents, then our best decision with these probabilities is the station-to-station call, because the expected average cost of the second alternative is only 35 cents, while for person-to-person calls the average cost of a completed call is 42 cents, since .40 of the time it costs nothing and .60 of the time it costs 70 cents.

FIGURE 9.2   Decision Making—Long Distance Calls

| | Contingencies | |
| **Alternatives** | **Person Being in Office** | **Person Being out of Office** |
	Probability = .6	Probability = .4
1. Person to Person	$.70	$.00
2. Station to Station	$.35	$.35

Expected Cost #1
      $(.6 \times .70) + (.4 \times .00) = -\$.42$
Expected Cost #2
      $(.60 \times \$.35) + (.4 \times \$.35) = -.35$

Another example is a common type of business decision (see fig. 9.3). The return from investment alternatives may be negative or positive, depending upon market or economic conditions for that year. Figure 9.3 shows that if the costs of two alternatives are the same, the best alternative with these particular probabilities for the states of nature will be the second alternative, since it will bring the greatest return on the average. Of course this assumes also that the decision maker here is trying to maximize his return.

Some decision makers may use a different set of decision criteria. For example, some may want to choose alternative 1 in figure 9.3 instead of alternative 2 because the loss cannot be greater than $500 in a particular year.

Decision Making under Uncertainty

In decision making under uncertainty, the decision maker is faced with the difficulties that arise from each alternative having a number of different consequences or payoffs, depending upon differences in the occurrence of states of nature (or contingencies) which may influence the decision. But, unlike decisions under risk, the probabilities of the states of nature cannot be determined. For example, a worker may have a choice among jobs which differ with respect to their average salary and their job security. The choice of the highest-paying job with lowest job security may be best in a time of economic growth and prosperity but the lowest-paying job with highest job security may be best if the economy is expected to take a downturn. Or a company may have several alternative advertising programs available to it. The payoff or consequences of each alternative will depend in part on the reactions of competitors to each of the alternatives and perhaps also to changes in consumer preferences, and to other variable factors. Since these events influencing the consequences of various alternatives are in the future, the decision maker is forced to deal with this uncertainty and may be unable to make acceptable probability estimates of each different state of nature occurring.

FIGURE 9.3 Dollar Returns From Investments

	Contingencies	
	Good Year	**Bad Year**
Alternatives	**Probability = .70**	**Probability = .30**
1. Buy Alternative 1	+$1,000	−$500
2. Buy Alternative 2	+$1,500	−$1,000

Expected Return, #1
$$(.7 \times \$1,000) + (.3 \times (-\$400)) = \$550$$
Expected Return, #2
$$(.7 \times \$1,500) + (.3 \times (-\$1,000)) = \$750$$

Some writers on decision making do not believe that this situation is common in managerial decision making (MacCrimmon, 1974). They feel that almost always the manager will be able to make some estimate of the probability of occurrence of the factors that influence decision outcomes, and therefore the approaches to decision making under risk will be applicable. In situations where the decision maker is unwilling to make such probability estimates, he can do several things. He can, for example, develop a payoff matrix and then assume the worst possible situation will occur. He then identifies the worst payoff for each alternative and chooses the strategy which gives him the highest return under the most adverse conditions. This is the criterion of pessimism, or the principle of *maximin*. The decision maker tries to maximize his gain under minimally favorable conditions.

Another suggested decision criterion is the opposite of the criterion of pessimism. It is the criterion of optimism, the *maximax* principle. Here the decision maker is optimistic and selects that alternative in which it is possible for the most favorable payoff to occur.

Another approach is to assume that the various states of nature that may affect the outcome of a choice among alternatives have an equal probability of occurring. Under this approach, the expected value of each alternative is calculated assuming each state of nature has an equal probability of occurring.

Decision-making approaches under uncertainty seem particularly important for the dynamic organization, when the environment of the organization is highly volatile, or uncertain. The approaches to making decisions under such conditions—those mentioned above, and others—are extensively considered in chapter 15.

Some Other Considerations in Comparing Alternatives

There is no easy way to select what criterion should be used in evaluating alternatives. Not every alternative considered by a manager is weighed against profits or costs. Often there are many criteria against which alternatives are evaluated (as in the Kepner-Tregoe heuristic). It is possible that the alternative must meet all the required standards, as would be the case where a decision maker lists the "must" criteria. However, often when an alternative is available, it may also be assessed against various other criteria, or "wants."

Compensatory and Noncompensatory Criteria. In establishing criteria, it is important to decide whether they are compensatory or not. If the criteria used are compensatory, then high scores on one criterion can offset low scores on another. Compensatory criteria are often applied to decisions to admit students to graduate programs; here, high test scores can often compensate for low undergraduate grades. The criteria for promotion to associate professor, on the other hand, are often teaching ability, scholarly accomplishment, and service to organization and community, but these are typically noncompensatory today. That is, insufficient publication, for example, will not be compensated for by high scores on teaching or service. An early illustration of a compensatory system for evaluation of alternatives is described in this passage from a letter from Benjamin Franklin to Joseph Priestley in 1772:

> When I have thus got them all together in one view, I endeavor to estimate their respective weights; and where I find two, one on each side, that seem equal, I strike them both out. If I find a reason pro equal to some two reasons con, I strike out the three. If I judge some two reasons con, equal to some three reasons pro, I strike out the five; and thus proceeding I find at length where the balance lies; and if, after a day or two of further consideration, nothing new that is of importance occurs on either side, I come to a determination accordingly.

Research on How Decisions Are Made.   Some research on how decisions are actually made indicates that the "satisficing" model is not descriptive of all decision makers. For example, a study of the job-selection decisions of graduate students in management at the Massachusetts Institute of Technology indicated that in making such decisions the students continued to search for information and alternatives even after a satisfactory alternative was found, and that much of the time they spent in decision making was to find support for an alternative favored very early in the process (Soelberg, 1966). Studies of employment interviewers' decisions have also shown that decisions are made quite early in the process—that the decision maker was not interested in obtaining as much information as possible about the various alternatives (Webster, 1964).

Other research shows that, in general, most decision makers seem to be more concerned about avoiding losses than making gains. One study indicated that a factor of importance is the system of rewards and punishments as they relate to the consequences of making certain decisions (Woods, 1966). For example, in making an investment decision, the typical decision maker is rewarded if the investment returns more than he estimated it would. Therefore, he is inclined to make a conservative estimate (even though an estimate is incorrect no matter in which direction the error is made). It is apparently more pleasant to do better than expected than to do worse than expected, and it seems that decision makers react accordingly. Decision makers may also be reluctant to change their personal probabilities, or their expectations, about uncertain events which may affect their decisions, even when new information indicates that this should be done. This is congruent with the finding that decision makers avoid information that tends to disconfirm the validity of a previous decision.

Other research shows that in dealing with uncertainty, the individual's psychological needs play an important role. He does not like uncertainty and does what he can to reduce the tension it creates. In decision-making situations, an individual often tries to appear, to himself and to others, to be an effective decision maker. This leads him to resist changing prior choices, to maximize the possibilities of receiving rewards, and to distort or ignore information which is incongruent with an image of a good decision maker. Research also shows that most managers are quite risk-averse, and are more concerned about the consequences of a decision for their own personal objectives than for the organization's (MacCrimmon, 1974).

Decision making, then, is the process of making a choice from among alternatives. We have emphasized the role of decision making as an important aspect of the problem-solving process. A critical aspect of decision making is isolating as precisely as possible the cause of the problem (problem identification). Only when this phase is completed successfully can an effective decision be made.

All of the different approaches to decision-making depend upon the degree of certainty that is present in the decision environment. In chapters 13 and 15 we will return again to these concepts because it is essential that managers in different types of organizations be familiar with them. For example, in hierarchical organizations, the manager must be familiar with decision approaches under conditions of certainty and risk. In other environmental conditions—for example, volatility—decision making under uncertainty is more likely to be the condition with which the manager must deal.

Discussion Questions

1. What is an "ill-structured" problem? Do you have any such problems in your life? How about a "structured" problem?

2. Under what conditions do you think a solution which is good (has high quality) would be rejected (has low acceptability)?

3. What are the dangers in using "experience" as a basis for solving problems?

4. Why would a manager want to have his subordinates make "programmed decisions"? Under what conditions would he not want to constrain them in such a fashion?

5. What is "expected value"? Are there any similarities between this concept and expectancy theory?

6. Is betting on the flip of a coin a decision under risk or a decision under uncertainty?

7. What is the difference between "maximin" and "maximax" approaches to making decisions?

Chapter 10

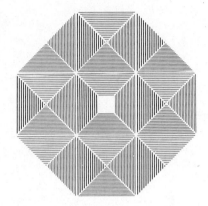

Objectives are basic to organizations. They affect an organization's
character in important ways, and they vary widely according to the
type of organization they serve. The goals of government agencies, for
example, often involve public service or regulation, while health-care
units or social agencies have goals which involve the delivery of
medical and health or social service to a community. As for business
organizations, they differ from one another in stated goals. In a survey
of 145 chief executives in business, the most frequently stated objective was to make profits or a living. To provide a good product or
service to the public was mentioned next most frequently, followed by
a concern for employee welfare, and finally, growth (Dent, 1959). Of
course, these were general rather than specific goals, and their relative
weight presumably reflects the bias of managers and owners. As we
will see, employees or customers often have a very different set of
objectives for business, and this will be an important consideration as
we analyze more specifically the nature of goals and the managerial
methods used to achieve them.

Though goals vary widely in kind, as well as in the purpose or
clientele they serve, managers must carry out certain fundamental
processes in order to direct the organization effectively toward
achieving its goals and in order to influence and monitor performance
to insure that events occur as intended. These fundamental processes
are those of *planning* and *control.*

Planning is the activity of determining what human and technological resources are required to reach a goal, when the resources will be
needed, and at what rate they should be used. Planning is future-
oriented. It may focus on the short range, from the present to one year,
or it may be concerned with the long run. Long-range planning covers

Resource Allocation

the proposed actions of an organization for periods beyond one year.

In planning, managers constantly make decisions about resource utilization—which to use and how to use them. These decisions are communicated to lower levels of an organization through budgets, rules, policies, and procedures, so that the probability of achieving goals is increased by increasing the likelihood of concerted action of all levels of the organization.

In today's turbulent economic and social environment, planning is becoming, if anything, increasingly complex and difficult. At one time, a planner may have been confronted with relatively discrete and manageable economic, market, and technological factors to weigh in making his plans, but the increased role of government and increasing social pressures in such areas as employment or pollution control are prime examples of the many additional variables which now have an impact on planning because of their potential effects on performance and profit. More "clients" are demanding an increasing number of goals from the organization.

For the very reason that the paths to goal achievement have become more complex, planning has become increasingly important, and managers recognize that this is so. As the world becomes more complex, and as resources become scarcer, better planning can increase the likelihood that complex goals can be met. Item 10.1 suggests ways in which a turbulent economic environment has affected corporate planning. It suggests, also, some of the ways organizations have moved to meet changing conditions through accelerated and flexible planning.

Control is concerned with insuring that events conform to plans. It is primarily a managerial function of attempting to ascertain where and how deviations from planned courses occur, so that corrective action can be taken. Control is closely related to planning. In planning, performance standards are set which become the criteria against which the execution of an activity is measured. For example, suppose we plan to achieve a 6 percent profit on sales. To do this, let us say that costs of $2.00 per unit become the cost control standard for the production department. When unit costs exceed $2.00, corrective action must be taken or the profit goal will not be reached.

For the purposes of control, mechanisms must be devised, especially in the maintenance and managerial subsystems of an organization, to monitor performance and feed back data which managers can use in identifying deviations from planned standards—such as excessive unit cost—and taking corrective action. Essentially, through planning, standards become the basis against which performance is judged. Reporting systems—whether simple or complex, and whether they deal with costs, machine accuracy, or human satisfaction, performance, or productivity—do nothing more than aid in control.

ITEM 10.1   Planning

Accurate Planning Has Never Been More Necessary Than in Today's Fast Changing Economic Environment

For corporate planners and the top executives who rely on their advice, the world has never looked as hostile or as bewildering as it does today. The very uncertainties, from the clouded economic outlook to the energy crisis, that make sophisticated forward planning more vital than ever before, also make accurate planning that much more difficult. "Annual financial plans for a number of companies are going to hell this year," says Jerome Jacobson, senior vice-president of Bendix Corp. "In a rapidly changing economic environment, some plans are out of date in three to six months."

So the very nature of corporate planning is undergoing a dramatic change, and the companies that fare best in coming years may well be the ones that adapt most quickly to the new styles in planning. Today's changes are most clearly visible in two areas:

Flexibility. Instead of relying on a single corporate plan with perhaps one or two variations, top management at more and more companies is now getting a whole battery of contingency plans and alternate scenarios. "We shoot for alternative plans that can deal with either/or eventualities," says George J. Prendergast, in charge of planning at chemical giant E. I. du Pont de Nemours & Co.

Speed. Companies are reviewing and revising plans more frequently in line with changing conditions. Instead of the old five-year plan that might have been updated annually, plans are often updated quarterly, monthly, or even weekly. Arizona Public Service Co. last year adopted a "dynamic" budget that looks ahead two years but is rolled over every month. At Ralston Purina Co., a 1% change in the price of a prime commodity kicks off a change in the company's cost models and the whole corporate plan may change accordingly.

This is heady stuff for corporate planners, because it was not so long ago that planning was a marginal blue-sky sort of operation that seldom got more than a nod from top management. But forward planning became a crucial function and the planner a central figure in the company in the complex, fast-changing business world of the 1960's and 1970's. "Planning has become intimately associated with the whole management process," says George A. Steiner, professor of management at UCLA.

And the role of planning will continue to grow because the outlook is so hazy—not just for business but for all society. What worked before may not work in the future, and a company's very survival may depend on how well it gauges the future. "Many companies feel we are moving into a new era," says Alonzo L. McDonald, managing director of McKinsey & Co. "The 1950-70 assumptions probably will not be good guidelines for the 1970's on."

Business Week, April 28, 1975

Goals and Planning

The existence of a goal, as we have seen, is inherent in the idea of planning. Goals, or objectives, are *desired end states*. An entity, or individual, directs efforts, activities, and energies to achieve the desired end state. But as we have suggested, the desired end state differs according to who is making the claim against the organization. Customers want the product at a reasonable price. Managers want salaries and security. Employees want jobs, equal opportunity, and wages. Suppliers want prompt payment of bills. For each of these demands, corresponding contributions are made by the different groups: workers supply labor; managers, administrative skills; owners, capital; and customers provide revenues. In planning, each of these important subgroups must be taken into account.

Organizational Goals and Individual Goals

Is it correct to say, then, that an organization has goals, since these are end states that are desired by individuals? Yes, because when we speak of organizational goals we mean what an individual, or group, desires—something that the system produces. As a customer, our goal for the local supermarket is that it has available the selection of foods we want when we want them. As an employee of the supermarket, we would expect reasonable wages and job security. *Organizational goals*, are what the *system* produces and how effectively it does so.

The Relationship of Goals to Plans

In the planning function, the manager must be concerned with determining what the goals are, what measures of goal achievement are appropriate, and how resources are to be allocated. This is no easy task. Take, for example, an advertising agency. Its stated organizational goal might be to provide high-quality service to clients. What does that mean, operationally? Is this goal measured best by the number of campaigns the agency conducts, its billing, or its profits? Each of these measures of goal achievement could lead to a different plan. For instance, if the number of campaigns is the measure, the agency might attempt to increase revenues by increasing its number of clients. With a profit measure as the primary objective, the firm might focus on cost-reduction strategies, at the expense of foregoing additional clients. All this is to say that the way the goals of an organization become specific for its members can markedly affect what they do.

Types of Goals

In our analysis, we will consider three types of goals: environmental goals, individual goals, and internal system goals.

Environmental goals

Environmental goal attainment is basic to the survival of an organization. Environmental goals are devised to meet the requirements, or demands, placed on the system from external sources. Groups beyond the boundaries of an organization, especially customers, expect products, services, or other relationships which provide utility, or value, to them. The customer is willing to pay for this utility. So long as utilities, or values, are provided to customers in appropriate quality, a firm can continue in existence.

Utilities may be products, such as refrigerators, pencils, buildings, clothing, and so on. They may also be services, such as health care, financial assistance, psychiatric help, and the like. So long as people wish to move from one place to another, there will be firms which build planes, automobiles, and bicycles. Fundamentally a firm must provide utilities to consumers to survive. *Environmental goal attainment comes first;* everything else derives from it.

Individual Goals

These are goals that individuals, or specifically identified subgroups, expect the organization to provide to them. Each person or group wants something slightly different than another in an organization. Workers want wages, managers want salaries, owners want profits. These are inducements which an organization must provide to obtain the contribution of these various groups. But to repeat: to achieve these individual goals, the environmental goal must be attained. Such a concept is based on March and Simon's (1958) inducement/contribution balance, which states:

1. An organization is a system of interrelated social behaviors of a number of persons we shall call *participants* in the organization.
2. Each participant in each group of participants receives *from* the organization *inducements* in return for which he makes to the organization *contributions.*
3. Each participant will continue his participation in an organization only so long as the inducements offered him are as great or greater (measured in terms of *his* values and in terms of the alternatives open to him) than the contributions he is asked to make.
4. Contributions provided by the various groups of participants are the source from which the organization manufactures the inducements offered to participants.
5. Hence the organization is "solvent"—and will continue in existence—only so long as the contributions are sufficient to provide inducements in large enough measure to draw forth these contributions.

Internal System Goals

Internal system goals are those of the subunits of the system. If the whole system is to achieve the environmental objective, every unit must have inputs from other units, and each unit must provide an output to be used by others. These are internal system goals. When an environmental goal is made operational, it is broken down into specific subgoals, and these are assigned to specific units of an organization as an internal system goal. Production output goals for a manufacturing unit, cost goals, market share goals, and efficiency objectives are all "end states" that are typically associated with a particular organizational unit (auditing, manufacturing, sales, and so forth). When a manager speaks about goals for his unit, he is talking about internal system goals. Because of the divergent interests of the various units of an organization, it is often difficult to successfully integrate the different points of view. Item 10.2 gives several useful suggestions to managers for keeping their planning on target.

An Example of the Goal Structure of an Organization

Consider a firm which manufactures and sells construction and power tools, such as drills, power saws, and the like. What would the structure of its objectives look like in terms of the types of objectives we have outlined?

ITEM 10.2   Planning

Ten Ways to Keep Your Planning on Target

Corporate planners, like other managers, can benefit from the experience of others. Here are 10 hints that may help your company's planning department stay on target:

Set goals for the planners. Guard against wasting time on nonessentials. William P. Frankenhoff, chairman of William E. Hill & Co., warns against "working things out to seven places." Says Stanford Research Institute's James E. Matheson: "People gather the information they know how to gather, rather than what is important. You need to put your effort where you are not expert."

Stay flexible. Dow Chemical Co.'s director of corporate planning, J. E. Mitchell, says too many plans "are too inflexible and involve too many numbers. We stress fast response time. We worry about getting too bureaucratic." Avoid communicating through computer printouts, says Mitchell. Use people-to-people contact instead.

Keep a balanced outlook. "The point is not to overreact, to understand that when the business cycle is at its maximum rate of change, it is probably the worst possible time to start making changes in your strategy," says General Electric Co.'s Reuben Gutoff. In a year like this, he says, the trick is to position yourself for an upturn in the economy.

Involve top management. Harvard's Professor James P. Baughman says the chief executive officer has more influence on the planning process than any other variable. "He can make or break a plan depending on the vibes he sends out in a crisis," says Baughman. Says Planmetrics, Inc.'s Gary L. Neale: "The real planner—whatever his title—should be reporting to the CEO, or be the CEO."

Beware of future spending plans. Managers always underestimate. "Operating guys never expect to be spending money two or three years from now," says Tyler Corp.'s C. A. Rundell, Jr., "If you look at a division's capital spending program, it will estimate $14-million this year, $8-million next year, but only $4-million for the three years after that."

Test the assumptions behind forecasts. "Operating people depend too much on trade association forecasts, and the economists that trade associations hire are too optimistic," warns Mead Corp.'s William W. Wommack. The problem is compounded, he says, because when "you get two sets of data you tend to believe the one you want."

Reward those who dispel illusions. "The toughest thing to get rid of is the Persian messenger syndrome, where the bearer of bad tidings is beheaded by the king," says William S. Woodside, American Can Co. executive vice-president. "You have to lean over backwards to reward the guy who is first with the bad news. Most companies have all kinds of abilities to handle problems, if they only learn about them soon enough."

Don't focus only on today's problems. "The thing that makes planning most difficult now is the recession," says Johns-Manville Corp.'s Andrew C. Boush. "Operating managers need to get away from everday firefighting."

Establish goals before you plan. Otherwise, short-term thinking takes over. "The pressure to show short-term earnings-per-share gains," says Cresap, McCormick & Paget, Inc.'s Donald Mill-

er, "is one of the biggest deterrents to effective long-range planning."

Let managers do their own planning. Too often operators are operators, planners are planners, and never the twain shall meet. Exxon Corp., says planner Brice A. Sachs, is moving more of the "hip shooters" (operators) into the ivory tower (planning department). This practice, he says, is one way to "inject into all those macro projections the vitality of real life."

Business Week, April 28, 1975

Reprinted from the April 28, 1975, *Business Week* by special permission. Copyright © 1975 by McGraw-Hill, Inc.

Environmental Goals

These would be primarily a function of the market: to provide power tools that are priced appropriately, relative to their quality and durability. To meet such a goal, a firm may take different approaches. It might for instance, build high-quality, durable tools selling at a reasonably high price for customers who use the equipment frequently and heavily. Or it might elect to build a product that is not so durable, but nevertheless very useful to customers who use the equipment less frequently. If it did the latter, the price could be substantially lower, but the product value high for the particular customer. The decision as to which of the two alternatives to take is a *strategy decision*.

Internal System Goals

The environmental goal is translated, through the strategy decision, into a more refined and specific objective for the various units of the organization. These may be *product goals, market share goals, productivity goals,* and *profitability goals.*

Product goals state the character of the output. How long should the product last? How should it look? What components are to be used in its manufacture?

The answers to these questions represent how the strategy decision is translated in the system; that is, what kind of product to make to achieve the environmental goal. Design standards, quality control levels, and manufacturing methods may all be thought of as forms of the product goal.

Market share goals specify at what particular group of tool users the product is aimed and what proportion both of the total market for power tools and of the particular market segment the firm believes it can obtain. Some customers, of course, will continue to demand high quality and durability, even though the price may be higher. Another group will want lower price and less durability. In opting for the high volume-low price segment of the market, the firm will consider the probable size of that market segment relative to the total market for power tools, as well as the total share of that market segment it is possible for the firm to obtain. Typically, they will then measure at least one aspect of market success by determining how much of the market they have relative to competitors, and their share currently relative to previous years.

Market share goals set the tone for the development of specific sales strategy and planning. What kind of advertising program is most likely to be effective in reaching the desired group of customers? Geographically, where are the majority of potential customers located? How can the sales staff sell most effectively? What channel of distribution is most efficient?

Productivity goals measure the efficiency with which resources are used. Productivity is defined as the output obtained relative to inputs. Productivity goals typically are expressed as ratios, such as sales per employee, or units produced per worker. Productivity goals may be set for manufacturing activities, marketing functions, and other areas of operation. Setting productivity goals is an attempt to give managers some idea of what they must achieve to contribute to the effectiveness of the whole system.

Productivity goals may be derived from a number of different sources—past ratios of outputs to inputs, for example. If previously 10 employees produced 1,000 units per day, then we would want to add 2 more employees if projected levels increased to 1,200. On the other hand, by adding only 1 more employee and improving the operation, perhaps we could still attain an output of 1,200 units; thereby we have improved productivity and very likely reduced costs.

Profitability goals are a form of productivity measure which refer to how well the organization has performed, overall. Typically, profitability goals are assessed by considering returns obtained on sales or investments. Profit as a percentage of sales or as a proportion of assets are common measures of profitability.

   Profitability goals focus less on how well a specific component of
the organization is doing and more on the whole firm, although it is
possible to devise such indexes for specific units. Profitability is
generally used as a measure of managerial effectiveness and may have
significant effects on the acquisition of capital. For example, investors
will be more willing to risk their funds in a firm that has higher profitability than another, presuming that both offer similar prospective
returns in the form of dividends to the investor.

Individual Goals

Individual goals are what *people* want. They are reflected in the
planning documents of an organization. Wage levels for example, will
be shown and used as estimates of part of the product cost. Profit
levels will be sought. The individuals and groups who expect payoffs
from the system will, of course, press to increase their return. Owners
will want higher profits and dividends, workers will want higher
wages. The final overall plan adopted by an organization will reflect
all of these subgroup goals. The final plan derives from the pressures
that each brings to bear on the others. In this sense, then, plans to
achieve objectives represent compromises among the subgroups.

The Planning Process and Objectives

One way to look at planning, then, is as a factoring, or breaking down,
of the environmental objective into system goals for both the long- and
short-range. Basically, strategic decisions are made about the nature of
products and markets. These are then translated into profit and cost
objectives for the total firm and the specific operating units. Figure
10.1 illustrates the planning and control cycle for an organization. For
the coming year it is necessary to develop specific goals and strategies
for marketing, production, and support functions. From these projections, standards are developed which become the basis for evaluating
how effectively the firm operates.

   At the same time that planning is being done for the short-run, long-
range considerations such as capital acquisition and new products
must be considered and evaluated. This long-range planning requires
an intimate knowledge of products and costs, as well as of strengths
and weakness of the firm. While planning staff units can be of great
help in processing information, as item 10.3 indicates, the process can
end up being a "study in arithmetic." Planning is an integral part of
the manager's job.

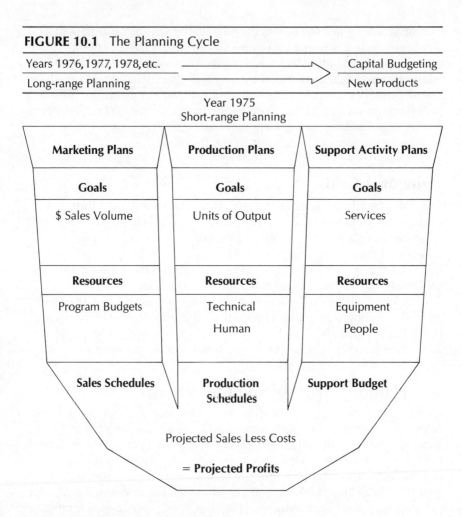

FIGURE 10.1 The Planning Cycle

Years 1976, 1977, 1978, etc. ——————————————⟶ Capital Budgeting

Long-range Planning ——————————————⟶ New Products

Year 1975
Short-range Planning

Marketing Plans	Production Plans	Support Activity Plans
Goals	**Goals**	**Goals**
$ Sales Volume	Units of Output	Services
Resources	**Resources**	**Resources**
Program Budgets	Technical	Equipment
	Human	People
Sales Schedules	Production Schedules	Support Budget

Projected Sales Less Costs

= **Projected Profits**

The Development of Plans

LAG Company manufactures a component for electronic calculators. In the past, they have found that their own level of sales bears a
fairly constant relationship to the level of sales for the entire industry,
about 1 percent. In order to plan, long-term and short-term, the
company bases a forecast on projected industry activity. In our hypothetical example, total demand is predicted to be as shown in table
10.1, along with the expected level of sales for LAG Company (1
percent of industry volume).

Figure 10.2 is a hypothetical projection of total industry sales derived from the data shown in table 10.1. Industry forecasts such as this are often prepared by organizations themselves, but are also available from trade associations, industry groups, and very often from governmental sources.

The plant has a capacity of producing 18,000 units per year, or 1,500 per month. It employs 10 managers, whose positions are given in the organization chart shown in figure 10.3.

ITEM 10.3   Planning

The Doers Should Be The Planners

Xerox' White and Hughes test their plans with word games. "The computers can't possibly handle things that have this many uncertainties," White says, so he assigns key headquarters staff members and a group of outside consultants of various persuasions to critique the plans. Adds Gould's Carroll: "Too often, when you ask for a plan, even a thoughtful guy will make it a study in arithmetic. If he isn't forced to say where he wants to end up, then he will tend to go along with existing products, and talk competitors rather than competition [for the consumer's disposable income]."

Forcing managers, not just planners, to look at "where they want to end up" is basic to most corporate planning. The idea is that the doers in the company should also be the planners, with the planning department acting as a kind of staff group. The planning itself is not an adjunct to management but an integral part of the business. The prevailing planning style in large corporations is that the goals come from the top of the organization to the bottom, but the plans—even long-term plans—go from the bottom up. And there is nothing in the new so-phisticated planning techniques that operator-planners cannot use at any level.

Alternate planning, for example, can be and often should be carried down to the individual business unit, since one part of a company frequently is thriving while another part is dying. At Dow Chemical, says corporate planner J. E. Mitchell, "There is constant contingency planning, product by product. Each major product line has three or four alternate scenarios." In some companies, operating units even make most of their own assumptions about the business environment—usually a function of the planning department. "Our operating officers," says Fluor Corp.'s manager of financial planning, James W. Street, "know as much about the political and economic climate in their areas as anyone in the company. We rely on their judgment in most cases."

Business Week, April 28, 1975

The president of the company is ready to plan for the coming year. He is about to determine what, when, how, and at what rate components will be manufactured and sold. His ultimate plan will also tell him something about whether he will have extra cash for particular periods during the year or need short-term financing. He will learn something about raw materials requirements, and how many employees he may have to add. From his final, comprehensive plan, he should be able to determine what the profit level is likely to be and, more important, whether or not it is satisfactory.

What does this executive know to begin with? First, he has a reasonably good estimate of what his sales levels will be in 1976, the coming year (15,000 units) and in the future if:

1. the industry forecast is fairly accurate;
2. he continues to operate (i.e., manufacture and sell) in the same industry;
3. there are no major changes, such as strong new competitor or a major technological shift.

He also knows a great deal about his costs of operations from previous years. Collecting historical cost information allows him to estimate the costs to produce a unit of product and to make a judgment about what level of sales are required to break even.

FIGURE 10.2   Hypothetical Projections of Industry Sales of Electronic Calculators and LAG Company Sales

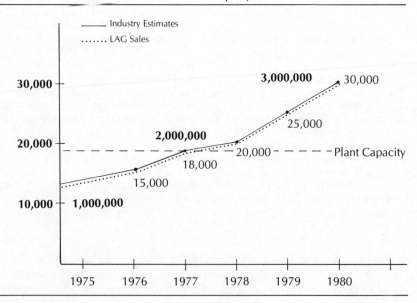

One other fact is evident. From figure 10.2 it can be seen that with plant capacity of 18,000 units, the firm will be unable to increase sales in year 1978 to the potential level of 20,000 components. So this year, the president must also make a capital investment decision for the coming year. Should he expand current facilities, add new ones, or simply stay the same size?

TABLE 10.1 Projected Industry and LAG Company Sales (in units)

Year	Industry Volume	LAG Company Volume (1%)
1976	1,500,000	15,000
1977	1,800,000	18,000
1978	2,000,000	20,000
1979	2,500,000	25,000
1980	3,000,000	30,000

FIGURE 10.3 Organization Chart of LAG Company

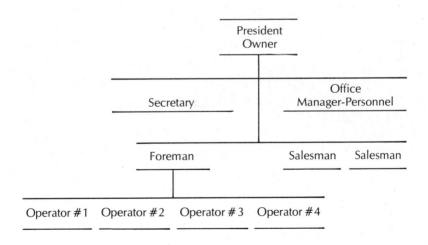

Break-even Analysis

Forecasts are estimates, and estimates may be inaccurate. It would be useful to know what the profit might be for various levels of sales. It would also be useful to know how much must be produced and sold in order to cover costs, or to break even. The break-even point is that point where sales and costs are equal. Break-even analysis shows the relationship between fixed costs, variable costs, and sales volume.

Fixed costs are those costs which are fairly constant and remain the same regardless of the level of production. Of course, all costs change over time and in this sense are not fixed, but for purposes of break-even analysis, it is safe to assume that at least for the planning period there will be such minor variations in these costs that they are, for all practical purposes, fixed. Rental or lease payments, interest charges, and executive salaries, are examples of fixed costs.

Variable costs, on the other hand, are those which change as the production level changes. They are costs incurred each time an additional unit is produced and/or sold. Materials, direct labor, portions of changes for utilities, and sales commissions, are examples of variable costs.

The total costs (TC) for a firm, at a given level of production are equal to the fixed costs plus the total variable costs (VC), or

$$TC = FC + (VC \text{ per unit} \times \text{number of units})$$

The total costs for a firm vary, based on the level of production. Assume that LAG Company has determined that fixed costs and variable costs can be estimated with reasonable accuracy as follows:

Fixed Costs (monthly)
Administration Costs	$2,500
Fixed Manufacturing Cost	1,000
Miscellaneous Costs	250
Monthly Fixed Costs	$3,750
Yearly Costs—$3,750 × 12 =	$45,000

Variable Costs per unit
Direct Labor	$2.00
Direct Materials	2.00
Variable Manufacturing	1.00
Marketing Costs	.50
Total Variable Cost Per Unit	$5.50

To estimate the total costs to the firm for a particular level of production, we use the formula given above ($TC = FC + [VC$ per unit $\times$ number of units]), so that at 18,000 units of production the total cost is:

$TC = \$45,000 + (\$5.50 \times 18,000)$
$TC = \$45,000 + \$99,000$
$TC = \$144,000$

At 8,000 units it is $89,000

$TC = \$45,000 + (5.50 \times 8,000)$
$TC = \$45,000 + 44,000$
$TC = \$89,000$

and if the forecast of 15,000 units is right, total costs will be

$TC = \$45,000 + (\$5.50 \times 15,000)$
$TC = \$45,000 + \$82,500$
$TC = \$127,500$

By examining the Total Costs line on the break-even chart (fig. 10.4), we can see how costs vary as a function of production level. The costs at the different production levels are marked (x) on the Total Costs line. At each point, it is clear on the break-even analysis chart of figure 10.4 what part of the total costs is the variable and what the fixed component.

But these costs are important in relation to the sales revenue of LAG. The sales revenue for particular sales levels is shown by the Revenues line, if we assume LAG sells each unit for $10.00. If LAG were to produce and sell its total production capacity (18,000), then it would have sales revenue of $180,000. Projected sales revenues for 8, 10 and 15 thousand units are:

18,000 units = $180,000
8,000 units = $ 80,000
15,000 units = $150,000

Profit levels can not be computed by simply deducting total costs from revenues. These are shown in table 10.2. Determining the specific level of sales at which the LAG company will break even can now be determined. The break-even point is the point where *revenues equal costs*. Since

Sales Volume = Price (P) $\times$ Number of Units (N)
Total Costs = Fixed Costs (FC) + Variable Costs (VC) $\times$ Number of Units (N)

TABLE 10.2 Profits (Loss) for LAG Company at Different Sales Levels

Production Level	Revenues	Less	Total Costs	Equals	Profit or Loss
18,000	$180,000		$144,000		$36,000
8,000	$ 80,000		$ 89,000		($9,000)
15,000	$150,000		$127,000		$23,000

The break-even point is where Sales Volume = Total Costs, or

$$P \times N = FC + (VC \times N)$$
$$(P \times N) - (VC \times N) = FC$$
$$N(P - VC) = FC$$
$$N = \frac{FC}{P - VC} \text{ , in this case}$$

$$\text{Break Even } N = \frac{\$45,000}{\$10 - \$5.50}$$

$$= 10,000 \text{ units}$$

FIGURE 10.4 Break-even Analysis for LAG Company

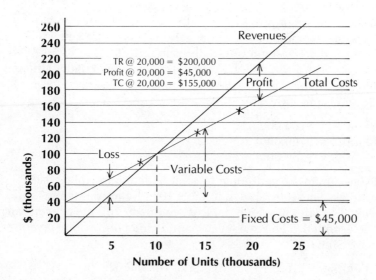

The firm breaks even when the difference between the price and unit variable costs $(P - VC)$ is enough to cover the total fixed costs. These relationships can be seen in figure 10.4. It shows that at a level less than 10,000 units, LAG experiences a loss; for example, at 8,000 units, a $9,000 loss is incurred. But profit begins to occur above 10,000 units.

Such an analysis performed for ABC-TV was an important factor in deciding to produce a morning show, *AM America*, to compete with NBC's *Today*. Some of the cost and revenue considerations are explained in item 10.4.

ITEM 10.4   Planning and Break-even Analysis

ABC's Costly Challenge to the *Today* Show

It is almost a certainty that if American Broadcasting Co., Inc., knew four years ago, or even one year ago, what it knows now about current economic conditions, it would not have laid plans to launch a new network TV show that will lose several million dollars next year. But unlike the marketer of a new product who can decide at the last minute to hold off until times are better, once ABC-TV announced that it intended to compete against NBC-TV's highly profitable *Today* show with a program called *AM America*, starting Jan. 6, 1975, it could do little else except move determinedly ahead.

• • • •

Following a five-year plan laid down by the network's former president, Elton Rule (now president of the parent company), and followed by his successor, James Duffy, ABC-TV improved its fortunes to a "parity" position with its rivals in such areas as news coverage, sports programing, daytime and late-night ratings, and children's shows.

Another consideration, however, went into the creation of *AM America:* the chance for profits. Relatively sold out at high prices until its recent nighttime rat-

ings slide, ABC-TV reasoned that it could offer another eight minutes of commercial time to advertisers if it added two hours of morning programming to its schedule. Five days a week, 52 weeks a year, the eight minutes could produce millions in revenue.

ABC had only to look at NBC's *Today* to see how profitable such a show can be. *Today*, which sells a minute for $12,000 on 218 stations, grosses about $25-million annually and is said to net more than $10-million. ABC concluded that *AM America* could draw business, particularly at an initial price of $3,000 per minute. The sales results so far are surprisingly encouraging, says George Newi, Network vice-president for daytime sales. General Foods and Colgate signed on for the full year, and Kellogg, Gillette, Sears, Nabisco, and Campbell Soups are among advertisers that already have bought more than 80% of the available commercial time in the first quarter.

Sales numbers. With its weekly production budget approximately that of *Today*, about $100,000, *AM America* is not expected to break even until its third year. To become profitable, it will have

to increase its audience well above its
initial target of some 2-million homes,
which will result in charter advertisers
paying a low $1.46 per each thousand
viewing homes. *Today,* which reaches
well over 5-million viewers each morning, not including an unmeasurable audience of several hundred thousand trav-
eling businessmen in hotel rooms, has a

cost-per-thousand figure of $2.80, al-
though discounts for quantity buys can
lower it to $2.10.

Business Week, Nov. 30, 1974

The Development of Operational Plans and Budgets

Knowing that the predicted sales level of 15,000 units will result in a
profit, the president of LAG must now translate this into more specific
plans. For example, 15,000 units will not be produced and sold in a
single day or week. The demand and production will be spread
somewhat reasonably over a year, revenues will flow in over the year
to produce total sales, and there will be a steady stream of payments
(for materials, labor, leases, etc.) throughout the year.

It becomes useful now for the manager to think about at what rate
sales will occur, revenues will be received, and payments will have to
be made and to plan for these eventualities. *Budgets* are such plans.
They are projected levels of revenues and expenditures which are
targets, or goals, that will, if achieved, result in the desired level of
performance.

There are many different types of budgets. Among those in use in
industrial organizations are the production budget, the materials
purchase budget, the budgeted income statement, the budgeted
balance sheet, the capital expenditure budget, the cash budget, and
the manpower budget. When the various budgets have been developed, they become the basis for other planning. For instance, the
production budget can be an important source of information for a
personnel manager because from it he can predict when to enter the
labor market to add new staff. The cash budget will show when shortages of funds will probably occur, so that the firm may be able to
anticipate and secure short-term loan commitments substantially in
advance of need.

If the president of LAG company feels reasonably sure that LAG
will sell 15,000 units in the coming year, this information can be
translated for use in other specific plans, or budgets. A complete
budget system, according to Weston and Brigham (1972), includes a
(1) production budget, (2) a materials purchases budget, (3) a budgeted
income statement, (4) a budgeted balance sheet and (5) a capital

expenditure budget. These plans can be used to estimate whether or not the firm can achieve its objectives and what spending limits must be maintained if it is to do so.

Sales and Profit Objectives

Suppose the president of LAG sets a profit objective of a 6 percent return on sales. The 15,000 unit sales prediction, and the 6 percent target become the bases for planning within shorter time spans of the year, say each quarter. Based on previous sales patterns, it is estimated by the planners that the 15,000 units are to be sold in the following quarterly pattern for the year:

Quarter	Volume
1	3,400
2	3,600
3	3,900
4	4,100

A set of budgets can be derived for each quarter (or, for that matter, for any time period). In the example that follows, the *illustrative* budgets show monthly estimates for the first quarter only, but it would be a simple matter to follow the procedure to develop similar ones for other quarters. Suppose first-quarter sales are broken down on a monthly basis as follows:

Month	Units	Unit Price	Sales Volume
January	1,000	$ 10.00	$ 10,000
February	1,200	$ 10.00	$ 12,000
March	1,200	$ 10.00	$ 12,000

Production Budgets

Assume that the estimated *standard* cost for each unit of product is $6.00. With such a cost assumption, and the monthly sales forecasts as noted above, a production budget for each of the months can be prepared. The production budget (table 10.3) shows the number of units to be produced and the amount required to be held in inventory. (In this example, it is assumed that the finished goods inventory is 50 percent of the following month's sales.)

Materials Purchases Budget

The materials purchases budget (table 10.4) shows the level of raw material requirements which must be maintained to meet the plans. Inventories of raw materials will depend on a number of factors, such as anticipated changes in price, reorder times, the storage space available, and the costs of money required to purchase inventories.

Cash Budgets

When production schedules, material requirements, and the manner in which sales dollars flow into the firm are known, the cash budget (table 10.5) can be prepared. These budgets show the flows of cash into and out of the organization. Preparing a cash budget allows the manager to estimate whether or not there will be excess cash (or a

TABLE 10.3   Production Budget for LAG Company

| | Monthly Average Last Year | Estimated This Year First Quarter | | | |
Item		First Month	Second Month	Third Month	Source of Data
1. Sales at $10 per unit	$ 10,000	$ 10,000	$ 12,000	$ 12,000	Assumed
2. Unit sales	1,000	1,000	1,200	1,200	Line 1 divided by $10
3. Beginning inventory (units)	500	500	600	600	One half of current month's sales
4. Difference (units)	500	500	600	600	Line 2 minus line 3
5. Ending inventory (units)	500	600	600	600	One half of next month's sales
6. Production in units	1,000	1,100	1,200	1,200	Line 4 plus line 5
7. Estimated cost of goods produced	$ 6,000	$ 6,600	$ 7,200	$ 7,200	Line 6 times $6
8. Burden absorption, under or (over)	0	(100)	(200)	(200)	Line 6 times $1 less $1,000 fixed mfg. expense
9. Adjusted cost of goods produced	$ 6,000	$ 6,500	$ 7,000	$ 7,000	Line 7 less line 8
9a. Adjusted cost per unit	$ 6	$ 5.91	$ 5.83	$ 5.83	Line 9 divided by line 6
10. Value of ending inventory (finished goods)	$ 3,000	$ 3,545	$ 3,500	$ 3,500	Line 5 multiplied by line 9a (rounded)

shortage) at the end of the period. This will allow for improved cash management, since borrowings, or investments, may be more rationally undertaken. It can be seen, in this budget, that LAG will have excess cash at the end of the third month of $3,100.

Budgeted Income Statements and Balance Sheets

With the materials purchases and cash budgets, a forecasted income statement and balance sheet can be prepared. The budgeted income statement indicates projected gross income from sales, minus the cost of goods sold, labor charges, depreciation and other expenses. This is shown in table 10.6 and it is derived following standard accounting practice. One adjustment, however, which must be made is the "cost of sales." This changes because of variations in inventory and production levels. This adjustment is shown in table 10.7. With this statement, the president of LAG can see what the estimated income will be for each month. This statement can also be used to assess whether or not the company can meet its objective of profit of 6 percent on sales. Total profits of $2,399 are shown for the three months for sales of $34,000; thus LAG's rate of profit is 7 percent.

The budgeted balance sheet (table 10.8) shows the future financial position of the firm; that is, the impact of the projected operations on LAG's assets and liabilities. This information is especially useful when a firm seeks to secure added funds from external investors.

TABLE 10.4 Materials Purchases Budget for LAG Company

Item	Monthly Average Last Year	Estimated This Year First Quarter			Source of Data
		First Month	Second Month	Third Month	
11. Production in units	$1,000	$1,100	$1,200	$1,200	Line 6
12. Materials used (units)	2,000	2,200	2,400	2,400	Line 11 times 2
13. Raw materials, ending inventory	2,200	2,400	2,400	2,400	Raw materials requirements next month
14. Total	4,200	4,600	4,800	4,800	Line 12 plus line 13
15. Raw materials, beginning inventory	2,000	2,200	2,400	2,400	Raw material requirements this month
16. Raw materials purchases	$2,200	$2,400	$2,400	$2,400	(Line 14 less line 15) times $1

Planning for Human Resources

From these data, other plans may be developed. For example, manpower needs may be forecast. LAG's organization chart (fig. 10.3) shows that four operators are employed. These four workers produce 1,000 units, or 250 units per worker monthly. If we assume this represents a normal output, then it is clear that in the second and third months of the quarter, LAG is in trouble, because the average production per worker must increase from 250 to 300 units.

TABLE 10.5 Cash Budget for LAG Company

| Item | Monthly Average Last Year | Estimated This Year First Quarter | | | Source of Data |
		First Month	Second Month	Third Month	
Receipts					
17. Accounts receivable collected	$10,000	$10,000	$10,000	$12,000	Sales of previous month
Disbursements					Raw materials purchases of previous month
18. Accounts payable paid	$2,000	$2,200	$2,400	$2,400	
19. Direct labor	2,000	2,200	2,400	2,400	Line 6 times $2
20. Indirect labor	700	700	700	700	Assumed
21. Variable manufacturing expenses	1,000	1,100	1,200	1,200	Line 6 times $1
22. Insurance and taxes	100	100	100	100	Assumed
23. General and administrative expenses	2,500	2,500	2,500	2,500	Assumed
24. Selling expense	500	500	600	600	5% of line 1
25. Total disbursements	$8,800	$9,300	$9,900	$9,900	Sum of lines 18-24
26. Cash from operations	$1,200	$700	$100	$2,100	Line 17 less line 25
26a. Initial cash	5,000	6,200	6,900	7,000	Preceding month, line 26b
26b. Cumulative cash	6,200	6,900	7,000	9,100	Line 26 plus line 26a
27. Desired level of cash	5,000	5,000	6,000	6,000	50% of current month's sales, approx. 4.2% of annual sales
27a. Cash available (needed) cumulative	$1,200	$1,900	$1,000	$3,100	Line 26b less line 27

TABLE 10.6 Budgeted Income Statement for LAG Company

| | Monthly Average Last Year | Estimated This Year First Quarter | | | |
Item		First Month	Second Month	Third Month	Source of Data
28. Sales	$ 10,000	$ 10,000	$ 12,000	$ 12,000	Line 1
29. Adjusted cost of sales	6,000	5,955	7,045	7,000	Line 54
30. Gross income	$ 4,000	$ 4,045	$ 4,955	$ 5,000	Line 28 less line 29
31a. General and administrative expenses	2,500	2,500	2,500	2,500	Assumed
31b. Selling	500	500	600	600	5% of line 1
32. Total expenses	$ 3,000	$ 3,000	$ 3,100	$ 3,100	Line 31a plus 31b
33. Net income before taxes	1,000	1,045	1,855	1,900	Line 30 less line 32
34. Federal taxes	500	522	927	950	50% of line 33
35. Net income after taxes	$ 500	$ 522	$ 927	$ 950	Line 33 less line 34

$$1,200 \text{ units} \div 4 \text{ workers} = 300 \text{ units per month}$$

It may not be economical to add another employee, however, since with an average output of 250 units, productive capacity would then be 1,250 units.

TABLE 10.7 Work Sheet to Adjust Cost of Sales for LAG Company

| | Monthly Average Last Year | Adjusted Cost of Sales Estimated This Year First Quarter | | | |
Item		First Month	Second Month	Third Month	Source of Data
50. Adjusted cost of goods produced	$ 6,000	$ 6,500	$ 7,000	$ 7,000	Line 9
51. Add: Beginning inventory	3,000	3,000	3,545	3,500	Line 10 lagged one month
52. Sum	$ 9,000	$ 9,500	$ 10,545	$ 10,500	
53. Less: Ending inventory	3,000	3,545	3,500	3,500	Line 10
54. Adjusted cost of goods sold*	$ 6,000	$ 5,955	$ 7,045	$ 7,000	Line 52 less line 53

*Note difference from line 9, adjusted cost of goods produced.

Thus, the production foreman must make some arrangement for overtime or develop some more efficient method of production.

Knowing that the average monthly production in the second quarter will be 1,200 units (3,600 ÷ 3), a fifth employee could be sought at the beginning of, say, March, so that in April he can be fully productive. This information is valuable to a personnel manager, since from it he can estimate how many production employees will be needed.

In similar fashion, the marketing staff may be increased. With two salesmen, the average monthly sales per employee is 500 units (1,000 ÷ 2). As the level of sales increases, the marketing staff will undoubtedly be working harder. Since an additional salesman will not be needed until the average monthly volume is 1,500 units, it may be

TABLE 10.8 Budgeted Balance Sheet for LAG Company

		Estimated This Year First Quarter			
Item	Monthly Average Last Year	First Month	Second Month	Third Month	Source of Data
Assets					
36. Cash	$ 5,000	$ 5,000	$ 6,000	$ 6,000	Line 27
37. Govt. securities					Sales of current
38. Net receivables	10,000	10,000	12,000	12,000	month
39. Inventories Raw materials	2,200	2,400	2,400	2,400	Line 13
Finished goods	3,000	3,545	3,500	3,500	Line 10
40. Current assets	$ 20,200	$ 20,945	$ 23,900	$ 23,900	Total lines 36 thru 39
41. Net fixed assets	80,000	79,800	79,600	79,400	$80,000 less $200 per month deprec.
42. Total assets	$100,200	$100,745	$103,500	$103,300	Total lines 40 and 41
Liabilities					
43. Accounts payable	$ 2,200	$ 2,400	$ 2,400	$ 2,400	Raw material purchases this month
44. Notes payable $3,200	2,000	1,300	2,200	100	$3,200 less line 27a
45. Provisions for federal income tax	500	1,022	1,950	2,900	Cumulation of line 34
46. Long-term debt	25,000	25,000	25,000	25,000	Assumed
47. Common stock, $50,000	50,000	50,000	50,000	50,000	Assumed
48. Retained earnings $20,000	$ 20,500	$ 21,023	$ 21,950	$ 22,900	Cumulation line 35 plus $20,000
49. Total claims	$100,200	100,745	103,500	103,300	Sum of lines 43 through 48

unnecessary to hire a new salesman next year. However, if the 18,000 units forecast for the following year become the sales objective, clearly an additional salesperson will be required, since average monthly sales are 1,500 units, enough to support 3 salesmen. For personnel planning, however, the search must begin in the last quarter of next year, probably in early November so that by January 1 the marketing group is fully staffed.

Capital Budgeting

The president of LAG must make a long-range planning decision: Should LAG expand its production facilities to seek the additional business possible?

The company president can see that his present plant capacity of 18,000 units is adequate for the next two years. However, if his current sales projection is correct, in year 1978 LAG could sell 20,000 units, 25,000 the following year, and 30,000 the following.

Let us assume the president has $50,000 available for investment. He must decide how to expend this amount to obtain the greatest return. For the sake of simplification, we will consider only two alternative investments.

The first is an addition of production facilities near the existing location. Production space is available near the existing plant. Due to space limitations, however, the maximum production capacity of the total facilities if the lease is taken will only be 28,000 units. In the first year after the lease begins, LAG capacity will increase to 23,000 units; the next year it will go to the 28,000 maximum. The cost will be $40,000.

The second alternative is to lease a new plant on the West Coast. But there will be no output from this facility until the second year, at which time total LAG capacity will be 30,000 units. The cost for this alternative is also $40,000. Table 10.9 gives some of the relevant data the president will consider. (We have made a number of simplifying assumptions here to show conceptually how such decisions can be made.)

Long-range Planning, Capital Budgeting, and Control

A wide range of factors, forces, and effects must be evaluated in the planning process. Product design, plant location, marketing strategies, corporate image, and the like are important considerations. Perhaps the most important set of considerations revolves around how, and if,

TABLE 10.9 Comparative Returns from Two Investment Alternatives

		Local Lease Increase			West Coast Lease[c] Increase		
Year	Sales Potential[a]	Sales	Units	Profits	Sales	Units	Profit
1978	20,000	20,000	2,000	$ 4,000	− 0 −	0	$ 0
1979	25,000	25,000	7,000	14,000	25,000	7,000	14,000
1980	30,000	28,000	10,000	20,000	30,000	12,000	24,000
1981	30,000[b]	28,000	10,000	20,000	30,000	12,000	24,000

a. From table 10.1.   b. Estimated; not Shown on table 10.1.   c. Estimated at $2.00 per additional unit.

an organization is going to make current expenditures for projects that have the promise of generating future returns. *Capital budgeting is the process of assessing the value of expenditures such as these to the firm.* If we build a new plant, the costs may be incurred over a short time, but the benefits may accrue for longer periods. Programs for research are similar investments that must be made currently, but which have long-run payoffs.

In the final analysis, when we have finally made decisions about (1) what products to produce—new and/or old, (2) where to produce them, (3) how they should be built, (4) how they should be marketed, and so on, commitments in the form of new equipment, facilities, and programs must then be made which begin to bind the firm to future courses of action.

For LAG Company the selection of either of the alternatives mentioned will have significant consequences. First, there will be loss of flexibility. Committing $40,000 to a lease means that the money cannot be spent elsewhere, in product development or advertising, say. It also means that for the life of the lease (five years), LAG has a fixed commitment that could seriously affect the profitability of the firm. Suppose, for instance, that the basic premise on which this decision is made is incorrect and that sales do not increase as predicted to 30,000 units by year 1980. Then LAG is stuck with capacity to produce something no one is buying.

Second, as the firm increases in size, it must begin to plan for other situations. Personnel must be added, distribution channels developed, additional related product lines considered. The future commitments that one makes can have important ramifications beyond the immediate problem. Even so, capital budgeting is of benefit to a firm. For example, by preparing market forecasts and comparing them with future and current production capacities, the construction of new facilities can be timed. Acquisition of land and financing can be obtained so that resources will be ready when needed, not too early and not too late. Some capital equipment, such as buildings and machines, take long lead times for acquisition.

Lenders and investors are more receptive to well-planned products. Capital budgeting will also be useful to the financial manager, making it easier for him to decide when he should enter capital acquisition markets to secure necessary funds.

Selecting from Alternative Proposals. The basic aim in the selection of a capital budgeting project is to choose those proposals which provide a return to the organization in excess of the cost of the capital of the firm. Funds that are used to obtain assets have a cost. Interest must be paid on loans and dividends to equity shareholders, and even funds generated internally (for example, through retained earnings) have alternative uses which can be viewed as a cost. These costs can be estimated and weighted to obtain a cost of capital for a firm.

Basically, the returns from any investment decision should exceed the costs of capital. In some rare instances, this may not be so, especially when external factors cause a firm to make an expenditure. For example, pollution controls may be expensive and generate few, if any, added returns, yet the firm may have to provide them. In such a case, the firm must raise prices, or perhaps be willing to accept a lower total return than in the past.

At any rate, the firm should select those investment proposals which exceed the costs of capital. A number of different methods of evaluating return on investment provide a basis for making capital budgeting decisions. All take the costs of capital into consideration. Rather than illustrating each of them by example, we will show how one of these methods would be used by LAG company to determine whether it should select the local lease of the West Coast lease.

Net Present Value Method. To use the net present value method, the costs of capital to the firm are used to discount the future stream of cash flows. The present value of these cash flows is obtained and then compared to the cost of the project. If the net present value is greater than the outlay, then the investment should be made. If there are two alternatives, then the alternative with the greatest net present value should be selected, if only one investment can be made.

The concept behind this method assumes that the cost of capital is determined. At LAG, for example, we assume it to be 12 percent. Then the value today (present value) of a future inflow of $1,000 in one year is less than $1,000, or $893. This amount ($893) invested at 12 percent will yield $1,000 in a year. One thousand dollars received two years from now has an even lower current value, $797, which is how much would have to be invested at 12 percent, compounded annually to yield $1,000 in 2 years. (Tables giving present values of $1.00 for different rates are given in most texts on financial management.)

Since the (assumed) cost of capital to LAG is 12 percent, we can now compute the net present value for each alternative investment. Table 10.9 shows the incremental profit for each year of the investment. The return for each year for each investment is multiplied by a discount factor from present value tables, and a total net present value is obtained. Table 10.10 shows this computation for the alternatives facing LAG. If the available funds are $40,000, then the most desirable alternative for LAG is the West Coast lease, since the net present value is $18,774 for this alternative compared to $14,410 for the local lease.

TABLE 10.10 Comparative Present Value

Local Lease	Discount Factor	Present Value	
1978 $ 4,000	.893	$ 3,572	
1979 $14,000	.797	$11,158	
1980 $20,000	.712	$14,240	
1981 $20,000	.636	$12,720	
		$54,410	Present Value of Returns
		$40,000	Cost of Lease
		$14,410	Net Present Value

West Coast Lease	Discount Factor	Present Value	
1978 $ 0	.893	$ 0	
1979 $14,000	.797	$11,158	
1980 $24,000	.712	$17,088	
1981 $24,000	.636	$15,264	
		$58,774	Present Value of Returns
		$40,000	Cost of Lease
		$18,774	Net Present Value

Alternative Methods of Capital Decision Evaluation   There are other ways to evaluate capital investment decisions. Basically, any one of three methods which take into account future cash flows and discount them will give similar results to the net present value method just discussed. The internal *rate of return* method and developing a *profitability index* would have yielded the same results; that is, the West Coast lease is the preferred alternative. Under some conditions, however, different results might obtain with the different methods. Weston and Brigham (1972) note these project characteristics which might yield different results using different methods:

1. if the projects have different lives;
2. if the costs of one project are higher than those of another;
3. if cash flows increase over time for one project, while they decrease for the other.

Another method for assessment of these projects—not recommended by finance experts, but widely used—is *payback*. The payback method simply determines which alternative returns the total invested amount to the firm first.

The Human Effects of Planning and Budgeting

There are human problems that result from the planning and budgeting processes. People are affected by plans. Plans mean more than just numbers—or standards—that are used for guiding the actions of organizations. When constraints such as plans are imposed, they cause people to react. In this section we will examine some possible human consequences of being involved in and affected by planning. To do this, we must consider the sequence of activities which produce the plans and budgets themselves and then their actual use by organizational members. The model in figure 10.5 shows this process and its effects.

The first stage (stage 1) covers those activities which produce the final documents. Managers meet with subordinates, and projections of expenditures are formulated, evaluated, consolidated, and coordinated. Competition occurs between units for the resources available.

FIGURE 10.5 Sequence of Planning Activities

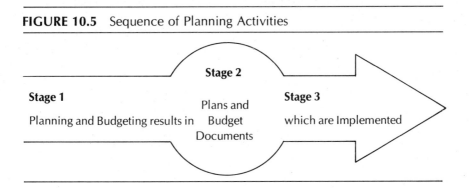

Stage 1

Planning and Budgeting results in

Stage 2

Plans and Budget Documents

Stage 3

which are Implemented

From this process, budgets and plans emerge. The budget (stage 2 in the model) is a set of quantified goals. It is used to provide guidance to subordinate units. The goals may be very specific or more general. The latitude a particular manager has over resources allocations may be narrow or broad. Plans may be more extensive than budgets, defining and clarifying how certain things should be done. Finally, the budget can be used (as in stage 3) as a standard of comparison to evaluate performance as a basis for rewarding managers.

Planning and Budget Development (Stage 1)

A budget is, after all, a document which allocates resources among different units in an organization. When resources are scarce there is likely to be competition among units for increased amounts, relative both to their past funding levels and relative to other units. In one study (Pfeffer and Salancik, 1974) the budgeting process at the University of Illinios was examined in an attempt to determine how resources were distributed among the university's departments. The study considered budget allocations, and examined their relationship to the power of the various departments, their work load, and their national reputation. The study found that to the extent that a department had power, measured by presence in university committees, it had an advantage in the budgetary process regardless of its work load and concluded that "subunit power affects the allocation of resources within the organization."

Anxiety from Budgeting and Planning   Another characteristic of the budgeting process which may cause problems is that budget negotiations are likely to be carried out in secrecy. This secrecy and the fact that budgetary allocations are likely to be based on power, as well as the amount of work to be done, may generate a high level of anxiety for those managers involved. If the planning and budgeting process leads to fear that there will be inequitable or inadequate distribution of resources, this can lead to one or more of the following reactions by managers:

1. Political Behavior.   Managers may attempt to increase their power in an organization by political behavior. They may, for instance, withhold important information until the last minute to magnify its significance. Or they may be excessively ingratiating toward superiors or those in positions of influence. Providing favors beyond the normal courtesies and requirements of the work assignment are also political.

2. Negative Reactions Toward Planning and Budget Units.
Perceived inequity of resource allocation may trigger negative reactions toward those units responsible for the collection of budget data and preparation. Personnel in the controller's office (probably a group of staff specialists) are likely to have the major responsibility for putting together a budget's final figures. They may end up bearing the brunt of criticism since they are more convenient targets than line managers. After all, an individual's superior will be responsible for promotion decisions, making it unwise to alienate him by directing aggression toward him.

If this mode of adaptation becomes at all widespread, it will hinder the planning group's effectiveness because it will become increasingly difficult to interact with other units to obtain accurate and timely information.

3. Overstatement of Needs. To protect his perceived equitable share of future resources, managers will sometimes pad estimated budgetary needs. They learn quickly that cuts are usually made in requested amounts and, in order to be equitable, all units have to experience relatively similar budget cuts. Therefore, the honest manager, estimating his needs with some degree of accuracy, is penalized. He quickly learns that an over-statement of requirements helps him secure his "fair" share.

4. Covert Information Systems. If there is a high degree of secrecy regarding budget allocations to other units, managers will seek to make some estimate of how they fare relative to others. They will probably overestimate the amounts obtained by other units. Nevertheless, because the allocations may represent something other than need —for example, the power one has—information will be sought about the amount received by others. Secretaries, staff members from the budget offices, and those with access to data will be prodded for information. A communication network may develop which provides some information, although it may quite possibly be inaccurate.

The Use of Participation for Anxiety Reduction. Acceptance of plans and budget requirements may be substantially increased through "participative management" strategies. March and Simon (1958) have concluded that participation may minimize problems when there is a "felt need for joint decision-making." Certainly if power is a major factor in determining budget allocations, then a participative strategy is warranted.

Participation is a decision-making process in which an individual or group can influence, or change, decisions. Of course, to move toward more participation in budget development and away from unilateral (or relatively so) determination of budget levels implies a redistribution of power to those groups involved.

Participation in the budgeting process is a promising method for anxiety reduction and increased involvement. The document that emerges will likely be more generally accepted if it is developed through a process in which line managers are involved and with overt, active support from top management.

Plans and Budgets (Stage 2)

The outcomes of the preparation stage are plans and budgets. Basically, a budget is simply a listing of physical and human resources with authorized expenditure levels which a manager uses in performing his job. It is a formal document which constrains or regulates an individual manager's behavior in such a way as to increase the predictability that subordinates will act in a particular way. There is a fundamental assumption that if resources are expended as allocated and plans carried out as developed, satisfactory performance will result.

Plans and Budgets as a Set of Goals Plans and budgets are goals for a manager. There is much empirical literature on the subject of goals that sheds some useful insights into how they affect performance.

Some of the most extensive work on the relationship between goals and performance has been reported by Locke (1968). He reasoned that if "goals regulate performance, then hard goals should produce high performance. . . ." The results of several studies he conducted, as well as other research he cites, leads him to conclude that "The results are unequivocal: The harder the goal, the higher the level of performance. . . ." However, and perhaps more relevant to the problem of plans and budgets, he found that when subjects had specific goals, they were more likely to do better than when they had general or nonspecific goals. Carroll and Tosi (1973) in their management-by-objectives research conclude that

. . . for all types of subordinates, the superior should make sure the goals established focus on significant and important areas of departmental need, are clearly stated, and the relative importance of goals pointed out.

The difficulty of goals, however [had different effects]. For example difficult goals were related to decreased effort in managers with low self-assurance and among less mature and experienced managers. However, difficult goals were associated with increased effort among managers with high self-assurance, managers who associated their performance with the reward system, and mature managers.

Turcotte (1974) conducted research comparing two state agencies which had different types of control systems, one having more specific goals than the other, and found that

Demanding objectives, quantitatively expressed and understood . . ., were essential foundations of the effectiveness of the high performing agency.

From these studies, it seems that the "motivating" effect of the budget derives primarily from the fact that it is a statement of explicit goals.

Budget Implementation (Stage 3)

Finally, the important question is how plans and budgets are used by the manager. He brings them to life, but the effects previously noted— anxiety in the preparation, the effects of goals, etc.—have taken place and are likely to form the perceptual base from which individual reactions will develop.

Both plans and budgets may be viewed as instruments which specify, at least partially, certain actions that a manager must take to achieve his goals. So the manager must use these instruments—make them work. Otherwise they will be useless.

The Budget and Performance Evaluation.   The seductive nature of plans and budgets is that they are "objective." Goals are quantified in a way that makes sense to the pragmatic manager—dollars and cents— and are likely to be a significant component in the evaluation of managerial performance. How budgets are used in performance evaluation is crucial, since a manager may—using them wrongly—reinforce behavior which can have negative effects on performance.

Learning theory, (chap. 3) postulates that when a behavior is reinforced (i.e., rewards or punishments are seen as its consequences), the probability that an individual will act similarly in later periods changes. Therefore, when a person is rewarded for, say, meeting a budget requirement, it can be predicted that he will later work to meet other budget requirements. It is important to ask the question, "What are we reinforcing when we use the budget as a basis for evaluation?" The answer is, of course, "It all depends."

Suppose the superior rewards or sanctions a subordinate based solely upon whether or not a budget requirement is met; for example, a subordinate who exceeds expenditures levels is not given a salary increase, while one who stays below budget is given a substantial one. *In this case, the reinforced behavior is achievement of a particular level of a measure.* It is possible that the methods used to achieve this goal may be organizationally suboptimal. For example, a manager may meet a budgeted maintenance expenditure by not having maintenance performed, or by having it done but arranging for billing in the next fiscal period. In either instance, what is intended may not be accomplished. When the superior's concern is with the budgeted level and it is used as described above, then those who have to live with the budget learn the ropes of manipulating outcomes with little regard for what is really intended as the purpose of the activity. This is because budgets, and most managerial controls, do not give any guidance on *how* to do something. Rather, they simply specify the approved level of resources to be used. Effectiveness depends both on the quantity of resources *and how they are used.*

To use plans and budgets effectively, then, a manager must go beyond them. He should, of course, communicate to his subordinates the intended level of achievement. But he must also monitor the way subordinates go about achieving that level. The manager may have to coach subordinates extensively about *how* to achieve goals. This means that performance evaluation must focus on both budget requirements *and* behavior so that, from a reinforcement point of view, the subordinate not only learns how much is expected, but how to do it.

Other Factors in Evaluation.   The utility of the budget as an evaluation device may be diluted by a number of other factors. First, the rewards for achievement of performance goals may not be seen as as valuable by the subordinate as by the superior. Second, the budget only contains one type of performance criterion, while overall performance may include more subjective facets. Third, the frequency of performance reviews is not great, generally once or twice a year. Such a schedule usually does not allow sufficient opportunities to link rewards strongly to performance measured against the budget. And, finally, some superiors simply may not regard the budget as a useful enough evaluative device to give it prominence in assessment.

In this chapter, we have treated planning and control, and budget development. Some effects of these processes on individuals have been discussed. It is, of course, another matter to implement decisions made in these processes so that they are carried out by the managerial staff of an organization. This question of implementation will be examined in the next chapter.

Discussion Questions

1. What is the relationship between planning and control?

2. Using the concepts of goals (environmental interest, system, and individual) write up goal definitions for some organization with which you are familiar.

3. Why is it important for line managers, rather than staff units to be extensively involved in planning?

4. Estimate the break-even point for Product Y. It sells for $10.00 per unit. Total costs for different sales levels are as follows:

Units	Total Costs
2,000	$40,000
4,000	50,000
6,000	60,000

5. Managers, we believe, can experience a great deal of concern and anxiety during planning and budgeting periods. Why does this happen? When it is said that "participative" management helps allay that anxiety, what does this mean? What in your own terms does "participative management" mean?

Chapter 11

In any organization, many decisions must be carried out by persons other than the decision makers, and there may be resistance to some of these decisions, a resistance which can take many forms—verbal protest, refusal to cooperate, work slowdowns. Resistance may be directed against decisions about work methods, assignments, organizational policy or structure, or salaries or benefits—in other words, changes which impinge upon the needs or personal objectives of organizational members. Or a change may increase insecurity when its effects are unknown, or because it is a threat to an organizational member's economic well-being, his status, or his social relationships, or because to comply would be an inconvenience, or simply because the change involves a conflict with employee attitudes or values. Thus any organizational decision must take into account not only the effectiveness of the alternative selected in reaching a goal or solving a problem, or its efficiency in the use of resources, but also whether or not it is acceptable to those who are to implement it.

Effective Decisions

In chapter 9 we introduced the notion by Maier (1963) that a decision can be evaluated in terms of the degree to which acceptability (A) is important as compared to the importance of quality (Q). The *quality* of a decision refers to the degree to which technical and rational factors govern in the selection of alternatives, while *acceptability* refers to the extent to which those who are ultimately going to carry out the decision are willing to implement in it a way which minimizes problems and maximizes implementation.

The Implementation of Decisions

An effective decision, according to Maier, takes both acceptance and quality into account as shown:

$$\text{Effective Decision} = \text{Quality} \times \text{Acceptance}$$

When either quality or acceptance is zero, (or not present if required), then a decision is a bad one. Quality is an objective characteristic which can very often be measured or assessed against some technical standard, but acceptance tends to be more of a subjective evaluation, more emotional and attitudinal.

Maier proposes three types of decisions using these dimensions. The first of these is Q/A, a decision that has *high quality but low acceptance requirements*. For these decisions, it is important that the alternative chosen is correct, since its quality has technical or economic significance for the organization. At the same time, the acceptability requirement is low, probably because the decision is not germane to the personal needs or objectives of the organizational members who are to carry it out. For example, the interest rate a bank chooses can have a significant effect on its economic situation, yet most of the bank's employees are indifferent to the choice.

A second type of decision, A/Q, is a decision in which *acceptability requirements are high but quality requirements are low*. Which of several qualified employees works on a Saturday overtime assignment is a decision of this type. Who works on Saturday is of great interest to the employees, but of little concern to management.

In an $A=Q$ decision, both the acceptability and quality requirements are high. An example of this type of decision would be the introduction of a new work procedure. It is important that the work procedure be acceptable since employees have a high degree of interest in it, and it is equally important that an efficient rather than an inefficient procedure be chosen.

How Quality / Acceptability Affects Decision Making

Obviously not all decisions made at higher levels create acceptance problems. Many fall within the "real" boundaries of the "psychological contract" (see chap. 8). Many actions taken by top management will be viewed as legitimate, and there will be little or no resistance, and often, as we have seen, the individual or group may be indifferent to a decision because it has little impact on personal needs and objectives. Many times, moreover, it is obvious to those who are to carry out a decision that very complex technical considerations beyond their competence enter the evaluation of alternatives. They will accept the advice of the "expert," or the person who "knows." When these conditions exist, the method for selecting alternatives should be the rational, systematic methods described in chapters 9, 10, 13, and 15.

It should be noted that rational decision strategies must often be used even where a decision—perhaps because it threatens an individual's or a group's security—has a high acceptance requirement. Such decisions may well meet resistance, and strategies must be employed to overcome or adjust to such resistance. For example, some industrial firms have overcome resistance to change in work procedures by providing economic guarantees to workers affected by the change. The employees, for instance, may be guaranteed their jobs or their incomes. This may be an effective way to obtain acceptability when the resistance is caused by perceived economic threat. In other cases, acceptance of alternative work procedures, policies, or other changes has been obtained by bargaining; that is, giving the employees something they want in exchange for acceptance of the change. This will be especially applicable when the employees are represented by a union. Other approaches for obtaining acceptance include making the changes tentative instead of final, consulting with employees in advance of making the change, or allowing those who will implement the change to participate in making it.

Participative strategies, decision making in which a person has an opportunity to influence the outcome of decisions, are appropriate when *acceptance* requirements are high. The effectiveness of participative strategies was dramatically illustrated in an early study by Coch and French (1948), which set out to discover the effects of different degrees of participation in the acceptance of technological changes which were needed to increase worker productivity. In the study, some employees were told by the firm's industrial engineers what the change in work methods was to be, a second group of employees elected a representative to discuss the proposed changes with the firm's representative, and a third group, the total participation group, met with the firm's representative and suggested changes themselves. Productivity fell in all three groups immediately after the changes were implemented, but fell significantly less in the total participation group than in the other two groups, and productivity 30 days after the changes was much higher in both participation groups than it was in the nonparticipation group. These results are consistent with a series of studies conducted by Kurt Lewin and his colleagues (1953) during World War II.

We will discuss such participative approaches, and the circumstances under which they should be used and how they are implemented, later in this chapter. We will also show how the implementation methods can be integrated in the system of administration called *management by objectives* (MBO), the system which is our next immediate topic.

Management by Objectives

In recent years, an approach known as management by objectives (MBO) has become popular as a means of implementing top management or company decisions. Under the MBO approach, an organization establishes goals and programs to attain these goals at the highest level of the organization and then carries out a process to help insure that lower levels of management understand, accept, and direct their efforts toward the accomplishment of these higher-level goals. Through the MBO process, general goals of the organization become internal system goals and eventually performance requirements for individuals.

MBO: A Definition

Under a management by objectives program, a superior and a subordinate attempt to reach a consensus of (1) what goals the subordinate will attempt to achieve in a given time period, (2) the plan or means by which the subordinate will attempt to accomplish the goals, and (3) the means by which goals progress will be measured and the dates for such measurements. After there is such agreement, the superior will periodically review performance. This may involve quarterly

performance reviews along with a final performance review at the end
of the year.

The heart of this process is *the objective* and *the action plan.*
Success depends on how well both the objective and the plan are
defined, communicated, and accepted. Objectives are goals (or ends);
action plans are the maps for reaching those objectives. Thus, MBO is
a process in which the individual members of an organization work
with one another to identify common goals and coordinate their
efforts in reaching them.

Objectives can be thought of as statements of purpose and direction.
They may be long-range or short-range. They may be general, to
provide direction for an entire organization, or they may be highly
specific, to provide detailed direction for an individual. MBO emphasizes the *what* and the *how* of the intended accomplishments.

It is important to take note of this fact that objectives may be
general, for a larger organization, or specific, for an individual,
because one purpose of MBO is to make it possible to derive specific
from general objectives, and to insure that objectives at all levels in
the organization are meaningfully located structurally and that they
are linked to each other. Sets of objectives for an organizational unit
determine its activities. A set of objectives for an individual determines his job description and can be thought of as a different way to
provide that job description. Once objectives are determined and
assumed by organizational units and by individuals, it is possible to
work out the means (performance) required for accomplishing the
objectives. (Objectives may or may not require change. The goal or
end-state may well be one of insuring that no change occurs—as, for
example, in maintaining the quality level of a product.)

MBO serves to document expectations in superior-subordinate relationships regarding what is to be done and the level of attainment for
the period covered, and accordingly carries such values as these: It
provides a base for developing and integrating plans and personal and
departmental activity. It serves as the basis for feedback and evaluation of subordinates' performance. It provides for coordination and
timing of individual and unit activities. It draws attention to the need
for control of key organizational functions. It provides a basis for
work-related rewards as opposed to personality-based systems. It
places an emphasis on change, improvement, and growth of the organization and the individual.

Under MBO the end result represents a condition or situation that is
desired, a purpose to be achieved. The concept of "end" is equated
with goal or objective. Objectives may be specific achievement levels,

such as product costs, sales volume, and so on, or they may be completed projects. For instance, the market research department may seek to complete a sales forecast by a particular date so that the production facilities can be properly coordinated with market demands. Objectives, or end states, are attained through the performance of some activity. These activities are the means to achieve the end.

The Cascading of Objectives

In chapter 10 we discussed environmental and internal subsystem goals. Environmental goals are synonymous with the basic purpose of an organization; they seek to meet the demands placed upon the organization for its product or service, delivered in a way which will satisfy the desires of the organization's clients. Internal system goals are the objectives which organizational subsystems must meet to accomplish environmental goals.

The responsibility for developing environmental goals is typically top management's—usually the chief executive's, in conjunction with the board of directors or a group of vice-presidents. Once these goals are developed, then internal subsystem goals (marketing, production, etc.) are stated, usually in the form of general plans. When these have been developed, they are communicated to the next-lower levels. This can be done by a series of cascading meetings between superiors and their subordinates and work groups, continuing from the top management level to the lowest point of supervision.

Initially, the corporate executive officer determines his objectives and general program. Then he meets with his immediate subordinates, including staff and operating executives in charge of major divisions. At this meeting he defines his objectives and plans for the group—a statement of what he believes to be the major activities and goal areas for the following year. The purpose of this meeting, for the subordinates, is informational. They are given the opportunity to increase their understanding of how the chief executive sees the direction, goals, and plans of the company. Negotiable and nonnegotiable areas and plans should also be discussed, because these will become operating constraints for lower-level managers. A nonnegotiable area is one in which the chief executive requires that a specific approach be taken. In these areas lower-level personnel have no discretionary power. For instance, the chief executive may insist that certain products not be produced, because he has been so directed by the board of directors. Negotiable areas represent activities and goals where the chief executive is willing to modify his positions.

At the first meeting, there is little emphasis on specific goals and objectives of the subordinates, but from the information received, each manager should be able to develop a plan of action, goals, and appropriate performance measures for each relevant organizational objective in his own unit or division. Then, in a private meeting with the chief executive officer he undertakes an assessment of his goals and what he will do to achieve them. When these goals and specific plans of action are agreed upon, specific goals and ways of achieving them exist for two levels of management.

Once a second-level executive knows what his objectives are, he schedules a meeting with his operating and staff personnel. At this meeting, he makes known to that group the goals and action plans that he has agreed to with his superior. This group meeting again is essentially an informational one, and subordinates are encouraged to ask questions and engage in discussion that will help them understand the kinds of commitments that have been made. The subordinate can then make a more accurate assessment of his discretionary areas, and those areas that are nonnegotiable, nondecision-making areas.

After this group meeting, each third-level executive individually prepares a set of action plans and objectives for himself and his unit and then meets individually with his superior. At this time the superior and the subordinate agree upon the goals, activities, and criteria for assessment of success.

When some consensus has been reached and the executive has his set of goals, he then schedules a meeting with his subordinates and the process continues as described. This cascading process proceeds to the lowest level of the organization at which it remains feasible. At each succeeding lower level, the range of individual discretion becomes less and less, of course. This may mean that for the lowest operating managerial level, the meetings are essentially communicational, with activities being specified and the subordinate being given a fairly well-developed set of operating measures and action plans that he must implement. The nature of the organizational beast is such that the lowest-level managers operate within tighter organizational constraints than managers at higher levels; the latter formulate the goals of the organization, and the former translate them into work.

Problems in Cascading Objectives

Some difficult problems must be resolved in this cascading process, or there will be a breakdown in MBO. The first is timing. For the cascading process to occur effectively, meetings between superiors and subordinates must be fairly tightly scheduled; otherwise, the goal setting process may extend over too long period of time. A specific, relatively limited period should be devoted to goal setting—perhaps the two-week period immediately following the final budget determination for the following fiscal year. If managers know that a particular time is scheduled for goal setting, they can schedule their own commitments appropriately.

Another problem in the cascading of objectives is the time involved in the determination of objectives and action plans. One general complaint voiced by managers is that MBO takes an inordinate amount of time. It is our contention that MBO is a way to be an effective manager, and managers who would use it effectively would adapt it into their regular work schedules, because MBO is part and parcel of the management process.

A third problem is the possibility of a break in the goal-setting chain. If, at any level, a manager fails to set goals, those at lower levels cannot effectively use MBO. This is perhaps the primary reason that goal setting should be done during a specific time period. Managers can then be held accountable for setting goals. One goal, in fact, that should be set for all managers by their superiors is the setting of goals for their subordinate groups. Their success in this area can be verified later in the evaluation of performance.

Scope and Type of Objectives

It would be difficult to develop objectives for a manager which would cover each and every area of his responsibility, for the structure of most jobs is too complex. Yet once objectives are set for a position, they should comprise the major description of the job, and their achievement in light of what is known about total job requirements should be assessed. Once objectives are set for a person, a basis exists for insuring that there is a "balance" of activities in his job; for example, that a worker is performing the normal duties, while at the same time growing and developing. Concurrently, the relative importance of objectives or failure to achieve them should be kept in mind. For example, a man who fails on a difficult creative objective should not be evaluated in the same way a man who fails to maintain a critical recurring operation. The former may have undertaken a high-risk project, at the suggestion of his boss, which would have had high payoffs. He may for example, have been attempting a revolutionary product design. The latter may simply be failing at meeting normal job requirements.

Performance Objectives

A performance objective is derived directly from the job assignment from the major areas of an individual's responsibility and activity. Included in these areas would be the maintenance of recurring or routine activities, the solving of problems, or the creation of innovative ideas, products, services. *Routine objectives* represent the normal requirements of the job, the kind of thing commonly found in a job description. Quantity requirements, the time one is supposed to come to work, normal deadlines for reports are all routine objectives. Other objectives, however, may take on special importance for a number of reasons—emergencies, change in priorities, or management decisions. These are called *special-project objectives*.

A special activity for one position may be routine for another. A special-project goal for a lower-level manager might be a routine goal for his superior. Developing a computer-based information system for personnel records might be a highly creative objective for the personnel department, yet would probably be considered a routine goal for a systems analysis group.

What an Objective Should Look Like

The first critical phase of objectives-setting is the statement which describes the end sought. This statement should be:

1. clear, concise and unambiguous;
2. accurate in terms of the true end-state or condition sought;
3. consistent with policies, procedures, and plans as they apply to the unit for which the objective is being set;
4. within the competence of the unit, or represent a reasonable developmental goal for it;
5. interesting, motivating, and/or challenging whenever possible.

Some examples of goal statements might be: "Increase sales 10 percent," "Reduce manufacturing costs by 5 percent," "Reduce customer complaints," "Increase sales by 5 percent by December 1," "Increase quality within a 5 percent increase in production control costs," "Develop understanding and implementation of computer techniques among subordinates."

Notice that most of these goal statements have at least two key components. First, each clearly suggests an area of activity in which accomplishment occurs. Second, four of the six clearly specify a level of achievement, the quantity or deadlines to be met. The desired level of achievement is the performance level.

The Action Plan

The "action plan" is the means by which an objective is attained. The action plan should summarize what is to be done. The action plan for a complex activity should be broken down into major subprograms and should represent the "best" alternative, of possibly many, which would achieve the goal level. The action plan provides an initial basis for a total action program for an individual or department. Action plans might be stated in the following manner:

1. *For a sales increase,* develop more penetration in a particular market area by increasing the number of calls to dealers there.
2. *For a reduction in manufacturing costs,* analyze the overtime activities and costs and schedule more work during regular hours.

Subordinates may base their own action plans on those developed by their manager, using his plan to guide their own roles in their unit's effort. Clear differentiation of means from ends allows lower-level use of the objectives process. Considering both means and ends permits comparing performance with some criteria and determining if events occurred which are presumed to lead to a desired outcome.

It is important to recognize the distinction between measuring an objective and determining if an event has occurred. If we are unable to measure or specify the goal level adequately, then we simply assume that the desired goal level has been achieved if a particular event or set of activities takes place. For example, while it is very difficult to measure whether or not a manager is developing the talents of subordinates, we can determine if he has provided them with development opportunities. If they have participated in seminars, attended meetings, or gone off to school, it can be assumed that the development activity is being properly conducted.

Some further benefits and opportunities provided by adequate attention to an action plan are these:

1. It aids in the search for better, more efficient methods of accomplishing the objective.
2. It provides an opportunity to test the feasibility of accomplishing the objective as stated.
3. It develops a basis to estimate time or cost required and deadline for accomplishment.
4. It examines the nature and degree of reliance on other people in the organization toward coordination and support needed.
5. It uncovers anticipated snags or barriers to accomplishment.
6. It determines resources (manpower, equipment, supplies, facilities) required to accomplish the objective.

7. It facilitates control if the performance is well-specified and agreed upon; reporting need only occur when problems arise in implementing. This is a form of planning ahead; when plans are sufficiently complete, only deviations from it need be communicated.
8. It identifies areas in which the superior can provide support and assistance.

Coordination Requirements

Success or failure in reaching an objective may depend upon the contribution and performance of other individuals or departments. Therefore, they must be considered. Some contingencies apply to all objectives, of course. For example, delays in the availability of resources, change in support or priorities from higher management, equipment failures, delayed information or approval, and the like, which are unplanned, should be taken into account when the assessment of objective accomplishment is made.

Other contingencies, specific to the objective, might be inadequate authority of the subordinate, lack of policy covering aspects of the objective, possible failure to gain cooperation from others, known delays in the system, and so on. Once these are uncovered, several actions are possible:

1. reexamination of the objective (e.g., alteration of a deadline) when and if the contingency occurs;
2. commitment of the superior to aid by overcoming or preventing the contingency;
3. revision of the performance required to accomplish the objective;
4. establishment of a new objective. If a contingency is serious enough, an objective aimed at overcoming the problem may be justified.

Constraints on Action Plans

Deadlines and budget constraints can and should be strictly specified in some cases, and not in others. A great deal depends on:

1. the importance of the objective;
2. the ability to determine the time or costs required in performance;
3. whether or not written plans or objectives of other people require coordinated completion dates;

4. the amount of time and money the subordinate will spend on the particular objective under discussion;
5. the predictability of problems or barriers to accomplishment.

Discussing these constraints furthers understanding between superiors and subordinates and establishes the constraint's use in evaluation. Expectations become known; realities can be tested. Deadlines and costs should be viewed as "negotiable." Deadlines especially should not be set simply to insure that action is initiated.

MBO and Managerial Control

An important managerial function, control, is accomplished through MBO. MBO requires that goals be set and that they be used for evaluation of performance and as a basis for providing feedback. This sets standards for improvement.

The importance of the development and use of sound criteria (objectives) for evaluation, appraisal, and feedback cannot be overemphasized. Sound criteria are essential if meaningful changes in behavior are to be achieved. "Hard" criteria must be used with extreme care. They are best viewed as ends or levels; they indicate nothing about attaining either. "Soft" criteria involve not a particular level of achievement, but determination that an event or condition has or has not occurred. Soft criteria are a vital and fundamental part of MBO. Without them, the approach cannot be well implemented.

To some managers, the development and communication of goals comes naturally. They are intuitively able to determine and specify appropriate measures, criteria, goals, and the most satisfactory methods for achieving them. They innately sense what must be observed and measured and can communicate this effectively to subordinates—and this is the behavior, of course, which management by objectives seeks to develop and reinforce.

Evaluating the Accomplishment of Objectives. Some goals lend themselves more easily than others to measurement—scrap rates, production costs, sales volume, and other "hard" measures. These measures pertain most to lower organizational levels and to areas such as production, marketing, or other major functional activities of the organization; they pertain least to most staff and specialist units. A distinction relevant to the measurement problem is the difference between routine and special project objectives.

Routine objectives are basic to the job, a core part of the job description. How should they be set and measured? The manager must tell the subordinate—early in the relationship—what the activities of the job are and what the desired level of performance is. Evaluation should not occur after a period of service unless there has been previous discussion of criteria.

At the same time that the criteria are being specified, acceptable tolerance limits should be developed. Assessment of routine objectives should be a major part of the objectives process, yet it should be of most concern *when performance falls outside levels;* thus minimum performance levels should be set for routine activities, and evaluation of routine goals should be by exception— that is, only when these standards are not met.

The ability to manage by exception demands good plans or clear standards from which exceptions can be specified in advance. Odiorne (1964) cites the following example:

> The paymaster, for example, may report that his routine duties cluster around getting the weekly payroll out every Friday. It is agreed that the measure of exception will be zero—in other words, the boss should expect no exceptions to the diligent performance of this routine duty. Thus, the failure any week to produce the payroll on Friday will be considered an exception that calls for explanation by the subordinate. If the cause were reasonably under his control or could have been averted by extra care or effort, the absence of the payroll will be considered a failure on the part of the subordinate.

Generally, routine job responsibilities or goals are expressed as job standards, or other "hard" performance measures. Although appraisal and evaluation essentially compare performance to the standard, this procedure may be relatively shortsighted and suboptimal. Recall that the manager should also evaluate the *manner* in which performance was carried out. For example, costs can often be reduced by foregoing certain expenditures, and a subordinate who realizes his performance is being quantitatively assessed may do this. But the expenditures foregone may be the very ones that enable a greater profit to be turned in the future—research and development expenses, for example—and thus the subordinate's "high" performance in the short run may have negative long-run effects. There can be substantial distortions of behavior when only quantitative criteria are used in measurement.

Problem-solving, special project, or creative objectives are more difficult to quantify than the essentially routine. If the ends are truly creative, determining an adequate performance level may necessarily rely on intuitive judgement. It is usually possible, however, to judge if an activity has been performed appropriately even though the ends, or the performance levels, are neither quantifiable nor measurable. Furthermore, constraints may be set on the activities. We can assess that they have occurred by some specific point in time or that a specific dollar amount has been expended. Thus, we are not only concerned with whether or not events have occurred, but also within some tolerance limit such as target dates, budget constraints, or a quality assessment by the manager. It becomes possible under these conditions to establish review points, thus giving attention to the outcomes of activities when they occur. Deliberations on these outcomes can serve to reevaluate both objectives and means. Thus changes are possible, and both flexibility and control are assured where they appear to be most needed—where predictions, plans, and standards cannot be specified or articulated in advance.

When and How to Use Participation

When acceptance is a critical component of a decision situation, it probably can best be achieved by involving the persons who will carry out the decision in the decision process. Obtaining acceptance through participation not only has the benefit of giving the participants a feeling of influence on the alternative chosen, but provides them with an understanding of the reasons for the change and what the change will require of them, which is important, since one of the chief reasons for resistance to change is the uncertainty associated with the potential effects of change.

Participation means that a person can influence—have something to say about—a decision that is beyond his formal authority range (the degree of discretion in his job). Participation is used for more than just gaining acceptance of a decision, however. For example, it is often necessary for subordinates to participate in the making of a decision because the decision maker needs their ideas or needs information that only they possess. Under these conditions, participative approaches also increase the quality of a decision.

Since MBO is intended to facilitate subordinate participation and involvement, the implicit nature of power and authority must be recognized. Unless they have the approval of their superior, lower-level managers cannot legitimately influence goal levels and action plans in areas in which they have no formal authority or discretion. Therefore, it is necessary to spell out areas in which subordinates have some latitude, so that they know what their decision limits are.

Otherwise they may unrealistically believe they can participate in
departmental and organizational decisions which are outside their
discretion area, that their superior will allow them more extensive
influence in a decision area than the superior actually will. When a
person expects to participate and then cannot, negative consequences
can occur.

One way to define discretion areas, or formal authority, is to determine whether or not an individual should influence the goal or action
plan. In a boundary-spanning activity affected by conditions outside
the organization, for example, the individual charged with performing
that activity may be the person in the best possible position to determine both the goals (or ends) and the most appropriate means to
achieve them, because external conditions may not be clearly known
to internal managers. For instance, marketing executives in constant
touch with the external environment are in a better position to determine possible sales penetration and programs than anyone else in the
organization. However, not having authority over goal levels should
not preclude involvement of a lower-level manager in goal setting.
Here the MBO process should focus on developing the best means for
goal attainment.

High levels of skill and technology required in a particular function
may make the specialist better able than a nontechnical person to
assess what can be done in a technical field. Thus, the specialist
should be involved in determining goal levels, as well as in carrying
out activities.

An important limitation on discretion, or formal authority, is organizational level. The lower the organizational level, the narrower the
zone of a manager's discretion. That is, managers at the lower levels
are responsible for fewer, more specific, and more measurable activities and can commit smaller quantities of resources than those at
higher levels.

Another factor which causes variation in the authority range for a
particular job is the changing competency levels of the incumbent. A
person learning a job may need a great deal of guidance from his
superior. As his skills increase, however, his superior may spend less
time with him since he can capably handle more activities and make
more decisions.

What about those decisions that fall outside the discretion limits? In
these, as we have seen, the subordinate's role may be that of contributing information and assistance, inputs to the decision-making
process of his superior, which the superior may choose to accept or
reject. But this type of activity must be differentiated from goal-setting

participation in which the individual has something to say about the final shape and form of the goals and activities.

Discretion boundaries are not rigid. While a particular decision may fall within the discretion range under normal circumstances, emergencies might develop which would result in the decision being made by the superior. These conditions cannot be foreseen, and consequently cannot be planned for.

Some Guides to Using Participative Methods

There are various degrees of participation possible. Subordinates may be allowed complete autonomy in making the decision, or the decision maker may consult with them and then make the decision himself. (See the discussion of leadership style in chap. 8.) Which of these alternative approaches is best in decision-making depends upon the situation and the type of decision to be made. Two approaches for deciding on the degree of participation required by the decision have been developed, one by Maier (1963), the second by Vroom and Yetton (1973), who extended Maier's approach.

Maier's Decision-Making Approach

As we have discussed, Maier classified decisions into one of three categories based on the decision's acceptance and quality requirements. For Q/A decisions—those where acceptance is of little importance and thus of little concern to the decision maker—the manager may make the decision, or it may be made by an expert in the field, and it is likely that the decision will be accepted with little or no problem. For A/Q decisions—those where acceptance requirements are high and quality requirements are low—the form of participation can of course vary, depending upon the type of decision that is involved. Extensive participation and subordinate influence is appropriate and should be allowed, since it does not matter to management which alternative the group chooses. In this situation the only criterion of effectiveness is to obtain a satisfactory decision for the group involved. One way to do this when the objectives to be achieved by a decision are specified is for the superior to give the "must" dimensions. (See the discussion of the Kepner-Tregoe heuristic in chap. 9.) The subordinates then can evaluate the "wants." In the case of the A = Q decision, however, it is important that the group choose an alternative which is high in both quality and acceptance. For the A = Q decision, Maier recommends that the decision maker play an active role in the decision-making process. This will help insure that a high-quality decision emerges.

For any problem in which a participation approach is used, Maier recommends that the leaders follow a set of principles derived from research on group problem solving. These same concepts also apply to participation with individuals. Maier has found that the *quality* of decisions is enhanced when:

1. A discussion leader participates in the discussion.
2. The discussion leader has been trained to lead a discussion group.
3. A "developmental" as opposed to "free" discussion mode is used. That is, the members do not simply discuss anything. Rather, they attempt to move from problem definition to cause to solution.
4. Effort is directed at overcoming surmountable obstacles, such as obtaining inputs from shy members.
5. All available facts are used.
6. Group members are prevented from progressing too rapidly toward a solution.
7. The "idea-getting" process is separated from the "idea-evaluation" process.
8. An emphasis is placed on the problems to be solved rather than the alternatives available.
9. The leader refrains from suggesting solutions himself.
10. Groups are required to work on a particular problem twice rather than once.

Maier's research also shows that the *acceptance* of decisions is enhanced when:

1. The individual has an opportunity to have his opinion reflected in the group decision itself.
2. The individual feels free to express his ideas about the issue.
3. The group leader does not dominate the discussion.
4. The group leader has been trained in group decision procedures.
5. An atmosphere of tolerance for the conflict of ideas exists.
6. The group makes a high-quality decision.
7. The group leader has positive feelings about the creativity of group members.

The Vroom-Yetton Model

There can be, as we have noted, several different levels, or degrees of subordinate involvement in decision-making. Vroom and Yetton

(1973), extending Maier's work, described different methods of decision making and devised an heuristic for deciding when and how
various decision strategies should be used. These range from making
the decision alone to allowing a group to make it, with the manager
serving as moderator of a group discussion. The alternative strategies
are described below. As the decision approach moves from *AI* toward
GII (*A* stands for autocratic; *C* for consultative; and *G* for group), the
amount of subordinate influence over the final decision increases.

AI   The manager makes the decision alone with currently available
     data.

AII Necessary information is obtained from subordinates, but the
     manager still decides alone. The role of the subordinates is input of
     data only. They have nothing to do with generating or evaluating
     alternatives.

CI   The manager discusses the problems with relevant subordinates
     individually. Then, without bringing them together, he makes a
     decision that may or may not reflect their input.

CII The manager shares the problem with subordinates in a group
     meeting, gathering ideas and suggestions. He then, alone, makes
     the decision which may, or may not, take the input of the group
     meeting into account.

GII Problems are shared with the group. The manager functions in the
     "participative" style described by Maier. His role is to provide
     information and help, facilitating the group's determination of
     their own solution, rather than his.

The Vroom-Yetton (V-Y) model takes into consideration a number
of factors which influence the degree of success in using a participative approach. (There is no *GI* in the V-Y model.) It is called a normative, or prescriptive, model because it describes how a decision
should be made. The appropriate method is contingent upon the
following properties of the situation in which the problem arises:

1. *Importance of the Quality of the Decision.* How important is it to
achieve a high-quality solution? If there is no quality requirement,
then any acceptable alternative will be satisfactory to management
and the decision becomes a relatively easy one to make and the group
can make the decision itself.

2. *Extent to which the Decision Maker Has the Information Necessary to Make Decisions.* Vroom and Yetton point out that there are

two kinds of information that may be necessary to make an effective decision. One type of information pertains to the preferences of subordinates about alternatives. The second type of information is whether or not there are rational grounds on which to judge the relative quality of alternatives.

When the leader is not aware of subordinates' preferences, he must obtain this information somehow, and participative approaches are one such means. If the leader has this information, however, and the problem is such that an individual decision is more likely to produce a better solution than that of a group, then clearly the situation calls for the manager to make the decision alone.

In what kinds of situation is a group likely to make a better decision than an individual? Research indicates that an individual can do as well as a group when either (1) the problem has a highly verifiable solution, or when (2) the solution requires thinking through complicated interrelated stages, keeping in mind conclusions reached at earlier times. This same research shows that a group is superior when the problem is complex, has several parts, and the group members possess diverse but relevant talents and skills. Insight and originality can then be more likely obtained from a group than from an individual (Kelley and Thibaut, 1969).

3. *Extent to Which Problem Is Structured.* As we noted in chapter 9, in structured problems, the alternatives or at least the means for generating them are known. In most organizations at least some use is made of standard procedures which give individuals all or most of the information necessary to take a previously planned action. In an ill-structured problem, on the other hand, the information may be widely dispersed through the organization, with a number of individuals each possessing a part. These individuals will probably have to be brought together to solve the problem or to make a joint decision.

4. *Extent to Which Subordinates' Acceptance Is Important.* Acceptance by subordinates is not critical where a decision will be implemented by someone outside the specific unit in which the decision is made or where it falls in the boundaries of the psychological contract. In the latter instance, carrying out the decision is a matter of simple compliance rather than a matter of the exercise of initiative, judgment, or creativity. The more commitment required from subordinates in the carrying out of a strategy, of course, the more important subordinate acceptance becomes.

5. *Prior Probability that an Autocratic Decision Will Be Accepted.* If a decision is viewed as the exercise of the legitimate authority of a manager, it will be accepted by subordinates without participation,

since it falls within the boundaries of the "psychological contract."'

6. *Extent to Which Subordinates Are Motivated to Attain Organiza-tional Goals.* Organizational members may have objectives in a partic-ular situation inconsistent with those of management. In such cases, participation in decision making in order to increase acceptance of a needed change may be more risky than in those situations where the goals of the two groups are the same. Thus, participative decision making could be expected to work best where there is mutual interest in the problem.

7. *Extent to Which Subordinates Are Likely to Disagree over Solu-tions.* Subordinates may disagree among themselves over prospective alternatives because of different gains or losses from an alternative or because of differences in values or other critical factors. The method used to reach a decision must facilitate resolution of the disagreement, and thus group involvement is necessary.

The Decision Factors and the Vroom-Yetton Model

All of these factors are presented in the form of questions in the Vroom-Yetton model in figure 11.1. The questions in that model are to be answered on a yes-no basis. The decision tree format establishes the sequence of the questions of concern to the decision maker in various situations. At the end of every path in the decision tree is one of 11 basic problem situations. Each of these situations gives the decision maker one or more alternative approaches for making the decision. According to Vroom and Yetton, the best method for making decisions can be determined with such an approach.

To illustrate, let us say that a manager wishes to change the work schedule so as to have at least one maintenance engineer on duty at all times between 9 A.M. and 9 P.M., six days a week, and that this represents a departure from previous work schedules. He has a number of alternative ways to make his decision. He starts with ques-tion A in figure 11.1, "Is there a quality requirement?" He decides that there is none since he will be satisfied with a wide variety of different work schedules so long as a maintenance engineer is on duty at all times between the hours of 9 A.M. and 9 P.M., six days a week. Because he answered No to question A, he must go to question D, "Is accept-ance of decision by subordinates critical to effective implementa-tion?" Suppose that in his opinion the answer to question D is Yes, since acceptance of the schedule is critical to its effective implementa-tion. (If he had answered question D No, the decision tree shows a type 1 problem situation, and any of the decision-making methods for

FIGURE 11.1 Decision-Process Flow Chart for Group Problems

A. Is there a quality requirement such that one solution is likely to be more rational than another?
B. Do I have sufficient information to make a high-quality decision?
C. Is the problem structured?
D. Is acceptance of decision by subordinates critical to effective implementation?
E. If I were to make the decision by myself, is it reasonably certain that it would be accepted by my subordinates?
F. Do subordinates share the organizational goals to be attained in solving this problem?
G. Is conflict among subordinates likely in preferred solutions? (This question is irrelevant to individual problems.)
H. Do subordinates have sufficient information to make a high-quality decision.

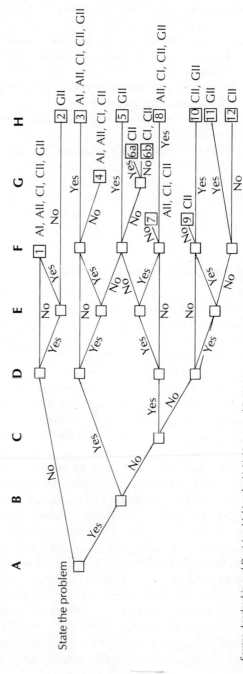

Source: *Leadership and Decision-Making*, by V. H. Vroom and P. W. Yetton (University of Pittsburgh Press, 1973). By permission of the authors and the publisher.

dealing with a group listed earlier—*AI, AII, CI, CII, GII*—could be used to deal with the problem.) Because he answers *Yes* to question *D*, he must next answer question *E*. Let us assume that he answers *No* to question *E*, "If I were to make the decision by myself, is it reasonably certain that it would be accepted by my subordinates?" A *No* answer to question *E*, according to the decision tree of figure 11.1, presents a type 2 problem situation. The recommended approach for making this type of decision is *GII*, which requires the decision maker to share the problem with the group and to agree to accept any alternative that the group supports. A *Yes* answer presents a type 1 problem situation, and any method can be used to deal with the problem.

In problem types where many alternative decision-making approaches exist, as is the case for problem types 1, 3, 4, and 8, the decision maker may want to use the alternative which requires the fewest number of man hours to make and to implement the decision— but here it should be remembered that although a manager may be able to make a decision more quickly alone, it may take more time in the long run to communicate that decision to subordinates and to achieve an understanding of what is required than would a participative decision.

Decision-making Behavior of Managers and the V-Y Model

A number of studies have been conducted by Vroom and Yetton to determine the extent to which managers use particular decision-making approaches, and the degree to which the V-Y normative model is descriptive of such strategies. In one study of 385 managers from more than 100 firms, it was found that these managers used all five of the decision-making approaches. The most frequently used styles appeared to be CI and CII, in which the manager shares problems with subordinates and then makes the decision himself. In studies of actual problems solved by more than 600 managers in many different organizations, it was found that most of the problems did not have a pressing time constraint and that most involved some degree of both quality and acceptance (Vroom and Yetton, 1973). Most managers felt that they lacked some of the information needed to make a satisfactory decision. To solve these problems, the managers used approaches CI, CII, and GII in about equal proportions. It was found that managers had a tendency to use participation more under circumstances where subordinates had necessary information, a quality decision was important, subordinates were trusted, and acceptance was considered important. There was also more participation when it was unlikely that subordinates would accept an autocratic decision. Several other studies have indicated that a continued use of participation is especially important in organizations in which individuals have become accustomed to it. In such instances, subordinates accept autocratic decisions far less readily than they do participative ones.

Vroom and Yetton (1973) also studied the decision behavior of eight different groups of managers from a variety of firms. They found that both the nature of the problem itself and the decision-making preferences of the managers influenced the degree to which participation was used. Situational factors, however, were much more important than individual preferences in determining the choice of decision-making approach. The research of Vroom and Yetton shows that middle and upper managers typically consult with their subordinates in decision making. Participation is not only used to obtain acceptance but also whenever subordinates have relevant information for the decision, when they are dealing with unstructured problems, when they need a high-quality decision, when the subordinates are not likely to accept autocratic decisions, and when the subordinates are trusted by the superior.

Dangers in the Participation Approach

Maier (1963) has suggested several reasons why managers may resist using the participative group decision approach to increase acceptance of decisions. First, the manager may fear that subordinates will reject the need for any change. Second, he may fear that subordinates will make a low-quality decision. Third, a manager may feel that subordinates may expect to participate in future decisions. Fourth, the supervisor may feel that respect for him will diminish, since as a supervisor his role is to lead, not follow. Fifth, many managers feel it is their responsibility to make the decisions and that subordinates do not wish to participate in the decision-making process. Many managers probably feel they do not have the ability to lead a group discussion and are uncomfortable in such a situation.

A few research studies support Maier's contentions. For example, one study seems to show that the participation approach will not be effective when the employees do not feel their actions are "legitimate" in the particular situation (French, Israel, and Aas, 1960); also when employees feel they do not have the necessary information or skills to contribute significantly to a decision-making discussion, they feel inferior and resent being placed in a situation they find uncomfortable

(Mulder and Wilke, 1970). In addition, those participating must be motivated to work on the problem; that is, it must be a problem they have an interest in solving.

Perhaps the most significant obstacle to the use of participation is "pseudo participation." Many managers theoretically acknowledge that decisions are more readily accepted when subordinates are "involved," so they bring together a group ostensibly to discuss a problem. After an airing of facts, there sometimes emerges a consensus among the group for an alternative unacceptable to the manager. He will then say, in effect, "Those are great ideas, but we have to do it another way." In reality, he expected the group to conclude for his alternative. Since they didn't, he overruled them. This tactic can only lead to problems for the manager. He will find it difficult to obtain much involvement later, since he will hardly be trusted.

Thus, there are certain prerequisites to making the participative approach work. These are that the problems suggested for discussion in the group should be appropriate in terms of their perceived legitimacy and with respect to the amount of interest the employees have in the problem. In addition, the manager should be trained in group discussion techniques, and he must match the amount and type of participation used to the expertise of the participants.

Values of Managing by Objectives

MBO is seen by many organizations to be the most objective way of evaluating managerial performance. It is also a practical method of introducing participative methods, and it is an aid in the planning process. But it is more than that. If a manager can "intuitively" function in an MBO style, there are other important advantages. These are outlined here.

Directs Activity Toward Organizational Goals. An organization exists in order to achieve certain goals, and individuals are hired because they can make a contribution toward the attainment of those goals. We cannot assume, however, that all work activity in an organization is directed toward organizational goals. MBO does not necessarily solve this problem, but if carried out properly it does provide a powerful stimulus for the integration of work activity with organizational objectives. Under MBO, managers must be able to relate their work activity to their specific performance objectives, which, in turn, are integrated with organizational goals.

Forces and Aids Planning.   The objectives approach forces all managers in the organization to plan, which benefits the organization, the units, and the individual managers. This may, in fact, be the most important benefit of MBO, since it forces managers to spend a significant amount of time on activities that will move the organization forward. Better planning has the following benefits:

1. It reduces the incidence of crash programs or emergency situations, which are usually the result of something's not having been done when it should have been.

2. Objectives are more likely to be clear, and this should lead to more rational work assignments. Improved planning also means fewer problems, less tension, and a more pleasant work environment.

3. Better utilization of scarce resources results from planning. Individuals, machines, or groups with special abilities but limited capacities can be allocated to the objectives that are most important or to which they can make the most significant contribution.

Provides Clear Standards for Control.   Intelligent decisions are based on clearly formulated standards and/or goals. (In any organization many different types of goals or standards are possible, be they qualitative or quantitative). With MBO, the average manager will have clear-cut objectives that he can use to control the activities and performances of his subordinates.

Improves Motivation Among Managers.   Specific goals mobilize and direct energy better than a more general directive to do one's best. Thus, the specific goals associated with MBO can serve as incentives, even though they may not be attached to any specific material rewards.

A superior can also improve the motivational level among his subordinates by setting (or allowing to be set) individual goals that are in line with their interests or perceived abilities. It is necessary, however, for the superior to know his subordinates well. He must have some awareness of each subordinate's personal goals, level of achievement needs, self-concept, including degree of self-esteem, interests, and expectancies concerning work assignments. This is obviously going to require time and effort and interest.

Provides Objective Appraisal Criteria.   In some firms, evaluation, which we will discuss more fully in chapters 12 and 14, is based on "trait" assessments. There are many limitations to the use of personality-trait ratings as an evaluation alternative. Under the objectives approach, however, recognition is given to the manager who gets things done, rather than to the manager who makes a good impression or who conforms to his superior's expectations as to how something should be done. Performance reviews should also be less threatening under MBO, since much of the mystery about what is expected is reduced, and the manager is more likely, of course, to identify positively with goals developed with his participation rather than with those imposed upon him. In addition, less defensiveness may be generated under MBO since the discussions are not person-centered. Maier reports research which shows that problem-centered discussions elicit less defensiveness than person-centered discussions (1963).

Facilitates Problem Recognition.   The frequent review sessions that should be part of the objectives approach will result in a better identification of problems. Problems, by definition, are barriers to goals. Increased superior-subordinate interaction to discuss goal progress should help to identify problems early. The presence of an experienced superior may result in the identification of problems of which the subordinate may not be aware.

Allows Use of Several Levels of Subordinate Influence.   In any job, there are several activity aspects. (We discussed this in chap. 5.) Some facets may be less important than others. Some may have a higher *quality* requirement than *acceptance;* others, just the reverse. When using an MBO approach, the manager has the opportunity to use *several* approaches in working with subordinates—to be flexible.

Management by Objectives—An Organization Philosophy

MBO is often suggested as a "program." Forms, procedures and other organizational devices are designed to make managers use it. While these are useful aids, MBO should actually become a normal managerial style without them; it should become as nearly as possible, intuitive. The degree of a subordinate's acceptance of MBO is related to his perception of its support and reinforcement from top management. The approach must be an intrinsic part of the job of managing. It must be related to other organizational processes and procedures, such as budgeting, it should be fundamentally incorporated into planning activities, and it should be one of the major inputs to the performance appraisal and evaluation process.

Participation and Organizational Types

Participative group decision approaches are more likely to be used in some organizations than in others and especially at certain levels in those organizations that use them. There is evidence from research that decision making becomes more participative at the higher levels of management (Heller and Yukl, 1969). This can be expected, since higher-level managers are often perceived to be more closely identified with the organization's goals, to be more worthy of trust because of higher competence, and to have the appropriate work values. They are more organizationalist in outlook. In addition, their decisions are more important and less structured, the necessary information for a decision is possessed by more people, and the implementation of decisions requires initiative and creativity from those executing the plan.

Organizations in different types of environments will differ with respect to the frequency with which participative decision-making approaches are used. Professionals and specialists can be expected to feel that they have a right to participate in the making of decisions and will be less accepting of autocratic decisions. Also, in dynamic organizations, problems become less structured, and the information relevant to solving the problem is dispersed among different specialists. On the other hand, organizations faced with environmental certainty will have more structured problems and more narrowly defined jobs with limited discretion than those faced with environmental uncertainty; this is likely to decrease the frequency with which participative and group decision-making approaches are used.

Environmental uncertainty has an important effect on the extent to which clear-cut goals can be set and communicated to the rest of the organization. In chapters 7 and 13 it is pointed out that the environmental goals of the bureaucratic organization are likely to be relatively stable over time. This will make it easier to break them down into goals for lower units. In dynamic organizations, where the environment is likely to change, goals are less well-fixed. So many factors will determine how to get effective implementation of decisions that a manager must not only have the technical expertise which enables him to make sound judgments, but he must also be skilled at analyzing the kind of problems faced, in order to get a decision implemented at the point where it will be carried out.

Discussion Questions

1. The chapter indicates that many decisions do not have acceptability requirements because they are not of concern to organizational members. List the decisions in a university that would have acceptability requirements for students but not for faculty. List the decisions that would have acceptability requirements for both students and faculty in an academic environment.

2. Some advocates of the use of participation argue that employees should be required to participate in the decision-making process even if they have no interest in doing so, as a means of improving their knowledge and competence. Do you agree? Why or why not?

3. Let us assume that the administration at your university decides to change the admission standards for entering a particular college on campus (assume the college of business administration). Should students participate in this decision? Why or why not? If so, to what degree should they participate? Why?

4. List the advantages and disadvantages of using the "management by objectives" (MBO) approach at your university for directing the activities of your faculty.

5. Under the Vroom and Yetton approach discussed in the chapter, it is recommended that when several decision-making alternatives are all equally feasible that the decision maker choose that which is least time consuming. This is typically the most autocratic method of making the decision. Do you agree with this strategy in these situations? Why or why not?

6. Write up a policy statement for an organization to use in guiding managers in situations involving the implementation of change.

7. Think of a recent situation in which you had a decision made which affected you? Was it a good decision? Was it an acceptance-dominated decision? Did you participate in making it?

8. The text makes it clear that in MBO there are some areas which are nonnegotiable between a superior and a subordinate. How does this fit with the concept of "participation"?

9. Why is goal-setting so important? Or is it? Under what condition?

10. "MBO moves the point at which subjectivity enters into evaluation to a different place. It does not make evaluation objective." Comment.

11. Compare the strategies for decision making proposed by Vroom-Yetton with the leadership styles studied by Lewin, Lippit, and White (chap. 8). Does this lead you to any conclusions about the advancement in the study of leadership in the last 25 years? What?

Part V

Managing Different Types of Organizations

Now we are going to reach out for the threads from parts II, III, and IV, pull them together, and weave them into managerial process contingency theory. In this part of the book we take the position that different types of organizations (part III) with different types of people (part II) require different management approaches (part IV). Basing our analysis on the theoretical formulations described in the preceding parts of this book, we now want to be as prescriptive as we can in proposing how managerial approaches can be adapted to the needs and character of each organizational type.

Many decisions in the stable organization are programmed, which means that once the necessary information about a problem has been gathered, there is a pre-established solution. Chapters 12 and 13 describe managerial strategies for the hierarchical organization.

Since the dynamic organization is continually faced with problems which—because they are nearly always new—require a great deal of problem exploration and the generation of alternative solutions, coordination of activities often takes the form of problem-solving meetings and informal contact among the organization's members. Suggested managerial strategies are discussed in chapters 14 and 15.

The problems of managing the mixed organization are considered in chapter 16. Basically it is one of integrating the two kinds of systems of managing already discussed—the hierarchical and the flexible. In the mixed organization, the resolution of conflict between departments is a vital skill which a manager must develop.

Chapter 12

In the last few chapters we have described the concepts underlying the basic functions of management. Leadership, decision-making, resource allocation, planning, and control are approaches and activities employed by all managers. Clearly, however, the effectiveness of a manager will turn on how well he understands the needs and values of the people carrying out the work in which his organization is engaged and on how well he selects and applies management techniques appropriate to the character of the organization, the context in which it operates, and the types of problems it faces.

In this chapter and the next we will consider how management techniques appropriate to hierarchical organizations are chosen and used. Chapter 13 will examine in greater detail some approaches to decision making which were introduced in chapter 9, with special attention to techniques for decision making under conditions of certainty and risk. In this chapter we will consider how a manager in a hierarchical organization can most effectively perform the following activities:

1. Selection	5. Leadership
2. Compensation	6. Managing Stress
3. Motivation	7. Managing Conflict
4. Performance Evaluation	

Selection of Personnel

Managerial control of performance is facilitated when there is a good match of people and jobs. To have a person working in a job which he likes and for which he has the competence and motivation saves a

Managing Human Resources in the Hierarchical Organization

supervisor much time. Having considered the different orientations of people to work organizations (chap. 3) and the different forms of organizations (chap. 7) we are in a position now to draw some general conclusions about what types of people we will find in hierarchical organizations, and on that basis we can suggest some effective selection techniques.

The Personnel Composition of Hierarchical Organizations.

In a hierarchical organization, the largest proportion of employees will be rank-and-file workers, for instance, blue collar in manufacturing and white collar in insurance companies or government agencies. Most of this rank-and-file group can best be characterized as having an external orientation, as described in chapter 3. They tend, in general, not to be highly ego-involved or committed to their work and/or the organization. They tend to seek psychological satisfactions outside the workplace. This is partly due to their narrow job definitions; that is, the tasks are not extremely challenging, and there is relatively little opportunity for advancement to positions where rewards are greater. One reason why promotion opportunities are limited is that there are fewer positions at the higher levels. Another is that often the requisites for advancement include advanced education, which the lower-level group is less likely to have. An external orientation should not be construed to mean an unwillingness to work, however. Rank-and-file workers will probably do what is expected of them, but they do not obtain their primary satisfaction from their work (Dubin, 1956; Kornhauser, 1965).

The middle management and specialist groups in the hierarchical organization will also contain a large number of externals—in this case, managers who have reached career plateaus and have little opportunity for advancement. They become increasingly committed to their life away from work rather than to the work or organization.

We can also expect, at the mid-levels to find a group of "organization-oriented" managers and specialists, people on the way up who seek the values and rewards of the system itself, high in achievement orientation and loyal to the organization. Figure 12.1 shows this general staffing configuration for the bureaucratic organization.

FIGURE 12.1   Orientations as a Function of Level in a Hierarchical Organization

---

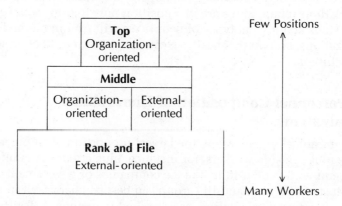

Selection Strategies in the Stable Organization

An organization will attempt to recruit individuals who appear to have the attitudinal orientation appropriate to itself. In a study of a bank, Argyris (1954) showed that it recruited individuals who were nonaggressive, and sought to avoid competition and conflict. He also showed that this type of personality was appropriate for all but the top-level jobs in the bank. There are other research studies which show that individuals tend to choose, and be selected by, organizations congruent with their personal goals (see for instance, Porter et al., 1975).

Selection involves choosing from a group of applicants those who appear most capable of performing the duties of a particular position.

Recruitment, of course, precedes selection. Recruitment is a positive process. It attempts to draw as many qualified applicants as possible to apply for the position. Selection is a negative process, inasmuch as an attempt is made to eliminate applicants from further consideration.

"Statistical" Selection for Hierarchical Organizations.   A number of different devices are used to aid a manager in reaching a good selection decision—the trial period, the application blank, references from former employers, the interview, and various psychological tests. These methods are typically used when the applicants are from outside the organization, but some of them are also used for internal selection, as in the case in which candidates are considered for promotion. If these tools are to be a part of the manager's kit, then they should have some utility; that is, they should work. For selection purposes, this means that tests, interviews and the like should have *validity*.

Personnel managers generally attempt to validate their selection methods, but the validation efforts have often been poorly designed. Today, however, the Equal Employment Opportunity Commission, established to enforce federal antidiscrimination laws requires that selection methods be validated. This means that the selection method must have predictive accuracy for a certain job. Thus, the selection requirements must be job-related. In a typical validation study the selection method, say a psychological test, is given to an entire group of applicants. Scores are calculated for each individual, but hiring is done *without reference to the score*. After the employees have been on the job for a sufficient period of time, their job performance is evaluated. The level of performance is then compared to scores on the selection method to see if there is a relationship between test scores and performance scores. An analysis of this sort might indicate, as it has in various selection studies, that applicants who are older, or who have lower education levels, or who have higher intelligence scores, or who have higher finger dexterity scores also tend to have higher job performance scores for particular jobs. Or the analysis might indicate that there is no consistent relationship between scores on a selection method and job performance scores.

When there is a relationship between scores on a selection method and job performance scores, a minimum score may be established which an applicant must attain before he is considered further. When there is no relationship between selection instrument scores and job performance, there is little value to using them. It may even be illegal to use the test if it discriminates against members of minority groups.

Such an approach to personnel selection is called the "statistical" approach. It is used to determine the validity of various selection techniques for different occupations. For example, thousands of studies have been conducted on the validity of psychological tests in selection. Currently, more than 60 million psychological tests are given each year. They measure such characteristics as intelligence, motivation, and personality traits, such as self-esteem or neuroticism, perceived to be important for the performance of certain tasks.

Statistical approach tests vary in the degree to which they are predictive of job success in different occupations. For example, Miner (1969) concludes that personality tests have been found to be useful in selecting salesmen, visual acuity and finger dexterity tests for selecting machine operators, and tests of achievement motivation to be more predictive of managerial success than for other occupational groups. Thus, which tests are most appropriate in a given organization will depend on the jobs to be performed and the occupational makeup of the organization.

The same is true of other selection instruments. The application blank has been more predictive of the behavior of office workers than of other groups (Dunnette, 1965). The research seems to show also that the interview and the reference check generally have low validity unless they are very carefully designed, structured, and utilized (Carlson et al., 1971).

The statistical approach is more useful in the hierarchical organization than in the dynamic organization, because it is more likely that an employee's output can be accurately measured and his performance scored if job duties are stable over time. In addition, there are likely to be a number of individuals performing the same job in the stable organization, and this situation permits comparison of large enough groups of "successful" to "unsuccessful" workers to determine whether or not any particular selection instrument distinguishes between "good" and "bad " performance on the job. Since it is probable that there will be more potential employees for most lower-level jobs, statistical decision strategies will simplify and increase selection effectiveness.

Selection of Managers.   The statistical approach may be of value for the selection of individuals for first-level managerial jobs so long as there is a large pool of applicants and there are a large enough number of positions to be filled.

Beyond the entry level, however, managerial jobs will be filled on the basis of two factors. One is the individual's performance in his present position, and the second is the fit between the perception that decision makers have of the individual's personal attributes and those they would like.

Most promotions in the stable organization will come from present staff; that is, there will be promotion from within. This is so for a number of reasons. First, because there are proportionately fewer managerial jobs, they will represent a valuable reward, or payoff. It would be demoralizing to lower-level personnel who have invested personal careers in a firm to see higher-level jobs, for which they believe they are in line, go to newcomers. Second, present managers will be known to the organization, both in terms of performance and of personality. However, though the stability of an organization and the relatively slow advancement it offers provide an opportunity to observe an individual's effectiveness over a substantial period of time and to make a reasonably good judgment about how well he does, such observation does not necessarily suggest how well he will do in future positions. Incumbents will have an opportunity to demonstrate competence, but only in a relatively narrow range of activity. Thus, decision makers cannot make good estimates of how well a person can perform in areas which have not been part of his job scope. In response to this problem, many organizations have in recent years developed "assessment centers" in which applicants from the organization for higher-level positions are given an opportunity to demonstrate their versatility and ability to perform effectively in a number of simulated managerial situations.

Much more than sheer competence of the persons being considered comes into play in making promotion decisions. Given that a number of candidates with acceptable levels of competence are available for a position, it is most likely that the one perceived as having values, attitudes, and behavior patterns congruent with those of top management will get the job. Generally, the bureaucratic organization's low or marginal performers will not be considered for advancement. However, they may, for reasons of their loyalty, be retained in the organization.

Favoring those with congruent values may not hamper organizational effectiveness if the persons selected for promotion are competent. Such selection tendencies do, however, naturally foster homogeneous attitudes among top management. In a bureaucratic organization this can become a problem if the environment changes substantially. Otherwise, it will mean a smooth-working managerial team.

Compensation

Employee compensation can be considered to include all valued
resources, such as hourly wage payments, salaries, and incentive pay,
given by an organization to employees as a return for their work.
Compensation also includes fringe benefits such as pensions, vaca-
tions, stock options, and employee discounts, all of which require
expenditures by the organization. Compensation programs in an
organization have several objectives: (1) maintaining competitive
labor costs, (2) attracting qualified human talent, (3) motivating
members to perform at a high level, (4) minimizing turnover by
maintenance of employee satisfaction, and (5) encouraging organizational members to improve their skills, abilities, and knowledge.
While the specifics of any compensation system, and the extent to
which it achieves these objectives, vary in different types of organizations, there are four general policy questions that any organization
must resolve and which apply in dynamic as well as bureaucratic
organizations. We discuss these below, and then describe more specifically how these decisions might be dealt with in a bureaucratic
organization.

The Wage-level Decision.   Wages must be high enough to attract and
retain personnel, but not so high that labor costs become excessive;
the organization can pay itself out of existence. Most organizations
use the wage survey to provide the information they need to determine the degree to which their wages and salaries conform to those
paid by their competitors for certain types of employees. A decision
may then be made to pay less, more, or the same as competitors.
Employee productivity, the proportion of total costs made up by labor
costs, and the ability to pass on wage-costs increases to the consumer
are among the important factors affecting the wage-level decision.

The Wage-structure Decision.   The second wage policy decision is to
determine how much each job is worth relative to the other jobs in the
organization. The wage structure is the system of wage relationships
among *jobs* (not people) in the organization. Since a sense of pay
equity is a determinant of the percieved fairness of compensation, this
is an important decision.

Several methods of job evaluation can be used to compare jobs in
terms of their complexity and difficulty in order to establish differences in base pay rates among them. A basic assumption in most
evaluation methods is that jobs which require more education, experience, judgment, and similar factors than others should be paid more.

The Individual Wage-differential Decision. The third wage decision has to do with choosing a method to establish compensation differentials among individuals on the same job. For motivational purposes it is important to insure that those who contribute more effort or perform at a higher level than others on a particular job should be paid more. Also, the organization may wish to pay a premium to those individuals on a particular job who have more potential, or who have been with the organization for a longer period of time. When there is a labor union, this area is the subject of negotiation between labor and management.

The Wage-method Decision. Employees may be paid based on time worked, such as by the hour or week. Or an organization may use incentive pay, which relates compensation to how much output is achieved. Some incentive plans are designed for a whole plant or organization.

Methods for Determination of Pay

Since the lower level makes up the largest number of people in the hierarchical organization, we will focus on methods of pay determination for that group in this chapter. Executive compensation will be discussed in chapter 14.

In the bureaucratic organization it is possible to use one of several well-developed job evaluation approaches, because the jobs tend to be well-defined, stable, and of relatively low complexity. All job-evaluation systems require specific job descriptions; thus jobs can be compared in terms of their content. Differences in pay are based on the level of the position in the hierarchy, and this presumably reflects the level of job difficulty.

The high proportion of lower-level employees in a bureaucratic organization means that it is much more likely to be unionized, leading to the use of uniform and consistent compensation procedures for the workforce. In addition, the stability of the external environment, its unionization, and the prospect of longer tenure of the workforce will mean there will be greater pressures for increased fringe benefits than in the dynamic organization, because workers may believe that they will be spending a long part of their life in the organization and need to have a secure future. Older workers are more concerned with fringe benefits, and unions generally seek security against the risks associated with loss of income due to retirement, unemployment, or health. Environmental stability makes it possible

for the hierarchical organization to obligate itself to provide future
benefits to its employees.

Job Evaluation.   Job evaluation is the determination of the relative
worth of a particular job as compared to other jobs, which offers a way
to approach the wage structure policy question. One method which
may be used in bureaucratic organizations is the *point system*. The
point system attempts to develop a score (based on points assigned to
different characteristics) for a job. After a general analysis of jobs in a
given class, a set of characteristics common to all jobs is derived.
These characteristics may be such things as amount of effort required,
the level of education required, the pleasantness of working conditions, the amount of responsibility attached to the job, and so forth.
Each of these factors can be weighted differently, depending upon
their differential importance. Because of the nature of jobs, it may be
possible to develop fairly accurate descriptions of different levels for a
factor. Education levels required in jobs, for instance, may be rated in
the following way:

Level of Education Required on the Job	Points Assigned
less than 5 years	1
5–12 years	3
12 or more years	5

If a job requires a high school education, then the job would receive
3 evaluation points. If education level was not critical for a job, that
job would get no points.

Once a list of factors common to jobs at a particular level has been
developed, the extent of the combined factors for each job is determined. The score each job receives is then obtained and compared to
others, which forms the basis for compensation level. For instance, a
clerk typist's job may have a score of 35 points while a clerical supervisor's score may be 57 points. This would mean the clerical supervisor would receive a higher base salary than the clerk typist.

After the jobs have been evaluated using this approach, they are
grouped together into "pay grades" on the basis of point similarity.
For example, all the jobs which have a point value ranging from, say,
50 to 75 points may make up a pay grade and may have an hourly rate
of pay ranging from $2.50 to $3.00. All jobs having point values from
75 to 100 may be authorized pay of $3.00 to $3.75 per hour. (Full
detail of compensation plans may be found in various books dealing
with personnel and compensation. See, for instance, Nash and Carroll,
1975).

There are other methods of evaluating jobs which a manager would find useful in a hierarchial organization. Though these are beyond the scope of our discussion, all of them measure essentially how much effort, skill, and related qualities are required to perform a job.

Individual Incentive-pay Systems.   Individual incentive-pay programs seek to tie pay levels to output. An employees pay is determined by how much he produces. High output means high wages, low output results in lower pay. Incentive pay systems are possible when the following conditions prevail:

1. the individual's work output can be easily identified and measured,
2. programmed tasks are performed repetitively, and
3. the individual controls the work pace.

Individual incentive-pay systems may be easier to use in a bureaucratic organization than in a dynamic organization, since there is more emphasis on the use of performance standards and standardized tasks —both prerequisities of this pay system. Nevertheless, the majority of employees in stable organizations are paid time wages at weekly or hourly rates, instead of incentive wages, because an incentive rate would require that the individual control his own work pace, that the individual's contribution to output be readily identifiable, and that the union and/or employees accept this approach to compensation. Usually all of these conditions cannot be met.

Motivation in Stable Organizations

Efforts to increase performance by stimulating individuals to do better and work harder are constrained in the hierarchical organization by the type of work (technological factors) and the characteristics of the people. As mentioned earlier, organizations tend to choose individuals who appear to have the motivations and personalities consistent with the job demands to be placed on them (Argyris, 1954), and individuals, in seeking jobs, look for organizations they think will fill their needs (Porter et al., 1975; Vroom, 1966; Super, 1972). Thus we would expect hierarchical organizations to attract individuals who prefer or can function well in a more highly structured work environment, with low needs for achievement and low scores on initiative measures. Some research has found that managers in the more stable and structured government organizations have higher security needs, and that this is especially true in the more structured units in the

organization (Paine, Carroll, and Leete, 1965). And we would expect
such individuals to perform best in that type of work environment.
There is research evidence from studies of several organizations to
support these assertions (Schneider, 1975). In a company studied by
the authors, managers scoring highest on needs for structure were
most satisfied with very well-defined goal assignments (Carroll and
Tosi, 1973).

This is not to say that an organizational member must be low in
achievement needs and high in need for structure in order to adapt
successfully to a stable organization. However, if a person has a low
tolerance, or need for, structure or unusually high achievement needs,
we would predict serious lack of congruence between the organization
and the individual.

Miner's role motivation theory (Miner, 1965) states that there are
certain common role requirements for managerial positions: (1) positive attitudes toward authority, (2) favorable disposition toward
engaging in competition with peers, (3) assertive behavior, (4) ability
to exercise power over subordinates without emotional difficulty, (5)
tendency to stand out from the group, in a position of high visibility,
and (6) ability to keep on top of routine job demands.

Research shows that individuals who behave and feel in these ways
tend to seek out managerial positions (Miner and Smith, 1969).
Research also shows that managers with these characteristics, attitudinal and behavioral, are more effective in more hierarchically structured managerial positions with more formalized procedures, relationships, and communication patterns (Miner et al., 1974). They are not
so effective in less rigid and less formal types of organizations.

For lower-level employees, we expect that they will be motivated by
extrinsic factors (those rewards controlled by others) such as pay,
status, and promotion opportunities, more than by intrinsic characteristics of the work itself (Kohn and Schooler, 1969).

Motivational Approaches in Hierarchical Organizations

In chapter 5, several different managerial motivation strategies, and
their advantages and disadvantages, were described, rated by different
occupational groups. Now let us consider their effectiveness in stable
organizations.

Fear or Threat.   The fear approach can be effective where organizational members have few alternative job opportunities. As the data
presented in figure 5.1 shows, more managers from the more struc-

tured organizations (such as bank managers and manufacturing foremen) rated the fear approach higher in effectiveness than did engineering managers. In this study, however, the preponderance of the managers from structured organizations did not rate this approach as effective, and probably rightly so. The use of the fear approach can induce anxiety and disrupt performance, and it loses whatever effectiveness it has when employees are protected by a strong union or tenure rights. It can contribute to aggressive tendencies which may result in acts of sabotage or other antiorganization or antisupervisory activity. We would expect greater use of the fear approach on lower-level employees in the stable organization. Coercion or bribery would be most commonly found where job incumbents had negative orientations and were alienated from their work.

Reciprocity.   The reciprocity approach involves the trading of privileges for high performance. Reciprocity will probably be most used where supervisors have little power to reward their subordinates differentially for performance and where intrinsic task motivation of the work group is low. The approach will work when the privileges that can be given are valued by the workers, but, as we have seen in chapter 5, it can cause problems. Some privileges come to be expected as normal practice. For example, one foreman allowed his men to wash up 10 minutes before quitting time so long as all the work was done. Since they finished early every day, they always left their work station early. When the foreman took away the privilege, requiring them to clean up *after* quitting time, a grievance was filed. The decision of the arbitrator was that the practice had become standard and could not be taken away from the employees.

Reinforcement Approach.   Under the reinforcement approach, rewards are given to individuals for superior performance. This is indeed an effective way to improve performance. Individuals who perceive a relationship between performing at a higher level and receiving rewards try to perform at the higher level. Perhaps the most basic problem is that there is a tendency to think of this method in terms of "material" rewards, such as increased pay, but if it is not possible to separate one employee's performance from that of another, then material inducements cannot be used. As we have seen, at lower levels in particular, pay systems will probably be designed to give all individuals in the same job class the same hourly rate, regardless of contribution.

Another important way to use this approach, however, is through social reinforcements. Managers can give recognition when a job is well done and withhold it when it isn't. A freight handling firm in which supervisors were taught to give subordinates positive social reinforcement reported striking improvements in quality of work (Organizational Dynamics, 1973). Kim (1974) reports that telephone company employees improved performance when provided with specific feedback and reinforcement about performance levels.

Ego-involvement. In the ego-involvement method, attempts are made to improve performance through obtaining personal commitments to reach higher levels. For the method to work, however, the individual must have confidence in his ability to attain a goal, and at the lower levels of the stable organization in particular, there may be many individuals who do not have such confidence in their own ability, or individuals may simply recognize that they are prevented from reaching higher goal levels because their success is too dependent on others who work on interrelated jobs, or because the capacity of the equipment is limiting.

Ego-involvement is also difficult to obtain because of the nature of certain kinds of work. It is unreasonable to expect a person to be deeply committed to a highly routine, repetitive, boring job.

Team Building. Team building seeks to foster the development of cohesive work groups committed to high performance. This would be appropriate when the task requires collective effort, and when good relationships among those doing the work can facilitate or hinder performance, but it is inappropriate if the tasks tend to be independent and coordinated by supervisors at higher levels. The team-building approach, where appropriate, can improve morale and increase the amount of helping behavior. There is, incidentally, the danger that strong groups (teams) which develop negative feelings about management could take concerted action against the organization.

Competition. Managers may attempt to motivate by inducing competition between individuals or groups. For competition to be effective, the following conditions must exist:

1. The work must be independent, not interdependent.
2. The rewards (material or social) must be attractive.
3. Participants must feel they have a chance to win.

It is not likely that all of these conditions can be met on an individual basis, but group competition, especially between departments, may work. Competition is especially effective when it arises from the members themselves, but it often is difficult for a manager to create a competitive environment, and managerial efforts to set up competition with small token rewards often do not work. In one plant, an effort was made to create a competition between departments for cost reduction. The winning groups would have a party, paid for by management. Most workers saw this as just another management effort to push them, and they did little to change their style of work.

Job Design.   Job design is perhaps the most fruitful way to improve performance in hierarchical organizations, especially if the capacity of equipment sets an upper limit on the level of performance. If, for example, an assembly line can produce 60 units per hour, then improved attitudes, morale, or whatever cannot raise output. If this is the case, performance may be increased by investing in new capital resources. The technological constraint cannot be overcome by any of the approaches already outlined, and the most important question is, "Do we have the technology capable of achieving the desired output?"

The job design approach can take two forms. One is restructuring the task activities to make more efficient groupings—the classic industrial engineering or scientific management approach. The second is changing the job scope, either increasing or decreasing a person's responsibility. Job enrichment is a method which falls into this second category. In job enrichment, the employee is given a bigger job to do and is allowed to manage the job, in the sense that he plans his work, executes the plan, measures how well he is doing, and takes corrective action as necessary. Research has shown that such job enrichment programs can improve performance, especially in terms of the quality of performance (Ford, 1973).

Possibilities for improvement in motivation through job enrichment are of course most likely to be found when the tasks are programmed and repetitive, a condition which is frustrating to individuals with needs for achievement and self-control. Simple, routine, and repetitive jobs, however, are not likely to attract or retain many people concerned about achievement and the assumption of higher levels of responsibility, unless they see some opportunities for advancement, and some research indicates that a significant proportion of the operative employees in the hierarchical organization may prefer more narrowly defined jobs (Hulin and Blood, 1968). Moreover, increasing discretion at lower levels of the organization may run contrary to the climate, atmosphere, or culture of the hierarchical organization. If such a counter-climate exists, job enrichment efforts are unlikely to have any beneficial effects unless a broader program of organization development is undertaken. Organization development approaches are discussed more extensively in chapter 18.

Motivation Strategies in Practice.   Our analysis here is intended to suggest the relative values of a number of approaches which can, of course, be used singly or in combination at various points in the organization. However, working toward improved performance by motivating both managers and workers requires a constant, consistent effort. Item 12.1 describes motivational efforts at General Motors. The reader should note how broadly based the approach is, but he should bear in mind that these approaches are used throughout the company. The task of the individual manager is to find the approach or combination of approaches that has the highest probability of success in his circumstances.

Performance Evaluation

In order to make decisions about such fundamental matters as salary increases and promotion, it is necessary that some judgment be made of how well a person has done his job. The process of making such a judgment is *performance evaluation.*In this section, we are going to present some general concepts of performance evaluation applicable to any type of organization. These will be relevant to the management of personnel in bueaucratic, mixed, or flexible organizations. Then, in the remainder of this section, we will suggest how performance appraisal can most effectively be done in the hierarchical, bureaucratic organization.

Periodically most organizations formally evaluate the performance of members. They do so for a variety of purposes. First, evaluation aids in allocating merit pay increases, because there is a general belief that exceptional performance should be rewarded when possible, and that some portion of the amount allocated for pay increases should be based on merit. While union contracts and salary ranges may make this hard to achieve for lower-level jobs, it is usually less difficult for higher managerial positions.

Formal rating systems also provide information on the training needs of organizational members, and by locating skills and abilities in the organization, they are useful for making transfer and promotion decisions.

In addition, performance evaluation serves a feedback function.

When an employee does his job well, and is told so by his boss, he receives positive reinforcement, while negative feedback about poor performance may help "extinguish" the undesirable work habits. Of course, this reinforcement function of evaluation occurs only if the person knows how he has been rated. Identification of the basis of a rating is of course an important value of MBO (chap. 11). In any case, discussion of ratings, and especially providing coaching in areas of deficiency, helps to identify job-related problems and is an important part of every manager's role. Performance ratings are also often needed to serve as a criterion, or the measure of performance, in selection studies, especially if there is no way of measuring employee output directly.

ITEM 12.1 Motivation

General Motors Strives to Motivate Its Workers

Grey-haired Thomas A. Murphy, newly appointed chairman of General Motors Corp. (GM), takes a practical and realistic approach to improving employee motivation.

• • • •

As the world's largest industrial company, GM treats new ideas in labour relations and work restructuring with a questioning and guarded enthusiasm. "Our top management has taken a clear decision in favour of experimenting with new ways of managing people," declares Stephen H. Fuller, vice-president of personnel administration and development.

• • • •

Although the lead comes from top management, the nature and location of experiments are decided not at corporate level, nor even national level in the 29 countries where GM now manufactures, but by the individual plants. Plant managers are encouraged to initiate whatever experiments they feel most suit the circumstances of their operation. "We have no standard formula or reci-

pe," says Fuller. "Each situation is unique."

The company's serious involvement in what the 59-year-old Murphy calls "people experiments" was highlighted by Fuller's appointment four-and-a-half years ago from an academic career.

• • • •

The company keeps a close eye on the progress of the experiments with regular meetings at executive level. For example, Morris says: "Every three to four months the executive vice-president responsible for the US car and truck body assembly divisions gets together with the general managers of his divisions, accompanied by their personnel directors and their OD specialists. At these meetings each division reports on what new people experiments they have launched as well as the progress of projects underway."

In addition, last year the company established a liaison committee with the United Automobile Workers, the largest union with which it has to deal in the US. This "quality of work life" committee, which consists of Morris and Fuller on one side and two senior union officials on the other, invites the managers of individual plants to talk about the progress of their projects. "We don't have any rigid format or pattern for these meetings, nor any rules or regulations on what the committee can do," says Morris. The quality of work life doesn't dictate to local plants how they should go about their projects. But it does encourage plants to take up new ideas.

· · · ·

To stress that the committee isn't applying pressure to local management, Fuller and Morris do not keep comparative records of how active plants are initiating experiments. It might not be fair to do so, indicates Morris. "After all, the plants that have had the best industrial climate may be doing less dramatic experiments than those who have problems," he says.

Fuller is adamant that the company is concerned to do more than just make jobs easier or more interesting. He declares: "Companies have been enriching jobs in this way for years. Other things are just as important, including giving workers the opportunity to contribute to the solution of problems found in their own work relationships with superiors, and the way in which their ideas are heard and acted upon. So are structural changes which reduce the number of levels in the organization, getting people closer to top managers."

Nevertheless, a number of experiments the company has carried out have been basically changes in the organization of work. For example, several plants have adopted pilot schemes to build some parts of vehicles in teams instead of on assembly lines.

Even so, Creason admits that some people in the group didn't like the new procedures. This is a point that all the GM executives are keen to hammer home. Group experiments may suit some people, but not all. Fuller cites several instances in US plants.

"The GM assembly division has built Chevrolet vans for many years, and this has become a fairly simplified product," he notes. "They took four men and women to a separate building and tried to educate them to build a van. They had the assistance of an engineer who worked with them to get them started. Building a van on the assembly line takes eight man hours per man. At first these people were taking 13 to 14 man hours. But eventually they got to the point where they could build the van in a little less than one and half hours per man. Finally we put that van assembly job in Detroit with another team alongside the ordinary moving assembly line."

Some people on the team soon decided they preferred working on the assembly line and the department had to juggle its personnel until it had a group that liked team work. Adds Fuller: "We intended to put the team building approach through the whole plant. But when we surveyed the workers, they just didn't want it."

This general apathy on the part of the employees led to the abandonment of a much publicized team experiment at GM's truck and coach division, according to Morris. In 1973 a number of workers were organized into groups of six to assemble the vehicle bodies and groups of three to assemble chassis, of mobile homes.

"We learned a lot from that," he admits. "For one thing we learned that if you are going to try the team concept of assembly, you had better try with something you know how to build, not a brand new product. We also found that the people, by and large, did not like the idea at all.

"In a typical assembly operation, the man has a fairly simple job assignment. He doesn't have a multiplicity of things to do. He can develop a style, a method and a rhythm which permit him to do the job in his own way and at his own pace.

"In a group system the individual has

a lot of things to do. The whole psychology of the job has been changed for him. He has a much greater responsibility than before and he finds it quite frustrating because instead of three elements to his operation he now has 20 or 30. When he gets to number 13 or 14 he starts to think: 'Oh my God did I do number seven?' The people told us they didn't like this extra responsibility."

While it would be unfair to say that GM regards team building experiments as a palliative towards industrial unrest, it is clear that the company sees only a limited future for them, if only on practical grounds. Explains Fuller: "In the Detroit team building experiment producing Chevrolet vans, the men performed about eight jobs an hour. On an assembly line there are 40 to 70 jobs an hour. Our Lordstown plant has run at 110 jobs an hour. You just couldn't build a plant big enough to handle that volume of production on a team basis."

One of the biggest problems is supplying materials and parts. A car may contain upwards of 15,000 parts. "How," asks Morris, "could you possibly store that many parts where they would be accessible to five or ten men?

"You can experiment with a group if it is a very simple vehicle and if the production volume is very low."

Adds the voluble and expansive Murphy: "I don't ever forsee the end of the assembly line. We may see different approaches to sub-assembly, to break down the job so that it can be done more effectively. But our experience in the plant is this: the greatest difficulty we have with our employees is not because the job is repetitive so much as the fact we have to change the job, which we frequently have to do because of product development or new investment."

Murphy and his colleagues show much more enthusiasm for projects which do not involve massive changes in the physical layout of the plant. Creason, for example, speaks glowingly

of the US assembly division's programme of "planned leadership." The programme, which has now spread to other GM plants as far away as Sao Paulo, Brazil, is aimed at releasing the foreman from many of his routine tasks. It also involves training all the workers to take over other jobs when necessary.

• • • •

At the Oldsmobile division in Detroit the employees themselves were asked to try to determine the cause of absenteeism. Some of the managers were dubious about involving the shop floor, says Fuller. But they agreed to let the scheme go ahead. The personnel staff first interviewed foremen and their bosses, the general foremen. Then they met with a number of employees who had particularly bad absenteeism records.

These interviews, which turned up some 70 contributory causes, were followed by interviews with a random sample of 200 newly hired workers. Several foremen attended courses in group problem solving, then got together with a number of workers to form a task force to tackle the question at shop-floor level.

Direct improvements occurred as a result of the interviews and discussions. They included a programme to ease new workers' orientation into the plants and some experiments in modifying less attractive jobs. The company claims the workers became enthusiastic at their involvement and that unofficial absenteeism fell in the plants by over 8%. In the rest of the division it rose by 25% over the same period. Turnover also fell by 38% in one plant and 25% in another, compared with a fall of only 14% in the rest of the division.

Giving employees the chance to discuss and influence decisions that affect their working conditions is becoming more and more common in GM, claims Murphy. However, he doesn't much like the idea of workers on the corporate board. "We have worker representation on the board of our German company. I think it may be right for Germany. But I'm not sure that it would be right for the US or other countries," he declares.

One of the most successful projects in worker involvement is at the Indiana plant of Delco Electronics, a division where employees participate in setting goals for their area. The goals involve, for example, absenteeism, quality levels and wastage. Each group of employees meets with its supervisor whenever a problem arises that affects its operation. The foremen have had training in group discussion techniques. So too have a number of long-serving workers who are appointed discussion leaders.

• • • •

The Adam Opel plant in West Germany took the opportunity to give a small group of workers similar control over their own workplace when it introduced job rotation to the cushion department. Many of the workers in this department were old or handicapped. The two shifts of seven people handled three operations: cutting and sewing, assembly and frame-making.

The management decided to make the cushion department workers responsible for their own production and quality control, as well as planning work schedules and ordering parts. The workers have also taken over some minor repair work to their machines.

The two foremen and their superintendent attended a short course in motivation theory, delegation and effective communications, before rearranging the workshop. They taught the employees to handle all three operations.

Ten weeks after the experiment started, the workers all declare they preferred the new work system and the foremen had overcome their initial scepticism. "Production and quality have been at least maintained," says Creason.—David Clutterbuck

International Management, 1975

Who Rates?   Performance evaluation may be done by one's superior, groups of managers at higher levels, subordinates, and peers. It has also been done by rating "experts" from the personnel department. For certain purposes, self-ratings have recently become popular. In self-rating, the individual assesses his own performance over a past period of time.

There are pros and cons for each of these methods. Subordinates may be most qualified to rate supervisory style, peers the competence of professionals, and supervisors the job performance of rank-and-file workers. If evaluation is intended to promote behavior change, there may be more acceptance of the need for change if self-ratings are used. In some organizations, a rating expert from the personnel department is used in order to achieve consistency in the ratings and to prevent favoritism and bias. The expert interviews the individual, his superior, and other organizational members who know the person well in order to arrive at an assessment.

Methods of Rating.   There are a variety of rating methods. The
graphic rating scale is the most popular and one of the earliest
approaches developed. With a graphic rating method, the person is
evaluated on the basis of a number of job-related and/or personal
characteristics such as quality of work, quantity of work, reliability,
cooperativeness, and so on. Typically, beside each evaluation factor is
a five-point scale representing different degrees of the factor (such as
"excellent," "good," "fair," "needs improvement," and "bad"). The
rater simply checks the word or phrase which he believes best applies
to the individual being rated.

With the *critical incidents* method, the supervisor keeps a record of
the positive and/or negative behaviors of each subordinate over a
period of time, such as six months or a year. The behavioral incidents
over the period provide the evidence for a high or low rating. They
also provide the basis for a discussion with the employee of his
performance during the period, and give specific cases to document
the rating.

Under the *work standards* approach, performance standards are
established for the tasks an employee performs. These standards may
be established from a systematic analysis of the task (such as motion
study) or on the basis of a past performance. The individual's performance is then evaluated against these standards. This approach was
emphasized by the early scientific management writers, as we
discussed in chapter 2.

Under *management by objectives,* the superior and subordinate
jointly establish performance objectives for the subordinate for a
particular time period, such as a year. The subordinate's performance
then is evaluated against these objectives at the end of the time
period. An attempt is made to identify the cause of any performance
failures, and coaching by the superior can be based on dealing with
these problems.

The *assessment center,* used to assess future potential, is a method
in which individuals are brought together to work on different types
of assignments while under continuous scrutiny by a group of
observers. Many of the center's exercises and assignments involve
simulations of real-life situations the employee might face if promoted
to a higher-level position, and performance in the assessment center
setting is evaluated and rated. Research indicates that assessment
center ratings correlate with later job performance, suggesting that this
may be a useful method of identifying potential managers.

No matter what the rating system, the final ratings should be as
accurate as possible, since they are often used as the basis for pay

increase or promotion decisions. To maintain morale and performance, it is critical that the best candidates be promoted.

To be acceptable the rating system must of course also be seen as valid and fair to the ratee; if it is not, the individual will not be motivated to change his behavior, and negative feelings may be generated against the supervisor and, perhaps, the organization.

Performance Evaluation in the Hierarchical Organization

Certain evaluation methods are especially applicable in hierarchical organizations and different approaches may be used for different purposes. Some rating systems emphasize the rating of performance only, and these may be most appropriate when using the ratings for purposes of allocating merit pay, for motivation, or when the ratings are used as criteria in research studies for organizational purposes. Other evaluation techniques attempt to identify strengths and weaknesses in terms of abilities and personality traits. These approaches are most useful when using the ratings as an inventory of talent for promotion or transfer.

Evaluating Worker Performance.   The work-standards approach is widely used where jobs are repetitive, because, first, there is general acceptance of the idea that an individual can be held responsible for his own actions or performance, and second, because the programmed and repetitive tasks characteristic of the stable organization make it relatively easy to establish performance standards.

Evaluating Managers and Professionals.   MBO, which also emphasizes performance, can be used as the evaluation yardstick for managers and professionals in the stable organization, since this approach works well under conditions of organization stability. However, there are problems in evaluating performance with MBO. Managers may incorrectly emphasize results, to the exclusion of the means by which goals are achieved, because there are likely to be output measures which are presented as "acceptable" standards. Excessive emphasis on objective performance standards in the stable organization can lead to dysfunctional behavior. For example, Blau (1955), in a study of a state employment agency, found that interviewers evaluated on the basis of the number of applicants processed paid little attention to successfully placing the applicants and in fact avoided those applicants who required more of their time and effort.

There are many other examples of how the establishment of "objective" performance standards against which individuals or groups were to be evaluated resulted in deliberate distortion of performance records, omission of information that would reflect adversely on performance, and the generation of false statistics.

Used correctly, MBO can be an effective device, however. If the manager both sets goals with subordinates, and develops with them acceptable means of achieving those goals, it can be determined both whether or not a goal was achieved and whether or not an action plan was carried out. The supervisor can focus on problems resulting from performance, rather than on personality deficiencies, and there should be less defensiveness than with the more traditional type of rating system. A systematic comparison of the MBO performance appraisal approach with that of an existing rating system at General Electric a number of years ago found that much better results were achieved with the MBO approach (Meyer, Kay, and French, 1965).

Participation by the subordinate in setting goals in MBO has been argued pro and con. In some cases it is necessary. In others it may not be, since both task requirements and technology are known in the stable organization to both the superior and his specialized staff. However, participation in setting work goals and objectives may still be desirable for purposes of achieving higher motivation and worker commitment. As we have seen in our studies of participative decision making some studies show that when a person participates, he is more committed to the decision (Maier, 1963). If participation clarifies goals, that is good, since it is goal clarity that is related to better performance (Locke, 1968; Carroll and Tosi, 1973).

Who Conducts the Evaluation? In the stable organization, the superior is in a position to make judgments about performance. He typically knows the task objectives and the best approach for achieving them. He is usually in frequent contact with the person being rated. The existence of objective performance data makes rating easier than in a more dynamic organization, and there is probably less of a need for the services of a staff rating expert. However, with a single rater the possibility of bias and favoritism is higher; a staff rating expert might prove useful in the stable organization to keep the superior "honest" in his ratings. On balance, however, it seems that the most preferable case is to have the supervisor himself conduct the rating and provide feedback so that an opportunity is provided to improve supervisory-subordinate relationships and to bring job-related problems to the attention of both the rater and ratee.

Leader Behavior in Hierarchical Organizations

As indicated in chapter 8, leadership is an influence process—one which affects both how one might react to his job and how well he might do it. Of course, as we have already noted, other factors, such as technological factors and group pressures, affect performance and attitude. And, as we have noted in chapter 8 also, some of the leader's behavior is affected by the group he supervises. When performance is low, a manager may exert more production pressure. When it is high, the supervisor may be more considerate (Lowin and Craig, 1968).

Task characteristics also are determinants of the most effective managerial behavior. For example, Morse and Lorsch (1970) studied two stable firms in the container industry, one successful and the other less successful, and found that different degrees of participation, or subordinate influence over decisions, were valued in the respective firms. In both firms, the tasks are programmed, and the work is mechanized and repetitive. The investigators found that the effective container manufacturer was characteristized by centralized management decision making and a basically authoritarian climate. Worker morale was apparently good. The less successful company was characterized by decentralized decision making and a more participative climate. Morale was lower than in the more authoritarian, more effective plant.

Results such as this suggest that in attempting to determine what a manager should do, we must take into account the characteristics of the situation. Fiedler's (1967) approach to leadership has this capability, and we use a variant of his model for our discussion. The concepts we will discuss in the section which follows are also applicable to the leadership problem in dynamic organizations, which we will consider in chapter 14.

Factors Affecting Leadership Effectiveness

Our approach takes into account leader behavior, characteristics of the situation, and the relationship between a leader and the group. There are two leader behavior factors (initiating structure and consideration), two situational characteristics (leader position power and task structure), and one group factor (work climate).

Leader Behavior.   Much research, cited in chapter 8, shows that leaders differ in their behavior patterns as perceived by those whom they lead, or supervise. Two behavioral patterns which seem to be very consistently found in the study of leaders are *initiating structure* and *consideration*.

1. Initiating Structure. This refers to behaviors of a leader directed at accomplishing tasks. It includes the assigning of tasks to individuals, letting group members know what is expected of them, and asking the group members to follow standard procedures. It involves planning and organizing the work. It is a task-oriented activity and similar to Fiedler's concept of low LPC (see chap. 8).

2. Consideration. This refers to the establishment of socioemotional relationships between the leader and the group members. Supervisors high in consideration create a climate of psychological support, warmth, and helpfulness. Such supervisors show concern and trust for others. This dimension of leader behavior is like the high-LPC leader described by Fiedler.

All managers exhibit both these behaviors to some degree, but some tend to emphasize one more than the other. Figure 12.2 illustrates the different emphases that may be possible. One manager may be high on consideration and another high on initiating structure.

FIGURE 12.2 Different Emphases on Initiating Structure and Consideration

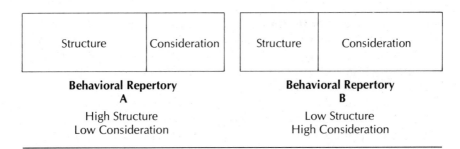

| Structure | Consideration | Structure | Consideration |

**Behavioral Repertory
A**

High Structure
Low Consideration

**Behavioral Repertory
B**

Low Structure
High Consideration

---

3. Position Power. In the leadership discussion in chapter 8, it was pointed out that influence is based on several different power bases. Position power, an important factor in Fiedler's theory, is *formal authority*, the organizationally designated discretion to decide who gets what.

4. Task Structure. Task structure, according to Fiedler, refers to the extent to which jobs are well-defined or ill-defined. Job requirements may be fairly well spelled out and relatively constant over time (as would be the case in hierarchical organizations) or they may not have clear requirements, as would be the case in a flexible organization.

5. Work Climate. Fiedler theorized that an important determinant of leader effectiveness is the relationship between the group members and the leader. When there is trust and confidence, the leader can be more *directive*. Otherwise, he should, according to Fiedler, demonstrate a stronger *consideration* orientation.

The work climate is the ambience that exists within the work group. It is the degree of trust that subordinates have in the leader, the level of group cohesiveness, the general satisfactoriness of leader and group relationships and the congruence between individual and organizational needs and values. There are two types of work climates that effect the appropriate leadership style, *relaxed* and *tense*.

Relaxed climates are those in which there is high satisfaction with work and with the superior. Individual values and attitudes of members do not conflict with those of the manager or the organization. In general, there is a great deal of mutual trust and respect, and good relations exist between the leader and the members of his organization.

In tense climates organization members have little trust in the leader's competence and fairness. Basically, there is disagreement between the leader and subordinates about the appropriate way to solve problems. Individual values are different from those that would make for a more smoothly running unit.

Managerial Behavior in Bureaucratic Organizations   The primary factor which differentiates the managerial position in the hierarchical organization from that in a dynamic one is the level of task structure. The production subsystem is likely to be repetitive, with jobs broken down into relatively narrow tasks, and organization structures will be fairly well fixed, with clear lines of authority, responsibility and job definition. Since goals are relatively stable, the work assignments will be fairly constant over time. There will be a fairly heavy investment in fixed, specialized resources capable of producing only a limited number of products.

If this is so, then the two factors which are determinants of how a leader should act to produce effective results are (1) his position power and (2) the work climate. Figure 12.3 shows the relationship between these two dimensions and leader behavior. This model is consistent with that of Fiedler (1967) and also that of House (1971). When the work climate is relaxed, and the leader is liked by his group, he can use his position to define the jobs more clearly, let his subordinates know what he expects, and give them guidance as to how to do it. House says that consideration will not have a positive effect on performance and satisfaction when the task is satisfying; therefore it seems that initiating structure would be the style to emphasize, as shown in figure 12.4. But House cautions against excessive use of initiating structure behavior, for if it becomes extreme, it will be viewed as too much pressure, and produce negative results. In essence, this means that if the pressure is too severe, it may cause the work climate to change from relaxed to tense, inducing poor results.

In a tense climate, consideration behavior should be emphasized, as shown in figure 12.5. High levels of initiating structure behavior will make an already unpleasant situation more intolerable. So the leader must take action to improve the attitudes of the group toward him and the situation.

FIGURE 12.3 Leader Behavior in Bureaucratic Organizations

High Task Structure

Climate	Position Power	
	Strong	Weak
Relaxed	Initiating Structure	Initiating Structure
Tense	Consideration	Consideration

FIGURE 12.4 Leader Behavior Reportoire
under Conditions of High Task Structure,
Relaxed Climate, and High or Low Position Power

Initiating Structure	Consideration

FIGURE 12.5 Leader Behavior Repertoire
under Conditions of High Task Structure,
a Tense Climate, and High or Low Position Power

Initiating Structure	Consideration

Why Position Power May Be Unimportant. Position power is organizationally based. It falls to whomever is in a particular job assignment. When position power is high, it means the boss can hire or fire, give salary increases and recommend and promote. When it is low, he cannot do these things.

In the bureaucratic organization, however, the use of position power, whether high or low, may be somewhat limited by other factors. If, as we have said in chapter 7, there are well-established control systems which use relatively objective or measurable output criteria, such as costs, number of units produced, and so forth, then a leader with high position power may be able to take action autonomously when performance falls below a particular level. But it is relatively difficult to justify a disciplinary action unless performance deficiencies can be adequately demonstrated.

Additionally, it is likely that if the work of subordinates is interdependent, as would be the case with long-linked technology, it may be extremely difficult for a supervisor to fix the responsibility for poor performance on a particular individual, making the use of sanctions difficult.

When position power of a superior is low, it is still possible that lower-level personnel may be subject to sanctions, because they may be imposed from elsewhere in the firm. An example of this would be the use of a disciplinary layoff for absenteeism. This discipline may be imposed by the personnel department, not the direct supervisor.

How a Manager Can Improve Performance

According to the model shown in figure 12.3, the performance of a work unit will be high when there is some congruence between climate, leader behavior, position power, and the level of task structure. In a hierarchical organization the task structure is fixed and well-defined by the work system; therefore top management has at least four possible strategies to consider in the event of poor performance.

1. Improve Technological System.   This strategy is basically one of job design or change. Suppose we find, in an assembly-line operation, that a relaxed climate is present. There are generally good relationships existing between the leader and his group. An analysis of the leader's behavior shows that his style is predominantly one of initiating structure, as shown in figure 12.3. Or, suppose that in the same type of job setting, we find a considerate leader in a tense climate. If, in either of these instances, poor performance occurs, it may be that the technological system needs to be redesigned. Improvements in efficiency may be made through methods study. Perhaps the jobs should be enriched, made more challenging. Or, perhaps they should be more narrowly defined. It may be that old equipment should be replaced.

Clearly the suggested alternative to improve the results of the organizational unit calls for working in the technological system, not trying to change leader behavior from initiating structure to consideration, or vice versa. When technological limitations are the cause of poor performance, trying to change how a manager behaves may only serve to aggravate the problem, since the upper limit of performance is the technological capacity.

2. Change Emphasis of Manager's Behavior. When the technology is adequate, performance deficiencies could be a result of the incongruency of the manager's style. If, for instance, the relationships that exist within the group are good (a relaxed climate) but the leader's behavior pattern is dominated by consideration, then he should attempt to move toward a style dominated by initiating structure. This can be done by employing a greater number of systemic factors available in an organization, such as budgets, procedures, and control mechanisms. The leader can increase initiating structure by planning more extensively, by making more decisions, letting others know precisely where they stand on particular problems, or by being in general more businesslike.

Being higher on initiating structure should not be confused with being more authoritarian, or autocratic. These terms imply extreme rigidity in holding to a position once taken, being unwilling to accept counterarguments when they make sense, or in general displaying an arrogant disregard for others. When we suggest that more initiating structure should be used, we mean that the manager should use the tools provided by the organization to facilitate his operations.

Neither is it suggested that the manager show no considerate dimension in his behavior. Certainly concern for others is an important human quality, and a highly regarded one. The manager simply changes the emphasis of what he does to provide greater guidance.

When the manager finds himself in a tense environment, where relationships are not so good, and the predominant style he exhibits is one of high initiating structure, he should move toward a more considerate stance, from the pattern shown in figure 12.4 to the one shown in figure 12.5. In the tense work climate the increased pressures associated with initiating structure may lead to lower performance or outright sabotage. Increased consideration will offset dissatisfactions that may arise from the work situation (House, 1971).

3. Change the Climate. Changing the climate as a strategy to obtain congruence between leader style and the situation may not be a practical alternative for the manager. It is only over time that a particular climate can develop, and it might take years, for instance, for a group of subordinates to develop a highly trusting, relaxed climate. Distrust, lack of cohesiveness, and negative attitudes could be a result of a long history of broken commitments, poor organizational practice, and bad management.

The manager who is high in initiating structure in a tense environment may attempt to shift it to the more supportive, relaxed climate. This may be done by exposing group members to awareness training, group discussion, and other group development processes. He can begin to operate in a more trustful, honest fashion, supporting the members in problems with other organizational units, seeking more benefits and resources for his group, and generally working to restore trust. But again, this is likely to be a longer-term approach to improving performance than if he elected to try a change in leadership style.

4. Change the Leader.   Suppose that an individual manager exemplifies either a predominant structure style or considerate style. If the climate is difficult to change, either because values of the work group are strongly entrenched and resistant to change efforts or because the climate is relaxed and there is a general unwillingness to induce a tense climate because it is less desirable to top management, then the most effective strategy is to remove the leader and replace him with one whose style is congruent with the situation.

Managing Organization Stress in the Bureaucratic Organization

Pressures and stresses in organizations frequently derive from the demands or expectations of others at different positions in the organization. For instance, a production unit supervisor may wish to have his foremen give workers a three-day disciplinary layoff for absences, while the personnel department expects the foremen to use such extreme discipline only for drastic infractions of company policy. The foremen are being asked to take two contradictory actions, and may, as a consequence, find themselves in role conflict. Other stress occurs when a person is uncertain of exactly what his job is or how his performance is to be evaluated. This is role ambiguity. Role conflict and role ambiguity singly or combined can cause severe problems for individuals.

Stress is perhaps always present to some degree in the work situation, and perhaps it has some value in stimulation and incentive to overcome problems, but excessive stress obviously can have dysfunctional, disruptive, and even dangerous consequences to both the organization and the individual.

Role Conflict. Among the dysfunctional consequences of role conflict are these: (1) intensified internal conflicts for the individual, (2) increased job tensions, (3) reduced job satisfaction, and (4) lessened trust in superiors and the organization. (Kahn et al., 1964).

Hamner and Tosi (1974), after reviewing some of the research on role conflict, concluded that its effects are not the same for all levels in an organization. Because lower-level managers and employees in hierarchical organizations are accustomed to clear authority relationships, they find it difficult to cope with role conflict. Role conflict may not be such a problem for top managers, because individuals at this level are likely to have been selected for their ability to deal with such pressures. We would expect, in bureaucratic organizations, to find the following forms of role conflict.

1. *Intrasender Role Conflict.* Intrasender role conflicts are inconsistent expectations from a single person. A manager, for instance, may expect his subordinates to increase production but does not give them added resources. Often managers resort to this kind of demand when there are cost-cutting drives, or other programs to increase efficiency, and extraordinary demands are being made of the manager.

2. *Intersender Role Conflict.* Intersender role conflict occurs when two different individuals place incompatible demands upon a person. For example, the quality-control manager of a plant expects the forman to reject more units of the product, while the production manager wants increased quantity and therefore fewer rejections.

3. *Interperson Role Conflict.* Interperson role conflict is a condition where organizational demands are in conflict with one's values. This is not likely to be a serious problem in the stable organization, since it tends to be staffed by organizationally-oriented types with value systems consistent with that of the organization.

Ways to Minimize Role Conflict

In order to reduce role conflict to an acceptable level, conflicting demands must somehow be reconciled or eliminated. Here are some ways which may be used by the manager to do this:

Eliminate Authority Overlaps.   An authority overlap occurs when two superiors have the formally designated right to dictate subordinate actions in the same area. In our example above, the production manager has the right to set production quotas, but the quality-control manager has the right to reject an unsuitable product. One way to eliminate such an overlap of authority would be to require the quality control manager to obtain the concurrence of the production manager on quality-control versus production problems, and vice versa; in other words, the conflicting managers reconcile their points of view before the problem reaches the foreman.

Clarify Authority Relationships.   Often a person experiences role conflict because he is not sure who has authority, and he responds to another who is in a higher position but outside his chain of command simply because of the other's status. By increasing the person's awareness of those to whom he should, or must, respond, some conflict may be reduced.

Insure that Superiors Maintain the Integrity of the Hierarchy.   This solution of course is related to clarifying authority relationships. The "territorial" imperative here for a manager should be not to allow intrusion by other managers outside the chain of command, unless appropriate. Whether or not an intrusion is appropriate is organizationally defined, as might be the case in the instance of the production supervisor and the quality-control manager.

Role Ambiguity

Role ambiguity is defined as uncertainty about what the individual is to do (task ambiguity), or uncertainty about how one is evaluated by others (social-emotional ambiguity). Role ambiguity has been found to be related to: (1) increased tension, (2) dissatisfaction with work, (3) reduced self-confidence, and (4) poorer relations with others (Kahn et al., 1964).

  After reviewing the research on role ambiguity, Hamner and Tosi (1974) suggest that it is most likely to be troublesome for higher organization levels than for the lower-level ranks, since top management jobs tend for the most part to be less structured. In a bureaucratic organization of course, there is likely to be less task ambiguity even at higher levels than is normally found in comparable jobs in dynamic organizations. The pressing problem is likely to be ambiguity deriving from uncertainty about performance evaluation.

Social-emotional Ambiguity. Social-emotional ambiguity may be a problem in the stable organization because, even though there are fairly well-defined measures for assessment of effectiveness, it is also likely that many rewards are allocated on the basis of background characteristics, personality, appearance, or general congruence of the employee's values with the organization's. Carroll (1966), for instance, has shown how appearance has affected success of an applicant in an interview regardless of his qualifications. In the stable organization there is often uncertainty about what one must do, or simply what one must be, to succeed in advancing. This is especially frustrating for the organizationalist, who seeks satisfaction from the organization. The presence of social ambiguity means that the signals about how to be "successful" are unclear. Organizationalists find this disconcerting.

Strategies to Reduce Role Ambiguity

To deal with role ambiguity, it is necessary to take two related steps:

1. *Define behavioral and output requirements.* Installing a management by objectives program is one approach for clarifying performance expectations, because the superior and the subordinate together determine the means of accomplishing the desired end result.

2. *Reward the achievement.* When the individual has been successful, the organizational reward system must be used to recognize it. Managers will thus communicate to subordinates what to do and what is important not only with words, but also through action. This will keep the level of role ambiguity low.

Managing Conflict in the Bureaucratic Organization

Often different parts of an organization have very different ideas about how things should be done—how the budget should be allocated, who should be appointed executive officer, what the objectives should be, how the goals should be accomplished, and so on. When there is lack of consensus, and different groups or departments attempt to have their points of view accepted over others, there is organization conflict.

Conflict causes difficulty because quite often managers don't know how to resolve it well, it is socially undersirable, and often it creates internal tension that makes it difficult to work. On the other hand, conflict can be valuable if it results in problem solutions that are valuable.

Sources of Conflict

Disagreement in any area that is important to individuals and groups can cause conflict to develop. There are some problems, however, that tend to be pervasive in bureaucratic organizations. These are:

Resource Allocation Decisions. Budgets are a frequent source of problems. The quantity of money, people, and resources available affects the ease with which a task can be accomplished. When resources are tight, managers must work harder to get the results that were more easily obtained with a larger budget. In order to make their jobs easier, increased resources are generally sought by supervisors of all organizational units.

Budgets can also be indicative of status in an organization. The larger a unit's budget, the more prestigious the unit. When a manager faces a budget cut relatively greater than others, or if his budget is reduced while another's is increased, these threats to status will be resisted.

The potential for conflict also exists when there is dependence by more than one unit on scarce resources. In bureaucratic organizations, resource allocation decisions may be made unilaterally, without lower-level participation. The budgeting unit, over time, will have developed "conversion factors" which can be used for allocation decisions. For example, it may have been determined from past experience that it takes one man hour to produce ten units. If the budgeting unit has a projected level of production, it can arrive at an allocated labor cost. It tells the manager of a department that he has, for example, a $150,000 labor budget, and he has no say in the matter. When this kind of environment exists, it induces distrust and anxiety. Yet the nature of budget preparation in bureaucratic organizations often fosters such feelings, and they lead to conflict.

Status Differences. The primary form of status differentiation in the bureaucratic organization is between organizational levels. There will be relatively sharp differences in privileges associated with the top management, middle management, lower management, and working levels. Workers may eat in cafeterias, lower and middle managers in large dining rooms, and top management may eat in the "executive dining room." Organizational conflict, however, is most likely to result from the distinction between management and operating levels. Since operating jobs are narrowly defined, with low skill and educational requirements, workers are easily replaced, and this, of course, is the principal basis of unionism, which provides an institutionalized system for resolving differences between management and the operating personnel.

Conflict between management levels will not be as overt as that between union-managment, because, once a person has moved into a management position, he usually modifies his attitudes to be consistent with the environment—to be those of management. Lieberman (1956), for example, found that when workers were promoted to foremen their attitudes shifted toward those of management.

There will, however, be some latent conflict between managerial ranks. Lower managers will feel that the status symbols, pay, and other benefits are not equitably distributed; that top management, receives a disproportionate share of the rewards. Whether their belief is well founded or not, there is no mechanism for reducing the inequity, especially since middle-level managers do not organize into unions (although there is a growing tendency for mid-level professionals, such as engineers, to do so).

This latent conflict in the management hierarchy of bureaucratic organizations exists partly because the environment is unchanging. Top management has long tenure as well as control of important information and resources. They will insure that they have adequate resources for their purposes *before* decisions are made about resource allocation for lower levels. There *is* inequity, it will be long-lasting, and this is a source of conflict.

Different Perceptions.   Dearborn and Simon (1958) have shown that different managers evaluating the same problem define the cause in a fashion consistent with their work assignments. The relatively stable organization structure of the bureaucratic organization will affect perceptions. When the firm is organized functionally (e.g., with departmental groupings based on the type of work: production division, marketing division, accounting division, and so forth), managers in each of these units will see problems and solutions in terms of their functional specialty. When departmentation is geographic (e.g., a western division, southern division, and so forth), the primary frame of reference will be geographic.

Another perceptual difference of importance flows from the union-management relationship. Managers and unions see one another as an adversary, and taking an adversarial position with another group can often be detrimental to the constructive resolution of conflict.

The Balance of Power

When groups are in conflict, it is often because one group has greater power than another; conflict seeks to bring about a change in this power relationship.

What factors affect the balance of power in a stable organization? Certainly economic factors and dependence are primary aspects of the union-management relationship. When economic conditions are favorable to a firm (high sales and profits along with high employment), the union is in the better position to assert its demands. If unemployment is high, the firm is in the stronger bargaining position.

Hierarchical status differences between management levels are maintained because of the nature of resource allocation decision processes in stable organizations. Resources are allocated from the top of the hierarchy down, and at each level how much is passed on to lower levels is usually a relatively unilateral decision. Managers are likely to hoard resources, maintaining discretionary funds where possible, which means that lower levels of management must constantly go to the higher levels to obtain additional resources. Since the organization is relatively stable, there are few external pressures to change this resource allocation process, and this leads to concentrations of power and to conflict.

Managers at higher levels also have a great degree of control over information that lower levels need. This information not only has to do with work activities, but also with important personal considerations (e.g., how one is evaluated and the likelihood of promotion). Information can be power, and like economic resources, may be hoarded at higher levels.

Power will be distributed among divisions and departments as a function of:

1. the unit's possession of important information;
2. the making of recommendations that are likely to be accepted;
3. the importance of the unit's function.

The Power of Information.   A person must understand his job before he can do it. He must know how decisions are made before he can influence them. He must know what criteria are used in making decisions before he can work to achieve them. In some organizations, budgeting units are extremely influential because they are the central point into which information from different units flows. This information is reshaped into budget proposals. It would be useful for a manager to have information about the budgetary allotments of other units in order to present his own case in the most favorable way. Because they hope to obtain such information, some managers will respond to demands from the budgeting unit that go far beyond its scope of formally defined authority.

The Power of Recommendation.   Certain individuals and departments develop, over time, the capacity to influence other's decisions. For example, the president of a major publishing firm relied heavily on advice from a trusted colleague who started the business with him but who, for personal reasons, never achieved high position. This confidante was at least four organization levels below the president, but when major decisions were under consideration, his advice was sought and usually heeded. This led many managers at all levels to seek the confidante's assistance in gaining the president's ear.

Personnel departments often have similar influence, especially in large, dispersed organizations. When the manager of the branch plant in Racine needs a production supervisor, he may turn to the personnel department for a list of potential candidates. Those who aspire to success in the firm know that the personnel department can be of great help to them. In many firms, personnel files are closely guarded to prevent individuals from learning how their performance is evaluated and what potentially they can expect in the way of promotions. This form of secrecy is not uncommon. When questioned about the reason for not telling an employee about what has been planned for him, a personnel executive said,

It can cause more headaches than it's worth. Suppose we think someone is capable of taking over the Birmingham plant in a year and it looks like the plant manager will be moved to make room. If the economy changes, or any number of things happen to freeze the present plant manager in his position, we can't promote the person. He'll be disappointed, frustrated, and may leave because he feels we haven't kept our promise, even though we never really made one.

The Importance of the Units' Function.   The balance of power between the production and boundary-spanning systems is an important relationship. Most organizations will find themselves in a situation in which one function is more critical than another, and the unit performing the critical function will generally have the most power. How can this happen in a stable environment, as we have defined it? Suppose that a firm has a captive market; suppose it is the primary producer of product A, and can sell all it can produce. So long as such demand exists, the production function will be the most powerful in the firm, especially if there are manufacturing problems which might limit output if not effectively overcome. The production function is the controlling factor, and thus the most powerful. In another firm, production problems may be minimal, while the chief problem will be to keep sales constant or growing. In such a firm, marketing will be the dominant unit.

Since the dominant unit will be more influential, it may receive proportionally larger budget allocations, and it may have access to important information. This advantaged position may cause those in other units to be more aggressive in their dealings with it, breeding discontent and coordination problems which hinder effective cooperation.

Resolution of Conflict in Stable Organizations

As we have suggested, conflict resolution should, generally, lead to improved performance. Assael (1969) notes that conflict will be beneficial if, when it is resolved, the following conditions exist:

1. critical review of past actions;
2. more frequent communications between disputants, and the establishment of outlets to express grievances;
3. more equitable distribution of system resources;
4. standardization of modes of conflict;
5. creation of balance of power within the system.

There are two kinds of mechanisms which facilitate conflict resolutions: (1) the improvement of the formal conflict resolution system, and (2) the nonstructural solution.

Formal Mechanisms

One of the main functions of organization structure is to resolve differences that arise among members. (The purpose of a labor relations department, for example, is to facilitate union-management relations.) Therefore, by definition, hierarchy can be used to resolve conflict. Managers can resolve conflicts among members by acting as an intermediary in discussion, by making the decision themselves, or by referring both parties to another location in the organization where the decision can be made.

Use of Formal Departments.   Union-management conflict is often handled by a department of the firm which has been formally assigned those functions. Other staff functions can also serve to reduce conflict. Accounting department personnel, for example, can show two conflicting managers the manner in which budget allocations were decided and why. The managers then may either prepare a stronger justification for their own cases or accept the decisions because they are better informed.

Use of Committees.   In some circumstances, committees may be able to resolve conflict. When a committee contains representatives of various groups, different points of view can be considered, and recommendations, proposals, or decisions made which can take the different points of view into account. Perhaps the greatest danger of this method is that the final determination may be one where everyone gets something, but no one gets all he needs. Compromises reached in committees are often alternatives which are not most effective from the point of view of the "best" way, but simply for keeping the internal peace.

Nonstructural Solutions

Quite often conflict must be treated by dealing with the people involved, rather than by using the structure of the organization. Some strategies that may be useful in the stable organization (as well as the dynamic) are increased participation in decision-making, the use of group development, and the replacement of personnel.

Increased participation in decision-making allows subordinates an opportunity to make recommendations. Discussing these recommendations with them individually and as a group will increase the information available and make them aware of potential problems. Increased participation, as we have seen in chapter 11, may take many forms, ranging from allowing the individual to make a decision to simply informing him of the grounds on which a decision has been made.

Group development and team-building training methods may also be useful in reducing conflict. With these methods individuals are brought together for the purpose of learning how to interact more effectively (see chap. 18).

Replacement of personnel is a technique to be used when the conflict can be traced to the obstinacy or personality of one or more members of a unit who are unwilling to change. It happens, though rarely, that a single individual causes many of the problems in a unit and is not willing to yield to the needs of others or the organization.

Intraorganization transfer to a more compatible climate or a job where there will be less interaction with others should be considered when the individual has skills that are valued by the organization. If he does not want to transfer, managers must then terminate his employment; that is, fire him.

In this chapter, we have analyzed some of the ways in which managerial techniques are applied in organizations of a certain type. As they examine any organizational situation, management students should bear in mind that the character of the organization, its environment, and the orientations of the people it attracts are the important determinants of how it will function. Many of the techniques suggested in this chapter will work in other situations as well. They are proposed here because we believe that they are most congruent and useful in organizations of a hierarchical character. They represent the starting point from which a manager can begin to analyze his problems and deal with them.

Discussion Questions

1. What do you think of the statement "Rank and file workers will do what is expected of them, but they do not obtain primary satisfaction from their work." If true, how will this affect an organization's productivity? What will a typical manager's reaction be to such a position?

2. "Statistical selection" means making a decision to hire someone based on whether or not a score they get on a "test" is above a cutoff point. Why should such an approach be used? Why not? Under what conditions might it be of great utility to a manager?

3. Have you ever been interviewed for a job that you did not get? What do you think the interviewer found wrong with you? List the factors on a sheet of paper. Are there some which you can easily change?

4. In this chapter we suggest several alternative ways a manager might "motivate" a worker or work group. From your experience, can you recall a time when such techniques were used on you? When you tried them on others? How did they work?

5. In our discussion of leadership, we suggest that one way for a leader to improve unit performance would be to change his style; for example, move from a "structure" emphasis to a "considerate" emphasis. There is an adage "A leopard can't change his spots." Can a manager change his behavior? How?

6. Why might role conflict have more potential impact on managers at lower levels of an organization?

7. What are some added forms that status differentiation takes in bureaucratic organizations beyond those noted in this chapter?

13. List the positive and negative aspects of working in a stable organization.

14. Indicate why *you* would or would not want to work in the stable organization.

15. Discuss strategies for a manager to follow in getting ahead in the stable organization.

Chapter 13

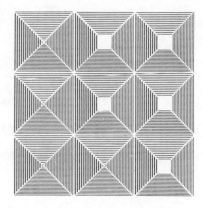

When the environment is well-defined, known, and relatively constant—as it is for hierarchical organizations, deterministic techniques can be applied to decision problems. The decision maker assumes that certain costs, conditions, and circumstances can be specified with accuracy. With such an assumption, various alternatives can be evaluated, and the one which best achieves the goal can be selected. This is called *decision making under certainty*.

Decision making under risk is also likely to be employed in hierarchical organizations. Often, even though a manager can't be certain about things, he may be in a position to make a probability estimate about them. As we noted in chapter 9, this may be because of his past experience, or perhaps because of data that have been collected and analyzed. These two approaches to decision making and resource allocation are the most prevalent in hierarchical organizations.

The Nature of Goals in Stable Organizations

In chapter 10, different types of goals are discussed. Of particular relevance to the decision-making process as discussed in this chapter are two types of goals: (1) environmental goals, and (2) internal systems goals. The character of the environmental goals, especially the rate and type of change in them, affect the way the internal system goals are set by decision makers. When the environmental goals are essentially unchanging, managers can develop, over time, organizationally acceptable measures of performance and ways of doing things. As time goes on, and activities within the system remain relatively unchanged, cost and performance measures will be developed which become the basis for planning and control.

Decision Approaches in Hierarchical Organizations

Environmental Goals

In stable organizations, goals will be fairly constant, over time, and can generally be considered as given, or having a great deal of certainty. But they take on this characteristic of certainty because we assume them to be so. We do this, for example, by examining the market environment and deciding that a particular group of customers exist and will demand our product. Suppose that the market for steel can be broken down into four general segments, automotive firms, appliance firms, defense firms, and others. A steel manufacturer may, strategically, decide to focus on only one of these. Which one he chooses is important to his success or failure. To say that there is certainty in any one market is obviously incorrect, but it is possible to say that a particular market has a probability of being a certain size. This means that the steel firm may set environmental goals using decision-under-risk approaches. We will describe an example of this approach in this chapter.

Internal System Goals

Let us say, then, that a firm may meet its environmental goal by manufacturing a particular product, or set of related products, say steel or aluminum for a segment of the market. Its customers expect, or demand, that these products meet certain requirements of quality and quantity that are similar to the nature of demand in previous periods. Goals of this type can easily be broken down, or factored, into subgoals for each organizational unit. One segment of the firm will be allocated the task of producing iron, another of rolling steel plate, another with the marketing function, and so on. These factored subgoals represent internal subsystem objectives. The internal subsystems (various divisions) know fairly well what they are to do. For them, the important thing is to know "how much" and at "what costs."

If there is stability in the environmental goals, then following from our analysis in chapter 7, we assume that a particular method of production (the means to achievement) has been developed. It is likely that a substantial investment has been made in plant and equipment, and fixed production processes of limited purpose have been devised. In a steel company, for example, the equipment produces only steel. In an automobile company, the production system can only produce cars.

To say thus that the means of achievement is fixed implies that there is only one way for the firm to operate. It will produce its products in a particular way, and similarly have a fixed system of distribution. There is little need for extensive discussion with lower-level managerial personnel for the purpose of finding a better way to produce.

Of course, this is not to say that lower-level personnel cannot help improve efficiency, but their help will come in trying to figure out how to do, at a lower cost, things which are already being done. The purpose of having lower-level staff involved and participating in decision making is primarily to *communicate* to them desired performance levels, or levels of achievement.

For the most part then, internal system goals in hierarchical organizations will be defined in terms of *level of achievement*, as opposed to the *means of achievement*. This is so because the means is already established, and there is little need for changing it.

The Characteristics of Controls.

For control purposes, measures of performance can be constructed from historical precedent; that is, the firm will have a fairly well-accepted, and predetermined set of control points developed from past experience. For example, it may be known that marketing activities can be effectively managed by monitoring orders received. When orders drop below a particular level, added sales or promotional activity will be necessary.

By knowing what to monitor, the firm can, by using historical data, remain aware of what levels are critical. Forecasts can be made of "order level activity" from previous years' experience, much as was done in the case of LAG Company described in chapter 10.

Also, desired profitability levels can be set by top management. If the firm desires a 25 percent return on capital, for instance, it can work backward through its cost and revenue structure to determine how much should be produced, when, and at what cost. Since the systems of the organization are fixed, the appropriate levels of work forces and required levels of sales can be determined.

One important characteristic of these subsystem goals is that they will be objective, in the sense that they can be acceptably—though not perfectly—quantified and measured. Scrap rates, sales per employee, return on investment, number of units produced are all less subject to disagreement than more subjective criterion such as "high quality," "effective sales methods," or "the impact of advertising expenditures."

Top management usually has the most influence in the determination of the goals of stable organizations. Since the question is one of what level of achievement is appropriate, and there are years of experience from which to extrapolate, goal levels are set by top management with the aid of accountants and production engineering staffs.

Fairly rigid standards will be set, and the primary method of managing activities will follow a *management by exception* mode, which means that only when deviations occur will they be called to the attention of top management for corrective action. Because strategic control points are defined by the system, and the desired goal levels are specified, particular points in the operation can be observed, and, if these stay within the control limits, adequate performance can be expected.

When rigid standards are built into goals, there will be close, tight control, and little deviation will be tolerated, because a small deviation can magnify into a serious problem. For example, in a firm which manufactures 5 million units per year, an upward cost deviation of only 10¢ per unit can mean $500,000 in increased costs.

Decision-making Approaches Under Risk

In chapter 9, we described the conditions for decisions under risk, in which a manager can make a decision when he is able to make some "acceptable" assessment of the amount of uncertainty involved. To examine more closely one such problem, let us suppose that you are the owner of a chain of small gift shops. You are planning to locate a new shop in a nearby college town. You have two alternative sites for your shop, one in the center of town and another in a new shopping center being constructed just outside of town. You are not certain what the future holds for the downtown business district nor for the shopping center. In any case you feel that you should seize a good opportunity if it arises.

You know that there are risks involved. Several things could happen which might make either alternative good or bad, and you must assess the risks and evaluate the alternatives.

States of nature are a way of conceptualizing the world, especially the relevant environment for persons making decisions. For your problem, your experience has led you to conclude that the relevant dimension is the movement of local population. You decide that three general population trends are possible:

1. people will move away from town;
2. people will stay where they are; or
3. people will move into town.

These are the states of nature for your decision problem. You believe that where people move will affect your profits and income.

In order to make the best decision, you must make some estimate of the probabilities of each of these states of nature occurring, so you turn to the local population experts (the Chamber of Commerce, the state department of commerce, consultants, etc.) and they tell you, "We can't be certain what will be the movement of the population in this town, but we have made some estimates of the probability of each of your three states of nature occurring." These estimates, as noted in chapter 9, are subjective probabilities, but you regard them as reasonably accurate. The probability estimates for the states of nature are as follows:

State of Nature	Probability
1. Away from town	.4
2. No change	.3
3. Movement toward town	.3

You are now able to prepare a payoff matrix. A payoff matrix is a way to represent a decision problem. Such matrixes are constructed with the states of nature in columns, the available strategies in rows. The payoff for a particular strategy and a given state of nature is the point where the row and column intersect. Figure 13.1 shows the payoff matrix for your problem. In the matrix are entered the various payoffs that would obtain. These payoffs are called *conditional values* (CV), or what you can expect if a particular strategy is chosen and a particular state of nature occurs. To arrive at the conditional values for our problem, you make, say, sales forecasts for each of the six cells in this matrix. For example, as shown in figure 13.1, the conditional value of the strategy "to locate in the center," if population moves away from town, is $60,000, or what the company would make if the strategy were selected and this state of nature occurred.

FIGURE 13.1 Payoff Matrix to Locate Gift Shop in Town or in Suburban Shopping Center

State of Nature / Strategy	Movement Away from Town p = .4	No Change p = .3	Movement Toward Town p = .3
Locate in Town	$25,000	$40,000	$50,000
Locate in Center	$60,000	$40,000	$20,000

Naturally it is important to specify conditional values as accurately as possible, since they are forecasts—what you will get if something happens. How can conditional values be developed? Basically, for your problem you would forecast your profits, or income, for each cell in the payoff matrix. This means that you must:

1. determine sales levels for each state of nature,
2. determine costs for each state of nature, and
3. compute the profit for each state of nature.

Once you have done this you can make your decision. In chapter 9, the idea of expected value (EV) was introduced. The rational decision maker will of course select the strategy which has the greatest expected value. Selecting this strategy will be the best decision.

The total expected value for each strategy is calculated by multiplying the probability of the state of nature times the payoff for that state, and adding these values for all states of nature for that strategy. This is shown in the formula

$$\Sigma EV = p_1(CV_1) + p_2(CV_2) + p_3(CV_3) + ..p_n(CV_n)$$

where ΣEV = the total expected value
$CV_1..CV\ n$ = conditional values of each state of nature, and
p = the probability

You are now in a position to compare the two strategies by computing the expected values of each. To compute the total expected value for each strategy, you multiply the conditional value by the probability for each state of nature and add them together. This is done for each alternative strategy. For the "locate in town" strategy the expected value is $37,000.

$$\Sigma EV = .4(25,000) + .3(\$40,000) + .3(\$50,000)$$
$$= 10,000 + 12,000 + 15,000$$
$$= \$37,000$$

For the "shopping center" strategy, the expected value is $42,000.

$$\Sigma EV = .4(\$60,000) + .3(40,000) + .3(20,000)$$
$$= \$42,000$$

Applying the rule of rational decision making, the best alternative is to move to the shopping center. The reason for this is that the decision maker when facing this decision a number of times will, on the average, be advantaged in the amount of \$5,000 (\$42,000 − \$37,000 = \$5,000) when selecting the shopping center over the in-town location.

Probabilities Mean Maybe

Is the decision maker absolutely better off by using such a strategy as just described? In the long run, yes. But it is possible to select an alternative which has a lower expected value than another and yet fare much better with it than one with a higher expected value. Suppose, for example, that an electronics manufacturer must decide between using his available resources to build a new computer or a new electric typewriter. If the states of nature are defined as two different conditions of demand, then the following payoff matrix represents the profits from each strategy.

	Demand I .5	Demand II .5	ΣEV
Computer	$1,000,000	$−300,000	$350,000
Typewriter	400,000	400,000	400,000

Clearly the rational decision would be to manufacture the new typewriter. But if the manufacturer decides to build the computer and the state of nature proves to be Demand I, he wins big. Do you feel lucky? Then build the computer. Rational? Manufacture typewriters.

Utility and Expected Value

To return to the gift shop problem, suppose that in order to locate in the shopping center, you must take a long-term lease, immediately paying $15,000 to the owners—but in town you need only take a monthly lease. In both cases you will still realize the returns in the payoff matrix of figure 13.1.

If the decision maker is not willing to risk, or spend $15,000, then clearly the other alternative is preferable. Another example may make the point more clearly. Suppose you are involved in a gambling game, flipping coins. You have been told that if you flip a head, you win $100 and if you flip a tail, you lose $50. Clearly the expected value is high; where .5 is the probability of a head appearing and a tail appearing, the expected value of the situation can be computed as follows:

$$.5(\$100) + .5(-\$50) = EV$$
$$\$50 - 25 = \$25$$

This means that on the average you are $25 ahead each time you flip a coin. But, suppose that you must bet only in $25 amounts, you only have $25, and have to pay that much for a bus ticket home. You can't afford to lose, therefore, you can't afford to bet. You can't make the "rational" decision, because the utility of having a sure way home is greater than the potential payoff.

A Planning and Control Approach for Hierarchical Organizations.

As we have said, a high degree of environmental certainty facilitates the use of decision strategies and resource allocation methods which are called "deterministic." In such decisions, chance elements do not exist; that is, the decision maker feels it is a realistic assumption to assume certainty, that certain situations, costs, and other conditions can be specified with accuracy. Starr (1971) gives the following example:

> Assume that an expansion in plant capacity is planned. Several strategic and tactical alternatives are considered. The possibilities are narrowed down and discarded until finally, a single plan of action is accepted. A final plan is detailed as though no worthwhile opportunities for deviating from the plan will occur.

Planning and resource allocation decisions of this type are generally preferred by managers because they offer several advantages, among which Starr (1971) notes the following:

Simple Formal Procedures Can Be Used.   There is lessened need for coordination between organizational units to develop the plans. Data such as costs and resource capacities are usually available from production units or cost accounting groups, or computer information systems may have information which is easily accessible. This facilitates the development of plans, since this information can be incorporated in existing planning models.

Efficient Logistical Support Is Possible.   Once the most efficient plan is formulated, it is relatively easy to obtain help, support, and coordination from other departments. The final plan can be quickly disseminated throughout the relevant units of an organization to become the basis for planning their activities.

Control Is Emphasized Rather Than Planning.   With deterministic methods the planning models, (e.g., linear programming) have already been developed. These models pinpoint strategic control points and provide the manager with a specification of *what* should be monitored, and also with specific amounts, or measures, to be achieved, such as the number of units to produce or the allowable costs which can be incurred without exceeding the limits.

No Recognition of Uncertainty Is Required.   It is easy to make a plan when the planner knows what is going to happen. In fact, somewhere along the line in every organization this assumption must ultimately be made in order for operations to continue, even in a volatile environment. For example, an airplane manufacturer must, in designing and building a prototype of a plane which is to be sold to the Defense Department, at some point give the go-ahead, even though the future sales depend on such unknown factors as the performance of the aircraft, approval by the military, and subsequent congressional approval.

Linear Programming

Of all the techniques suggested for improving decision making which have emerged from the quantitative, or operations research approach (see chap. 2) perhaps the one of greatest utility to managers is linear programming.

Linear programming is a technique which maximizes, or minimizes, some objective function of an organization—such as profit or cost— through the solving of a set of simultaneous linear equations which represent constraints, or limitations, relative to the function. It has a number of applications in decision-making situations where it is possible to define relationships among the factors in the form of linear equations. The complexity and subtleties of this method are extensive, but a simple illustration can show its conceptual underpinnings.

Suppose the ABC Company manufactures stereos and TV sets. Its plant has four departments: (1) a speaker assembly group that can build either 500 stereo speakers, 400 TV speakers, or some combination not to exceed either of these levels; (2) a components manufacturing section which can build 600 TV units, 400 stereo units, or some combination; (3) a stereo assembly department which can build 350 stereos per day, but no TV sets; and (4) a TV assembly unit which can build 350 TV sets, but no stereos.

The finance group estimates that the profit returned for each TV set is $20 per unit and the profit from a stereo unit is $40. Figure 13.2 summarizes this information.

The ABC Company wants to obtain the maximum level of profit. The capacity of each department represents restrictions, or constraints. The components shop, for instance, can produce 400 stereo components, but not 600. Assembly for TV sets cannot exceed 350 units, although it can be less. It cannot be less than zero, however, since there is no negative production.

The ABC Company's level of profit is given by the equation:

$$20x + 40y = \text{Profit}$$

FIGURE 13.2 ABC Company

Constraints	TV (x)	Stereo (y)	Linear Equation
Components Department	600	400	2x + 3y = 1,200
Speaker Department	400	500	5x + 4y = 2,000
TV Assembly	350	—	x = 350
Stereo Assembly	—	350	y = 350
Profit	$20	$40	20x + 40y

This equation is called the *objective function* or the factor (in this case profit) to be maximized. Objective functions can also be minimized, as in the case where one might seek a least cost solution. To simplify finding a solution, the departmental capacities given in figure 13.2 can be represented as linear equations. They can be computed simply. The method for determining a linear equation is given by the formula where x_1, x_2, and y_1, y_2 can be determined

$$\frac{y - y_1}{x - x_1} = \frac{y_2 - y_1}{x_2 - x_1}$$

The equation representing the components constraint can be determined in the following manner:

If $y_1 = 0$, then $x_1 = 600$
If $y_2 = 400$, then $x_2 = 0$

This is so because, the way the problem is stated, if ABC produces 600 TV components (x_1), then it can produce no stereo components (y_1). If ABC produces 400 stereo components (y_2), then it can produce no TV components (x_2). These two points are shown on figure 13.3 as points N and O. When these values are put in the general equation given above, the specific linear constraint for the components department is found.

$$\frac{y - 0}{x - 600} = \frac{400 - 0}{0 - 600}$$

$$-600y = 400x - 240,000$$
$$-6y = 4x - 2,400$$
$$2x + 3y = 1,200$$

FIGURE 13.3   Components Department Constraint

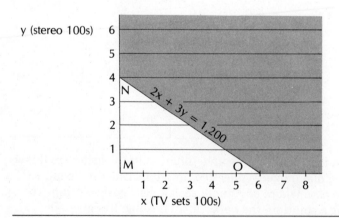

y (stereo 100s)

$2x + 3y = 1,200$

x (TV sets 100s)

Figure 13.3 shows that ABC can produce any number of components so long as they fall within or along the boundaries of the triangle denoted by M, N, O. It cannot produce 800 TV components and zero stereo components. Neither can it produce 400 TV *and* 400 stereo components.

There are other limitations to ABC's level of production. The speaker constraint also acts to reduce the *feasibility area* within which ABC can produce. The linear equation for this department is shown in figure 13.2

$$5x + 4y \leq 2,000$$

This equation can be derived in the same fashion as that for the components assembly department. Figure 13.4 shows how this constraint limits further the *feasible* production of ABC. It can be seen that the feasibility area in figure 13.3 is further reduced by the area designated P, O, Q in figure 13.4.

But we have not yet finished considering the limitations which must be taken into account for ABC Company. In figure 13.2, it is also shown that two other departments, TV assembly and stereo assembly, impose constraints. In the case of ABC, the stereo assembly constraint is given as $x \leq 350$. This means that this department as presently constituted is not set up to assemble TV sets, and is capable of assembling up to, but not more than, 350 units of stereo equipment. The

FIGURE 13.4 Components and Speaker Department Constraints

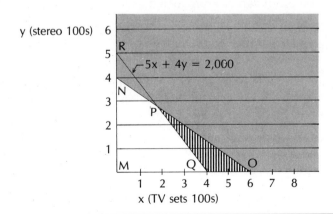

departmental constraint is shown on figure 13.5 along with that of the TV assembly department.

The TV assembly department is also unique, as is the stereo assembly department. Its resources are not transferable; thus, it has a capacity of zero stereo assembly, but up to 350 TV sets. This constraint is given as $y \leq 350$.

This produces the feasibility area by the amount (N, S, T) to account for the stereo assembly constraint ($x \leq 350$) and (U, V, Q), which eliminates some capacity due to the stereo constraint ($y \leq 350$). This gives the feasibility area shown in both figures 13.5 and 13.6 (M, S, T, Q, U, V). The ABC Company can produce any combination of TV sets and stereos which fall within this polygon, or on any of its boundaries.

But we still have not answered the most important question, "How many of each?" The answer to this question is found by considering the relationship of the *objective function*, the function to be maximized, to the feasibility area of production. The objective function, in this case, is a profit relationship and is

$$20x + 40y = \text{Profit}$$

Determining the maximum profit level for ABC can be accomplished by examining a family of lines given by the objective function relative to the feasible production capacities. Suppose for example, a profit level of $80,000 is projected. By constructing an *iso profit* line on figure 13.6, it can be see that $80,000 can be obtained if ABC produces at any point on line 1, figure 13.6. An iso profit line is one which any combination of TVs and stereos will result in the same profit. The iso profit line for $80,000 profit can be constructed as follows:

$$20x + 40y = \$80,000$$
When $x = 0, y = 200$ and
when $x = 400, y = 0$

It can be seen, by examination of figure 13.6, that there is still a great deal of feasible capacity. If the projected profit is set at $100,000, the iso profit line would be given as line 2 in figure 13.6, or

$$20x + 40y = \$100,000$$
When $x = 0, y = 2,500$, and
when $y = 500, x = 0$

The maximum profit is obtained when the iso profit line reaches a point away from the origin of the graph (M) so that it is still tangent to the feasibility area. This occurs when the line given by the objective

FIGURE 13.5 Components, Speaker, TV Assembly, and Stereo Assembly Constraints

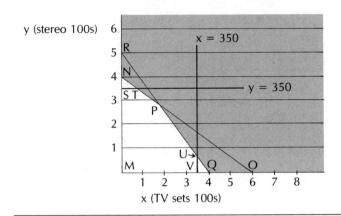

FIGURE 13.6 Maximizing the Objective Function (20x + 40y = profit)

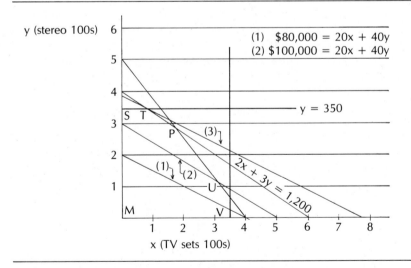

function (20x + 40y) passes through point (T) in the feasibility area, or line 3 on figure 13.6. It is impossible to produce above the line at this point because that would be *outside* the feasibility area. To produce below the line leaves unused capacity. This point (T) can be easily found. It is located at the point where the stereo assembly constraint $(y \leq 350)$ intersects with the speaker assembly constraint $(2x + 3y = 1,200)$. This is shown below

$$\text{stereo assembly } y \leq 350$$
$$\text{components } 2x + 3y = 1,200$$

This problem is solved by substituting the value of y (350) from our first equation above into the second equation.

$$2x + 3(350) = 1,200$$
$$2x = 1,200 - 1,050$$
$$x = 75 \text{ units}$$

The maximum profit appears, then, when ABC produces 75 TVs and 350 stereos. The amount of profit is

$$\$20 \ (75) + \$40 \ (350) = \text{profit}$$
$$\$1,500 + \$14,000 = \$15,500$$

Is this the maximum level of profit? Consider what happens if ABC produces elsewhere within the feasibility constraints. If it moves back along the constraint, $y \leq 350$, to produce one less TV set (74), the profit is reduced by $20. If it produces one less stereo (349), the profit is reduced by $40. What would the profit be at another point in the feasibility area, say U? This point U is located where the components constraint $(2x + 3y = 1,200)$ intersects with the components assembly constraint $(x \leq 350)$. Thus, it is located where these equations are equal. To find the number of stereos and TVs at point U, we begin with the two constraints

$$\text{components } 2x + 3y = 1,200, \text{ and}$$
$$\text{TV assembly } x \leq 350$$

Since we now have a value for x, it can be substituted in the components constraint $(2x + 3y = 1,200)$ and yield a value for y.

$$2(350) + 3y = 1,200$$
$$3y = 1,200 - 700$$
$$y = 166\tfrac{2}{3}$$

Therefore, point U is located where the production levels would be 350 TV sets and 167 stereos. By substituting these production level values in the objective function, the profit is given as

$$\$20x + \$40y = \text{Profit}$$
$$\$20 \ (350) + \$40 \ (167) = \$13,880$$

Thus, ABC obtains maximum profit when it produces at point T.

Assumptions of Linear Programming. Two important assumptions that lie behind this approach are (1) additivity and (2) divisibility. Wagner (1969) defines additivity to mean the "total amounts of each input and associated profit are the sums of the inputs and profits for each individual process." Divisibility means for "each activity, the total amounts of each input and the associated profit are strictly proportional to the level of . . . each activity [being] capable of continuous proportional expansion or reduction." He goes on to state that

> The assumptions of divisibility and additivity are equivalent to stating that the underlying mathematical model can be formulated in terms of linear relations. Strictly interpreted, the axioms imply constant returns to scale and preclude the possibility of economies or diseconomics of scale (in both the technology and profit aspects). Suitable mathematical devices of an advanced nature often make it possible to introduce economies and diseconomies into a modified linear model. In real situations the above two postulates may hold only approximately, but nevertheless well enough, to permit useful application of the linear approach.

Some Other Uses of Linear Programming. The resource allocation problem as shown above in simple form is probably the most frequent illustration of linear programming. The method can be used to determine the most efficient way to allocate production facilities when the objective is to maximize profits or minimize costs. For instance, a plant might have several departments, each with different capacities to produce different combinations of several products. Knowing the true profit contribution of each product, it can determine how many of each to produce.

What we have shown in this chapter are the general approaches that a manager in a hierarchical organization can take when faced with decision situations. These are methods to facilitate the decision process in a stable environmental situation.

Discussion Questions

1. Suppose you had a small plant with 3 departments. Department A could assemble 400 washers, but no dryers. Department B could assemble 500 dryers, but no washers. Department C could produce 600 washers or 600 dryers, or

some combination, not to exceed a total of 600 units. What would be the production levels that yield a maximum profit if:

a. The dryers yielded $40 unit profit and washers yielded $80?
b. The dryers yielded $70 per unit and washers yielded $30?
c. The dryers yielded $50 and the washers yielded $50?

2. How does the relatively stable character of the environment affect the specific type of control standards in a hierarchical organization?

3. What is the "rational" decision if you have the following payoff matrix

	States of Nature		
	(1) $p=.5$	(2) $p=.3$	(3) $p=.2$
Strategy 1	$2,000	$10,000	$12,000
Strategy 2	4,000	11,000	8,000

4. Why is it necessary for a manager to take a position, as Starr states in this chapter, that in the final analysis a plan "is detailed as though no worthwhile opportunities for deviating from the plan will occur"?

5. What is a deterministic decision approach?

Chapter 14

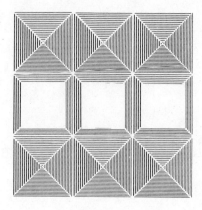

In this chapter and the next, we turn our attention to the dynamic organization. Chapter 15 considers problems of decision making and resource allocation in an organization faced with an uncertain environment. This chapter considers the same topic areas as did chapter 12, except it suggests strategies or approaches for dealing with the human resources of a more flexible, project-management oriented, organization. The following areas again are discussed:

1. Selection
2. Compensation
3. Motivation
4. Performance Evaluation
5. Leadership
6. Managing Stress
7. Managing Conflict

In dynamic organizations, these activities take a different shape than that of their counterparts in hierarchical organizations. The turbulent environment of the dynamic organization requires much more flexibility in relationships among members so that the system can adapt more readily.

Selection of Personnel

The selection of personnel is important in a different way in the dynamic organization than it is in the stable organization. There are not only initially higher recruitment, assessment, orientation, and training costs to be considered, but also higher potential costs should a wrong selection decision be made. If the professional hired proves to be inadequate, for example, and fails to complete a project on time, a dynamic organization may lose many hundreds of thousands of

Managing Human Resources in a Dynamic Organization

dollars through, say, the loss of a market to a competitor. Conversely, a rejected applicant who is hired by a competitor and is successful there can be very costly to the firm which rejected him.

In volatile environments, there is a high level of turnover of professional and managerial staff, since as demands for skills change, certain professionals become expendable and must be replaced by others. The more variable the tasks over time, the higher the rate of staff change.

A reduction in the volume of work at a firm may also force the layoff of many qualified professionals who must later be replaced if the volume of work increases. An aerospace firm, for example, may have to lay off large numbers of talented professionals because of lack of work for them, only to be forced to recruit furiously a month later if it receives a large contract.

Turnover can be a problem if an organization loses someone with a particular skills configuration and must find a replacement with the same configuration, since the number of qualified applicants is usually smaller for the dynamic organization than it is for a hierarchical organization. This is so because the members of dynamic organizations must at one and the same time be highly versatile and yet possess highly specialized skills.

The Mixture of Organization Types

In the dynamic organization the mixture of organizational orientations will tend to be as shown in figure 14.1. At the lowest level of the organization there will be a professionally-oriented group of specialists, highly trained and skilled. The externalists will probably be a smaller group of operating personnel charged with carrying out routine tasks. They will be longer-term employees.

At the mid-levels, the mixture of types changes. Two groups of roughly the same size will be found, one of organizationally-oriented managers and one of professionally-oriented managers. The organizationalists will be administrators who are making a managerial career, with success defined by their organization's achievement of primary work goals. The professionally-oriented group will be specialists who have been promoted to managerial positions because of their high competence, but who have retained their original value system.

The distribution of types changes again at the top level, which will have a preponderance of organizationalists. This occurs because selection decisions for higher managerial ranks are made by those already in high positions, and they are likely to place more value on the organization as such than on professional commitment. Technical skills are still important at this level, however, and some of the top management group will have a professional orientation.

Selection in the Dynamic Organization

The selection of personnel in dynamic organizations is more difficult than it is in stable organizations because, in the former, members do different kinds of tasks from one period to another and their tasks are often not well-defined. Therefore it is difficult to find specific predictors of effectiveness. In addition, jobs in dynamic organizations tend to have higher skill requirements than in hierarchical organizations, since a higher proportion of managers and professionals are

FIGURE 14.1   Representation of Different Orientations as a Function of Organization Level in the Dynamic Organization

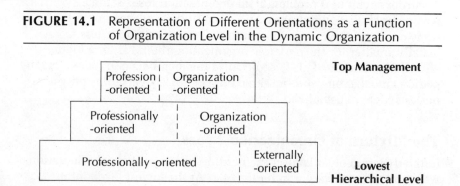

employed. Therefore, in dynamic organizations selection will tend to be based on the clinical approach (discussed below), rather than the statistical, because the jobs are more individualized. For example, a dynamic organization may need a person to assume responsibilities for several different projects. This person may need to have the abilities to perform a number of different specialized functions, and also to have the kind of personality that fits in with other project team members. Such characteristics are difficult to measure—as well as being in short supply.

The Clinical Approach.   In the dynamic organization, then, a more individualized approach to selection, called the "clinical approach," is used (Dunnette, 1966). In the statistical approach, an applicant is at least initially accepted or rejected on the basis of some score, or combination of scores, received on a test. In clinical selection, tests may be incorporated along with other important data, such as experience and education. However, clinical selection is also much more subjective. The person, or group, making a clinical decision combines the data about an applicant based on a judgment of how all the predictors of job success should be weighted and evaluated, based on the evaluator's own experience with the job.

The clinical approach to selection is suited to the dynamic organization for two reasons. First, there simply are too few jobs and too few applicants to allow an effective validation study which might insure the utility of, say, specific cut-off scores on a particular test. This means that the selector must do this intuitively. Second, there are important data which are difficult to value quantitatively but which would be useful in a selection decision; for example, the applicant's responses and behavior in an interview. This information may be important and should not be ignored, but it can only be included judgmentally.

Compensation in the Dynamic Organization

In the dynamic organization, the general problems of compensation policy are those described in chapter 12: the *wage-level* decision, the *wage-structure* decision, the *individual wage-differential* decision, and the *wage-method* decision. The approaches to solving these policy questions, however, must be different than those discussed in chapter 12, because the work of specialists in the dynamic organization is highly complex, the jobs are usually ill-defined, and they do not lend themselves to the precision of the evaluation methods

described in chapter 12. Because of the variability of task requirements within and between professional specialties, it is difficult to
make internal comparisons to determine the relative worth of different
jobs.

As mentioned, the dynamic organization has a much higher proportion of managers and professionals than the hierarchical organization,
and compensation for this group will be lower in importance relative
to other job factors. The lack of definition of tasks characteristic of this
group makes it difficult to use individual incentive plans in which it
is necessary to measure output precisely and where each individual
must have control over the level of output himself. We would expect
greater use of the group incentive plans and the plant-wide incentive
plan in the dynamic organization. If an incentive plan is to be used
with professionals, it often involves payment of a bonus to a team if a
particular project is completed by a certain date and is of a satisfactory quality level.

Maturity Curves

Since the tasks in a dynamic organization are not programmed and the
professional shifts from task to task on different projects, it is almost
impossible to establish base rates for professional jobs through the job
evaluation approaches described in chapter 12. As a substitute for job
evaluation, the pay for professionals can be established using "maturity curves" developed from an analysis of salary levels attained by
professionals of a certain type after certain time periods upon
receiving their final college degrees. For example, the organization
may subscribe to a survey which indicates the average compensation
for chemical engineers for certain years after graduation. An overall
judgment is then made of the quality of a particular individual chemical engineer in the company. If he is of average quality, he is paid
what the average chemical engineer in that industry with a similar
amount of experience is paid. If he is superior, he may be paid a
certain percentage more than the base rate of the average chemical
engineer.

The Classification Method

This method seeks to group different jobs into classes, or grades,
based on the amount of difficulty, challenge, authority, or other
important factors. This method has been used in government agencies
for years. It is also used in private industry. In the federal government

it is known as the *GS system*. Under this approach, various job grades are established. Each job grade, such as GS 1, GS 5, or GS 9, has a description in general terms of the characteristics of jobs in that group. For example, the jobs in grade GS 1 are described as involving "little or no latitude for the exercise of independent judgment," while those in grade GS 5 have "limited latitude," and those of GS 9 require "the exercise of independent judgment in a limited field." Whenever a new job is created and it is necessary to determine a wage rate for it, the description of the job is compared to the various grade descriptions to identify the one in which it belongs. The salary range for that grade is then authorized for the job. All the jobs within a certain grade are supposed to be similar with respect, for example, to the amount of latitude allowed the job incumbent. The classification method may be useful in dynamic organizations if the job characteristics represent, for example, level of training, experience, responsibility for projects, or other criteria of value in an organization of this type.

Executive Compensation

In chapter 12, we did not discuss pay methods for managers. That is because the approaches to evaluating executive and managerial positions are similar to those described above for dynamic organizations. Classification systems and maturity curve approaches are often used to determine base pay levels for executives. However, stock option plans, bonuses, and profit-sharing programs are an important part of many excutive compensation plans. They may account for as much as 50 percent of a manager's pay. While we will not go into these in detail, all of them generally seek to link pay with performance. To do this, some reasonably systematic approach to evaluation is required. The reader who carefully followed the discussion of MBO (chap. 11) can see the utility of this method for dealing with these aspects of executive pay.

Performance Evaluation in the Dynamic Organization

Performance evaluation in the dynamic organization is also different from that in the hierarchical organization because more individuals perform a greater variety of tasks that are nonprogrammed and nonrepetitive. In addition, many organizational members, such as the professionals, are assigned to various work teams where they work with different individuals and for different supervisors.

Evaluating Worker Performance

There may be some lower-level jobs in the dynamic organization that can be routinely defined. When this is so, employees in these positions may be evaluated using the work standards approach which we saw in chapter 12. In other nonroutine and nonspecialist jobs at lower levels, the use of critical incidents (see chap. 12) may facilitate evaluation. The use of these methods, however, must be based on the existence of a clear understanding between the individual and his superior about the job requirements and how the tasks should be performed. When using the critical incidents method, the evaluator must be careful that the incidents recorded represent a true sample of the worker's behavior. That is, he must not record only the wrong things done; he must also be aware of, and record, the positive contributions of a worker so that the method does not become a "black book" of negative performance.

Evaluating Managers and Professionals

Because relatively objective output measures are difficult to obtain in the dynamic, flexible organization, management by objectives must be undertaken on a different basis than it is in the stable organization. End results (objectives) may be specifiable only in general terms; for example, increased quality or production of a low-cost unit. But since neither quality nor cost level can be precisely defined, MBO must concentrate on the definition of means for goal achievement.

In developing a basis for evaluation with MBO in a dynamic organization, then, the general objective is stated, and an action plan is given in detail. When an individual is evaluated, the focus is on whether or not he is carrying out the action plan, and it is *assumed* that if he is, the objective will eventually be reached. In effect, this strategy attempts to get employees to go through the steps that are assumed to lead toward the goal. For example, suppose a project group has the following goal: "To develop a new product that performs better than Competitor A, and at a lower price." Such a project may take two or three years to complete. But in the interim period, the individuals assigned to it expect promotions, wage increases, and other rewards. About all that a manager can do in such a case is to make sure that the project group members are engaging in the activities which, based on experience, are most likely to achieve the desired result. The action plan for such an objective might be given in the following steps.

1. Analyze the competitor's product's characteristics.
2. Determine this company's capacity to produce a similar product.
3. Redesign the product with less expensive components.
4. Test the product for performance.
5. Prepare plans for a pilot test of the product in the market place.
6. Transfer the design to the manufacturing division for production.

If such an action plan takes three years to carry out, then a manager evaluating the performance of the project group must determine whether or not the group is carrying out the elements in the plan, and he must do this at regular intervals long before the achievement of the objective can be measured in the market place. So, periodically, the manager assesses whether or not: (1) the competitor's product was analyzed, whether or not (2) a study of capacity was conducted, and so forth, step by step through the action plan.

Participation in setting objectives of this type requires extensive involvement of those who will carry out the action plan. The supervisor may not have the technical competence needed to develop an action plan for activities which are not so routine and will vary from project to project. He often does not know what subordinates do nor how they do it, and therefore he must solicit their ideas in establishing work objectives for both individuals and project groups. Thus, because subordinates often know more about what it is possible to achieve than their superior, in the flexible organization they should have more to say about goals and action plans than would be the case in a hierarchical organization.

Who Conducts the Evaluation?

The superior in the dynamic organization will be directing individuals who are using skills and knowledge unfamiliar to him, and therefore it is difficult for him to judge their performance. In addition, if he is directing higher-level personnel who are individually working on different projects with different task teams, he will not have the knowledge—or the time—to evaluate their performances. Thus, in the dynamic organization, inputs for evaluations are more likely to come from a group of professional peers and/or the various supervisors or project team members with whom the organizational members work. While the supervisor may himself provide feedback directly to subordinates, he must rely on these other sources of information for much of that feedback.

Some Cautions about MBO.   In the dynamic organization, the MBO
approach may have to be used on a group basis, rather than on an
individual basis, since the group's work is interdependent and the
projects are often assigned to teams. Additionally, if goals are changed
too often in the MBO system (because of the necessity to adapt to a
rapidly changing situation), organizational members may lose confidence in it, with a resulting loss of motivation. Thus, when goals
change, any documents that have the obsolete goals written in them
should also be changed.

Motivation in the Dynamic Organization

Individuals seek organizations which provide satisfaction of needs.
Because they do, we expect the dynamic organization to attract
managerial and professional types with high needs for achievement,
high initiative, and low needs for a structured work environment
(Lorsch and Morse, 1974). And it does. Managers, professionals and
technicians—those who make up the largest proportion of workers in
this type of organization—generally are high in initiative, decisiveness
and self-confidence and not so concerned with security needs (Ghiselli, 1971; Pelz and Andrews, 1966; Kornhauser, 1960). They also
tend to be more concerned with higher-order needs, such as self-
actualization. Further, a national survey of various occupational
groups shows that managers and professionals rate money (an
extrinsic motivator) lower relative to other job factors than do operative workers (Nash and Carroll, 1975).

However, there is a distinction, as noted earlier, between *how*
managers and professionals want to achieve—be successful. Managers
are more likely to be organization-oriented than professionals, and
will seek recognition of their achievement through the attainment of
organizational status, power, and position. The professional, who
regards achievement highly, may seek recognition from fellow professional colleagues both in and out of his own organization.

Managers and professionals, then, have high intrinsic motivation to
do well, as a group. In addition, tasks in the dynamic organization
tend to be more complex, challenging, and interesting than in the
hierarchical organization, and this, coupled with the orientation of a
large group of employees who prefer such tasks, means that motivation is not a critical problem. Most individuals with such needs and
who are performing tasks which are challenging will be motivated to
high performance, the level of that performance being largely determined by their competence. If a highly competent staff can be

selected, the chances for survival and profitability of a dynamic organization are greatly increased. This is especially so when the individual
can see the relationship between effort and results and between
results and rewards, whether the rewards are based on organizational
payoffs or on professional recognition.

Failure to see this relationship, however, can result in goal blockage
and frustration (see chap. 3). When goal blockage occurs frequently for
important personal goals, a person may become sufficiently frustrated
to give up and become de-motivated. He may decrease his efforts
and/or seek to leave. Blocks to goal progress can arise from a number
of sources in the dynamic organization. Where the work is highly
interdependent, frustrations can easily arise when one individual's
lack of progress leads to goal blockage of another. In addition, among
scientists, professionals, and technicians, equipment failure or inade-
quacies in the qualities of materials may induce performance-gener-
ating frustration. Thus, in the flexible organization, it is especially
important that emphasis be placed on task facilitation activities, such
as providing help and resources when needed. Managerial strategy
should be directed toward removing goal obstacles.

Managerial Approaches to Motivation in the Dynamic Organization

As in chapter 12, some of the managerial strategies used for motivation are discussed below. Here, however, the focus is on how they
may be used in the dynamic organization.

Fear or threat.   Since fear or threat can only be effective when the
subject has limited job alternatives, it seems to be of little value to the
manager in a dynamic organization, especially in periods of growth,
when the services of specialists are in demand elsewhere. Also, the
use of such pressure is inconsistent with the value orientations of
professionals, and may increase their dissatisfaction with the organization to the point where they will look elsewhere for a more condu-
cive, compatible work environment.

Threat may have some short-run effect when there is a declining
market for specialist services, but as table 5.1 in chapter 5 shows,
engineering managers rated the use of this approach as less effective
than managers from more structured organizations.

Reinforcement.   It will be difficult to use reinforcement approaches
in the flexible organization. First, professionals may find more rein-

forcement, both positive and negative, from their colleagues than from management. Since many of their professional peers will be outside the organization, a manager cannot influence the manner in which reinforcement is applied. For example, a university professor's work may be highly regarded by professors at other universities, and he may receive rewards and recognition from them. His superiors at his own univeristy can do little to alter these rewards. About all they can do is to make his work easier so that he increases his probabilities of success. If the work the professor does is valued by the organization, then there will be no problem, but often this is not the case, especially when professional activities impinge disproportionately on teaching, committee assignments, and other organizational work.

Since much of the work in a flexible organization is done on a group project basis, it is difficult to pinpoint a particular individual's contribution, and this makes it difficult to reward them on an individual basis. In such a setting, it is appropriate to establish a group reward system. When this strategy is used, however, there still remains the problem of obtaining a distribution of the group reward to members of the group. This problem can be solved by having group members decide how much each should get. This is the method used to distribute playoff rewards—world series shares, for instance—by professional sports teams. Typically, the decision is that all members, ranging from the team's superstars to the least-used man of the roster, share equally.

Team Building.   The team-building approach is one in which cohesive work groups with high standards of performance are formed. Engineering supervisors, however, rated team building less effective than did supervisors from more structured organizations (table 5.1, chap. 5), a judgment that may reflect some of the difficulties of tying together the activities of a diverse set of specialists with different interests. In the company from which the sample was taken, project teams were not used frequently, and each specialist worked in a group of similarly trained personnel, rather than in an integrated task team.

Where integrated task teams of a highly interdisciplinary nature are used, team building will foster group cohesiveness and cooperation within the team. However, it may also serve to increase the potential for conflict between groups.

Ego-involvement.   Engineering supervisors rate the ego-involvement approach higher than do other types of supervisors (table 5.2, chap. 5). This follows, since professionals and specialists are likely to be more personally involved in their work because they have spent years attaining their competency, and thus their work becomes an important aspect of their psychological make-up. If it is possible to show how their work is connected with organizational success and, at the same time, allow such groups to become more extensively involved in the planning and design of activities, performance gains will probably occur.

Job Design. Attempting to increase performance through job re-design is a useful approach in the dynamic organization. Since care must be taken to insure that a specialist's job activities draw upon his strengths, the specialist's job can be studied to identify its routine and clerical activity component, and these can be transferred to other positions. Positions such as the engineering assistant—an assistant brought in to free the professional's time so that more of the profes-sional's time can be spent on the task itself—are already utilized in the aerospace industry, for example. In the health field, paramedics aid the physician, and the expanded-duty auxiliary performs many technical functions for the dentist.

Job enrichment of the type described in chapter 12 will have very little effect on an employee's ego-involvement, since in the dynamic organization, jobs are already filled with variety, challenge, and autonomy.

The Suggested Method—Increase Ability. Perhaps the most effective way to improve performance in the dynamic organization is to raise ability levels, especially since the personal motivation is already there. One way to increase competence is through additional training and education.

Organizations may send their specialists back to school for advanced study, seminars, and other specialized training. Many firms bring in instructors to offer advanced work on the job site.

Another way to increase the competence level of an organization is through the judicious replacement of subpar personnel. An organiza-tion may find it more effective to replace personnel with others of higher competence than to try to train present personnel up to compe-tence because, according to the motivation model presented in chapter 5, both the human and technical input factors affecting perfor-mance will be high, raising the probability of getting good results. Peter Drucker, a noted management writer, comments in item 14.1 about some of the critical problems of managing the motivational setting of the workforce of a dynamic organization.

ITEM 14.1   The Motivational Setting

Managing the Knowledge Worker

Direct production workers—machinists, bricklayers, farmers—are a steadily declining portion of the work force in a developed economy. The fastest growing group consists of "knowledge workers"—accountants, engineers, social workers, nurses, computer experts of all kinds, teachers and researchers. And the fastest growing group among knowledge workers themselves are managers. People who are paid for putting knowledge to work rather than brawn or manual skill are today the largest single group in the American labor force—and the most expensive one.

The incomes of these people are not, as a rule, determined either by supply or demand or by their productivity. Their wages and fringe benefits go up in step with those of manual direct-production workers. When the machinists get a raise, the foreman's salary goes up by the same percentage more or less automatically—and so does everybody else's in the company right up to the executive office.

But whether the productivity of the knowledge worker goes up is questionable. Is there reason to believe, for instance, that today's school teachers are more productive than the teachers of 1900—or today's engineer, research scientists, accountant or even today's manager?

At the same time the knowledge worker tends to be disgruntled, or at least not fully satisfied. He is being paid extremely well. He does interesting work and work that does not break the body as so much of yesterday's work did. And yet the "alienation" of which we hear so much today (I personally prefer to use the good old word "distemper") is not primarily to be found in the working class. It is above all a phenomenon of the educated middle class of employed knowledge workers.

Two Needs We do not know how to measure either the productivity or the satisfaction of the knowledge worker. But we do know quite a bit about improving both. Indeed the two needs: the need of business and the economy for productive knowledge workers and the need of the knowledge worker for achievement, while distinctly separate, are by and large satisfied by the same approaches to managing the knowledge worker.

(1) We know first that the key to both the productivity of the knowledge worker and his achievement is to demand responsibility from him or her. All knowledge workers, from the lowliest and youngest to the company's chief executive officer, should be asked at least once a year: "What do you *contribute* that justifies your being on the payroll? What should this company, this hospital, this government agency, this university, hold you accountable for, by way of contributions and results? Do you know what your goals and objects were? And what do you plan to do to attain them?"

Direction of the knowledge worker toward contribution—rather than toward effort alone—is the first job of anyone who manages knowledge workers. It is rarely even attempted. Often the engineering department only finds out, after it has finished the design, that the product on which it has been working so hard has no future in the marketplace.

(2) But at the same time, the knowledge worker must be able to appraise his contribution. It is commonly said that research is "intangible" and incapable even of being appraised. But this is simply untrue.

Wherever a research department truly performs (an exception, alas, rather than the rule), the members sit down with each other and with management once or twice a year and think through two questions: "What have we contributed in the last two or three years that really made a difference to this company?" and "What should we be trying to contribute the next two or three years so as to make a difference?"

The contributions may indeed not always be measurable. How to judge them may be controversial. What, for instance, is a greater "contribution": a new biochemical discovery that after five more years of very hard work may lead to the development of a new class of medicinal compounds with superior properties; or the development of a sugar-coated aspirin without great "scientific value" that will improve the effectiveness of pediatric medicine by making the aspirin more palatable for children, while also immediately increasing the company's sales and profits?

In fact, unless knowledge workers are made to review, appraise and judge, they will not direct themselves toward contribution. And they will also feel dissatisfied, non-achieving and altogether "alienated."

(3) Perhaps the most important rule— and the one to which few managements pay much attention—is to enable the knowledge workers to do what they are being paid for. Not to be able to do what one is being paid for infallibly quenches whatever motivation there is. Yet salesmen, who are being paid for selling and know it, cannot sell because of the time demands of the paperwork imposed on them by management. And in research lab after research lab, highly paid and competent scientists are not allowed to do their work, but are instead forced to attend endless meetings to which they cannot contribute and from which they get nothing.

The manager may know the rule. But rarely does he know what he or the company does that impedes knowledge workers and gets in the way of their doing what they are being paid for. There is only one way to find out: Ask the individual knowledge worker (and the knowledge-work team he belongs to): "What do I, as your manager, and what do we in the company's management altogether, do that helps you in doing what you are being paid for?" "What do we do that hampers you?" "Specifically, do we give you the time to do what you are being paid for, the information you need to do it, the tools for the job?"

(4) Knowledge is a high-grade resource. And knowledge workers are expensive. Their placement is therefore a key to their productivity. The first rule is that opportunities have to be staffed with people capable of running with them and of turning them into results. To make knowledge workers productive requires constant attention to what management consulting firms and law firms call "assignment control." One has to know where the people are who are capable of producing results in knowledge work—precisely because results are so very hard to measure.

Effective management of the knowledge worker requires a regular, periodic inventory and ranking of the major opportunities. And then one asks: "Who are the performing people available to us, whether they are researchers or accountants, salesmen or managers, manufacturing engineers or economic analysts? And what are these people assigned to? Are they where the results are? Or are their assignments such that they could not produce real results, no matter how well they perform?"

Unless this is being done, people will be assigned by the demands of the organization—that is by the number of transactions rather than by their importance and their potential of contribution.

In no time they will be mis-assigned. They will be where they cannot be productive, no matter how well-motivated, how highly qualified, how dedicated they are.

One also has to make sure that knowledge workers are placed where their strengths can be productive. There are no universal geniuses, least of all in knowledge work, which tends to be highly specialized. What can this particular knowledge worker do? What is he doing well? And where, therefore, does he truly belong to get the greatest results from his strengths?

Most businesses and other organizations as well spend a great deal of time and money on the original employment of people who, it is hoped, will turn into knowledge workers. But at that stage one knows very little about the future employes—beyond the grades he got in school, which have little correlation with future performance capacity. The true personnel management job, in respect to knowledge workers, begins later, when one can place the worker where his strengths can be productive because one knows what he or she can do.

Skills and Ability Manual strength is additive. Two oxen will pull almost twice the load one ox can pull. Skill is capable of subdivision. Three men, each of whom has learned one aspect of a skill, e.g. glueing the legs to a table, can turn out far more work of equal skill than one man skilled in all aspects of carpentry. But in knowledge work two mediocre people do not turn out more than one man capable of performance, let alone twice as much. They tend to get in each other's way, and to turn out much less than one capable person. In knowledge work, above all, one therefore has

to staff from strength. And this means constant attention to placing the knowledge worker where what he can do will produce results and make a contribution.

Knowledge is perhaps the most expensive of all resources. Knowledge workers are far more expensive than even their salaries indicate. Each of them also represents a very sizable capital investment—in schooling and in the apprentice years during which the worker learns rather than contributes (such as the five years which every chief engineer knows will be needed before the young graduate can truly be expected to earn his salary). Every young engineer, every young accountant, every young market researcher represents a "social capital investment" of something like $100,000 to $150,000 before he starts repaying society and his employer through his contributions. No other resource we have is equally "capital intensive" and "labor intensive." And only management can turn the knowledge worker into a productive resource.

But also, no one expects to achieve, to produce, to contribute quite as much as the knowledge worker does. No one, in other words, is more likely to be "alienated" if not allowed to achieve.

Not to manage a knowledge worker for productivity therefore creates both the economic stress of inflationary pressures and the highly contagious social disease of distemper. We can indeed measure neither the productivity nor the satisfaction of the knowledge worker. But we know how to enrich both.—Peter Drucker

The Wall Street Journal, Nov. 7, 1975

Leader Behavior in Dynamic Organizations

In the dynamic organization, the leader contributes to performance and satisfaction to a greater extent than in the hierarchical organization. This is because the work is not so preplanned and because so many problems arise which require cooperation to solve. In addition, providing information to organizational members on the goals and activities of other employees and units facilitates task performance. Finally, as we have said, performance is the product of motivation and ability. If ability is high, potential performance is high. The supervisor's responsibility is to insure that the potential is achieved— that human resources are used to capacity.

How can a leader be effective in a dynamic organization? The reader is urged to be familiar with the content of chapter 8, "Leadership," and also to review the section in chapter 12 where we defined the factors that seem to be important in determining effective leadership style. They are briefly noted here:

1. *Initiating structure.* Behavior of a manager, or leader which emphasizes task direction, planning, organizing and controlling.

2. *Consideration.* Behavior which demonstrates concern for others.

3. *Work Climate.* Two types of work environments were proposed. A relaxed climate is high on trust and group cohesiveness. Tense climates are more negative in the sense that there is lack of consensus, at least between the leader and the group.

4. *Leader position power.* There are rights and prerogatives that individuals have by virtue of the fact that they have a particular job assignment. High position power is present when the manager can make and implement decisions without seeking approval from his superior. Low position power occurs when either the leader can be replaced if the group chooses to do so, or the manager must clear minor decisions with others in the organization.

The primary factor that must be taken into account when considering leadership style for a dynamic organization is that the tasks are primarily unstructured.

Low Task Structure in Dynamic Organization

In dynamic organizations, professionals and managers are often shifted from one project to another as they are needed. We have defined the nature of project management in chapter 7. Because of the volatile environment of a dynamic organization, projects will change periodically, and member of such organizations will sometimes find themselves in ambiguous situations. They will, perhaps, not know how to do a particular job or solve a new problem. This can occur when they are not sure what skills are required or, if they do know,

FIGURE 14.2 Leader Behavior in a Dynamic Organization

| | Low Task Structure | |
| | Position Power | |
	Strong	Weak
Relaxed Climate	Consideration	Initiating Structure
Tense Climate	Initiating Structure	Consideration

they do not possess them. Another possibility is that an individual may not know how his particular competence fits with others in the organization. For example, suppose one employee is an expert on propulsion systems and another is an electronics communications specialist. Both of these persons may be extremely competent in their own fields of specialization, but if a project requires interdependent effort, then some way to integrate and coordinate their work must be devised. If they themselves are uncertain as to how to proceed, they will not function at maximum efficiency. Under the conditions of low task structure—when there is a high level of task ambiguity—the selection of leadership style can be facilitated by the model proposed in figure 14.2, adapted from Fiedler (1967).

This model shows that leader behavior is affected by both the degree of position power and the climate of the group. Position power has been found elsewhere to be a factor which affects how leader behavior affects performance and satisfaction (House, 1971).

Under a relaxed climate condition, when the leader has a great deal of autonomy (position power), the best approach is one which emphasizes consideration behavior, as in figure 14.3.

FIGURE 14.3 Leader Behavior Repertoire under Conditions of Low Task Structure and either (1) Strong Position Power and Relaxed Climate, or (2) Weak Position Power and Tense Climate

Consideration	Initiating Structure

When a tense climate exists, then initiating structure will have desirable effects on performance and satisfaction when the leader has high position power. House (1971) suggests that this is because where "tasks are varied and interdependent and where teamwork norms have not developed within the group, initiating structure and close supervision will regulate and clarify path-goal relationships," or show the staff the way that the job should be done. Thus, in a dynamic organization, a manager with high power and tense climate must exhibit a behavioral style that is more directive, and work-oriented. He should focus on defining subordinate tasks, fixing responsibilities, planning, budgeting, and controlling. This will impose performance pressures on the group, and so long as these pressures are not intense enough to induce dissatisfaction, good results will be obtained. Figure 14.4 illustrates the behavioral style appropriate under conditions of high position power and a tense climate.

When the position power is weak, the manager cannot impose sanctions or exert pressures because he lacks control over rewards and sanctions. If, however, the climate is relaxed, then the group members will respond to the structure-emphatic style (fig. 14.4). The leader provides task-oriented information and direction to the group, which facilitates improved performance.

However, as House (1971) has pointed out, when the working situation is unsatisfying, then initiating structure behavior may be seen as undesirable pressures which compound the already negative character of the tense climate. Therefore the leader must use a consideration emphasis, as shown in figure 14.3.

Ways That a Manager Can Improve Performance

Figure 14.2 suggests a number of possibilities for dealing with poor performance in the dynamic organization, and here we will analyze some of the possibilities and suggest the circumstances under which they are most likely to be effective.

FIGURE 14.4 Leader Behavior Repertoire under Conditions of Low Task Structure and either (1) Strong Position Power and Tense Climate, or (2) Weak Position Power and Relaxed Climate

Consideration	Initiating Structure

Replace Members with Others of Greater Ability

Whereas in the bureaucratic organization, technology, plant, and equipment are important, individual skill and ability are critical in the flexible organization. When there is congruence between leader style, work climate, and position power, and performance is still low, then it may be that employees, either managerial or professional, must be terminated and more competent ones hired. Of course, it may not be necessary to replace whole units. The least competent should be replaced. Because some other employees will be retained, it may be that the new personnel will not sufficiently change the climate from relaxed to tense, or vice versa, so that the climate, behavior, and power congruence still remains. The general competence level of the group presumably will increase, however, leading to better performance.

Change Position Power

When the members of the work group possess the necessary competence to do the job, but acceptable results still are not achieved, one alternative would be to change the level of position power for the manager. If a manager is high on the consideration dimension (fig. 14.3), with high position power, and in a tense environment, then according to the model in figure 14.2, reducing the position power would probably increase effectiveness. The same strategy can be used for the high initiating structure leader (figure 14.4) with strong position power in a relaxed environment.

How to Weaken Position Power.   There are a number of ways that position power can be reduced. These generally focus on redefining the character of the mangerial position description by reducing the discretion and autonomy a manager has. Some ways of doing this are:

1. *Reduce the size of the manager's budget.* Basically this will require the manager to go to higher authority to get increased resources. He may have the same level of total resources to perform his job, but he will be limited with regard to what he can spend at his own discretion. He will have to check more frequently with his superior.

2. *Reduce his authority in specific matters.* Suppose it has been normal practice for the manager to make the final hiring decision on the recommendation of others. Requiring the manager to seek approval from the personnel department for hiring or firing a partic-

ular person reduces his discretion and his position power.

3. *Increase the authority of subordinates.* It may be possible to add to the responsibility and authority of subordinates, thus bringing subordinate position power to a level more equal to the managers'.

There are some problems, of course, in the matter of reducing position power. Obviously, it threatens the status of an individual, and may have unforeseen or undesired consequences; for example, a competent manager may see his position to be so threatened that he will resign. The problems of coping with status reduction must be considered when the strategy of reducing position power is to be taken.

How to Increase Position Power.   When the high initiating structure leader (figure 14.4) is in a tense climate and has low position power, or the high consideration leader (figure 14.3) has low position power in a relaxed climate, one remedy could be to increase the leader's position power. There are a number of ways to increase position power.

1. *Increase the discretion of the manager.* Eliminating review of decision by higher-level managers increases a person's freedom of action. This can be accomplished, for example, by allowing a manager to spend larger portions of a budget without seeking approval. In one major manufacturing firm, for example, department managers must obtain approval for any expenditure in excess of $1,000. If the limit were raised to $2,000, position power would be increased.

2. *Decrease the scope of responsibility of subordinates.* A manager can decrease the discretion of subordinates by changing their job descriptions so that they must clear more decisions with him before acting or in such a way that their job assignments are restructured and narrowed. In one firm, project managers once responsible for both the design of a new tool and the development of manufacturing plans for it had their responsibilities changed to cover only the design activity. The development of manufacturing plans was shifted to another unit, reducing the authority of the project managers.

3. *Raise the status of the position.* While this may not have a direct effect on position power, it is possible that differences between managers and their groups may be increased by raising the status of the manager, while doing nothing for the group. Increasing the manager's participation at higher levels, providing him with a better office, offering him participation in executive compensation plans are all ways to increase his status.

Change Leader Behavior Style

The leader may be able to shift his behavioral repertoire in order to obtain the required congruence. When a considerate leader (figure 14.3) is in a relaxed climate with weak position power or in a tense climate with high position power, improved results will be obtained if the behavioral style becomes higher in initiating structure (fig. 14.4). A manager may demonstrate more initiating structure behavior by emphasizing the following behaviors:

1. Pay more attention to the formal structure of the organization, such as emphasizing the importance of deadlines, budget constraints, and adherence to policy.

2. Schedule more meetings to develop plans for units at lower levels.

3. Take a more active part in the redefining of tasks and the design of projects, taking more firm stands on positions, making subordinates more aware of the differentiation in organization levels that exists between superiors and subordinates.

4. Actively engaging in coaching functions, helping subordinates understand their job better.

Conversely, the leader should become more considerate (move from a style in fig. 14.4 to that in fig. 14.3) when he is high on the initiating structure dimension and in either a relaxed climate with strong position power or a tense climate with weak power. A manager may show greater consideration by engaging in some of the activities listed below.

1. *Show greater concern for personal problems.* This can be done, for example, by being willing to discuss how off-the-job problems affect the work of a subordinate.

2. *Representing the interests of the employee to top management.* Going to bat for members of the group or showing an interest in their advancement in the organization is a way to demonstrate concern for the individual.

3. *Increase the degree of subordinate participation in decision making.* There are usually opportunities for subordinate involvement that managers do not use. More frequent group meetings to solve problems not only may be a way to get better, more useful inputs, but could also be a demonstration of a considerate behavioral style.

Change the Climate

Attempting to change the climate is again a long-term strategy. It is probably not wise to attempt to change from a relaxed to a tense climate, since that would mean inducing distrust and reducing group cohesiveness. The alternatives suggested above seem more appropriate.

However, when a tense climate is present and the leader style is incongruent—that is, a high consideration leader with strong position power, or a high initiating structure leader with weak position power —then group development efforts may be undertaken to raise the level of trust, cohesiveness and satisfaction of the members. Ways of accomplishing group development are discussed in chapter 18.

Managing Organizational Stress in the Dynamic Organization

The concepts of organization stress, role conflict and role ambiguity are discussed extensively in chapters 4 and 12. Role ambiguity is likely to be a particular problem in the dynamic organization, because the uncertainty rising out of the complex and volatile nature of the environment pervades the nature of the tasks.

Role Ambiguity

Role ambiguity has two dimensions. The first, *task ambiguity,* is uncertainty about what a person should do. The second, *social-emotional ambiguity,* occurs when a person is uncertain about how he is evaluated. Two general conditions which generate role ambiguity are characteristic of the dynamic organization:

(1) *Organization Complexity.* As the organization achieves moderate size, it may be increasingly difficult for an individual to see how his work is related to that of others.

(2) *Rate of Organizational Change.* When the environment changes, internal relationships among jobs will change. Thus, different performance criteria may become important at different points in time (Kahn et al., 1964).

The effects of role ambiguity are increased tension, dissatisfaction with work, increased distrust, and poor relationships with others. As Hamner and Tosi (1974) note, role ambiguity may be more of a problem at higher levels than at lower. It is also more pervasive in the dynamic organization than in the bureaucratic one.

Task Ambiguity. In the bureaucratic organization, more precise task definition often flows from the narrowness of the job requirements and the stability of the organization. In the flexible organization, on the other hand, the configuration of activities (tasks) required to achieve an objective or complete a project changes over time. Since dynamic organizations are usually staffed primarily by highly trained people, including professionals, these employees will know how to do certain things well, but even though they will know how to do their own tasks, there may be a great deal of ambiguity arising from their job's relationship to other jobs. The research scientist may be extremely skillful in studying the physical properties of electrons, for example, but may not be able to understand how her work ties in with an entire project. In short, ambiguity may develop because personnel do not know the goals to which their activities should be directed.

Another type of task ambiguity may face the project manager responsible for bringing together experts from different disciplines to solve a problem. He may be uncertain of what different competencies should be brought in; his problem is one of determining which config- uration of skills is required. Only after this decision is made can thought be given to the problem of integrating and coordinating their effort.

Social-emotional Ambiguity.   Social-emotional ambiguity stems from lack of awareness of the criteria used in evaluation. In most flexible organizations, individuals are assessed on the basis of how well the project turns out and/or how well they carry out their tasks. When the project life does not coincide with budget and planning cycles or compensation review periods, this kind of assessment can present a problem. If a project is completed in mid-February, say, but the personnel review period is set for mid-June, months may pass before a superior makes a determination of what the success or failure of the project means in terms of promotions or changes in pay. It will there- fore be difficult to link rewards and performance, since they are separated so far in time.

Strategies for Reducing Role Ambiguity

There are a number of methods by which a manager in a dynamic organization can reduce role ambiguity.

1. *Clarify the path-goal relationship.* In his path-goal theory of motivation, House (1971) emphasizes that the manager's role is one of insuring clarity of the relationship between the goal (expected results) and the path (how it should be done). Since the expert, or profes- sional, in the dynamic type of organization knows how to perform (the path), the manager must do his best to state *expected goals* as

clearly as possible. If this is done, the professional can then assess whether or not, with the competence he possesses, he has a reasonable likelihood of reaching the goal.

2. *Define expected work behavior.* Some consensus should be achieved between the manager and the subordinate about how the work will be done—unless the manager is willing to let the employee make this decision. If such an approach is taken, however, the manager must be willing to trust the judgment of the expert. He should not continually be monitoring what is being done.

If the manager has preconceived notions about the best way to accomplish an activity, whether it comes from past experiences or from his own personal bias, he should let the subordinate know his preferences.

3. *Assess performance on the consensus criteria.* If assessment is based on an agreement between the superior and subordinate on how the task is to be done, then the question becomes "Was it done as agreed?" The level of success or failure is secondary, from an evaluation point of view.

These suggested strategies for dealing with role ambiguity, the reader will note, follow closely the MBO strategy suggested in chapter 11, as well as in the early part of this chapter.

Role Conflict

The negative effects of role conflict are intensified internal conflict, increased job tension, reduced job satisfaction, and low trust. In the flexible organization the role conflict will take the following forms:

Intersender Role Conflict.   This type of role conflict, caused by inconsistent demands from two or more sources, will not be as frequent a problem in the dynamic organization as in the bureaucratic organization, because under a project management type of structure it will be necessary to constantly redefine superior-subordinate relationships so that the individual will know, as a result of recent project change, to whom he is responsible in carrying out certain duties and assignments.

Interperson Role Conflict.   Interperson-role conflict occurs when organization demands conflict with an employee's basic values. As we have seen, it may not occur to an important extent in hierarchical organizations, but it will present a special problem when a member of an organization has been trained and indoctrinated in a profession with high ethical standards and feels that the organization requires actions that are below this standard, or where the person has learned certain specific ways of doing his job. When this is the case, and demands conflict with these points of view, individual problems will be aggravated to the point where employees may elect to leave. Research on attitudes of professionals and scientists indicates that they often feel that managers act in unethical ways (Moore and Renck, 1955).

Interrole Conflict.   When an individual is subject to incompatible pressures because he has more than one role, interrole conflict is present. A scientist who is also a supervisor may face contradictions in his feelings about his responsibilities to the organization and to his professional field. The college professor who identifies more strongly with his professional colleagues than with his school, or the lawyer who identifies more strongly with the legal profession than with his firm, both find themselves in a position where other professionals expect a particular behavior from them which is difficult to perform because of organizational demands.

Strategies for Dealing With Role Conflict

Since there are individuals who place a high value on their professional roles, provision must be made to give them—as part of their jobs—some opportunity to feel that their work has this value. Here are some strategies to reduce role conflict and to instill such a feeling.

Clearly define project structures.   The manager should spend time developing the authority-responsibility relationships for projects. Not only is it necessary to determine what should be done, but also who in the organization is responsible for doing it. Then this information must be communicated to those who will do the work. It will usually also be useful to specify the length of time an individual will be assigned to a project. Such time limits provide important information about *who* can initiate action for him, for what period of time. For example, an engineer on a project team to develop a new communications system for a satellite may be assigned to it for a six-month period. During that time the project chief is his superior. Unless the project assignment is then extended, at the end of six months, the engineer should count on returning to his regularly assigned department.

Set aside time for professional activities.   If the person is an active professional whose external relationships represent legitimate demands, time should be allowed to maintain those external relationships. Work can often be scheduled around these, and the organization may even pay for part of the expenses connected with attending such meetings.

Select those who have values compatible with the organizational requirements.   Interperson-role conflict can be minimized by careful screening of job candidates. If, for instance, a firm is a major defense contractor, it should, of course, screen out applicants who have strong antimilitary tendencies. Screening, however, can be overly careful. The flexible organization needs different skills and inputs, and excessive care in a selection strategy can result in the hiring of applicants whose points of view are so narrow they limit the creativity required to adapt successfully to a volatile environment.

Assign people to permanent "groups."   One way to resolve inter-sender conflict is to assign each employee to a group, or department, with someone in charge. They may be loaned to other projects as needed, but they should always have a departmental contact. An engineer may be assigned to the Communications Systems Department, for instance, but could be loaned to different projects as necessary.

Managing Conflict in the Dynamic Organization

The management of a conflict can be especially important in a dynamic organization, partly because it is important to retain people who have special skills and partly because there are special causes of conflict in dynamic organizations.

Sources of Conflict

Resource allocation problems are found in dynamic organizations, just as in hierarchical organizations, but two other problems surface as well. The first arises from differences between professional groups. The second is conflict between specialists and managers.

Resource Allocation.   In flexible organizations, budgets are likely to be drawn according to particular projects rather than departments. A project budget is one in which resources are allocated on the basis of a particular set of activities for the purpose of the achievement of a project goal. Project managers will of course compete for additional shares of a scarce resource, and since projects generally represent new or different endeavors for an organization, those who know how to plan and execute them will have more power, based on expertise, than the budget group, who must rely on the experts' recommendations. Project directors may tend to overestimate resource requirements to avoid being caught short—a kind of competition that bids up project cost and can be very dysfunctional for the organization.

As is the case with bureaucratic organizations, budget allocations in dynamic organizations are also thought of as indicative of the status and priority of an activity. This being so, project managers will generally seek to raise the level of this indicator to increase their own and their unit's importance. Conflict is especially likely when there appears to be an excessive level of support for one project and only minimal support for another.

Status Differences.   Among professionals in dynamic organizations, status problems are more likely to exist between different professional and technical groups—that is, horizontally—than between levels, as is the case in bureaucratic organizations. Status differences may also reflect the priority of different projects in the organization.

If a dynamic organization is staffed with professionals and technical experts who have invested much personal time in the development of their competence (which is usually the case), differences in status associated with intraprofessional rivalry will exist, because in their training they are likely to have been indoctrinated with values stressing the importance of their own group.

On the other hand, differences in status associated with priorities assigned to different projects is an organizationally-induced condition. In any firm, some activities are clearly defined as having higher priority than others, while at the same time, *all* projects are likely to be staffed by individuals who believe their skill and competence are important. They will be highly committed to a professional area of expertise, and yet they see that this area is not considered as important organizationally as some others. Differences between an individual's self-perceived status and the priorities associated with projects give rise to feelings of resentment.

Specialist/Administrative Conflict.   The problem of authority is difficult in the flexible organization because the specialist, or professional, possesses technical expertise (a form of power) and is probably more capable of making decisions within his sphere of competence than the manager in charge of his organizational unit. Yet the line manager is still "responsible" to higher organization levels for the operation of a unit. Victor Thompson (1963) calls this "specialist/ administrative conflict." It is a common problem in both flexible and mixed organizations. Advances in technology and market volatility make it difficult for those in higher-level positions who are no longer working directly in the technical field to maintain their high skill levels in those fields, and since organizations attempt to manage lower levels from higher levels, this difference in competence between lower and higher levels, and the right to make a decision and the ability to make it, causes conflict.

The feasibility of tentative goals of an organization are often technical questions. Thus they are best evaluated by specialists, although the superior in an organization has the right to approve or object to such tentative goals. The utility of a goal is a matter best left to the judgment of technical specialists, yet they do not have the power of decision. In large, complex organizations, the problem is made still more complex by the need to involve many specialists, or departments of specialists, in problem solving with managers. This problem of the "right to decide" causes both the specialist and the administrator to resort to the use of role defense mechanisms.

Specialist role defenses are oriented primarily toward the profession or the skill area in which the specialist functions or operates. He may seek peer support. The role defense of those in hierarchical positions is somewhat different. The administrator may make appeals to organizational loyalty or attempt to assert the power of his hierarchical position.

The Balance of Power

In the flexible organization, power will be based primarily on one or more of these factors: (1) technical expertise, (2) being in a role in a critical boundary position, (3) the amount of ownership interest one has in the organization, and/or (4) the priority of a project.

Expert Power. A dynamic organization succeeds or fails depending on whether or not the technical competence is present to perform the work. The organization may be more dependent on the expert than vice versa. Additionally, we have seen that it is unlikely that managers possess the technical skill required to evaluate alternatives and design projects well, because, even though they may have had technical competence early in a career, moving into an administrative job makes it difficult to maintain competence in rapidly developing and changing fields. This leads, in dynamic organizations, to the relegation of hierarchical (formal position) power to a secondary status.

Boundary Positions.   Those positions in an organization which inter-face with the external environment are called "boundary positions." Individuals in boundary positions must possess the ability to interpret changing environmental conditions and translate them into mean-ingful objectives for the organization. Such individuals will have a great deal of power because of the importance of their ability to the organization. They may very well experience high levels of role conflict because of different demands from the external sector and the internal organization, but they will still have a significant effect on the determination of what the organization will ultimately do.

Financial Interest.   In a smaller organization, where the ownership is not broadly dispersed to a large number of small shareholders, finan-cial interest can be especially powerful. That is, an owner can exert a great deal of influence on the setting of organizational objectives—and he may do this completely arbitrarily, with only rudimentary compe-tence.

The Priority of a Project.   The priority assigned a project can be another base of power. Managers who are in charge of a project which is assigned a high priority will have a great deal of influence (power) in the organization. For example, a firm may have three projects under way simultaneously. One may involve several millions; the other two, only several hundreds of thousands of dollars each. Obviously, the success of the firm economically is more contingent on the first than on the last two, and the manager of the first will have much more organizational power than the manager of the last two.

Resolving Conflict in Flexible Organizations

In an organization using project management, it may be difficult to create interdependencies between main projects in such a way that they will increase organizational cohesiveness. For instance, the work of a group working on project A may have no relation to the work done by the project B group. The success of either group in achieving project objectives may be independent of the other, and yet conflict arising from status differences between the two project groups may be hampering total effectiveness. Two approaches are suggested by Margulies and Wallace (1973) to resolve this problem. They are the use of team-building approaches and/or exchange of members.

Team Building.   The negative stereotypes of one group concerning another may lead to ineffectiveness. In team building an effort is made to increase the accuracy of both groups' perceptions. Each group initially meets separately to compile a list of reasons why they can't interact effectively with the other—to identify the causes of the problem. The groups then meet jointly, exchange lists, and discuss them. Margulies and Wallace (1973) say:

> Reactions and questions are responded to at length, though a ground rule limiting debate helps avoid rationalizations and justifications, facilitates the process of getting data out, and establishes a norm of *listening,* a critical factor in effecting change in the relationship. At this point careful *differentiation* of the groups, their needs and their perceptions is important. It often helps to have the groups meet separately to discuss discrepancies in perceptions and the quality of the differences between groups.

Margulies and Wallace go on to say that after differentiation has occurred, the integrating process can begin. This can be started by having selected members from both groups meet to form a new group and devise strategies for solving the problems, plans for implementing the strategies, and a way to follow up to see that the solutions are implemented.

This method can be effective, according to Margulies and Wallace, when the conflict is creating critical problems, when key members of both groups are willing to face the issues, when there is acceptance between the groups of a third-party facilitator, and when there is a general agreement to utilize and follow up on the solutions proposed.

Exchange of Members.   One reason why conflict often persists is that members of a specific group never leave that group and never operate in other groups. Thus, over time, they build up a loyalty to their own group and develop distorted perceptions of others. It may be possible to reduce some conflict situations by exchanging members of the two groups; for example, by transferring some staff from project A to project B, and vice versa. Such reassignment can have the effect of introducing different viewpoints into both groups, and of correcting misconceptions.

Margulies and Wallace suggest that this strategy will be effective under the following conditions:

1. There are persons [in both groups] whose technical competences overlap.
2. The difficulties are not rooted in deep-seated hostilities, prejudices and biases toward others.
3. Preliminary diagnosis indicates that the problems arise out of lack of understanding and appreciation of the other groups.

Other Approaches.   Some of the techniques noted in chapter 12 may be as useful in the flexible organization as in the bureaucratic. For the most part, however, the use of formal hierarchical mechanisms and formal departments is an ineffective approach in the dynamic organization. In fact, their use often increases difficulties. The use of committees, increased participation, and replacement of personnel, however, may have beneficial effects in the dynamic organization.

As with the suggested approaches to managing hierarchical organizations in chapter 12, the techniques outlined in this chapter seem especially congruent for the dynamic organization. However, they may have some utility in other organization settings for they represent, we believe, a point of departure toward solving human problems.

Discussion Questions

1. Performance evaluation for professionals in the dynamic organization focuses on means, not ends. Discuss this point of view.

2. What are the inherent problems with peer evaluation of performance? What are the advantages?

3. Why is reinforcement, as a managerial motivation strategy, not effective in a dynamic organization?

4. Can you specify the conditions under which an effective leader (say high in initiating structure behavior) in a dynamic organization would be effective in a hierarchical one?

5. Specialist/administrative conflict exists when the professional (with the skill to make a decision) has to deal with a manager (who has the right to decide). Why

can such a problem exist in an organization in which everyone works toward the same goal? Or does it?

6. One suggested approach to improving leadership is to "change the level of position power." What kind of problems do you expect to have to deal with if you reduce someone's position power?

7. List the positive and negative aspects of working in the dynamic organization.

8. Indicate why *you* would or would not want to work in a dynamic organization.

9. Some dynamic organizations eventually become more stable. Describe some of the problems that might be anticipated if this occurs.

10. What performance appraisal techniques would seem to be most useful to the organization in the dynamic organization? Which is most acceptable to the managers and professionals in this type of organization? Why?

Chapter 15

The manager in the dynamic organization faces a much less certain decision environment than in a hierarchical one. In a dynamic organization, he may not be able, or willing, to assign *risk* (or probability) to various states of nature, and he therefore is likely to make use of techniques for decision making under conditions of *uncertainty*. In this chapter, we will explain in more detail the concepts of decision making under uncertainty which were introduced in chapter 9, as well as some specific techniques for making such decisions.

Environmental Goals in Dynamic Organizations.   By definition, environmental goals for a dynamic organization will be constantly changing. The same general objective of survival is present as for the hierarchical organization, but the manner in which this goal is met varies. For example, an electronics firm may, in one time period, be producing a component for a space project, while at another time it may be building components for a computer manufacturer, and at still another time, it may be producing a device for hospitals.

Thus the product goal in the dynamic organization is not constant, since what the firm produces will vary from period to period, and consumer requirements in terms of type, quality, and quantity will keep changing. This makes it difficult to factor, or break down, these goals in similar ways over time. An appliance manufacturer, for example, may produce the exterior of refrigerators and stoves with minor changes in design in the same unit year after year. In a dynamic organization, however, there may be no set production system, except for the life of a project. When the project changes, the production system is redesigned and the staff reconstituted both in size and in the combination of skills required to satisfy the new conditions.

Decision Approaches in Dynamic Organizations

Internal System Goals.   In the dynamic organization, *internal systems goals* will be defined in two dimensions: both by level of achievement and means of achievement. Because each project must be designed substantially differently from previous projects, extensive coordination and cooperation will be required from lower-level personnel in order to find out what they can do, how long it will take, and when it can be done. If there are a large number of different units involved, one of the primary tasks of top management will be to perform this integrating function. Having lower-level personnel involved in these work activities necessitates that their inputs, in the form of proposals and design, be considered significantly, since they possess the technical expertise and are likely to be the most competent group to provide this information. In the stable organization, lower-level participation serves a communication function; in the dynamic organization, these groups will actually influence the way things are to be done. They will be extremely helpful in project design and in determining how a specific objective should be achieved. Item 15.1 describes the planning process in dynamic organizations. It shows the need for lower-level involvement in planning—but with a need for some centralized control.

The Characteristic of Controls

Thus, in the dynamic organization, the focus of control will be different for different projects because the dimensions of level and means of achievement will vary from project to project. It is necessary to define the *means of achievement* for projects, since in many cases, the manager will be unable to determine, during the actual conduct of the project, whether or not costs are at an acceptable level or whether or not the product performs adequately. In a steel plant, for example, performance may be monitored as the production process goes on by quality and cost measures, but in the aerospace industry about all a manager can do is determine whether an activity is completed on time and whether those who performed it have done it in a way that is generally acceptable.

ITEM 15.1   Resource Allocation

A Focal Point of Planning

If planning is now working its way up from the bottom in most large companies there still is a focal point of planning at the corporate level that is becoming increasingly significant—resource allocation among the units of a company. Frequently this is the key to the corporation's centralized authority.

At GE, for example, planning is carried out simultaneously but with a different perspective at corporate headquarters and in its 43 strategic business units. "Some type of corporate glue was necessary to tie these pieces together," says GE's Gutoff. "That recognition led to the planning work that pulled together these decentralized businesses. The business units were charged with doing their own planning, but overlaying that was planning at the corporate level, where we're going to have to make some tradeoffs, some resource allocations. It's really the interplay of these two activities that led to the functioning of the whole GE system."

Corporate planning at RCA Corp. also emphasizes determining which businesses will grow and which will not. "The top-down look on the businesses is as competitive investments," says George C. Evanoff, vice-president for corporate development at RCA, which has five major operating groups and 15 primary profit centers. "We're putting more emphasis on where the resource should be placed than how it should be applied. For example, do we back domestic satellites? Our essential plan is an articulation of strategies saying this area should receive more attention, this one less in terms of resource allocation."

This twin-planning technique—in which diverse business units plan their own futures but with an override by the corporation—may be the most effective answer yet to the increasingly knotty control problems facing complex companies spanning several industries. Professor James P. Baughman of Harvard Business School maintains that as business redefines its post-World War II assumptions, there is a rush away from decentralization to more centralized decision-making. Until recently, decentralization has been gospel and most middle managers were weaned on the concept. Now with the tightening of control, division managers in many corporations are beginning to complain about loss of autonomy. "It's cultural shock for a great many divisional executives," who see their previously delegated power eroding and even their pay threatened, says Baughman. "But it's also cultural shock for the top managers who aren't familiar with this sort of decision making."

Business Week, April 28, 1975

Thus, because middle management and professional groups have the technical expertise, middle and lower-level management in the dynamic organization will be more extensively involved in setting both end result and activity goals than in the stable organization, and evaluation will proceed according to these goals. Of course, top management evaluates and approves the goals, but they will need to use more participative management strategies than is usually true in the hierarchical organization.

The primary mode of management in a dynamic organization will be project management (see chap. 7). Under project management, an executive's influence and authority is much more fluid than in the stable organization, changing with each project. Cleland (1967) notes that

> project management—molding the organization around a specific task or project—is the concept that has been developed to deal with situations where production and marketing strategies for new projects do not fit into a purely functional type of organization.
>
> The project manager works across functional . . . and organizational . . . lines to bring together activities required to accomplish a project. . . .
>
> Authority in project decisions may be indifferent to the order of hierarchical affairs. . . .project authority depends heavily on the personality of the project manager and how he sees his role in relation to the project environment.

Decision Making under Uncertainty

The difficulties with which organizations operating in a volatile environment must cope arise from the fact not only that changes in the external environment must be perceived and assessed, but also that the changes themselves often alter the organization's methods of goal achievement. This means that organizations operating in a volatile environment must have a flexible structure, one in which both human and technical resources are adaptable to changing tasks. Since the opportunities to develop fixed production systems that are present in the stable organization are not present in the dynamic organization, resources in the latter must be kept mobile.

What the manager in the dynamic organization must do is adopt planning strategies for short time periods, recognizing that subsequent periods may require vastly different organizational activities. Starr (1971) addresses this problem by noting that one

approach is to speed up management's response rates and to plan
for periods that are short enough to be relatively stable. Short planning periods have all the dangers of suboptimization. . ., but, if
consecutive periods are relatively independent, then a good deal
can be gained from faster decision making, more rapid action, and
so on. Speed is accomplished largely through increased experience. . . .

The emphatic thrust, then, in dynamic organizations will be to
make decisions about what environmental goals should look like,
based on the changes that managers feel will occur, and to focus on
the development, design, and effective managing of project-like task
activities.

The manager in the dynamic organization therefore needs to know
how to make decisions when there is high uncertainty in the environment. He must deal with two problems: (1) selecting a strategy likely
to be successful in an unpredictable environment, and (2) implementing the strategy. Item 15.2 describes GE's approach for evaluating
various strategies. It shows the "subjectivity" involved in strategy
decisions in a dynamic organization.

The following discussion of decision making under uncertainty
introduces the ideas that are helpful in approaching decision problems in unpredictable circumstances. Suppose MVR Company is an
electronics firm which manufactures solid state electronic components, transistors, and quartz crystals. Their primary market has been
to produce these components for other firms, acting as a main
supplier for companies which manufacture and market digital
watches and electronic calculators. After evaluating the success of
these firms, MVR's president and executive committee decide that it
may be profitable for them to enter one or more of these watch and
calculator fields. The executive committee meets and proposes four
strategies for MVR. It is equally open to the four strategies and is
meeting to decide which way the company should go. The strategies
are:

S1. To manufacture and market medical technology
S2. To manufacture and market electronic calculators
S3. To manufacture and market digital watches
S4. To remain in the current business

Today the planning group is meeting with the executive committee
to present the results of their study of each of these alternatives. They
were asked to forecast the returns to MVR for each of these different

strategies so that the executive committee could select the "best"
alternative. Due to the innovative character of each of these strategies

---

ITEM 15.2   Planning

General Electric's 'Stoplight Strategy' for Planning

General Electric Co. thinks it has found at least a partial solution to an age-old corporate planning problem: how to put a value on those critical elements in planning it is impossible to attach a number to. In a decision on whether a product will live or die, for example, the value of a patent or the impact of social change cannot be quantified. By using its Strategic Business Planning Grid, or "stoplight strategy," GE can at least evaluate such factors with something more than just a gut reaction.

"It's the best way we've found to sort disparate businesses," says GE planner Reuben Gutoff. "You eventually have to make a subjective decision, but you put into it all the hard information you can. It's one way to compare apples and oranges."

GE, with 43 distinct businesses, has a lot of apples and oranges. In every annual planning review, each individual business is rated not only on numerical projections of sales, profit, and return on investment, but also on such hard-to-quantify factors as volatility of market share, technology needs, employee loyalty in the industry, competitive stance, and social need. The result is a high,

---

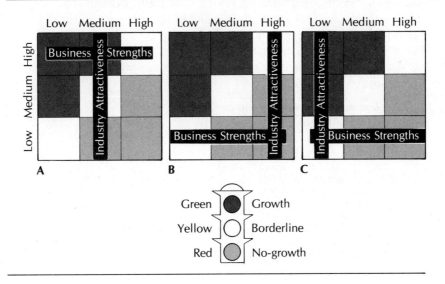

General Electric's "Stoplight Strategy" for Planning

medium, or low rating on both attractiveness of an industry and GE's strengths in the field.

How it works. If industry attractiveness is seen as medium and GE's strengths as high (Chart A), an "invest and grow"—or green light—decision would result, because the evaluation bars cross in a green square. Both industry attractiveness and business strength are low in Chart B, indicating a red light strategy, or a business which will continue to generate earnings but no longer warrants much additional investment by GE. Chart C represents a business with high industry attractiveness but low GE strength—a "yellow" business that might go either way.

A green business is expected to grow. A red operation's strategy, on the other hand, may involve consolidation of plants, limited technology infusion, reduced investment, and strong cash flow. A yellow business could be borderline, or the business—say, electronic

components—could be diverse enough to have both red and green units.

"We don't give definitive weights to the non-numerical factors," says Gutoff, "but they do have weights. At the end of our discussion there is a good consensus on what's green, red, or yellow." The result, he says, is "semiquantitative." After three or four critiques at various levels, the final grids—and decisions—are made by the corporate policy committee—the chairman, three vice-chairman, five senior vice-presidents, and the vice-president for finance.

The process is not just window dressing. It may prevent costly mistakes. "Interestingly," says one GE planner, "the financial projections are often best on businesses that turn up worst (in the red) on the grid."

Business Week, April 28, 1975

(except S4), no one is really willing to make any guesses about the probabilities of market changes which might affect the profits. No one, then, feels he can make a good estimate of the different states of nature which might occur. Yet, the planning group has made some projections based on certain possible market conditions (but not whether or not these will occur, or their probabilities). These states of nature are:

N1. Increased demand in the medical field
N2. Increased demand for electronic calculators
N3. Increased demand for digital watches
N4. No change in the current demand state

The resulting forecast for each strategy and the return (conditional value) for each state of nature is shown in figure 15.1 as a payoff matrix with the conditional values (the entries) representing changes in projected profits for MVR (given in millions of dollars). Note that these decision makers are faced with a substantially different problem than the one faced by the gift shop in chapter 13, since they cannot, or will not, make probability estimates about the states of nature. The

FIGURE 15.1 Payoff Matrix for MVR Company

Strategy	States of Nature			
	Market Conditions			
	N1	N2	N3	N4
	Increased Medical	Increased Calculator	Increased Watches	No Change
S1. Enter Medical Field	300	250	100	-100
S2. Enter Calculator	100	400	200	-150
S3. Enter Digital Watch	50	300	600	-300
S4. Stay the Same	-50	-75	-100	150

expected value (EV) for each strategy cannot be computed since $EV = (p)(CV)$. So, how can a "rational" decision be made?

Problems of this type are called *decisions under uncertainty*. Miller and Starr (1960) say that   .

> one of the most interesting results of decision theory has been the discovery that there is no one best criterion for selecting strategy. Instead, there are a number of different criteria, each of which has a perfectly good rationale to justify it. The choice among these criteria is determined by company policy and/or the attitude of the decision maker.

When these different criteria are applied to a decision under conditions of uncertainty, it is possible that any of a number of different strategies may be selected. Here are several of these decision criteria as they apply to the MVR Company.

The Pessimistic Criterion

The decision maker may adopt an attitude that is pessimistic, that the worst is likely to happen. Given this set of assumptions, the decision maker should select the strategy which returns to him the greatest amount under the worst conditions. Consider the problem of the MVR Company. For each strategy, we find the *lowest*, or minimum payoff. These are shown for the MVR Company in figure 15.2, the payoff matrix.

Now assuming that the worst will happen, if we select the strategy

FIGURE 15.2 Payoff Matrix for MVR Company

| | States of Nature | | | | |
| | Market Conditions | | | | |
Strategy	N1 Increased Medical	N2 Increased Calculator	N3 Increased Watches	N4 No Change	Worst Pay Off
S1. Enter Medical Field	300	250	100	(-100)	-100
S2. Enter Calculator	100	400	200	(-150)	-150
S3. Enter Digital Watch	50	300	600	(-300)	-300
S4. Stay the Same	-50	-75	(-100)	150	-100

Decision using Pessimistic Criterion:
Stay in same business or enter medical field.

FIGURE 15.3 Payoff Matrix for MVR Company.

| | States of Nature | | | | |
| | Market Conditions | | | | |
Strategy	N1 Increased Medical	N2 Increased Calculator	N3 Increased Watches	N4 No Change	Best Pay Off
S1. Enter Medical Field	(300)	250	100	-100	300
S2. Enter Calculator	100	(400)	200	-150	400
S3. Enter Digital Watch	50	300	(600)	-300	600
S4. Stay the Same	-50	-75	-100	(150)	150

Decision using Optimistic Criterion:
Enter digital watch field.

no *change* in product structure (S4), then we will obtain the maximum minimum payoff. This same outcome will occur if we enter the medical field (S1). This criterion for making decisions is called *maximin.* If our conditional values are correctly forecasted, then the worst that can happen to MVR is that they will not lose more than

$100 million if they stay in the same business (S4) or enter the medical field (S1).

The Optimistic Criterion

Just as one could assume the worst might happen, it could also be assumed that the best might occur. The decision maker may feel fortunate, rather than unfortunate. The *maximax* criterion selects the strategy which has the greatest payoff. This approach, of course, is just the opposite of the pessimistic criterion. To determine the best decision using the *maximax* or optimistic criterion, the decision maker determines the largest payoff for each strategy. For the MVR Company, these are shown in figure 15.3.

In this case, the MVR Company would select the alternative of entering the digital watch market (S3). If the assumption about good fortune holds, then the company will make $600 million.

The Regret Criterion

There is another way to look at the problem. Once we make a decision, and know the results, it may be that we would have been better off if we had done something else. The regret criterion is based on the idea that

the decision maker should attempt to minimize the regret which he may experience. Exactly what is his regret? It appears to be the fact that he may not have selected the best strategy in terms of the particular state of nature that did, in fact, occur. Savage suggests that the amount of his regret might be measured by the difference between the payoff he actually received and the difference between the payoff he actually received and the payoff he could have received *if he had known the state of nature that was going to occur* [emphasis ours] (Miller and Starr, 1960).

Making these assumptions, it is possible to construct a *regret matrix* for MVR Company. The entries are the "amount of regret" for each strategy and each state of nature (figs. 15.4 and 15.5). First consider what the best strategy would be in the event of the occurrence of the state of nature (N1), increased medical product demand. Examining that row in the payoff matrix, it is clear that the medical field strategy (S1) would be best. If we select that alternative, we would be most satisfied and have no regrets ($300 − $300 = 0). This was computed

FIGURE 15.4   Payoff Matrix for MVR Company

| | States of Nature | | | |
| | Market Conditions | | | |
Strategy	N1 Increased Medical	N2 Increased Calculator	N3 Increased Watches	N4 No Change
S1. Enter Medical Field	300 (-300)	250 (-400)	100 (-600)	-100 (-150)
S2. Enter Calculator	100 (-300)	400 (-400)	200 (-600)	-150 (-150)
S3. Enter Digital Watch	50 (-300)	300 (-400)	600 (-600)	-300 (-150)
S4. Stay the Same	-50 (-300)	-75 (-400)	-100 (-600)	150 (-150)

by taking the highest payoff for that state of nature ($300) from the payoff for the medical field entry alternative.

We can continue in the same fashion to obtain a regret measure for the "calculator" alternative for the same state of nature (increased medical demand—N1). MVR would have made $100 million if they had decided this way, but they could have made $300 million if they had done something else (entered the medical field, S1). They would have lost the opportunity to make $200 million—$100 million (the calculator payoff) which they received, less $300 million (the medical field alternative), which they did not get. The regret for the other two strategies (S3 and S4) if the market increases in medical technology is given at $250 million and $350 million (see fig. 15.5).

Now consider the regret computations for another state of nature, for example, if the market shift is to "increased demand for digital watches" (column N3 in the payoff matrix). If this state of nature occurs, then MVR would experience no regret (0) if they "enter the digital watch market" (S3). But, if N3 does occur and they have selected S1, then they would experience $500 million worth of regret. This means they made $100 million but lost the opportunity to make $600 million. The $500 million is obtained by subtracting $600 million (payoff for S3, N3) from the $100 million (payoff for S1, N3). By continuing with computations such as these, the regret matrix in figure 15.5 is constructed.

We are not yet finished, however, for MVR wants to select the strategy which leaves them with the least regret. MVR management can now examine each strategy, and find the greatest regret score for it. The strategy selected using this criterion is to enter the calculator market (S2), since MVR would experience the least amount of regret ($400 million) if they did this.

The Rational Criterion

This approach is based on the idea that for decisions under conditions of uncertainty, it is impossible to make a reasonably adequate estimate

FIGURE 15.5 Payoff Matrix for MVR Company

| | States of Nature | | | | |
| | Market Conditions | | | | |
Strategy	N1 Increased Medical	N2 Increased Calculator	N3 Increased Watches	N4 No Change	Maximum Regret
S1. Enter Medical Field	0	-150	-500	-250	-500
S2. Enter Calculator	-200	0	-400	-300	-400
S3. Enter Digital Watch	-250	-100	0	-450	-450
S4. Stay the Same	-350	-475	-700	0	-700

Decision using Regret Approach:
Enter digital watch field.

FIGURE 15.6 Payoff Matrix for MVR Company.

| | States of Nature | | | | |
| | Market Conditions (p = .25) | | | | |
Strategy	N1 Increased Medical	N2 Increased Calculator	N3 Increased Watches	N4 No Change	ΣEV
S1. Enter Medical Field	300	250	100	-100	137.5
S2. Enter Calculator	100	400	200	-150	137.5
S3. Enter Digital Watch	50	300	600	-300	162.5
S4. Stay the Same	-50	-75	-100	150	-18.75

Decision using Rationality Criterion:
Enter digital watch field.

of the probability of a particular state of nature occurring, but that if there is no cause to believe that one state of nature is more likely to occur than another, it can be reasonably assumed that they are equally likely to occur.

Making this assumption means that for a decision problem under uncertainty (where we apply no probability estimates), we assign equal probabilities to all states of nature. In the case of MVR Company, this means that we assign probabilities of .25 (¼) to each state of nature. When this is done, then it is possible to compute the total expected value for each strategy, and this leads to the decision to enter the digital watch market (S3). This computation is shown in figure 15.6.

A Planning and Control Approach in Dynamic Organizations

Planning and control in dynamic organizations must take into account the uncertainties involved. The dynamic organization must rely on less accurate estimates of project time and costs than the stable firm. In planning and control in the dynamic organization, the control process can be facilitated by giving managers some idea about what aspects of the project are critical in order to pinpoint strategic control points. These points can then be monitored to see that events are conforming to plan. The following example shows how this can be accomplished using the method known as PERT.

PERT (Project Evaluation and Review Technique)

Suppose you are a project manager for the MLZ Aerospace firm. You have just been told that the company is going to embark on the design and construction of a space-landing vehicle. While MLZ has been active in the space program, it has never been involved with a project quite like this. You have virtually no experience with landing vehicles, but the company has successfully produced other equipment which is similar but still substantially different enough so that you, as a manager, feel somewhat uncertain about how long such a project will take.

In cases like this, PERT is a useful planning and control device, since it introduces the concept of probability estimates, which have some utility when planning is done in a relatively uncertain environment. To use PERT for this project, you must:

1. identify each task required;
2. obtain time estimates for each task; and
3. determine the sequencing and relationship of each task to the others.

Figure 15.7 shows the basic network design for this project. Each task (or activity) is designated by an arrow (→), and represents some relatively discrete part of the work on the project. Each activity starts and stops with some identifiable event and is designated by a circle (○), so that an activity event chain will look like this, A→B, where the activity (1) can be clearly identified by a beginning and an end point. An example might be the activity (1) of *going to work*. It is preceded by the event *leave home* (A) and followed by the event *arrive at work* (B). For each activity, a time estimate is made. For example, you might estimate that, based on past experience, it will take you 35 minutes to get to work.

FIGURE 15.7 Basic PERT Network for Space-landing Vehicle Project

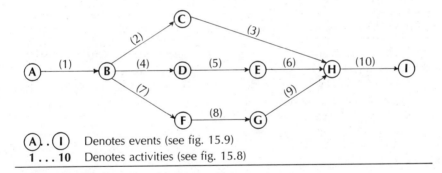

(A)..(I) Denotes events (see fig. 15.9)
1 ... 10 Denotes activities (see fig. 15.8)

Time Estimates

Network diagrams have been used extensively prior to the development of PERT. The Gantt Chart, for example (mentioned in chap. 2), is a planning, scheduling, and control device similar to PERT, but constructed without the use of time probability estimates. The time estimate is the significant component of the PERT approach.

Figure 15.8 lists the activities that you, the project manager, know will be required to complete the space vehicle. Figure 15.9 is a list of events that designate the starting and ending of each of these activities.

FIGURE 15.8 Activity Time Estimates

Activities	Optimistic (a)	Most Likely (b)	Pessimistic (c)	Activity Time Estimate (Te)
1. Approve Specifications	2	2.5	6	3
2. Develop Recruiting Plans	1	3	5	3
3. Hire Work Force	3	4.5	9	5
4. Design Power System	4	5.5	10	6
5. Build Power System	8	11	14	11
6. Test Power System	4	6	8	6
7. Design Frame	3	4.5	9	5
8. Build Frame	9	9.5	13	10
9. Test Frame	1	3	5	3
10. Assemble and Test Vehicle	4	6	8	6

FIGURE 15.9 Events for Space-landing Vehicle Project

A. Receive Specifications
B. Begin Project
C. Begin Recruiting
D. Begin Power System Construction
E. Begin Power System Test

F. Begin Frame Construction
G. Begin Frame Test
H. Assemble Frame and Power System
I. Deliver Vehicle

Also shown in figure 15.8 are the time estimates which are necessary to construct the PERT network. For each activity, three time estimates are obtained, the *optimistic, most likely,* and *pessimistic.*

1. *optimistic time (a).* In the event that the work proceeds without any problems, interferences, or obstacles, what is the least time that the activity would take?

2. *The most likely time (b).* What would the manager expect the activity time to be under normal circumstances? Realistically, how much time is required to complete the activity?

3. *The pessimistic time (c).* What is the maximum time that the activity would require if things go very wrong? Given the worst of conditions, how much time should the project take?

These times are shown in the columns in figure 15.8. In order to calculate a time estimate for an activity (Te), these times are weighed in the following fashion.

$$Te = \frac{a + 4b + c}{6}$$

These weights are values derived from a Beta distribution and when used with the three time estimates provide, some planners think, optimum accuracy in estimating (Starr, 1971).

As the project manager, you go to each section chief responsible for the designated activity and ask for each of these time estimates. Suppose you get, from the head of power system design (activity 4) the following time estimates.

        a. Optimistic design time = 4 weeks
        b. Most likely design time = 5.5 weeks
        c. Pessimistic design time = 10 weeks

Using the formula for computing Te, we find that the estimate used in our network is 6 weeks.

$$Te = \frac{4 + 4(5.5) + 10}{6} = \frac{36}{6} = 6 \text{ weeks}$$

FIGURE 15.10 PERT Network for Space-landing Vehicle Project Showing Estimated Activity Times and Critical Path

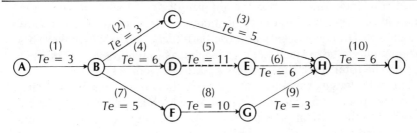

Path Times   ------ Critical Path

By obtaining similar estimates of each of the activities listed in figure 15.8, the manager constructs the network shown in figure 15.10. Figure 15.10 is a representation similar to figure 15.7, but the activity times (Te) have been entered above the arrows.

The Critical Path

By examining figure 15.10, you can see that there are three main branches, or paths, in this project.

1. $A \rightarrow B \rightarrow C \rightarrow H \rightarrow I$ = 17 Weeks
2. $A \rightarrow B \rightarrow D \rightarrow E \rightarrow H \rightarrow I$ = 32 Weeks
3. $A \rightarrow B \rightarrow F \rightarrow G \rightarrow H \rightarrow I$ = 27 Weeks

The longest of these is called the *critical path*. Knowing the *critical path* can be of great help to the manager.

1. *It is the longest path in the project.*
2. *It is the shortest time in which the project can be completed.* If our estimates of time are correct, it will be impossible for MLZ to build the space vehicle in less than 32 weeks, as resources are currently allocated.
3. *It identifies strategic control points.* The manager is able to identify which parts of the project should be observed most closely. If activities along the *critical* path take more time than estimated, then we can be certain that the length of the project time will be extended.

There is, once the project starts, no leeway in time on the critical path. On the other paths, however, there is some leeway. This leeway is called "slack time," and is the amount of time that we have that is, in a sense, noncritical to the project target date. As figure 15.10 shows, the path BCH takes 8 weeks and the path BDEH takes 23 weeks. This means that we have slack time, or leeway as to when event C must begin. The total slack time on this path is 15 weeks.

The knowledge of where slack time exists is important because it identifies pockets of potential resources which conceivably could be diverted to the critical path to shorten it. To compute slack time, two other concepts are needed in PERT.

Earliest Possible Time (EPT).   This is the earliest, or soonest, that an activity can begin. It takes into account the times for all activities in the PERT network that precede it which are linked to it in sequence. In the example, for instance, the earliest possible time for event C is 6 weeks after the project begins. This is so because activities (1) and (2) each take 3 weeks.

Latest Allowable Time (LAT).   This is the latest time at which an activity can begin in order to meet the time requirements of the critical path. It can be seen from figure 15.10 that the latest allowable time for event C is 5 weeks before the event H. Figure 15.11 illustrates these concepts. By computing the time required for path *ABDEH* on the critical path (26 weeks), and subtracting the time required for activity (3), "Hiring the Work Force," which takes 5 weeks, the latest allowable time for event C is 21 weeks (26 − 5). In figure 15.11, latest (LAT) times and earliest (EPT) times are illustrated for both paths in the project other than the critical path.

Figure 15.12 is a summary table in which the slack time (LAT − EPT) is computed for each event in the network. It is constructed in the following manner. The first event (A) is designated as time 0, or the start of the project; the LAT and EPT are the same. The EPT for event B is three weeks after the project begins, since this is our estimated project time. The latest allowable time is also three weeks, because event B is on the critical path. Each event on the *critical path* has been identified in figure 15.12 with an asterisk (*). LAT and EPT for events on the critical path are the same; therefore, there is no slack time for any of them. This is shown by the zero in the "Slack Time" column of figure 15.12.

The manager can now proceed to compute the EPTs for all events not on the critical path. By beginning at the start of the project and adding the activity time for all activities preceding an event, the EPTs are determined. Event C has an EPT of six weeks after project start. Event F's EPT is eight weeks ($A \xrightarrow{3} B \xrightarrow{5} F$). Event G's EPT is 18 weeks ($A \xrightarrow{3} B \xrightarrow{5} F \xrightarrow{10} G$).

The latest allowable times are computed by working back along the noncritical paths from a point where they meet an event on the critical path. It has been shown that the LAT and EPT for event H is 26 weeks. Since we have made a time estimate of 3 weeks for activity 9, "Testing the Frame," the LAT for event G is 3 weeks *before* event H, or 23 weeks (26 − 3) after the start of the project. The slack time for event G is five weeks.

$$\text{LAT} - \text{EPT} = \text{slack time}$$
$$23 - 18 = 5 \text{ weeks}$$

Figure 15.13 illustrates the notion of slack time on noncritical

---

FIGURE 15.11 Slack Time Computation for Space-landing Vehicle Project

---

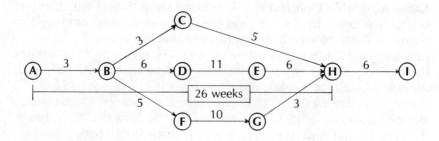

Event C: Latest Allowable Time, 26 - 5 = 21 weeks
          Earliest Possible Time, 3 + 3 = 6 weeks
Event G: Latest Allowable Time, 26 - 3 = 23 weeks
          Earliest Possible Time, 3 + 5 + 10 = 18 weeks
Event F: Latest Allowable Time, 26 - 3 -10 = 13 weeks
          Earliest Possible Time, 3 + 5 = 8 weeks

FIGURE 15.12 Computation of Slack Times for Events
              in Space-landing Vehicle Project

Events	Latest Allowable Time (LAT)	Earliest Possible Time (EPT)	Slack Time (LAT - EPT)
A. Receive Specifications*	0	0	0
B. Begin Project*	3	3	0
C. Begin Recruiting	21	6	15
D. Begin Power System Construction*	9	9	0
E. Begin Power System Test*	20	20	0
F. Begin Frame Construction	13	8	5
G. Begin Frame Test	23	18	5
H. Assemble Frame and Power System*	26	26	0
I. Deliver Vehicle*	32	32	0

*Denotes event on critical path.

paths. Events along them may, in effect, be slid forward to the LATs for events C and G. Events on these paths may start any time after EPT, but begin no later than the LAT. It is, in this sense, that slack time is leeway for the project.

FIGURE 15.13 Slack Times for Space-landing Vehicle Project

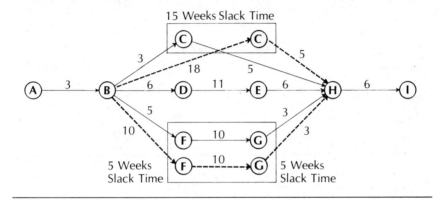

Redesigning the Project.   Having gone through the analysis of the project, the manager decides that the project time of 32 weeks is unacceptable. The deadline is 30 weeks from project start, not 32. Knowing where slack time exists permits him to shift resources to the critical path, or to move activities off the path.

Faced with the dilemma of a deadline that cannot be met with the current plan, one possibility would be to move events off the critical path. If, for instance, the path BCH was some activities other than recruiting, and activity six not dependent on activity five, one alternative might be to move activity six as shown in figure 15.14. This changes the critical path, as shown, and reduces planned project time to 27 weeks. This is not a likely alternative for MLZ because of the nature of the project, but it is one solution to other network problems.

Perhaps the most realistic alternative for the project manager in this case would be to use some of the slack resources on path ABFGHI. Assume that these activities are technical engineering functions performed in different departments. If frame design engineers also have competence in designing power systems, it may be possible to transfer some of these people to the power system design and construction stage. Let us do that and assume that the times for the following activities on the critical path become these:

FIGURE 15.14   Revised Network with Events and Activities Moved off
Critical Path to Locations where Slack exists

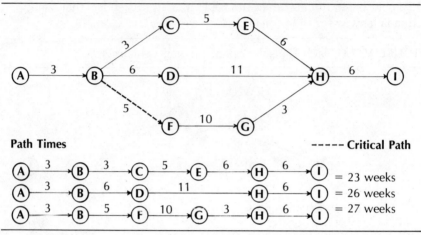

Path Times   ----- Critical Path

A —3→ B —3→ C —5→ E —6→ H —6→ I = 23 weeks
A —3→ B —6→ D —11→ H —6→ I = 26 weeks
A —3→ B —5→ F —10→ G —3→ H —6→ I = 27 weeks

FIGURE 15.15   Revised Network Showing Critical Path when Resources
Are Shifted from Frame Division to Power System Division

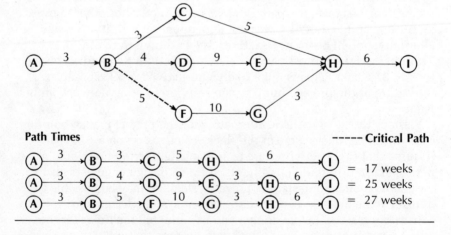

Path Times   ----- Critical Path

A —3→ B —3→ C —5→ H —6→ I = 17 weeks
A —3→ B —4→ D —9→ E —3→ H —6→ I = 25 weeks
A —3→ B —5→ F —10→ G —3→ H —6→ I = 27 weeks

Activity	Te
4. Design Power System	4 weeks
5. Build Power System	9 weeks
6. Test Power System	3 weeks

These reduced activity times have been obtained because resources have been directed to the critical path. The new network is shown in figure 15.15. The new critical path is *ABFGHI* and is 27 weeks.

Some Applications of PERT

There have been a number of different applications of the PERT technique to management decision problems. It has been used, for example, in the construction industry for the planning of large-scale projects such as buildings, dams, and roads. It has been used to plan and control major defense projects such as the building of the Polaris submarine. To make an assessment of the costs for a project, instead of time estimates, a manager can use the most likely cost, the least cost, and the highest cost for activities. Then the manager can proceed as described in the time estimate example above.

Perhaps the most important point of this chapter is that there are ways to manage in the uncertain environment. They require different techniques than might be useful in the stable organization, but the manager faced with uncertainty should find some comfort in knowing that approaches exist which can be of help to him.

Discussion Questions

1. What are the primary differences between the various approaches to decision making under uncertainty (e.g., optimistic, pessimistic, etc.)? What would you think to be the primary determinant of which one you would use?

2. Construct a PERT network for some project which you are planning in the future, say a vacation. Where is the slack time? What is the critical path?

3. In chapter 13, Starr was quoted as saying that in the final analysis, "a plan is detailed as though no worthwhile opportunities for deviating from the plan will occur." Is this true for dynamic organizations? Why? What are the differences between the dynamic and hierarchical organizations with respect to this statement?

4. Suppose you have the following payoff matrix:

	States of Nature		
	(1)	(2)	(3)
Strategy 1	$2,000	$10,000	$12,000
Strategy 2	4,000	11,000	8,000
Strategy 3	9,000	8,000	6,000

a. What is the decision that the "optimist" would make?
b. The "pessimist"?
c. To minimize "regret"?
d. The "rational" manager?

Chapter 16

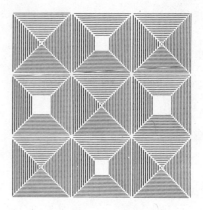

By definition, the mixed organization contains subunits which have stable environments and subunits which have volatile environments —the level of environmental stability, of course, being relative. That is, classifying environments as *either* stable *or* volatile oversimplifies reality but is necessary for purposes of analysis and discussion.

In the market-dominated mixed (MD-mixed) organization, the market is volatile and the technological sector is stable. Lawrence and Lorsch (1969) describe a container company which had an uncertain market environment, since demand for their product (corrugated boxes for poultry, citrus fruits, beer, etc.) varied with changing geographic demand, weather conditions, and competitor actions. On the other hand, the processes for manufacturing these containers did not change significantly in any short period of time.

Conversely, the technologically-dominated mixed (TD-mixed) organization has a volatile technology but a stable market. In one firm of moderate size which manufactures picture tubes for television sets, there were some startling technological advances over a short period of time. "Quick heat," which allowed the tube to project a picture more quickly than before, was introduced, as were new methods of safeguarding tubes against the possibilities of fire or explosion. The product changed and the technology had to change to keep pace. On the other hand, the customers (manufacturers of television sets) were limited in number and readily identifiable, and demand for the new type of tube was highly predictable.

Under conditions such as this there is a need to recognize that the structure of the different parts of the organization must vary—each unit must be appropriate for the level of uncertainty of the environment with which it interfaces. We have pointed out in previous

Managing the Mixed Organization

chapters the managerial processes that are the most appropriate in stable organizations and in dynamic organizations. The discussion in those chapters is relevant to the mixed organization also, since the management processes appropriate to the stable organization are also appropriate to the stable organizational units in the mixed organization, and those appropriate to the dynamic organization are appropriate to the dynamic organizational units in the mixed organization.

Many managers in mixed organizations do not understand the necessity of such a differentiation in terms of structures and management. One large company in another country, for example, is composed of a number of subsidiary companies organized into an appliances division, an electronics division, and an industrial goods division. The practice in the organization was to require all subsidiary companies to adhere closely to the organization's personnel policies even though this caused problems for certain units. For example, the technologically advanced companies had to promote from within and were not allowed to hire individuals with advanced technological training and experience, even though this was necessary to keep abreast of changing scientific and technological developments. As a result, the more technologically-sophisticated subsidiaries were falling behind competitively. In addition, the decision-making structure, supervisory style, performance-evaluation procedures, and personal characteristics of employees were not differentiated among the appliance companies (in stable environments) and the electronic and industrial goods companies (in dynamic environments). Top management felt that one particular managerial approach would be effective in *all* the subsidiaries. Similarly, Lawrence and Lorsch (1969) report that several U.S. companies they consulted were not

aware of the importance of establishing the appropriate type of differentiation, given a particular state of uncertainty. Thus, a lack of
awareness by managers of the research on organizational design, along
with a belief in "universal" managerial principles, contributes to
continued managerial problems rising simply from the existence of
ineffective structures of organization.

Figure 16.1 represents the mixed organization we have been
discussing. It shows two organizational units, one flexible and one
bureaucratic. Manager X of the flexible unit will need to operate with
a loose structure, make decisions under uncertainty, and often must
manage highly trained personnel such as engineers, or marketing
professionals. On the other hand, it is likely that manager Y of the
bureaucratic unit will find that he is responsible for a highly routine
system with well-defined decision rules and policies. These differences between the organizational units may create problems for
manager X and manager Y—and also for manager Z who must manage
the interface between the units.

FIGURE 16.1   The Interface Problem in the Mixed Organization

---

The factor determining the severity of this interface problem is the
amount of interdependence between the units. In the mixed organization, it is likely that in some units the work flow requires that two
units must work closely together. Obviously the greater the interdependence, the higher the need for integration. In the same organization, however, still other units may have little contact.

The achievement of integration between diverse organizational
units is a worthwhile goal, since high degrees of integration are associated with high economic performance. The most integrated firms are

the most successful—where integration between units is necessary because of their interdependence (Lawrence and Lorsch, 1967).

Successful integration is not necessarily a matter of avoiding conflict in all situations. Conflict between two organizational units may be reduced or eliminated, and yet the units may not work together productively in achieving organizational objectives. We know also that conflict among or between organizational units may actually be useful in terms of organizational goals if it stimulates creativity. This is an especially important factor in volatile organizational settings, particularly where the fostering innovation is important.

In addition, since all organizations have multiple objectives, many of which do not fit together neatly, some means must be found to satisfy all of an organization's objectives to at least some degree, and this occurs often through conflict and then compromise. For example, if an organization wants to produce a product where the objectives of cost, production ease, and technological sophistication are all important, conflict between the marketing department (concerned with price), the production department (concerned with manufacturing efficiencies), and the research and development unit (concerned with emphasizing technological sophistication) may have beneficial effects, since a compromise embodying all of these considerations may result.

At the same time, conflict can be harmful if it takes certain forms. This is why in the rest of this chapter the emphasis is on the positive management of conflict, in contrast to allowing conflict to occur without taking action to channel it into behaviors that are not harmful to the organization. In any organization, efforts should be made to integrate the activities of various organizational units—most especially those with interdependent work, but before we begin to link differentiated systems together, we should be aware of the causes of problems that must be solved.

Causes of Integration Difficulties

There are some natural pressures which will drive the hierarchical unit to be separate, or differentiated, from the flexible unit of the mixed organization. As we have seen (chap. 14), the organization unit at the volatile boundary will be most influential in terms of company policy and strategy. There is some support for the notion that when one group dominates another consistently and imposes its views consistently over time, the less powerful group's negative reactions tend to produce conflict (Walton and Dutton, 1969). These differences lead to differentiation, both formal and informal, of the hierarchical and dynamic units. For example, a relationship which was strained and obviously unsatisfactory to both parties is that described between a company's engineering and marketing departments in Hampton, Summer, and Webber (1973). The situation began to develop when an engineering department was criticized for low productivity. The engineers blamed their low productivity on the time they had to spend consulting with members of the marketing department about price quotations to customers. The engineering department initiated a procedure to keep track of the amount of time they were spending with marketing personnel. The procedure, resented by marketing department representatives, required them to sign in and out of the engineering department. Although some marketing managers did sign the register, many refused to do so and the number of contacts with engineers dropped off significantly. Some marketing personnel then refused to provide information to engineers. This, of course, reduced the cooperation between the units.

In general, individuals will increase interactions which in the past have been pleasant to them and will try to avoid interactions which are emotionally distressing. Feelings of exploitation can easily arise when one individual or group feels that they are providing more benefits to another party than they are receiving in return.

Feelings of inequity which can create strong behavioral reactions in individuals can also contribute to poor relations among groups. If one group feels that another group is being unfairly favored in an organization, it may do what it can to make the other group look bad and to suggest that the favored treatment is unjustified (Seiler, 1963). A group may be favored by top management because it performs functions perceived to be very important to the organization, but in this situation other organizational units are of course likely to feel that their activities are undervalued by top management, especially if the favored groups are composed of highly specialized and educated individuals competing with the less-favored line management groups for recognition.

When groups compete against one another they tend to develop distorted and inaccurate perceptions of themselves and the other group. The differences between them are exaggerated, and the similarities are overlooked. Negative stereotypes are formed of the other group and positive stereotypes of an individual's own group, and it becomes increasingly difficult for a group to see merit in another group's ideas or position on an issue. Each group becomes more susceptible to influence from its leaders, and if such influence is directed at maintaining the conflict situation, this adds to the conflict reinforcement resulting from the perceptual distortions. The question is, what are the causes of these difficulties and how can they be treated managerially?

Organizational Differences

Figure 16.2 shows some of the differences between the internal structures of the hierarchical and dynamic units. Such differences have been shown in some research (Lorsch and Morse, 1974; Hall, 1973), and while it is true that any particular organization may not have exactly these characteristics, they seem to be very prominent generally. Specifically, there will be differences in these units in their (1) general structure, (2) objectives, (3) bases of authority, (4) bases for compensation, (5) evaluation criteria, (6) organization climate, and (7) organization status.

FIGURE 16.2 Organizational Differences Between the Hierarchical and Dynamic Units

Factor	Hierarchical	Dynamic
General Structure	Emphasis on Rules More Formality Limited Autonomy in Decisions Narrow Job Definition	Less Rigid Structure Fewer Rules and Policies Greater Discretion in Decisions More Job Scope
Objectives	Short-range/ Cost	Long-range/ Development
Bases of Authority	Position Power Commitment to Organization Centralization	Skill and Expert Power Commitment to Self and Discipline Decentralization

Bases of Compensation	Level and Relative
	    Importance of the Position
	Increases Based on
	    "Merit" and Tenure
		Quality of Training
		    and Experience
		Increases Based on
		    Experience in Area of
		    Competence (Maturity Curves)

Evaluation Criteria	Objective Measures
	Focus on Results as Outcomes
	Short Time Span between
	    Performance and Results
		Subjective Criteria
		Focus on Activities
		    rather than Results
		Long Time Span between
		    Performance and Results

Organization Climate	Rules-oriented Formalism	Innovation-oriented
Status	Lower	Higher

Objectives.   Different organizational groups have different assigned objectives, and these become the objectives of the individuals in those units. The manufacturing unit is concerned about production efficiency, downtime, and scrap, for example. The marketing unit is concerned about customer satisfaction through service and prompt delivery. The research group may be primarily concerned with product quality and performance. The time span for objectives also differs. The production unit tends to have short-range objectives, while the research group has long-range objectives. These different sets of objectives contribute to a great deal of disagreement among such organizational units.

Differences in objectives also contribute to differences in the way causes of problems are perceived. Dearborn and Simon (1958) showed that even though executives when faced with a problem evaluated the same set of facts, the *cause* of the problem was attributed to different difficulties. The sales executives tended to see a sales problem, the production executives saw a need to clarify the organization, and the personnel managers saw human relations problems.

Authority Differences.   There is some evidence that in the better-performing organizations, power or influence resides at higher management levels in the stable organizations or units and at lower management levels in the dynamic organizations or units (Lawrence and Lorsch, 1969; Lorsch and Morse, 1970). These differences in power may in themselves contribute to conflict, and they presumably relate to differences in the origin of power and influence in the stable and dynamic units. In the stable organization we find power and influence based on position power or control over resources, while in the dynamic organization, knowledge of how to do the job is most critical and influence arises out of personal skill and expertise (Friedlander, 1970).

The five types of power listed by French and Raven (1959) are: reward power, coercive power, legitimate power, referent power, and expert power. (We have discussed variants of these in chap. 8.) Some research shows that organizational members in dynamic units are likely to respond best to expertise rather than to the other bases of influence (Miner, 1973). In the more stable line departments, however, legitimate, reward, and referent power are more important (Miner, 1973).

Thus, at the interface between the hierarchical and dynamic organizational units of an organization, one group may not respond well to the influence attempts of another group because each is using an appeal which is acceptable to its members but not to the other. Other problems at the hierarchical/dynamic interface arise because authority in the stable unit tends to be concentrated at the top—exercised in a hierarchical format—while in the dynamic unit authority is dispersed among many individuals and is weighted by the technical expertise of the individual. This situation often creates serious frustrations for personnel in the stable organizational units because they have difficulty in identifying the individuals in the dynamic unit who are appropriate to contact in terms of the required authority.

Authority differences also cause difficulties because as an organization has more specialists (professionals) with technical expertise, line managers may feel a sense of frustration—of loss of control. Victor Thompson (1963) sharply makes this point:

> Modern bureaucracy attempts to fit specialization into the older hierarchical framework. The fitting is more and more difficult. There is a growing gap between the right to decide, which is authority, and the power to do, which is specialized ability. This gap is growing because technological change, with resulting increase in specialization, occurs at a faster rate than the change in cultural definitions of hierarchical roles. This situation produces tensions and strains the willingness to cooperate. Much bureaucratic behavior can be understood as a reaction to these tensions. In short, *the most symptomatic characteristic of modern bureaucracy is the growing imbalance between ability and authority.* . . .

Compensation Bases.   For an organization with components in two different environments, we can expect two different bases for the determination of pay. In the flexible units, the quality of a person's training and experience is important. What he has done, where he has been to school, and his achievements in other organizations will be critical in determining his basic pay rate. In addition, increases in compensation may come from an assessment of how well the individual is recognized in his professional area of competence.

On the other hand, traditional methods of determining pay levels may be used in the stable sector. The background of the individual is much less an important determinant of salary level than is the level and relative importance of the position held by the individual, as determined through job evaluation procedures. Increases in compensation will be based on merit (which is more likely to be assessed in terms of hard measures of performance), as well as tenure.

When different systems of compensation are used, feelings of inequity may arise. If line managers in production groups are paid bonuses on the basis of profits of their unit, and specialists and staff personnel are paid bonuses on the basis of subjective appraisal, individuals who do badly under the pay system used for them (whichever it is) will believe the other system would be more appropriate for their situation.

Performance Evaluation Criteria.   The bases for evaluating the performance of organizational members in the stable and the dynamic units of a mixed organization will probably differ. In fact, they probably should differ, since if the evaluation system is not considered appropriate for the task, the individual performing that task tends to be dissatisfied (Scott et al., 1967). In dynamic units, composed of professionals or highly-specialized managers, performance evaluation will lean toward the subjective. It is less easy to quantify output measures in such units, so the focus of concern must be on whether or not a particular individual has gone through the steps required to complete a particular task. Since the results of the task may not be seen for a long time (i.e., there is a longer time span between performance and results), managers in the flexible unit are faced with the problem of determining whether or not an individual's—or group's—activities are likely to yield desired results. It may also be necessary to use outsiders (in addition to insiders) as evaluators—as is done, for example, in evaluating university professors—since higher-level managers do not have the technical competence to make such judgments.

In the stable units, the superiors can typically carry out the evaluations themselves without the aid of others. In one mixed organization, a group of supervisors and peers in the research and development department evaluated the effectiveness of the technical personnel. When a management by objectives program was introduced into the company, one of the reasons for its rejection by the research and development unit was that the system did not provide for a group evaluation of the performance of the technical personnel, and their immediate superior felt he was unable to make such a judgment. In this instance, some personnel in the stable departments of the company felt that the dynamic department was simply being contrary in its opposition to the new program. They did not realize that the new performance evaluation system failed to accommodate the needs and special evaluation problems of the unit involved.

Differences in the methods of evaluation used may lead to feelings of inequity, especially when such methods influence pay. They may also lead to feelings of jealousy between groups, especially on the part of those whose performance is rated low, and this can lead to conflict.

Organization Climate.   The organization climate refers to how an organization's practices and procedures are perceived by organizational members, and the relationship of such perceptions to ways of thinking about the organization and subsequent behavior (Schneider, 1974). Members of an organizational unit tend to agree on their climate perceptions, and they do, in fact, behave in ways which are congruent with their perceptions of the kinds of behaviors supported or rewarded by the organization (Litwin and Stringer, 1968).

The climate of an organizational unit will also affect certain types of orientations of organizational members (Litwin and Stringer, 1968). Higher perceived amounts of structure, or formalism, have a tendency to arouse power needs and to reduce achievement and affiliation needs for individuals. Thus, in stable organizational units we would expect higher concerns about power than in the dynamic units. On the other hand, in dynamic units where there is informality in structure, high standards of performance, encouragement of innovation, and toleration of conflicts, the need for achievement is aroused. So, organization climate can be expected to affect the way representatives of various groups think, behave, and attempt to solve problems when working together in an interface situation.

Status Differences.   The status of individuals is their hierarchical ranking in a group. Individuals have high or low status depending on their relative ranking against others in the same group. Within an organization, groups also will have different status levels. In general, units operating in the more volatile boundary of an organization will have the highest status because they are the units (and individuals) upon whom the organization must depend for adaptation to change. The dynamic unit will also tend to have highly educated specialists in it, since such personnel are needed to cope with its environmental uncertainties (Thompson, 1967). This means, often, that the specialist is in a situation where his skills and ability are very important, and he is less dependent on the organization than it is on him. Such persons may enjoy more organizational privileges than others. Some of the factors which reflect status differences are shown in figure 16.3.

Usually, persons with high status, or those from high-status organizational units, feel it appropriate for other units or persons to acknowledge their superior status. Thus, where the market forces involve much uncertainty, the marketing units will attempt to dominate. When the technology is volatile, the technology or production units will try to exert influence over the more stable units. For example, in a small company manufacturing soaps and detergents, the production technology was fairly stable, but competition with other firms in the industry was very keen. Profits of the firm depended, to a considerable extent, on the effectiveness of the advertising and sales promotion programs. In this company, the marketing deparment dominated both the production and the research departments. On the other hand, in a company which manufactured electronic test equipment for industrial customers, successful competition was based on performance characteristics of the equipment as compared to other equipment available in the market. In this company, the research department was the highest-ranking organizational unit and it imposed its desires on all other departments (Seiler, 1963).

FIGURE 16.3 Factors Likely to Result in Status Differences Between Flexible and Hierarchical Units in a Mixed Organization

Stable (low status)	**Factor**	**Flexible** (high status)
Less Years of Formal Education	Education	More Years of Formal Education
Functional Training		Technical Training
Greater Restrictions, Adherence to Rules, Policies, and Procedures	Organizational Privileges	More Freedom, Travel, Benefits, Autonomy
Individual More Dependent on Organization	Direction of Dependence	Organization More Dependent on Individual

For a variety of reasons, there may or may not be acceptance of the dominance by the higher-status group. For example, there may be a time lag in the acceptance of a lower status on the part of a department. In one company, the production department's status had declined relative to marketing as production techniques became more standardized. But the production units refused to accept fully the higher status of sales until after the older production managers retired and were replaced by new personnel.

If a lower-status department attempts to influence a higher-status department, this violates the higher-status group's expectations of what is appropriate behavior for a lower-status group. For example, in a company making diesel engines, the product design engineering group refused to accept suggestions from the drafting section, even though the draftsmen provided a useful source of good design ideas (Lawrence et al., 1965).

In the company mentioned earlier which manufactured electronic test equipment, new product ideas were developed in the research and development department (Seiler, 1963). The research design then went to production engineering where the blueprints were drawn, specifications determined, and parts lists developed. Then the product went to production for a test run, and finally to full production. Relations between production engineering and production were not cooperative, however, and there was much delay in putting new products on the market. Certainly part of the reason for the poor relationship between these two departments was the perceived lower-status production engineering staff, who seemed to be telling production what to do, when the production staff felt no sense of inferiority to the engineers.

Differences in Individuals

Lorsch and Morse (1974) conducted a major study which shows that different kinds of organizations will attract and retain individuals with different kinds of value orientations. Figure 16.4, which is based on this research, summarizes some of the differences between individuals in different groups. We would generally expect such differences to exist between hierarchical and dynamic units in mixed organizations.

FIGURE 16.4 Some Individual Differences Between Members of Stable and Dynamic Organizational Units

Stable	Factor	Dynamic
Low	Tolerance for Ambiguity	High
Low	Integrative Complexity	High
Toward Position Power	Attitudes Toward Authority	Toward Autonomy
Low	Individualism	High
Low	Outside Reference Groups	High
Low	Professional Values	High

Integrative Complexity. Integrative complexity is an individual's capacity to deal with a variety of information, understand it, and integrate it in order to solve problems. Lorsch and Morse found that in plants (hierarchical organizations), managers generally scored low on the measure of integrative complexity. On the other hand, managers of research laboratories (dynamic organizations) had high levels of integrative complexity.

Tolerance for Ambiguity.   Tolerance for ambiguity is an individuals's capacity to function in uncertain situations. High tolerance for ambiguity means that a person is capable of operating without precise job definition and with unclear authority responsibility relationships and high degrees of uncertainty about evaluative criteria. A person with a low tolerance for ambiguity has a need for structure and definition of activities. Lorsch and Morse found that R & D managers have high tolerances for uncertainty, while plant managers have low.

Attitudes Toward Authority.   If it is true that individuals in flexible organizations will have higher educational levels than those in hierarchical organizations, then we can expect their attitudes toward authority to be different than those of people in hierarchical organizations. In general, those with high educational levels are less tolerant of directive leader behavior. Thus, Lorsch and Morse found that managers in dynamic units tended to have a preference for more autonomy than those in stable units. On the other hand, managers in hierarchical organizations seemed to have a preference for strong authority relationships, or high position power. Hall (1973) found professionals to be high in preferences for autonomy, especially those professionals who work in informally structured organizations.

Attitudes Toward Individualism.   Lorsch and Morse also measured the degree to which individuals prefer to work alone or with others. They found that in production plants, managers wanted more extensive involvement with others and to work in groups. The characteristics of members in the research laboratory were quite different. Their preference was to operate alone.

Orientation to Outside Reference Groups.   Managers and professionals with an inside-the-organization orientation are sometimes referred to as "locals," while those who identify with outside reference groups are called "cosmopolitans." The cosmopolitans are influenced by outside groups. They attempt to adhere to what they perceive to be the values of their profession, and they therefore are less loyal to their employing organization than the locals. This contributes to value conflicts between the two groups.

Value Differences. Some research shows that differences in what is valued contribute to high conflict and low integration (Seiler, 1963). Other research has illuminated these value differences between professionals and line managers (Moore and Renck, 1955; Danielson, 1960; Pelz and Andrews, 1968; Litterer, 1970). Professionals and scientists are concerned less with money and promotions than are managers, and more with the intrinsic nature of their tasks. In addition, professionals and scientists tend to have a longer time perspective than line mangers and are more concerned with product quality and being candid in presenting information than are managers. The specialists and professionals place a higher value on research than do line managers, and value the scientific approach more than the line manager. This can create hostility, as Moore and Renk (1955) indicate in their study of the satisfactions of professionals in industry:

> It seems clear from the evidence available that the professional is job-oriented. He is concerned primarily with competent performance in his chosen field. He seeks status through specialization. . . . General management, on the other hand, takes pride in its integrative skills and its ability to move about freely in a variety of fields. From management's standpoint, the specialist often appears to be overelaborating the obvious. . . . It is frustrating to management representatives who must try to simplify the environment and cut through a mass of detail to be confonted by specialists who seem equally bent on complicating the environment beyond reason.

> From the professional's standpoint, there is often the feeling that management does not know what it is doing. The analytical mind finds the integrative mind somewhat inconceivable, perhaps even a little obnoxious. The ability to reach decisions on the basis of partial information and what might appear to be flimsy evidence is not held in high esteem by the professional. In fact, in professional circles, this borders on charlatanism.

Integration in the Mixed Organization

Perhaps the most effective way to approach the problem of integrating units with divergent tasks, values, and people is to have the appropriate form of organization structure. The primary coordinating mechanism in any organization is the managerial subsystem. A manager's responsibility is to effectively integrate the interdependent groups under his level and to resolve conflicts that occur among them.

A superior can be effective in resolving conflict by persuasion if the conflict is not too serious and if the superior is esteemed by the groups involved. If the groups are not too differentiated and if both groups identify with the same objectives, the task is easier. Of course, a superior can use his authority or use sanctions to force one or both groups to take particular actions, but this can lead to enduring feelings of resentment or a perception that a superior was unfair or arbitrary. One approach to the design of structure for the mixed organization is the matrix form.

Matrix Organization

The matrix form of organization has been found useful when it is necessary to integrate the activities of many different specialists while at the same time maintaining specialized organizational units (see fig. 16.5). The two alternatives to the matrix form are usually *functional organization*, in which organizational units are formed of different specialists, and *product organization*, in which all the different specialists needed to produce a given product are in the same unit. The former approach obviously makes it difficult to achieve the integration of the different specialists, while the latter does not allow specialists sufficient access to other specialists and often results in too many specialists of a certain type working at less than their capacity on a particular product.

FIGURE 16.5 A Matrix Organization (Adapted from Galbraith, 1973)

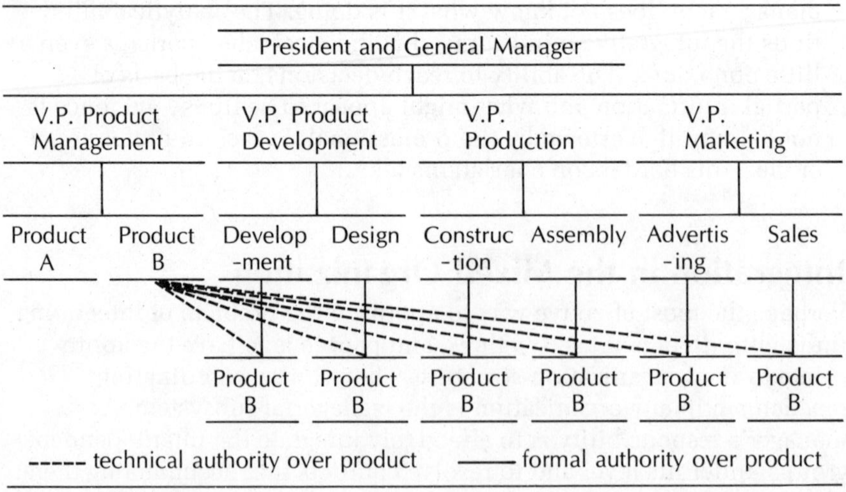

President and General Manager			
V.P. Product Management	V.P. Product Development	V.P. Production	V.P. Marketing
Product A / Product B	Develop-ment / Design	Construc-tion / Assembly	Advertis-ing / Sales
	Product B / Product B	Product B / Product B	Product B / Product B

----- technical authority over product   ——— formal authority over product

In the matrix organization (like the project management form discussed earlier), specialists from specialized organizational units are assigned to one or more project teams to work together with other specialists. For example, chemical, mechanical, industrial, and electronic engineers may work together in a team with physicists, accountants, human engineers, and other professionals to develop a new product. Each member of the team is subject to dual authority. He takes orders from the project manager and from the manager of his specialized department. The goals of each of these managers may be different. In the aerospace industry, for example, the project managers tend to be concerned about meeting schedules within budgetary limitations and in producing output within previously planned specification (Galbraith, 1973). The specialized unit managers, on the other hand, are primarily concerned with full utilization of existing resources and the long-term development of such resources and high technical performance (Galbraith, 1973). The individual members of the project team should be able to integrate their efforts better within a group than when they are merely the representatives of their own specialized groups. Retention of the specialized organizational units, however, enables the individual specialist to obtain help from professional colleagues on technical problems and gives him the opportunity to identify with his professional group and to learn and grow in his profession with the help of others. The use of specialized organizational units also makes for more efficient utilization of human resources for the organization and less duplication of resources.

An example of a matrix organization is given in figure 16.5. In it the specialized departments are development, production, and marketing. These, in turn, are further divided into the more specialized departments of development and design for development, construction and assembly for production, and advertising and sales for marketing. There are two product departments, A and B. Some managers from each of the six specialized departments are assigned to the product B group. Thus they report to two different supervisors.

The matrix form of organization is also used outside industrial settings. For example, one college of business administration uses a matrix form of organization. Faculty members are assigned to their specialized departments such as marketing, finance, management, accounting, and so on. Then there are program managers for the undergraduate program, the graduate program, the management development program, and so on. Each faculty member may work for the several program managers for varying amounts of time.

While effective, the matrix form is not a panacea. Disagreements occur between managers of different projects and between project managers and managers of specialized departments. In addition, the members of the project team themselves often receive incompatible requests from their two superiors and therefore, experience considerable role conflict and stress. They also often experience insecurity because they are working on temporary projects.

Even though the matrix form of organization may be the most appropriate way to structure a mixed organization, there will still be integration problems stemming from the structural and individual differences we have noted earlier in this chapter. The manager of the mixed organization may find the following approaches useful in addressing these difficulties: (1) system re-design, (2) confrontation approaches, (3) appeal systems, and (4) the use of superordinate goals.

System Redesign.   If integration problems are due to the design of the work system, then the system can be restructured and the conflict reduced. For example, if the problem is that a lower-status group is initiating action for a group which perceives itself to have a higher status, the problem might be alleviated by using a liaison individual or group to coordinate both groups, by re-designing the work flow so that the lower-status group does not impose its wishes on the higher-status group, by transferring certain elements or personnel in the lower-status group into the higher status group, or by combining the two groups into one.

Some of these possiblities are shown in figure 16.6. Let us assume that work flows from unit A to unit B and from unit B to units C and D, as shown in example 1. Let us further assume that the relationship between units B and C is quite poor. This could be true for a number of reasons. Perhaps the quality of work performed by unit C depends upon the quality of the work received by it from unit B and this dependency is resented by C. Or perhaps unit C's personnel consider themselves to be superior to the personnel of unit B, but unit B's personnel seem to be giving them orders. For whatever reason, the relationship between B and C is quite unsatisfactory, as shown in example 1, figure 16.6

In example 2, direct contact between units B and C has been avoided by placing a liaison between them. Research shows that this individual (it can be a group) is most effective if he has values approximately midway between the values of the personnel in the two units to be integrated (Lawrence and Lorsch, 1969). The title of the liaison, or integrator, commonly varies according to the kind of organization in which it is found. In an organization with many products, for

---

FIGURE 16.6   Examples of Possible System Relationships

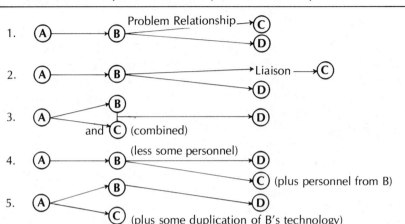

instance, the liaison may be called "product manager," and be in charge of coordinating all of the various specialized units which produce particular products. The liaison individual should be a person who has high influence in the organization, which gives him power, and he should also be expert enough in the areas he is coordinating to know when one group attempts to mislead others. The integrator is also more effective if he has the behavioral skills to be a good conference leader and if he has the reputation of operating in the interests of the organization as a whole. In some organizations, the integrator has only informal authority, but in others he has formal authority and can employ sanctions against those who are not cooperative. For example, he may be given a budget and therefore some control over resources (Galbraith, 1973).

In example 3, units B and C have been combined, a strategy that takes advantage of the fact that most individuals feel inclined to help fellow group members, as we stated in chapter 4.

In example 4, a segment of unit B has been transferred to unit C. The new personnel in unit C now no longer represent unit B but identify with their new group, unit C. Of course, there will not be an immediate identification, but it will come with time, especially if the new personnel are treated with respect by the original members of unit C. This approach was used with some success in a chemical company when chemical engineers were transferred from a research unit to an engineering unit with other types of engineers (Seiler,

1963). The chemical engineers moved from a low-status position in a high-status organizational unit to a high-status position in a lower-status organizational unit.

Example 5 shows a situation in which interactions between units B and C are no longer necessary because unit C has duplicated, within itself, those activities formerly performed by unit B. Unit C might establish its own production subunit, for example, or its own product-planning subunit, which would make it unnecessary for it to have any interaction with unit B. In many companies this kind of a situation evolves naturally when the relationships between groups become so unpleasant there is strong motivation to stop all interaction (Seiler, 1963). This approach can be taken by management consciously in a reorganization program, or informally by the parties themselves, provided they can obtain the necessary resources. Seiler reports several instances in which scientists in research departments set up and ran their own production equipment to avoid interactions with a production department.

Sometimes a procedural change, rather than a change in the structure of organizational units, can solve the problem. For example, conflict between two groups can be the result of one group frustrating another group in the latter's attempts to achieve its objectives. This frustration leads to aggressive feelings and behaviors directed at the other group. In one company, the marketing group, after receiving orders from customers, found that the credit department often did not allow certain orders to be shipped when the order exceeded the customers' credit lines with the company. The marketing personnel—not knowing a customer's credit standing—had already counted on receiving credit in the bonus system for the sales and were naturally angered by this. The situation was improved by having the orders sent to the credit department for approval *before*, rather than after, they were sent to the marketing department (Chapple and Sayles, 1961).

Confrontation Approaches.   In some organizations, there seems to be a belief that if conflict is ignored—or suppressed—it goes away. There are unwritten norms against raising issues that are particularly troublesome to members. Usually problems won't go away; they need more than aspirin and rest. One way to resolve conflict is by confrontation—to face up to the conflict and allow each party to express its hopes and views. One study of six firms in the plastics industry showed that the more successful firms used confrontation more extensively than did the less successful firms in dealing with conflict (Lawrence and Lorsch, 1967).

If there are differences between the hierarchical and dynamic units of the kind shown in figure 16.2, we might then expect confrontation to be more tolerable in the dynamic unit because disagreement and conflict are considered to be part of the course of scientific investigation. In the hierarchical unit, harmony, compliance, and formality might lead to less tolerance of confrontation. If so, such differences with respect to the desirability of conflict and confrontation can create difficulties at the hierarchical/dynamic interface.

The nature of the issues in the conflict are of great importance. Research has shown that conflict over technical issues (such as differences in opinion on product design) is related to high performance, but that interpersonal conflict (based on personality factors or styles of behavior) contributes to lower performance (Miner, 1973). In confrontation it is important to keep the discussion impersonal and focused on the problem to be solved or the task to be done—not on the parties involved.

Various confrontation approaches are used in organizations in dealing with conflict. An older approach is bargaining, and there are two forms of this approach—*distributive bargaining* and *integrative bargaining*. Distributive bargaining involves a situation where one party's loss another's gain. Conflict over the allocation of limited resources is an example of such a situation. Here the objectives of the conflicting parties are contradictory and some type of compromise is usually worked out. In integrative bargaining, on the other hand, there is the possibility of a solution that will benefit both parties. This is most likely when one group has too many resources and another not enough, or two groups can reduce costs or increase revenue by sharing.

A more recently developed confrontation approach—encounter groups—has been found to be useful in improving the relationship between two or more groups, especially where perceptual distortion and the development of negative stereotypes within each group have exaggerated group differences and provided a justification for the resulting dysfunctional interaction patterns. In the encounter group resolution approach, the conflicting groups are brought together to discuss the weaknesses in their relationship and to work out a new relationship. For example, two groups of female professionals were in conflict in a health facility. Both groups were brought to a conference site for a period of two days. The first day each group met separately to discuss the weaknesses and strengths in its own group as well as its perception of the other group. Each of the groups then selected a spokesman to communicate this perception to the other group. The groups were then brought together to provide feedback to each other on how they perceive their present relationship. Then they met separately again to discuss this feedback and to work out a plan for a better relationship.The two groups then met together once more and devised a plan to develop an improved relationship with one an other. The initial reaction after such an experience was that satisfaction with the group relationship improved as a result of the encounter-group experience. After a period of six months, however, the attitudes had started to regress toward their old levels, perhaps because no changes in the structure of the organization were made, and the underlying problem (inequitable treatment of the two groups) remained. Only some of the perceptual distortions were changed by the experience. Thus, in using this approach, there must be a real change in the organizational or social system itself if relationships are to be significantly improved over the long run.

Although the research evidence supports the personal confrontation approach as a means of improving organizational effectiveness (Blake, Shepard, and Mouton, 1964; Lawrence and Lorsch, 1967), it is not easy for a manager to use this technique. Generally most people wish to avoid open conflict, avoid expressions of emotional feelings, and not openly show antagonisms toward others. Furthermore, the candid expression of feelings and individual perceptions is often seen as quite risky by the parties concerned, since they become vulnerable because of their disclosures.

Personal confrontation is most likely to be effective when certain conditions exist (Walton, 1969). First, both parties must be motivated to eliminate or reduce the conflict, and it is best if both are motivated to use this approach at the same time. Next, the organizational power of each party should be equal. In addition, the conflict dialog should contain a time period or an opportunity for both parties to describe the points of disagreement and to express their feelings about them, and then a time period when the parties can express their similarities and common goals and their wish to more effectively manage their disagreements. Results are also likely to be better when the participants know how to provide interpersonal feedback and reassurance, clearly understand what the other party is saying, and maintain a productive level of tension (neither too high nor too low) during the dialog. Managers should be taught these skills in organizations where integration problems are common and where confrontation is established as the procedure for resolving conflicts.

Appeal Systems.   In many companies, formal appeal systems have been established so that organizational members can obtain another judgment on a dispute not successfully solved at a lower level (Scott, 1965). Typically, however, such appeal systems are for rank-and-file employees and not for higher-level personnel such as managers and professionals. A common approach is to send the appeal to a higher organizational level until it is either solved to the satisfaction of the parties or they accept the situation. The sequence is often this: to the supervisor, to the department head, to the personnel department, and finally to the president (Scott, 1965). In companies with unions, formal grievance procedures usually are used. The union will process a grievance for any employee at a particular level, such grievances usually involving a disagreement between the company and an employee about the employee's rights as specified in the labor contract.

Use of Superordinate Goals. Sometimes relationships between groups in conflict can be improved through the establishment of superordinate goals (Sherif, 1961), goals which are desired by two or more groups but can only be reached through cooperation of the groups. For example, the replacement of a departmental bonus system with a plant-wide bonus system may help induce the various departments in the plant to work together more effectively. Suppose that managers in a production department manufacturing a home appliance are paid a bonus based on lowering of production costs. This department is not cooperative with the marketing department, however, in its attempts to service important customers and in obtaining the cost estimates needed to provide bids to customers. The conflict between the departments could be improved if the company would shift from a "cost center" bonus system to a "profit center" bonus system in which the amount of sales and the price received for the product influence the amount of bonus that the manufacturing managers receive. The new system rewards the manufacturing managers as well as the sales managers for obtaining new customers and servicing customers more effectively.

Integration has historically been a concern of management. The degree of integration generally refers to the amount of collaboration among organizational units or the unity of effort available for the achievement of organizational goals. Integration is especially difficult to achieve in the mixed organization because the subunits have diverse characteristics. In this chapter, we have discussed integration problems and how they might be solved. The same techniques can be used in the hierarchical and dynamic organizations discussed in previous chapters, or when there is an integration problem between two stable organizational units or two dynamic organizational units.

Discussion Questions

1. Provide some examples of a market-dominated organization and a technologically-dominated mixed organization.

2. Discuss the "images" the organizational members in the stable and dynamic units in the mixed organization would have of each other. What would be some of the consequences of these images?

3. Openly confronting conflict is often recommended today. What are some of the advantages and disadvantages of this? If differences among organizational members or between groups are to be discussed openly, what rules or procedures may minimize the difficulties associated with this approach?

4. Is your university a mixed organization? Why or why not? Give examples.

5. Will increased communication between organizational subunits decrease conflict and increase cooperation? Why or why not?

Part VI

Organization Change

Because organizations must adapt to the environment, they must change. When there are external pressures for flexibility, looseness must somehow become characteristic of the system, and vice versa. Chapter 17 talks about this process—the changing of the structure of an organization to adapt most effectively to an environment.

In Chapter 18, internal change processes are considered. The idea underlying chapter 18 is that the structure is adequate, but that performance can be fine-tuned by improving skills and abilities or changing attitudes of members. Methods for inducing such changes are discussed in chapter 18.

Chapter 19 discusses issues and problems that organizations will have to relate to in the future to remain effective.

Chapter 17

In chapters 6 and 7 we showed how the organization's structure is related to the nature of the technological and market environment in which it operates. Those structures, of course, should be considered only as models of particular types, not as unchangeable absolutes. The relationship between groups and departments, even in bureaucratic organizations, changes. In the bureaucratic organization the change is less rapid, more predictable, and takes place in smaller degrees than it does in the dynamic organization, but there is change.

In this chapter we examine ways in which the organization may change, with special concern directed at the formal structure. The basic idea is this: If an organization's structure is a function of the environment, as we have said, then when the environment changes, the structure must also change if the organization is to survive.

What causes the structure of an organization to change? First, a major change takes place when the organization grows. Everyone has seen a church group or a civic association which began as a small informal group of interested people, for some reason become popular and attract membership. Growing pains follow. Rules develop, formal procedures for the election of officers must be designed, and so forth. Business firms are no exception to this rule of change.

Secondly, major changes in the structure of an organization result from changes in its relationship to the environment. Taking the model for understanding the relationship presented in chapters 6 and 7 as representative, then if the environment of a dynamic organization becomes more stable, it must begin to take on more bureaucratic characteristics. Conversely, when the stable environment of the bureaucracy becomes more uncertain, there is no choice but to loosen up the fixed rules, policies, and guides that govern the system.

Changing Organization Structure

In this chapter we are concerned with the adaptation of an organization to the external environment and the changes in structure that follow from that adaptation. We will discuss four aspects of structural development and change: first, how structure, both formal and informal, develops; second, the problems associated with change in organization structure in growth periods; third, problems that an organization must face when it finds environmental circumstances changing; finally, how an organization can attempt to influence the conditions of the environment so that its existing structure is compatible with it.

The Emergence of Organization Structure

A narrow view of organization structure is to define it in terms of formal, written factors such as procedures, job descriptions, policy manuals, and organization charts. These devices prescribe behavior for workers and managers. However, they only partially explain member behavior. A more comprehensive and appropriate view is to consider organization structure as the pattern of interaction relationships among organizational members, and to analyze the degree to which behavior is predictable. When there are very stable, enduring, and clear behavioral patterns, we can say that the organization structure is rigid or "tight." The structure is easy to observe and probably simple for new members to comprehend. They can come into the organization, read the appropriate job and procedural description, and begin to contribute very rapidly.

When the pattern is not so stable and clear, or when it changes in short intervals of time, the organization structure can be described as "loose," or flexible.

Not all the patterning of behavior comes from the formal definitions prescribed in manuals, job descriptions, and procedures. As we have seen, much of it, even in bureaucratic organizations, stems from the individual characteristics of the members and pressures from groups. This is especially true in new or small organizations. Organizations represent an accommodation to members as well as to environmental demands, especially when there are changes in key members.

In newly-developing organizations, predictable patterns of behavior emerge as members interact with each other over time and find that certain behaviors are accepted by others, make their own work easier, or simplify problems of dealing with others. Consider what happens when two strangers are brought together, for whatever reason, to work on an activity. Without guidance from a third party, they will work out who should do what and when. Over time, if they continue to work together, they will begin to interact in a routine way. As new people are added to work on the activity, they will, initially, have to fit into the existing pattern. But that pattern will change over time to accommodate the new members. Regular interaction patterns will appear. Behavior will be as predictable and stable as if there were written specifications such as job descriptions and procedures. Think about a time when you were in a large class. Initially, you might not have been assigned a seat by the instructor. But after a short period of time, you find that you come to class with certain people. As the term progresses, seating patterns become fairly stable. You sit in, or close to, the same seat most of the term, and you may find that you regularly interact with certain people in certain ways. Predictable behavior patterns have emerged even though there have been no efforts to impose any structure on the group.

In most behavioral systems there will always be some changes in membership. New people come in as old members leave. If the system is a small company, it will be easier to bring in new employees if there is a written description of the expected behavior of members (norms). Otherwise, each time a new person is employed he must spend a great deal of time learning his job, what others are doing and how things get done. Written job descriptions, policies, and procedures simplify initiation, and so they are written. And multiply and multiply—and this happens in growing organizations.

Organization Growth and Structure Change

What happens to the structure of an organization when it goes through a growth period? One of the more developed approaches to this situation has been formulated by Filley (1962). Growth, to Filley means an "increase in absolute increments of change in growth indexes, principally sales, assets and employment—generated from internal sources" (Filley and House, 1969). Growth, in this view, is defined as an increase from the firm's own operations, not as a result of acquisition and merger. There are three stages of growth: Stage 1, "The Small Firm"; Stage 2, "Dynamic Growth"; and Stage 3, "Rational Administration." Organizations in each of these three stages are different. When certain conditions occur in the environment, an organization may move to the next stage. Figure 17.2 summarizes characteristics of organizations at these different stages.

Stage 1: The Small Firm

Initially, when the firm is small, the owner-manager does nearly everything. He may produce the product, market it, and arrange for financing. He plans, organizes, and controls the operation alone, performing himself all the managerial functions described in chapter 1. As the market for the product grows, with a corresponding increase in production, help must be obtained from others. New personnel are hired and assigned work. This represents the initial differentiation, or separating, of activities. In the small firm, this differentiation is likely to take the form of a split between the managerial functions (planning, organizing) and the operating activities. The new personnel will be responsible for doing the work, but very little of the managing. For example, a small book publisher manages the business, but is also actively engaged in the operational functions of manuscript acquisition, editing, producing, and marketing. When he adds his first permanent staff, their assignments may be copy editing or proofreading and carry no managerial responsibilities.

The second stage of differentiation in the small firm will be a separation among the operating activities. Marketing will be separated from production, and the beginning of formal departmentalization will occur. Probably the owner-manager will still continue to perform the control function and the acquisition of both physical and human resources. The financial control activity will be the last to be completely differentiated in the small firm. The owner-manager will keep his hand on the helm of the ship.

In a small organization, relationships between employees and the manager are likely to be highly personal. In this stage, there are few of the written, formal aspects of organization structure found in larger organizations. Assignment of responsibilities is usually done verbally,

FIGURE 17.1 Growth Stages of an Organization

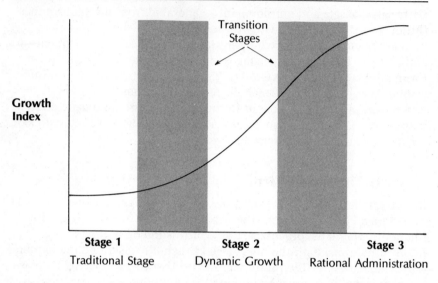

Stage 1	Stage 2	Stage 3
Traditional Stage	Dynamic Growth	Rational Administration

thus providing flexibility so that employees can be easily shifted from one job to another, providing the owner with a way to maintain a high level of operating efficiency. What formal structure there is will probably be imposed by governmental requirements for record keeping, such as the maintenance of wage records for social security purposes, reports that may have to be submitted to comply with health and safety laws, and financial reporting for tax purposes.

The objectives of the small firm will be a reflection of those of the owner-manager. The owner-manager expects a reasonable income and living standard (which may be quite high), and at the same time an opportunity to be independent, working for himself in a job which he likes.

A firm may remain small (in stage 1) if the owner-manager does not want to become involved with, or feels he cannot manage, the problems associated with managing a complex organization. For example, suppose the owner-manager of a small electronics component firm who supplies highly-specialized circuitry for the space program could triple his sales and profits, but only by adding more technical and managerial staff, moving to a different part of the country, and reducing the personal control which he has over the business. Even though there is a high potential for growth, if the owner is not the kind of person who wants to take advantage of it, he may elect to stay small. Many owners of small firms have made such conscious choices, even though the conditions for growth were present.

The Transition to Growth. If an organization is to experience rapid growth, then a number of conditions must exist. Unless they are present, Filley believes, the firm cannot enter stage 2, "Dynamic Growth." The following circumstances facilitate rapid expansion.

1. *Innovation.* Something must occur which makes larger markets available. A new product may be introduced, or an old product may acquire a new potential. A firm may discover a new production method which substantially reduces costs. An invention may provide the innovation necessary.

2. *Significant Returns for Risk.* With innovation, there is usually high risk. There are many innovations that are useful to a small number of people but do not seem to have the potential of large-scale returns. Thus, the risk of undertaking the production and marketing of them may not seem worthwhile. The owner-manager of a small firm

---

FIGURE 17.2 Critical Factors in Stages of Growth

Continua of Growth	1	2	3
Objectives	Comfort-survival	Personal Achievement	Market Adaptation
Policy	Traditional	Personal	Rational
Leadership	Craftsman	Entrepreneur	Professional
Work-group bonds	Fixed Roles	Interaction-Expectation	Homogeneity
Functional development	Single	Successive Emphasis	Full Development
Structure	Power Levels	Field of Force	Rational Hierarchy
Staff	Housekeeping	Technical-Personal	Technical-Coordinative
Innovation	No Creativity	Innovation	Development
Uncertainty-risk	Nonrisk	Uncertainty	Risk
Growth-size economies	Size Benefits	Growth-Size Benefits	Size Benefits

Source: Filley, A.C., and R.J. House. *Managerial Process and Organizational Behavior.* Glenview, Ill.: Scott, Foresman and Company, 1969.

must see the potential pay-off of an innovation as far exceeding the risk involved before he will consider expansion and growth.

3. *Entrepreneurial Orientation.* The entrepreneur is an innovator willing to assume risks for expected returns. The owner-manager of the small firm must have an entrepreneurial orientation—that is, he must be willing to take risks—in order to obtain the returns associated with growth. The comfort-survival objective of the owner of a small firm must change; if the opportunities are present but the owner-manager is not entrepreneurially oriented, he will not make the decisions required to move into the second stage.

4. *Additional Resources.* In the dynamic growth stage (stage 2), substantially greater resources will be required to both produce and distribute the product. Often the firm, at this stage, does not have the capacity to generate enough resources to take advantage of the innovation and its potential. An outside source of capital must be found. If this capital comes from borrowing (which will heavily commit the owner to financial institutions) the lending institutions themselves must see an opportunity for return.

These are the conditions which must be present if an organization is to grow. If it does, then its relatively informal atmosphere will change.

Stage 2: Dynamic Growth

The organization grows because it exploits an innovation in an increasingly larger marketplace. Sales rise, new employees are added, production increases. Growth may be very rapid, initially occurring at an increasing rate. For example, in the first stage, growth may occur at a constant rate of, say, 5 percent annually, but if the firm moves into the dynamic growth stage it may be 6 percent in the first year of stage 2, 7 percent in the second year, 8 percent in the third year, and so on. In later periods of the dynamic growth stage, the rate of growth may begin to slow down. It may move, for instance, from 10 percent in one year to 8 percent the next year, to 7 percent the following year, and so on (see fig. 17.1).

The character of leadership in the dynamic growth stage will be different from that in the first stage. It will still be highly personal, but of course more entrepreneurial and charismatic. This atmosphere will pervade the organization, especially those members close to the chief executive. It is possible that in this second stage, the leader must be someone other than the owner-manager of stage 1. While the owner-manager in stage 1 may be willing to enter the growth stage, he may find difficulties in managing a growing organization. He may want to make policy, but not get involved in the management of it. He may step aside to become the chairman of the board and hire an entrepreneurially-oriented president. He can set the tone, make policy, and handle the more ceremonial, ritualistic activities. The actual operation of the firm will be in the hands of the entrepreneur-president.

The objectives of the organization in this stage are likely to remain a reflection of those of the key executive, who of course is the entrepreneur-president. Filley (1962) describes the president's goal as "personal achievement." Growth, success, and its attendant status and prestige are reflections of the personal needs of the entrepreneur. *Playboy*, the magazine phenomenon of the '50s and '60s was successfully launched by Hugh Hefner on a relative shoestring. As its appeal grew, the organizational and entrepreneurial talents of A. C. Spectorsky provided the advertising program and nationwide distribution that allowed the magazine to convert that appeal to a spectacular success.

As the organization grows in size, and has to add new staff members, new personnel will be heavily influenced by the charismatic personality of the leader. They will be, like him, concerned with growth and willing to take risks for the possibility of substantial long-term payoffs. In the initial phase of the dynamic growth stage, while the organization is still relatively small, new members may be simply an extension of the personality of the leader. He will, through them, manage the growing organization. It is likely that they will make decisions in a fashion consistent with his beliefs, attitudes, and general policies.

During the early phase of stage 2 managers will devote their energies toward exploiting external opportunities, rather than on internal problems of efficiency and effectiveness. This lack of attention to internal managerial problems may impose a cost later, but at the time it can be ignored. For instance, both human and capital resources may lag substantially behind the level that is necessary to adequately support sales. Too, the production system may be extended beyond its capacity in order to meet market needs, thus foregoing necessary maintenance of equipment, which of course could result in earlier equipment replacement. There is a cost when a firm has to replace a capital asset before it would have had to if proper precautions had been taken.

Often at this stage decisions are made to acquire capital resources to support a projected level of activity that in the end proves unrealistic. When this happens, the organization will find itself with excess resources that become a critical managerial problem when it reaches the third growth stage. For instance, during the late 1950s and early '60s, university enrollments were expanding rapidly. During that time, many classrooms and dormitories were built on the assumption that ever-increasing enrollments would require these facilities. The buildings took 3 to 4 years from planning to completion, and during that period of rapid growth classrooms and housing facilities were crowded. The resource base lagged behind the level required. In more recent years, however, enrollments have tapered off, and now many universities have excess classroom and dormitory space.

During periods of rapid growth, the large inflow of revenues from increasing sales provides a cushion for internal inefficiencies. High sales and income can cover up many managerial mistakes. If, for example, costs increase more than they might where there was more planning and control, it may be relatively easy to pass these increases on to the consumer. This is especially true of a growing firm which has a monopoly on a particular innovation through patent control or simply because there are few other firms in the industry or market.

Changes in Structure.   As the organization continues to grow it will be necessary to add more personnel, and as more and more people are brought in, it is less likely that those selected will be reflective of the character of the leader and his initial associates. In an effort to insure consistency of decision-making, policies and procedures will have to be formalized (written) to provide guidelines for the growing number of new people, and it will not be possible completely to permeate the growing organization with the strong personality of the entrepreneur. Thus, the *structure* of the organization will begin to emerge more formally and clearly. The informality of earlier periods will give way to job descriptions, organization charts, and policy manuals.

The maintenance and managerial subsystems (the authority relationships) described in chapter 7 will become more pronounced and clearly separate from the production and boundary-spanning units. Greater predictability of actions from organizational members will be sought by the development of guidelines which delineate the form of the organization's structure relationships between individuals. Employees will then know what kind of decisions to make under what circumstances, to whom they must report, and the general scope of things for which they are accountable to their superior.

In the dynamic growth stage, the status system in an organization will become obvious. Those close to the leader will have access to a larger proportion of organization benefits and prerogatives, both formally and informally, than those not close to him. At the same time, as the organization develops, it may be difficult to determine exactly who is close to the leader and who is not. Some lower-level managers may misrepresent their relationship to the leader in order to enhance their own status.

Policy and procedures will become increasingly evident in order to obtain predictability and control. But their proliferation may be the beginning of such a reduction in the organization's members' freedom that the organization cannot take full advantage of the growth situation. Individuals will begin to be constrained by job descriptions, hierarchical relationships, procedural rules, and control systems. They will be reluctant to go beyond them. One reason for this is that the staff added later in the growth stage will not have an opportunity to get to know the entrepreneur personally, and if they are not as risk-oriented as he is to begin with, they will tend to stay within their position guidelines in order to avoid the risk of failure, with subsequent job loss.

The Transition to Rational Administration. As the organization moves up the growth curve, it may begin to experience competition from other firms. The market, which was once its own, is now invaded by others who see the opportunities for growth and profitability. The firm begins to lose its market advantage. As the market begins to be shared with others, profits begin to diminish. Because of competition, it is more difficult to pass on increased costs to the consumer. Growth begins to slow down because of the external factor of competition—but also because the existence of the more formal structure begins to set the organization in its ways. It becomes less able to capitalize on outside opportunities because it has built up an investment in human and physical resources with particular skills.

The transition period to stage 3 begins as market growth starts to slow. The assets begin to catch up with the output and pressures emerge for more efficient use of resources. To continue to operate at a relatively acceptable level of profit, the organization is forced to look inwardly for effectiveness. That means making better, more efficient, use of its resources. *Playboy's* successes of the '60s brought competition in the form of other publications directed at a similar market. *Playboy*, once the daring innovator, suddenly found that a shift in tastes had occurred. Other magazines were successful in their appeal to the market, reducing *Playboy's* market share. Playboy clubs were in financial trouble, the price of Playboy stock dropped rapidly and profits suffered. The management of *Playboy* responded by moving toward a more stringently controlled operation. It "tightened up."

During such a transition period, the formal structure of an organization begins to become very clear and well-defined. Policies, rules, job descriptions, and the authority structure become fairly firmly set. Managerial and maintenance subsystems to support the production and distribution functions set in place earlier in the life of the organization become more important. This is because many of these subsystem activities will have access to and control over the necessary information and technical competence required to support the increased effectiveness of internal resource utilization.

An important change in the nature of the managerial style begins to occur. In the dynamic growth period, the firm is dominated by the entrepreneur. As the organization moves to the third stage of growth, the managerial style becomes more professional, shifting toward a more impersonal form evidenced by the use of more bureaucratic structure. "Successfully achieved, the move into rational bureaucracy provides the firm with a defensive posture against decline, allowing it a solid and stable base upon which to expand further" (Filley and House, 1969).

Stage 3: Rational Administration

When the organization enters the rational administration stage, it has the characteristics of the bureaucratic form described in chapter 7. It will be structured by a well-defined set of tasks with explicit job definitions, authority-responsibility relationships, and a clear hierarchy of authority and responsibility. The managerial emphasis will be to plan, organize, and control activities in such a way as to insure long-term survival. Such a shift in strategy can be seen in item 17.1, which describes how Polaroid is moving, under its new president, toward a greater emphasis on long-range planning.

In stage 3 the rate of increase in organization size will be relatively modest compared to stage 2 rates. By now, the opportunities for rapid growth created by the existence of innovation in the early stage will be gone. Growth will slow down and markets will become more stable. Because of the stability of the external market and technological sectors, along with the internal rigidities from the development of the bureaucratic formal structure, it is unlikely that the firm will experience a rapid, dynamic growth period again. It may be too large with too much capital investment in resources that cannot be shifted easily to new and different markets where there may be extensive opportunities. If an organization in stage 3 is to experience the rapid growth of stage 2 again, it may have to do so through the process of acquisition and merger. It will likely have to join with other organizations which are in the dynamic growth stage and integrate them into the existing structure of the firm. This will often pose difficult problems of integration of the two different organizations, but it may well be the only way that rapid growth can again occur.

ITEM 17.1   Transition to Stage 3

The Team Builder

Transition—After a Genius. Shortly after William J. McCune, Jr., became president of Polaroid Corp. February 18, he had one wall of his office moved four feet to make more room for meetings. But he wouldn't let the workmen repaint the old walls to exactly match the new one.

"Bill tends to run a fairly frugal show," one Polaroid executive says. "He simply isn't one for flourishes."

Indeed he isn't. Mr. McCune has always stayed so far back in the shadows of more flamboyant Polaroid executives that he is practically unknown outside a close coterie of scientists, engineers and top executives. He joined Polaroid 36 years ago, just two years after its founding, and since 1950 he has headed all Polaroid engineering.

• • • •

Appointment Unexpected. Hardly anyone expected Mr. McCune to become Polaroid's president. He had been executive vice-president since 1969, but he had been talking about retiring since 1965. Polaroid's reclusive, 65-year-old founder, Edwin H. Land, had always been chairman, president, chief executive, chief operating officer and director of research. And even though he had repeatedly talked Mr. McCune out of retiring, most people thought one of two senior vice presidents would someday succeed Mr. Land. (Polaroid has no mandatory retirement age).

• • • •

"Traumatic" News. The news sent shock waves through Polaroid's ranks, already demoralized by a cost-cutting drive, widespread layoffs, pay freezes and rumors of further cutbacks to shore up the company's profits. "It was rather traumatic," one officer says.

Mr. McCune's promotion has only begun a probably prolonged and painful management realignment. Polaroid is a prime example of a company that has grown too big for one or two men to run but has failed to build a strong second tier of management to succeed its aging founder when he finally steps aside.

"It's one of the most difficult kinds of succession situations," a longtime Polaroid executive says. "It's the classic business school case, but it's next to impossible for an outsider to imagine how difficult the transition is going to be."

One outsider who thinks he can imagine is Eugene C. Jennings, a professor at Michigan State University's Graduate School of Business Administration. "Land is a genius, but the time has come for him to get the hell out," says Mr. Jennings. "He's going the way of Juan Trippe at Pan American, Eddie Rickenbacker at Eastern Air Lines, Al Sloan at General Motors, and other builders who stayed too long.

"The most competent people in Polaroid are those just below the top ranks," Mr. Jennings adds. "They've got some very good captains and majors there, excellent people, but their morale and team spirit have deteriorated badly. The company is at a point where it could go downhill very rapidly from here, or it could snap back and go on to much bigger things."

Profits have toppled 60% from their 1969 peak, and the company nearly lost money on U.S. operations last year. Total 1974 earnings plunged 45%, to $28.4 million, or 86 cents a share, on sales of $757.3 million. First quarter profit fell 17% from the year-ago period, to $8.2 million, or 25 cents a share, on sales of $142.6 million. Polaroid's stock hit a low of $141.25 last year, down from a 1973 high of $143.50. It closed yesterday on the New York Stock Exchange at $30.125.

Sales of Polaroid's instant SX-70 folding cameras and film, which produce dry, litter-free color prints, have fallen far short of projections, while U.S. demand for its peel-apart film products has slumped. Soaring manufacturing costs have shriveled profit margins, and technical problems still bedevil production of the film-pack batteries that power the complex SX-70.

Moreover, formidable competition looms. Eastman Kodak Co., with six times the sales and twice the assets of Polaroid, is readying its own instant cameras and instant film, perhaps for introduction next year.

In short, Polaroid is at a crucial juncture—probably its most crucial since it created instant photography with the first Land camera in 1948.

Sudden Changes Unlikely. Mr. McCune isn't likely to order sudden sweeping changes, but his new authority is being felt throughout the company. "He has known for years that certain things needed to be done around here, and now that he's got the charter he's doing them," one executive says.

"We had been trying to get certain product decisions for as long as two years before Bill became president," the executive adds. "The routine had been that one top guy thought this and another top guy thought that and the boss (Mr. Land) was waffling. So we'd go back and get more data and do it all over again. Now Bill just says, 'Okay, do it.'"

Mr. McCune is pushing decision-making to unprecedently low echelons. "You should have seen the faces of some of the nonengineering guys the first time Bill asked them, 'Why the hell are you asking me that? Why don't you just go do it?'" an engineering man says.

• • • •

Stress on Planning. Mr. McCune confirms that the marketing people failed to lower some sales targets fast enough. "But if you talk to marketing people you'll find they had some difficulties with some projections they had from the engineering side, too," Mr. McCune says. "One of my objectives is to try to smooth that up some."

He is also emphasizing long-range planning. "A lot of people think planning is a process by which you prematurely make decisions," Mr. McCune says. "I think of it as a way to look at your options and keep those options open."

What Mr. McCune has already done "that is terribly important and terribly promising," says Mr. Wensberg, the 45-year old senior vice president of marketing, "is to lay out in a very orderly fashion the problems and the opportunities the company is facing and set people to work on them." Another officer adds, "Up to now, all the long-range planning here has been contained in Dr. Land's cranium."

"Bill's pulling people together, getting some teamwork established," says George H. Fernald Jr., 48, the assistant vice-president responsible for film manufacturing. "But we're a lot of highly motivated, bright, stubborn, opinionated people. How do you get them together?". . . .—Richard Martin

The Wall Street Journal, April 25, 1975

Relationship to Organization Models

How do the ideas of growth described above fit the organization models outlined in chapters 6 and 7? One way to look at this is to think of the small firm (stage 1) as in the quadrant with the volatile market and the volatile technology (see fig. 6.6). As the organization grows in size, it moves away from that quadrant toward the greater stability associated with either the stable market or the stable technology. Organizations in general will move toward, although they may never reach, the quadrant characterized by both a stable market and a stable technology.

Knowing something about the various stages of growth, along with the characteristics of an organization in each of the stages, permits better planning in organizations at various points in the growth cycles. Such knowledge can be critically needed by a firm in the dynamic growth stage passing to the third stage, rational bureaucracy. In this transition period, it is necessary for a stable, well-designed structural system to cope with the problems of the stable environment. The firm that can adapt most effectively will be the most successful and profitable in its industry.

Adapting to Environmental Changes

Since the environment is composed of organizations and groups outside the boundaries of the firm, there may well be changes in it over which the internal management of an organization has little or no control. A dynamic organization may find its market and technological sector becoming more stable. Or a bureaucratic organization may find that its environment is becoming increasingly unpredictable. Environments may change as result of several different sets of conditions; innovation, for example, or market saturation, or changing consumer preferences, or changes in legal requirements, or actions of other organizations, or effects of pressure groups. These causes of organizational change are reasons why an organization's structure must change. Later in this section we will show how structures can be changed to adapt to changed environments.

Innovation. We have seen how innovation is necessary for growth to occur. In some instances innovation changes the competitive character of the environment to which an established organization must adapt. For instance, the development of high-speed transportation, along with refrigeration capabilities in trucks and rail cars, made it possible to provide off-season fresh vegetables and produce nation-wide. This changed the marketing patterns of both producers and processors. The development of microcircuitry made possible both cost reduction and size reduction of computers. They are now more readily available to smaller firms. The development of scanners to read data from food packages makes it possible to use data processing and computers at supermarket checkout counters. The implications of such a move in the supermarket industry are enormous. The nature of the checker's job is changed. Inventory managers must revise their systems to use the new technology; inventory levels may be determined almost instantaneously. Ordering can be more responsive to sudden shifts in demand. Such an innovation not only has implications for the supermarket and the customer, but also for the manufacturers of the scanning equipment, who must develop different sales strategies and programs to support the use of this equipment by the customer. New marketing strategies must be devised to deal with the problem of initiating and integrating a new organizational unit into the existing structure of the computer firm as well as insuring that the sales function is handled well.

Market Saturation.   A firm in a dynamic market and with a dynamic technology with control of innovation may find, over time, that the market becomes more stable as demand begins to peak out. Or that the technological advantage it possessed because of patent control diminishes as other competitors develop similar processes or products.

As products become widely distributed in the hands of most potential users, then, eventually the demand may slow down to a point where the market is primarily a replacement market. Then growth will come from replacement and increases due to changes in population levels. As this happens, the managerial strategy of the firm may become more inward-looking, seeking ways of increasing profitability through internal efficiencies. This will be manifest in tighter procedures and controls.

Changing Consumer Preferences.   The character of the market may change with shifts in consumer tastes. The women's fashion industry has long been cited as an example of changing consumer tastes with attendant impacts on the operating effectiveness of clothing manufacturers. This same kind of phenomenon seems to be emerging in men's fashions. Clothing styles are much more varied for men than they have been in the past. Such volatility makes it difficult for manufacturers of men's suits, for example, to predict sales levels as accurately as in the past. Production methods, procurement, and purchasing have to be more responsive to shifts in taste.

Changes in Legal Requirements.   Often the environment is changed by action of the government. These changes sometimes cause a firm to shift its method of production. For example, current legislation requires automobile engines to produce lower emissions of certain chemical compounds. These requirements mean a change in the design of automobile engines which necessitates changes in production methods. Or, as another example, the Food and Drug Administration often requires pharmaceutical manufacturers to take certain drugs off the market, or imposes stricter controls on the distribution of these drugs. The subsystems of the drug company's organizational structure must respond—adapt—to these changes in their environment.

There have been instances where certain products have simply been made illegal. Perhaps the classic example is the prohibition of alcoholic sales during the late 1920s and 1930s. The ban on cigarette advertising on television forced advertisers to look for new media.

Other Firms' Action.   Changes for a particular organization may be induced by what other firms in that environment do. High profitability and growing markets may bring about the entry of other firms into an area, and as competition begins to develop, prices, as we have seen, may begin to drop. The market may become saturated, bringing about a degree of market stability. Or new manufacturing processes may be developed by other firms. Or more efficient ways of production may be developed by a competitor. Or a competitor may locate its production facilities closer to the market. To all of these environmental disequilibriums organizations must adjust.

Pressure Groups.   In some cases, changes in the internal structure of an organization are brought about by interest groups outside the organization. These groups may feel they should be able to affect the decision making of a particular firm. The ecology movement in the United States is an example of such an activity. Another is reflected in the study of the TVA by Philip Selznick (1953). He shows how local governments and citizens' groups applied pressure to the Tennessee Valley Authority. These pressures resulted not only in a change in the TVA's policies of operation, but also a change in its structure. Selznick describes one method for adapting to pressure groups which he calls "co-optation." Co-optation consists of absorbing the external group into the policy- and decision-making structure of the organization.

Direction of Environmental Changes

The environment can change in two directions. It can increase in uncertainty—that is, move from stable to volatile—or it can increase in certainty—move from a volatile to a stable condition.

From Volatile to Stable.   There will be a "natural" tendency for all organizations to move toward a hierarchical organizational structure. This effect is similar to changes in structure that occur with growth (which we discussed in the first part of this chapter). The maintenance subsystem will attempt to increase the degree of predictability of members' behavior. Those in the adaptive sector will seek ways to reduce variance in the volatile environment. The maintenance and managerial subsystems will develop record systems to keep track of both people and resources for internal control purposes. Procedural mechanisms such as governmental reporting requirements on tax withholding and social security will require regular reports which begin to regularize behavior. As the number of systems and procedures increase and become more permanent, the organization structure becomes less flexible.

If the environment is becoming progressively more stable, then the organization should increase the degree of specificity and rigidity of its structure. Jobs should be defined more exactly, more permanent authority-responsibility relationships should be established, and the degree of freedom of organization members to make decisions should be restricted. There will be a need for greater coordination with other units as work becomes more interdependent, and this creates a situation where it is especially important to be able to rely on another person to do his job. Thus it becomes less efficient to allow people to decide how and what to do. They must have operating definitions of their work.

The major concern in this situation, as we suggested earlier, must be the congruency between the rate of the development of structure with the changing environment. The development of a more rigid structure must keep pace with the changing, reduced, degree of volatility of the environment, but if it becomes too inflexible too soon, it may stifle creativity. A high volatility environment will not turn into a stable one overnight. The change will be gradual and thus the increasingly rigid organizational structure should also arise gradually. For example, as the rate of technological change begins to slow, the production subsystem may become more hierarchical and its methods more routine. But if the market is still volatile, the structure of the marketing department should remain flexible. It should move toward more specificity only in concert with the external environment.

The information for making such changes comes from adaptive subsystems. The market research group, for example, can tell the decision makers about the market. The engineering research group can monitor the technological sector. If the organization proceeds too swiftly in imposing structural rigidity, it may find itself disadvantaged because it cannot cope effectively in an environment that is still fairly volatile. For example, suppose a firm manufactures several lines of specialized furniture. It may decide to standardize production for a mass market. If the market isn't there, losses will occur. On the other hand, if organization structure lags substantially behind the rate of environmental change, then the organization may find itself at a competitive disadvantage. If, for example, more efficient, standardized operations can produce similar products at lower costs, then the firm that moves quickest to standardize operations will have the competitive advantage.

From Stable to Volatile.   If the environment shifts rapidly from stability toward volatility, there may be great difficulty in adjusting. The stable bureaucratic organization, with a substantial investment in both people and physical resources, will find a great deal of internal resistance to change. The large organization in a stable environment will thus attempt to minimize the possibility of such a shift.

One way to minimize this possibility is through the control of technology. The large firm will control technological breakthroughs which might be transformed into useful products and will introduce them into the product line gradually. To do otherwise would require dismantling of the capital assets and an enormous reinvestment. For example, the automobile industry introduced the change from the standard transmission to the automatic transmission gradually. At General Motors, it first became available in one line, the Oldsmobile, and then in another as retooling took place. It would have required a substantial investment if the changeover had been made across the whole product line. By controlling the rate of introduction of new products, the organization is not only able to experiment, but is also able to make the change slowly enough to avoid major reshuffling of the production side of the firm.

It can be seen, then, that the rate of introduction of new products is controlled—or an attempt is made to control—because even though changing over to a new product may be technologically feasible, economically it isn't. The auto industry moved in a similarly cautious fashion in introducing small cars to meet the competition of European and Japanese imports. The market was obviously there, but the industry felt it had to make the changeover at a rate that was economically feasible. A company that may have waited too long is discussed in item 17.2. (Meanwhile, General Motors' tiny new Chevette took off faster than any other new model in the company's history: 6,100 of 19,000 available 1976 Chevettes were sold in the first 8 days the car was marketed.)

ITEM 17.2   Environmental Change

Chrysler Midgets Send Imperial to Graveyard

Detroit—Chrysler Corp. has scrapped the Imperial from its 1976 lineup of new cars but two new compacts have emerged to take the big car's place.

Later next year, a new Japanese-made subcompact, the Plymouth Arrow, will make its debut as hard-pressed Chrysler Corp. attempts to expand its small-car offerings.

The two new U.S.-built compacts— Plymouth Volare and Dodge Aspen— "will be the family cars of the future," Sydney L. Terry, vice president-public responsibility, told a press conference Wednesday.

• • • •

Chrysler dropped the 50-year-old Imperial in the face of sharply falling sales. In the first nine months this year, the auto maker sold only 4,035 Imperials, down more than 50 per cent from a year ago. Most of the market for the luxury car disappeared two years ago when the Imperial's outward design was made nearly identical to other full-sized cars.

Over-all Chrysler new-car sales tumbled 25.2 per cent in the first nine months this year, compared with an industry average of 12.4 per cent. Dodge bore the brunt of the skid, tallying a 32.9 per cent plunge, while Plymouth scored a 20.3 per cent drop.

That performance triggered four straight quarters of losses totaling $243.3 million for Chrysler Corp., and the company has said the Sept. 30 quarter loss

will top the $58.7 million deficit in the previous quarter. Chairman Lynn Townsend resigned, and the new chairman, John Riccardo, said the company will be in the black in the final 1975 quarter.

Most of Riccardo's hope is riding on the compact Plymouth Volare and Dodge Aspen, available in two-door, four-door and stationwagon models and covering a wide range of prices.

More than half the industry's 1975 sales were small cars, including subcompacts, compacts and imports, and Chrysler is predicting the total will rise to 55 percent for 1976. Compacts alone will account for more than 20 per cent of the market, according to Richard B. McLaughlin, vice president for automotive sales.

The subcompact Plymouth Arrow is built by Mitsubishi of Japan on the same chassis as the hot-selling Dodge Colt but will be available only in a sporty hatchback model.

• • • •

The compact-sized wagons are expected to be the sleepers of the industry McLaughlin said. The American Motors Hornet Sportabout is the only other U.S.-built compact wagon offered, and the Sportabout has become one of the industry's all-time success stories.—Dan Miller

Chicago Daily News, Oct. 15, 1975

It is more than likely that a change to a more volatile environment will be faced by industries which are composed of a large number of small organizations. For example, in the restaurant industry there were once a large number of small independents who operated in a traditional fashion. Then the rapid development of quick food service franchises, such as McDonald's and Kentucky Fried Chicken, caused a major change in the nature of the industry. The small, traditional firms were not able to take advantage of the opportunities and have found themselves losing the competitive battle with the quick food franchises. The calculating equipment industry is another example. Prior to the development of integrated circuitry, adding machines and calculators were largely mechanical, relying on electrically-driven gear mechanisms. Suddenly the development of integrated circuitry made possible extremely rapid calculation with smaller and more reliable equipment. Manufacturers of adding machines and calculators were faced with the problem of surviving in a market which was substantially changed by innovation.

There are three things that a firm can do when its environment becomes more volatile than it has been. First, it can *change its strategy* to take advantage of the new opportunities. Second, it can seek *merger* with or *acquisition* of an organization currently capable of functioning in that environment. Third, it can elect to *withdraw* from the volatile segment of the environment.

Changing strategy requires a shift in the way a firm is managed as well as in the technological processes of production and distribution. The product may be redesigned to more closely parallel that of competitors. This new design may change the way the product works, or it may simply be a change in appearance. If there has been a shift in the way the product is built (as in the case of electronic calculators), the organization may not have either the production methods or the staff to operate under the new system, and so it must acquire the services of a new group of product engineers capable of dealing with the change. If the change is a style change (as might be the case in men's fashions), new designers must be obtained. When the change in strategy requires a change in production methods, the organization will have to invest heavily in the new technology, scrapping the old production system and replacing it with a new one. The substantial investment involved, along with the attendant risk, requires a decision that should be very seriously evaluated before the change is undertaken.

Merging with a firm which is already successfully operating in the volatile environment, or one which has the technical capability but perhaps has not been profitable due to limited resources, is another way to deal with environmental change toward volatility. The joining of the two organizations is likely to produce a synergistic effect which will substantially increase the resource base and, if the fit is a good one, potentially increase the returns of both organizations involved. When this method for adapting to the environment is the one chosen, the organization which emerges will have to face the difficulties of managing the mixed organization, as discussed in chapter 16.

To withdraw from the volatile segment of the environment and continue to produce and market existing goods and services is a third possibility. The organization may elect to stay as it is, but it will face problems of managing in a retrenching position, since a segment of the market is gone. If the new environment is stable and the market is large enough, in absolute terms, however, effective managers may continue to operate a firm profitably. The remaining customer segment in the industry may be large enough for a few, but not many firms. As the less profitable and inefficient competitors who remain in the stable sector begin to drop out, the remaining firms may increase internal efficiencies to be acceptably profitable, still operating as they did in the past.

Attempting to Change the Conditions of the Environment

One should not come away with the impression that an organization in its environment is like a cork passively bobbing on the waves. Organizations need not simply react to changes in the environment; they can undertake to influence the external circumstances that directly affect them. Most organizations, either individually or collectively, as an industry or interest group, try to influence the environment, smoothing out fluctuations in demand by increasing marketing efforts during slack periods. Price policies often have the same objective. By offering discounts during periods of low demand, consumers may be induced to purchase the product or service at a time when the sales level of an organization might otherwise be low.

An obvious example of change tactics are lobbying efforts designed to yield legislation making external conditions more favorable. Agricultural groups, for example, press for government programs to insure stable prices and stable farm income in the face of foreign competition and the vagaries of nature. The meat industry seeks protective tariffs, one purpose of which is to minimize competition from imports.

Firms may use different approaches when attempting to influence the environment, but the objective is essentially the same. They seek to induce changes in the broader segment of society which will make the environment more compatible with their own method of operation.

Increasing Market Volatility. A firm may find itself selling its product or services to a set of consumers which is fairly well-defined and not increasing greatly in size. The volatility of a market may be increased by generating demand for the product in other segments of the population where the product is not used extensively. For example, Black and Decker, a manufacturer of power tools, has consistently in the recent past reduced the price of power drills. Several years ago these tools were bought primarily by professional tradesman in the construction industry and by hobbyists who used them frequently. Through the development of more efficient production systems and product redesign using less expensive components, Black and Decker was able to reduce the price of its power drills to a point where they become inexpensive enough to be bought by those who make only intermittent use of them. Thus the company made its product attractive to a larger number of consumers and substantially increased the market. Applying this same strategy to other products, such as circular saws, Black and Decker experienced very rapid growth in sales and profits from 1967 to the present. Its products have essentially the same functions as they did when they were first introduced. The market shift was caused by their strategy of cost and price reduction.

Increasing Technological Volatility. In some cases it is possible to develop a product that performs the same function as another, but uses a different technology. Electronic calculators were cited as an example earlier. Another example is the development of microwave ovens by manufacturers of kitchen equipment.

Such technical innovations can be made only if a firm is willing to expend vast amounts for research and development, at a corresponding risk. Because of the cost and risk involved, it is likely that most organizations will seek to adopt new technology after it has been developed, rather than attempt to find a significant breakthrough itself. This is especially likely to be the case where the current technological formation of a firm, or industry, represents a large investment in capital resources. Firms in the automobile or basic steel industry, for example, will not introduce technological changes which alter the basic nature of their production processes in a short time period. As

we have noted, their strategy is more likely to be one of gradual introduction of the new technology.

Select a Compatible Environment.   It is possible that an organization
may have the capacity to function effectively within a particular
environment, but for a number of reasons may choose to operate in a
different one. For ease of analysis, environments were described in
chapter 6 in rather sharply defined terms. Actually, of course, in the
real world there is a continuum of environments. As figure 17.3
shows, there are different degrees of stability and volatility. Suppose
that firm X_1 is representative of a type of firm found most commonly
in an industry. It could, for example, be an automobile manufacturer.
Firm X_2 in figure 17.3 may also manufacture automobiles. Their
product, however, may be specialized sports cars, or racing automobiles made for a very specific clientele, with the most recent technological advances built into the product. Under these circumstances,
the structure of the two firms will be quite different.

FIGURE 17.3   Continuous Nature of Environmental Variability

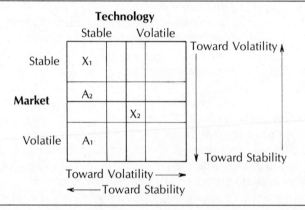

A_1 designates a firm in a volatile market with stable technology. The
example cited earlier of a type of organization in this environment
was a manufacturer of women's fashions, and the organizational type
is characteristic in particular of the houses of certain designing
manufacturers like Yves St. Laurent, or Rudy Gernriech, who attempt
to remain at the forefront of the industry by introducing radical or
even shocking change in each new fashion season. One reason why
the market is so volatile is that this condition is fostered by designers

themselves. There are, however, firms which manufacture more "traditional" clothes for women. Chanel and the Villager are noted for classic designs which do *not* change markedly from year to year. These houses, of course, would be in sector A_2.

Item 17.3 describes the strategy of the Rucker Company in selecting a compatible environment. In the early 1960s Rucker acquired a number of firms, increasing its asset base markedly. But the problems associated with managing so many diverse organizations (see chap. 16 for some of these problems) led to a decision to divest and return to a more familiar scope of operation.

ITEM 17.3 Moving to a More Compatible Environment

How Rucker Cured Its Conglomerate Fever

Clarence J. Woodard, the 51-year-old chairman and chief executive officer of Oakland-based Rucker Co., knows something about the perils of conglomerate fever. In the go-go years of the 1960s, he acquired 26 companies in a half-dozen industries, a strategy that boosted sales of his tiny systems engineering company to $110-million in 1969, or a ten-fold increase in only four years. Unfortunately, Rucker's earnings disappeared in the process, as one acquisition after another failed to live up to expectations.

When Rucker lost $2-million in 1970, Woodard tried another tack, more in tune with the conventional wisdom of the 1970s. He began divesting, so Rucker could concentrate on its single, most successful operation: oil-well drilling equipment and services. With his new strategy, earnings now are beginning to keep pace with sales. As oil exploration boomed in 1974, Rucker's revenues increased 49% to $127-million and earnings more than doubled to $8.2-million.

• • • •

Control. Ironically, Rucker is emphasizing management control more now,

when it has only one basic venture, than it did when it had dozens of unrelated operations. "We are considerably more sophisticated as a company now," says Woodard. "We've gone through a maturing process. We have evolved the management philosophy that we will not invest in products where we can't achieve a significant market share, with a chance to be the leader."

That is a far cry from Woodard's scattergun approach of the 1960s, when the company was in everything from computer software to irrigation hardware. Rucker's goals, strategies, management structure, and managers have largely changed, along with the change in the nature of its operations. According to Edward M. Gibbs, a former McGraw-Edison engineer who joined Rucker as executive vice-president in 1968 and became president in 1972, there was "no instant decision one bright and sunny morning to cut the company down." The strategy just evolved, he says, as the importance of market share became clear.

• • • •

The most successful acquisitions gave Rucker a specialty in equipment for difficult drilling situations—the type of gear that could be expected to generate the biggest profits. It acquired Hycalog, a maker of diamond drill bits; Shaffer Tool Works, which produces the kind of blowout preventers used to control pressures on virtually every well drilled nowadays; and Acme Tool, a major tool rental and service company. These ventures now form the nucleus of Rucker's operations.

The slide. Yet when Woodard tried to duplicate the company's success in drilling equipment by expanding into such fields as aerospace controls and plastics molding equipment, Rucker reaped one failure upon another. It bought an aircraft controls manufacturer, for example, in 1967—just before that industry went into a tailspin. It jumped into computer software mainly to bolster a sagging systems division, than had to pick up a data processing operation to bolster the software effort.

Performance. Rucker's success in drill-

ing equipment last year made its stock—which more than doubled—one of the top performers on the New York Stock Exchange. It was one of the few companies that managed to sell new equity. Still, the current share price of $15 is only eight times last year's earnings, a long way from the dizzying multiples of the 1960s, and well below those of other drilling equipment companies.

Woodard has no intention of returning to the diversification tactics of the past. "As you concentrate your resources, the span of control is also concentrated so the company becomes more manageable," he says. "We are not going to divert any resources or management time outside the petroleum industry. It has all the opportunities we can handle."

Business Week, April 17, 1975

As organization structure changes, the processes of management must also change. When the environment shifts from volatile to stable, the firm must move from the managerial techniques outlined in chapters 14 and 15 to those described in chapters 12 and 13. Decision making will shift from decisions under uncertainty to decisions under certainty or decisions under risk. As an organization's structure becomes more rigid, with more specific job descriptions, different personnel with different attitudes, needs and motivation should be recruited. Of course in the event the change is in the other direction (from stable to volatile), the managerial strategies should shift accordingly from those in chapters 12 and 13 to those of 14 and 15.

A change in the structure of an organization will create different role pressures on incumbents, and they must adapt to these if the organization is to survive and survive efficiently. Some of these structural changes can be anticipated, though not easily influenced by the firm. Other structural changes may be planned and implemented in order to increase the effectiveness of the organization within its current operating environment. Organizations interact with the environment; they do not simply react.

In this chapter we have described several ways in which the external environment may change, bringing about *corresponding* internal changes of the organization. There are many current trends which will influence organization structure in the future. Some will act to increase formalization and predictability and contribute to more of a bureaucratic design for organizations, while others will contribute to less formalization and to more of a dynamic design for organizations.

Discussion Questions

1. Why do people who continually interact with each other over time develop stable, predictable behavior patterns?

2. What is the effect of a change in the environment on structure, say as when the federal government began to impose safety legislation?

3. What kinds of decisions can an organization make which will affect the environment to make it more compatible with the organization?

4. What happens, when rapid growth occurs, to managers of small organizations?

5. It seems implicit that a person who starts a business that becomes exceptionally successful and large will have to step aside if the success is to be continued—or does it?

Chapter 18

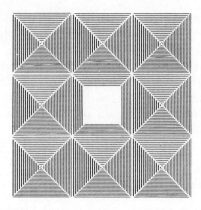

In Chapter 17 we noted that organizational structure must change in response to changes in the environment. At the same time, we recognized that some changes in organizational structure occur because the organization finds itself forced (for reasons of survival) to accommodate itself to the demands of its members. The reverse also holds true: members of an organization—who stay in the organization—accommodate themselves to the demands of the organization (to keep their jobs; to win promotions).

Pressures for such accommodations—for changing people—stem chiefly from management's dissatisfaction with their organization's level of effectiveness, and low levels of effectiveness are, as we have said in chapter 5, attributed by management to deficiencies in human skills, motivation, or behavior, even though inadequate resources or structure may be wholly or partly to blame.

Cultural forces operate also. Western civilization has traditionally seen as its mission the changing of the environment and of people. Nature must be transformed to serve the purposes of organizations, of society as a whole, or individuals. People must be changed as well—to conform to what some group or organization believes is suitable behavior or performance. Every organization—educational, governmental, and business—expends a large part of its efforts toward changing people for the possible enhancement of the objectives and values of the organization.

In the past few years, because of the growth of what has been called the "human potential" movement, some organizations have tried to effect change and growth on an individualized basis. That is, in some organizations programs for change try to create more diverse, rather than homogeneous individuals. The approach taken by an organiza-

Changing People in Organizations

tion is determined by what it needs. If the organization perceives its need as the development of individuals who must fit into a specific role, change is directed toward developing homogeneous people. If the organization perceives its need as diversified individuals, however, who are creative and adaptable, its emphasis will be on individualized change. There is some research evidence that the structured or stable organization emphasizes standardization in its change efforts, while the dynamic organization emphasizes change programs that encourage diversity with growth (Friedlander, 1971).

When change efforts are organizationally planned and authorized, there is the strong implication that someone in the organization desires a change in performance. But exposing an individual to a situation that induces him to change, and then placing him in an organizational setting that supports and reinforces former behavior or attitudes leads to frustration, disappointment, and bitterness. This is most likely to happen if the systemic factors in the organization—policies, rules, procedures, job descriptions—are not structured to reinforce the change on a continuing basis.

A great deal of recent theory and research has led to the conclusion that change efforts must be more broadly based than they have been and consist of more than mere classroom exercises. Many have stressed the need for designing change efforts to be compatible with the organizational climate (Schein, 1961; Sykes, 1962; House and Tosi, 1963). This means that the management group must be willing to support change efforts with organizational reinforcements. Only when this is done can management expect change efforts to result in the kinds of behavior intended. This support can only be provided in the form of specific top management decisions and practices. It is not enough for management to "verbally" support development. They must do it with their practices and policy making.

Organization Development.   Our perspective on these efforts to change individuals is our version of *organization development* (OD). Beckhard (1969) defines organization development as

> an effort planned, organization wide, and managed from the top to increase organizational effectiveness and health through planned interventions in the organization's processes, using behavioral science knowledge.

This view leads us to consider any particular type of training (such as specific skills in mathematics, or computer programming, or interpersonal relations), or the redesign of organization structure to be more consistent with the outside environment, as part of OD. The essential aspect is that the particular approach be planned, based on the needs of the organization, and integrated with other efforts.

This view is broader than the narrow meaning of OD given it by some training faddists. This narrower view, which grew out of sensitivity training programs, stresses humanistic values. The emphasis is on providing opportunities for human beings to realize their potential, and for allowing organizational members to influence the decision-making process, the objective being to establish open and candid human relationships.

When it was found that providing managers with a course of training and then sending them back into the existing social system where newly learned behaviors were not supported or reinforced was ineffective in obtaining change, it became evident that a systems approach was needed, that change efforts must be directed at more than just the attitudes of individuals. Relationships among individuals and among groups must also be the target of change attempts, and these relationships are affected not only by the unique personalities of people, but also by the structure of the organization.

Organization development is *not*, therefore, a particular type of training method. It includes a wide variety of methods and uses whatever is necessary to accomplish the desired change. Two factors loom large in OD. The first is whether or not the people who are the targets of change can change or are willing to change; the second is that there must be some assessment of what the change requirements are. An assessment of these factors can be made through organization planning.

Prerequisites of Change

Before individuals or groups can be changed, certain conditions must
be present. First, the causes of the present unsatisfactory state of
knowledge, behavior, or attitudes must be understood. If change in an
individual or group is desired, it is because behavior or attitudes are
not what they should be. Change attempts have the best chance of
success when the causes of present behavior and attitudes can be
determined. Second, the obstacles standing in the way of change must
not be insurmountable. If there is to be a change in knowledge, for
example, certain minimum levels of learning abilities must be present,
since limits in individual learning abilities place limits on the amount
and type of material that can be learned. Certain behavior patterns or
attitudes are so deeply ingrained and are so important to the functioning of the individual that they can be changed only with great
expenditures of time and energy, if at all. A third prerequisite of
change is motivation to change. An individual—or group—must be
motivated to change an existing level of knowledge, behavior patterns,
or attitudes, or the influence programs will fail. Fourth, defensiveness
must be minimized. Since most individuals have a favorable self-
image, they are not inclined to accept information about themselves
which is at variance with this favorable self-image. Organizational
members who perform at an unsatisfactory level, for example, are
likely to shift the blame to other people or the situation, such as a lack
of resources. In general, they refuse to acknowledge that their
preformance is unsatisfactory or that their errors are serious. All of
this hampers change.

Some research has been carried out to identify the situational
factors which are related to a positive reaction to training by the
participant; some of these factors have been identified in studies in
two organizations of the reactions of foremen to management development training (Carroll and Nash, 1975). In these studies it was found
that foremen reacted more positively to the training program if they
believed that good performance would result in pay increases or
promotions: when they desired a promotion; when they were relatively satisfied with their jobs and the organization; when they felt
that the company was supporting the program; when they felt their
superior was supporting the program; when they perceived they had
the power to make changes in their jobs; and when they perceived the
content of the program to be related to the solution of their current
problems. In other words, participants are more favorable toward
change efforts when they see them as a means of accomplishing
personal objectives. Those who react most favorably to a program

expect that it will help them attain outcomes they consider important (promotions, pay increases, solution of current problems). Also, those employees favorable to the company are more favorable toward training programs that the company endorses than those not favorable to the company, and those who feel they have the power to utilize the training on their jobs are also positive in attitude about the programs.

Behavioral scientists believe that if an individual participates in the making of a change, he is predisposed to accept the change. Why? First, because he has a greater understanding of it, and thus less uncertainty, which is a source of resistance to change. Second, with participation the individual (or group) becomes ego-involved with the change. If a person makes a suggestion, and if he believes it is a good suggestion, he will be motivated to try to make it work. If he does not try to make it work, and if the suggestion ultimately proves to be no good, that will be a negative reflection on him as a person, and he will have to reevaluate his opinion of himself. Third, if a person commits himself to successful accomplishment of a change, he will be motivated to make it succeed, because people see themselves as individuals who keep their word, and they try to live up to this aspect of their self-concept. Finally, in a group setting, the individual perceives that the change is being accepted by his peers, whose opinion he values.

Participation does not always overcome resistance to change, however. As pointed out in chapter 11, participation is generally not effective when the individuals involved do not have the competence or information needed to contribute to the development of the change, or when they lack motivation or interest in the subject of concern, or when they do not consider their participation in the change decision appropriate.

Determination of Developmental Needs

Without the foundation of organization planning, organization development efforts cannot be related to the long-range performance requirements of the organization.

Organization planning consists of making projections of what the organization will look like in the future—three, five, or even ten years hence. These projections can be constructed from data available from more extensive planning, such as long-range building or capital expansion projects. Thus, we can arrive at an "ideal" organization structure for some point in time in the future.

To bridge the gap between the ideal and the present organization structure, the use of "phase plans" is appropriate. Phase plans are intermediate plans or steps to achieve the desired structure on a sound and practical basis. The projected structure is broken down into phases with respect to time and organizational units. For example, at stated future times, certain subunits may be split off and reorganized in an orderly manner. The various phases may be timed to coincide with major additions, planned operational changes in plant and equipment, introduction of new products, and the planned retirement of executives. The final form of organization at a given point in time will no doubt differ from the ideal structure originally conceived for that time, but the use of phase plans allows for revision of the long-range plan and forces planners to consider changes in economic conditions, product line, span of control, or loss of key personnel.

Forecasting organizational requirements pinpoints the primary considerations in planning the future organization structure of the firm and should result in several benefits: (1) because the personnel selection program can be based on the future requirements of the firm, the general skill requirements of future executives can be determined; (2) promotion decisions will be improved, since individuals can be directed into positions for which they are most qualified or for which they have the capability of being trained; (3) for those engaged in the planning of developmental efforts, organization planning provides a basis for establishing developmental objectives. Perhaps the greatest value of organization planning is the knowledge gained about the existing structure and members of the organization. Problems that need immediate attention may be uncovered. When sound organization planning is the foundation on which development programs rest, the company can avoid initiating them in response to the whims of executives or to training fads.

Requirements for Future Performance. Requirements for future performance can be inferred generally from the long-run organization plan. For example, if we assume that in the future decision making will require increased use of operations research and information technology—tools based on mathematical skills—the fundamental mathematics can be taught immediately. Then managers can be prepared for advanced training in specific applications in a relatively short time. Training in specific applications of these tools may then be included in development programs concurrently with the fundamental concepts of managing and organizing human behavior.

While there is little question of the difficulty of making determinations for specific positions, Mann's conceptual framework offers some aid for the organization planner (Mann, 1965). Basing his conclusions on a number of field studies of several levels in organizations, he concludes that managers must have technical skill, human relations skill, and administrative skill.

Technical skill is the specialized knowledge needed to perform the major functions and tasks associated with a position. Human relations skill is the capacity to work with people and motivate them in such a way that they want to perform well. Administrative skill, as we have noted in chapter 8, is the ability to make decisions and conceptualize relationships directed toward organizational goal achievement, rather than toward maximizing return to some specific subunit of the firm. These skills, of course, necessarily include the ability to plan, organize, and control the functioning of the organizational system and structure.

Mann makes two important points regarding the skills mix. There are different skill requirements for different organizational levels. At the lower supervisory levels, technical and human relations skills are primarily important. At the higher levels, administrative skill assumes major importance. Mann proposes also that the skills mix differs for different stages of organization growth and development. Therefore, as a person progresses through a career in an organization, the nature of his development experiences should change. Also, as discussed in chapter 17, as an organization progresses through various stages of growth, skill requirements can be anticipated. For example, before the firm moves into the stage of "rational bureaucracy," managers can be given training in systematic management processes.

Such an organizational planning effort will provide the overall framework for specific developmental or training experiences. In most organizations, training and development programs emerge from specific short-range situations. For example, when civil rights employment legislation made it legally necessary that more women and minority group members be moved into managerial positions, many firms attempted to reduce the resistance of the incumbent work group with training. It is important, though, that long-range organization planning be undertaken, because then it is possible to consider every training effort as it fits into an overall theme.

Development Techniques

Organizations have used many methods to change individuals and groups. These methods are the technology of the trainer. They are teaching techniques, activities which are intended to bring about a change in another. Part of the problem in doing this is overcoming resistance to change. Some of the ways industry uses these methods are discussed in item 18.1. Here we will review various off-the-job and on-the-job training methods, review what is known about their effectiveness in accomplishing various kinds of change, and then discuss how they may be applied to general programs of organizational development including the programs of Blake and Mouton and of House.

Off-the-job Methods

Off-the-job methods are learning environments other than in the work setting. Typically they present, in a classroom situation, particular training content. This content can range from typing classes to lectures and discussion of such subjects as human relations theory or quantitative decision-making techniques.

Lecture. Perhaps the most common form of training is the standard lecture, in which someone competent in a particular topic area presents a set of concepts and ideas to a group. While it is true that often questions and answers are used to determine understanding, the lecture is generally considered an "instructor-centered" method.

Films and Videotape. Another instructor-centered method is the use of film or TV. Sometimes the instructor appears on the screen and presents material in much the same fashion as in a lecture, and sometimes he is interviewed. Usually, questions and answers are not used unless someone, such as a trainer, is present and using the film as a vehicle to stimulate discussion. Sometimes the film presents dramatization of certain incidents in order to provide examples of the concepts being taught.

Programmed Instruction. Programmed instruction is also an instructor-centered approach. However, it is at the same time interactive, in the sense that the learner moves at his own pace, not advancing to a more advanced set of concepts until he has mastered a preliminary set. With conventional programmed instruction, concepts are presented to the learner, and then a series of diagnostic questions are asked. If all questions are answered correctly, the learner moves on to the next concept. If questions are answered incorrectly, the learner is directed to additional material on the subject. Programmed instruction is theoretically based on principles of reinforcement, the

ITEM 18.1   Management Development

How Companies Raise a New Crop of Managers

Eli M. Black, chairman, president, and chief executive officer of United Brands Co., who committed suicide last month, not only ran a one-man show but failed to groom a successor. The board is still searching for a replacement, while two committees run the company.

That kind of transition problem ought to be lesson enough for any company. Yet in today's recession, management development programs, which are supposed to provide in-depth backup at every level and facilitate the transfer of power at the top, are on nearly every corporate cost cutter's list. General Motors, Chrysler, Corning Glass, First National Bank of Chicago, and New York Telephone, for example, already are pruning long-established programs.

• • • •

Management development is vulnerable because it is expensive, time-consuming, and complex to administer. It means, almost by definition, having a managerial surplus. IBM, for example, has three or four potential replacements for each of several hundred top jobs. It also means moving managers in and out of jobs, sometimes just when they are beginning to make a contribution, to give them breadth of experience. That kind of talent transfer can be expensive not just because it temporarily drags down efficiency but because the physical moves that accompany many such job changes are today more costly than ever.

For all the trouble and expense of the development programs, many large corporations see no real alternative, even in today's economy. A growth company like Xerox, with sales of $3.58-billion last year, may still have to go outside to fill its management ranks, but mature companies prefer to provide for their own needs. Moreover, it is probably more than coincidence that companies dominant in their industries, such as Exxon, AT&T, IBM, and Citicorp, often have the most effective programs. Exxon Chairman John K. Jamieson, AT&T Chairman John D. deButts, IBM Chairman Frank T. Cary, and Citicorp Chairman Walter B. Wriston have all had 20 or more years of service in their companies and are products of their companies' systems.

An effective program can pay enormous dividends. It can boost morale at every level, help companies hold good men, and prevent the dislocations that come with moving an outsider in at the top. "When a chief executive is brought in from the outside," says one executive who has seen several such changes, "he brings in 50% of his staff from the outside, and they bring in 50% of theirs from the outside, and so on down the line. By the time the results are in a couple of years later it may be too late to save the company."

No two companies approach development the same way, but some common threads run through programs considered most effective:

. . . They are built deep into the system, involving all levels of management and affecting the way the organization works. "We don't hire management trainees," says Edward F. Krieg, IBM director of management development. "We go after competent people and provide a crucible where they can evolve into managers."

. . . Management development is part of every manager's job. Each executive is responsible for grooming his subordinates, and his salary and promotions are based partly on their success.

. . . Top management support and a long-term commitment to the program are unwavering. Otherwise, movement of executives in and out of learning jobs comes to an end.

To provide constantly challenging jobs and promotions requires that older workers must retire and mediocre ones must leave. Exxon, for one, tries to keep the top 10% of its management talent moving up by weeding out the bottom 10%. "The life-blood of our management development system is the rate at which we can move talent through the management ranks, always providing a greater challenge," says Frank Gaines, Jr., executive development coordinator at Exxon.

Citibank uses much the same approach. For nearly 40 years, the bank has relied less on formal training than on hiring people with strong academic credentials, thrusting responsibilities on them, and closely watching their performance. "There is no alternative for doing," says Thomas C. Theobald.

Theobald likes to take people right from school, give them such rudimentary tools as cash flow accounting, and put them to work under close supervision. "We set goals for our people and they are reviewed formally every few months, but informally every few hours," he says. "The idea is to find out who can make sensible judgments and who can't, and then give those who can lots of opportunity."

He likes to "take a roll" occasionally, too, gambling on a younger person. But he monitors the person's performance through the four division heads and four staff heads reporting to him. "I spend about half my time coaching people and making judgments about them," Theobald says. "And I read every single performance report on the 300 officers in the group and see every salary action."

Companies have developed varied techniques to hasten the learning process. Some attempt to compress work experience by giving developing managers short-term special assignments on high-level task forces or making them assistants to division or corporate executives. For example, Stanley Rosenthal, now a 34-year-old partner at Peat, Marwick, Mitchell & Co. in Chicago spent two years in the company's department of professional practices in New York. The department's 12 partners and 30 managers have no direct client responsibility but work on quality control and advise the operating offices on knotty accounting problems. "You get two years of intensive problem solving and when you return to your office you are recognized as being current in SEC matters and accounting practices."

Course work. Some companies combine course study with work experience. Since 1967, The First National Bank of Chicago has tapped 167 liberal arts graduates for its First Scholar program. First Scholars attend graduate business school at nights for two and a half years and work in various line and staff jobs at the bank for from one to six months.

"It's a fast track," says Robert Bourke, 23, a First Scholar for the past 20 months. "They slot you right into the management mode and give you wide experience right away. The business school and the work mesh well so that the learning curve is straight up."

First National has retained about 82% of its scholars, and they have gone into all phases of the bank's management, where they have easily held their own with the MBAs the bank has hired fresh out of business school.

Outside course work comes in for praise as well as criticism. Peat, Marwick runs a two-week refresher course at Stanford University for partners, who may be in their 30s, 40s, and 50s, to keep them abreast of new developments in business economics and management science. And many companies send executives to the 13-week advanced course at Harvard, MIT, and other B-schools. "They are good for compressing experience and giving our people exposure to executives of other companies," Gaines of Exxon says. But Paul Anderson, vice-president of Booz, Allen & Hamilton, Inc., says that courses are "only good as supplements to work experience." Adds E. H. Clark, Jr., chairman of Baker Oil Tools, Inc.: "I send a guy to school when he's screwed up and I want to get him out of my hair."

Coordinated program. When management development fails, it is most often because top management is not directly involved. Contrast, for example, the experience at American Airlines with that at Exxon. American's program experiments lacked strong support from top management and were wiped out during economic slumps. "We were never able to give development the proper emphasis," says Gene E. Overbeck, senior vice-president at American. The airline now has a new program in the works, and it has the strong endorsement of American's new president, Albert V. Casey. Making room for the young talent, however, may not be easy.

By contrast, at Exxon, management development is already closely monitored from the top. Chairman Jamieson, President Clifton C. Garvin, Jr., and the seven other inside directors constitute a compensation and executive development committee (curiously the acronym is COED—although there are no women members), which meets each Monday to review the development programs in each of Exxon's 12 major operating units.

These units in turn have their own COEDs reviewing fast-rising managers in the affiliates reporting to them. "Every man on the board is a product of the system so he believes in it," Gaines says.

Exxon's program is closely coordinated with the company's business plan. Each line manager must draw up a long-range plan for the replacement needs of his organization. In it he must appraise all his key executives, forecast job openings for the next five years, and assess the most likely candidates to fill them.

Plans for more than 3,000 executives are reviewed at successively higher levels. Ultimately, the corporate COED reviews and comments on every appointment for the 250 most senior jobs and keeps track of another 500 jobs to insure adequate depth in the management ranks.

If most companies concede that management development is expensive, few can pinpoint exactly how much it costs. Many companies such as Exxon claim that it is so much a part of the management structure that the cost cannot be calculated. Peat, Marwick, however, estimates that it spends at least $10-million annually for training, including time lost during the course work. And First National Chicago calculates that it spends about $31,000 for each First Scholar.

Cutbacks. That kind of expense is an obvious target when companies start cutting back as they are doing today. First National Chicago's Scholars program, for example, is being reduced to 12 people this year, from 28 in 1974. At some companies the cutting is far more severe.

At Corning Glass Works, which since last July has laid off 9,000 employees, or nearly one-fifth of its worldwide work force, development has slowed perceptibly.

• • • •

Less drastic cutbacks in development programs are commonplace. New York Telephone Co. has reduced its work force in the last three years from 105,000 to 85,000. One result: managers are now moved laterally instead of being promoted.

Still, many companies with traditionally strong development programs are preserving what they can even in the face of deep sales slumps. GM is moving managers infrequently and has curtailed recruiting. But some of the management development survives. "Results of the program have changed," says William B. Chew, director of GM's human resources management activity, "but that

doesn't change the need for the program."

Business Week, March 10, 1975

Reprinted from the March 10, 1975, *Business Week* by special permission. Copyright © 1975 by McGraw-Hill, Inc.

reinforcement ostensibly coming from the satisfaction of answering the diagnostic questions correctly.

Simulations—Business Games. The simulation is an attempt to involve the learner in a learning situation which approximates the real world. In most simulations the learner is faced with a series of decisions that must be made—for example, decisions about resource allocations. These decisions are then fed into computer models and their effects are shown. Simulations may be extremely complex, or very simple, and they may deal with a wide variety of problems— manufacturing, retailing, or even governmental management.

Case Studies. The case is a narrative, written presentation of a set of problem facts that the student analyzes and then solves. Cases are used to stimulate discussion of topics of all types. Like simulations, they can be simple or complex.

Conference (Discussion) Methods. The conference method may be used with or without cases and simulations. Students may be assigned material for reading and the instructor will then use a series of questions to stimulate discussion. The conference method is intended to involve the participant more extensively in the learning process than do lectures or films. It is a group-centered method of instruction, one in which the participants extensively engage, along with a conference leader, in the development of ideas that can lead to greater understanding of what is being taught.

Role Playing. Role playing is an experiential, student-centered method of instruction. In role-playing, the student (learner) is asked to act as another person. For example, in a management training program, a labor-management role play may be used. One participant assumes the role of a company negotiator while another acts as a union representative. Each has received a set of facts and is instructed to represent his side in determining the final form of a labor contract.

Other problem areas—such as worker motivation, or the effect of different leadership styles and different modes of participation in decision making—may also be highlighted through role playing. Role playing is especially useful in developing interpersonal skills, in showing the consequences of behaving in different ways, and in developing an understanding of the perspectives of others.

Sensitivity Training.   Sensitivity training generally focuses on exploring the nature of interpersonal relationships. Individuals are brought together in groups which have little or no structure. Group members, in an ambiguous situation, must work out, under the guidance of a leader, their own structure.

In sensitivity training there is an attempt to foster greater understanding of the participants themselves, and of other people, and an attempt to increase the interpersonal skills of the participants. It is generally felt that such objectives are achieved when the individuals become more accepting of feedback from others, more candid about expressing their own feelings, more trusting, more spontaneous, more flexible, more sincere, and more willing to face up to conflict and personal problems.

Sensitivity training sessions generally try to establish a learning atmosphere in which self-examination and criticism is rewarded, where constructive feedback is given others, and where social support is given for change efforts. Various experiential exercises, tests, and role models are also frequently used to facilitate such learning.

The Effectiveness of Off-the Job Methods

Programmed instruction, sensitivity training, computer games, television, and role playing have been widely used in training only in recent years. These newer techniques, along with more traditional methods such as the lecture, conference method, films, and case study method provide a number of training and education alternatives to use in a particular situation. While availability of resources (money, time, and personnel) play a significant part in the choice of one training method or another, another important criterion must be the relative effectiveness of the training method being considered for a particular training objective. In chapter 3 we presented a "model" of the individual, composed of the following facets:

1. skills, ability, and knowledge;   4. values;
2. self-concept;   5. needs and motives.
3. attitudes;

We can think of development as an effort to change these character-istics. However, it is unlikely that any technique noted above that is used in the work setting is powerful enough to change strongly-held values, the self-concept, or needs and motives. These characteristics are probably resistant to these change methods because they are embedded in the human personality. However, it is possible with these training techniques to change some skills, ability, knowledge, and attitudes. This conclusion is based on fairly extensive research which has been done on training methods.

Acquisition of Knowledge. Research indicates that programmed instruction is effective for knowledge acquisition. In 20 studies which compared programmed instruction to conventional lecture and discussion in an industrial situation, it was found that immediate learning was at least 10 percent higher under programmed instruction in 7 comparisons, and there was not a practical difference between the conventional and programmed instruction in 13 comparisons (Nash, Muczyk, and Vettori, 1971). Nash and his colleagues, however, have pointed out that most of the studies involving a comparison of programmed with conventional instruction have not used a well-planned and well-carried out conventional class as the basis for comparison (Nash et al., 1971).

Lectures are also effective in knowledge acquisition. Four extensive reviews of the literature where the subjects were primarily college students all concluded that on the basis of research comparisons made, lecture and discussion methods are equally effective for the acquisition of knowledge (Buxton, 1956; Dietrick, 1960; Stovall, 1958; and Verner and Dickinson, 1967).

Research results, with students as subjects, generally show no significant differences between television lecture courses and conven-tional lecture courses. For example, Schramm (1962b) in summarizing 393 studies of the amount learned in television courses versus conventionally-taught courses. found that in 65 percent of the comparisons there were no differences, in 21 percent of the compari-sons the television approach was more effective, and in 14 percent of the comparisons the participants in the television courses did worse. Andrew (1954) found the lecture was superior to a film for imparting knowledge to adult subjects.

In a well-controlled study where a class taught by the case method was compared to a class taught by a lecture-discussion approach, the case-study section scored significantly higher on achievement tests (Butler, 1967).

Changing Attitudes. In two fairly well-controlled studies where the
lecture and discussion approaches were compared in situations
involving attitude change among adults (prisoners and executives),
the discussion approach was more effective (Butler, 1966; Silber,
1962). In five controlled studies involving changes in behavior of
adults, the discussion approach was more effective than the lecture
method in changing behavior (Bond, 1956; Levine and Butler, 1952;
Lewin, 1958). Some of these comparisons were not entirely fair to the
lecture method, however, since in the discussion groups the participants were usually asked to commit themselves to future actions
while the subjects in the lecture groups were not asked to do this. In
spite of this, it appears that the discussion approach is superior to the
lecture in changing attitudes and behavior.

Several studies conducted among students show that role playing
can be quite effective in changing attitudes (Festinger and Carlsmith,
1959; Harvey and Beverly, 1961). Role playing seems especially effective if the subjects participating in the role-playing situation are asked
to take the point of view opposite to their own and to verbalize this
opposite point of view to others (Culbertson, 1957; Janis and King,
1954; King and Janis, 1956; Janis and Mann, 1965).

Sensitivity training is fairly effective in changing attitudes. Four
studies using control groups have been conducted with adults where
an attempt was made to see if behavior was changed as a result of
sensitivity training (Boyd and Ellis, 1968; Bunker, 1965; Miles, 1965;
Underwood, 1965; and Valiquet, 1968), and these studies did find
behavioral changes. With respect to attitude change, two studies using
a before-and-after measure without controls and with student and
adult participants found attitude changes as a result of sensitivity
training (Schutz and Allen, 1966; Smith, 1964). Although there were
certain methodological deficiencies in these studies, on balance the
results show that sensitivity training can result in at least short-run
behavioral and attitudinal change, although such change may not be
related to greater job effectiveness (Campbell and Dunnette, 1968).

Problem-solving Skills. Unfortunately, the research on the effectiveness of the case study as a training device to improve problem solving
is very limited. Only a few studies were found that involved more
than an attempt to obtain testimonials from course participants. Fox
(1963) found that about one-third of the students exposed to case-
study analysis improved significantly in their ability to handle cases,
about a third made moderate improvement, and a third made no
improvement. Solem (1960) found that both the case-study method

and role playing were effective in learning how to derive solutions to problems but felt that role playing was better for teaching participants how to gain acceptance of solutions.

More evidence is available on the effectiveness of role playing in developing problem-solving skills. In addition to the study by Solem (1960), studies by (Maier, 1953), Maier and Maier (1957), Maier and Hoffman (1960a; 1960b), and Maier and Solem (1952) indicate that problem-solving skills can be improved for both students and managers with the use of role playing. Two studies (Parnes and Meadow, 1959; Cohen, Whitmyre, and Funk, 1960) found that training in brainstorming could improve problem-solving ability. Brainstorming could be taught by means of role playing.

As with the case-study method, there is little research or analysis on the effectiveness of business games as a method for teaching problem-solving skills. Dill and Doppelt (1963) conducted a student self-report study which indicated that the students did not seem to learn much about specific problem-solving solutions or strategies that could be used in other situations. Raia (1966) found that experience with a business game did not improve the ability to handle cases. McKenney (1962) found that students in sections with games plus lectures understood the interrelationship between organizational factors better than students in sections with cases plus lectures.

Interpersonal Skills.   Most of the research which has concerned itself with the effectiveness of training methods in developing interpersonal skills has been on sensitivity training. Six studies of sensitivity training indicate that participants describe others in more interpersonal terms than people without such training (Campbell and Dunnette, 1968). However, research specifically measuring changes in perceptual accuracy of others as a result of sensitivity training has been inconclusive.

Some research on the development of interpersonal skills has examined role playing. A study by Bolda and Lawshe (1962) showed that role playing can be effective in increasing sensitivity to employee motivations if the participants become involved in the role play. Another study indicated that role playing can be effective in improving interviewing skills (Van Schacck, 1957). In addition, studies by Maier (1953), Maier and Hoffman (1960a), and Maier and Maier (1957), show that role playing can be used to improve group leadership skills (which are a form of interpersonal skills).

Participant Acceptance.   What methods are preferred by the people who are in training? Several studies on managerial acceptance of the lecture versus the discussion approach indicate a preference among managers for the lecturer or more leader-centered approach (Anderson, 1959; Filley and Reighhard, 1965; House, 1962; Mann and Mann, 1959). Two other studies of managers and a study of adults found no difference in reactions or attitudes to the use of the lecture and discussion approaches (Hill, 1960; House, 1965).

Reviews of research on television lectures by Kumata (1956 and 1960; and Schramm, 1962a) show that television has fairly high acceptance among adults as a training method and with young children, and a much lower acceptance among high school and college students.

Raia (1966) found that business students in sections of a course which used a business game did not differ in attitudes toward the course from students who had sections without the business game. Rowland, Gardner, and Nealey (1970) found that only a few of the students participating in a business game felt that the game was a valuable learning experience and that attitudes toward the course were not improved as a result of the addition of the business game.

A series of studies in six organizations by Bolda and Lawshe (1962) indicated fair acceptance for role playing by managerial personnel. The training directors also rated the case study method as high on participant acceptance. A study by Fox (1963) found that attitudes toward the case study method in the form of student testimonials were favorable. However, Castore (1951) found interest in cases dwindled after a period of exposure to them. That programmed instruction is preferable to the lecture method is supported in a study conducted at IBM (Hughes and McNamara, 1961), and in a study by Neidt and Meredith (1966), but several studies show that participant acceptance of a training approach is a function of their experience with it (Guetzkow, Kelly and McKeachie, 1954; Harris, 1960; and Hughes, 1963).

Retention of Knowledge.   There has not been much research on the retention of knowledge for the different methods. The research that has been completed has been primarily with college students and has shown no clear superiority for the lecture or discussion methods as compared with each other (Dietrick, 1960; Verner and Dickinson, 1967), for the movie film as compared with the lecture and discussion methods (Sodnovitch and Pophorn, 1961; VanderMeer, 1948; Verner and Dickinson, 1967), for the television lecture as compared to the conventional lecture or discussion approach (Kumata, 1960; Klausmeir, 1961), or for programmed instruction as compared to the conventional lecture or discussion methods (Nash, Muczyk, and Vettori, 1971). The research reviews generally conclude that the amount of material retained is proportional to the amount learned (Dietrick, 1960; Vernor and Dickinson, 1967).

On-the-job Methods

Some feel that experience is the best teacher—that putting a manager into a situation where he can sink or swim is the best approach to development. When this approach is taken in a systematic way the developmental methods are "on-the-job." Not only can an employee learn the content of his job, but he has the opportunity to observe others at higher-level managerial positions and so can pattern his behavior after them.

Members of any organization can learn from watching others and modeling their behavior. Human beings can learn from observation and/or direct experience. As Bandura (1969) concludes:

Research conducted within the framework of social-learning theory demonstrates that virtually all learning phenomena resulting from direct experiences can occur on a vicarious basis through the observation of other persons' behavior and its consequences for them.

Organizations hire certain individuals—for example, "rate busters," or someone who exceeds the production norms (in the Soviet union, such workers are called "Stakhanovites")—and place them in a group as an example to be emulated by others in an attempt to change behaviors. Research on behavior modeling shows, however, that such models will not be imitated unless the individuals to be changed are motivated to learn by, and have some respect for, the model (Bandura, 1969). The authors conducted a research study in a manufacturing organization and concluded that managers model their behavior on that of superiors when a situation has forced them to take some kind of action and they do not have previous experience to apply to it (Carroll and Tosi, 1973).

There are at least three types of experiences that can be classified as on-the-job development: (1) job rotation, (2) special assignments, and (3) delegation and coaching.

Job Rotation.   With job rotation—a fairly common method—an individual is systematically moved from one position to another in an organization for the purpose of learning something about each of the positions and what the purpose and function of various organizational units are, relative to each other.

The sequence of different positions is planned in advance, with both the individual's and the organization's needs in mind, so that not always do two people get exactly the same experience. In one major aircraft company, for example, a new trainee worked for six months in production at Los Angeles, four months in the finance division in Seattle, and another six months in the marketing division in Washington, D.C. Then the employee selected the division in which she wanted to work and, after consultation with supervisors in each, the personnel department assigned her a position.

Another type of job rotation system is career progression planning. Rather than a horizontal series of jobs, a vertical sequence is planned as the individual moves up the hierarchy of the organization. For instance, the first position may be as an assistant foreman in manufacturing, then foreman. From there he may move to a higher-level position in the personnel department, after which he may be promoted to assistant plant superintendent. This type of job rotation system is usually used with employees who are considered to have high potential; that is, those destined for high managerial positions.

Special Assignments.   An individual may also undergo development through special assignment. For example, a manager may be assigned the responsibility of evaluating the organization's compensation program. In completing this assignment, the manager learns a great deal about compensation. Or a marketing manager may be assigned to a production committee to obtain a better appreciation of the problems in the production area. Such assignments are often tailored to the needs of the individual.

Delegation and coaching.   Delegation and coaching are also traditional developmental methods which can be quite effective. The subordinate is assigned—delegated—responsibility for a particular task, which he then carries out. He learns how to carry it out both by doing and by consulting with his superior when problems arise. Such a method works most effectively when the assignments made are challenging and when the superior spends sufficient time on coaching and provides useful feedback about the subordinate's performance. Research has shown that, as would be expected, a climate of helpfulness and supportiveness contributes to the effectiveness of coaching sessions (Carroll and Tosi, 1973), and that supervisors will do a better job of coaching when they receive credits or rewards for their efforts and when they have received training in conducting performance appraisal interviews (Douglas and Crain, 1975).

Effectiveness of On-the-job Methods

There has been no research comparing the use of the various on-the-job methods in terms of which might be better than another. Neither has there been any systematic assessment of these techniques compared to off-the-job methods. Organizations must, therefore, assess whether or not the costs of learning on the job are excessive. If so, then some sort of training away from work must be devised.

There are some problems that must be considered. Perhaps much of the value of on-the-job development comes from the "modeling" effects noted earlier. Thus, careful selection of the model and the situation in which it is hoped modeling behavior will occur can contribute to improved outcomes.

The primary problem with such a development strategy is the variability of supervisors under whom an individual will work. One may be very strong developmentally, another weak, so that the progress of the trainee is impeded. It can also happen that if supervisors are given the responsibility for such "temporary" employees they may not spend adequate developmental time with them, since they know that the employee's ultimate assignment will be elsewhere than their own units.

Some Integrated Approaches to Development

Now that we have described a fairly wide range of developmental methods and some general conditions under which they might work effectively, the question is how a manager can make use of them. He must, of necessity, understand something about how human beings change and how this can be accomplished organizationally.

Schein (1961) has analyzed a number of successful change programs in order to identify elements which such programs have in common and which can provide guides for the establishment of successful development. The change process, according to Schein (1961) and Lewin (1957), involves three basic stages: (1) unfreezing, (2) changing, and (3) refreezing.

Unfreezing.   The first step in the change process is unfreezing. At this stage attempts are made to motivate the target person to change before the actual change is introduced. Common to the unfreezing stage is the removal of social support to the individual for the old behavior or attitudes by insulating him from his habitual social system. For example, when trying to change attitudes, it may be useful, at least initially, to take the person away from his normal work setting, where he may be finding strong reinforcement of his present attitudes, to a location where he may obtain a new perspective. Next, rewards for willingness to change may be introduced, along with punishments for lack of willingness to change.

Changing.   Schein outlines two processes that seem especially effective in change programs. The first of these is *identification,* in which the target person identifies with one or more role models in his environment and thus tries to behave as they do. That is to say, the provision of appropriate role models facilitates change, since the role models exemplify the new behavior in their actions. The other effective change process is that of *internalization,* by which the target person discovers for himself that the new behavior or attitude solves his personal problems. Obviously this second change process is difficult to establish and control.

Refreezing.   In this stage, the newly acquired behavior or attitude must be supported by the social system in which the person normally functions if it is to become a part of the target person's normal behavioral patterns.

There are several "strategies," or suggested ways of going about this process described by Schein. Three of these are considered below. What is important about each of these is that they are systematic, planned ways to induce change.

The Grid-OD Program

The Blake and Mouton (1969) approach to organizational development emphasizes changing the whole organization in a series of six sequential steps. Each step represents a particular phase of the total program.

Phase 1.   This phase involves introducing managers to the managerial grid program. Phase 1 involves approximately five days of training. During this training period, managers participate in various exercises which illustrate group and intergroup problems and the advantages of certain problem-solving techniques which primarily emphasize involvement and participation. These problems focus on how other groups solve problems and what the difference is between high- and low-effectiveness groups. In addition, the group members receive feedback from the other participants as to their participant grid style. The managerial grid as an approach to describing leader behavior was discussed in chapter 8. Each person in the training is described by the other participants as having exhibited one of the five grid styles during the week of training. Each participant compares this evaluation with his self-evaluation. Then, the gap between this style and the 9.9 style (which represents excellence) is considered. An effort is made to get individuals to commit themselves to closing the gap between their present style and the 9.9 approach. During this phase, each participant also evaluates the general leader behavior patterns (a sort of leader culture) as they exist in his company.

Phase 2. In this stage, teamwork development is emphasized. An analysis of all work groups is made. Here each team member evaluates his group at work and then meets with the other members of the group to discuss their perceptions of the work culture of the group. Each member's grid style is assessed, primarily on how he relates to the group. Also, the group meets to study and attempt to resolve problems of operating together. A project, derived from some specific difficulty in the workplace, is initiated and investigated by the group. Phase 2 starts with the top group in the organization and slowly works down to the lower-level work groups.

Phase 3. In this step of the grid program, all groups review their external relationships and identify other groups with which they have problems of coordination, cooperation, or conflict. The emphasis is on developing intergroup relations. Key members of the groups with unsatisfactory intergroup relationships then meet to identify the type of relationship they actually have. They attempt to define the ideal relationship that should exist between their groups and develop a plan for overcoming the difficulties.

Phase 4. In this phase, a top management team designs an ideal strategic corporate model. This defines what the organization would be like if it were truly excellent. Consideration is given to the type of structure, the type of personnel, problems, and so on. The design team completes various instruments developed from the grid approach to help them in their task. After a long period of analysis, the model is developed and can then be evaluated by other organizational members and units.

Phase 5. Now comes the implementation of the ideal model. In this stage the organization is broken down into component parts and a planning team is created to help implement the model in each part, with the assistance of an overall phase 5 coordinator. Each team must of course implement the model with consideration for the unique character of its own organizational component.

Phase 6. This phase involves a critique of the whole OD program. Instruments are used to determine how the organization has changed since the OD program was initiated. Problems uncovered in phases 1 through 5 which hamper effectiveness are raised and form the bases for new ways of doing things.

   Blake and Mouton believe that eventually such methods will become the "normal" way to do things in an organization. There will be no need to use crutches such as training sessions or analytical paper-and-pencil instruments to describe the people or the organization.

House Management Development Model

One of the most useful and well-integrated models for understanding the prerequisites for change has been developed by House (1967). He presents a systematic approach to the problem which seeks to specify the minimum conditions required for successful change efforts. This model is shown in figure 18.1. The objectives of development, which represent the kind of changes that are typically sought when development programs are instituted, are given, together with the input factors that are likely to affect the change and the types of conditions required to achieve a particular developmental objective.

The Input Factors. House lists five key variables which affect the outcomes of developmental efforts. Four of these represent the context in which the change effort must operate. These are the characteristics of the participants, the organizational culture, the leadership climate, and organizational structure. The fifth is the developmental method itself, which is the stimulus used to induce change in the individual.

1. Participant Characteristics. We have already noted that particular types of individuals will predominate in different types of organizations. The organizationalist, the professional, and the externalists all have significantly strong but different attitudinal orientations. These different orientations must be taken into account in developmental

FIGURE 18.1 Conditions Required to Induce Change Through Development

Source: *Managerial Process and Organizational Behavior*, by Alan C. Filley and Robert J. House. Copyright© 1969 by Scott, Foresman and Company. Reprinted by permission of the publisher.

Conditions	Objectives				
	Change in Knowledge	Change in Attitude	Change in Ability	Change in job Performance	Change in End-Operational Results
Participant Characteristics	Sufficient motivation	Flexible attitudes on part of participants; Agreement with spirit of the material to be learned	Non-conflicting habits or personality traits		
Developmental Effort	Direct method of instruction (programmed learning, lectures, films, reading, and so on); Competent instruction	Discussion of on-the-job applications and personal benefits	Practice of desired abilities; Corrective training (therapy to correct undesirable habits and behavioral patterns)	Opportunity for on-the-job practice of newly acquired abilities	
Leadership Climate		Neutral or positive attitude of superior toward development	Superior's attitude and example consistent with desired change	Coaching, counseling, and periodic performance review by superior consistent with desired performance	Performance appraisal by the superior based on practices taught in the learning phase
Organizational Structure		Goals, top management philosophy, and policies consistent with learning phase		Philosophy, practices, and precedents of the policymaking executives consistent with desired manager performance	Top management active support and interest in development; Incentive system designed to reward practices taught in the learning phase
Organizational Culture		Cultural conditions and social beliefs consistent with desired attitudes		Informal group rules and standards consistent with desired change	Positive employee and informal group attitudes toward desired change

efforts. For example, training intended to change the attitudes toward the firm of externally-oriented members of an organization may encounter difficulty. If a program is intended to increase understanding of a particular managerial technique, however, this should not be a problem, since—for the most part—the level of intelligence of managers and professionals is above average.

2. Developmental Effort.   We have detailed several of the strategies used to induce change (on- and off-the-job types) earlier in this chapter. House believes that certain techniques are more likely than others to be effective, depending on the objective of the developmental effort.

3. Leadership Climate.   The climate of leadership in an organizational unit emerges from the interaction of leader (superior) and subordinates. There are two aspects of leadership of particular relevance to House's model of development. The first is the congruency of the leader's attitude with the general objectives of a particular training effort. This is especially relevant to attitude and skill change efforts, because the trainee should return to a work environment which supports the changes so that they receive reinforcement. The leader's behavior is the second important aspect. In the House model, the leader must provide guidance, counseling, coaching, and performance review based on developmental objectives.

4. Organizational Structure.   The formal structure of the organization is composed of goals, policies, procedures, job descriptions, compensation systems and so on. We have already extensively discussed variations in structure in chapter 7. It would be fruitless to attempt to teach managers in a bureaucratic organization to restructure their own units as dynamic organizations when the external environment is highly stable. The structure is an important limiting factor in performance.

5. Organizational Culture.   In chapter 4 we discussed the effects of groups and group norms on individuals. The culture of the organization can be defined as the values and norms that exist within a unit. It exists because of local cultural effects, the ethnic background of members, and the general social context of the location of the organization, as well as because of the structural and environmental characteristics of the organization itself.

This factor is not one easily changed by management efforts. If the culture is antithetical to organizational objectives, it can probably be changed only by mass replacement of personnel or by relocating the firm. In most instances, however, organizational culture will not be a *severe* limitation on training efforts. It is, however, a factor that must be analyzed, and the developmental content of training programs must be prepared in a way that is consistent with the culutre.

Objectives of Development.   The goals of development vary. Sometimes the intent is merely to increase knowledge. Often the goals are more ambitious, such as improved organizational results. House has attempted, after an extensive review of research on change efforts, to describe the minimum conditions which must be present to induce changes in (1) knowledge, (2) attitudes, (3) abilities, (4) job performance, and (5) end-operational results.

1. Knowledge Change.   Knowledge change goals are considered to be independent of skill and ability change goals. They refer simply to the level of information a person has. As a developmental objective, for example, it may be desired to make employees more aware of certain technical or management techniques, such as capital budgeting or linear programming, or it may be that a developmental objective is to increase an employee's understanding of current theory about managerial practice and behavior.

According to figure 18.1, to increase knowledge the participant must be willing to learn (be motivated) and be exposed to instructor-centered methods such as lectures, tapes, textbooks, and so on. So long as the instruction is competent (contains the necessary information), it is likely that one will learn.

One problem with such development is that even when these conditions (learner motivation and competent instruction) are present and people do learn, managers (or those who are responsible for development) expect other outcomes (e.g., improved job performance). It is like expecting all those who understand and appreciate Bach to be able to play his fugues.

2. Attitude Change.   In chapter 3 we defined an attitude as a predisposition to act in a certain way, an emotional feeling about something. Many firms have undertaken efforts to change attitudes of both workers and managers not only toward the company, but also toward women or minorities. They have done the latter to facilitate affirmative action programs, as well as to minimize problems in the workplace when women or minorities are hired.

For attitude change to occur, student-centered development methods are used. These are such processes as role-playing, sensitivity training, or group discussion methods in which the participants have an opportunity to consider how their current attitudes affect their work, and if and how changing them may improve the job situation. In development efforts in the organization, however, rigid attitudes—or those that are very important to the individual's psychological adjustment—will be difficult to change.

After the training, the environment to which the person returns is important. He should find a sympathetic leader, group norms that are not conflicting, and organization policies which do not make it difficult to change. For example, if the goal is to change attitudes of male managers toward women executives, then it would be necessary to have nondiscriminatory selection and promotion policies.

3. Abilities Change.   If a person learns capital budgeting theory, will he be able to prepare a long-range facilities program? That is, does a knowledge change alter behavioral ability? In the House model, skills change is considered to take place in the training program itself, not necessarily on the job. A person in a training program may learn how to program a computer or run a group meeting more effectively, but whether or not these skills are used at work is determined by the job. One problem with skills training is that sometimes the new skill is not needed in the workplace, and this of course, frustrates the one who has acquired it. For example, many organizations recommend that managers earn advanced degrees, such as the MBA. Often these degrees require courses in financial planning, but the graduate may not, for a long time, carry out this activity.

To change abilities, the developmental effort must be experiential; that is, the person must be able to practice the activity. For example, he must formulate a plan, solve a problem, run a meeting. Such techniques as role playing and group discussion often provide interpersonal skill development. Business games, (simulations) and obviously on-the-job methods such as special assignments and job rotation fall into this category.

Behavioral modeling is an important factor here. The superior must do the things he is seeking to develop in the subordinate. Or, if he does not have the capacity to do so, then he should give the subordinate the opportunity to use the skill. For example, the goal of development might be to improve computer-programming skills. The superior may not need such capacity in his own work and may have no ability to program, but he can make available to the subordinate every opportunity to use these abilities in problem solving.

4. Change in Job Performance.   There may be a wide gulf between having a skill and using it at work. The question with this objective is "How can we bring skills, knowledge, abilities, or attitudes developed away from work to the job?" For this objective of development, we expect that the subject will possess the requisite competence, and the responsibility of the manager and the organization is to incorporate the ability into the work situation.

The appropriate developmental method is to provide the opportunity to use these capacities on the job. The trainee must be permitted to make mistakes. The leader must offer coaching and guidance, providing help, support, and feedback about how well the subordinate is doing. Organization structure factors must be consistent with the desired performance. For example, in promotions, we must recognize the need to fail, and not pass over a manager simply because he may have had some very important and useful failure experiences from which he learned, early in his career. This approach will work effectively in conjunction with MBO (see chap. 11 and the section following in this chapter).

5. Change in End-Operational Results.   House does not expect improved results to be obtained unless the system (the structure) is designed so that it supports such results. For example, the compensation system must pay, not penalize, good performance. Managers must be able to reinforce subordinates with both objective and subjective rewards. All this must be consistent with, not contradictory to, the organizational culture.

Steps Involved in Development.   Like Blake and Mouton, House also suggests a series of steps to move from the objective of knowledge change to organizational results. Basically, his suggestion is to progress sequentially.

After a person has increased his knowledge, he can then think about what he has learned, reconsidering his attitudes and rationally changing them, if necessary. If a change in attitudes has made him more receptive, he can be exposed to skills training. When he returns to the job with these new skills, he should then have help from his superior in the form of stated objectives and feedback about his performance to reinforce his new behavior.

If such an approach is taken at several points of an organization, and all the developmental efforts are conducted, then improved overall performance can be expected.

This is a long sequence. The costs of development are high both in terms of money and commitment. Managers must, for example, be willing to make alterations in the organization structure; for instance, changing the methods by which people are paid. Some of these changes, as we noted earlier, will meet much resistance. It is often more comfortable to go through developmental motions (offer seminars and so on), than to approach development systematically with the objective of real change.

MBO as Development

It would be more desirable not to have to resort to programs or strategies, as outlined above, but rather to build development into everyone's job. With management by objectives (MBO) this is done, because emphasis is placed on establishing goals, developing ways to achieve these goals, and providing feedback about how well someone has done. We discussed this approach in detail in chapter 11. There, however, we only examined performance objectives, which have to do with the work itself. Of course, this is developmental to the extent that a manager develops goals with his subordinates that represent learning experiences for them. In addition to setting performance goals, however, MBO should take a more pointed orientation toward development. Managers should work out, with subordinates, personal development goals.

A personal development goal is an objective which has increased human potential as an end. It should focus on improving skills and abilities, attitude change, or better interpersonal relationships. As stated, MBO builds development into everyone's job. Every manager can work out, when needed, personal development goals for those who work for him.

It is important to stress that these goals be based on problems or deficiencies, current or anticipated, in areas such as technical skills or interpersonal problems. They may also be aimed at developing a subordinate for movement within the organization. The importance of these objectives lies in their potential for combating obsolescence, given our rapid expansion of knowledge, for preparing people for increased responsibility, and for overcoming problems in organizational interactions.

Setting development goals is probably more difficult than setting performance goals, since they are personal in nature and, as such, must be handled with care and tact. This difficulty of course may be avoided by simply not setting them, and it could be argued that they should be avoided, since they are an intrusion into an individual's privacy by the superior or the organization. However, when perceived personal limitations hinder effective performance, the problem must be treated.

Thus, if at any time the superior believes an individual's limitations stand clearly in the way of the unit's goal achievement, that should be made known to the individual. He may not be aware that he is creating problems and would gladly change—if he were aware. Many technically competent people have been relieved from positions because of human problems they create. Many might have been retained had they only known that problems existed or were arising.

When there is a need for them, personal development objectives should be a basic part of the MBO program. If there is no real need, then an effort to set them probably will produce general and ambiguous objectives, tenable only if the organization wishes to invest in "education for education's sake." Personal objectives should attack deficiencies related to performance, containing specific action proposals for solving the problems. This may be done in the following manner.

Pinpoint a Problem Area. Persons involved in goal setting should continually be alert to negative incidents resulting from personal limitations. It is particularly important that the manager recognize problems. When situations occur which he believes are due to either personal or technical limitations, he should be aware of who was involved and make some determination of the cause of the problem. Other individuals in the unit may be helpful in identifying problems; those with whom an individual interacts, for example, may be in a reasonably good position to judge his technical competence or to determine when problems are due to his behavior. If colleagues continually complain about another person, additional investigation into the problem is warranted. The most important source for identifying negative incidents may prove to be the person responsible for them. He may be very aware of problems in which he is involved and by discussing them may get at the primary cause.

To be worthy of attention as a problem area, these negative incidents should be significant in effect and frequency. This does not mean, however, that an important incident which occurs only once should be overlooked if it suggests serious deficiencies.

There are several areas in which personal development objectives could be set. Self-improvement goals may be assigned to improve current performance or skills, or may be specifically designed to develop skills required at higher levels or in future jobs (where it may be impossible at the present to describe the end state of affairs to be achieved).

1. *Improve interpersonal relations.* Inability to maintain reasonably effective working relationships may be due to a person's lack of awareness or his inability to cooperate. This may arise from personality deficiencies or simple lack of awareness of his impact upon others. He may be unable to recognize that he is precipitating problems.

2. *Improve current skills.* A manager may, for instance, be unable to prepare a budget or to engage in research because he has not had adequate training in these areas or because his training is not up-to-date. His general performance may be acceptable, but his skills should be improved.

3. *Prepare for advancement.* Another possibility covers either technical or human skills required for different or higher-level positions. These are truly developmental goals which focus on preparation for advancement. There are many ways in which they may be achieved. In some cases the individual may be given advanced work assignments; in others, they may be achieved by exposure in training situations to new concepts. In any event, they represent a *potential* problem area.

Assess the Causes of the Problem.   Once it has been established that a problem exists, the cause needs to be determined. Causes should be sought jointly, a result of investigation and discussion by both the superior and subordinate after both have thought of possible causes.

The possible causes of problems may be grouped into three general categories:

1. *Procedures and structure.* The structure of the organization itself may induce disturbances. Interpersonal conflict may develop because of the interdependence of work activities. For instance, if formal requirements cause a delay in information transmission, those who need it may develop negative attitudes and feelings.

2. *Others with whom an individual must work.* Problems with subordinates or managerial peers of the goal setter may be caused by personality incompatibility or lack of certain technical skills. While this may represent an important cause of problems, it is too easy to blame negative incidents on others.

3. *The person himself*. The individual may have habits and characteristics which are not congruent with those of subordinates or colleagues. Or he may lack the technical skills requisite to carry out certain responsibilities.

Attempting to define problems and causes facilitates converting development objectives into achievable goals. Like other objectives, they can be general (attend a sensitivity training course or role-playing seminar), or more specific (attend XYZ course in financial planning, use PERT techniques on Project X).

For assessing the achievement of development objectives we can rely simply upon the determination that the action plan has been carried out and that the individual has learned something. Suppose, for instance, that a development goal for an engineer destined to be a supervisor reads as follows: "To meet with members of the financial, marketing, and production groups in order to learn how product release schedules affect their areas." Currently, he may have to know little about this since he may now have little impact on product release schedules. The question is, how do you know that the activity produced the desired learning? You don't. At some point in time, the superior, who presumably has some knowledge in the goal area, should discuss the results of the meeting with the subordinate, emphasizing particularly the important points that should have been learned. Thus, the subordinate acquires both the learning experience of the meeting and reinforcement from the discussion.

We have made the point that development must be planned. It must be pointed at fairly specific objectives, based on problems which must be solved, and the methods used should be adequate.

Dalton (1970) found a number of factors to be associated with successful development, and these are identified in figure 18.2. First, he found that successful change is preceded by internal tensions which seem to produce a receptive environment for change efforts. A problem must exist. Second, the push for change should come from a respected or authoritative source. This also contributes to a successful change attempt since it gives credibility to the need for change. Third, it is more likely that change objectives will be achieved if they are specific rather than general. When specific development goals are known, as in the House model, then the development strategy can focus on what techniques are most likely to be effective.

The breaking off of old social relationships and the establishment of new ones also seems to facilitate change, as in the case in which people are placed in a new work environment in early stages of devel-

FIGURE 18.2 A Model of Induced Change

Tension Experienced within the System	Intervention of a Prestigious Influencing Agent	Individuals Attempt to Implement Proposed Changes	New Behavior and Attitudes Reinforced by Achievement, Social Ties, and Internalized Values—Accompanied by Decreasing Dependence on Influencing Agent
	Generalized objectives established	Growing specificity of objectives establishment of subgoals	Achievement and resetting of specific objectives
Tension within existing social ties ——→	Prior social ties interrupted or attentuated	Formation of new alliances and relationships centering around new activities	New social ties reinforce altered behavior and attitudes
Lowered sense of self-esteem ——→	Esteem-building begun on basis of agent's attention and assurance	Esteem-building based on task accomplishment	Heightened sense of self-esteem
——→	External motive for change (New schema provided)	Improvisation and reality-testing	Internalized motive for change

opment. Another factor which seems important is growing self-confidence and esteem which emerges as organizational members feel they are making progress in solving their problems. A factor which is especially valuable but correspondingly difficult to achieve, is that of internalizing the change, in which individuals accept the change because they see it as valid. Finally, the change must receive reinforcement in the social system to survive. This is to say that the structure of the organization must be congruent with environmental requirements and that the people in it be capable of coping with that state of the organization. These circumstances are extensively examined in chapters 6, 7, 12, 14, and 16.

Change is proceeding at an increasingly rapid rate in our economy today and organizations must change to survive. The successful management of change is indispensable, especially in the dynamic and mixed types of organizations. All organization types, but in particular the dynamic and mixed, must give the subject of change more attention than they have in the past.

Discussion Questions

1. Using the House model of management development, what is the most likely effect of courses which you have taken in college on your performance later at work?

2. Changing organizations is an extremely expensive process. Comment. What are the costs?

3. What is the basic difference between off-the-job methods and MBO as a strategy for changing people?

4. How do personal development goals differ from work or performance goals? What responsibility does a supervisor have in setting them? Should he have any?

5. How should the environment of an organization affect the training and development strategy of an organization?

Chapter 19

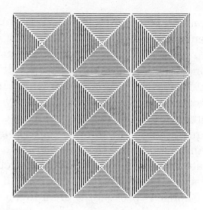

Organizations pervade all of modern life, and where the beginning and end points are to be found is something no one can say. In various ways, organizations serve the interests of all classes of people—the owners and investors, the members of the organization, and its various publics, from consumers to those who simply have concern for the ways in which the organization and its various outputs may directly or indirectly affect the qualities of their lives.

Viewed in this way, organizations become the most significant of social institutions. Our concern in this book has been to provide the best of contemporary understanding of how organizations can be effectively managed to meet their goals.

It remains in this final chapter to address two quite fundamental questions about the character of organizations and their relationship to society. One question has to do with the goals themselves. It would indeed be difficult to define precisely the appropriate goals for any organization, but in this chapter we can perhaps clarify certain of the pressures, from within and without, which suggest the directions in which organizational goals are cast, now and for the future. We would approach this question by analyzing in more detail the question of whom the organization serves.

A second question has to do with environmental forces, inside and outside the organization, which tend further to define the types of people who are likely to be associated with organizations in the future.

Throughout this book, we have stressed that the nature of the external environment will define the structure of the organization, and that as a general rule the people who are attracted to a particular type of organization are likely to be those whose outlooks and needs

The Effective Organization: Present and Future

are congruent with that organization. As is the case for every generation, however, we live in a time of social change. As social conditions change, so—too—do the outlooks, needs, and requirements of members of the society. If the outlooks of organizational members will change, organizations to be effective must adapt to those outlooks, or find other ways to be congruent with the needs of its members. In this chapter, we will look briefly at some of the social forces which presently are interacting in an important way with the character of organizations.

Organization Effectiveness

First, let us consider the nature of organizational effectiveness and some common measures of this quality in an organization. The purpose of managing—of obtaining congruence among the environment, structure, people, and process—is, of course, to increase the level of an organization's effectiveness, and of course the basic measure of an organization's effectiveness is survival. In order to serve its various publics, it must survive, and, conversely, if it does not serve them well, it will fail.

Various observers have attempted to factor the basic areas of effectiveness which contribute to survival. Parsons (1956), a sociologist, states that effective organizations adapt to their environment, know their goals, and achieve behavioral integration of personal goals of organizational members with organizational goals. In a study of 100 Texas firms, Friedlander and Pickle (1968) hypothesized that the effective organization was one which provided satisfaction of owners (through profits), satisfaction of customers (through speed of service, quality and quantity of goods and services, and the helpfulness of the staff), satisfaction of employees, satisfaction of suppliers and creditors (with fair treatment and prompt payment of accounts), and satisfaction of the community (through good citizenship). Of these, only satisfaction of owners, satisfaction of customers, and the providing of certain satisfactions to employees were related to financial success for the 100 firms.

Some studies have sought to identify indicators of organizational effectiveness by surveying large numbers of managers. A study of 283 organizational units in private industry by Mahoney and Weitzel (1969) found that organizations which used and developed their human resources effectively, which had good planning, which emphasized task accomplishment, which constantly initiated improvements in their operations, and which had cooperation among organizational units were very likely to be effective according to the ratings of practicing managers. A similar study by Paine (1970) of government units indicated that effective government organizations were those which had clear goals, good planning, good cooperation between units which rewarded ability, and where superiors provided support to subordinates.

Such lists of characteristics of effective organizations are indicative, but still quite general. They beg the question of how an organization achieves effectiveness. One study by Thune and House (1970) points to the importance of planning; it shows that increased time and emphasis placed upon planning is related to effectiveness for organizations, but Mintzberg (1973) suggests further that, as we have stated throughout this book, the planning process of different organizations varies with changes in their environment and with their stages of growth. That is, planning techniques vary in utility, depending upon the environment, structure, and personnel. The approach to the utilization of human resources must vary by type of organization, since employees in different types of organizations have different values, motives, and expectations. Thus, any discussion of organizational effectiveness without reference to type of organization is too abstract and general to be of practical importance.

Measures of organizational effectiveness have always been important. If, however, it is true, as the popular press every week reports, that people are becoming disaffected with work—or with a "bureaucratic" society in general—then the rather narrow traditional views of effectiveness are less useful.

Perhaps for this reason, writers on organizational effectiveness lay increasing stress on the importance of meeting the needs of organizational members, or of using human resources in such a way as the maximize their potential. For example, Bass, as early as 1952, argued that the worth of the organization to its members should be considered as a measure of organizational value along with existing indicators of effectiveness. Caplow (1964) argues the importance of high levels of "voluntarism" (the ability of the organization to satisfy its members and their desire to participate in the organization) and "integration" (the organization's ability to control internal conflict, to increase communication about problems and procedures, and to achieve more consensus among its members about the organization's problems). Argyris (1964) has also emphasized the successful blending of individual needs and organizational goals as indicators of effectiveness, showing that achieving top-management goals at the expense of personal goal achievement leads to ineffectiveness. McGregor (1960) stresses the importance to organizational effectiveness of integrating personal and organizational goals, as have Blake and Mouton (1964) and Hill (1969). All of these writers point out that organizational members as individuals and groups must bargain with the organization in order to achieve an integration of organizational goals and personal motives.

Satisfaction of the personal psychological needs of members is increasingly viewed as an indicator of organizational effectiveness, whether such satisfaction contributes to the organization's task goals or not. The achievement of personal goals of employees is viewed as important for its own sake, and thus participation is seen not only as an effective way of obtaining acceptance of change but as an approach which is congruent with the inherent dignity of the individual.

The extent to which an organization is socially responsible is also seen more today than in the past as an indicator of effectiveness. Bass (1952) was an early advocate of the position that the worth of an organization to society must be considered in determining overall organizational value. Many critics of business have argued that responsibility to the general public—for example, in product quality or impact on the physical environment—must take precedence over concern for profits or stockholder interest. In addition, it is increasingly proposed that the private sector of the economy should carry a more significant part of the burden in helping the disadvantaged, rebuilding slums, reducing crime, improving education, and seeking other social gains (Henderson, 1968). Some surveys (Baumhart, 1961) show that managers increasingly accept responsibility in these areas and no longer see profit as their *only* concern, though profitability and responsibility to stockholders remain, not surprisingly, their most important concern (Lorig, 1967).

Managing in the Changing World

The world is constantly changing—politically, socially, and technologically—and these changes seem to have accelerated in recent history. Individuals, groups, and organizations adapt to this change in a dynamic way, with social and political change encouraging techno-logical developments and these in turn contributing to further social and political change.

Some of the primary change forces with which managers must cope in the near future will be increases in foreign competition, growth of the multinational organization, continuing rapid growth of technical knowledge, growing power of government, political instability, increases in organization size, changing composition of the labor force, changes in the values of organizational members, and continued improvements in opportunities for minority group members. Such changes can well be considered as representative of the changes in environment cited throughout this book, and many of the organiza-tional adaptations we have discussed will be in response to just such changes as these. As we discuss these environmental changes in greater detail, the reader should consider how the nature of these adaptations will be reflected in the organizational dynamics detailed in this book.

Growth in Size of Organizations

Perhaps the first factor that will be relevant to future managerial effec-tiveness is the sheer size of organizations. We can expect organiza-tions in the future to be larger than they are today (Bennis, 1970). In 1947 the largest 200 corporations in the United States produced 30 percent of the value added to manufacturing output, but by 1970 the top 200 produced 43 percent of the value added (Burck, 1975). Greater size of course suggests greater formalization; whether such organiza-tions will need greater differentiation in their own structures, however, to meet increased environmental pressures is a question for future analysis.

Increased Foreign Competition

United States firms are facing increased foreign competition. At the present time, a significantly higher proportion of the automobiles, sewing machines, binoculars, musical instruments, electrical motors, television sets and radios, clothing and shoes, bicycles, motorcycles, and other products that are sold in this country are made by foreign manufacturers than was the case a few years ago. The rapidly improving quality of some of these goods, as well as effective price competition, have made this competition difficult to cope with. Many domestic industries have been seriously affected by it in recent years, and even the U.S. automobile industry has suffered significant economic losses. Foreign competitors often have very efficient modern plants, built since the Second World War, and they have taken very quickly to modern management methods developed chiefly in the United States in the past 20 years. Their labor forces are highly motivated and often willing to work at low wages.

Increased foreign competition requires more attention by domestic producers to costs and technological improvements, and, where the technology is volatile, more specialists and more market research techniques and activities are needed. Such competition also increasingly involves the government, since economic actions, especially on the part of large firms or industries, may have an impact on national policy, imports and exports, foreign-exchange relationships, and currency reevaluations, all of which play a significant role in prices in the product or factor markets.

Growth of the Multinational Organization

In the past two decades, large firms all over the world have opened operations in other countries or have entered into joint ventures or licensing arrangements with firms in other countries. Virtually every large business enterprise in the United States has overseas operations at present; one major toolmaker, for example, has plants in England, France, Italy, Japan, Mexico, Germany, and Australia. In the past few years, Japanese firms have opened several plants in the United States as well as in other countries. A firm in Taiwan has formed relationships with dozens of firms from other countries. The growth of U.S. industry abroad has been so great that in 1968, J. J. Servan-Schreiber, a French writer and political figure, said, "Fifteen years from now it is quite possible that the world's third greatest industrial power just after the United States and Russia will not be Europe, but American industry in Europe."

There are many reasons for this expansion. Transportation cost for many products are simply too high to ship long distances and still sell products at a competitive price. New foreign markets are not perhaps as saturated with products as domestic markets, making it possible to sell the product more readily at a higher price than in the domestic market.

Foreign operations obviously create much more environmental uncertainty than do domestic operations. Market forces as well as government actions must be predicted, and this may be difficult in countries without a stable political structure or mature economy. Cultural Differences and differences in needs and values of local employees suggest the need for different leadership and decision strategies. Some observers feel, for example, that the ability of middle managers or foremen in underdeveloped countries may be lower than that of the typical American manager (Carroll, 1976). If true, this would necessitate more centralization in decision making in such operations. Intensive social change and shifts—in the value of currencies, for example—produce a very uncertain environment in many aspects of foreign operations.

Technological Change

Technology has advanced extremely rapidly in recent years, and this trend can be expected to continue. To keep abreast of such advances, firms obviously need large numbers of highly specialized professionals with knowledge of such changes and their significance for marketing and production methods.

Of significance to the business firm is the time required for ideas to be converted to products. Figure 19.1 shows the relationship of basic research to the development, distribution, and eventual death of a product. Basic research of course is not carried out to produce specific new products, but typically produces new concepts, ideas, or modifications of existing models or theories. In the applied research stage, the new idea is tested in terms of its specific product application, and technological advantages are considered for the first time, while in the product development stage, the product is developed, evaluated, and subjected to cost analysis.

Research and development expenditures in the United States have steadily increased on an absolute basis every year and are significantly higher than in any other country in the world. However, research and development expenditures are not rising as fast as gross national product. In Europe and Japan, on the other hand, the percentage of national income devoted to research and development is rising, a development which has worried a number of analysts (Dean, 1974; Boretsky, 1974), though it should be noted that Japan and the European nations started at a very low base rate. However, U.S. firms

FIGURE 19.1 Product Life Cycle

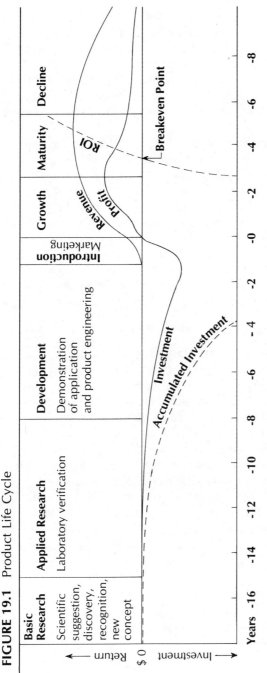

The product life cycle represents the history of a commodity or service from the time of its initial conception to its ultimate withdrawal from the market because of inadequate profit margin. There are four distinct phases of the life cycle after the initial introduction to the market: introduction, growth, maturity, and decline. Profit during these phases may be defined as the margin realized after both fixed and variable costs have been covered. The return on investment (ROI) does not begin until breakeven on the total accumulated investment is realized. The position of the breakeven point is determined by the effectiveness of management in controlling the investment prior to market introduction and in providing a correct pricing policy thereafter.

Source: McLoughlin, W. G. *Fundamentals of Research Management*. New York: American Management Association, 1970, p. 17.

often have access to technological developments from other countries through joint ventures, licensing agreements, or imitation, and the reverse is also true. Clearly, the fact that other nations are investing more heavily in research and development accelerates product change, making the technological environment of firms ever more volatile. Some of the nations which formerly imported technology, such as Japan, are now exporting it, particularly to the less-developed nations (Ozawa, 1973).

There is some disagreement among authorities over how long it takes a new concept or idea to be developed into a marketable product. Some say the period averages 14 to 19 years (McLoughlin, 1970) but others believe that the time has shortened in recent years. Ayres (1969) believes both that the lead time has shortened and that new technological processes saturate an industry much more rapidly than was the case a few years ago. Thus, today it is more important than ever for an industrial organization to be able to discern new technological and scientific developments quickly and to convert them to products or new technology. The boundary-spanning and adaptive subsystems are of course especially critical to this process.

Changing Composition of the Labor Force

The relative proportions of different occupational groups in the U.S. labor force has changed over the years, and this is perhaps not surprising in the light of both technological and social change. Presently, the number of professional and technical workers is increasing the fastest, with an estimated increase of 50 percent between 1968 and 1980 (Bureau of Labor Statistics, 1971). The number of service, clerical, and sales workers is also increasing more rapidly than such occupational groups as craftsmen, foremen, and factory workers. The average educational level of a United States employee is above 12 years of school, and white-collar workers now constitute just about 50 percent of the labor force. This change in composition in the labor force of course has implications for management in terms of effectiveness. It is also important to note that the advantages of job opportunities are not uniformly available to all Americans.

Employment of the Disadvantaged Worker

As a concluding note in this book, let us consider some of the challenges and responsibilities confronting managers in the matter of equal opportunities and, finally, how certain changes in societal values may further affect the design of organizations and approaches to managing them.

Pressures have increased upon every organization to employ more disadvantaged workers. In considering this question, it is fundamental to examine the socialization that has affected the attitudes and position of persons who are disadvantaged in the U.S. labor force. For our purposes, the disadvantaged are defined basically as ethnic or other groups who historically have not enjoyed the same educational and social opportunities as other Americans. Because of this long history of reduced participation in U.S. society, the disadvantaged often have low levels of self-esteem (Ausubel and Ausubel, 1969; Coleman, 1966). Such persons tend to have a short-run perspective and do not expect future benefits to result from current behaviors (Rosen, 1959). As personal frustrations increase, they become less optimistic and less motivated to find a job or to exert effort on a job (Means, 1966). Lack of success at work contributes further to reduced self-esteem and a feeling of irrelevance (Liebow, 1967). Money may not be an effective motivator for such groups because their pay checks often are spoken for in advance by creditors, relatives, or friends; they are expected to share whatever they have with those close to them and thus cannot fully utilize the fruits of their own labor (Davis, 1964).

The employment of disadvantaged workers unquestionably constitutes a contribution to the community and an appropriate exercise of corporate responsibility. It calls for a number of adjustments in management technique. The outlook of such individuals, for example, clearly calls for new motivational approaches, such as one proposed by Porter (1973), which calls for daily pay and attendance rewards. Perhaps special confidence-building programs and greater job security might work better, since they would address themselves to some of the primary problems involved. Special training programs have been launched in a number of companies (Doeringer, 1969), and some positive results have been obtained when the proper "supportive" climate has been established (Friedlander and Greenberg, 1969). Special training is needed not only for the disadvantaged employees themselves, but for the personnel who will carry out programs for the disadvantaged, since those people seem most resistant to changing company procedures or policies in order to meet the special needs of the disadvantaged (Goeke and Weymar, 1969).

Increased Employment of Minority Group Members in Higher-Level Management Positions

There is considerable evidence of discrimination against blacks and other minorities and women in compensation and promotion (Commerce Clearing House, 1972; Matich, 1970; Upjohn Institute, 1973; Cates, 1973; Equal Employment Opportunity Commission, 1972). Government and private groups in the past have placed substantial pressures on organizations to eliminate such discriminatory practices. Initially, conciliation procedures were used, but these have not been effective, and more stringent procedures are now in effect (Adams, 1972). The number of blacks and women in management and professional positions has slowly increased, but there is still resistance to their employment in such positions. Part of the bias lies in sexual and racial stereotypes which result in negative evaluations by incumbent managers (Rosen and Jerdee, 1974a). It does not appear that such stereotypes are disappearing quickly. Some research shows that even female managers are likely to favor males over females in promotion, selection, and placement decisions (Schein, 1975).

There seems to be no empirical justification for such general discrimination at work. Research has indicated a great deal of overlap among the white male group and female, black, and other minorities on various abilities relevant to job performance (Tyler, 1965). Research also shows no differences in personality factors, values, and job satisfactions between white males and minority group members that cannot be accounted for by variations in social situations (Tyler, 1965). Research also shows, finally, that minority group members have lower job satisfaction than the dominant white male group (O'Reilly and Roberts, 1973), which could be accounted for largely by differences in social situations facing the respective groups. In sum, this line of research suggests strongly that competent employees can be found for any job among members of various minority groups.

There are some average differences in values and motives of males and females, but these differences may simply reflect tendencies for men and women to fulfill various sex roles imposed by the culture (Tyler, 1965). It is possible that organizations are forcing women managers to adopt for themselves the male role stereotype (Schein, 1975). Perhaps, as we discussed in chapter 3, individuals are often forced to adapt to the organization's value system.

Changing Societal Values

There is, finally, growing evidence that the younger age groups in our society are changing their values, particularly those values that interface the world of work. As compared to previous generations, today's high school students put less emphasis on security and promotions and more on autonomy and interesting work. They are also less accepting of authority today than in the past (Sheppard and Herrick, 1972). Miner (1973) has found the same to be true of college students. He has found that there are fewer individuals with positive attitudes toward those holding positions of authority, who are competitive with peers, and who are willing to exercise power over others—all factors, obviously, which would be associated with attraction to management as a career, especially in structured organizations.

Business executives themselves predict a shift in national ideology in the United States by 1985 (Martin and Lodge, 1975). Among 1,800 executives surveyed, there was a preference for the traditional U.S. emphasis on individual rights and responsibility. The vast majority, however, predicted a new dominant ideology by 1985 which would stress rights stemming from the group and the use of property according to the goals of the community. If these studies reflect a coming permanent shift in values, contemporary management strategies must change. Newer motivational and leadership approaches will be needed.

Effect on Management

In this chapter, we have outlined briefly some of the major conditions that will impact organizational structure and management style in the future. Other factors—the effects of pollution, for example—are perhaps too evident from the information we receive daily to warrant discussion here, but the discerning reader will see their relevance to our theme.

The various environmental changes taking place today will have consequences that can hardly be predicted with accuracy, but which can be analyzed to some degree in the light of contingency framework set forth in this book. Clearly, certain of the changes will contribute to increased stability of certain types of organizations; for example, increases in sheer size may in many cases result in increasingly stable organizations, and whether this will be an advantage or a disadvantage, in view of changing social values, is something that remains to be seen. Certainly, managers will find it necessary continually to reassess the relationship of their organization structures and its goals to the values of the various publics, internal and external, with which it interfaces. One assumption might be that increasing environmental pressures of the kind outlined in this chapter will result overall in substantially greater differentiation among organizational subunits with respect to structure, personnel, and the way the managerial process is carried out.

The applied behavioral sciences will become increasingly important in management, since human resource problems in organizations will be more complex. The tremendous increase in the literature of applied behavioral science and a similar increase in management training and consulting programs are also indicative of this trend. The trends will continue, and knowledge in the behavioral area, as well as other areas of management, can be expected to increase as greater resources are committed to its development. This will mean that certain portions of this book—and others like it—will quickly become dated. Advances in management techniques will be required to sustain and increase managerial effectiveness. For these reasons, we expect to meet many of our readers again.

Discussion Questions

1. If the changes in values and personnel take place as predicted in this chapter, and management becomes more participative and humanistic, what will be the consequences of this for the increased international competition that is also predicted? Give reasons for your answers.

2. It is predicted that relationships among organizations will become increasingly important in the future. How can such relationships be improved?

3. Make a list of the technological developments which will have occurred by 2025. How will these influence the management of organizations?

4. Evaluate the various criteria of organizational effectiveness cited in this chapter. Were any important characteristics left out? Which ones? Why are they important?

5. As indicated in this chapter, many U.S. companies are establishing branches or subsidiaries in other countries and other countries are now operating in the United States. Make a list of the responsibilities that such companies have to the people and government of the foreign country in which they are located.

6. Some critics of current writings on the social responsibilities of a business say that the only responsibility of a business is to perform an economic function to society. Providing quality goods and services at the lowest possible cost should be the only concern of management. Do you agree or disagree? Why?

7. Write up a policy statement on social responsibility for a business organization. Do the same for a government organization. Discuss these.

References

Adams, A. V. "Toward fair employment and the EEPC: A study of compliance procedures under Title VII of the Civil Rights Act of 1964. EEOC Contract 70-15." Equal Employment Opportunity Commission. Washington, D.C., 1972.

Alderfer, C. P. *Existence, relatedness, and growth: Human needs in organizational settings.* Free Press, 1972.

Allison, D. "The motivation of the underprivileged worker," in W. F. Whyte (ed.), *Industry and society.* McGraw-Hill, 1964.

Anderson, R. C. "Learning in discussions: A resume of the authoritarian-democratic study," *Harvard Educational Review,* 29 (1959): 201–15.

Andrew, G. "A study of the effectiveness of a workshop method for mental health education," *Mental Hygiene,* 38 (1954): 267–78.

Argyris, C. "Human problems with budtets," *Harvard Business Review,* 1953.

———. *Organization of a bank.* Labor and Management Center, Yale University, 1954.

———. *Personality and organization.* Harper & Bros., 1957.

———. *Integrating the individual and the organization.* Wiley, 1964.

Asch, Solomon E. *Social psychology.* Prentice-Hall, 1952.

Assael, H. "Constructive role of interorganizational conflict," *Administrative Science Quarterly,* 14 (1969): 573–83.

Atkinson, J. W. *Introduction to motivation.* Van Nostrand, 1964.

———. "Motivational determinants of risk taking behavior," *Psychological Review,* 64 (1957): 359–72.

Ausubel, D. P., and P. Ausubel. "Ego development among segregated Negro children," in A. Ferman, J. L. Kornbluh and J. A. Miller (eds.), *Negroes and jobs.* Univ. of Michigan Press, 1969.

Ayres, R. U. *Technological forecasting and long range planning.* McGraw-Hill, 1969.

Bales, R. F., and P. E. Slater. "Role differentiation in small groups," in Parsons, T. R. et al. (eds.), *Family, socialization, and interaction process.* Free Press, 1955.

Barnard, C. *The functions of the executive.* Harvard Univ. Press, 1938.

Bass, B. M. "Ultimate criteria of organizational worth," *Personnel Psychology,* 2 (1952): 157–73.

Baughman, J. P. *The history of American management.* Prentice-Hall, 1969.

Beckhard, R. *Organization development: Strategies and models.* Addison-Wesley, 1969.

Bendix, R., and L. N. Fisher. "The perspectives of Elton Mayo," *Review of Economics and Statistics,* 31, 49, 312–21.

Bennis, W. G. "Toward a truly scientific management: The concept of organizational health," in Ghorpade, J. (ed.), *Assessment of organizational effectiveness: Issues, analysis, readings,* Goodyear Publishing, 1971. 116–43.

Blake, R. R., and J. S. Mouton. *The managerial grid.* Gulf, 1964.

Blake, R., and J. Mouton. *Building a dynamic corporation through GRID organizational development.* Addison-Wesley, 1969.

Blake, R. R., H. A. Shepard, and J. S. Mouton. *Managing intergroup conflict in industry.* Gulf, 1964.

Blake, R. R., J. S. Mouton, J. S. Barnes, and L. E. Greiner. "Breakthrough in organization development," *Harvard Business Review,* 42 (1964): 133–55.

Blau, P. *The dynamics of bureaucracy.* Univ. of Chicago Press, 1955.

Blauner, R. *Alienation and freedom.* Univ. of Chicago Press, 1964.

Bolda, R. A., and C. H. Lawshe. "Evaluation of role playing," *Personnel Administration,* 25 (1962): 40–42.

Bond, B. W. "The group discussion-decision approach: An appraisal of its use in health education," *Dissertation Abstracts,* 16 (1956): 903.

Boyle, B. "Equal opportunity for women is smart business," *Harvard Business Review,* 53 (1975): 85–95.

Boretsky, M. "U.S. technology-trend and policy issues," in *Twenty-Seventh National Conference on the Administration of Research.* Denver Research Institute: Univ. of Denver, September, 1973.

Boyd, J. B., and J. D. Ellis. *Findings of Research into Senior Management Seminars.* Toronto: The Hydro-Electric Power Commission of Toronto, 1962. Cited by J. P. Campbell and M. D. Dunnette, "Effectiveness of T-group experiences in managerial training and development," *Psychological Bulletin,* 70 (1968): 73–104.

Bunker, D. R. "Individual applications of laboratory training," *Journal of Applied Behavioral Science,* 1 (1965): 131–48.

Bunker, D. R., and G. W. Dalton. "The comparative effectiveness of groups and individuals in solving problems," in Lawrence, P. R., and J. A. Seiler (eds), *Organizational behavior and administration.* Dorsey Press, 1965.

Burek, "The intricate 'politics' of the corporation," *Fortune,* April, 1975.

Burns, T., and G. Stalker *The management of innovation.* Tavistock, 1961.

Butler, E. D. "An experimental study of the case method in teaching the social foundations of education," *Dissertation Abstracts,* 27 (1967): 2912.

Butler, J. L. "A study of the effectiveness of lecture versus conference teaching techniques in adult education," *Dissertation Abstracts,* 26 (1966), 3712.

Buxton, C. E. *College teaching: A psychologist's view.* Harcourt-Brace, 1956.

Cameron, J. "Black America: Still waiting for full membership," *Fortune,* 91.

Campbell, J. P., and M. D. Dunnette. "Effectiveness of T-group experiences in managerial training and development," *Psychological Bulletin,* 70 (1968): 73–104.

Caplow, T. *Principles of organization.* Harcourt, Brace and World, 1964.

Carey, A. "The Hawthorne studies: A radical criticism," *American Sociological Review,* 32 (1967), 408–16.

Carlson, R. E., P. W. Thayer, E. C. Mayfield, and D. A. Peterson "Improvements in the selection interview," *Personnel Journal,* 50 (April, 1971): 268-75, 317.

Carman, H. J. and H. C. Syrett. *A history of the American people.* Knopf, 1955.

Carpenter, C. R., and L. Greenhill. "An investigation of closed circuit television for teaching university courses," *Instructional Television Project Report #2,* University Park, Pennsylvania: Penn State Univ., 1958.

Carroll, S. J. "The relationship of various college graduate characteristics to recruiting decisions," *Journal of Applied Psychology,* 50 (1966): 421-23.

―――. "Effectiveness ratings of motivational methods by different groups of supervisors." Unpublished study, Univ. of Maryland, 1973.

―――. "Two cases of failure in using competition for motivation." Unpublished study, Univ. of Maryland, 1973.

―――. "Factors related to job involvement of dental assistants." Unpublished study, Univ. of Maryland, 1974.

―――. "Chungwham Picture Tubes Co. Ltd." in Carroll, S. J., F. P. Paine, and John B. Miner (eds.), The managerial process. Cases and readings. Macmillan, 1976.

―――, and H. Tosi. Management by objectives: Applications and research. Macmillan, 1973.

Carzor, R. "Organizational realities," Business Horizons, Spring, 1961, 95–104.

Castore, G. F. "Attitudes of students toward the case method of instruction in a human relations course," Journal of Educational Research, (1951): 201–13.

Cates, J. N. "Sex and salary," American Psychologist, 28 (1973): 929.

Chapple, E. D., and L. R. Sayles. The measure of management. Macmillan, 1961.

Cleland, D. "Understanding Project Authority," Business Horizons, 10, (Spring, 1967): 63-70.

Coch, L. and J. R. P. French, "Overcoming resistance to change," Human Relations, 1 (1948): 512–32.

Cohen, D., J. W. Whitmyre, and W. H. Funk. "Effect of group cohesiveness and training upon creative thinking," Journal of Applied Psychology, 44 (1960): 319–22.

Coleman, J. S. Equality of educational opportunity. U.S. Department of Health, Education and Welfare; Office of Education; and U.S. Government Printing Office, Washington, D.C., 1966.

Commerce Clearing House. Employment practices guide. Washington, D.C., 1972.

Costello, T. W., and S. S. Zalkind. Psychology in administration. Prentice-Hall, 1963.

Culbertson, F. "Modification of an emotionally held attitude through role playing," Journal of Abnormal and Social Psychology, 54 (1957): 230–33.

Cummings, L. L., and D. P. Schwab. Performance in organizations: Determinants and appraisal. Scott, Foresman, 1973.

Dalton, G. W., "Influence and organizational change," in Dalton, G. W., Laurence, P. R., and Greenier, L. G. (eds.), Organizational Change and Development. Dorsey Press, 1970.

Danielson, L. Characteristics of engineers and scientists. Ann Arbor, Mich.: Bureau of Industrial Relations, Univ. of Michigan, 1960.

Davis, A. "The motivation of the underprivileged worker," in W. F. Whyte (ed.), Industry and society. McGraw-Hill, 1964.

Davis, R. C. The fundamentals of top management. Harper, 1951.

Dean, R. C., Jr. "Why is U.S. technological prominence withering?" in Twenty-Seventh National Conference on the Administration of Research. Denver Research Institute: Univ. of Denver, September, 1973.

Dearborn, D. C., and H. A. Simon. "Selective perception: A note on the departmental identification of executives," Sociometry, 21 (1958), 140–44.

Dietrick, D. C. "Review of research," in R. J. Hill (ed.), A Comparative Study of Lecture and Discussion Methods. Pasadena, Calif.: The Fund for Adult Education, 1960.

Dill, W. R. and N. Doppelt. "The acquisition of experience in a complex management game," *Management Science,* 10 (1963): 30–46.

Doeringer, P. B. *Programs to employ the disadvantaged.* Prentice-Hall, 1969.

Douglas, J., and C. Crain. "Activity reaction forms: Measurement of dyadic perceptions of managers using a management by objectives program." Working paper presented at Midwest Academy of Management. Univ. of Michigan, Ann Arbor, Mich., April, 1975.

Dunnette, M. D. *Personnel selection and placement.* Wadsworth, 1965.

Dunnette, M. D. "Predictions of executive success," in F. Wickert and D. McFarland (eds.), *Measuring executive effectiveness.* Appleton-Century-Crofts, 1967.

Dunnette, M. D., J. P. Campbell, and K. Jaastad. "The effect of group participation on brainstorming effectiveness for two industrial samples," *Journal of Applied Psychology,* 47 (1963): 30–37.

Dunnette, M. D., R. D. Arvey, and P. A. Banas. "Why do they leave?" *Personnel* (1973): 25–39.

Durbin, R. "Industrial workers' worlds: A study of the central life interests of industrial workers," *Social Problems,* 3 (1956): 131–42.

"At Emery Air Freight: Positive reinforcement boosts performance," *Organizational Dynamics,* Winter, 1973.

Equal Employment Opportunity Commission. *Promise vs. performance.* An Equal Employment Opportunity Commission report, Washington, D.C., 1972.

Erikson, E. "Identity and the life cycle," *Psychological Issues,* 1 (1959).

Evan, W. M. "Conflict and performance in R and D organizations," *Industrial Management Review,* 7 (1965): 37–45.

Evans, M. G. *The effects of supervisory behavior on worker perceptions of their path goal relationships.* Doctoral Dissertation, Yale Univ., 1968.

Fayol, H. *General and industrial management,* C. Storrs (trans.). Sir Isaac Pitman and Sons, 1949.

Fernandez, J. P. *Black managers in white corporations.* Wiley, 1975.

Festinger, L. *A Theory of cognitive dissonance.* Row, Peterson, 1957.

———, and J. Carlsmith. "Cognitive consequence of forced compliance," *Journal of Abnormal and Social Psychology,* 58 (1959): 203–10.

Fiedler, F. *A Theory of leadership effectiveness.* McGraw-Hill, 1967.

Filipeti, G. *Industrial management in transition.* Irwin, 1946.

Filley, A. C. *A theory of small business and divisional growth.* Ph.D. Dissertation, The Ohio State Univ., 1962.

———, and R. J. House. *Managerial process and organizational behavior.* Scott, Foresman, 1969.

Filley, A. C., and F. H. Reighard. "A preliminary survey of training attitudes and needs among actual and potential attendees at management institute programs," Madison: Univ. of Wisconsin, 1962, cited in R. J. House, "Managerial reactions to two methods of management training," *Personnel Psychology,* 18 (1965): 311–19.

Fleishman, E. A. "Leadership climate, human relations training and supervisory behavior," *Personnel Psychology,* 6 (1953): 205–22.

Ford, R. "Job enrichment lessons from AT&T," *Harvard Business Review,* 1973 (Jan.-Feb.): 96–106.

Fox, W. M. "A measure of the effectiveness of the case method in teaching human relations," *Personnel Administration,* 26 (1962): 53–57.

Franklin, B. "How to make a decision," 1772, as quoted in MacCrimmon, K. R., "Managerial decision making," in Joseph W. McGuire (ed.), *Contemporary management: Issues and viewpoints*. Prentice-Hall, 1974.

French, J. R. P., and B. Raven. "The bases of social power," in D. Cartwright (ed.), *Studies in social power*. Research Center for Group Dynamics, Univ. of Michigan, 1959.

French, J. R. P., Jr., J. Israel, and D. Aas. "An experiment on participation in a Norwegian factory," *Human Relations*, 13 (1960): 3–19.

Fretz, C. F., and J. Hayman. "Progress for women—men are still more equal," *Harvard Business Review*, 51 (1973): 133–42.

Friedlander, F. "The relationship of task and human conditions to effective organizational structure," Bass, B. M., R. Cooper and J. A. Haas (eds), in *Managing for accomplishment*. D. C. Heath, 1970.

Friedlander, F. and H. Pickle. "Components of effectiveness in small organizations," *Administrative Science Quarterly*, 13 (1968): 289–304.

Friedlander, G. and S. Greenberg. "Work climate as related to the performance and retention of hard-core unemployed workers," *Proceedings of the 77th Annual Convention*, American Psychological Association, 1969.

Galbraith, J. *Designing complex organizations*. Addison, Wesley, 1973.

George, C. S. *The history of management thought*. Prentice-Hall, 1968.

Georgopoulos, B. S., and A. S. Tannenbaum. "A study of organizational effectiveness," *American Sociological Review*, 22 (1957): 534-40.

Ghiselli, E. E. *Explorations in managerial talent*. Goodyear, 1971.

Gibb, C. "Leadership," in *Handbook of Social Psychology*, vol. 2. Addison Wesley, 1954.

Goeke, J. R., C. S. Weymar. "Barriers to hiring the blacks," *Harvard Business Review*, 47 (1969).

Gollin, E. S., and M. Moody. "Developmental psychology," *Annual Review of Psychology*, 24 (1973): 1-52.

Goode, W. J., and I. Fowler. "Incentive factors in a low morale plant," *American Sociological Review*, 14 (1949): 619-24.

Gordon, W. J. J. *Synectics*. Harper and Row, 1961.

Gouldner, A. "The role of the norm of reciprocity in social stabilization," *American Sociological Review*, 15 (1960): 161-78.

Graen, G., K. Alvares, J. B. Orris, and J. A. Martella. "Contingency model of leadership effectiveness: Antecedent and evidential results," *Psychological Bulletin*, 74 (1970): 285–96.

Greene, C. N. "Causal connections among managers' merit pay, job satisfaction and performance," *Journal of Applied Psychology*, 58 (1973): 95-100.

Greene, Charles "The path-goal theory of leadership: A replication and analysis of causality," *Proceedings*, Academy of Management, 1974.

Greiner, L. E. "Patterns of organizational change," in G. W. Dalton et al (eds.), *Organizational change and development*, Dorsey Press, 1970.

Grove, B. A., and W. A. Kerr. "Specific evidence on origin of halo effect in measurement of employee morale," *Journal of Social Psychology*, 1951, 165–70.

Guetzkow, H., E. L. Kelly, and W. J. McKeachie. "An experimental comparison of recitation, discussion, and tutorial methods in college teaching," *Journal of Educational Psychology*, 45 (1954): 193–207.

Hackman, R., and E. E. Lawler, III. "Employee reactions to job characteristics," *Journal of Applied Psychology* monograph, 55 (1971): 259–86.

Haire, M., E. Ghiselli, and L. Porter. *Managerial thinking: An international study.* Wiley, 1966.

Hall, D. T., and K. E. Novgaim. "An examination of Maslow's need hierarchy in an organizational setting," *Organizational Behavior and Human Performance,* 3 (1968): 12–35.

Hall, R. H. *Organizations: Structure and process.* Prentice Hall, 1972.

——. "The concept of bureaucracy: An empirical assessment," *American Journal of Sociology,* 69 (1973): 32–40.

Hammond, L. K., and M. Goldman. *Sociometry,* 24 (1961): 46–60.

Hamner, W. C., and H. Tosi. "The influence of role conflict and ambiguity on the relationship of various role involvement measures," *Journal of Applied Psychology,* Fall, 1974.

Hampton, D. R., C. E. Summer and R. A. Webber. *Organizational behavior and the practice of management.* Scott, Foresman, 1973.

Harrell, T. W., and M. Harrell. "Army general classification test scores for civilian occupations," *Educational and Psychological Measurement,* 5 (1945): 231–32.

Harris, C. W. (ed.). *Encyclopedia of educational research.* Macmillan, 1960.

Harvey, E. "Technology and the structure of organizations," *American Sociological Review,* 33 (1968): 247–59.

Harvey, O., and G. Beverly. "Some personality correlates of concept change through role playing," *Journal of Abnormal and Social Psychology,* 63 (1961): 125–30.

Heckhausen, H. *The anatomy of achievement motivation.* Academic, 1967.

Heller, F. A., and G. Yukl. "Participation, managerial decision making and structural variables," *Organizational Behavior and Human Performance,* 4 (1969): 227–41.

Helmreich, R., R. Bakeman, and L. Scherwitz. "The study of small groups," *Annual Review of Psychology,* 24 (1973): 337–54.

Henderson, H. "Should business tackle society's problems?" *Harvard Business Review,* 46 (1968): 77–85.

Herzberg, F., B. Mausner, and B. Snyderman. *The motivation to work.* Wiley, 1959.

Hilgard, E. R., R. C. Atkinson, and R. L. Atkinson. *Introduction to psychology.* Harcourt, Brace, 1971.

Hill, R. A. *A comparative study of lecture and discussion methods.* The Fund for Adult Education, 1960.

Hill, W. "The goal formation process in complex organizations," *Journal of Management Studies,* 6 (1969): 198–208.

Hoagland, J. "Historical antecedents of organization research," in W. W. Cooper et al. (eds.), *New perspectives in organization research.* Wiley, 1964.

Homans, G. C. *The human group.* Harcourt, Brace and World, 1950.

House, R. J. "An experiment in the use of management training standards," *Journal of The Academy of Management,* 5 (1962): 76–81.

——. "Managerial reactions to two methods of management training," *Personnel Psychology,* 18 (1965): 311–19.

——. *Management development: Design evaluation implementation.* Bureau of Industrial Relations, Univ. of Michigan, 1967.

——. "A path goal theory of leader effectiveness," *Administrative Science Quarterly,* 16, 1971.

————, and H. L. Tosi. "An experimental evaluation of a management training program," *Academy of Management Journal,* 6 (1963): 303–15.

Hughes, J. L. "Effects of changes in programmed text format and reduction in classroom time on achievement and attitudes of industrial trainees," *Journal of Programmed Instruction,* 1 (1963).

Hughes, J. L., and W. J. McNamara. "A comparative study of programmed and conventional instruction in industry," *Journal of Applied Psychology,* 45 (1961): 225–31.

Hulin, C., and M. Blood. "Job enlargement, individual differences and worker responses," *Psychological Bulletin,* 69 (1968): 41–55.

Industrial Research. $33 Billion for research," *Industrial Research,* 16 (1974): 38–41.

Industrial Research. "Europe not catching U.S. in R & D yet," *Industrial Research,* 16 (1974): 24.

Inkeles, A., and P. H. Rossi. "National comparisons of occupational prestige," *American Journal of Sociology,* 61 (1956): 329-39.

Ivancevich, J. M. "A longitudinal assessment of Management by Objectives," *Administrative Science Quarterly,* March, 1972, 126–35.

Janger, A. R., and R. G. Schaeffer. "Managing programs to employ the disadvantaged," *Personnel policy study 219.* New York: National Industrial Conference Board, 1970.

Janis, I., and B. King. "The influence of role playing on opinion change," *Journal of Abnormal and Social Psychology,* 49 (1954): 211–18.

Janis, I., and L. Mann. "Effectiveness of emotional role-playing in modifying smoking habits and attitudes," *Journal of Experimental Research in Personality,* 1 (1965): 84–90.

Jarrett, H. (ed.). *Science and resources: Prospects and implications of technological advance.* The Johns Hopkins Press, 1959.

Jasinski, Frank J. "Technological delimitation of reciprocal relationships: A study of interaction patterns in industry," *Human Organization,* 15, 1956.

Jeswald, T. A. "The cost of absenteeism and turnover in a large organization," in W. C. Hamner and F. L. Schmidt (eds.), *Contemporary problems in personnel.* St. Clair Press, 1974.

Jones, E. W., Jr. "What it's like to be a black manager," *Harvard Business Review,* 51 (1973): 108–16.

Kahn, R., D. Wolfe, R. Quinn, and J. Snoek. *Organizational stress: Studies in role conflict and ambiguity.* Wiley, 1964.

Katz, D., and R. Kahn. *The social psychology of organizations.* Wiley, 1966.

Kelley, H. and J. Thibaut. "Group problem solving," in Lindzey, G. and E. Aronson (eds.), *Handbook of social psychology,* vol. 4. Addison-Wesley, 1969.

Kepner, C. H., and B. B. Tregoe. *The rational manager: A systematic approach to problem solving and decision making.* McGraw-Hill, 1965.

Kerr, Clark. "What became of the independent spirit?" *Fortune,* 48 (1953): 110–11.

Kilbridge, M. D. "Reduced costs through job enlargement," *Journal of Business,* 33 (1960): 357–62.

————. "Do workers prefer larger jobs?" *Personnel Journal,* 1960, 45–48.

Kim, J. "Effect of feedback on performance and job satisfaction in an organizational setting," unpublished doctoral dissertation, Michigan State Univ., 1974.

King, B., and I. Janis. "Comparison of the effectiveness of improvised vs. non-improvised role playing in producing opinion changes," *Human Relations,* 9 (1956): 177–86.

Klausmeir, H. J., *Learning and human abilities.* Harper, 1961.

Kohn, M. L., and O. Scheeler. "Class, occupation and orientation," *American Sociological Review,* 34 (1969): 659–78.

Korman, A. K. "Self esteem as a variable in vocational choice," *Journal of Applied Psychology,* 50 (1966): 479–86.

Kornhauser, A. *Mental health of the industrial worker.* Wiley, 1965.

Kornhauser, W. *Scientists in industry: Conflict and accommodation.* Univ. of California Press, 1960.

Krasner, L. "Behavior therapy," *Annual Review of Psychology,* 22 (1971): 483–519.

Kumata, H. *An inventory of instructional television research.* Ann Arbor, Michigan: Educational Television and Radio Center, 1956.

———. "A decade of teaching by television," in W. Schramm (ed.), *The impact of educational television.* Univ. of Illinois Press, 1960.

Landsberger, H. A. *Hawthorne revisited.* Cornell Univ., 1958.

Latham, G. P., and S. B. Kinne, III. "Improving job performance through training in goal setting," *Journal of Applied Psychology,* 59 (1974): 187–91.

Lawler, E. E. *Pay and organizational effectiveness: A psychological view.* McGraw-Hill, 1971.

———, and J. L. Suttle. "A causal correlational test of the need hierarchy concept," *Organizational Behavior and Human Performance,* 7 (1972): 265–87.

———. "Expectancy theory and job behavior," *Organizational Behavior and Human Performance, 9 (1973):* 482–501.

Lawrence, P. R., and J. W. Lorsch. *Organization and environment: Managing differentiation and integration.* Graduate School of Business Administration, Harvard University, 1967.

———. *Developing organizations: Diagnosis and action.* Addison-Wesley, 1969.

Leiberman, S. "The effects of changes in roles on the attitudes of role occupants," *Human Relations,* 9 (1956): 385–402.

Levine, J., and J. Butler, "Lecture vs. group decision in changing behavior," *Journal of Applied Psychology,* 36 (1952): 29–33.

Lewin, A. Y., and R. L. Weber. "Management game teams in education and organization research: An experiment on risk taking," *Academy of Management Journal,* 12 (1969): 49–58.

Lewin, K. "Studies in Group Decision," in D. Cartwright and A. Zander (eds.), *Group dynamics.* Row Peterson, 1953.

———. "Group decision and social change," in E. E. Maccoby, T. Newcombe, E. L. Hartley (eds.), *Readings in social psychology.* Holt, 1958.

Liebow, E. *Talley's corner: A study of streetcorner men.* Little, Brown, 1967.

Lippit, R., and R. K. Whyte. "An experimental study of leadership and group life," in E. E. Maccoby, T. H. Newcomb, E. L. Hartley (eds.), *Readings in social psychology.* Holt, 1958.

Litterer, J. A. "Research departments within large organizations," *California Management Review,* 12 (1970): 77–84.

Litwin, G. H., and R. A. Stringer, Jr. *Motivation and organizational climate.* Graduate School of Business Administration, Harvard Univ., 1968.

Locke, E. A. "Personnel attitudes and motivation," *Annual Review of Psychology,* 26 (1975): 457–80.

Locke, E. "Toward a theory of task motivation and incentives," *Organizational Behavior and Human Performance,* 3 (1968): 162.

Lorig, A. W. "Where do corporate responsibilities really lie?" *Business Horizons,* 10 (1967): 51–54.

Lorsch, J., and J. Morse. *Organizations and their members: A contingency approach.* Harper & Row, 1974.

Lowin, A., and J. Craig. "The influence of level of performance on managerial style: An experimental object lesson in the ambiguity of correlational data," *Organizational Behavior and Human Performance,* 3 (1968): 440–58.

McClelland, D. C., J. Atkinson, J. Clark, and E. Lowell. *The achievement motive.* Appleton-Century-Crofts, 1953.

MacCrimmon, K. R. "Managerial decision making," in McGuire, Joseph W. (ed.), *Contemporary management: Issues and viewpoints.* Prentice-Hall, 1974.

McGregor, D. *The human side of enterprise.* McGraw-Hill, 1960.

McGuire, J. W., and J. B. Parrish. "Status report on a profound revolution," *California Management Review,* 13 (1971): 79–86.

McKenney, J. L. "An evaluation of a business game in an MBA curriculum," *The Journal of Business,* 35 (1962): 278–86.

McLoughlin, W. G. *Fundamentals of research management.* American Management Association, 1970.

Mahoney, T. A., and W. Weitzel. "Managerial models of organizational effectiveness," *Administrative Science Quarterly,* 14 (1969): 357–65.

Mahoney, T. A., T. H. Jerdee, and S. J. Carroll. *Development of managerial performance: A research approach.* South-Western, 1963.

———. "The job(s) of management," *Industrial Relations,* 4 (February, 1965): 97–110.

Maier, N. R. F. "An experimental test of the effect of training on discussion leadership," *Human Relations,* 6 (1953): 161–73.

———. *Problem-solving discussions and conferences: Leadership methods and skills.* McGraw-Hill, 1963.

———. *Problem solving and creativity in individuals and groups.* Brooks-Cole, 1970.

———, and L. R. Hoffman. "Quality of first and second solutions in group problem solving," *Journal of Applied Psychology,* 44 (1960a): 278–83.

———. "Using trained 'developmental' discussion leaders to improve further the quality of group decisions," *Journal of Applied Psychology,* 44 (1960b): 247–51.

Maier, N. R. F., and R. A. Maier. "An experimental test of the effects of 'developmental' vs. 'free' discussions on the quality of group decisions," *Journal of Applied Psychology,* 41 (1957): 320–22.

Maier, N. R. F., and A. R. Solem. "The contribution of the discussion leader to the quality of group thinking," *Human Relations,* 3 (1952): 155–74.

Maier, N. R. F., L. R. Hoffman, J. J. Hooven, and W. H. Read. "Superior-subordinate communication in management," *American Management Association,* 1961, 9.

Mann, F. "Toward an understanding of the leadership role in formal organization," in R. Dubin et al. (eds.), *Leadership and productivity.* Chandler Publishing, 1965.

Mann, J. H., and C. H. Mann. "The importance of group tasks in producing group-member personality and behavior change," *Human Relations, 221 (1959): 75–80.*

March, J. and H. Simon. *Organizations.* Wiley, 1958.

Margulies, N., and J. Wallace. *Organization change: Techniques and applications.* Scott, Foresman, 1973.

Margulies, S., and L. D. Eigen. *Applied programmed instruction.* Wiley, 1962.

Marija, M. "The sexual barrier: Legal and economic aspects of employment, *"part III: Differences in pay.* College of Law, Univ. of California at Hastings, 1970.

Marriott, R. *Incentive wage systems.* Staples Press, 1968.

Martin, W. F., and G. C. Lodge. "Our society in 1985—Business may not like it," *Harvard Business Review,* 53 (1975): 143–50.

Maslow, A. H. "A theory of human motivation," *Psychological Review,* 50 (1943): 370–96.

Means, J. E. "Fair employment practices legislation and enforcement in the United States," *International Labor Review,* 93 (1966): 211–47.

Merton, R. K. *Social theory and social structure.* Free Press, 1957.

Meyer, H., E. Kay, and J. R. P. French. "Split roles of performance appraisal," *Harvard Business Review,* 43 (1965): 123–29.

Miles, M. B. "Changes during and following laboratory training: A clinical-experimental study," *Journal of Applied Behavioral Science,* 1 (1965): 215–42.

Miller, D. and M. Starr. *Executive decisions and operations research.* Prentice-Hall, 1960.

Miller, D. W. and M. Starr. *The Structure of Human Decisions.* Prentice-Hall, 1967.

Miller, L. K., and R. L. Hamblin. "Interdependence, differential rewarding, and productivity," *American Sociological Review,* 28 (1963): 768–77.

Miner, J. B. *Studies in management education.* Springer Publishing, 1965.

———. *Personnel psychology.* Macmillan, 1969.

———. "The real crunch in managerial manpower," *Harvard Business Review,* September-October, 1973, 146–58.

———. *The management process: Theory, research and practice.* Macmillan, 1973.

———, and H. P. Dachler. "Personnel attitudes and motivation," *Annual Review of Psychology,* 24 (1973): 379–402.

Miner, J. B., and N. R. Smith. "Managerial talent among undergraduate and graduate business students," *Personnel and Guidance Journal,* 47 (1969): 995–1000.

Miner, J. B., J. R. Rizzo, D. N. Harlow, and J. W. Hill. "Role motivation theory of managerial effectiveness in simulated organizations of varying degrees of structure," *Journal of Applied Psychology,* 59 (1974): 31–37.

Mobley, W. H. "An interorganizational test of a task-goal expectancy model of work motivation and performance," Ph.D. thesis, Univ. of Maryland, 1971.

Moore, D. G. and R. Rench. "The professional employee in industry," *Journal of Business,* 28 (1955).

Morse, J. J., and J. W. Lorsch. "Beyond theory Y," *Harvard Business Review,* May-June, 1970, 61–68.

Mott, P. E. *The characteristics of effective organizations.* Harper and Row, 1972.

Mulder, M. "Power equalization through participation?" *Administrative Science Quarterly,* 16 (1971): 31–38.

Mulder, M., and H. Wilke. "Participation and power equalization," *Organizational Behavior and Human Performance,* 5 (1970): 430–48.

Myers, C. A., and G. P. Schultz. *The dynamics of a labor market.* Prentice-Hall, 1951.

Nash, A. N., and S. J. Carroll, *The management of compensation.* Wadsworth, 1975.

Nash, A. N., J. P. Muczyk, and F. L. Vettori. "The relative practical effectiveness of programmed instruction," *Personnel Psychology,* 1971, 397–418.

Neidt, C. O., and T. Meredith. "Changes in attitudes of learners when programmed instruction is interpolated between two conventional instruction experiences," *Journal of Applied Psychology,* 50 (1966): 130–37.

Nord, W. R. "Beyond the teaching machine: The neglected area of operant conditioning in the theory and practice of management," *Organizational Behavior and Human Performance,* 5, 1969.

Odiorne, G. *Management by objectives.* Pitman, 1964.

O'Reilly, C. A., and K. H. Roberts. "Job satisfaction among white and nonwhites: A cross-cultural approach," *Journal of Applied Psychology,* 60 (1975): 340–44.

Osborn, A. F. *Applied imagination: Principles and procedures of creative thinking.* Scribner's, 1957.

Ozawa, T. *Transfer of technology from Japan to developing countries.* Unitar Research Report No. 7. United Nations Institute for Training and Research, 1973.

Paine, F. T., S. J. Carroll, and B. Leete. "A study of need satisfactions in managerial level personnel in a government agency," *Journal of Applied Psychology,* 50 (1966): 247 –49.

Paine, F. T. "Organizational assessment dimensions as related to the overall effectiveness of assessment terms," in Frey, W. (ed.), *Management Research and Practice,* in *Proceedings of the Seventh Annual Conference,* Eastern Academy of Management, Univ. of Massachusetts, Amherst, Mass., 1970, 114–123.

Parnes, S. J., and A. Meadow. "Effects of brainstorming instructions on creative problem solving by trained and untrained subjects," *Journal of Educational Psychology, 50 (1959): 171–76.*

Pelz, D. C., and F. M. Andrews. *Scientists in organizations: Productive climate for research and development.* Wiley, 1966.

Perrow, C. *Complex organizations.* Scott, Foresman, 1970.

———. *Organizational analysis: A sociological view.* Wadsworth, 1970.

Pfeffer, J., and G. Salancik. "Organizational decision making as a political process: The case of the university budget," *Administrative Science Quarterly,* 19 (1974): 135–51.

Porter, L. W., and E. E. Lawler, III. *Managerial attitudes and performance.* Irwin-Dorsey, 1968.

Porter, L. W., and R. M. Steers. "Organizational work and personal factors in employee turnover and absenteeism, *"Psychological Bulletin,* 80 (1973): 151–76.

Porter, L. W., E. E. Lawler, III, and J. R. Hackman. *Behavior in organizations.* McGraw-Hill, 1975.

Raia, A. P. "A study of the educational value of management games," *The Journal of Business,* 39 (1966): 339–52.

Rice, A. K. "Productivity and social organization in an Indian weaving shed," *Human Relations,* 6, 1953.

Ritti, R. R. "Job enrichment and skill

utilization in engineering organizations," in Maher, J. R. (ed.), *New perspectives in job enrichment*. Van Nostrand Reinhold, 1971.

Rizzo, J., House, R. J., and Lirtzman, S. "Role conflict and ambiguity in complex organizations," *Administrative Science Quarterly*, 15 (1970): 150–63.

Roethlisberger, F. J., and W. J. Dickson. *Management and the worker*. Harvard Univ. Press, 1939.

Rosen, B. and T. H. Jerdee. "Sex stereotyping in the executive suite," *Harvard Business Review*, 52 (1974): 133–42.

Rosen, N. *Leadership change and group dynamics: An experiment*. Cornell Univ. Press, 1969.

———. *Supervision: A behavioral view*. Grid, 1973.

Rowland, K. M., D. M. Gardner, and S. M. Nealey. "Business gaming in education and research," in *Proceedings of the 13th Annual Midwest Management Conference Academy of Management*, Midwest Division, East Lansing, Mich., April, 1970.

Schachter, S. *The psychology of affiliation*. Stanford Univ. Press, 1959.

Schein, E. "Management development as a process of influence," *Industrial Management Review*, May, 1961, 59–76.

———. "How to break in the college graduate," *Harvard Business Review*, 42 (1964): 68–76.

———. "Organizational socialization and the profession of management," *Industrial Management Review*, 9 (1968), 1–16.

———. *Organizational Psychology*. Prentice-Hall, 1970.

Schein, V. E. "Relationships between sex role stereotypes and requisite management characteristics among female managers," *Journal of Applied Psychology*, 60 (1975): 340 –44.

Schramm, W. *The research on programmed instruction: An annotated bibliography*. Stanford, Calif.: Institute for Communication Research, 1962a.

———. "What we know about learning from instructional television," in *Educational Television–The Next Ten Years*. Stanford University Press, 1962b.

Schreisheim, C., R. J. House, and S. Kerr. "The effects of different operationalizations of leader initiating structure: A reconciliation of discrepant results," *Academy of Management Proceedings*, 1975.

Schutz, W. C., and V. L. Allen. "The effects of a T-group laboratory on interpersonal behavior," *Journal of Applied Behavioral Science*, 2 (1966): 265–86.

Scott, W. G. *The management of Conflict: Appeal systems in organizations*. Irwin, 1965.

Scott, W. R., S. M. Dornbusch, B. C. Busching, J. D. Laing. "Organizational evaluation and authority: Incompatibility and instability," *Administrative Science Quarterly*, 12 (1967): 105–16.

Searfoss, D., and R. Monczka. "Perceived participation in the budget process and motivation to achieve the budget," *Academy of Management Journal*, Dec. 1973, 541–54.

Seashore, S. E. *Group cohesiveness in the industrial work group*. Survey Research Center, Univ. of Michigan, 1954.

Seiler, J. A. "Diagnosing interdepartmental conflict," *Harvard Business Review*, 41 (1963): 121–32.

Selznick, P. *TVA and the grass roots*. Univ. of California Press, 1949.

Shepherd, C. R. *Small groups. Some*

sociological perspectives. Chandler, 1964.

Sheppard, H. L., and N. Q. Herrick. *Where have all the robots gone? Worker dissatisfaction in the 70's.* Free Press, 1972.

Sherif, M. "Superordinate goals in the reduction of intergroup conflict," *American Journal of Sociology,* 63 (1958): 349–56.

Silber, M. B. "A comparative study of three methods of effecting attitude change," *Dissertation Abstracts,* 22 (1962): 2488.

Simon, H. A. *Models of man.* Wiley, 1957a.

———. *Administrative Behavior.* Macmillan, 1957b.

———. *The new science of management decision.* New York Univ. Press, 1960.

Smith, A. *An inquiry into the nature and causes of the wealth of nations.* Strahan and T. Cadell, 1793. The Modern Library, 1937.

Smith, P. N. "Attitude changes associated with training in human relations," *British Journal of Social and Clinical Psychology,* 3 (1964): 104–13.

Sodnovitch, J. M., and W. J. Pophorn. *Retention value of filmed science courses.* Kansas State College of Pittsburg, 1961.

Soelberg, P. "Unprogrammed decision making," *Papers and Proceedings, Academy of Management,* 26th Annual Meeting, 1966.

Solem, A. R. "Human relations training: Comparisons of case study and role playing," *Personnel Administration,* 23 (1960): 29–37.

Starr, M. *Management: A modern approach.* Harcourt Brace Jovanovoch, 1971.

Stedry, A. A., and E. Kay. *The effects of goal difficulty on performance.* General Electric Company: Behavioral Research Service, 1964.

Stedry, A. C., and E. Kay. "The effect of goal difficulty on performance: A field experiment," *Behavioral Science,* 11 (1966): 459–70

Stogdill, R. M. *Individual behavior and group achievement* New York: Oxford University Press, 1959.

———. *Handbook of leadership: A survey of theory and research.* The Free Press, 1974.

Stovall, T. F., "Lecture vs. discussion," *Phi Delta Kappan,* 39 (1958): 225–58.

Super, D. E. *The psychology of careers.* Harper & Bros., 1957.

———. *Occupational psychology.* Wadsworth, 1972.

Sykes, A. J. N. "The effects of a supervisory training course in changing supervisors' perceptions and expectations of the role of management," *Human Relations,* 15 (1962): 227–43.

———. "Economic interest and the Hawthorne researches," *Human Relations,* 18 (1965), 253–63.

Taylor, C. W. *Creativity: Progress and potential.* McGraw-Hill, 1964.

Taylor, F. W. *Scientific management.* Harper, 1947.

Thompson, J. *Organizations in action.* McGraw-Hill, 1967.

Thompson, V. *Modern organization.* Knopf, 1967.

Torrance, E. P. "The Minnesota studies of creative behavior: National and international extensions," *Journal of Creative Behavior,* 1 (1967): 137–54.

Tosi, H. L. "A reexamination of personality as a determinant of the effects of participation," *Personnel Psychology* 23 (1970): 91–99.

———. "Organization stress as a moderator of the relationship between influence and role response," *Academy of Management Journal,* 14 (1971), 7–22.

———. "The human effects of budgeting systems on

management," *Business Topics,* Autumn, 1974, 53–63.

————, and Stephen J. Carroll. "Some structural factors related to goal influence in the Management by Objectives process," *MSU Business Topics,* Spring 1969, 45–51.

Tosi, H. L., L. Baird, and L. Foster. "Relationships between different levels of superior and subordinate performance and subordinate attitudes and perceptions of leader behavior in the work setting," *Proceedings, Academy of Management,* 1975.

Tosi, H. L., R. J. Chesser, and S. J. Carroll. "A dynamic model of certain aspects of the superior/subordinate relationship," *Proceedings Eastern Academy of Management,* Annual Meetings, Boston, 1972.

Trist, E. L., and K. W. Bamforth. "Some social and psychological consequences of the long wall method of coal getting," *Human Relations,* 4 (1951): 3–38.

Turcotte, W. "Control systems, performance and satisfaction in two state agencies," *Administrative Science Quarterly,* March 1974, 60 –73.

Tyler, L. *The psychology of human differences.* Appleton-Century-Crofts, 1956.

Underwood, W. J. "Evaluation of laboratory method training," *Training Directors Journal,* 19 (1965): 34–40.

W. E. Upjohn Institute *Work in America.* MIT Press, 1973.

U.S. War Department. *What the soldier thinks: A monthly digest of War Department studies on the attitudes of American troops.* Army Services Forces, Morales Services Division, I, 1943, 13.

Valiquet, I. M. "Contribution to the evaluation of a management development program,"

Unpublished master's thesis. Massachusetts Institute of Technology, 1964. Cited by J. P. Campbell and M. D. Dunnette, "Effectiveness of T-group experiences in managerial training and development," *Psychological Bulletin, 70 (1968): 73–104.*

VanderMeer, A. W. *Relative effectiveness of exclusive film instruction, films plus study guides, and typical instructional methods. Progress report #10.* Instructional Film Program. Pennsylvania State College, 1948.

Van Schacck, H., Jr. "Naturalistic role playing: A method of interview training for student personnel administrators," *Dissertation Abstracts,* 17 (1957): 801.

Verner, C., and G. Dickinson. "The lecture, an analysis and review of research," *Adult Education,* 17 (1967): 85–100.

Vroom, V. H. *Work and motivation.* Wiley 1964.

————. "A study of pre- and post-decision processes," *Organizational Behavior and Human Performance, 1 (1966), 212 –25.*

————. and P. W. Yetton. *Leadership and decision-making.* Univ. of Pittsburgh Press, 1973.

Wagner, H. *Principles of operations research.* Prentice-Hall, 1969

Wainer, H. W., and I. M. Rubin. "Motivation of research and development entrepreneurs," *Journal of Applied Psychology,* 53 (1969): 178–84.

Walker, C. R., and R. H. Guest. *The man on the assembly line.* Harvard Univ. Press, 1952.

Walton, R. E. *Interpersonal peacemaking: Confrontations and third party consultation.* Addison Wesley, 1969.

————, and J. M. Dutton. "The management of interdepartmental conflict: A model and review," *Administrative Science Quarterly,* 14 (1969): 522–42.

Walton, R. E., and R. B. McKersie. *A behavioral theory of labor negotiations.* McGraw-Hill, 1965.

Weber, Max. *The theory of social and economic Organization,* (T. Parsons, trans.). The Free Press, 1947.

Webster, E. (ed). *Decision making in the employment interview.* Montreal: Eagel, 1964.

Weiss, D. J., R. V. David, G. H. England, and L. H. Lofquist. *The measurement of vocational needs.* Bulletin 39, Industrial Relations Center, Univ. of Minnesota, 1964.

Weston, J., and F. Brigham. *Managerial finance.* Holt, Rinehart, 1972.

Whitehill, A. M., Jr., and S. Takezawa. *The other worker.* East-West Center Press, 1968.

Wild, R., and Kempner, T. "Influence of community and plant characteristics on job attitudes of manual workers," *Journal of Applied Psychology,* 56 (1972): 106 –13.

Witkin, H. A., R. B. Dyk, H. F. Faterson, D. R. Guodenough, S. A. Karp. *Psychological differtiation.* Wiley, 1962.

Woodward, J. *Industrial organization.* London: Oxford University Press, 1965.

Wyatt, S., and R. Marriott. *A study of attitudes to factory work.* London: Medical Research Council, 1956.

Yuchtman, E. and S. E. Seashore. "A system resource approach to organizational effectiveness," in Ghorpade, J. (ed.), *Assessment of organizational effectiveness: Issues, analysis, readings,* Goodyear, 1971.

Zaleznik, A., C. R. Christensen, and F. J. Roethlisberger. *The motivation, productivity, and satisfaction of workers: A prediction study.* Division of Research, Harvard Business School, 1958.

Zalkind, S. S., and T. W. Costello. "Perception: Some recent research and implications for administration," *Administrative Science Quarterly,* September, 1962, 227–29.

Zimbardo, P., and E. B. Ebbesen. *Influencing attitudes and changing behavior.* Addison-Wesley, 1970.

Name Index

Aas, D., 226
Adams, A. V., 550
Alderfer, C. P., 75, 76
Allen, V. L., 520
Anderson, R. C., 522
Andrew, G., 519
Andrew, F. M., 408, 468
Argyris, C., 51, 118, 344, 351, 543
Arvey, R. D., 92
Assael, H., 378
Atkinson, R. C., 133
Ausubel, D. P., 549
Ayres, R. U. 547

Bakeman, R., 110, 133
Banas, P. A., 92
Barnard, C., 42, 49, 50, 158, 209
Barnes, J. S., 225
Bass, B. M., 543
Beckhard, R., 508
Bell, D., 39
Bendix, R., 48
Bennis, W. G., 544
Beverly, G., 520
Bissell, G., 30
Blake, R. R., 23, 224, 225, 231, 476, 526, 533, 543
Blau, P., 363
Blauner, R., 187
Blood, M., 355
Bolda, R. A., 521, 522
Bond, B. W., 520
Boretsky, M., 546
Boyd, J. B., 520
Brigham, F., 294, 305
Bunker, D. R., 520
Burck, C. G., 544
Burns, T., 54, 55, 180, 189
Butler, J. L., 519, 520
Buxton, C. E., 519

Cameron, J., 550
Campbell, J. P., 521
Caplow, T., 543

Carey, A., 48
Carlsmith, J., 520
Carlson, R. E., 346
Carroll, S. J., 7, 12, 79, 122, 132, 134, 137, 139, 146, 149, 150, 226, 227, 232, 309, 350, 352, 363, 373, 408, 509, 523, 525, 546
Castore, G. F., 522
Cates, J. N., 549
Chapple, E. D., 474
Chesser, R. J., 150
Christensen, C. R., 111
Coch, L., 314
Cohen, D., 521
Coleman, J. S., 549
Costello, T. W., 65
Craig, J., 230, 364
Crain, C., 525
Culbertson, F., 520
Cummings. L. L., 150

Dachler, H. P., 143
Dalton, G. W., 537
David, R. V.,
Davis, A., 549
Davis, R. C., 15, 43, 158
Dean, R. C., Jr., 546
Dearborn, D. C., 98, 114, 375, 462
Dickinson, G., 519, 523
Dickson, W. J., 45
Dietrick, D. C., 519, 522, 523
Dill, W. R., 80, 521
Doeringer, P. B., 549
Doppelt, N., 521
Dornbusch, S. M.,
Douglas, J., 525
Drucker, P., 411
Dunnette, M. D., 92, 220, 260, 346, 403, 520, 521
Dutton, J. M., 459
Dubin, R., 344
Dyk, R. B., 80

Ebbesen, E. B., 72

Ellis, J. D., 520
Erikson, E., 66
Evan, W. M., 166
Evans, M. G., 227

Fayol H., 32, 39, 40, 42, 50
Festinger, L., 72, 520
Fiedler, F., 226, 227, 228, 231, 364,
    365, 366, 367, 416
Filley, A. C., 483, 487, 490, 522
Fisher, N., 48
Fleishman, E. A., 226
Ford, R., 355
Fowler, I., 137
Fox, W. M., 522
Franklin, B., 273
French, J. R. P., 217, 226, 314, 363, 462
Fretz, C. F., 550
Friedlander, F., 263, 462, 507, 541, 549
Funk, W. H., 521

Galbraith, J., 471, 473
Gantt, H. L, 33, 36
Gardner, D. M., 522
George, C. S., 24, 32
Ghiselli, E. E., 79, 220, 408
Gibb, C., 220
Gilbreth, F., 33, 36, 38, 39
Gilbreth, L., 33, 38
Goeke, J. R., 549
Goode, W. J., 137
Goodenough, D. R., 80
Gordon, W. J. J., 260
Gouldner, A., 115, 138
Graen, G., 228
Greenberg, S., 549
Greene, C. N., 121, 230
Greiner, L. E., 225
Guetzkow, H., 522

Hackman, R., 76, 132
Hall, D. T., 79
Hall, R. H., 461
Hamblin, R. L., 146
Hamner, W. C., 371, 372, 421
Hampton, D. R., 460
Harvey, E., 169

Harvey, O., 520
Hayman, J., 550
Heckhausen, H., 132
Hefner, H., 487
Helmreich, R., 110, 133
Henderson, H., 543
Herrick, N. Q., 188, 550
Herzberg, F., 124, 125, 127
Hilgard, E. R., 146
Hill, J. W., 522
Hill, R. A., 543
Hoagland, J., 24
Hoffman, L. R., 521, 522
Homans, G. C., 99
Hooven, J. J.,
House, R. J., 151, 226, 227, 229, 367,
    369, 417, 422, 483, 490, 507, 522,
    528, 531, 533, 542
Hughes, J. L., 522
Hulin, C., 355

Inkeles, A., 80
Israel, J., 226

Janis, I., 520
Jerdee, T. H., 7, 12, 550
Jeswald, T. A., 122

Kahn, R., 106, 111, 156, 164, 212, 231,
    371, 372, 421
Karp, S. A., 80
Katz, D., 106, 111, 156, 164, 212
Kay, E., 149, 232, 363
Kelley, H., 330
Kelly, E. L., 522
Kempner, T., 132
Kepner, C. H., 237, 238, 239, 240,
    263, 264
Kerr, C., 48
Kilbridge, M. D., 188
Kim, J., 134, 354
Kimball, D., 33
King, B., 520
Kinne, S. B., III,
Klausmeier, H. J., 523
Kohn, M. L., 352
Korman, A. K., 81, 146

Kornhauser, A., 188
Kornhauser W., 344, 408
Krasner, L., 139
Kumata, H., 522, 523

Landsberger, H. A.,
Latham, G. P., 134
Lawler, E. E., III, 76, 129, 132, 139, 148
Lawrence, P. R., 55, 168, 456, 457, 459,
    462, 467, 473, 474, 476
Lawshe, C. H., 521, 522
Leete, B., 352
Lenin, V. I., 40
Levin, H., 119
Levine, J., 520
Lewin, A. Y., 520
Lewin, K., 315, 525
Lieberman, S., 72, 98, 375
Liebow, E., 79, 549
Lippit, R., 221, 222
Litterer, J. A., 468
Litwin, G. H., 465
Locke, E. A., 125, 126, 127, 232,
    308, 363
Lodge, G. C., 551
Lorig, A. W., 543
Lorsch, J. W., 55, 169, 364, 408, 456,
    457, 459, 461, 462, 467, 468, 473,
    474, 476
Lowin, A., 230, 364

McClelland, D. C., 132
MacCrimmon, K. R., 272, 274
McGregor, D., 50, 543
McKeachie, W. J., 522
McKenney, J. L., 521
McKersie, R. B.,
McLoughlin, W. G., 547
McNamara, W. J., 522
Mahoney, T. A., 7, 12
Maier, N. R. F., 99, 134, 238, 312, 313,
    327, 328, 334, 337, 363, 521, 522
Maier, R. A., 521, 522
Mann, F., 520, 522
Mann, J. H., 511, 512, 522
March, J., 15, 44, 50, 59, 281, 308
Margulies, N., 429, 430

Marriott, R., 146, 188
Martin, W. F., 551
Maslow, A. H., 74, 75, 93, 131
Mauser, B.,
Mayfield, E. C.,
Mayo, E., 46
Meadow, A., 521
Means, J. E., 549
Meredith, T., 522
Merton, R. K., 180
Meyer, H., 363
Miles, M. B., 520
Miller, D., 51, 52, 267, 441
Miller, L. K., 146
Miner, J. B., 143, 258, 346, 352, 462,
    475, 550
Mobley, W. H., 150
Moore, D. G., 424, 468, 469
Morse, J. J., 364, 408, 462, 467, 468
Mouton, J. S., 23, 224, 225, 231, 476,
    526, 533, 543
Mulder, M., 226, 334
Muczyk, J. P., 519, 523
Myers, C. A., 81

Nash, A. N., 79, 122, 139, 350, 408,
    509, 519, 523
Nealey, S. M., 522
Neidt, C. O., 522
Nixon, R. M., 214
Nougaim, K. E., 79
Nord, W. R., 62, 140

Odiorne, G., 324
O'Reilly, C. A., 550
Osborn, A. F., 260
Ozawa, T., 547

Paine, F. T., 80, 352, 542
Paterson, D. R., 80
Pelz, D. C., 408, 468
Perrow, C., 16
Pfeffer, J., 306
Pickle, H., 541
Pophorn, W. J., 523
Porter, L. W., 76, 79, 110, 148, 344,
    351, 549

Presthus, R. V., 83, 84, 85
Priestley, J., 273

Raia, A. P., 521, 522
Raven, B., 217, 462
Reighard, F. H., 522
Renck, R., 424, 468, 469
Rice, A. K., 102
Rizzo, J. R., 44
Roberts, K. H., 550
Rockerfeller, J. D., 30
Roethlisberger, F. J., 45, 46, 111
Rosen, B., 549
Rosen, N., 230, 550
Rossi, P. H., 80
Rowland, K. M., 522

Salancik, G., 306
Sayles, L. R., 474
Schachter, S., 111
Schein, E. H., 90, 91, 93, 115, 208
Schein, V. E., 507, 525, 526, 550
Scherwitz, L., 133
Schramm, W., 519, 522
Schultz, G. P., 81, 520
Schwab, D. P., 150
Scott, W. G., 463
Scott, W. R., 476, 477
Seashore, S. E., 110, 224
Seiler, J. A., 466, 468, 474
Selznick, P., 32, 53, 495
Servan-Schreiber, J. J., 545
Shepard, H. A., 476
Sheppard, H. L., 188, 550
Sherif, M., 146, 477
Silber, M. B., 520
Simon, H. A., 15, 44, 50, 59, 98, 114, 234, 238, 255, 281, 308, 375, 462
Smith, A., 27, 28, 30
Smith, N. R., 520
Sodnovitch, J. M., 523
Soelberg, P., 274
Solem, A. R., 521
Spectorsky, A. C., 487
Stalker, G., 54, 55, 180, 189
Starr, M., 51, 52, 267, 389, 435, 439, 440

Stedry, A. A., 149, 232
Steers, R. M., 110
Stringer, R. A., 465
Stogdill, R. M., 108, 220, 221, 222, 223, 224
Stovall, T. F., 519
Summer, C. E., 460
Super, D. E., 81, 351
Suttle, J. L., 76, 129, 139
Sykes, A. J. N., 48, 507

Takezawa, S., 73, 79
Taylor, C. W., 258
Taylor, F. W., 5, 24, 32, 33, 36, 37, 38, 39, 258
Thibaut, J., 330
Thompson, J., 171, 172, 184, 190, 203
Thompson, V., 54, 55, 154, 160, 427, 463, 465
Torrance, E. P., 258
Tosi, H. L., 44, 79, 134, 149, 150, 226, 227, 230, 232, 309, 352, 363, 371, 372, 421, 507, 523, 525
Tregoe, B. B., 237, 238, 239, 240, 263, 264
Turcotte, W., 309
Tyler, L., 69, 550

Underwood, W. J., 520

Valiquet, I. M., 520
VanderMeer, A. W., 523
Van Schacck, H., JR., 522
Verner, C., 519, 523
Vettori, F. L., 519, 523
Vinci, Leonardo da, 24
Vroom, V. H., 110, 121, 138, 146, 238, 327, 329, 330, 331, 333, 334, 351

Wallace, J., 429, 430
Walton, R. E., 459, 476
Watt, I., 27
Webber, R. A., 460
Weber, M., 49
Webster, E., 274
Weitzel, W., 542
Weston, J., 294, 305

Weymar, C. S., 549
Whitehill, A. M., Jr., 73, 79
Whitmyre, J. W., 521
Whyte, R. K., 221, 222
Wild, R., 132
Wilke, H., 335
Witkin, H. A., 80
Woodward, J., 54, 55

Wyatt, S., 188

Yetton, P. W., 238, 327, 329, 330, 331, 333, 334

Zaleznik, A., 108, 111
Zalkind, S. S., 65
Zimbardo, P., 72